INTERNATIONAL COMPETITION LAW

Should an international competition agreement be incorporated into the World Trade Organisation? Taylor examines this question, arguing that such an agreement would be beneficial. Existing initiatives towards the regulation of cross-border, anti-competitive conduct have clear limitations that could be overcome by an agreement, and the WTO would provide the optimal institutional vehicle for it. At a practical level, Taylor points out, an international competition agreement could address under-regulation and over-regulation in the trade–competition regulatory matrix, realising substantive benefits to international trade and competition. This book identifies the appropriate content and structure for a plurilateral competition agreement and proposes a draft negotiating text with accompanying commentary, and as such will be an invaluable tool for policy-makers, WTO negotiators, competition and trade lawyers, and international jurists.

MARTYN D. TAYLOR specialises in competition law, international economic law, telecommunications law and media & technology law, and has advised a diverse range of clients in a number of jurisdictions. He has worked or studied in the UK, Canada, Australia, New Zealand, China, Japan, Singapore and Hong Kong and he holds a PhD, LLM, BSc, LLB (Hons) and BA(Economics)(Hons) with first class honours. Dr Taylor has spoken at a number of international conferences and has published extensively, including as a contributor to *Merger Control Worldwide* (Cambridge University Press, 2005).

INTERNATIONAL COMPETITION LAW

A New Dimension for the WTO?

MARTYN D. TAYLOR

CAMBRIDGE
UNIVERSITY PRESS

CAMBRIDGE UNIVERSITY PRESS
Cambridge, New York, Melbourne, Madrid, Cape Town, Singapore, São Paulo

Cambridge University Press
The Edinburgh Building, Cambridge CB2 8RU, UK

Published in the United States of America by Cambridge University Press, New York

www.cambridge.org
Information on this title: www.cambridge.org/9780521863896

© Martyn D. Taylor 2006

This publication is in copyright. Subject to statutory exception
and to the provisions of relevant collective licensing agreements,
no reproduction of any part may take place without the written
permission of Cambridge University Press.

First published 2006

A catalogue record for this publication is available from the British Library

ISBN 978-0-521-86389-6 hardback

Transferred to digital printing 2008

Cambridge University Press has no responsibility for the persistence or accuracy
of URLs for external or third-party Internet websites referred to in this publication,
and does not guarantee that any content on such websites is, or will remain,
accurate or appropriate.

To my beautiful wife, Meena, and our daughters, Maya and Tara.
In loving memory of my mother.

CONTENTS

List of tables and figures   page xii
List of abbreviations   xv

1   Introduction   1

PART I   An International Competition Agreement is Desirable

2   Is competition law beneficial?   7
  2.1   What is competition law and what is its rationale and philosophy?   8
  2.2   Distributional fairness as a co-objective of competition law   24
  2.3   How does competition law relate to other governmental laws and policies?   28
  2.4   Conclusion: competition law is beneficial   33

3   Is an international competition agreement desirable?   34
  3.1   The globalisation of competition   35
  3.2   Extraterritoriality and jurisdictional conflict (a 'non-co-operative' approach)   53
  3.3   Conclusion: an international competition agreement is desirable   69

4   Is there a sufficient basis for an international competition agreement?   71
  4.1   Competition laws within the Asia-Pacific Economic Community   72
  4.2   Macro issues: objectives, methodology and structure of competition laws   76
  4.3   Micro issues: particular content and application of competition laws   79
  4.4   Regulation of market structure – merger laws   84

4.5   Regulation of unilateral conduct – anti-monopoly laws   89
4.6   Regulation of concerted conduct – horizontal and vertical agreements   93
4.7   Exemptions from the application of competition laws   97
4.8   Administration and enforcement of domestic competition laws   100
4.9   Conclusion: there is a sufficient basis for an international competition agreement   103

5   Have existing cross-border initiatives proved sufficient?   106

5.1   A network of bilateral competition agreements   107
5.2   The current momentum towards plurilateral agreement   122
5.3   Current initiatives towards the realisation of multilateral agreement   129
5.4   Insights into an international competition agreement   139
5.5   Conclusion: existing initiatives towards the regulation of cross-border conduct have clear limitations that could be overcome by an international competition agreement   142

PART II   The WTO Would Provide a Suitable Institutional Vehicle

6   Would the WTO provide a suitable institutional vehicle for an international competition agreement?   147

6.1   Historical relationship between trade law and competition law   148
6.2   Are international trade law and international competition law complementary?   163
6.3   Can international trade theory and international competition theory be reconciled?   176
6.4   Conclusion: the WTO could provide a suitable institutional vehicle for an international competition agreement   183

7   Would a WTO competition agreement promote international trade?   185

7.1   The effects of anti-competitive practices on international trade   187

- 7.2 The *Kodak-Fuji Film* case – application of WTO law to anti-competitive conduct   191
- 7.3 To what extent do domestic competition laws otherwise prevent such conduct?   201
- 7.4 International Conduct   212
- 7.5 Existing WTO provisions regulating Domestic Conduct and International Conduct   217
- 7.6 Conclusion: an international competition agreement would promote international trade   221

8 Would competition regulation of trade measures promote competition?   224
- 8.1 The effects of trade measures on international competition   226
- 8.2 Domestic Measures   232
- 8.3 International Measures   241
- 8.4 Government Commercial Activities   251
- 8.5 Conclusion: competition regulation of trade measures would promote competition   257

9 Should competition principles be introduced into anti-dumping law?   260
- 9.1 The basis and purpose of modern anti-dumping law   261
- 9.2 International competition law as an alternative to anti-dumping law   271
- 9.3 Conclusion: competition principles should be introduced into anti-dumping law   283

PART III The Optimal Form for a WTO Competition Agreement

10 What are the optimal objectives and principles for a WTO competition agreement?   289
- 10.1 What would be the optimal institutional vehicle for an international competition agreement?   289
- 10.2 Existing proposals for a WTO competition agreement   298
- 10.3 The objectives for a WTO competition agreement   315
- 10.4 Core principles for a WTO competition agreement   318
- 10.5 Conclusion: the WTO is the optimal vehicle for an international competition agreement   334

CONTENTS

11 **What is the optimal content for a WTO competition agreement?** 336
- 11.1 To what extent should any WTO competition agreement seek to achieve harmonisation of domestic competition laws? 337
- 11.2 To what extent should any WTO competition agreement seek to proscribe minimum international standards? 348
- 11.3 To what extent should the provisions of a WTO competition agreement be legally enforceable as binding precepts of international law? 355
- 11.4 Amendments to existing WTO trade rules 365
- 11.5 Conclusions on optimal content and approach for a WTO competition agreement 368

12 **What is the optimal structure for a WTO competition agreement?** 370
- 12.1 What would be the most appropriate institutional basis for a WTO competition agreement to promote effective compliance with its substantive obligations? 371
- 12.2 What would be the most appropriate institutional basis for a WTO competition agreement to *mitigate* potential international competition disputes? 378
- 12.3 What would be the most appropriate institutional basis for a WTO competition agreement to *resolve* international competition disputes? 383
- 12.4 Would the suspension of trade concessions be an appropriate sanction for a failure to comply with a WTO competition agreement? 389
- 12.5 Conclusions on optimal institutional structure for a WTO competition agreement 393

13 **Would a WTO competition agreement be politically achievable?** 395
- 13.1 The negotiation of a WTO competition agreement 395
- 13.2 Meeting the concerns of developing countries 413
- 13.3 Four-point incremental strategy for realising a WTO competition agreement 417
- 13.4 Conclusion: a plurilateral WTO competition agreement is politically achievable 421

14 Conclusion: a plurilateral competition agreement should be incorporated into the WTO   423
   14.1   Summary   423
   14.2   Conclusion   434

APPENDIX: Draft negotiating text for a plurilateral WTO competition agreement   435

Index   483

TABLES AND FIGURES

1	Structure of this book	3
2	Neoclassical (Marshallian) graphical representation of a market	10
3	Neoclassical representation of monopoly pricing	17
4	Cumulative causation cycle of economic growth	22
5	Representation of the grand utility possibility frontier and identification of the socially optimal point	25
6	Diagram illustrating the relationship between competition law and competition policy	30
7	Three principal modes of supply into foreign markets	38
8	Diagram illustrating application of domestic competition law to cross-border *inter*-firm commerce from Figure 7	39
9	Diagram illustrating application of domestic competition law to cross-border *intra*-firm commerce from Figure 7	41
10	Conceptual diagram illustrating under-regulation	45
11	Conceptual diagram illustrating over-regulation	47
12	Conceptual diagram illustrating system frictions	49
13	Welfare consequences of under-regulation, over-regulation and system frictions	50
14	Relationship between competition law enforcement and content	82
15	Continuum of behavioural thresholds	91
16	Forms of business combination and their regulation by competition law	93
17	Taxonomy of vertical agreements	96
18	Continuum of international agreements	107
19	Four principal elements of the First Generation Agreements	109
20	Six principal elements of the Second Generation Agreements	111
21	Six principal elements of the Third Generation Agreements	116
22	Procedural issues addressed by the ANZ Agreement	119

23	Competition co-operation agreements within APEC	125
24	Competition issues addressed by the WTO Working Group	137
25	Institutional structure for the world economy proposed at Bretton Woods (1947)	149
26	Existing competition law provisions in the WTO agreements	160
27	Matrix illustrating objectives of international trade policy and international competition policy	168
28	Comparison between international trade law and policy and international competition law and policy	171
29	Cross-perspectives between international trade law and international competition law	177
30	Potential overlap between trade law and competition law	179
31	Venn diagram of relationship between barriers to trade and barriers to market entry	181
32	Trade-competition regulatory matrix, showing regulatory 'loopholes'	189
33	Diagram illustrating analysis undertaken in Chapter 8	227
34	Governmental trade measures considered in Chapter 8	231
35	Application of a VER	242
36	Application of a VIE	247
37	Dumping occurs where the export price is less than normal value	262
38	Effectiveness of each institutional structure	292
39	Scope of each institutional structure	293
40	Context for each institutional structure	295
41	Achievability of each institutional structure	299
42	Ranking to identify most suitable institutional vehicle for an international competition agreement	300
43	Continuum indicating the extent to which the WTO could be amended to incorporate competition rules	301
44	Convergence-harmonisation continuum illustrating terminology	338
45	Illustration of marginal benefits in cost-benefit assessment	341
46	Illustration of marginal costs in cost-benefit assessment	345
47	Optimal extent of convergence of domestic competition laws	346
48	Indicative statistical distribution of domestic competition laws with and without a minimum standard	349
49	Indicative distribution of domestic competition laws with and without convergence to a minimum standard	358

50 Continuum of regulatory approaches   364
51 Potential coercive relationships   372
52 Characteristics of the three principal types of competition
    disputes   379
53 Negotiating positions of nations at the Doha Ministerial   406
54 Proposed modalities set out in draft Cancún Declaration   410
55 Negotiating positions of nations after the Cancún Ministerial   411

ABBREVIATIONS

ABA	American Bar Association
ACP	African, Caribbean and Pacific Group (Lomé Convention)
ANZ	Australia and New Zealand
APEC	Asia Pacific Economic Co-operation
ASEAN	Association of Southeast Asian Nations
CEECs	Central and Eastern European Countries
CER	Australia–New Zealand Closer Economic Relations Trade Agreement
DC	Developing country
EC	European Commission
ECOSOC	Economic and Social Council of the United Nations
EPG	APEC Eminent Person Group
EU	European Union (officially 'European Communities' in the WTO)
FDI	Foreign direct investment
FTAIA	(US) Foreign Trade Antitrust Improvements Act
FTC	(US) Federal Trade Commission
GATS	General Agreement on Trade in Services
GATT	General Agreement on Tariffs and Trade
GDP	Gross Domestic Product
GNP	Gross National Product
GSP	Generalised System of Preferences
GUPF	Grand Utility Possibility Frontier
IAA	International Antitrust Authority (as proposed by the Munich Group)
IAEAA	International Antitrust Enforcement Assistance Agreements
IAEA Act	(US) International Antitrust Enforcement Assistance Act 1994
IBRD	International Bank for Reconstruction and Development (World Bank)

LIST OF ABBREVIATIONS

ICJ	International Court of Justice
IIE	Institute of International Economics
IMF	International Monetary Fund
ITO	International Trade Organisation (never established)
JFTC	Japanese Fair Trade Commission
KHE	Kaldor-Hicks efficiency
LDCs	Less developed and developing countries (for this book)
MFN	Principle of most favoured nation treatment
MLAT	Mutual Legal Assistance Treaty
MTN	Multilateral trade negotiations
NAFTA	North American Free Trade Agreement
NT	Principle of national treatment
OAS	Organisation of American States
OECD	Organisation for Economic Co-operation and Development
OPEC	Organisation of Petroleum Exporting Countries
PECC	Pacific Economic Co-operation Council
S&D	Special and differential treatment
SCP	Structure-conduct-performance
STE	State Trading Enterprise
TPRB	Trade Policy Review Body
TPRM	Trade Policy Review Mechanism
TRIMS	Trade-Related Investment Measures
TRIPS	Trade-Related Aspects of Intellectual Property Rights
UN	United Nations
UNCTAD	United Nations Conference on Trade and Development
USTR	United States Government Office of the Trade Representative
VER	Voluntary export restraint
VIE	Voluntary import expansions
VRA	Voluntary restraint agreement
WTO	World Trade Organisation
WTO DSB	World Trade Organisation Dispute Settlement Body

1

Introduction

Modern business operates in a world that is highly economically integrated, but that remains politically, culturally and legally diverse. Notwithstanding globalisation, law and politics is still organised primarily on the basis of nation-states. National laws reflect significant social and political differences between nations. A fragmented international regulatory environment has evolved in which each government has developed its own unique approach to the regulation of conduct that affects its territory, often without regard to the effect of that regulation on other nations.

Competition law (or 'antitrust law' as it is known in the United States) is one form of such regulation. Competition law involves laws that promote or maintain market competition by regulating anti-competitive conduct. However, modern competition laws have traditionally evolved to promote and maintain competition in markets principally within the territorial boundaries of each nation-state. Domestic competition laws are not usually concerned with activity beyond territorial borders unless it has significant domestic effects.

This limited territorial approach has created difficulties in an increasingly globalised world in which transactions subsume multiple territorial spaces. Anti-competitive conduct may have adverse economic effects in multiple jurisdictions, unconfined by territorial boundaries. In this manner, while competition law remains essentially national, competition issues have become increasingly international, creating a regulatory disjunction. To the extent the effect of anti-competitive conduct crosses territorial boundaries, it may escape effective regulation.

On the one hand, *under-regulation* may occur. Anti-competitive conduct may not be prevented due to ineffective regulation, particularly as firms have every incentive to structure their arrangements to arbitrage cross-border regulatory differences. Conversely, *over-regulation* may occur. Legitimate competition may be impeded by excessive regulation, particularly where regulation aggregates over multiple jurisdictions.

Historically, to address perceived under-regulation of anti-competitive conduct, nations commenced applying their domestic competition laws on an extraterritorial basis to regulate foreign anti-competitive practices with adverse effects on their domestic markets. As identified in Chapter 3 of this book, such extraterritorial application of competition laws remains limited and has created significant jurisdictional conflict.

More recently, to address both under-regulation and over-regulation, nations have sought to negotiate bilateral co-operation agreements in relation to competition law matters. As identified in Chapter 5 of this book, while such bilateral agreements clearly assist, they do have clear limitations. As a result, international attention has turned to the possibility of negotiating a multilateral agreement on competition law, referred to in this book as an 'international competition agreement'.

Historically, the potential for an international competition agreement has been recognised by several initiatives. In 1945, in negotiations preceding the adoption of the General Agreement on Tariffs and Trade ('GATT'), limited international competition obligations were proposed within the *Charter for an International Trade Organisation*. While these obligations were not adopted within the GATT at its inception in 1947, a number of attempts were subsequently made to incorporate competition provisions. In 1994, with the conclusion of the Uruguay Round of GATT Multilateral Negotiations, the World Trade Organisation ('WTO') was created. The *Agreement Establishing the WTO* included a range of limited provisions addressing various cross-border competition issues on a sector-specific basis

Following further consideration of international competition issues, a formal WTO Working Group on the Interaction Between Trade and Competition Policy was established by a WTO Ministerial Conference in Singapore in 1996. The WTO Working Group has investigated various issues relating to the incorporation of competition law and policy into the WTO. Other organisations, such as the World Bank, the Organisation for Economic Co-operation and Development ('OECD'), and the International Bar Association, have also contributed to the analysis under a variety of different initiatives. More recently, WTO Ministerial Conferences in Doha (2001) and Cancún (2003), have contemplated formal WTO negotiations on competition law and policy.

Accordingly, international competition issues now have a prominent position on the international trade policy agenda.

With this background in mind, this book proposes that an international competition agreement should be incorporated into the WTO in the form identified in this book.

INTRODUCTION

	Proposal
	A plurilateral competition agreement should be incorporated into the WTO in the form identified in this book.

Parts of this book	Chapters of this book
An international competition agreement is desirable (*Part I*).	An international competition agreement is desirable and would be welfare-enhancing relative to the status quo (*Chapters 2 and 3*).
	There is a sufficient basis for an international competition agreement (*Chapter 4*).
	Existing initiatives towards the regulation of cross-border anti-competitive conduct have clear limitations that could be overcome by an international competition agreement (*Chapter 5*).
The WTO could provide a suitable institutional vehicle for an international competition agreement (*Part II*).	The WTO could provide a suitable institutional vehicle for an international competition agreement. The relationship between international trade law and international competition law can be reconciled at a theoretical level by the concept of market contestability (*Chapter 6*).
	At a practical level, an international competition agreement could address under-regulation and over-regulation in the trade-competition regulatory matrix, realising substantive benefits to international trade and competition (*Chapters 7, 8 and 9*).
The optimal form for an international competition agreement at the present time would be a plurilateral WTO agreement in the form identified in this book (*Part III*).	The WTO would provide the optimal institutional vehicle for an international competition agreement (*Chapter 10*).
	The optimal content, approach and structure for a WTO competition agreement can be clearly ascertained (*Chapters 10, 11 and 12*).
	A multilateral WTO competition agreement would not be politically achievable at the present time. However, a plurilateral WTO competition agreement would be politically achievable (*Chapter 13*).
	Bearing the above in mind, a plurilateral agreement should be incorporated into the WTO in the form set out in the Appendix to this book (*Chapter 14, Appendix*).

Figure 1: *Structure of this book*

In order to work through these issues systematically, this book is divided into three main parts as identified in Figure 1:

- Part I of this book identifies that an international competition agreement is desirable. Such an agreement would be welfare-enhancing and would address externalities in the cross-border regulation of competition. There is a sufficient basis for such an agreement. Existing initiatives towards the regulation of cross-border anti-competitive conduct have clear limitations that could be overcome by such an agreement.
- Part II of this book identifies that the WTO could provide a suitable institutional vehicle for an international competition agreement. The relationship between international trade law and international competition law can be reconciled at a theoretical level by the concept of market contestability. At a practical level, an international competition agreement could address under-regulation and over-regulation in the trade–competition regulatory matrix, realising substantive benefits to international trade and competition.
- Part III of this book identifies that the optimal form for an international competition agreement would be a plurilateral WTO agreement. A multilateral WTO competition agreement would not be politically achievable at this time. This book concludes by identifying the appropriate content and structure for a plurilateral WTO competition agreement and proposes a draft negotiating text with accompanying commentary.

This book is intended to make a substantive contribution to knowledge in this area with the intention of assisting policy-makers, lawyers, diplomats, officials, academics, jurists and experts alike in identifying the basis for, and formulating, an international competition agreement.

PART I

An International Competition Agreement is Desirable

2

Is competition law beneficial?

> Of all human powers operating on the affairs of mankind, none is greater than that of competition.
>
> (Henry Clay, 1832) [1]

Part I of this book establishes that an international competition agreement is desirable.

An important first step in analysing the desirability of an international competition agreement is to determine the extent to which competition law is beneficial. While it is widely assumed that competition law is beneficial, the precise causal reasons why (and the magnitude of those benefits) are not widely understood. This chapter addresses these issues in the following manner:

- Section 2.1 examines the theoretical rationale, modus operandi and philosophy underlying modern competition law. Modern competition law is principally concerned with economic goals, namely promoting the efficient operation of markets in order to maximise social welfare. Section 2.1 concludes that the welfare benefits of competition law are significant.
- Section 2.2 identifies that the efficiency objective of competition law may be complemented by distributional objectives. Such distributional objectives are controversial. Modern competition laws often attempt to reconcile inherent tensions between the objectives of economic efficiency and distributional fairness.
- Section 2.3 examines the relationship between competition law and other economic policies. Competition law is the principal instrument of competition policy and creates an environment conducive to sectoral deregulation. Section 2.3 identifies that such deregulation itself has a significant impact on economic welfare.

---

[1] Henry Clay, American statesman, Secretary of State and Presidential Candidate, *Speech to the American Senate*, 1832.

Chapter 2 confirms that competition law has a significant positive effect on economic welfare. Competition law deters anti-competitive conduct that may otherwise result in welfare losses to society. Competition law also supports sectoral deregulation, which may have significant positive welfare effects. In this manner, competition law is clearly beneficial.

2.1 What is competition law and what is its rationale and philosophy?

2.1.1 The role of competition in promoting market efficiency

It is common knowledge that competition law is concerned with the promotion and maintenance of competition for the benefit of society. However, the precise rationale, philosophy, modus operandi and causal theory behind competition law are relatively complex and not so well known. An understanding of this background is essential when determining whether competition law is, in fact, beneficial.

The intellectual foundation and conceptual framework for competition law is provided by neoclassical microeconomic theory. As such, the rationale, philosophy and causal theory underlying competition law closely reflect the assumptions, reasoning, and philosophy underlying neoclassical microeconomic theory. Indeed, the starting point for an understanding of the rationale behind competition law is to understand the microeconomic theory concept of a 'market', the perceived benefits of market efficiency, the role of competition, and their causal inter-relationship. In particular, it is necessary to understand that:

- markets allocate scarce resources between competing end uses;
- economic efficiency refers to the optimal use and allocation of such resources by markets, thereby maximising social welfare;
- competition enhances market efficiency;
- market power is anathema to competitive processes and, in the presence of market power, markets may not maximise social welfare; and
- competition law regulates market power in order to promote competition, thereby enhancing economic efficiency and increasing social welfare.

Each of these elements are considered in turn below.

Markets allocate scarce resources between competing end uses   At its most basic level, the discipline of economics involves the study of the allocation of society's scarce resources between competing end uses and

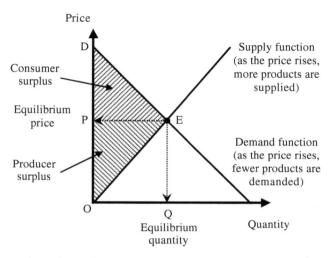

Figure 2: *Neoclassical (Marshallian) graphical representation of a market.*[6]

The market demand function will change over time for such reasons as changes in real disposable consumer income and changes in consumer preferences.

The market model used by neoclassical economics involves the realisation of a market equilibrium (E) by the interaction of consumer demand with producer supply. The equilibrium price (P) and quantity (Q) occur where the level of supply meets the level of demand such that an equilibrium number of market transactions occur.

Producers realise area (PEQO) in revenue to cover their costs and make a profit; equivalent to the total amount paid by consumers. Consumers realise a surplus utility after paying producers equivalent to triangle (DEP), known as 'consumer surplus'. Producers realise a surplus equivalent to triangle (PEO), known as 'producer surplus'.

In neoclassical microeconomic theory, a market transaction occurs when a particular producer and consumer agree on a price for a particular product. The point of coincidence of demand by consumers with supply by producers is known in neoclassical microeconomic theory as the 'market equilibrium' (E), as illustrated by Figure 2, and is the point at which an equilibrium number of transactions occur in the market.[7]

---

[6] A similar diagram can be found in almost any basic economics textbook and dates from Alfred Marshall's *Principles of Economics* (1890).

[7] The Marshallian model set out in Figure 2 is a *partial* equilibrium model, as it identifies the equilibrium in a single market, not the full economy.

This market equilibrium has two effects:

- first, it allocates supply to those producers that use the least resources; and
- second, it allocates consumption to those consumers that value the product the most.

The equilibrium price (P) acts as a signal to influence future production and consumption decisions.

A 'market' is then defined as the geographic field of rivalry between producers (or consumers) in respect of the supply (or demand) of the product over a particular time period. Furthermore, 'competition' is usually defined as the extent of actual and potential rivalry between producers for the patronage of consumers within this market in price and non-price terms.[8] Essentially, a market is the conceptual space–time arena for competitive behaviour.

A branch of microeconomic theory known as 'welfare economics' takes this analysis a step further and identifies the *welfare effects* of this market mechanism.[9] In Figure 2, the difference between the amount paid out to producers by consumers (area PEQO), and the total utility gain realised by consumers (area DEQO) is known as 'consumer surplus' and is the net welfare benefit accruing to consumers from the market transactions (i.e., area of triangle DEP).[10] The converse of consumer surplus is 'producer surplus' (i.e., area of triangle PEO) and is the net welfare benefit accruing to producers.[11] The aggregate of the consumer surplus and producer surplus is known as 'total surplus' and is the traditional welfare economics measure of welfare gains arising from market transactions.[12]

Economic efficiency refers to the optimal allocation of resources The concept of 'economic efficiency' refers to the optimal and timely allocation and use of society's scarce resources to maximise social welfare. If every market were efficient, the combination of outputs with the highest attainable social value would be produced from society's available

---

[8] Competition can also be used to refer to rivalry between consumers.
[9] Welfare economics is a normative branch of microeconomic theory concerned with the manner in which economic activity *ought* to be arranged to maximise economic welfare.
[10] Consumer surplus represents the additional utility gain by consumers arising because some consumers pay less than they were willing to pay.
[11] Producer surplus represents a revenue gain by producers above the amount they would have otherwise have been willing to accept. Producer surplus is often defined as the difference between aggregate producer revenue and the variable costs of production.
[12] These measures are controversial. If income effects are significant, an income-compensated demand curve must be used.

resources, maximising the 'total economic welfare' of society and eliminating any waste.

The standard economic concept of efficiency is 'Pareto efficiency' which refers to a situation where it is impossible to make a 'Pareto improvement': a reallocation of resources that would increase the welfare of at least one person without decreasing the welfare of anyone else.[13] A Pareto improvement is possible if an economy has idle resources or market failures. However, the concept of a Pareto improvement has minimal practical application as it does not recognise net welfare effects. Accordingly, economists developed a more sophisticated concept, known as a 'Kaldor-Hicks efficiency improvement' ('KHE improvement').[14] A KHE improvement refers to a reallocation of resources where those gaining welfare could hypothetically fully compensate those losing welfare, yet still benefit from a net welfare improvement. KHE improvements provide the underlying rationale for the 'cost–benefit' analysis in widespread use by policy-makers today. Importantly, every KHE improvement increases total economic welfare.[15]

There are three fundamental types of economic efficiency recognised by modern neoclassical microeconomic theory. Microeconomic theory reasons that a net improvement in any of these kinds of efficiency will improve the level of total economic welfare of society via a KHE improvement:

- *Allocative efficiency* is achieved where market processes lead resources to be allocated to their highest valued use among all competing uses. Accordingly, suppliers will allocate products to those consumers willing to attribute the highest value to them, maximising the welfare of both producers and consumers.[16] This is illustrated by Figure 2 in which the 'total surplus' (area DEO) is maximised once the market reaches equilibrium. An improvement in allocative efficiency will involve products being allocated to a more valued use, thereby increasing welfare.

---

[13] See, for example, the discussion on the concept of Pareto efficiency in J. Oser & S. L. Bruce, *The Evolution of Economic Thought* (Jovanovich, San Diego, 1988).
[14] The concept of 'Kaldor-Hicks efficiency' is defined as a situation in which it is not possible to make a KHE improvement, being a narrow definition of efficiency. The broader and more practical concept of 'Pareto efficiency' is therefore favoured as a more appropriate efficiency objective.
[15] Every Pareto improvement is necessarily a KHE improvement.
[16] Specifically, consumer welfare is optimised when, for each product, the price is equal to the lowest real resource cost of supplying that product, including a normal profit to suppliers (typically Price = Marginal Cost).

- *Productive efficiency* is achieved where products are produced at the minimum possible total cost with available technology. Production is thus undertaken by least-cost firms using as few resources in production as possible.[17] Productive efficiency involves both an optimal mix of cost-minimising inputs (technical efficiency) and maximum effort to ensure cost-minimisation (behavioural efficiency or X-efficiency). An improvement in productive efficiency will reduce production costs and shift the supply function in Figure 2 to the right, thereby increasing the 'total surplus'.
- *Dynamic efficiency* usually refers to the rate of technological innovation. Producers can utilise new technology to improve the quality of their products and increase productive efficiency. Dynamic efficiency ensures that firms continually innovate and develop better technologies to reduce costs over time.[18] An improvement in dynamic efficiency boosts the rate of innovation and accelerates the rate of realisation of productive efficiency gains over time.

Competition enhances economic efficiency In microeconomic theory, competition is viewed as the prime mechanism for promoting economic efficiency. However, the issue arises, exactly *how* does competition and competition law promote each kind of efficiency? The answer to these issues is not straightforward and Professor Scherer, in a leading article in this area in 1997, described this issue as 'hopelessly difficult'.[19] Yet a general understanding of the casual relationship between competition and efficiency is critical to the analysis whether competition law is beneficial, underpinning the desirability of any international competition agreement.

Initially, one can identify static effects. Producers have an incentive to maximise producer surplus and therefore continually strive to optimise production while minimising production costs. Producers with the lowest production costs will be rewarded with the greatest producer surplus so will have the greatest incentive to produce. Consumers who most value the product will benefit from the greatest gain in consumer surplus so will have the greatest incentive to consume. Rivalry between producers for the patronage of consumers will ensure that products are offered to

---

[17] Specifically, in the longrun the average cost of production of each producer is no greater than the minimum long-run average cost of production.
[18] See, for example, discussion in J. Schumpeter, *Capitalism, Socialism and Democracy* (3rd edn, Harper & Brothers, New York, 1950).
[19] See F. M. Scherer, 'Antitrust, Efficiency and Progress' (1987) 62 *New York University Law Review* 998.

consumers at an equilibrium price that balances production costs against consumers' willingness to pay. Allocative and productive efficiency are therefore promoted by competition. The process of competitive rivalry leads to KHE improvements.[20]

In the 1950s, new mathematical approaches enabled the development of economic theorems to model more precisely the causal relationship between competition and efficiency. The 'First Fundamental Theorem of Welfare Economics' postulates that a competitive equilibrium will *always* be Pareto efficient in circumstances of perfect competition if various assumptions hold.[21] In such theoretical circumstances, the relative prices of resources will precisely indicate their relative scarcity, and products will be produced at the lowest possible cost only to the extent they are valued by consumers, so no waste will occur.

However, in practice markets rarely, if ever, operate perfectly, but instead have inherent structural weaknesses (or 'market failures') that impede them from achieving an efficient outcome, including externalities, imperfect information and imperfect competition.[22] Indeed, the criteria required for perfect competition are so stringent that it is unlikely any real-world market could ever satisfy them; rather *imperfect* competition is ubiquitous.

Economists have sought to understand the implications of imperfect competition and utilised the 'Theory of Second Best'. The Theory of Second Best provides the insight that where market imperfections occur in *any* market, the equilibrium conditions may change in *all* markets.[23] Furthermore, while government regulatory intervention has the *potential* to offset market imperfections and restore equilibrium conditions as close as possible to their optimal result, the Theory of Second Best suggests that there remains an inherent risk that intervention to correct market imperfections in one market may exacerbate market imperfections in other markets: a dilemma for policy-makers. The Theory of Second Best

---

[20] Competition has two principal benefits: (a) it creates continued incentives for market participants to act in a manner consistent with greater efficiency; and (b) it ensures that any efficiencies are passed through the supply chain to benefit end-consumers.

[21] These assumptions include: utility maximisation by consumers; stable preferences; rational profit maximisation by producers; stable technologies; perfect information; costless transactions; perfect competition; homogeneous products; no barriers to entry; a complete set of markets; and that producers are price takers.

[22] See, for example, R. H. Coase, 'The Problem of Social Costs' (1960) 3 *Journal of Law and Economics* 1.

[23] See R. G. Lipsey & K. Lancaster, 'The General Theory of Second Best' (1956) 24(1) *Review of Economic Studies* 11–24.

has therefore led policy-makers to conclude that governments should exercise caution when intervening in markets and should only intervene where such intervention can accurately identify and optimally address the offending market imperfections.

Given the difficulty in accurately identifying the optimal regulatory intervention in a 'second best' world, modern regulatory theory adopts an approach based on approximation and general presumption. Simplistically, this typically involves the 'cost–benefit' ranking of regulatory policies based on their potential for maximising KHE improvements. Modern regulatory theory generally concludes that the most beneficial strategy for policy-makers is to remove market imperfections by the most direct means to reduce unintended adverse spillover effects on other markets and maximise KHE improvements.[24]

Consistent with this strategy, the modern theory of industrial organisation suggests that, as a general presumption, the more *competitive* a market, the more *efficient* that market will be.[25] This conclusion indicates a positive correlation between competition and efficiency and suggests a role for governments in regulating imperfect competition to achieve more competitive market outcomes, thereby realising KHE improvements.

Accordingly, such theories and general presumptions collectively establish the theoretical justification for modern competition law and its objective of promoting competition to increase economic efficiency.

2.1.2 Competition law enhances static efficiency and increases economic welfare

'Competition law' may be perceived as a policy instrument premised on microeconomic theory in which the government deliberately intervenes in the economy to enhance market efficiency by correcting market failures. Competition law is justified by policy-makers on the basis that if governments did not intervene, competition would be sub-optimal and therefore markets would not operate as efficiently as they otherwise could. The optimal extent of regulatory intervention remains controversial and is subject

---

[24] See, for example, discussion in J. Bhagwati, 'The Generalised Theory of Domestic Distortions and Welfare' in J. Bhagwati (ed.), *Trade, Balance of Payments and Growth* (OUP, New York, 1971).

[25] This conclusion represents the aggregation of results from a diverse array of economic models relating to imperfect competition, as supported by empirical evidence. See discussion in F. M. Scherer & D. Ross, *Industrial Market Structure & Economic Performance* (3rd edn, Houghton, New York, 1990), which establishes the case for competition law.

to several competing schools of thought. For example, while the 'Chicago School' has traditionally advocated minimal regulatory intervention, the 'Harvard School' has usually advocated greater intervention.[26]

More specifically, competition law is intended to regulate against the aggregation of market power. Market power is a result of imperfect competition and a cause of market failure. Increased market power provides market participants with an increased ability to influence the market price for their own profit-maximising benefit, to the detriment of market efficiency. In *Mexico – Measures Affecting Telecommunications Services* the WTO Panel reasoned:[27]

> A firm has market power if it has the ability profitably to maintain prices above competitive levels for a significant period of time . . .

Competition law assumes that the behaviour of market participants must be regulated so that they do not seek to increase their individual or collective market power by engaging in anti-competitive behaviour, known as 'behavioural regulation'. Competition law also assumes that firms must be prevented from merging with other firms in a manner that unduly increases their market power, known as 'structural regulation'. As the potential for anti-competitive conduct exists in all markets, competition law is usually given generic application across all markets to prevent such conduct.

Modern competition law therefore utilises a blend of behavioural and structural regulation to regulate:

(a) the use of existing individual market power (known as 'anti-monopoly laws');
(b) the concerted behaviour of market participants, thereby regulating their use and acquisition of collective market power (known as 'concerted conduct laws'); and
(c) the merger of market participants, therefore regulating their structural acquisition of market power (known as 'merger laws').

The theoretical basis for each form of regulation is set out below and is discussed in detail in Chapter 4 of this book.

Anti-monopoly laws Historically, Adam Smith was one of the first to articulate that competition could be thwarted by *'the great engine of* . . .

---

[26] See, for example, R. A. Posner, 'The Chicago School of Antitrust Analysis' (1979) 127 *University of Pennsylvania Law Review* 935.
[27] See *Mexico – Measures Affecting Telecommunications Services*, WT/DS204/R, Report of the WTO Panel, 2 April 2004, para. 7.153.

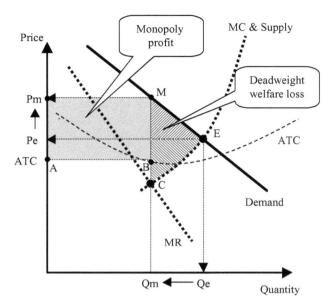

Figure 3: *Neoclassical representation of monopoly pricing*

monopoly.[28] His insight was that excessive market power may lead the market mechanism to fail to allocate scarce resources as efficiently as it otherwise could.

In particular, firms with substantial market power have a greater ability to influence prices within a market as their production will represent a significant proportion of market supply and they will be less subject to competitive constraints imposed by rivals. In an extreme situation of absolute market power, a monopolist can deliberately reduce production (Qe→Qm) and raise its prices to meet demand at that level of production (Pe→Pm), without fear of competition, as illustrated by the neoclassical representation of monopoly pricing in Figure 3. Accordingly, the monopolist may increase the market price, and reduce quantity supplied into the market, to a level that realises its own profit-maximising objective. Such behaviour diverts welfare from consumers to the monopolist (i.e. consumer surplus is converted to producer surplus). More importantly, such behaviour causes a deadweight loss in social welfare, as illustrated by the shaded triangle (area CME) in Figure 3, which represents a loss

---

[28] See A. Smith, *An Inquiry into the Nature and Cause of the Wealth of Nations* (1776), Book I, ch. 10, para. IV.7.175 (5th edn annotated reprint, Methuen, London, 1904); published on the internet at http://www.econlib.org/library/Smith/smWN.htm

in allocative efficiency because the market no longer reaches competitive equilibrium.

In the presence of competition, the market equilibrium would be E (Pe, Qe).

A monopolist maximises its profits by reducing the quantity it supplies from Qe to Qm, being the point at which the marginal revenue (MR) it realises from an additional unit equals its marginal cost of producing that unit (MC). The monopolist is the only supplier, hence the market supply function is equivalent to the monopolist's supply function.

In the absence of competition, the monopolist can increase its prices from Pe to Pm to meet demand at quantity Qm giving a new equilibrium M (Pm, Qm). As the new price is significantly above its average total cost B, the monopolist realises a monopoly profit (rectangle PmMBA). This behaviour also causes a 'deadweight loss' in total surplus (triangle MEC), indicating a loss in allocative efficiency and welfare.

The quantum of the aggregate loss in *allocative* efficiency associated with monopoly pricing in the United States economy was famously calculated by Harberger in 1954 at 0.1% of Gross National Product (GNP).[29] Subsequent studies have been inconclusive in validating these findings, although the general consensus in the literature is that the magnitude of allocative efficiency losses associated with monopoly pricing in the US economy are typically between 0.5% and 2% of GNP.[30] Based on such studies many theorists challenged why competition law was necessary given that such amounts appeared trivial.

However, welfare losses do not arise from allocative efficiency losses alone. Net productive efficiency losses associated with monopoly pricing have been estimated as being significantly greater in magnitude than allocative efficiency losses. Productive efficiency losses may include poor behavioural incentives to reduce costs, known as 'X-inefficiency', leading to technical inefficiency.[31] Productive efficiency losses may also arise from rent-seeking and defensive behaviour by the monopolist, involving the expenditure of resources on non-productive activities such as government lobbying, litigation and advertising to protect monopoly positions. While the literature indicates such costs are difficult to accurately quantify,

---

[29] See A. Harberger, 'Monopoly and Resource Allocation' (1954) 21 *American Economic Review* 77.

[30] See, for example, D. A. Kamershen, 'An Estimation of Welfare Losses from Monopoly in the American Economy' (1966) 17 *Western Economic Journal* 221.

[31] See, for example, H. Leibenstein, 'Allocative Efficiency vs X-Efficiency' (1966) 56 *American Economic Review* 392.

Scherer and Ross tentatively concluded in 1970 that the likely technical efficiency costs of monopoly pricing to the US economy were in the magnitude of 3% to 12% of GNP.[32]

Importantly, anti-monopoly laws do not usually directly regulate monopoly pricing to prevent such conduct. Rather, anti-monopoly laws usually prevent firms unfairly increasing their market power, reducing the potential for such pricing. Anti-monopoly laws therefore minimise the scope for the welfare losses identified above. Anti-monopoly laws achieve this by preventing firms with existing substantial market power from using that market power to impede market entry or unfairly damage existing competitors. The characteristics of anti-monopoly laws are outlined in Chapter 4 of this book.

Concerted conduct laws and merger laws Some degree of co-operation is an important facet of modern business organisation. Individuals and businesses must co-operate to some extent to co-ordinate their business activities and achieve their commercial objectives. However, such co-operation is anathema to market competition as it reduces the level of rivalry between firms in the market. By co-operating, firms may be able to increase their market power and thus engage in the same kind of conduct that a firm with significant market power can engage in, including monopoly pricing. A merger may be viewed as an extreme form of co-operation in which co-operative conduct is internalised within a single legal entity.

The incentives towards anti-competitive conduct should not be underestimated. As Adam Smith cynically commented in 1776: 'People of the same trade seldom meet together, even for merriment and diversion, but the conversation ends in conspiracy against the public, or in some contrivance to raise prices'.[33] With this in mind, competition law seeks to determine the appropriate mix between competition and co-operation in the economy by identifying the legal parameters for co-operative activity. Merger laws regulate the internalisation of co-operative activity. The characteristics of concerted conduct laws and merger laws are outlined in Chapter 4 of this book.

However, in regulating co-operative activity, competition laws should be careful not to prohibit inadvertently co-operative conduct that increases net welfare. Co-operative activity, for example, may enable firms

---

[32] See F. M. Scherer & D. Ross, *Industrial Market Structure & Economic Performance* (3rd edn, Houghton, New York, 1990), ch. 18, p. 678.
[33] See Smith, above n. 28, Book I, ch. 10, para. I.10.82.

to realise economies of scope and scale, thereby reducing their production costs and increasing productive efficiency. In this manner, the task of competition law under a comparative static efficiency analysis has been perceived as maximising total surplus via a KHE improvement: requiring that any gain in total surplus due to net productive efficiency gains exceeds any loss in total surplus due to allocative efficiency losses.

A number of empirical surveys have sought to quantify the detriments of collusive conduct and concentrated markets and the corresponding benefits of concerted conduct laws and merger laws.[34] A study of industries in six developed countries by Caves in 1990 concluded, for example, that increased market power associated with greater industry concentration caused a material reduction in productive and allocative efficiency.[35] The OECD noted in 2000 that it has proved impossible to date to quantify reliably the global welfare losses caused by collusive conduct, although such losses are generally regarded as significant.[36] Other research has identified that the presence of competition law promotes competition and reduces efficiency losses.[37]

In summary, competition law acts as a statutory mechanism to preserve and promote market competition and prevent the aggregation of excessive market power. There is clear empirical evidence that excessive market power leads to welfare losses as a result of allocative and productive inefficiency. There is corresponding empirical evidence that competition law is beneficial in reducing the scope for welfare losses by preventing excessive aggregation of market power.

2.1.3 Competition law enhances dynamic efficiency and increases economic growth

In addition to these static effects, excessive market power has significant dynamic effects. As identified by the World Bank, UNCTAD and the WTO, competition law can act as an important catalyst for long-term

---

[34] See, for example, UNCTAD, 'Empirical Evidence of the Benefits from Applying Competition Law and Policy to Economic Development in Order to Attain Greater Efficiency in International Trade', UNCTAD Discussion Paper, TD/B/COM.2/EM/10/Rev.1, 25 May 1998, para. 11.
[35] See R. E. Caves, *Industrial Efficiency in Six Nations* (MIT Press, Cambridge, 1992).
[36] See OECD, *Hard Core Cartels* (OECD, Paris, 2000), p. 7.
[37] See, for example, G. J. Werden, 'A Review of the Empirical and Experimental Evidence of the Relationship Between Market Structure and Market Performance', US Department of Justice, EAG Discussion Paper, 91–3.

welfare accumulation and sustainable economic growth by preventing the accumulation of excessive market power and promoting competition.[38] The precise causal mechanism by which increased competition impacts upon economic growth is beyond the scope of this book, but can be perceived in terms of three inter-related steps, forming a cumulative causation cycle:

- *Increased rate of technological progress* Markets motivate the behaviour of producers by rewarding good performance and penalising poor performance in a process akin to Darwinian natural selection. The hope of gain and the fear of loss continually guide producers to optimise production, to reduce costs and to invent and innovate. Competition motivates greater entrepreneurial activity as firms seek to obtain a strategic advantage over their competitors.[39] Invention and innovation is a key driver of economic growth.
- *Increases in productive and allocative efficiency* Similarly, competition ensures that producers continually improve their productive efficiency over time by continually reducing costs.[40] Competition also ensures that price signals remain optimal and assist market responsiveness in achieving allocative efficiency by ensuring production is continually optimised in line with the changing demands of consumers. Incremental improvements in productive and allocative efficiency will compound over time.[41]
- *Capital accumulation and cumulative causation* The efficiency gains identified above drive economic growth via a process of cumulative causation. Increases in consumer surplus lead to real welfare gains to consumers, permitting increased savings and further driving demand. Increases in producer surplus lead to greater profits by producers and permit reinvestment in human and physical capital, leading to greater

---

[38] See WTO, 'Synthesis Paper on the Relationship of Trade and Competition Policy to Economic Growth', WTO Paper, WT/WGTCP/W/80, Geneva, 18 September 1998. See *The East Asian Miracle: A World Bank Policy Research Report* (World Bank, Oxford University Press, 1993). See also UNCTAD, *The Development Dimension of Competition Law and Policy* (UNCTAD, Geneva, 1999).
[39] See, for example, J. A. Schumpeter, *Capitalism, Socialism and Democracy* (Harper & Brothers, New York, 1942). Intellectual property laws may be necessary to reward invention via appropriable profits.
[40] See, for example, J. L. Anderson, *Explaining Long-term Economic Change* (Macmillan, London, 1991).
[41] See R. M. Solow, 'A Contribution to the Theory of Economic Growth' (1956) 70 *Quarterly Journal of Economics* 65.

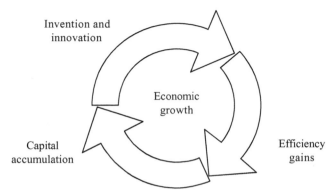

Figure 4: *Cumulative causation cycle of economic growth*

capital accumulation.[42] Capital accumulation enables greater research and development, promoting innovation and technological change and hence the realisation of efficiency gains, in a virtuous cycle, as illustrated by Figure 4.[43]

Dynamic efficiency affects the speed of this causation cycle. Higher economic growth *rates* (i.e. real GDP per capita growth) result from greater dynamic efficiency. The causal benefits of competition in increasing dynamic efficiency, and thus economic growth, have been subjected to detailed empirical analysis.[44] By way of example:

- In the United Kingdom, an empirical study of 670 companies by Nickell in 1996 determined that greater market power led to lower productivity growth, while increased competition promoted higher rates of productivity growth.[45] Similarly, as the World Bank recently identified in its *World Development Report 2002*, a number of other studies concentrated on industrial countries have found a positive relationship between competition, efficiency and the rate of productivity growth.[46]

---

[42] See, for example, discussion in D. C. North, & R. P. Thomas, 'An Economic Theory of the Growth of the Western World' (1970) 2 *Economic History Review* 23.
[43] See T. W. Swan, 'Economic Growth and Capital Accumulation' (1956) 32 *Economic Record* 334.
[44] See, for example, OECD, 'Innovation, Firm Size and Market Structure: Schumpeterian Hypothesis – Some New Themes', OECD Economics Department Working Paper No. 161, OECD, Paris, 1996.
[45] See S. Nickell, 'Competition and Corporate Performance' (1996) 104 *Journal of Political Economy* 4.
[46] See World Bank, *Building Institutions for Markets: World Development Report 2002* (World Bank, Washington DC, 2001), ch. 7.

- A study by the World Bank and European Bank for Reconstruction and Development in 1999 involved 3,000 small and medium enterprises in 20 transition economies. This study determined that competition from one to three rivals was important in explaining innovation, including a firm's decision to launch new products.[47]
- Empirical research has identified a negative correlation between market power and the rate of price adjustment. Oligopolistic markets, for example, suffer from more sluggish price responses than competitive markets and more frequently suffer excess capacity. Increases in market concentration and market power have been empirically determined to dampen innovative activity.

Furthermore, the specific effects of competition *law* on economic growth have also been assessed by various studies:

- A World Bank study in 2000 concluded that the effectiveness of competition law enforcement was positively correlated with long run economic growth to a high degree of statistical significance.[48]
- Empirical research has concluded that competition law has a significant positive impact on dynamic efficiency. Data relating to the telecommunications industry in OECD countries has confirmed that competition law has promoted competition and led to significant levels of technological innovation.[49]
- More significantly, in 1987, Scherer undertook an extensive review of the available empirical evidence and concluded that dynamic efficiency gains from competition law would, in most instances, be greater than any productive or allocative efficiency gains.[50] Furthermore, the cumulative nature of economic growth would mean that reductions in productivity due to dynamic inefficiency would otherwise be compounded over time, amounting to a very significant welfare loss.

The empirical evidence in a dynamic context therefore indicates that the welfare benefits of competition law are significant. Such welfare effects arise from the maintenance of competition in the face of incentives for firms to engage in anti-competitive conduct. Welfare effects are compounded over time and are critical to economic growth.

---

[47] See European Bank for Reconstruction and Development, *Transition Report 1999: Ten Years of Transition* (EBRD, London, 1999).
[48] See M. A. Dutz & A. Hayri, 'Does More Intense Competition Lead to Higher Growth?', World Bank Research Paper No. 2320, World Bank, Washington DC, April 2000.
[49] See OECD, *Regulatory Reform, Privatisation and Competition Policy* (OECD, Paris, 1992).
[50] See Scherer, above n. 19, at 1010 to 1018.

In summary, competition law may prevent anti-competitive conduct that may otherwise reduce or prevent competition. In doing so, competition law directly prevents welfare losses associated with excessive market power and reduced incentives to innovate. The empirical evidence indicates that the static and dynamic benefits of competition law are significant.

2.2 Distributional fairness as a co-objective of competition law

2.2.1 Social choice theory, social justice and distributional equity

While the principal objective of competition law is to promote economic efficiency, competition laws may also be used by governments as a policy vehicle to achieve distributional objectives simultaneously so as to achieve greater 'social equity'. Such distributional objectives remain controversial. Furthermore, different governments give different weight to considerations of efficiency and equity when formulating their respective competition laws depending on their political preferences. United States competition law arguably gives pre-eminence to considerations of economic efficiency. European competition law arguably has a greater tendency to reflect considerations of social equity and distributional fairness.

Insights into distributional issues are provided by modern welfare economics which conveniently separates objectives of economic efficiency from more controversial (and political) issues regarding the appropriate distribution of welfare within society. Modern welfare economics reasons that a conceptual 'Grand Utility Possibility Frontier' ('GUPF') can be identified for a production economy, defining the utility-maximising set of Pareto-efficient points that can be achieved by the economy. Each point on the GUPF represents a potential competitive equilibrium that maximises productive and allocative efficiency, hence maximising total economic welfare, as depicted in Figure 5.

The tangency point between the Social Welfare Function and the GUPF is the socially optimal point (S). The Second Fundamental Theorem of Welfare Economics indicates that this socially optimal point can be achieved as a general competitive equilibrium by lump sum transfers of wealth between individuals.

Accordingly, economists developed the 'Second Fundamental Theorem of Welfare Economics' which identifies that an economy may select which general competitive equilibrium it will achieve by way of lump

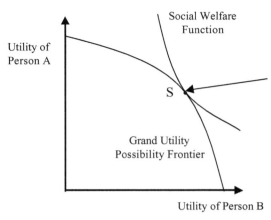

Figure 5: *Representation of the grand utility possibility frontier and identification of the socially optimal point*

sum transfers of welfare between individuals.[51] The method of selecting that general competitive equilibrium is known as 'social choice theory'. Social choice theory relies on a number of competing theories of social justice to select the socially optimal point on the GUPF.[52] The objective of social choice theory is to achieve an allocation of resources that is not only Pareto efficient, but is also socially optimal consistent with a society's prevailing distributional ideals.

Modern regulatory theory concludes that the least distorting, and hence most efficient, way to achieve distributional objectives is via lump sum welfare transfers by the most direct policy instrument. Modern government policy therefore gives effect to social choice theory by directly transferring welfare by such mechanisms as taxation and social welfare handouts. However, as welfare distribution issues weigh heavily on government policy, policy instruments primarily intended to promote economic efficiency objectives, including competition laws, may often incorporate secondary distributional objectives. The tendency to

---

[51] The theorem reasons that if household preferences and firm production sets are convex, if there is a complete set of markets with publicly known prices, and if every agent acts as a price taker, then any Pareto optimal outcome can be achieved as a competitive equilibrium if appropriate lump sum transfers of wealth are arranged.

[52] Influential modern theories of social justice have been proposed by such theorists as John Rawls (1971), Amartya Sen (1970), James Buchanan (1990), and Robert Nozick (1993). See, for example, J. Rawls, *A Theory of Justice* (Harvard UP, Cambridge, 1971). See also R. Nozick, *The Theory of Rationality* (Princeton UP, Princeton, 1993). See also A. K. Sen, *Collective Choice & Social Welfare* (Holden Day, San Francisco, 1970).

incorporate such distributional objectives is greater where such laws are enacted or administered by governments at the left end of the political spectrum.

In a competition law context, such secondary distributional objectives may reflect three distinct types of social justice:

- *'Producer-producer' equity* refers to the redistribution of welfare between different types of producers. Competition laws may be applied in a manner that protects particular types of competitors, for example, such as small and medium-sized enterprises. Competition laws may also prevent conduct by firms that is perceived as commercially 'unfair', even though it may lead to KHE improvements.
- *'Producer-consumer' equity* refers to the redistribution of welfare between producers and consumers. Competition laws may regulate conduct such as price discrimination that would otherwise enable producers to capture a greater proportion of total surplus in the form of producer surplus. Competition law may also increase the relative power of consumers by permitting such conduct as collective bargaining.

  The market mechanism itself distributes welfare between producers and consumers. Increased competition improves allocative efficiency, ensuring that producers do not capture all productive efficiency gains as producer surplus; rather, productive efficiency gains are partly transferred to consumers via reduced prices. However, governments may have different views on the extent to which producers should capture the benefits of productive efficiency gains and may trade-off consumer welfare against producer welfare by permitting greater market concentration.
- *'Consumer-consumer' equity* refers to the redistribution of welfare between different types of consumers. Competition laws can include provisions intended to benefit particular types of consumers disproportionately. However, this is uncommon and usually an indirect result of wider producer-consumer equity issues.

2.2.2 Tensions between the objectives of competition policy

Most commonly, distributional objectives are incorporated into competition laws via the subjective concept of 'fairness'. While the concept of efficiency has a reasonably clear objective economic meaning, the concept of 'fairness' is inherently subjective and is internationally nuanced and culturally distinctive. Different nations emphasise different aspects of fairness in accordance with their different social values, norms, customs and collective preferences. These differences may lead to tensions between different nations as to the appropriate objectives of competition laws.[53]

The historical tensions between the United States and Japan are illustrative.[54] Arguably, the United States has historically been more concerned to promote allocative efficiency and competition, favouring consumer surplus. Japan has historically favoured industrial policies to increase productive efficiency and market concentration, favouring producer surplus.[55] Such international differences inevitably lead to international conflict, as exemplified by the United States allegations in the late 1980s that Japanese competition laws at that time were not being properly enforced.[56]

Furthermore, it is a trite statement that competition law does not operate in a constitutional, political or social vacuum. Competition law complements the overall framework of laws and regulations that seek to promote the general public interest, including product standards, environmental requirements, intellectual property rights, and social welfare programmes.[57] Governments may consider that broader societal considerations require that competition laws are subordinated to long-term social objectives, including full employment, diffusion of economic power and regional development. Common social objectives influencing competition policy have included greater market integration, market opportunities for medium-sized enterprises, the deconcentration of economic power, and furthering a pluralistic economy and society. Competition law may also be affected by various 'populist' political goals.[58]

Given such divergent distributional influences, it is not surprising that the objectives of economic efficiency and distributional fairness frequently conflict and tensions arise. Distributional objectives may not necessarily lead to KHE improvements and can introduce market distortions that reduce total welfare. Modern competition laws often require governments to make difficult trade-offs between social and economic objectives and

---

[53] See M. E. Porter, 'Michael Porter on Competition' (1999) 22 *Antitrust Bulletin* 841.
[54] See discussion in C. F. Bergsten & M. Noland, *Reconcilable Differences: United States–Japan Economic Conflict* (Institute for International Economics, Washington DC, 1993).
[55] See D. E. Rosenthal & M. Matsushita, 'Competition Law in Japan and the West: Can the Approaches be Reconciled?' (1996) 19 *World Competition* 5.
[56] See W. A. Wallis, 'Economics, Foreign Policy and United States–Japan Trade Disputes' (1989) 22 *Cornell International Law Journal* 381, 382.
[57] See E. U. Petersmann, 'The Role of Competition Policy in Providing a More Equitable Playing Field in Globalising Markets: A Challenge for Governments and Multilateral Organisations', Paper presented at pre-UNCTAD X Seminar on the Role of Competition Policy for Development in World Globalising Markets, Geneva, July 1999.
[58] See, for example, the discussion in OECD, *Trade and Competition Policies: Comparing Objectives and Methods* (OECD, Paris, 1994).

attempt to reconcile inherent tensions between these objectives. Yet notwithstanding these complications, competition laws in almost all jurisdictions are recognised as primarily intended to increase economic efficiency by promoting and maintaining competition.

2.3 How does competition law relate to other governmental laws and policies?

There are two distinct mechanisms by which competition law may contribute to greater economic welfare:

- *Direct welfare effects*   As identified in detail above, competition law may prevent anti-competitive conduct that may otherwise reduce or prevent competition. In this manner, competition law directly prevents welfare losses associated with excessive market power and reduced incentives to innovate. The direct welfare effects of competition law were identified above as significant.
- *Indirect welfare effects*   However, competition law may also create an environment conducive to the adoption of deregulatory competition policies and removal of excessive regulation. As identified below, in many cases the adoption of competition law is a pre-condition for such competition policies. These competition policies may also have significant beneficial welfare effects. In this manner, competition law is *indirectly* responsible for some of the welfare gains realised from such competition policies. The indirect effects of competition law are identified below to illustrate further the manner in which competition law is beneficial.

2.3.1 Competition law as the principal instrument of competition policy

The question arises: *what is competition policy?* There are a variety of circumstances beyond competition law alone in which policy-makers have reasoned that government intervention is essential to promote competition in the public interest. These circumstances fall within the domain of government economic policy known as 'competition policy'. The concept of 'competition policy', at its broadest level, encompasses any government policy that addresses the extent, nature and scope for competition in the economy.[59]

---

[59] See, for example, discussion in P. J. Lloyd & K. M. Vautier, *Promoting Competition in Global Markets: A Multinational Approach* (Edward Elgar, UK, 1999).

As with competition law, the *raison d'être* of competition policy is to promote the efficient operation of markets in order to maximise economic welfare. Competition policy thus plays an integral part in the broad set of government policies that aim to enhance market structures and improve the operation of markets so as to improve social welfare. The ideological stance behind competition policy is that markets, when freed from market-obstructing government intervention, achieve a reasonable degree of allocative efficiency while creating the necessary incentives for increased productive and dynamic efficiency.

As such, competition policy is *inherently deregulatory* in character. Competition policy promotes the removal of excessive government regulation from all sectors of the economy so as to promote free markets and greater competition. In doing so, competition policy seeks to substitute heavy-handed government regulation for a light-handed minimalist approach and to shift the economy towards regulatory systems organised to a large extent around competition.[60]

Yet the ideological stance of competition policy is not purely laissez-faire. Competition policy recognises a role for government by acknowledging that market failures do occur, including via imperfect competition. Competition policy therefore endorses minimalist regulation, via competition law and sectoral regulation, to address those market failures, but only to the extent considered necessary in the particular circumstances.[61] To the extent sectoral regulation is required to address particular market failures, competition policy seeks to ensure such regulation remains consistent with the maintenance of market incentives associated with competition.

Elements of competition policy With the above analysis in mind, 'competition policy' thus comprises two essential elements as illustrated by the diagram in Figure 6:

- *Competition law* is focused on the regulation of market power and usually has generic application across all markets. Competition law is the principal legislative instrument for furthering competition policy.[62]

---

[60] See discussion in R. S. Khemani, J. W. Rowley & L. Waverman, 'Competition Policy, Accountability and Economic Adjustment' (1999) *International Business Lawyer* 482.
[61] See, for example, the discussion in World Bank, *Competition Policy in the Global Economy* (World Bank, Washington DC, 1998) regarding the appropriate role of competition policy.
[62] See M. D. Taylor, 'Looking to the Future: Towards the Exclusive Application of Competition Law', Paper presented to the International Bar Association Competition Conference, Budapest, May 2003.

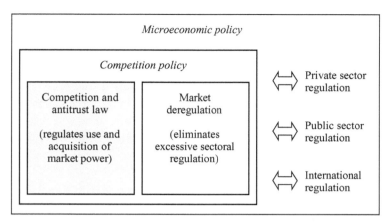

Figure 6: *Diagram illustrating the relationship between competition law and competition policy*

- *Market deregulation* (also known as market liberalisation) is focused on the elimination of excessive government regulation in particular sectors of the economy. Market deregulation gives effect to the conclusion identified above that governments should exercise caution when intervening in markets given the potential for sub-optimal regulation to reduce economic welfare.

Importantly, competition law is complementary to market deregulation:

- Market deregulation provides the means to reduce inefficient governmental regulation, thereby enabling firms to compete without adverse state intervention. Market deregulation is necessary to implement structural reforms that competition law alone would be unable to achieve.
- Competition law provides a means to combat anti-competitive behaviour, ensuring that market competition minimises deadweight welfare losses while redistributing welfare from producers to consumers.

Market deregulation in the absence of competition law creates risks that firms may exploit the absence of regulation to engage in anti-competitive practices that increase market power at the expense of competition. Conversely, the introduction of competition law without market deregulation would simply introduce a further level of regulation that would tend to overlap and replicate existing regulatory structures.

2.3.2 Empirical evidence of the benefits of competition policies

An extensive body of empirical evidence exists indicating that deregulatory competition policy has a significant positive impact on economic welfare by removing excessive regulation. The costs of such excessive regulation have been identified by the literature as significant. Country studies of the United States, Australia and Canada, for example, have concluded as follows:

- Hopkins calculated in 1992 that the net efficiency costs of excessive regulation in the United States were roughly 9.5% of real GDP per capita.[63]
- The OECD calculated in 1996 that the net efficiency costs of excessive regulation in Australia were between 9% and 19% of real GDP per capita.[64]
- Milhar calculated in 1996 that the net efficiency costs of excessive regulation in Canada were roughly 12% of real GDP per capita.[65]

A number of sectoral studies have also identified significant net efficiency costs from excessive regulation, although the extent of these costs is widely variable between nations, depending on the particular regulatory regime adopted for each industry. In the United States, for example, economic regulation associated with international trade, the telecommunications sector, and agricultural price supports, was calculated in 1988 as imposing the greatest regulatory burden.[66]

Against this backdrop of pre-existing costly regulation, the *benefits of deregulation* have been identified as significant.[67] By way of example:

---

[63] See T. D. Hopkins, 'Costs of Regulation: Filling the Gap', Report prepared for the Regulatory Information Service Centre, Washington DC, as referred to by J. L. Guasch & R. W. Hahn, 'The Costs and Benefits of Regulation: Implications for Developing Countries' (1999) 14(1) *World Bank Research Observer* 137.

[64] See OECD, 'Regulatory Reform: A Country Study of Australia', OECD Doc., PUMA/REG(96), OECD, Paris, 1996.

[65] See F. Milhar, 'Regulatory Overkill: The Costs of Regulation in Canada', Research Paper, Fraser Institute, Ottawa, Canada, 1996.

[66] See R. W. Hahn & J. Hird 'The Costs and Benefits of Regulation: Review and Synthesis' (1991) 8 *Yale Journal on Regulation* 233.

[67] Importantly, these studies do not suggest that deregulatory competition policies should completely eliminate regulation. Rather, these studies suggest that more efficient and less interventionist regulations should be adopted so as to reduce distorting effects on market incentives.

- The OECD calculated in 1997 that market deregulation could increase real GDP per capita in the long run by 1% in the United States, 3.5% in the United Kingdom, and 6% in France, Germany and Japan.[68]
- More generally, a comparative review of various European countries in 1993 concluded that there existed a positive correlation between relatively less regulation of product markets, productivity growth and overall economic growth.[69]
- The Australian 'Hilmer' competition policy reforms from 1994 were estimated by the Industry Commission to the Council of Australian Governments as increasing real Australian GDP per capita by 5.5%, while benefiting Australian consumers by almost AU$9 billion.[70] While other commentators have claimed the actual benefits of these reforms amounted to 1% of real GDP per capita, such benefits are still significant in welfare terms.

There are also numerous sectoral studies concluding that removal of excessive regulation may realise significant welfare benefits. These studies generally conclude that the benefits of deregulation are greatest in those sectors historically subject to the most pervasive regulation, namely finance, telecommunications, transportation and energy. The deregulation of seven major United States service industries during the 1980s, for example, was estimated as generating an increase of US$32 billion to 42 billion in consumer surplus and US$3.2 billion in producer surplus, resulting in a real 7% to 9% per capita improvement in that part of GDP affected by the reforms.[71] Agriculture is another sector where significant gains could be realised. Again, a range of anecdotal evidence supports such findings.

In summary, a brief survey of the literature indicates that the welfare costs of excessive regulation are significant. Welfare benefits can be realised by reducing excessive sectoral regulation. While these benefits are associated with deregulatory competition policies, not competition law, they are partially attributable to the existence of underlying competition law. Accordingly, in an indirect causal way, the adoption of competition law is

---

[68] See OECD, *The Economic Effects of Regulatory Reforms* (OECD, Paris, 1997).
[69] See K. Koedijk & J. Kremers, 'Market Opening, Regulation and Growth in Europe' (1992) 23 *Economic Policy* 443.
[70] See Industry Commission to the Council of Australian Governments, *The Growth and Revenue Implications of the Hilmer and Related Reforms* (Australian Government, Canberra, 1995).
[71] See C. Winston, 'Economic Deregulation: Days of Reckoning for Microeconomists' (1993) 31 *Journal of Economic Literature* 1263.

partly responsible for some welfare benefits of deregulatory competition policies.

2.4 Conclusion: competition law is beneficial

In summary, modern competition law is a form of government intervention in the economy that is principally intended to increase economic efficiency so as to increase the total economic welfare of society. Competition law regulates the excessive aggregation of market power via anticompetitive behaviour, ensuring that firms are continually subject to the disciplines of competition. Competition in turn maximises allocative, productive and dynamic efficiency. While empirical evidence of the welfare benefits of competition law is difficult to obtain, the available evidence suggests such benefits are significant.

This economic efficiency objective of competition law may be complemented by distributional objectives. These distributional objectives are diverse and often controversial, but are intended to result in a fairer distribution of welfare in society. Modern competition laws often attempt to reconcile inherent tensions between the objectives of economic efficiency and distributional fairness.

Competition law also has indirect welfare benefits. Competition law may create an environment conducive to the adoption of complementary competition policies. Deregulatory competition policies are intended to reduce excessive governmental regulation that may otherwise reduce competition or distort market incentives. Such competition policies may materially contribute to economic growth and increased social welfare. The benefits of such competition policies have been empirically quantified and are usually significant.

Chapter 2 therefore concludes that competition law is beneficial.

3

Is an international competition agreement desirable?

> We have seldom seen neighbourhood affection among nations. The reverse is almost the universal truth.
>
> (Thomas Jefferson, 1803)[1]

Chapter 2 concluded that competition law is beneficial. Chapter 3 now considers whether an international competition agreement would be desirable. Chapter 3 undertakes this task in the following manner:

- Section 3.1 outlines how trends in globalisation and multinational corporate expansion have exacerbated the risk of cross-border anti-competitive conduct. Such conduct is not currently regulated effectively on an international basis. Section 3.1 identifies that cross-border spill-overs (or 'externalities') provide an important policy justification for an international competition agreement.
- Section 3.2 identifies the current approach of the international community to the regulation of cross-border anti-competitive conduct, namely via the extraterritorial application of competition laws. Section 3.2 identifies inherent difficulties in an extraterritorial approach, including jurisdictional conflict.

While beyond the scope of this book, this chapter also identifies a number of economic models which conclude that greater international co-ordination of competition law would be welfare enhancing where each nation enforces its competition laws on an extraterritorial basis in accordance with its national self-interest. Chapter 3 therefore establishes that an international competition agreement is desirable and would be welfare enhancing relative to the status quo.

---

[1] Letter from Thomas Jefferson to John Breckridge, 12 August 1803.

3.1 The globalisation of competition

3.1.1 Globalisation of the international economy

Over the last three decades the world has experienced a period of unprecedented economic integration. World trade as a proportion of global production increased from some 10% in 1970, to 34% by 2000.[2] Annual foreign direct investment ('FDI') flows have increased by over 20% per annum over the last two decades and peaked in 2001 at US$1.3 trillion, indicating a significant increase in the international activity of corporations.[3] Meanwhile, capital markets have become globally integrated. Capital mobility has increased to the extent that 98% of the average US$1.2 trillion per day crossing the foreign exchange markets of the world is divorced from trade transactions.

During the 1970s and 1980s, this spread of economic activity across national boundaries was termed 'internationalisation'.[4] During the late 1980s and early 1990s, a deeper and more advanced stage of internationalisation was recognised in which economic activity became increasingly functionally integrated on an international basis. The OECD commented in 1994, for example:[5]

> The word 'internationalisation'... has proved too limited... Globalisation is a more recent phenomenon, a more advanced and complex form of internationalisation which implies a degree of functional integration between internationally-dispersed economic activities.

The term 'globalisation' was first applied to this phenomenon in 1985 by Theodore Levitt in *The Globalisation of Markets*.[6] Levitt adopted the term 'globalisation' to describe the process of realising a borderless global economy in which firms engage in international commerce with little regard to national frontiers. The OECD subsequently explained this concept in 1996 in the following terms:[7]

---

[2] See OECD, 'Investment Patterns in Longer-Term Perspective', Working Paper on International Investment No. 2000/2, OECD, Paris, April 2000.
[3] See, e.g. UNCTAD, *World Investment Report 2001* (UNCTAD, New York, 2001).
[4] See, e.g. discussion in P. Dicken. *Global Shift: The Internationalisation of Economic Activity* (The Guilford Press, New York, 1992).
[5] See OECD, 'Globalisation and Local and Regional Co-operation', Working Paper No. 16, OECD, Paris, 1994, p. 7.
[6] See T. Levitt, *The Globalisation of Markets* (OUP, New York, 1985).
[7] See OECD, *Globalisation: What Opportunities and Challenges for Governments* (OECD, Paris, 1996).

> As an economic phenomenon, globalisation is manifested in a shift from a world of distinct national economies to a global economy in which production is internationalised and financial capital flows freely and instantly between countries. Multinational enterprises wield vast economic power, while anonymous institutional investors influence currency rates, the availability and price of international capital, and interest rates.

While the term 'globalisation' is used imprecisely in the literature, it is most commonly attributed to the increasing organisation and integration of economic activity on an international basis, particularly the increasing role of globally-integrated cross-border corporate networks in the process of production and distribution. The concept of 'globalisation' recognises that firms are increasingly organising their business activities on an international basis to realise global scale efficiencies and rationalise production. The concept recognises that such firms can readily migrate their activities between nations to exploit market opportunities, obtain a strategic advantage and leverage a global brand. The concept thus contemplates the integration of a cross-border dimension into the very nature of the organisational structure and strategic behaviour of firms. Accordingly, the term 'globalisation' inherently recognises that rivalry between firms has an important cross-border dimension and that market competition has assumed a transnational character.

3.1.2 The rise of multinational corporations and cross-border alliances

Modern globalisation has had a profound influence on international trade and commerce with both beneficial and detrimental effects. On the one hand, firms must now operate in markets that are highly globally-integrated so have adopted business strategies, relationships and structures that have enabled them to organise their affairs on a transnational basis and respond to greater international competition. Hence globalisation has promoted the emergence of a greater diversity and volume of cross-border business arrangements, promoting competition in international markets. Yet on the other hand, such cross-border arrangements have also provided firms with a greater ability to circumvent domestic competition laws and to exploit differences between the competition laws of different nations. Globalisation and multinational corporate expansion have thus exacerbated the risk of cross-border anti-competitive conduct. In this manner, competition problems have increasingly assumed a cross-border dimension, creating a need for effective cross-border competition regulation.[8]

The critical question therefore arises, *are modern cross-border business arrangements effectively regulated by existing competition laws?* To answer this question, it is useful to categorise cross-border business arrangements into three principal modes of supply into foreign markets:[9]

- *Inter-firm commerce*   An exporter may enter into a conventional cross-border export-import relationship with a local importer, so that the international transaction is *inter*-firm, constituting cross-border inter-firm commerce.
- *Intra-firm commerce*   An exporter may acquire a stake in a local importer, or otherwise establish a foreign affiliate, creating a multinational enterprise. In this manner, the international transaction is intra-firm, typically by way of a combination of FDI and intra-firm commerce.
- *Strategic alliances*   An exporter may seek a degree of control over a local importer without acquiring it as a subsidiary, so may utilise a more sophisticated legal structure, such as a joint venture or franchising relationship. The international transaction may then constitute a combination of FDI and inter-firm commerce.

These three modes of supply are illustrated by Figure 7.

Each of these modes of supply is regulated on a slightly different basis by domestic competition laws, as discussed below. Importantly, the particular mode of supply influences the underlying transaction structure which, in turn, affects the ability of domestic competition laws to regulate the cross-border business arrangement effectively.

Importantly, the analysis below indicates that *all three* modes of supply into foreign markets would be under-regulated by existing domestic competition laws, *unless* such laws were given full extraterritorial application. However, even in circumstances of full extraterritoriality, the level of regulation may still not be sufficient given difficulties with cross-border investigation and enforcement. The key insight provided by the analysis below is that each nation will enforce its competition laws with regard

---

[8] See, for example, discussion in D. J. Gerber, 'Antitrust and the Challenge of Internationalisation' (1988) 64(3) *Chicago-Kent Law Review* 689. See also comments in K. M. Vautier & P. J. Lloyd. *International Trade and Competition Policy: CER, APEC and the WTO* (VUW Press, Wellington, 1997), p. 4.
[9] See, for example, A. Bollard & K. M. Vautier, 'The Harmonisation of Competition Policy and Law Under APEC', PAFTAD 23 Conference, Taipei, Taiwan, 9 December 1996, p. 4.

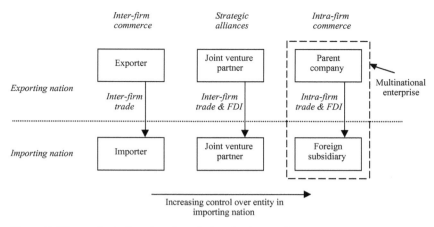

Figure 7: *Three principal modes of supply into foreign markets*

to its own domestic self-interest and will not usually be concerned with effects on foreign markets.

Inter-firm commerce[10]   The first mode of supply into foreign markets comprises cross-border *inter*-firm commerce, typically via a traditional export-import relationship in which the exporter retains little or no control over the actions of the importer. The cross-border transaction in such circumstances is governed primarily by contract law and trade law and involves the cross-border transfer of goods and services, usually by way of contract.

While domestic competition laws apply to such cross-border transactions, they apply predominantly on a territorial basis. As identified by Figure 8, the domestic competition laws of a nation are typically ineffective in regulating foreign anti-competitive behaviour by an entity located outside the territorial jurisdiction of that nation. Furthermore, the foreign nation in which the anti-competitive behaviour actually occurs may have little incentive to take action if the anti-competitive behaviour does not adversely affect its own markets. These territorial differences mean that anti-competitive conduct may escape effective regulation, providing an important justification for an international competition agreement.

- *Example*   Foreign exporters may engage in certain conduct that harms domestic Australian markets, such as by forming a foreign price fixing

---

[10] Inter-firm commerce is broadly consistent with the General Agreement on Trade in Services ('GATS') mode of supply known as 'cross-border supply', as set out in Art. I:2(a) of the GATS.

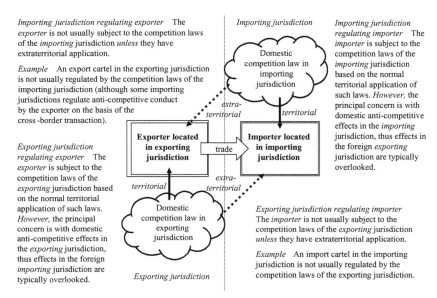

Figure 8: *Diagram illustrating application of domestic competition law to cross-border inter-firm commerce from Figure 7*

cartel for goods supplied into Australia. In such circumstances, Australia (i.e. the importing jurisdiction in Figure 8) may have little means under Australian competition law to prosecute that foreign cartel.[11] The cartel members may not be incorporated in Australia or carrying on business in Australia and may have no assets in Australia, being the principal means by which a jurisdictional nexus is usually established under Australian law. The powers of the Australian competition regulator to investigate that cartel would be hampered by territorial limitations on its powers.[12] Australia would therefore be heavily reliant on investigatory and enforcement action undertaken by the governments

---

[11] Sections 5 and 6 of the Trade Practices Act 1974 (Cth) do give Australian competition law some degree of extraterritorial application. However, the extent of that application is limited. Typically it requires jurisdiction to be exercised on the basis of incorporation, carrying on business in Australia, or assets located in Australia. However, in the case of exclusive dealing and resale price maintenance, the Act expressly applies to situations of cross-border supply.

[12] The information gathering powers of the Australian Competition and Consumer Commission under section 155 of the Trade Practices Act 1974 (Cth) are unlikely to have extraterritorial application, as evidenced by the need for section 155A providing power to obtain information in New Zealand.

of the nations in which the cartel was carrying on business (i.e. the exporting jurisdiction in Figure 8).

Intra-firm commerce[13] The second mode of supply into foreign markets comprises cross-border *intra*-firm commerce. A firm may engage in intra-firm commerce by establishing a foreign affiliate, creating a parent-subsidiary relationship. The decision whether to establish a foreign affiliate provides the basis for the modern theory of the multinational enterprise.[14] In its simplest form, this theory postulates that a firm will prefer intra-firm commerce, and thus establish a foreign affiliate, if:[15]

(a) one or more stages of production can be undertaken locally, or a strategic advantage can be obtained by establishing a local distribution network; and
(b) internalisation of supply would realise net benefits, including from vertical integration, retaining control over intellectual property, protecting or leveraging branding, or avoiding costly regulation.

There are essentially two principal mechanisms for a firm to establish a foreign affiliate, namely via greenfields entry or by acquiring a stake in an existing entity. Over the last two decades, acquisition has been increasingly preferred as it enables a firm to expand rapidly into new geographic markets to achieve a critical mass at a reduced cost.[16] Importantly, once the parent firm controls more than 10% of the equity of a foreign affiliate it falls within the United Nations and OECD definition of a 'transnational corporation'.[17] UNCTAD has estimated that there were upward of 63,000 transnational corporations in existence in 2001.[18] In that year, these firms controlled approximately 800,000 foreign affiliates and accounted for approximately one-third of world trade.

---

[13] Intra-firm commerce is broadly consistent with the GATS mode of supply known as 'commercial presence', as set out in Art. I:2(c) of the GATS.
[14] See J. R. Markusen, 'The Boundaries of Multinational Enterprises and the Theory of International Trade' (1995) 9 *Journal of Economic Perspectives* 169.
[15] See, e.g. W. J. Ethier, 'The Multinational Firm' (1986) 101 *Quarterly Journal Economics* 805.
[16] See P. M. Mehta, 'Foreign Direct Investment, Mega-Mergers and Strategic Alliances: Is Global Competition Accelerating Development or Headings Towards World Monopolies?', Paper at pre-UNCTAD X Seminar on the Role of Competition Policy for Development in World Globalising Markets, Geneva, July 1999.
[17] See, e.g. UNCTAD's definition of 'transnational corporations' in UNCTAD, 'FDI Geography and the New General of FDI Promotion Policies', UNCTAD, TAD/INF/PR23, 18 September 2001.
[18] See UNCTAD, *World Investment Report 2001* (UNCTAD, Geneva, 2001), p. 8.

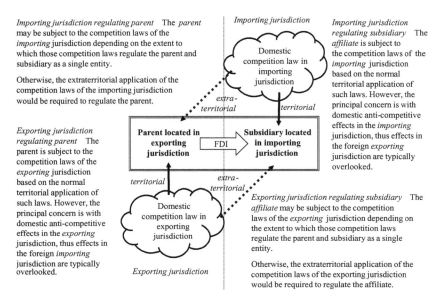

Figure 9: *Diagram illustrating application of domestic competition law to cross-border intra-firm commerce from Figure 7*

Modern globalisation has increasingly encouraged firms to adopt more sophisticated cross-border relationships, resulting in a trend away from traditional *inter*-firm commerce towards *intra*-firm commerce and strategic alliances. As a result, trade flows have been increasingly supplemented, even replaced, by FDI. UNCTAD commented in 1994, for example, that:[19]

> ... the sales of foreign affiliates have surpassed exports as the principal vehicle to deliver goods and services to foreign markets. This alone – and even without taking into account the linkage between FDI and trade as well as the dissemination of knowledge – makes FDI one of the most important mechanisms of international economic integration ...

Unlike inter-firm commerce, intra-firm commerce is regulated principally by corporate, foreign investment, and merger laws. While domestic competition law applies to such intra-firm commerce it faces the same territorial limitations as with inter-firm commerce, as identified in Figure 9 (although such extraterritoriality is now also influenced by the extent to

---

[19] See UNCTAD, *World Investment Report 1994* (UNCTAD, Geneva, 1994), p. 10.

which parents and their affiliates are considered to be the same regulated entity for the purposes of the competition regulation). In addition, multinational enterprises frequently have a greater ability to arrange their affairs to circumvent domestic competition laws. Again, certain anti-competitive conduct may thus escape effective regulation.

- *Example* Two multinationals could enter into a cartel, but this cartel could be agreed and documented in a nation without competition law and unlikely to assist with foreign discovery requests or extraterritorial enforcement.
- *Example* A multinational enterprise could engage in anti-competitive conduct in a nation with weak or non-existent competition laws and avoid regulation even though such conduct may have adverse effects on the markets of other nations.

Strategic alliances The third mode of supply into foreign markets comprises strategic alliances. Such strategic alliances typically assume the form of joint ventures and franchising arrangements.[20] Strategic alliances are particularly prevalent in high-technology industries as they enable a firm to reduce the risk of losing valuable intellectual property, while avoiding the costs of establishing foreign subsidiaries. Strategic alliances have also proved useful for penetrating 'difficult' markets where different business cultures and long-term relationships make the assistance of an astute local partner essential. Such structures may be commonly utilised where local laws prohibit certain levels of foreign ownership or investment, such as in China.

Strategic alliances may be regulated by contract, trade, foreign investment or corporate laws, depending on the particular legal structure adopted. Such arrangements more frequently give rise to competition concerns given that they often involve agreements between competitors and involve more flexible legal structures that can be tailored to circumvent domestic competition laws. The application of domestic competition law to strategic alliances follows the same pattern as identified in Figure 8 and Figure 9.

Again, domestic competition law is limited by its territorial application. While many nations give their competition laws some degree of extraterritorial application to regulate strategic alliances that involve domestic entities but which are concluded offshore, the application and enforcement of domestic competition laws in such circumstances remains exceptionally

---

[20] These include, for example, bilateral supply and distribution agreements, equity sharing arrangements and incorporated/unincorporated joint ventures.

difficult. Furthermore, as with cross-border inter-firm commerce, the nation in which the anti-competitive behaviour occurs may have little incentive to take enforcement action if the anti-competitive behaviour does not adversely affect its own markets. Again, certain anti-competitive conduct may escape effective regulation.

Summary The above analysis suggests that cross-border anti-competitive conduct is currently not regulated effectively on an international basis:

- While intra-firm commerce is usually regulated more effectively than inter-firm commerce, effective regulation will depend on the full extra-territorial application of the domestic competition laws of each jurisdiction to regulate foreign conduct that is adversely affecting the domestic market. However, even in circumstances of full extra-territoriality, the level of regulation may still not be sufficient given difficulties with cross-border investigation and enforcement.
- Strategic alliances generally comprise a hybrid of intra- and inter-firm commerce, so the effectiveness of the regulation will depend on the particular structure adopted.

The key insight provided by this analysis is that each nation will enforce its competition laws with regard to its own domestic self-interest and will not usually be concerned with effects on foreign markets. This insight is important to the policy justification for an international competition agreement.

3.1.3 *Cross-border competition regulation and economic externalities*

The analysis set out above identifies the difficulties inherent in the territorial application of competition laws and hints at the policy justification for an international competition agreement. However, a more sophisticated level of analysis is required, with reference to economic theory, to develop this policy justification further. Such economic analysis confirms the conclusion above that *insufficient* regulation of cross-border anti-competitive conduct is one policy justification for an international competition agreement (i.e. '*under*-regulation'). However, it also highlights that the converse is true and *excessive* regulation of such cross-border conduct provides a further policy justification (i.e. '*over*-regulation').[21]

---

[21] See the detailed discussion on under-regulation and over-regulation in Professor A. R. Guzman, 'The Case for International Antitrust' (2004) 22 *Berkeley Journal of International Law* 355, 359.

In particular, each nation has formulated its competition laws from a *national* perspective. Each nation has acted rationally in its national interest to maximise its domestic welfare, without full regard to the impact of its laws and enforcement conduct on the welfare of foreign nations or the collective international community. This focus of nations on maximising their national welfare, rather than collective global welfare, creates what is known in microeconomic theory as an 'economic externality'.

Economic externalities can assume a negative or a positive form:

- A *negative* externality is an economic spillover effect that *harms* a third party not directly involved in the relevant activity.
- A *positive* externality is an economic spillover effect that *benefits* a third party not directly involved in the relevant activity.

Economic externalities can also arise in the context of underlying conduct, as well as in the regulatory decisions that permit or prevent such conduct:

- Externalities in *underlying conduct* arise where the conduct of firms in one nation may have positive or negative effects on the markets of nations, hence may involve negative or positive externalities, respectively.
  - *Example*   An example of a positive externality in underlying conduct is a domestic merger that benefits foreign shareholders.
  - *Example*   An example of a negative externality in underlying conduct is an export cartel that increases prices paid by foreign consumers.
- Externalities in *regulatory decision-making* arise where the decisions made by a regulator in one nation have positive or negative effects on the markets of nations, hence may involve negative or positive externalities, respectively.
  - *Example*   An example of a positive externality in regulatory decision-making is a regulatory decision which permits a domestic merger to occur that, in turn, benefits foreign shareholders.
  - *Example*   An example of a negative externality in regulatory decision-making is a regulatory decision which *prevents* that domestic merger. Another example is a regulatory decision which fails to prevent anti-competitive conduct such as the export cartel identified above, leading to increased prices paid by foreign consumers.

Bearing these concepts in mind, the types of economic externalities arising in the context of 'under-regulation' and 'over-regulation' can be precisely identified. This is demonstrated by speculating what *enforcement* activity each nation would undertake, consistent with its national self-interest,

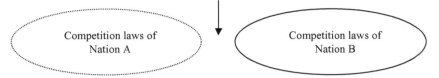

Figure 10: *Conceptual diagram illustrating under-regulation*

against certain underlying conduct that itself has cross-border positive or negative externality effects.

Under-regulation   If a nation were to undertake enforcement activity consistent with its national self-interest, it would usually *permit* conduct that had no adverse effects on its national markets, regardless of whether or not that same conduct had significant adverse spillover effects on other nations. An export cartel, for example, would be permitted by that nation even though that cartel restricted the supply of goods and services into the markets of other nations.[22] In certain circumstances, the adverse spillover effects on other nations from that export cartel would outweigh the benefits to the particular nation of permitting that cartel. Accordingly, the cartel would be permitted by that nation even though it resulted in a net detriment to collective global welfare.

This result can be classified as 'under-regulation' as the national competition laws of that nation would *permit* anti-competitive conduct that was ultimately welfare-*reducing* to the overall global community. Such under-regulation occurs either where the coverage of domestic competition laws is incomplete so that anti-competitive conduct is not regulated at all, or where the relevant anti-competitive conduct is regulated by national competition laws but the level of regulation is below the globally optimal level. Under-regulation is illustrated by Figure 10.

In economic terms, under-regulation occurs where the *underlying conduct* itself has a negative spillover effect on other nations (i.e. involves a

---

[22] If the domestic competition laws of those other nations cannot adequately regulate the transaction (such as via extraterritoriality), then those other nations will suffer a consequent welfare loss.

negative externality), so the *decision not to regulate* permits the continuance of that negative spillover effect, itself comprising a negative externality. Accordingly, a *negative* externality in the underlying conduct is perpetuated by a *negative* externality in regulatory decision-making.

- *Example* An example of under-regulation is a regulatory decision which fails to prevent anti-competitive conduct, such as an export cartel, leading to increased prices paid by foreign consumers. This involves a negative externality in regulatory decision-making.

Over-regulation Conversely, if a nation were to undertake enforcement activity consistent with its national self-interest, it would usually *prevent* conduct that adversely affected its national markets, regardless of whether or not that same conduct had significant beneficial spillover effects for other nations. A cross-border merger that adversely affected that nation, for example, may be prohibited by that nation even though it had significant benefits for other nations. In certain circumstances, the beneficial spillover effects for other nations of the relevant conduct may outweigh the detriments to the particular nation of preventing that conduct.[23] Accordingly, the merger may be prevented by that nation even though it resulted in a net benefit to collective global welfare.

This result can be classified as 'over-regulation' as the national competition laws of that nation would *prevent* anti-competitive conduct that was ultimately welfare *enhancing* to the overall global community. Such over-regulation occurs where one or more competition laws impose a level of regulation above the collective globally optimal level, including in circumstances where the domestic competition laws of different nations overlap. Over-regulation is illustrated by Figure 11.

In economic terms, over-regulation occurs where the *underlying conduct* itself has a *positive* spillover effect on other nations (i.e. a positive externality), so the *decision to regulate* prevents the realisation of that positive spillover effect, itself creating an opportunity cost in the form of a negative externality. Accordingly, a *positive* externality in the underlying conduct is prevented from realisation by a *negative* externality in regulatory decision-making.

- *Example* An example of over-regulation is a regulatory decision which prevents beneficial conduct, such as a merger benefiting foreign

[23] A nation may prevent conduct due to perceived adverse effects on that nation, even though the transaction may have positive spillover effects on other nations and, as a whole, be globally welfare enhancing.

Over-regulation occurs where one or more competition laws impose a level of regulation above the globally optimal level, including in circumstances where the domestic competition laws of different jurisdictions overlap

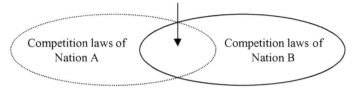

In economic terms, a *positive* externality in the underlying conduct is prevented from realisation by a *negative* externality in regulatory decision-making.

Figure 11: *Conceptual diagram illustrating over-regulation*

shareholders, that would otherwise realise positive externalities in favour of those shareholders. This also involves a negative externality in regulatory decision-making.

Summary   In summary, positive and negative externalities in underlying conduct interact with negative externalities in regulatory decision-making leading to under-regulation and over-regulation in the following manner:

- In the context of under-regulation, a nation does not recognise the costs that its *failure to regulate* causes for other nations, such costs arising in the form of negative spillover effects of anti-competitive conduct.
- In the context of over-regulation, a nation does not recognise the costs that its *excessive regulation* causes for other nations, such costs arising in the form of opportunity costs created by preventing positive spillover effects of positive conduct.

The underlying cause of the negative externality in regulatory decision-making in both circumstances is the fact that each nation acts in its own national interest without regard to the interests of other nations. A nation may thus *permit* conduct that decreases collective global welfare because that same conduct may benefit that nation alone, resulting in *under*-regulation relative to the globally optimal level. Conversely, that nation may *prevent* conduct that increases collective global welfare because that same conduct may harm that nation alone, resulting in *over*-regulation relative to the globally optimal level.

While complex, this economic reasoning provides the simple and important insight that while domestic competition laws and their enforcement may be optimal from a national welfare perspective, they may not be optimal from a collective global perspective. Such a divergence of regulatory interests reflects the existence of the negative externality in regulatory decision-making.[24] An international competition agreement could address that negative externality by requiring each nation to take into consideration the welfare consequences on other nations of its regulatory decisions. More specifically, an international competition agreement should seek to ensure that *cross-border conduct that increases global welfare is permitted, but cross-border conduct that decreases global welfare is prevented*. An international competition agreement is therefore justifiable in economic policy terms on the basis that it could correct the underlying negative externality by aligning domestic regulatory decision-making with the globally optimal result.

Further effects of over-regulation   Importantly, *over-regulation* has two further associated economic effects. First, it may lead to increased transactions costs for firms when engaging in cross-border conduct. Secondly, over-regulation in the context of the extraterritorial application of competition laws may lead to 'system frictions'. Both economic effects are considered in detail below and are detrimental to global welfare. Again, both economic effects could be mitigated by an international competition agreement.[25]

- *Transactions costs*   Over-regulation may impose significant transactions and compliance costs on firms, given that firms must comply with multiple layers of regulation from different national regimes, as each nation seeks to regulate the transaction in a different manner.[26] Similarly, different jurisdictions may impose different remedies that are each optimal from their own perspective, but when aggregated together are sub-optimal from a collective perspective, resulting in over-regulation. Such over-regulation may distort the efficient flow of international goods and services by inducing firms to arrange their international transactions in a manner that minimises their regulatory risks.

---

[24] See, for example, A. Sykes, 'Externalities in Open Economy Antitrust and their Implications for International Competition Policy' (2000) 23 *Harvard Journal of Law & Public Policy* 89.

[25] Regulatory differences between nations may be legitimate. A global competition agreement would aim to reduce differences that are caused by the negative externality and that have no other legitimate basis.

[26] See, for example, E. U. Petersmann, 'Legal, Economic and Political Objectives of National and International Competition Policies: Constitutional Functions of WTO "Linking Principles" for Trade and Competition' (1999) 34 *New England Law Review* 145.

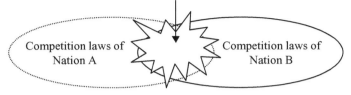

Figure 12: *Conceptual diagram illustrating system frictions*

Cross-border mergers and acquisitions, in particular, are highly sensitive to such over-regulation given that they are often time critical.[27] The increased transaction costs of over-regulation (including the cumulative effect of remedies imposed by several jurisdictions) may ultimately outweigh the benefits which the transaction parties had hoped to attain, or may significantly delay the transaction, leading to its ultimate abandonment. Such vulnerability may also enable particular jurisdictions to exert disproportionate leverage when seeking remedies. It is not uncommon for remedies to be sought which themselves have adverse spillover effects for other jurisdictions, as illustrated by the Boeing/McDonnell Douglas merger discussed below.

- *System frictions* In addition to such transactions costs, over-regulation in the context of the extraterritorial application of competition laws may lead to 'system frictions' with broader adverse systemic effects. In circumstances where a nation has the ability to apply its competition laws on an extraterritorial basis, that nation may seek to prevent that anticompetitive conduct in foreign jurisdictions which it believes is harmful to its national interest even though that conduct would otherwise be permitted under the competition laws of those foreign jurisdictions. Such regulatory differences between nations may lead to jurisdictional conflict, or 'system frictions'. System frictions occur when two or more domestic competition laws applied to the same cross-border conduct lead to inconsistent results and, potentially, jurisdictional conflict, as illustrated by Figure 12.

---

[27] International mergers and acquisitions are frequently highly time sensitive and vulnerable to regulatory uncertainty. See United States Department of Justice, 'International Competition Policy Advisory Committee Final Report', International Competition Policy Advisory Committee, United States Department of Justice, Washington DC, 28 February 2000, ch. 2.

Difficulty	Consequence for global welfare
Under-regulation	• Globally welfare reducing conduct is permitted, reducing global welfare.
Over-regulation	• Globally welfare enhancing conduct is prevented, reducing potential global welfare gains. • Transactions and compliance costs are increased, reducing global welfare.
System frictions (as a more severe form of over-regulation)	• Globally welfare enhancing conduct is prevented, reducing potential global welfare gains. • Transactions costs (including risk) are significantly increased, reducing global welfare. • Jurisdictional conflict may spillover into international policy, resulting in trade sanctions and other broader adverse systemic effects, reducing global welfare.

Figure 13: *Welfare consequences of under-regulation, over-regulation and system frictions*

In the worst instances, system frictions may become highly politicised and trigger trade disputes, potentially leading to the destabilisation of international diplomatic and trade relations. Jurisdictional conflict may thus spillover into international trade policy, resulting in trade disputes and economic sanctions between nations.[28] Several examples of system frictions and their adverse effects are discussed in detail below, providing further justification for an international competition agreement.

Welfare consequences   The welfare consequences of under-regulation, over-regulation and system frictions (as a more severe form of over-regulation) are summarised in Figure 13. To date, such welfare costs have been most apparent in the context of the over-regulation of international mergers and acquisitions. In such circumstances, a transaction has typically been challenged by some, but not all, reviewing jurisdictions and different remedies have been imposed by different jurisdictions.

---

[28] See, for example, discussion in A. N. Campbell & M. J. Trebilcock, 'International Merger Review: Problems of Multi-jurisdictional Conflict' in E. Katzenbach, H. E. Scharrer & L. Waverman (eds.), *Competition Policy in an Interdependent World Economy* (Nomos Verlagsgesellschaft, Baden-Baden, 1993), ch. 9.

A number of significant transactions in recent years clearly illustrate the potential for system frictions to arise as a result of over-regulation. These notably include:[29]

(a) the successful Boeing/McDonnell Douglas merger of 1997;
(b) the successful MCI/Worldcom merger of 1999; and
(c) the unsuccessful GE/Honeywell merger of 2001.

In all three examples, the relevant merger involved entities domiciled in the US and merging under US domestic law, yet subsidiaries of the merging entities had sufficient sales in markets in the European Union ('EU') to trigger the application of the EU merger law on an extraterritorial basis.[30] In all three examples, US competition authorities approved the mergers, yet the Competition Directorate-General of the European Commission ('EC') threatened significant adverse regulatory measures if its concerns were not addressed.[31] In the case of Boeing/McDonnell Douglas and GE/Honeywell, this extraterritorial intervention led to accusations by the US of unwarranted interference, leading to diplomatic conflict and tacit or overt threats of retaliatory trade sanctions. In the case of Boeing/McDonnell and MCI/Worldcom, the merging parties in the US agreed to make significant concessions to EU interests. Of these three examples, the Boeing/McDonnell Douglas example was the most concerning and is considered in detail below.

3.1.4 Case study: Boeing/McDonnell Douglas merger

The Boeing/McDonnell Douglas merger involved the US$16 billion acquisition of McDonnell Douglas by the Boeing Company, both firms being well-known multinational aircraft manufacturers with operations located principally in the United States.[32] Airbus Industrie, a European rival

---

[29] Other examples include Ford/Mazda; Compaq Computers/Tandem Computers; KPMG/Ernst & Young; Price Waterhouse/Coopers & Lybrand; Ciba Geigy/Sandoz; Montesdin/Royal Dutch Shell. See, for example, UNCTAD, 'Competition Cases Involving More Than One Country', UNCTAD Paper, TD/B/COM.2/CLP/9, Geneva, 7 June 1999.
[30] EU merger laws are based on the Control of Concentrations Between Undertakings Regulation, Council Regulation 139/2004, OJ 2004 No. L24 and Commission Regulation 802/2004, OJ L133 (of the same name), by the EU Council, 21 December 1989.
[31] The EU has no formal jurisdiction to prevent a merger involving two foreign firms, However, it has legal authority and power to impose limitations on their activities in the EU. For example, it can impose extra taxes, penalties, or even bar the merging firms from doing business in Europe.
[32] See E. M. Fox, 'Lessons From Boeing: A Modest Proposal To Keep Politics Out of Antitrust' *Antitrust Report*, 19 November 1997. See also, e.g. http://www.boeing.com.

aircraft manufacturing consortium involving four European governments, vigorously opposed the merger.

The US Federal Trade Commission ('FTC') approved the Boeing/McDonnell Douglas merger on the basis that the merger was necessary to the long-term survival of McDonnell Douglas which, without the merger, purportedly would not have remained as a significant competitor.[33] However, while the merger occurred in the United States, it had potential adverse effects on European markets given that Boeing and McDonnell Douglas both had European operations. As sales by Boeing and McDonnell Douglas in the EU exceeded the thresholds of the EU merger regulation, having a 'community dimension', the EC determined that it had jurisdiction over the merger based on effects in EU markets. The EC contradicted the FTC and challenged the acquisition on the basis that it strengthened Boeing's dominant market position in the international jetliner market.[34]

While the different results between the EU and US were principally attributable to the stricter treatment of vertical agreements by EU competition laws, this did not prevent the rapid politicisation of the EC challenge to the acquisition.[35] This politicisation was particularly acute given that Boeing and Airbus were considered the respective national champions of the US and EU aircraft manufacturing industries, both realising hundreds of millions of dollars of revenue and generating significant employment for their respective nations. Further friction resulted when the EC admitted that it had no direct jurisdiction to block the US transaction, rather the EC threatened to levy crippling fees on the sales of Boeing aircraft in Europe if the transaction occurred. At the height of US–EU tensions, the US House of Representatives voted 416 to 2 to warn the EC against '*an unwarranted and unprecedented interference in a US business transaction*'.[36] President Clinton of the United States also telephoned the President of the European Commission to underline American concern. Meanwhile, US diplomats warned of trade sanctions if the EU did not capitulate to US interests.

---

[33] See *Statement of Chairman R Pitofsky and Commissioners JD Steiger, RB Starek III and CA Varney in the Matter of The Boeing Company/McDonnell Douglas Corporation*, File No. 971–0051, 27 July 1997.

[34] See *Boeing/McDonnell Douglas*, EC Case No. IV/M.877 (30 July 1997). See also J. T. Dahlburg, 'Europeans Object to Boeing Takeover of McDonnell-Douglas', *Los Angeles Times*, 5 July 1997.

[35] See discussion in A. F. Bavasso, 'Boeing/McDonnell Douglas: Did The Commission Fly Too High?' (1998) 19(4) *European Competition Law Review* 243.

[36] See 'A Warning Shot to EU Over Boeing-McDonnell', *Business Week Online*, 9 July 1997.

American interests viewed the EC decision with considerable suspicion, particularly as Airbus was accorded a prominent role in the EC review process. The US portrayed the EC as partial to the effect of the acquisition on Airbus, rather than considering the long-term benefit of the acquisition to international aircraft consumers.[37] This view was not assisted by the perception of politicisation of the issue within the EU itself. Eventually, international tensions between the US and EU dissipated when Boeing negotiated a package of remedial measures with the EC, including modification of long-term supply contracts, patent sharing arrangements and the continued separation of Boeing and McDonnell Douglas until 2007.[38]

While the potential for US–EU jurisdictional frictions on competition issues has now been mitigated to some extent by the conclusion of a further trans-Atlantic co-operation agreement, as discussed in Chapter 5 of this book, the potential still remains for jurisdictional conflict. This potential was clearly illustrated by the proposed merger of General Electric with Honeywell in early 2001 in which the EC blocked the US transaction on the basis of negative effects on European markets, again provoking uncompromising diplomatic rhetoric from the US. President Bush, at that time in the early months of his Presidency, declined to give effect to congressional pressures for US trade sanctions against the EU and the proposed merger was eventually abandoned as a result of the EC intervention. Accordingly, the potential for trans-Atlantic frictions clearly remains.

3.2 Extraterritoriality and jurisdictional conflict (a 'non-co-operative' approach)

3.2.1 The extraterritorial application of competition laws

As noted above, the critical difficulty arising in the regulation of cross-border anti-competitive conduct is that domestic competition laws principally have only territorial effect. Anti-competitive conduct beyond national borders may escape regulation if the foreign nation in which the conduct occurred has ineffective laws or no incentive to regulate. As a solution to this territoriality issue, and in the absence of a truly

---

[37] See E. M. Fox, 'Lessons From Boeing: A Modest Proposal To Keep Politics Out of Antitrust' *Antitrust Report*, 19 November 1997.

[38] See *Boeing/McDonnell Douglas*, EC Case No. IV/M.877 (30 July 1997) and *The Boeing Co., et al., Joint Statement closing investigation of the proposed merger and separate statement of Commissioner Mary L. Azcuenaga*, FTC File No. 971–0051 (1 July 1997), reported at (1997) 5 *Trade Reg Rep* (CCH) ¶24,295.

international competition law, the United States historically sought to apply its competition laws on an extraterritorial basis to regulate foreign anti-competitive conduct where such conduct had adverse effects on US domestic markets. Other nations have now followed this approach to varying degrees. Such extraterritoriality has therefore evolved as the de facto mechanism to regulate cross-border anti-competitive conduct in the absence of an international competition agreement.

However, extraterritoriality has a number of inherent difficulties. Most critically, extraterritoriality undermines the fundamental precept of territorial sovereignty in international law. Indeed, the extent to which a nation is permitted to assert its jurisdiction internationally is heavily circumscribed by international law.[39] The limits of state jurisdiction are generally established by internationally accepted customs and practices which define the parameters within which a nation may enforce domestic law without violating or infringing upon the sovereignty of another state. As such, the principle of jurisdiction represents a careful attempt to balance the competing interests of sovereign nations so as to mitigate the potential for international conflict.

A fundamental measure of jurisdiction is provided by the principle of territoriality. This principle recognises a nation's sovereign right to exercise legitimate jurisdiction over the acts of all persons performed within its territory.[40] The basic presumption of customary international law is that territoriality and jurisdiction are co-extensive. International jurisprudence then recognises a limited range of circumstances in which a nation may assert jurisdiction over activities conducted beyond its territorial boundaries in the form of 'extraterritorial' jurisdiction. The nationality principle, for example, may permit a nation to assert extraterritorial jurisdiction on the basis of the allegiance that a person owes to their nation notwithstanding that the relevant conduct occurred in a foreign territory.[41] Customary international law also accepts a principle of universal jurisdiction by nations over a limited class of criminal matters regardless of where the act is performed, notably piracy. Most other principles for exercising extraterritorial jurisdiction remain highly controversial and are either not widely accepted or accepted only in a limited range of circumstances.

---

[39] See *Nottebohm Case (Second Phase)* [1955] ICJ Reports 4.
[40] See *Lotus Case (France v. Turkey)* [1927] Pub PCIJ Series A No. 10. See also *Compania Naveira Vascongado v. Cristina SS* [1938] AC 485, 496–7. See also *United States v. Baker* (1955) 22 ILR 203.
[41] See *Passport Seizure Case* (1955) 22 ILR 73. See also *Lotus Case*, above n. 40.

IS AN INTERNATIONAL AGREEMENT DESIRABLE? 55

In general, international jurisprudence requires that a claim of extraterritorial jurisdiction must be premised on a substantial and genuine connection between the subject matter of the claim of jurisdiction and the reasonable legitimate interests of the nation seeking to exercise jurisdiction.[42] Any claim of extraterritorial jurisdiction is then subject to the requirement that the claim of jurisdiction does not interfere with the legitimate affairs of the nation in whose territory the claim is made.[43] This requirement ensures extraterritoriality claims do not encroach upon the sovereign right of a nation to manage its territorial affairs.[44]

Accordingly, extraterritorial jurisdiction is a delicately balanced construct as it inherently involves a nation asserting jurisdiction over a matter that also falls within the territorial jurisdiction of another nation, thereby infringing upon the territorial sovereignty of that other nation.[45] Yet as nations such as the United States have sought to regulate cross-border anti-competitive conduct, they have pushed the concept of extraterritorial jurisdiction to the limits of international acceptability. Not surprisingly, extraterritoriality in the context of competition law enforcement has resulted in frequent jurisdictional conflict.

Jurisdictional conflict in competition law most frequently arises where the anti-competitive conduct in question is considered unlawful by the nation seeking to exercise extraterritorial jurisdiction, but is considered lawful in the nation where the conduct occurred. In such circumstances, the extraterritorial application of the laws of one nation to the business practices within another nation may well amount to an infringement of the latter nation's sovereignty and territorial integrity. The potential for such jurisdictional conflict is acute given that significant differences remain between the competition law regimes of different nations, based on legitimate differences between their relative economies, cultures, societies and customs. The English House of Lords has astutely commented, for example, that:[46]

---

[42] See *Barcelona Traction Case* [1970] ICJ Reports 248. This maxim is known as *extra territorium jus dicenti impune non paretur*.
[43] This is known as the 'objective territoriality' principle. See *Service of Summons Case* [1927] ILR 38. See also *Lotus Case*, above n. 40.
[44] See, for example, Judge Fitzmaurice's separate opinion in *Barcelona Traction* [1970] ICJ Reports 105.
[45] See *Fisheries Case* [1951] ICJ Reports 116. See also *Nottebohm Case (Second Phase)* [1955] ICJ Reports 4.
[46] Per Lord Frazer in *Rio Tinto Zinc Corporation v. Westinghouse Electric Corporation* [1978] 2 WLR 81, 125.

> ... claims to extraterritorial jurisdiction are particularly objectionable in the field of [competition] legislation because, among other reasons, such legislation reflects national economic policy which may not coincide, and directly conflict, with that of other states.

Two of the most notorious instances of jurisdictional conflict occurred in 1978 and 1984 in the *Uranium* litigation, and *Laker* litigation, respectively. In both cases, jurisdictional conflict clearly infringed sovereignty and, as a result, precipitated an international diplomatic incident and adverse retaliatory measures (i.e. 'system frictions', as discussed previously).

3.2.2 Case study: Uranium litigation

In the *Uranium* litigation, Westinghouse Electric Corporation of the United States was sued by 27 electricity utilities for breach of contract in relation to its failure to honour fixed-term uranium supply contracts for various nuclear power stations.[47] Westinghouse faced an estimated US$2 billion in damages with the litigation described at the time as '*the highest price package of private lawsuits in US history*'.[48] A court order for performance would have rendered Westinghouse insolvent. Westinghouse was thus in a desperate position and its survival depended on offsetting that litigation.

In its defence, Westinghouse alleged that its uranium supply contracts were commercially incapable of performance by reason of a shortage of uranium and steeply rising prices, partly attributable to the activities of an international cartel of uranium producers.[49] Westinghouse simultaneously commenced litigation in the US District Court, alleging a violation of US antitrust laws by 29 domestic and foreign conspirators in this cartel, including foreign uranium producers from Australia, Britain,

---

[47] Westinghouse Electric Corporation was a major supplier of nuclear power plants to public utilities and had entered into a number of contracts with electric utilities to construct nuclear facilities. The contracts required Westinghouse to supply the facilities with uranium fuel for a fixed term at a set price, subject to inflation adjustment. Westinghouse had not covered itself with futures contracts.

[48] See 'Westinghouse Faces Devastating Litigation', *Business Week*, 26 September 1977.

[49] By 1975, the price of uranium had quadrupled and the price had doubled again by 1978. Accordingly, Westinghouse notified the electric utilities that it could no longer honour the supply contracts due to commercial impracticability. The electric utilities sued Westinghouse for damages. The federal cases were consolidated into one action in the Eastern District of Virginia. See re *Westinghouse Electric Corporation Uranium Contracts Litigation* 405 F Supp 316 (Judicial Panel on Multidistrict Legislation 1974).

South Africa and Canada.[50] Westinghouse sought US$6 billion in punitive and compensatory damages for losses incurred as a result of the activities of the cartel.[51] Meanwhile, the US Department of Justice initiated its own criminal investigation of the alleged uranium cartel, partly as a result of the associated publicity.

Westinghouse next embarked on a far-ranging inter-jurisdictional discovery effort with the assistance of US courts.[52] The breadth of the US jurisdiction alleged in the proceedings raised considerable alarm among the governments of Australia, South Africa, the United Kingdom and Canada who perceived it as a 'fishing expedition'. In response, Australia, South Africa and Canada each adopted legislative measures prohibiting compliance with the discovery requests.[53] Simultaneously, the British House of Lords refused the requests (via letters rogatory) of the US courts and deferred to the British government's view that British sovereignty would be infringed if such requests were granted.[54]

During trial, the foreign defendants each refused to recognise the jurisdiction of the US courts and filed *amicus curiae* briefs arguing lack of subject matter jurisdiction.[55] The US Seventh Circuit Court of Appeals treated these briefs with disdain and entered default judgments against the non-appearing foreign defendants, permitting Westinghouse to calculate its financial loss. Westinghouse subsequently commenced debt recovery proceedings. Eventually, various claims by Westinghouse against these foreign defendants were settled by the parties via million dollar payments and cut-price uranium ore deliveries. The Department of Justice terminated its criminal investigation without taking any action.

The particularly troubling feature of the Westinghouse litigation was that the international uranium cartel had been formed in response to the United States Atomic Energy Commission's protectionistic closure of the US domestic uranium market to foreign uranium producers. As the US market represented approximately 70% of the world market for uranium at that time, this closure had caused serious economic hardship

---

[50] The defendants included Conzinc Rio Tinto, Queensland Mines, Mary Kathleen Uranium, Pancontinental Mining (Australia), Rio Tinto Zinc Corp (Britain), Nuclear Fuels Corp, Anglo American Corp (South Africa), and Rio Algom (Canada).
[51] *Re Uranium Antitrust Litigation* 480 F Supp 1138 (ND Ill, 1979).
[52] *Re Uranium Antitrust Litigation* 473 F Supp 393, 400–6 (1979).
[53] Foreign Proceedings (Excess of Jurisdiction) Act 1984 (Cth) (Australia). The Act authorised the Australian Attorney-General to prohibit the giving of evidence or production of documents to a foreign tribunal on the basis of protecting the national interest.
[54] *Rio Tinto Zinc Corporation* v. *Westinghouse Electric Corporation* [1978] 2 WLR 81.
[55] *Re Uranium Antitrust Litigation* 617 F 2d 1248 (7th Cir 1980).

to the foreign uranium producers. In 1972, the producer countries had therefore agreed to make a joint stand against the US trade boycott. The relevant uranium producers of these nations agreed to form a defensive cartel with floor price arrangements, delivery rules and quota allocations in respect of the supply of uranium. The governments of Australia, Britain, South Africa and Canada allegedly encouraged the formation of this cartel to 'stabilise' world uranium prices.

The uranium antitrust litigation therefore represented, in part, a jurisdictional challenge by the US courts to the sovereign right of the governments of Australia, Britain, South Africa and Canada to determine their own domestic policies. Each of these four nations responded to this challenge by enacting legislation to block the extraterritorial jurisdiction asserted by the US courts. This legislation became known as 'blocking' legislation and assumed two forms:[56]

(a) discovery blocking statutes, which restricted the extent to which foreign litigants such as Westinghouse could obtain evidence or compel production of commercial documents for use in foreign proceedings; and
(b) judgment blocking statutes, which blocked, in whole or in part, the enforcement of foreign judgments considered offensive to the national interest.

Nations that have now enacted such blocking statutes, for example, include Australia, New Zealand, Britain, South Africa, Netherlands, Denmark, Finland, France, India, Norway and Sweden.

Such blocking legislation has proved effective. A special Australian Parliamentary Committee, established in 1983 to consider the problem of the extraterritorial application of US antitrust laws in the context of the Westinghouse litigation, and the benefits of the Australian blocking legislation, relevantly commented:[57]

> Despite firm Australian representations to the US administration opposing US attempts to regulate the legitimate interests of Australian companies, the US administration and courts showed no serious concern for Australia's expressed interests. It was not until the Foreign Antitrust Judgements

---

[56] See R. E. Price, 'Foreign Blocking Statutes and the GATT: State Sovereignty and the Enforcement of US Economic Laws Abroad' (1995) 28 *George Washington Journal International Law & Economics* 315.

[57] See Joint Committee on Foreign Affairs and Defence, *Australian-United States Relations: The Extraterritorial Application of United States Laws* (Australian Government, Canberra, 1993), ch. 3.

(Restriction of Enforcement) Act was enacted in 1979 that the Westinghouse case was settled out-of-court, even then involving US$11 million payable by the Australian defendants (together with extremely high legal costs).

Notwithstanding such blocking legislation, there remained a risk that US antitrust judgments could be enforced against the US assets of foreign firms. Australia and Britain therefore developed a third form of blocking legislation that provided Australian and British defendants with a 'clawback' right to recover losses suffered by way of a foreign judgment executed against their foreign assets. This loss was recoverable against the assets of a judgment creditor from that foreign jurisdiction located in a local jurisdiction. In Britain, only the excess of compensatory damages (i.e. punitive damages) can be recovered by such a 'clawback' action. In Australia, the Attorney-General may specify which part of a foreign judgment may be subject to such a 'clawback'.[58]

However, these three forms of blocking legislation further exacerbated the jurisdictional quagmire and created greater scope for 'system frictions'. This was illustrated by the Laker litigation in 1984.

3.2.3 Case study: Laker litigation

The Laker litigation involved the application of a blocking statute by the British government against the US courts. Laker Airways, a British cut-price airline competing on the trans-Atlantic route, had expanded its operations to meet rapidly increasing demand, by purchasing additional aircraft from McDonnell Douglas in the United States. However, when the exchange rate of the pound against the dollar declined precipitously, Laker encountered severe financial difficulties. The airlines competing with Laker allegedly used that moment to undertake significant and predatory price reductions. Laker was eventually placed in liquidation in 1982.[59]

Laker, via its liquidator, subsequently commenced civil litigation against eight American, British and European airlines, and McDonnell Douglas, alleging violations of US antitrust laws.[60] Laker sought US$700 million in damages alleging, in particular, collusive predatory

---

[58] Foreign Proceedings (Excess of Jurisdiction) Act 1984 (Cth)(Australia), section 10.
[59] See M. Leigh, 'Laker Airways Ltd v Pan American World Airways Inc' (1985) 79 *American Journal International Law* 1069.
[60] *Laker Airways Ltd* v. *Pan Am World Airways*, No. 82–3362 (DDC filed 24 November 1982). *Laker Airways Ltd* v. *Sabena Belgian World Airlines*, No. 83–0416 (DDC filed 15 February 1983). *Laker Airways Ltd* v. *Pan Am World Airways*, 559 F Supp 1124, 1137 (DDC 1983).

pricing, payment of secret commissions to travel agents and undue pressure on Laker's aircraft financiers. Laker asserted that the US court could exercise jurisdiction on the basis of Laker's operations in the US, the effect of the defendants' conduct on those operations and the fact that Laker's liquidation creditors were principally based in the US.

Each of the defendants defended the action in their home jurisdictions as well as in the US. This created direct jurisdictional conflict, as each court sought to pre-empt the other's jurisdiction. British Airways, for example, obtained anti-suit injunctions in Britain restraining Laker from continuing its action in the United States. At Laker's request, the United States District Court then granted injunctions preventing British Airways from obtaining further similar relief.[61] As a result, the English Court of Appeal granted anti-suit declarations, permanently injunting Laker from proceeding with its antitrust claims against British Airways in the United States.[62] Finally, at the request of British Airways, the British Secretary of State for Trade and Industry invoked the British blocking statute.[63] Further litigation ensued as Laker Airways sought to overturn the decision of the British Secretary of State by judicial review, while appealing the antisuit injunctions and declarations.[64]

After further protracted legal wrangling, the British House of Lords ruled that British Airways had voluntarily entered the US market and had obtained licences to operate scheduled services under US domestic laws and relevant international treaties. In doing so, British Airways had submitted voluntarily to US domestic law. The House of Lords also reasoned that Laker's allegations did not disclose a cause of action under English law, but did disclose a cause of action under American law, hence the American court was the only forum of competent jurisdiction. The Laker jurisdictional conflict was thus resolved when the British courts deferred to US jurisdiction.[65]

Interestingly, if the Laker approach were to be applied by all nations, then the nations with stricter competition laws would tend to prevail. The decision in *Laker Airways* therefore represents a move towards

---

[61] *Laker Airways Ltd v. Sabena Belgian World Airlines* 731 F 2d 909 (DC Cir 1984).
[62] *British Airways Board v. Laker Airways Ltd* [1983] 3 WLR 413, CA.
[63] On 27 June 1983 the British Secretary of State for Trade and Industry invoked the Protection of Trading Interests Act 1980 (UK) and issued directions prohibiting compliance with the US antitrust measures. See Protection of Trading Interests (US Antitrust Measures) Order 1983 (SI 1983 No. 900).
[64] See discussion in A.V. Lowe, 'Blocking Extraterritorial Legislation: The British Protection of Trading Interests Act 1980' (1981) 75 *American Journal of International Law* 257.
[65] *British Airways Board v. Laker Airways Ltd* [1984] 3 WLR 416, HL.

over-regulation of international transactions. The decision also illustrates the potential jurisdictional quagmire associated with extraterritoriality in the context of cross-border competition law proceedings and the scope for significant system frictions.

3.2.4 The 'effects doctrine' and United States extraterritoriality

The Uranium and Laker litigation clearly illustrates that the extraterritorial application of competition laws may provoke considerable international tension. As a result, it is typically the more powerful nations that have utilised extraterritoriality given their greater ability to withstand such tensions. The US, in particular, is the nation that has most frequently and aggressively applied its domestic competition laws on an extraterritorial basis over the past five decades, partly because it adopted the most expansive view of extraterritorial jurisdiction of any nation and partly due to its status as an international superpower. Indeed, the Uranium and Laker jurisdictional conflicts each involved attempts by US litigants to invoke US extraterritorial jurisdiction against foreign nationals.

The historical experiences of the US provide a number of insights into the difficulties with extraterritorial enforcement and are therefore briefly summarised below. The scope of extraterritorial application of US domestic competition laws expanded significantly from 1945 until 1982 by way of judicial decision, but was curtailed by legislative intervention from 1982 following significant international criticism. US courts have subsequently refined jurisdictional jurisprudence determining the appropriateness of extraterritoriality.

The extraterritorial application of US antitrust laws has evolved over nearly a century. Over that period, the extent of that extraterritoriality has altered considerably, impacting on the underlying effectiveness of extraterritoriality as a mechanism for international competition law enforcement by the US. This evolution has largely been a product of differences in judicial interpretation. In particular, US extraterritoriality was initially derived from the expansive wording of section 1 of the Sherman Act which reads:[66]

> Every contract, combination . . . or conspiracy, and restraint of trade of commerce . . . *with foreign nations* is declared to be illegal. (emphasis added)

---

[66] Sherman Act 1890, reprinted at 15 USC 1–7 (1994).

When the US Supreme Court first ruled on section 1 in 1909, it was not construed as covering conduct occurring outside the US.[67] However, this ruling was short-lived and in 1927 the Supreme Court held that US courts had subject matter jurisdiction over an international cartel involving both Mexican and US sisal traders.[68] As the US emerged as the dominant world power following World War II, the US apparently sought to assert its dominance over world affairs and the doctrine of strict territoriality was replaced by an emphasis on the extraterritorial application of US antitrust law. In the well-known *Alcoa* case of 1945, Judge Learned Hand famously reasoned that the Sherman Act extended to govern the restrictive business practices of foreign firms if those practices generated effects within the US. Relying on the protective basis of jurisdiction, he wrote:[69]

> We should not impute to Congress an intent to punish all whom its courts can catch, for conduct which has no consequence within the United States . . . On the other hand . . . it is settled law . . . that any state may impose liabilities, even upon persons not within its allegiance, for conduct outside its borders that has consequences within its borders which the state reprehends . . .

This *Alcoa* principle subsequently became known as the 'effects doctrine'. Following *Alcoa*, the US commenced a period of aggressive extraterritorial antitrust enforcement.[70] The most extreme example of the application of the effects doctrine involved an unsuccessful antitrust challenge by an American labour union against the international OPEC oil cartel.[71] Another notorious example included a successful antitrust challenge against a Swiss and American association of watch manufacturers which effectively forced the restructuring of the domestic Swiss watch industry.[72] Examples in the Australasian region included investigations by the US Department of Justice into international shipping arrangements and various producer boards, leading New Zealand to follow Australia and enact blocking legislation. At its most potent, the effects doctrine proved

---

[67] *American Banana Co* v. *United Fruit Co* 213 US 347, 355–6 (1909).
[68] *United States* v. *Sisal Sales Corp* 274 US 268 (1927). Sisal is a plant used to make rope.
[69] *United States* v. *Aluminium Co. of America (Alcoa)* 148 F 2d 416 (2nd Cir 1945) at 443.
[70] See D. P. Wood, 'The Impossible Dream: Real International Antitrust' (1992) *University of Chicago Legal Forum* 277, 280.
[71] *International Association of Machinists* v. *OPEC* 477 F Supp 553 (CD Cal, 1979), aff'd 649 F 2d 1354 (9th Cir 1981), cert. denied, 454 US 1163 (1982).
[72] *United States* v. *Watchmakers of Switzerland Information Centre Inc* 1963 Trade Cases 70,600 (SDNY, 1965).

highly controversial and was strongly resisted by many nations on the basis that it exceeded the limits of international acceptability.

Due to the severity of jurisdictional conflicts caused by the effects doctrine, as demonstrated by the Westinghouse litigation and the *Swiss Watch* case, the US Congress determined that legislative intervention was necessary. The Foreign Trade Antitrust Improvements Act 1982 (' FTAIA') sought to address foreign governments' concerns over perceived excesses of jurisdiction by codifying the 'effects doctrine' and restricting its application. The FTAIA provided that US antitrust law only extended to conduct involving commerce with foreign nations to the extent that such conduct had a '*direct, substantial, and reasonably foreseeable effect*' on US domestic or import commerce, or export commerce by domestic firms.[73] The FTAIA also ensured, perhaps hypocritically, that US antitrust laws could not be invoked by foreign firms that were being injured by US parties in foreign markets.

Concurrently with the development of this legislation, the US courts also fashioned a 'jurisdictional rule of reason' based on international comity and conflicts of laws principles. This approach expressly recognised the adverse effects of extraterritoriality on foreign nations. The US Court of Appeal in the *Timberlane* case, for example, reasoned that extraterritorial jurisdiction should not be exercised in situations where 'the interests of the United States were too weak and the foreign harmony incentive for restraint too strong to justify an extraterritorial assertion of jurisdiction'.[74] In the 1993 *Hartford Firecase* case, the US Supreme Court clarified that such comity considerations were not applicable unless there was a 'true conflict' between domestic and foreign law such that a firm could not simultaneously comply with the laws of both nations.[75] In essence, the *Hartford Fire* decision provides that if the laws of the United States and the laws of another country regulate the same activity, the stricter of the laws will apply to the extent of any inconsistency.[76] This approach clearly facilitates the potential over-regulation of international transactions.

---

[73] Foreign Trade Antitrust Improvements Act 1982, 15 USC 6a, 45(a)(3) (1988).
[74] See *Timberlane Lumber Co* v. *Bank of America*, 549 F 2d 597, 609 (9th Cir 976), on remand, 574 F Supp 1453 (ND Cal, 1983), aff'd 749 F 2d 1378 (9th Cir 1984), cert. denied, 472 US 1032 (1995).
[75] See, for example, S. A. Burr, 'The Application of US Antitrust Laws to Foreign Conduct: Has Hartford Fire Extinguished Considerations of Comity?' (1994) 15 *University Pennsylvania Journal of International Business Law* 221, 223.
[76] See *Hartford Fire Insurance Co.* v *California* 509 US 764 (1993); 113 S Ct 2891 (1993).

In this manner, while the US has relied on the extraterritorial application of its competition laws to protect its own domestic interests, it has also recognised that such extraterritoriality has clear limitations. The 'aggressive' extraterritoriality of the 1970s and 1980s has now been replaced by a more conciliatory approach, sympathetic to the interests of other nations. The current approach governing the extraterritorial application of US antitrust laws is summarised in the *Anti-trust Enforcement Guidelines for International Operations 1995* issued by the US Department of Justice and the US Federal Trade Commission. While acknowledging the FTAIA requirements, these guidelines adopt the essence of the *Hartford Fire* decision and provide that extraterritorial jurisdiction may be exercised where:

(a) the conduct involves anti-competitive activities that violate US antitrust laws;
(b) the conduct has a direct, substantial and reasonably foreseeable effect on US domestic or import commerce, or export commerce by domestic firms; and
(c) US courts have jurisdiction over foreign firms engaged in such conduct (requiring an analysis of considerations of international comity).

However, the US is not alone in applying its antitrust laws extraterritorially. Other nations have also pursued extraterritoriality to varying degrees to protect their domestic interests. As one would expect, the extent of extraterritoriality by each nation has been closely correlated with the relative status and economic power of that nation. The EU, for example, rivals the US in terms of economic power and has thus adopted a similarly expansive extraterritorial approach. In the *Dyestuffs* and *Wood Pulp* cases, for example, the European Court of Justice recognised that it could assert jurisdiction on the basis of a limited form of 'effects' doctrine, subsequently known as the 'implementation' doctrine, which enabled the EU to assert jurisdiction over firms without any presence in the EU. The precise extent of EU extraterritoriality remains controversial.[77]

Most other nations have adopted a more restrictive approach to the extraterritorial application of competition laws. Australia, for example, has legislation which is drafted to avoid any general application of

---

[77] See *A. Ahlstrom Osakeytio v. Commission* (1988) 4 CMR 14,491 ('*Woodpulp* case'), See also *IBM v. Commission* [1981] ECR 2639 ('*Dyestuffs* case').

the 'effects' doctrine, as noted above. Australian extraterritorial jurisdiction is not usually asserted unless the relevant firm is incorporated in, or carrying on business in, Australia or has assets in Australia, with some notable exceptions. New Zealand and Canada adopt a similar approach. Full extraterritoriality remains essentially limited to the economic superpowers and is currently the exception, rather than the rule.[78]

3.2.5 Is extraterritoriality sufficient to regulate cross-border competition effectively?

In circumstances where competition has become increasingly globalised, the extraterritorial application of competition law is, to a degree, inevitable. Without such application, firms could arrange their affairs such that any anti-competitive conduct occurred where those nations with competition laws did not have jurisdiction, but those nations with jurisdiction did not have the laws, means or incentives to take enforcement action. As such, nations such as the US and EU arguably have had little choice but to apply their competition laws to foreign conduct where such conduct harms their respective economies.

In theory, in a perfect world with full extraterritoriality by all nations, one would expect that all anti-competitive conduct would be regulated, as any nation that suffered from anti-competitive activity could apply its domestic competition law on an extraterritorial basis to that conduct. The question therefore arises: to what extent is the extraterritorial enforcement of competition laws an effective solution to the correction of the negative externalities identified previously, namely under-regulation and over-regulation? In this regard, it is clear that extraterritoriality is a potential solution only to *under*-regulation. Yet extraterritoriality does not correct the underlying negative externality in regulatory decision-making and, in fact, may *exacerbate* over-regulation and cause system frictions, as identified below.

Does extraterritoriality correct under-regulation? Extraterritoriality may correct under-regulation, but the correction is by no means perfect. This is attributable to two key factors:

---

[78] However, versions of the 'effects' doctrine test have been endorsed by numerous nations including Austria, Belgium, Canada, Denmark, Finland, Germany, Greece, Japan, Luxembourg, Norway, Portugal, Spain, Sweden and Switzerland. See, for example, discussion in D. J. Gerber, 'The Extraterritorial Application of the German Antitrust Laws (1983) 77 *American Journal of International Law* 756.

(a) extraterritoriality does not sufficiently address the negative externality in regulatory decision-making that leads to under-regulation, although extraterritoriality does provide a crude mechanism for one nation to influence the decision-making process of another; and
(b) extraterritoriality is incomplete and is hindered by procedural issues in enforcing competition laws in foreign jurisdictions.

The logic behind the first factor is intuitive. When a nation applies its domestic competition law on an extraterritorial basis, that nation is inherently motivated by national self-interest.[79] Similarly, the underlying basis for extraterritoriality remains legislative and it is highly unlikely that the welfare of foreign citizens would be weighted equally with the welfare of domestic citizens in the domestic legislative and political process.[80] With this in mind, the extraterritorial application of competition laws is not likely to lead to optimal regulation of anti-competitive activity from the point of view of the collective global interest, given that the self-interest of the enforcing nation will continue to diverge from the collective global interest. Rather extraterritoriality is, at best, a crude mechanism for one nation to influence the decision-making process, although it may provide a means to prevent under-regulation.

In relation to the second factor, it is clear that even when competition laws are given extraterritorial application, this does not necessarily guarantee successful enforcement action to correct circumstances of under-regulation. Extraterritorial enforcement of competition laws is notoriously difficult and is not practicable or appropriate in many cases, particularly where evidence cannot be obtained from a foreign jurisdiction. Such enforcement usually requires jurisdiction over foreign firms, which is frequently difficult to obtain. Similarly, appropriate remedies may not be available or enforcement may not be possible due to differences in legal systems between nations.

International discovery in the course of extraterritorial antitrust litigation has caused considerable difficulties for the US in exercising extraterritorial jurisdiction, as with other nations. Most nations have had little sympathy with the use of extensive pre-trial discovery mechanisms

---

[79] Likewise for a private party of that nation undertaking extra-territorial enforcement action.
[80] A government seeking to maximise the welfare of its own citizens is unlikely to consider the costs or benefits of its laws on citizens in foreign nations, hence the negative externality in regulatory decision-making identified previously is unlikely to be corrected. See A. O. Sykes, 'Externalities in the Open Economy Antitrust and Their Implications for International Competition Policy' (1999) 23 *Harvard Journal of Law & Public Policy* 89, 92.

by the US legal system. A desire to frustrate what have been described as 'global fishing expeditions' by US litigants was another of the major motivations behind the enactment of blocking statues by Britain, France, Australia and New Zealand, as discussed previously. Insufficient access to witnesses and documentary evidence may thus prevent extraterritorial enforcement, particularly where blocking legislation has been enacted or applied. While the Hague Convention on the Service of Process and the Hague Evidence Convention have both ameliorated this problem to some extent between signatory states, serious impediments remain with respect to non-signatory jurisdictions.[81]

Most nations, including the US, now recognise that the extraterritorial application of competition laws is exceptionally difficult without the co-operation of the respective foreign governments. Accordingly, most nations have sought to increase the level of co-operation in competition law enforcement by entering into bilateral co-operation agreements, as discussed in Chapter 5. However, such co-operation is still limited on an international basis, so many of the difficulties identified above remain.

Does extraterritoriality correct over-regulation? Extraterritoriality does not correct over-regulation. Rather, extraterritoriality is itself another tier of regulation so is likely to exacerbate or result in over-regulation. This can be illustrated by a simple example:

- *Example* We assume that a particular international merger results in net benefits to the international community as a whole, but net detriments to a particular nation. In circumstances of full extraterritoriality *every* nation has the potential ability to block that merger by applying its competition laws extraterritorially, hence regulatory approval from *every* affected nation would be required for the transaction to proceed. However, given that a particular nation suffers a net detriment, that nation would not grant regulatory approval, regardless of the net benefits to the global community as a whole. Hence, the merger would be blocked, resulting in over-regulation.

This example illustrates that in order for a transaction to proceed in circumstances of full extraterritoriality, the transaction must improve the welfare of every nation affected by the transaction. As a consequence, such

---

[81] See The Hague Convention on the Service Abroad of Judicial and Extra-judicial Documents in Civil and Commercial Matters (1969) 20 UST 361, 15 November 1969. See also The Hague Convention on the Taking of Evidence Abroad in Civil and Commercial Matters (1970) 23 UST 2555, 27 July 1970.

a requirement implies over-regulation in which potentially efficient transactions from an international viewpoint are prevented simply because one nation is adversely affected so would block the transaction. This may have been the case for the GE/Honeywell merger discussed previously: the EU acted in its own self-interest to block the merger at the expense of the US.

Does extraterritoriality mitigate system frictions? As noted previously, system frictions are a form of over-regulation which arise as a result of extraterritoriality. Accordingly, extraterritoriality does not mitigate system frictions, rather it is the underlying *cause* of such system frictions.

As illustrated by the historical experience with the 'effects' doctrine of the US, extraterritoriality may frequently trigger jurisdictional conflict and, in some circumstances, serious diplomatic disputes. The exercise of extraterritorial jurisdiction may arouse resentment in target nations and have a destructive impact on global co-operation and international diplomatic relations. Such resentment can be acute given that each nation's competition laws are usually tailored to the particular domestic circumstances of that nation and are not necessarily appropriate to the foreign circumstances of the target nation. While the welfare consequences of such international conflict are difficult to quantify, such conflict may have potential spillover effects in terms of delaying or thwarting other co-operative initiatives between nations that would otherwise have significant positive welfare effects. Such conflict may also lead to welfare-destroying retaliatory measures and trade sanctions, destabilising the WTO.

Similarly, considerations of international comity are critically important in ensuring that nations continue to have confidence in each other's judicial systems and the international legal system. However, the extraterritorial application of competition laws, particularly in the case of the US, has frequently challenged considerations of international comity, undermining confidence in the international legal system. In addition, when extraterritorial action is taken by private companies, these companies are usually unconstrained by political and diplomatic considerations and may act in their own interests at the expense of other nations or the global community. The prevalence of blocking statutes is symptomatic of the difficulties arising in such circumstances.

Summary Extraterritoriality does not effectively correct under-regulation of cross-border anti-competitive conduct. Furthermore, it may exacerbate over-regulation and system frictions, with resulting welfare losses. Extraterritoriality is therefore not an effective solution to cross-border competition issues.

3.3 Conclusion: an international competition agreement is desirable

In summary, domestic competition law is inherently territorial in its approach, creating difficulties in an increasingly globalised world in which transactions subsume multiple territorial spaces. Anti-competitive conduct is currently regulated on an ineffective and inconsistent basis across jurisdictions using domestic laws. However, the application of domestic competition law in an international context is influenced by economic externalities which result in over-regulation and under-regulation. This situation has been exacerbated in recent decades by globalisation, greater economic integration and multinational corporate expansion, as illustrated by the Boeing/McDonnell Douglas merger and the GE/Honeywell merger.

While the extraterritorial application of domestic competition laws has provided a de facto mechanism for nations to regulate cross-border anti-competitive conduct in the absence of international competition laws, such an extraterritorial approach has clear deficiencies. Such extraterritoriality controversially impinges on state sovereignty and may trigger serious diplomatic disputes, as illustrated by the *Laker* and *Uranium* cases. Nations have also enacted blocking legislation to thwart such extraterritoriality, generating further system frictions. Extraterritoriality does not address the underlying negative externality and may in fact exacerbate over-regulation and system frictions by providing a mechanism for one nation to interfere in the domestic affairs of another.

While beyond the scope of this book, a number of economic models have concluded that greater international co-ordination of competition law would be welfare enhancing relative to a situation in which each nation enforces its competition laws on an extraterritorial basis in accordance with its national self-interest.[82] Empirical evidence quantifying these

---

[82] See detailed analysis and economic model in M. D. Taylor, 'International Competition Law: A New Dimension for the World Trade Organisation?', PhD thesis, Law Faculty, University of Sydney (2005), Appendix 1 and Appendix 2. In the interests of brevity and given its highly mathematical nature, this material is not addressed in further detail in this book.

benefits is difficult to obtain, but the conclusions from Chapter 2 regarding the welfare benefits arising from competition law and policy suggest that the welfare benefits of an international competition agreement would be significant.

Chapter 3 therefore concludes that an international competition agreement is desirable and would be welfare enhancing relative to the status quo.

4

Is there a sufficient basis for an international competition agreement?

> APEC economies have long recognised the strategic importance of developing competition principles to support the strengthening of markets to assure and sustain growth in the region.
>
> (Asia Pacific Economic Co-operation, Shanghai, 2001)[1]

Following from the conclusion in Chapter 3 of this book that an international competition agreement is desirable, Chapter 4 considers whether there is a sufficient basis for an international competition agreement.

Chapter 4 identifies whether there is sufficient commonality between the competition laws of a sample group of nations which otherwise exhibit considerable diversity, namely the 21 nations of the Asia Pacific Economic Co-operation ('APEC').[2] By analysing the extent of convergence of the competition laws of these APEC nations, Chapter 4 seeks to identify common themes upon which an international competition agreement could be based. Chapter 4 also seeks to distil a set of commonly accepted principles that may provide the basis for any international competition agreement and makes a number of preliminary recommendations for the content of such an agreement.

Chapter 4 concludes that, notwithstanding such diversity, there is sufficient commonality among nations to provide a basis for an international competition agreement.

---

[1] See 'APEC Economies – Breaking Down the Barriers, Case Studies in Administrative and Regulatory Reforms', Report Prepared for the APEC Economic Leaders Meeting in Shanghai, APEC, 2001, p. 24.

[2] The 21 nations are: Australia, Brunei, Canada, Chile, People's Republic of China, Hong Kong, Indonesia, Japan, Malaysia, Mexico, New Zealand, Papua New Guinea, Peru, Philippines, Russia, Singapore, South Korea, Taiwan, Thailand, United States and Vietnam.

4.1 Competition laws within the Asia-Pacific Economic Community

4.1.1 APEC as a proxy for the international community

In order to identify whether there is a sufficient basis for an international competition agreement, it is necessary to consider the extent to which the existing domestic competition laws of different nations are similar or dissimilar. An international competition agreement should ideally build upon similarities while reducing dissimilarities, furthering the evolution of an 'optimal law' which addresses the economic externalities identified in Chapter 3. However, rather than considering every nation in the world, it is useful to consider a sample group of nations which exhibit considerable diversity and that are sufficiently representative of international differences. Such a sample is provided by the 21 nations of APEC. These 21 nations account for roughly half of global trade.

APEC was inaugurated in 1989 as a Ministerial dialogue group between the nations of the Asia-Pacific region, recognising their growing economic inter-dependence. APEC has subsequently evolved to become the primary institutional vehicle for promoting free trade and practical economic co-operation within the Asia-Pacific region. Over the past decade, the APEC nations have embraced a series of visions and action plans, an important element of which has been the adoption of effective competition policies and the promotion of competition policy co-operation. Accordingly, the extent of competition policy co-operation between the APEC nations remains advanced by world standards.

However, notwithstanding such co-operation, harmonisation of competition laws has not been an objective of APEC, thus significant differences remain between the competition laws of APEC nations. Furthermore, the APEC nations exhibit a diversity of cultures, institutions, social and economic policies, and stages of economic development. Given such diversity, the APEC nations may be perceived as a microcosm of, and therefore proxy for, the international community. Consequently, the differences between the competition laws of APEC nations provide insights into the likely differences that one would encounter within the wider global community.

Importantly, three APEC nations do not yet have generic competition laws. These nations are representative of the roughly 50% of nations that do not have generic competition laws within the wider international community.

4.1.2 APEC nations without competition laws

The issue arises why competition law is not yet ubiquitous. The APEC experience provides a number of insights. The APEC nations *without* competition laws form three groups.

Group One This group comprises nations that have so far deliberately chosen not to enact generic competition laws on the basis that an absence of trade barriers is sufficient to promote competition. Hong Kong and Brunei are the only remaining Group One nations after Singapore enacted competition legislation in 2004.

The Group One nations recognise that competition law corrects market failures, but challenge the orthodox view that market failures are pervasive. In particular, these nations view generic competition law as unnecessary in circumstances where international trade places constraints on the domestic market power of firms. Rather, these nations favour sector-specific minimal competition laws to address particular circumstances where domestic market power is unlikely to be constrained by international trade, such as in network industries.[3] While the approach of these nations remains controversial, the World Bank has commented that this approach may be uniquely appropriate for open-market entrepôt nations exposed to intense international competition.[4] Any international competition agreement would most likely endorse the World Bank's view as to the limited applicability of this approach, particularly as the economic literature has generally concluded that the removal of trade barriers is at best an imperfect substitute for competition laws.[5]

Group Two This group comprises nations that intend to adopt competition laws, but have been delayed from doing so due to internal opposition. Malaysia is currently the only remaining Group Two nation, as Vietnam enacted competition legislation in 2004.

The Malaysian government has historically been suspicious of generic competition laws, believing they favour multi-national corporations and

---

[3] Hong Kong, for example, has sector-specific telecommunications competition laws set out in licences granted to telecommunications operators by the Telecommunications Authority of Hong Kong.
[4] See World Bank, 'Competition Policy in a Global Economy: An Interpretative Summary', Global Forum for Competition and Trade Policy Conference, New Delhi, India, March 1997.
[5] See, for example, H. Hohn & J. Levinsohn, 'Merger Policies and Trade Liberalisation', Research Seminar in International Economics, Discussion Paper No. 420, University of Michigan, Ann Arbor, 11 June 1997.

disadvantage developing nations.[6] However, Malaysia has indicated that it intends to enact a generic competition law once threshold political support has been achieved. Any international competition agreement should recognise that many nations in the wider global community remain in a similar situation. Technical assistance would be necessary to assist such nations to develop competition laws appropriate for their particular circumstances.

Group Three This group comprises nations that do not intend to adopt competition laws due to their less-developed status. Papua New Guinea was historically the only member of this group in APEC but enacted competition legislation in 2002.[7] Papua New Guinea historically claimed that it lacked the necessary institutions and resources to enforce a competition law effectively and perceived a competition law as less beneficial than other potential economic development initiatives.

Papua New Guinea's historic stance recognises that an important precondition for competition law is an effective institutional setting and threshold level of economic development. Where this pre-condition is not satisfied, as in the case of many less developed nations, the World Bank has recommended that such nations should concentrate on institutional strengthening rather than enacting competition laws that may be misunderstood or improperly enforced. Alternatively, such nations should introduce less sophisticated competition laws tailored to their particular needs. This suggests that any international competition agreement should identify any institutional pre-conditions for the enactment of competition laws and should recommend institutional strengthening where these pre-conditions are not met.

4.1.3 *APEC nations with competition laws*

The earliest known competition laws were promulgated in China by the Tang dynasty in AD 737.[8] The first reported competition case was *Darcy*

---

[6] See, for example, an article by an employee of the Malaysian Ministry of Domestic and Consumer Affairs: J. Govindan, 'Malaysia: Concerns About Competition Law' (1999) 25(10) *International Business Lawyer* 466. However, Malaysia has recently indicated its willingness to enact a competition law.

[7] Independent Consumer and Competition Commission Act 2002 of Papua New Guinea.

[8] Article 33 of the Tang Code of AD 737 prohibited price fixing. See L. S. Liu, 'Efficiency, Fairness, Adversary and Moralsuasion: A Tale of Two Chinese Competition Laws' in C. K. Wang, C. J. Cheng & L. S. Liu (eds.) *International Harmonisation of Competition Laws* (Martinus Nijihoff, Dordrecht, 1995).

v. *Allen* in England in 1603 in which a monopoly granted by the Crown was struck down for violating Magna Carta.[9] In 1624, the English Parliament enacted a Statute of Monopolies which deemed all laws creating monopolies to be 'utterly void', with exceptions for temporary patents and inventions.[10] However, modern competition law was established principally by the enactment of the Sherman Act in the United States in 1890 following similar legislation enacted in Canada in 1889.[11] Notwithstanding this lengthy history, most of the roughly 80 nations with competition laws in the global community have enacted their competition laws only within the past few decades.[12] Accordingly, the widespread international adoption of competition law is essentially a recent phenomenon.

As microeconomic theory and business practices have evolved over the past century, so modern competition laws have evolved to reflect these changes. Indeed, modern competition laws remain in a process of continual evolution and refinement as competition laws are modified to address new and innovative business structures, economic theories and competitive techniques. Given the evolutionary nature of competition law, modern competition statutes (as those of the APEC nations) tend to incorporate an eclectic mix of proven traditional approaches, carefully crafted modern provisions and ad hoc governmental responses to perceived competitive unfairness.

Those APEC nations that have enacted competition laws tend to have competition laws that are surprisingly similar in general content and structure. These similarities reflect commonly-accepted underlying microeconomic theories and principles, common underlying notions of fairness and commonly accepted precedents established by the earliest statutory formulations of competition law, such as the Sherman Act. These similarities also reflect the common historical origins of competition laws within APEC and common cultural and economic influences between APEC nations.

---

[9] *Darcy* v. *Allen* (1603) 77 Eng Rep 1260, 11 Co Rep 84.
[10] Statute of Monopolies (1624) 21 Jac 1 c 3: 'all monopolies . . . are contrary to the laws of the realm, and so are and shall be utterly void and of [no] effect and in no [way] to be put into use or execution'.
[11] While Canada enacted a competition statute in 1878, the United States Sherman Act of 1890 (codified at 15 USC 2) is generally considered to have provided the foundation for modern competition law. Prior to 1890, various US states had passed similar laws, but they were limited to intra-state business.
[12] In the 1960s, for example, only 24 nations had competition laws. See discussion in M. R. A. Palim, 'The Worldwide Growth of Competition Law: An Empirical Analysis' (1998) 16 *Antitrust Bulletin* 105.

However, notwithstanding similarities in content and structure, considerable differences remain between APEC nations in the application of their competition laws. Indeed, each APEC nation has enacted its own unique formulation of competition law which has been tailored to its particular institutional and economic setting. Each formulation reflects the particular concerns of each nation and the different weighting each nation has given to various economic and social policy trade-offs. Each formulation also reflects the particular legislative and institutional context of the nation and the extent to which competition laws have evolved over time in that nation. Accordingly, each APEC competition law remains culturally nuanced and nationally distinctive. Harmonisation of competition law between nations has, until recently, remained rare.

The uniqueness of each nation's competition laws suggests that any international competition agreement should remain necessarily general in application, thereby leaving scope for the retention of national differences. Any international agreement that attempted to harmonise competition laws without regard to national differences would not receive international support. Accordingly, any international competition agreement should initially seek to establish broad principles to guide the content and application of national competition laws, rather than, for example, prescribing an international competition law with supranational application. This conclusion is considered in greater detail in Chapter 11 of this book.

Any international competition agreement would have the unenviable task of reconciling these different approaches. In considering the scope for such reconciliation, this chapter broadly categorises the relevant issues as:

- 'macro issues', concerning the objectives of APEC competition laws and their methodology and structure; and
- 'micro issues', concerning the substantive content, application and enforcement of APEC competition laws.

This chapter considers the macro and micro issues, in turn, below in the context of a detailed analysis of the extent of commonality between the competition laws of APEC nations.

4.2 Macro issues: objectives, methodology and structure of competition laws

Significant macro issues associated with APEC competition laws involve their objectives, general methodology and overall structure. These issues

IS THERE SUFFICIENT BASIS FOR AN AGREEMENT? 77

are each considered below and are revisited in Chapter 10 of this book in the context of the draft WTO plurilateral competition agreement set out in the Appendix to this book.

4.2.1 Objectives of APEC competition laws

In a joint study undertaken in 1999, the World Bank and OECD identified a clear convergence of international opinion as to the principal objective of competition law, namely to maintain and encourage competition in order to promote economic efficiency.[13] This economic objective is broadly consistent with the approach adopted by all APEC nations. Such consistency suggests that any international competition agreement would most likely follow the World Bank and OECD's recommendations that the greatest weight should be given to considerations of economic efficiency when designing competition laws.

However, the wording and interpretation of this overriding economic objective has many different national permutations among APEC nations.[14] Furthermore, each APEC nation has tempered this economic objective by different incidental considerations of distributional fairness, consistent with the different approaches identified by the ABA. The different relative weighting of such economic and social objectives between APEC nations and the diversity of social objectives has created significant differences in the application of national competition laws. However, the World Bank and OECD identified in their 1999 study that social objectives are usually secondary in importance to economic objectives.[15]

---

[13] See World Bank & OECD, *A Framework for the Design and Implementation of Competition Law and Policy* (World Bank, Washington DC, 1999), ch. 1.

[14] In Australia, for example, the objective of the Trade Practices Act 1974 is to: 'enhance the welfare of Australians through the promotion of competition and fair trading and the provision for consumer protection'. In contrast, Canada's Competition Act 1985 provides: 'the purpose of this Act is to maintain and encourage competition in Canada in order to promote the efficiency and adaptability of the Canadian economy, in order to expand opportunities for Canadian participation in world markets while at the same time recognizing the role of foreign competition in Canada, in order to ensure that small and medium-sized enterprises have an equitable opportunity to participate in the Canadian economy and in order to provide consumers with competitive prices and product choices'.

[15] Chinese competition laws, for example, heavily emphasise wider social objectives under the rubric of protecting the public interest, including the elimination of corruption and profiteering. See Law of the People's Republic of China for Countering Unfair Competition 1993, Art. 8.

4.2.2 Methodology and structure of APEC competition laws

The competition laws of APEC nations exhibit common underlying principles and concepts, reflecting their common methodology and structure. For example, all APEC competition laws recognise the concepts of 'market' and 'market power'. These principles and concepts reflect the common microeconomic foundations of competition law and reflect precedents established by the competition laws of influential nations, such as the US. These principles and concepts could provide a basis for the initial standardisation of competition principles and concepts within an international competition agreement.

Similarly, the competition laws of APEC nations exhibit a common content and structure, comprising three general elements (as identified in Chapter 2 previously):

- *Merger laws* Substantive provisions that regulate market structure, usually in the form of merger and acquisition prohibitions which are intended to prevent excessive market concentration.
- *Anti-monopoly laws* Substantive provisions that regulate unilateral market conduct, usually in the form of prohibitions against the misuse of market power by powerful firms.
- *Concerted conduct laws* Substantive provisions that regulate concerted conduct, usually in the form of prohibitions against certain vertical or horizontal agreements with collusive or exclusive effects.

This tripartite structure reflects an important causal relationship between market structure and market conduct derived from the theory of industrial organisation and known as the 'structure-conduct-performance' (or 'SCP') paradigm.[16] The SCP paradigm proposes a causal sequencing of factors that determine the level of competition in a market, with market structure determining market conduct and thus the level of competition. Merger laws are perceived as necessary to regulate one aspect of market structure, while anti-monopoly laws and concerted conduct laws are perceived as necessary to regulate market conduct, with the objective of increasing competition.

The SCP paradigm was historically the dominant paradigm of the theory of industrial organisation, but is less widely used today given the

---

[16] Edward Mason initially developed the SCP paradigm in the 1930s. See E. Mason, 'Price and Production Policies of Large-Scale Enterprise' (1939) 29 *American Economic Review* 61.

evolution of game theory and contestability theory and with the identification of other determinants of market conduct beyond market structure alone. However, the SCP paradigm does provide important insights into the similarities and differences between competition laws given its historical role in shaping the evolution of those laws.

The two elements targeted by competition law are market structure and market conduct:

- *'Market structure'* describes the environment within which firms in a particular market operate. The principal determinants of market structure are product differentiation, market concentration, and barriers to entry. Market structure is considered by the SCP paradigm to be an indirect causal determinant of the extent of competition in a particular market. The SCP paradigm reasons that the regulation of market structure will reduce the potential for anti-competitive behaviour. Merger laws regulate market structure by regulating market concentration as well as some aspects of market conduct.
- *'Market conduct'* refers to the behaviour of the firms in a market, focusing on the degree of co-operation permitted between firms and any behavioural constraints placed on a firm's ability to exercise its market power. Market conduct is considered by the SCP paradigm to be a direct causal determinant of the extent of competition in a particular market, and is itself influenced by market structure. The SCP paradigm reasons that provisions regulating market conduct will directly regulate anti-competitive behaviour by firms competing within that market. Anti-monopoly laws and concerted conduct laws are the principal forms of competition law regulating market conduct.

The widespread international acceptance of the tripartite structure of merger laws, anti-monopoly laws, and concerted conduct laws, and the SCP paradigm upon which it is based, suggests this tripartite structure could be endorsed by any international competition agreement.

4.3 Micro issues: particular content and application of competition laws

A range of micro issues arise when considering the similarities of APEC competition laws. These micro issues relate principally to different regulatory approaches, institutional influences, and key underlying concepts (such as market definition and market power). Again, each are considered below and are revisited in Part III of this book.

4.3.1 'Conduct-oriented' and 'result-oriented' approaches

The competition laws of APEC nations, as with the competition laws of most nations, incorporate a blend of conduct-oriented and result-oriented provisions which reflect a different regulatory approach to different types of anti-competitive conduct:

- *Conduct-oriented* (or per se) provisions absolutely prohibit certain conduct without any consideration of the effects of this conduct on competition. Per se provisions are characterised by clear rules for contravention with little scope for consideration of mitigating circumstances. Such provisions reduce compliance costs by enabling the prompt determination of the legality of particular conduct. However, the inherent inflexibility of such provisions may sometimes lead to the inadvertent prohibition of pro-competitive conduct, with adverse welfare consequences. The exact character of such per se provisions differs between APEC nations. For example, US per se provisions are typically judicial in origin and US courts retain a degree of flexibility to recognise exceptional circumstances. However, Australian per se provisions are legislative in origin and tend to remain inflexible.[17]
- *Result-oriented* (or rule of reason) provisions require a court or adjudicator to assess certain conduct by reference to its effect on competition. Rule of reason provisions provide greater scope for recognition of welfare enhancing conduct, but create compliance uncertainty due to the complex competition analysis required and the high degree of discretion given to enforcement authorities. This uncertainty may be reduced if guidance is given as to the interpretation and application of such provisions, such as via case law or administrative guidelines.

In summary, while the particular detail of conduct-oriented (per se) and result-oriented (rule of reason) provisions may differ between nations, all nations accept the existence of these two different approaches and the rationale underlying them. Accordingly, the existence of these two alternative approaches could be endorsed by an international competition agreement.

---

[17] Australia's Trade Practices Act 1974 contains per se prohibitions against, for example, third line forcing (s. 47(6)) and exclusionary provisions (s. 45). See also *News Ltd* v. *Australian Rugby Football League Ltd* (1996) 64 FCR 410; 139 ALR 193; ATPR 45-421.

4.3.2 Institutional influences on APEC competition laws

The particular combination of conduct-oriented and result-oriented provisions incorporated within the competition laws of each APEC nation reflects a variety of underlying institutional, historical and social influences.[18] Of these influences, the APEC experience suggests that *institutional* influences are particularly important.

In a world with perfect enforcement of competition laws, a nation would ideally prefer result-oriented (rule of reason) provisions, and would apply conduct-oriented (per se) provisions only to conduct considered so obviously anti-competitive that a rule of reason assessment was unnecessary. In this manner there would be little risk of inadvertently prohibiting welfare enhancing competitive conduct. However, given that competition law enforcement is imperfect, deviations from this ideal are the norm. As a general rule, the greater the extent to which a nation's institutions cannot accurately undertake a complex rule of reason analysis, the greater the extent to which that nation would deviate from this ideal and prefer conduct-oriented per se provisions.

Any international competition agreement should recognise that the relative use of conduct-oriented provisions is, to some extent, influenced by the prevailing enforcement conditions of each nation, as illustrated by Figure 14. This, in turn, is influenced by the degree of institutional development of each nation. Intuitively also, the degree of sophistication of a nation's competition laws should reflect the ability of that nation to manage such sophistication competently, which further favours the greater use of less sophisticated per se provisions by less developed nations. This suggests that any international competition agreement should therefore treat nations differently depending on their degree of economic and institutional development.

4.3.3 Market definition and market power under a rule of reason analysis

Where the competition laws of APEC nations involve a conduct-oriented rule of reason approach, they usually require the application of a three stage process:

---

[18] See APEC, *Study of Competition Laws for Developing Economies* (APEC, Singapore, 1999), pp. 17–19.

Quality of institutions and competition law enforcement	Appropriate emphasis of competition law	Relevant APEC nations
Judicial enforcement Enforcement via the courts or a quasi-judicial independent competition authority	Predominantly 'rule of reason' result-oriented provisions given the high level of institutional expertise	United States, Australia, New Zealand, Canada, Japan
Quasi-executive enforcement Enforcement via a government agency with some independence	Mixture of result- and conduct-oriented provisions, as determined by the quality and independence of the relevant enforcement institutions	Peru, Chile, Russia, Korea, Mexico, Indonesia
Executive enforcement Enforcement via non-specialist government ministries	Predominantly per se conduct-oriented provisions given the lower level of institutional expertise	Philippines, Thailand, China

Figure 14: *Relationship between competition law enforcement and content*

- First, the relevant markets are defined, also known as market definition.
- Secondly, the degree of 'market power' of the relevant firm is assessed.
- Thirdly, the competitive consequences of the conduct in question are then analysed.

As indicated in Chapter 2, the concept of 'market', and the associated concept of 'market power', are both universally accepted competition law principles based on microeconomic theory that may provide a basis for initial international agreement. The concept of the 'market' is inherently multi-dimensional. The market dimensions recognised by most jurisdictions are the dimensions of product, geographic space and, sometimes implicitly, functional level. A fourth temporal dimension is also recognised in some jurisdictions. The first three market dimensions could potentially be recognised by an international competition agreement, while the fourth dimension could remain discretionary.

The concept of product substitutability, in particular, could be endorsed as a basis for market definition given its near universal acceptance. This was illustrated by the decision *Mexico – Measures Affecting Telecommunications Services* in which the WTO Panel commented:[19]

> For the purposes of this case, we accept the evidence put forward by the United States, and uncontested by Mexico, that the notion of demand substitution – simply put, whether a consumer would consider two products as 'substitutes' – is central to the process of market definition as it is used by competition authorities.

As identified in Chapter 2 of this book, a 'market' is an important conceptual instrument employed by competition law to define and analyse the field of rivalry between firms and to identify their relative 'market power'. 'Market power' is defined in most APEC nations as the ability of a firm to maintain prices profitably above competitive levels for a significant period of time, consistent with the reasoning of the WTO Panel in *Mexico – Measures Affecting Telecommunications Services* and the economic basis for market power identified in Chapter 2 of this book. A high level of market power signifies a lack of effective competitive constraints on a firm and therefore an absence of effective competition.

Since a principal purpose of defining markets is to enable an inference to be made as to the existence of market power, markets are usually defined in such a way that they provide a reliable index to the degree of market power present. As is well known to competition lawyers, markets that are defined too narrowly will typically overstate the degree of market power present by ignoring important sources of competition. Markets that are defined too broadly will typically understate market power by including perceived sources of competition that in reality impose little constraint on market power. However, market definition necessarily involves some degree of judgment. As a result, it is common for similar markets to be defined differently between the competition laws of APEC nations. For this reason, it is not proposed that any international competition agreement would seek to achieve uniformity of market definition between nations.

Rather, any international competition agreement should endorse the concepts of 'market definition' and 'market power' as fundamental conceptual tools in competition policy analysis. Any international competition agreement should ideally endorse the recognised dimensions of a market, particularly the near universal concept of product substitutability.

---

[19] See *Mexico – Measures Affecting Trade in Telecommunications Services*, WT/DS204/R, Report of the WTO Panel, 2 April 2004, para. 7.152.

In this manner, competition law would have a commonly-accepted methodological basis enshrined in international law. This methodology would also prevent nations from disconnecting competition law from its microeconomic foundations. In turn, this would ensure competition law remained resistant to welfare-reducing influences, including rent-seeking and corruption.

4.4 Regulation of market structure – merger laws

At a greater level of detail, the key elements of each of the three principal forms of competition law (merger laws, anti-monopoly laws and concerted conduct laws) can each be analysed to determine similarities between the APEC nations. First of these are *merger laws*, which are principally associated with the regulation of market structure. Almost all competition law regimes seek to regulate market structure, reflecting the methodology of the SCP paradigm. The single aspect of market structure that is most commonly regulated by competition law is market concentration, although merger laws are usually formulated to address behavioural considerations jointly as well. Market concentration measures the number of firms within a market and their relative market shares. The level of market concentration provides a useful proxy for the likely intensity of market competition.

The concern of competition law is that a high degree of market concentration may be associated with increased market power, reduced competition and reduced competitive constraints on existing firms. Such effects may arise in two principal ways:

- First, higher concentration may result in an individual post-merger firm having *excessive* market power. Such high levels of market power may enable more powerful firms to acquire greater producer surplus at the expense of consumer surplus and total economic welfare, as identified in Chapter 2 of this book.
- Secondly, higher concentration may result in an increased likelihood of the post-merger firm co-operating either expressly or tacitly with other firms so that together they can reduce quantity supplied into the market, particularly in more concentrated oligopolistic market structures.

Merger law is the principal mechanism used by APEC nations to regulate market structure. Merger laws are mostly framed so as to prohibit a firm from acquiring an asset or business where the acquisition would unduly increase the market power of that firm. However, merger laws rarely seek to remedy pre-existing high levels of market concentration. Rather, merger laws have a ratchet effect by preventing unwarranted increases in market concentration relative to pre-existing levels. Where APEC nations have sought to reduce market concentration, they have typically enacted industry-specific competition reforms. In some nations, competition authorities may have remedial powers to break-up monopolies.[20]

Not all APEC nations with competition laws have merger laws, including Chile (although Chile applies its concerted conduct provision to mergers), China and the Philippines. Yet there are risks associated with regulating market conduct without regulating market structure. If anti-cartel law is applied without merger law, for example, cartel parties could simply internalise their cartel by merging, leading to overly concentrated markets.[21] Any international competition agreement should recognise that merger laws are complementary to laws regulating market conduct, so nations should ideally enact both types of competition laws simultaneously.

Three key elements of merger laws are:

- notification procedures;
- merger thresholds; and
- any public benefit assessment.

Each are considered below.

4.4.1 Notification procedures

Merger control laws differ between nations and are insufficiently harmonised at present to enable a 'standardised international merger law' to be drafted.[22] However, common principles and themes are recognisable. The merger laws of APEC nations, as with most nations, typically involve a procedure whereby firms notify a competition authority of mergers and acquisitions that may create excessive market concentration or otherwise

---

[20] Structural separation has been used most frequently as a remedy by the US, the most important cases being: *Standard Oil* v. *US* (1911) 221 US 1; *US* v. *American Tobacco* (1911) 221 US 106; *US* v. *Aluminium Company of America* (1945) 148 F 2d 416 (2nd Cir); *US* v. *Paramount Pictures* (1948) 334 US 131; *US* v. *United Shoe Machinery* (1954) 347 US 521; *US* v. *AT&T* (1983) 160 US 1001.
[21] See E. Cruz, 'Mergers in the Inter-Island Shipping Industry: The Philippine Experience', International Training Programme on Competition Policy, Seoul, August 1997.
[22] See, for example, detailed discussion in OECD, 'Report on Notification of Transnational Mergers', OECD Paper, DAFFE/CLP(99)2/FINAL, OECD, Paris, 23 February 1999.

adversely impact on competition.[23] The competition authority of each APEC nation then assesses such mergers and acquisitions against structural or behavioural thresholds to determine their legality. Most APEC nations regulate both share and asset acquisitions.[24]

In almost all APEC nations, the emphasis is on pre-merger notification (also known as 'pre-notification'). Post-merger notification (or 'post-notification') is generally considered undesirable as it creates compliance uncertainty and unscrambling a merger is often extremely difficult. India (a non-APEC nation), for example, has found its historical post-notification regime to be highly problematic for this reason.[25]

Two principal types of pre-notification regimes are used by APEC nations:

- *Voluntary pre-notification*, in which each firm decides whether it should seek clearance or authorisation from a competition authority. The firm faces a risk of subsequent legal challenge if it does not obtain clearance and the merger is subsequently found to be anti-competitive (e.g. Australia, New Zealand).
- *Mandatory pre-notification*, in which all mergers and acquisitions above a certain statutory threshold must be notified to the competition authority before the relevant transaction occurs. The competition authority then determines whether any competition law issues arise. The thresholds for mandatory pre-notification vary widely between APEC nations and include, for example, various combinations of market share thresholds (e.g. Peru), monetary value thresholds (e.g. Canada), voting thresholds (e.g. Russia) and shareholding thresholds (e.g. Mexico).

While a voluntary pre-notification regime shifts compliance risks to the industry participants and thus reduces the role of competition authorities, such a regime also reduces the flow of information to competition authorities. A mandatory pre-notification regime is therefore preferred by most APEC nations on the basis that it enables the competition authority to capture more information and thus undertake more effective

---

[23] The widely different notification requirements for different nations create considerable compliance costs for firms. See comments, for example, in R. D. Paul, 'The Increasing Maze of International Pre-Acquisition Notification' (1990) 23 *International Company and Commercial Law Review* 43.

[24] See, for example, E. J. Mestmacker, 'The Concept of Merger in Merger Control Legislation' in C. J. Cheng, L. Liu & C. K. Wang (eds.) *International Harmonisation of Competition Laws* (Martinus Nijihoff, Dordrecht, 1995), p. 27.

[25] See J. W. Rowley, 'Competition Policy in a Global Economy – A Question for India' (1997) 23(11) *International Business Lawyer* 436.

enforcement.[26] However, the mandatory notification thresholds must be set at a level that does not burden the regulator with excessive volumes of information. Unduly burdensome mandatory pre-notification regimes may also impose considerable compliance costs on merging entities.[27]

A mandatory pre-notification regime does not preclude voluntary pre-notification as these regimes are not mutually exclusive and may co-exist. Mandatory notification requirements could, for example, be set at a high threshold to catch the worst mergers and acquisitions, while all other mergers and acquisitions are subject to voluntary pre-notification.[28] As a hybrid approach adopts the best aspects of both regimes, any international competition agreement should ideally promote a hybrid pre-notification approach.

4.4.2 Merger thresholds

In all APEC nations, mergers and acquisitions are prohibited only where they exceed a particular statutory threshold. There are three principal types of statutory thresholds used by APEC merger laws:

- Structural thresholds, in which mergers are prohibited if they result in a firm achieving a threshold market concentration (e.g. Taiwan).
- Behavioural thresholds, in which mergers are assessed to determine if they may lead to a threshold reduction in market competition (e.g. Australia, Canada, Japan, Mexico).
- Hybrid behavioural and structural thresholds, whereby certain threshold market concentrations are deemed anti-competitive, while other mergers and acquisitions are assessed under a rule of reason approach (e.g. Russia, Korea, Chile).

---

[26] A 2001 survey by White and Case determined that the most common merger notification system is mandatory pre-notification, which is required by forty-five jurisdictions. By contrast, five countries require both pre- and post-merger notification, three require post-notification only, one (Brazil) allows notice to be filed either pre- or post-merger, eleven countries permit voluntary notification, and two (Malta and Pakistan) have a required registration procedure. See 'White & Case Survey Shows No Let-up of Spreading Worldwide Maze of Merger Control Laws', *White & Case Newsletter*, Washington DC, 9 May 2001.

[27] See discussion in J. B. Kobak & A. M. D'Irio, 'The High Cost of Cross-Border Merger Reviews' in G. Meric & S. E. Nichols (eds.), *The Global Economy at the Turn of the Century* (MIT, Massachusetts, 1998).

[28] This is the approach used by the United States within its Hart-Scott-Rodino Antitrust Improvements Act, 15 USC 18a, S. Rep. No. 94-803 (1976).

Structural thresholds Structural thresholds suffer from the same difficulties as other conduct-oriented (per se) provisions, as discussed previously. A structural threshold prohibits a merger without considering the actual impact of the merger on competition and instead uses market concentration as a proxy for determining likely anti-competitive effects. This creates a risk that certain mergers harmful to competition may be permitted, while other mergers with net benefits may be prohibited. A hybrid threshold approach reduces this risk by applying structural thresholds only to clearly anti-competitive market concentrations. Accordingly, behavioural or hybrid thresholds are favoured by almost all APEC competition laws and only Taiwan continues to utilise structural thresholds alone.

Behavioural thresholds Two distinct behavioural thresholds are identifiable among the merger laws of APEC nations:

- 'Substantial lessening of competition' or 'restriction or prevention of competition', which is a lower threshold applying to situations of market oligopoly, as well as single-firm dominance and near-monopoly (e.g. Australia, Singapore, Papua New Guinea).
- 'Acquisition of market dominance', 'creating a monopoly' or 'creating monopolistic power', which is a higher threshold applying only to situations of single-firm dominance and near-monopoly (e.g. New Zealand prior to 2001).

The higher threshold of 'acquisition of dominance' was historically used by New Zealand on the basis that New Zealand's smaller economy required higher levels of business concentration to achieve minimum efficient scale.[29] New Zealand lowered its merger threshold to the 'substantial lessening of competition' level in May 2001 to harmonise its threshold with Australia.

The APEC experience suggests that any international competition agreement should encourage the use of behavioural thresholds to the extent each nation's institutional structure permits. The exact behavioural threshold will tend to reflect political choices within each nation as to the desired level of market concentration, but as a general rule only smaller economies should set higher behavioural thresholds.

---

[29] See R. S. Khemani, *Merger Policy and Small Open Economies* (Competition Bureau, Ottawa, 1991). See also the detailed discussion in M. Gal, *Competition Policy for Small Market Economies* (Harvard University Press, Cambridge, MA, 2003).

4.4.3 Public benefit assessment

An important incentive for businesses to acquire or merge with other businesses are the synergies and productive efficiencies that result from such mergers and acquisitions. In some circumstances, such benefits may outweigh anti-competitive detriments as discussed in Chapter 2 of this book. In particular, gains in technical efficiency arising from a merger may outweigh reductions in allocative efficiency and x-efficiency, leading to a KHE improvement which increases the total economic welfare of society.

Australia and New Zealand, for example, have enabled merger synergies and efficiencies to be expressly recognised by permitting statutory authorisation of mergers on the basis of a net public benefit test. A number of other APEC nations also enable public benefits to be considered during any competition assessment, although less formally.

The APEC experience suggests that public benefit assessments reduce the risk of inadvertent prohibition of mergers and acquisitions that may have significant net public benefits. However, as Canada has argued, such assessments also risk prejudicing the autonomy of competition authorities by requiring them to consider political matters. Accordingly, any formal public benefit assessment should remain politically transparent and should involve the application of narrowly prescribed statutory criteria. Any international competition agreement should seek to establish general principles of clarity and transparency to guide such public benefit tests, preferably referring to net efficiency improvements.

4.5 Regulation of unilateral conduct – anti-monopoly laws

As noted above, merger laws are not usually concerned with situations of pre-existing high market concentration. Rather, competition law regulates situations of pre-existing high market concentration by regulating market conduct, particularly by regulating the behaviour of firms with considerable market power via 'anti-monopoly laws'. In accordance with the SCP paradigm, regulation of market conduct ensures competition is maintained and thus market efficiency and fairness is enhanced. All APEC competition laws include anti-monopoly laws. Such anti-monopoly laws are the second of the three principal forms of competition law identified above and are analysed below for the APEC nations.

While pure monopoly is extremely rare, a firm may have sufficient market power in a concentrated market to enjoy many of the benefits available to a true monopolist. These benefits include, for example, the ability of the firm to raise its prices to extract monopoly profits from consumers and to use its market power to eliminate competitors or to impose barriers to competition. Accordingly, where a firm has excessive market power it may act in a manner harmful to the efficient operation of markets, as discussed in Chapter 2 of this book. Anti-monopoly laws aim to prevent such behaviour.

As with merger laws, anti-monopoly laws have several key features, namely a threshold of dominance, particular prohibitions and, in some cases, natural monopoly regulation and price controls. Each are considered below.

4.5.1 Threshold of dominance

The anti-monopoly laws of APEC nations define the level of market power at which a firm is subjected to anti-monopoly laws, usually known as the 'threshold of dominance'. A firm passing the threshold of dominance is considered to have insufficient competitive constraints on its pricing and other behaviour. Anti-monopoly laws address this market failure by prohibiting certain harmful conduct that could be undertaken by this firm. As with merger laws, the APEC thresholds of dominance comprise two general types:

- Structural thresholds, which are focused on market structure, such as possessing a defined market share. Structural thresholds vary widely, with Taiwan using a 70% market share, Korea and Indonesia using a 50% market share, and Russia using a 35% market share, for example.
- Behavioural thresholds, which are focused on market conduct, such as possessing substantial market power or a dominant market position.

Behavioural thresholds involve the consideration of a broader range of factors than structural thresholds and are therefore more result-oriented (rule of reason). The features of result-oriented and conduct-oriented provisions discussed previously, apply equally to the selection of structural or behavioural thresholds for anti-monopoly laws.

As illustrated by Figure 15, the behavioural thresholds of competition laws fall along a continuum. The higher thresholds on the right-hand side are typically used for merger control and anti-monopoly laws. The lower thresholds on the left-hand side are typically used for concerted conduct laws. The anti-monopoly laws of APEC nations are concerned with more concentrated market structures to the right of the continuum and generally adopt one of three approaches:

IS THERE SUFFICIENT BASIS FOR AN AGREEMENT? 91

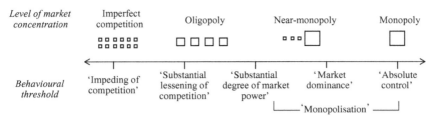

Figure 15: *Continuum of behavioural thresholds*

(a) a lower behavioural threshold of 'substantial degree of market power' (e.g. Australia, Mexico, New Zealand, Papua New Guinea);
(b) a higher behavioural threshold of 'market dominance' or 'dominant market position' (e.g. Canada, Peru, Indonesia, Russia, Singapore, Vietnam); and
(c) a similarly high behavioural threshold of 'monopolisation' or 'monopolistic status' (e.g. China, Japan, Philippines, United States).

As a general rule, one would expect that the selection of a particular behavioural threshold by each nation would tend to reflect a number of policy choices, including pre-existing levels of market concentration and the perceived harm caused by powerful firms. The APEC experience suggests that threshold selection is also heavily influenced by historical influences and political preferences.

Furthermore, there is no common approach to interpreting the wording of each threshold (particularly the concept of 'monopolisation'), so the actual threshold of dominance may vary widely between different APEC nations even where the wording is apparently similar. Accordingly, any international competition agreement should not prescribe an 'ideal' threshold of dominance, but should rather identify that any threshold of dominance could be set at least at the 'substantial degree of market power' level.

4.5.2 Particular prohibitions

APEC anti-monopoly laws generally fall into three broad categories:

- 'Conduct-oriented' provisions, where certain conduct of firms with threshold market power is prohibited on a per se basis, whether or not that firm has an anti-competitive purpose (i.e. China).[30]

---

[30] See China's Law of the People's Republic of China Countering Unfair Competition 1993, Art. 6 which sets out a per se prohibition against forcing of goods and services.

- 'Culpability-oriented' provisions, where certain conduct of firms with threshold market power is prohibited if the firm has an anti-competitive purpose (e.g. Mexico, New Zealand, Australia). The procedures used to determine an anti-competitive purpose differ widely between nations and are influenced by rules of evidence.
- 'Result-oriented' provisions, where certain conduct of firms with threshold market power is prohibited only if it has a threshold anti-competitive effect based on a rule of reason analysis (i.e. Australia, Canada, Chile, Peru).[31]

Unlike result-oriented provisions, all conduct-oriented and culpability-oriented provisions must necessarily prescribe the types of prohibited anti-competitive conduct. The particular types of prohibited anti-conduct differ considerably between APEC nations. For example, Chinese anti-monopoly laws contain specific prohibitions against certain types of exclusionary conduct and pricing below cost.[32] Korean anti-monopoly laws prohibit such matters as unreasonable controls on the sale of goods, interfering with the business activities of competitors, and engaging in threats to restrain competition.[33] These specific prohibitions tend to reflect the particular concerns of competition policy-makers within each nation, but usually are intended to protect smaller competitors from abuses of market power by larger competitors.[34]

As a general rule, the more specific the particular prohibitions are, the greater the scope for a firm to avoid the application of anti-monopoly laws. Accordingly, any international agreement should ideally favour broadly-expressed prohibitions.

The divergent approaches of APEC nations suggest that it would be difficult to achieve any standardised international anti-monopoly law. However, any international competition agreement could recognise and endorse commonly-accepted conceptual parameters or principles, including, for example, that anti-monopoly law should have a threshold of dominance and should apply to abuses of market power.

---

[31] See Australia's Trade Practices Act 1974 (Cth), s. ISI AJ (2). See Canada's Competition Act 1985 s. 79. See Peru's Legislative Decree 701, 1991, Arts. 4 and 5. See Chile's Decree Law No. 211 of 1973, Art. 6.
[32] See China's Law of the People's Republic of China for Countering Unfair Competition 1993, Arts. 11, 6.
[33] See Korea's Monopoly Regulation and Fair Trade Act 1980, Art. 3–2.
[34] See, for example, T. Näcke, 'Abuse of Dominant Positions: Recent World Developments' (1995) 23(10) *International Business Lawyer* 458.

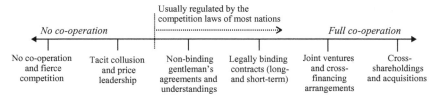

Figure 16: *Forms of business combination and their regulation by competition law*

4.6 Regulation of concerted conduct – horizontal and vertical agreements

The last of the three principal forms of competition law are concerted conduct laws, which are analysed below for the APEC nations.

Concerted conduct is prohibited by APEC competition laws where such conduct is perceived as interfering in the competitive process, thereby preventing the efficient operation of markets. Concerted conduct enables firms to co-operate to increase their collective market power. Accordingly, it may create the same types of market failure as are associated with firms misusing their market power in concentrated markets. Certain concerted conduct may also be prohibited by competition law due to wider social concerns of 'unfairness'.

Concerted conduct requires some form of agreement between firms, ranging from tacit collusion and non-binding 'gentlemen's agreements' through to sophisticated joint venture agreements and long-term contracts, as illustrated by the continuum in Figure 16. However, concerted conduct laws may only be applied where sufficient evidence of an agreement exists. Accordingly, the application of the concerted conduct laws of each APEC nation is constrained by the rules of evidence within each nation. For example, Russian cartel cases have historically required the Russian competition regulator to identify evidence of a formal written agreement, impairing the effectiveness of Russian competition laws in regulating informal cartel behaviour.[35]

Concerted conduct laws are principally intended to prevent agreements between firms that may have collusive or exclusive effects:

- Collusive effects reduce the level of competitive rivalry between firms, thereby reducing competitive incentives and restraints and causing

---

[35] See P. Joskow, R. Schmalensee & T. Tsukanova, 'Competition Policy in Russia During and After Privatisation' (1994) 42 *Brookings Papers in Economic Activity: Microeconomics* 1.

economic inefficiency. The most common collusive effects are associated with such agreements as cartels or market sharing agreements.
- Exclusive effects result in discrimination against third party rivals to provide the firms with a relative competitive advantage in the market. The most common exclusive effects are associated with exclusionary agreements, such as market boycotts or exclusive marketing arrangements.

Concerted conduct laws are further categorised into laws regulating horizontal agreements and laws regulating vertical agreements. Horizontal agreements tend to have collusive effects while vertical agreements tend to have exclusive effects, although there are numerous exceptions. Concerted conduct laws regulating horizontal agreements and vertical agreements are each considered below.

4.6.1 Horizontal agreements

Horizontal agreements refer to concerted behaviour between two or more firms competing within the same functional markets. Horizontal agreements subject to concerted conduct laws include price fixing agreements, output restrictions, market sharing agreements, customer allocation agreements and collusive tendering.

The competition laws of APEC nations generally utilise a combination of rule of reason and per se provisions to regulate horizontal agreements, although the particular mix and phraseology of these provisions differs significantly between nations. As a general rule, horizontal agreements are treated with suspicion by most APEC nations as they necessarily involve agreements between competitors and are thus more likely to be anti-competitive. Accordingly, certain horizontal agreements are commonly regulated by per se provisions notably 'hard core' cartel conduct, such as price fixing, output agreements, market division agreements and bid rigging.[36] Most APEC nations, for example, prohibit price fixing on a per se basis. These per se prohibitions are typically statutory, but may also be developed by case law (e.g. the US), or promulgated by way of regulation (e.g. Korea). However, other forms of horizontal agreements are not usually treated as strictly and are commonly subject to a rule of reason approach.

---

[36] See discussion in OECD, *Hard Core Cartels* (OECD, Paris, 2000).

IS THERE SUFFICIENT BASIS FOR AN AGREEMENT? 95

Almost all APEC nations regulate horizontal agreements via a conduct-oriented rule of reason approach. This approach imposes liability on the basis of breach of a behavioural threshold associated with the effect or intended effect of the horizontal agreement on competition. However, the application of this behavioural threshold to particular factual situations may be highly complex and this complexity has led to considerable divergences in approach between APEC nations.

There are two distinct conduct-oriented approaches adopted by APEC nations:

(a) 'combinations in restraint of trade', which is a concept equivalent to unreasonable suppression of competition (e.g. United States, Japan, Philippines);[37] and
(b) 'substantial lessening of competition' or 'practices affecting, diminishing or impairing free competition' (e.g. Australia, Canada, Russia).[38]

The differences between these two approaches are historical in origin, but both essentially employ the same behavioural threshold.

As discussed previously, the risk associated with per se prohibitions is that they may inadvertently prohibit pro-competitive conduct. Accordingly, any international competition agreement should urge nations to adopt rule of reason provisions to the extent that the institutional structure of each nation permits. The APEC experience further suggests that each nation should concentrate per se prohibitions only against cartel-like activities, with exemptions for genuine joint ventures. The relevant behavioural threshold accepted by almost all APEC nations is based on a lessening of competition of a predetermined amount or threshold. Any international competition agreement could adopt these common principles.

---

[37] See the US's Sherman Act 1890, s. 1 which refers to 'combination in the form of trust or otherwise, or conspiracy, in restraint of trade or commerce'. See also Japan's Antimonopoly Act 1947, ss. 2(6), 3 which refers to 'unreasonable restraint of trade'. See also the Philippines' Revised Penal Code RA 3815, 1930, Art. 186 which refers to 'combinations in restraint of trade'.
[38] See, for example, Australia's Trade Practices Act 1974, s. 45 and New Zealand's Commerce Act 1986, s. 27 which both refer to 'substantial lessening of competition'. See also, for example, Canada's Competition Act 1985, s. 45 which refers to the restraining, lessening or restricting of competition *unduly* in various circumstances.

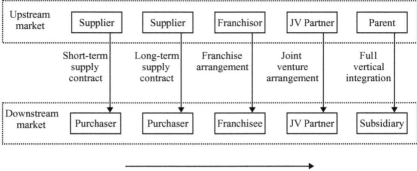

Figure 17: *Taxonomy of vertical agreements*

4.6.2 Vertical agreements and vertical restraints

Vertical agreements involve agreements between firms at different levels of the product supply chain, usually between firms competing in different functional markets. Vertical agreements range from single transactions between completely independent enterprises at different stages of the distribution chain, to the vertical integration of such stages within a single enterprise, as illustrated by Figure 17. Concerted conduct laws are mostly concerned to prohibit 'vertical restraints', which are exclusionary in effect and involve the use of contractual arrangements to restrict the freedom of firms to contract with third parties, including via tying, exclusive dealing, and territorial restraints.[39]

In most cases, the same behavioural threshold and conduct-oriented approach that each nation uses for the regulation of horizontal agreements is also applied to the regulation of vertical restraints. Accordingly, the same issues arise as discussed previously.

Vertical restraints on prices, or 'resale price maintenance', tend to be universally prohibited by all APEC nations on a result-oriented per se basis. However, the use of per se prohibitions is less common for other types of vertical restraints although most APEC nations retain per se prohibitions against specific vertical restraints that are considered particularly

---

[39] See, for example, G. A. Hay, 'Vertical Restraints' in C. J. Cheng, L. Liu & C. K. Wang (eds.), *International Harmonisation of Competition Laws* (Martinus Nijihoff, Dordrecht, 1995), p. 189.

troublesome.[40] These prohibitions tend to reflect political preferences within each nation so even similar nations have different per se provisions. New Zealand, for example, specifically prohibits exclusionary provisions, price fixing and resale price maintenance,[41] while Australia also specifically prohibits such matters as secondary boycotts and exclusive dealing.[42]

Over the past two decades, economic theory has recognised that many vertical agreements may have net benefits to society and the continued validity of prohibiting vertical restraints on a per se basis has been increasingly questioned. Accordingly, any international agreement would ideally encourage the use of a rule of reason approach in the regulation of vertical restraints to the extent that the institutional structure of each nation permits.

4.7 Exemptions from the application of competition laws

In addition to a consideration of each of the three types of competition law, as set out above, it is also necessary to consider the scope of such laws and their particular administration and enforcement. The scope of competition laws is necessarily determined by the extent of exemptions from those laws. In this regard, all APEC nations utilise exemptions from the application of their competition laws. These exemptions are specific to the public policy concerns of each nation, although the underlying justifications for particular types of exemptions are very similar.

The APEC experience suggests that such exemptions fall within three broad categories:

(a) exemptions for state-entities;
(b) exemptions for public-interest cartels; and
(c) exemptions for particular industries and industry sectors.

Each are considered, in turn, below.

---

[40] Note, however, that this per se prohibition is controversial. See, for example, discussion in J. Bork, *The Antitrust Paradox* (Basic Books, New York, 1978), p. 288. See also discussion in F. Comanor, 'Vertical Price Fixing, Vertical Market Restrictions, and the New Antitrust Policy' (1985) 98 *Harvard Law Review* 983, 1001–2.
[41] See, for example, New Zealand's Commerce Act 1986, s. 29 (exclusionary provisions), s. 30 (price fixing), and s. 37 (resale price maintenance).
[42] See the Australian Trade Practices Act 1974 (Cth), ss. 45D and 45, respectively.

4.7.1 Exemptions for state entities

Many APEC nations have an exemption or partial exemption for government entities. This exemption is common in circumstances where state-owned entities are prevalent within an economy. Accordingly, an exemption for government entities is common for APEC nations that have not fully deregulated their economies or retain significant sectors of the economy in government ownership, including Thailand, Korea and Chile.[43]

However, exemptions for government entities are risky given that such entities typically have considerable market power and could use this market power to harm competition. Most nations with state exemptions from competition laws have sought to mitigate these risks by requiring state entities to conduct any commercial activities in a manner consistent with wider public policy objectives. Any international competition agreement could promote a principle of competition accountability for state enterprises on this basis.

4.7.2 Exemptions for public interest cartels

Public interest cartels are, by definition, cartels that are specifically exempted from competition laws on the basis that they are perceived to have net public benefits. They are generally of four types:

(a) import cartels, where collusion is permitted in order to countervail the market power of foreign exporters;
(b) export cartels, where collusion is permitted in order to countervail the market power of foreign importers;
(c) rationalisation cartels, where collusion is permitted in order to assist in the restructuring of particular industries; and
(d) depression cartels, where collusion is permitted in the interests of assisting firms to overcome sector-specific or economy-wide depressions.

In each case, these cartels are tolerated as a necessary evil in the interests of promoting domestic economic prosperity. However, such exemptions from competition laws have remained controversial and many economic theorists have challenged whether such cartels are in fact beneficial, as

---

[43] See S. Supanit, 'Thailand: Implementation of Competition Law' (1999) 27(11) *International Business Lawyer* 497.

discussed in Chapters 7 and 8 of this book. A principle that is generally accepted within most APEC nations is that such cartels should be subject to exemption on a case-by-case basis where there are net public benefits (although the assessment of these benefits is typically subject to a high degree of political influence). At present there appears to be a trend towards a more restrictive approach to the granting of such exemptions within APEC, as exemplified by Japan's recent repeal of its extensive cartel exemptions on the basis that such exemptions were causing more harm than good. Any international competition agreement may wish to highlight this trend and recommend that all cartel exemptions should be assessed against clear and transparent public benefit criteria.

4.7.3 Exemptions for particular industries and sectors

Almost all APEC nations have exemptions for particular industries and sectors from their competition laws. Many of these exemptions are associated with an overlap between competition law and alternative regulatory regimes. For example, shipping is regulated under an alternative competition regime in many nations, including New Zealand and Australia, so is frequently subject to specific exemptions from generic competition laws.

Almost all APEC nations have a specific exemption for their intellectual property laws, although this exemption usually relates specifically to the conferral of monopoly rights to patent holders.[44] Other common exemptions apply to trade unions and agricultural producer associations. Many exemptions tend to be specific to the particular economic and social policies of APEC nations, such as Canada's exemption for amateur sport and New Zealand's exemption for its government pharmaceutical-purchasing agency. Any international competition agreement could establish a principle that all such exemptions should be non-discriminatory and strictly limited in scope.

---

[44] See, for example, New Zealand's Commerce Act 1986, s. 45 which excludes a variety of intellectual property rights from the application of New Zealand's competition law, although it ensures that such intellectual property rights remain subject to regulation under New Zealand's anti-monopoly laws. In this manner, a refusal to grant a copyright licence, for example, could still constitute an anti-competitive abuse of market power consistent with the *Magill* case before the European Court of Justice: *Radio Telefix Cierann and Independent Television Publications Ltd* v. *Commission of the European Communities* [1995] All ER 416 (EC).

4.7.4 Issues for any international competition agreement

An important characteristic of competition law is that it should remain generic and comprehensive in its application so as to reduce compliance and enforcement costs, and to ensure that distortions are not created within an economy. Furthermore, if competition law is limited in its scope and applicability via the extensive use of exemptions, it is likely to lose credibility and its role in economic policy will be reduced. On this basis, any international agreement should discourage the use of exemptions.

However, competition law does not exist in a political vacuum and the APEC experience suggests that exemptions remain an integral part of modern competition laws. The World Bank has also highlighted that it is preferable to have a limited competition law (subject to a number of exemptions) rather than no competition law at all.[45] Accordingly, any international competition agreement should recognise that exemptions are necessary to address particular national concerns. Yet any such agreement could also establish the principle that any exemptions should be no greater in scope than is necessary for the particular national concern to be addressed.

Where a nation has extensive exemptions within its competition laws to an extent that contradicts any rules or principles set out in any international competition agreement, the nation should be encouraged to use the international trade law concept of 'derogations', rather than not ratifying any international competition agreement at all. Hong Kong and Singapore, for example, could use a derogation to exempt the application of an international competition agreement to the extent that the markets of both nations are open to intense international competition, as discussed previously. The appropriateness of this approach and similar alternative mechanisms are discussed in the commentary accompanying the draft WTO plurilateral competition agreement set out in the Appendix to this book.

4.8 Administration and enforcement of domestic competition laws

As noted above, a final element of APEC competition laws that requires examination involves differences between administration and enforcement. This necessarily requires consideration of the appropriate role of administrative agencies and the nature of enforcement and remedies.

---

[45] See World Bank, above n. 13.

4.8.1 Appropriate role of administrative agencies

Almost all APEC nations have created a specific competition agency, or have assigned a specific branch of a government ministry, to oversee their competition laws. All APEC nations except the Philippines and the US have allocated responsibility for competition law administration and enforcement to one agency which then prioritises and co-ordinates its activities subject to its budgetary constraints. The US utilises two agencies, which co-operate to ensure their activities do not overlap or conflict. The Philippines relies on multiple government agencies to enforce competition laws within their particular areas of speciality. The Philippine experience is instructive, as industry-specific responsibility for enforcement and administration has caused competition laws to be applied strictly in some areas but not in others, creating inconsistencies.[46]

The exact role and function of these competition authorities varies widely within each APEC nation. In many APEC nations, the competition authority is involved in wider competition policy development. In Mexico, for example, the Federal Competition Commission has contributed towards the adoption of privatisation policies and regularly participates in inter-ministerial committees.[47] Similarly, in Korea, the Chairman of the Korean Fair Trade Commission is also the chairman of the Economic Regulatory Reform Committee and may present opinions at Cabinet meetings and economic ministerial meetings.[48] However, the danger in such an approach is that the independence of the competition agency may be compromised. Some analysts have observed that the Korean and Mexican competition agencies were subject to a degree of political influence.[49]

As the World Bank and OECD have recommended, the institutions used by nations to administer and enforce competition laws should be tailored to the particular circumstances of each nation with regard to fundamental principles of institutional design. The APEC experience provides several insights into critical principles of institutional design that should guide the establishment of competition agencies. By way of example:

---

[46] See G. T. Santos Jr, 'The Philippines: Competition Policy Developments in the Service Sector' (1997) 25(11) *International Business Lawyer* 468.

[47] See S. Levy & R. de Villar, 'Contribution of Competition Policy to Economic Development: The Case of Mexico', OECD Documents, OCDE/GD(96)59, 1996.

[48] See W. Cho, 'Korea's Economic Crisis: The Role of Competition Policy' (1999) 27(11) *International Business Lawyer* 495.

[49] See discussion in APEC, *Study of Competition Laws for Developing Economies* (APEC, Singapore, 1999).

- Some analysts have observed that the Chinese and Russian competition agencies were historically subject to a high degree of political influence, reflecting the role of the state in the socialist market economy model. Both nations have subsequently sought to give their competition agencies a higher degree of political independence.
- Similarly, some analysts observed that the decisions of the Japanese, Korean and Thai competition authorities historically tended to lack transparency, reflecting the close relationship between business and government in these nations. All three nations introduced competition law reforms to address these issues, although continuing concerns have been expressed in relation to enforcement of Thailand's competition laws.[50]
- All APEC nations have acknowledged that effective staffing of any competition agency is essential. There is a risk that if too much power is entrusted to an inexperienced competition agency, that agency may do more harm than good.

Accordingly, the APEC experience suggests that the most crucial principles for ensuring effective competition law administration and enforcement are political independence, decision-making transparency, accountability, and adequate resourcing. Any international competition agreement could outline these fundamental principles of institutional design to guide the establishment of national competition agencies.

4.8.2 Enforcement and remedies

Enforcement mechanisms and remedies differ widely between APEC nations and tend to reflect the particular legal system within each nation. In general terms, competition law may be enforced:

(a) directly by governmental agencies, with these governmental agencies having quasi-judicial powers to impose administrative remedies or penalties, such as fines;
(b) indirectly by governmental agencies, with these governmental agencies able to take action before the courts to seek remedies or penalties; and/or
(c) by private individuals, with these individuals able to take action before the courts to seek damages, remedies or penalties.

---

[50] See, for example, discussion in M. Williams, 'Competition Law in Thailand: Seeds of Success or Fated to Fail?' (2004) 27 *World Competition* 459.

In the case of governmental enforcement, some APEC nations empower their respective competition agency to initiate action proactively on its own accord, while other nations require their competition agency to react to industry complaints. In the case of private enforcement, different nations impose different requirements for jurisdictional standing. In Japan, for example, private enforcement may only be undertaken if permitted by the relevant competition agency, the Japanese Fair Trade Commission. Furthermore, the remedies for breaches of competition law also differ widely between APEC nations. Remedies include, for example, imprisonment, fines, injunctions, divestiture, damages and compensatory orders.

Any international competition agreement would need to recognise these different enforcement practices, institutions and remedies between nations. The proposed remedies for breaches of competition law should accord with the particular remedies usually applied to similar conduct in the relevant nation. Accordingly, international competition agreements should avoid detailing specific remedies, although certain types of remedies and punitive principles could be recommended. For example, most APEC nations agree that the principal method for deterring anti-competitive conduct should involve the imposition of monetary penalties. Most APEC nations also agree that penalties should be set at levels that reflect the costs to society of anti-competitive conduct and that have a sufficient deterrent and punitive value.

4.9 Conclusion: there is a sufficient basis for an international competition agreement

The APEC experience provides a number of insights into the likely content of any international competition agreement. Initially any such agreement should not be overly ambitious and should simply seek to establish principles to guide the content and application of national competition laws.

First, any international competition agreement should recognise institutional pre-conditions for the enactment of competition laws and should recommend institutional strengthening where these pre-conditions are not met. Similarly, any agreement should recognise that the particular mix between conduct- and result-oriented competition law provisions is influenced by the ability of institutions to manage sophisticated rule of reason analyses competently. Accordingly, the effectiveness of competition laws is dependent on effective institutions.

Secondly, any international competition agreement should promote economic efficiency as the objective of competition law, but should also recognise that social and distributional objectives may be important to particular countries. In realising these objectives, any agreement should encourage the simultaneous enactment of merger laws, anti-monopoly laws and concerted conduct laws, as follows:

- Merger laws should ideally involve behavioural thresholds and hybrid pre-notification procedures. The exact behavioural threshold will tend to reflect political choices within each nation, but as a general rule only smaller economies should set higher behavioural thresholds. Principles of clarity and transparency should guide any public benefit exemptions for mergers above this threshold.
- Anti-monopoly laws should ideally involve a behavioural threshold of dominance set at least at the 'substantial degree of market power' level. If culpability or conduct-oriented provisions are used, these should be broadly expressed.
- Concerted conduct laws should ideally involve rule of reason provisions. Per se prohibitions should be limited to the worst instances of horizontal collusive behaviour and should be applied sparingly to vertical exclusive behaviour.

Finally, any international competition agreement should recommend that national competition laws should be enforced by a single agency which is independent, transparent, accountable and adequately resourced. Penalties should be set at levels which reflect the costs to society of anti-competitive conduct and which are sufficient to have both a deterrent and punitive effect. Exemptions should be discouraged and should be no greater in scope than is considered necessary in the circumstances.

In summary, there is sufficient commonality among the competition laws of different nations to support an international competition agreement, notwithstanding considerable diversity, as illustrated by a sample group of nations comprising those nations within APEC. An analysis of the competition laws of APEC nations indicates that commonly accepted principles can be readily distilled. An international competition agreement could be based on these principles. However, there also remain areas where considerable differences are apparent and where international consensus would be unlikely to be achieved at the present time.

Competition laws have similar efficiency objectives and a common structure, but may have diverse distributional objectives. Competition laws are based on commonly accepted economic concepts of markets and market power. Competition laws typically adopt a tripartite structure involving merger laws, anti-monopoly laws and concerted conduct laws, but the particular formulation of these laws may differ considerably. So while many of the broad features of competition laws are similar across jurisdictions, the particular nuances and specific detail of competition laws in each jurisdiction differ widely, as does their particular factual application.

The APEC analysis suggests that any international competition agreement should not be overly ambitious and could simply establish broad principles to guide the appropriate content of national competition laws. A range of insights and common themes can be identified in relation to merger laws, anti-monopoly laws and concerted conduct laws that would enable a competition agreement to be adopted based on broad principles without proscribing specific formulations of law. Any such agreement should also recognise the institutional pre-conditions for competition laws and the need to recognise legitimate diversity sufficiently, resource limitations and competition law experience. With this in mind, a broad framework for an international competition agreement can be identified. There is therefore a sufficient basis for an international competition agreement.

5

Have existing cross-border initiatives proved sufficient?

> The derivation of a common antitrust standard among nations – a truly international antitrust law – does not arise simply through legislative act. It must be the logical culmination of the economic, political, and social development of a nation or groups of nations.
>
> (Kintner, 1973)[1]

Chapter 5 of this book analyses existing initiatives at the bilateral, plurilateral and multilateral levels relating to the regulation of cross-border competition. Chapter 5 considers whether these initiatives alone may already be sufficient to address the externalities identified in Chapter 3 of this book. Chapter 5 has three principal sections:

- Section 5.1 considers the nature of bilateral competition agreements and their limitations. Section 5.1 examines the evolution of such agreements from 'first generation' to 'fourth generation' agreements over the past three decades and identifies current initiatives towards increased bilateral co-operation. Section 5.1 also identifies positive comity and negative comity as important mechanisms to address the externalities identified in Chapter 3 of this book.
- Section 5.2 identifies two important plurilateral competition initiatives, namely within the EU and APEC. Section 5.2 analyses the advantages and disadvantages of both of these initiatives and their current limitations. Section 5.2 identifies elements of plurilateral initiatives that could have multinational application and considers whether plurilateral initiatives alone would sufficiently regulate cross-border anti-competitive conduct.
- Section 5.3 identifies existing multilateral competition initiatives, including initiatives within UNCTAD, the OECD and the WTO. Section 5.3 identifies the limitations of these initiatives and whether

---

[1] See E. W. Kintner, *Primer on the Law of Mergers* (Macmillan, New York, 1973), p. 63.

HAVE EXISTING INITIATIVES PROVED SUFFICIENT? 107

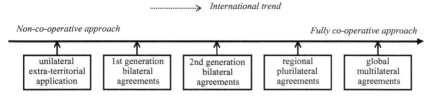

Figure 18: *Continuum of international agreements*

they could provide a vehicle for the development of a multilateral competition treaty.

Chapter 5 concludes that the existing cross-border initiatives have clear limitations and are not sufficient on their own to address the externalities identified in Chapter 3. An international competition agreement would be necessary to address these issues. Chapter 5 concludes that a combination of the existing initiatives with an international competition agreement would sufficiently regulate cross-border competition.

5.1 A network of bilateral competition agreements

Approaches to the cross-border regulation of international competition may be perceived as falling along a continuum from 'non-co-operative' approaches to 'co-operative' approaches, as illustrated by Figure 18. At the non-co-operative (left) end of the continuum, each nation may unilaterally seek to apply its domestic competition laws on an extraterritorial basis regardless of the views of other nations, as discussed in Chapter 3 of this book. At the fully co-operative (right) end of the continuum, nations will co-operate on cross-border competition law enforcement and maintain similar competition laws in accordance with their obligations under a multilateral agreement. Over time, the level of cross-border co-operation has increased and hence the international community has incrementally progressed along the continuum to the right.

5.1.1 First generation bilateral competition agreements

Given the difficulties associated with non-co-operative (extra-territorial) approaches to the regulation of cross-border competition, as identified in Chapter 3 of this book, nations have increasingly favoured a co-operative approach. Bilateral competition agreements, in particular, have provided an important mechanism for mitigating jurisdictional conflict and promoting cross-border co-operation on competition law enforcement.

Indeed, such bilateral agreements may be perceived as establishing the de facto international standard for cross-border competition law enforcement in the absence of an overriding multilateral framework for the regulation of cross-border competition.

Bilateral competition agreements have largely been confined to date to circumstances in which two jurisdictions with similar competition laws and similar views on competition law enforcement have found it expedient to co-operate and formalise such co-operation. Mutual confidence between nations regarding their respective competition enforcement policies and procedures has remained an important pre-condition for such agreements. Moreover, the greater the degree of confidence and similarity between nations in relation to their respective competition laws and enforcement policies, the more likely it is that these nations will favour sophisticated bilateral agreements, and the greater the degree of corresponding bilateral co-operation. As nations have gained greater confidence in each other's competition law enforcement mechanisms, so these bilateral agreements have become increasingly ambitious.

In this manner, bilateral competition agreements have undergone four distinct evolutionary phases over the past thirty years with each successive evolutionary phase involving a more sophisticated and ambitious form of bilateral co-operation:

(a) 'passive co-operation' agreements, from 1976 ('*First Generation Agreements*');
(b) 'negative comity' agreements, from 1988 ('*Second Generation Agreements*');
(c) 'positive comity' agreements, including international antitrust enforcement assistance agreements, from 1995 ('*Third Generation Agreements*'); and
(d) 'extension of jurisdiction' agreements, which remain rare ('*Fourth Generation Agreements*').

First Generation Agreements   Important catalysts for the negotiation of First Generation Agreements were a series of formal policy recommendations promulgated from 1967 by OECD. In these recommendations, the OECD proposed that advanced industrialised nations should co-ordinate their competition law enforcement activities to reduce the economic costs of inter-jurisdictional conflict. The OECD recommendations therefore contemplated a form of 'passive co-operation'.

The First Generation Agreements embodied this concept of passive co-operation but otherwise remained basic in nature, containing four principal elements as outlined in Figure 19. Co-operation and consultation

Element	Description
Notification	Limited notification requirements required each nation to notify the other nation before it commenced a competition law proceeding that affected the significant interests of that other nation.
Information exchange	Limited information exchange requirements required each nation to exchange limited information on request for the purposes of competition law enforcement, subject to confidentiality considerations.
Co-operation	Passive co-operation requirements required the competition authority of each nation to respond to requests for limited co-operation from its foreign counterpart.
Consultation	Limited consultation procedures required the competition authorities of each nation to consult with each other over enforcement investigations and actions with a view to avoiding jurisdictional conflict.

Figure 19: *Four principal elements of the First Generation Agreements*

requirements were intended to mitigate inter-jurisdictional conflict associated with extraterritorial enforcement of competition laws. Notification and information exchange requirements were intended to promote consultation between national competition authorities to avoid duplication of effort when investigating cross-border anti-competitive conduct. The First Generation Agreements included, most notably, agreements between the US and Germany in 1976,[2] the US and Australia in 1982,[3] the US and Canada in 1982,[4] and France and Germany in 1987.[5]

Importantly, the First Generation Agreements did not seriously contemplate reciprocal cross-border law enforcement or substantive

---

[2] See Agreement Between the Government of the US of America and the Government of the Federal Republic of Germany Relating to Mutual Co-operation Regarding Restrictive Business Practices, Bonn, 23 June 1976, 27 UST 1956, (1976) 15 ILM 1282.

[3] See Agreement Between the Government of the United States of America and the Government of the Commonwealth of Australia Relating to Co-operation on Antitrust Matters, 29 June 1982, 34 UST 3888, (1982) 21 ILM 702.

[4] See Agreement Between the Government of the US of America and the Government of Canada Relating to Mutual Co-operation Regarding Restrictive Business Practices (1982) 23 ILM 702.

[5] See Agreement Between the Government of France and the Government of the Federal Republic of Germany Relating to Mutual Co-operation Regarding Competition Law (1987) 26 ILM 531.

cross-border competition laws. Moreover, they permitted each ratifying nation to overlook any anti-competitive effects of particular conduct within its jurisdiction on the markets of the other ratifying nation, so did not address the negative economic externalities identified in Chapter 3 of this book.

5.1.2 Second generation bilateral competition agreements

As confidence grew, and the limitations of the First Generation Agreements became apparent, the US and the EC (as the world's competition law heavyweights) sought to negotiate a more sophisticated bilateral agreement which introduced novel concepts of 'comity'. The resulting US-EC Agreement was concluded in 1991, was subsequently struck down by the European Court of Justice, but was reinstated with retrospective effect in April 1995.[6] The EC-US Agreement remains in effect today and extends considerably further than its predecessors so may be considered the first 'Second Generation Agreement'. Subsequent Second Generation Agreements have been concluded between a number of countries, including, more recently, the US and Israel in March 1999, the US and Japan in October 1999, the US and Brazil in October 1999, and the US and Mexico in July 2000.

These Second Generation Agreements expand the four principal elements of the First Generation Agreements identified in Figure 19, but also adopt two innovative principles of 'negative comity' and 'positive comity', as identified in Figure 20. Importantly, the comity provisions provide a mechanism to address the economic externalities identified in Chapter 3 of this book.

- *Negative comity* The principle of 'negative comity', in a competition context, refers to an obligation placed on an enforcing nation to consider the interests of an affected nation when enforcing its domestic laws and to refrain from taking enforcement action that adversely affects the interests of that affected nation.

    Negative comity therefore partly mitigates the *over*-regulation identified in Chapter 3 of this book by requiring an enforcing nation to factor into its enforcement decisions any adverse impact on other nations.

---

[6] France successfully challenged the European Commission before the European Court of Justice for signing the agreement without prior approval from the European Council. See Case C-327/91, *French Republic* v. *Commission of the European Communities*, [1994] ECR I-3641.

Element	Description
Notification	Stringent notification requirements (in addition to those of the First Generation Agreements), require each nation to notify the other of any significant information bought to its attention that could warrant enforcement activity by the other.
Information exchange	Stringent information exchange requirements require each nation to exchange information on general matters relating to the implementation of its competition laws and enforcement activities that affected the important interests of the other nation. This includes information relating to the activities of private sector entities, although constraints preserve the confidentiality of private sector information.
Co-operation	Full co-operation obligations require each competition authority to assist its foreign counterpart to the fullest extent consistent with its laws, important interests and reasonable available resources.
Consultation	Consultation procedures required regular meetings between the personnel of each nation's competition authority and with co-ordinated law enforcement where both nations pursue enforcement action against related anti-competitive conduct.
Negative comity	Full 'negative comity' obligations require each nation to consider the important interests of the other nation when it enforces its competition laws. Negative comity provisions mitigate over-regulation by requiring a nation to refrain from measures which detrimentally affect the interests of the other nation, as discussed in greater detail above.
Positive comity	Limited 'positive comity' obligations permit each nation a limited right to request the other nation's competition authority to initiate appropriate enforcement action, if it believes that anti-competitive activity carried out on the territory of the other nation adversely affects its important interests. Positive comity provisions mitigate under-regulation by an enforcing nation and may be perceived as creating a form of deputised law enforcement.

Figure 20: *Six principal elements of the Second Generation Agreements*

The negative comity obligations in Second Generation Agreements expressly require the enforcing nation to consider the effect of any anti-competitive conduct in its territory on the markets of the affected nation and to:[7]
  (a) notify the affected nation when the enforcing nation's enforcement proceedings affected the important interests of the affected nation; and
  (b) give full and sympathetic consideration to possible ways of fulfilling the enforcing nation's enforcement needs without harming the important interests of the affected nation.
- *Positive comity*   The principle of 'positive comity', in a competition context, refers to an obligation placed on an enforcing nation to consider express requests for enforcement action made by an affected nation to the extent that conduct in the territory of the enforcing nation is adversely affecting the affected nation.

Positive comity therefore partly mitigates *under*-regulation by requiring an enforcing nation to take enforcement action where there is an adverse impact on another nation. The positive comity obligations in Second Generation Agreements expressly required the enforcing nation to:
  (a) give full and sympathetic consideration to the affected nation's request; and
  (b) take whatever remedial action the enforcing nation deemed appropriate on a voluntary basis and in considering its legitimate interests.

Accordingly, while negative comity procedures contemplate notification by a party when taking enforcement action, positive comity procedures enable nations proactively to request enforcement action by foreign nations. These twin principles of comity expressly recognise that anti-competitive conduct in one nation can be harmful to the markets of another nation and provide an instrument for nations to influence the enforcement activity of other nations.

However, a significant limitation on the type of bilateral co-operation contemplated by existing Second Generation Agreements is their restriction on the sharing of private sector confidential information between national competition authorities. Each nation's competition authorities remain bound by domestic laws preserving confidentiality and this restricts their ability to co-ordinate cross-border competition law

---

[7] See OECD, 'CLP Report on Positive Comity', OECD Paper, DAFFE/CLP(99)19, 10 June 1999.

enforcement. In nations frequently undertaking criminal prosecutions for breaches of competition law, such as the US, this has proved particularly troubling due to the stricter burden of proof associated with criminal enforcement. Under Second Generation Agreements, private sector confidential information may typically only be shared between competition agencies if an investigated firm gives its prior written consent to any cross-border information exchange. However, it would not usually be in the interests of a firm to do so, particularly in circumstances where the firm could face substantial criminal sanctions.

Second Generation Agreements do not create substantive binding cross-border competition laws or a cross-border jurisdiction to apply the laws of one nation within the territory of the other. However, they do create a framework that national competition authorities can use to influence competition law enforcement in foreign jurisdictions, notably via comity provisions. The pre-conditions for the negotiation of Second Generation Agreements are low, not requiring the degree of similarity of competition laws or the degree of mutual institutional confidence that more advanced bilateral agreements require. For this reason, Second Generation Agreements remain the favoured form of bilateral agreement between nations that have not previously co-operated on competition law matters.

5.1.3 Third generation bilateral competition agreements

Since the 1970s, the US Department of Justice and State Department have negotiated a number of treaties known as mutual legal assistance treaties ('MLATs'). These MLATs are intended to assist cross-border criminal law enforcement between the US and foreign governments. Such treaties permit the sharing of investigative information and the obtaining of documents and evidence located in foreign nations for use in criminal prosecutions.[8]

Under a typical MLAT, each nation agrees to use its investigative powers to obtain information for criminal investigations conducted by the other nation, when requested to do so. While the initial MLATs were intended only for use in conventional criminal prosecutions, the scope of MLATs has progressively expanded over time and some of the more recent MLATs expressly contemplate competition law criminal prosecutions.[9]

---

[8] See T. Ellis & E. Pisani, 'The US Treaties on Mutual Assistance in Criminal Matters: A Comparative Analysis' (1985) 19 *International Lawyer* 189.

[9] See, for example, US–Switzerland Treaty on Mutual Assistance in Criminal Matters, entered into force 23 January 1977, 27 UST 2019, TIAS 8302.

In 1990, within the context of an expansive MLAT, Canada and the US expressly sought to share confidential information on competition law enforcement thereby seeking to overcome some of the limitations with Second Generation Agreements by forming the first 'Third Generation Agreement'.[10] Previously, the competition authorities of both nations had been significantly constrained in their cross-border enforcement activities due to their inability to exchange confidential information or seize evidence for the benefit of their foreign counterpart. The sharing of confidential information between Canada and the US permitted by the MLAT enabled a number of successful cross-border criminal prosecutions against cartel behaviour. Canadian prosecutions of cross-border cartels uncovered by the US Department of Justice, for example, led to the imposition of Canadian fines of nearly US$100 million over the next decade. An important attribute of these cartel cases was that enforcement would have been impossible in the absence of the enforcement co-operation permitted by the MLAT.

International Antitrust Enforcement Assistance Building on the success of the US–Canada MLAT, the US sought to extend its ability to enter into competition law MLATs with other nations.[11] In November 1994, at the behest of the Clinton administration and with widespread bipartisan support, the US Congress enacted the International Antitrust Enforcement Assistance Act 1994 ('IAEA Act').[12] The IAEA Act mandates US competition authorities to enter into reciprocal 'International Antitrust Enforcement Assistance Agreements' ('IAEAAs') for the purposes of cross-border competition law enforcement and exchanges of confidential information. Under each IAEAA, the US competition authorities may co-operate and exchange private sector confidential information on a case-by-case basis with each foreign competition authority that has agreed to do likewise.[13]

To address the concerns of US business interests that IAEAAs might endanger the confidentiality of corporate information, the US Congress incorporated numerous safeguard provisions. These provisions ensure that a prerequisite for the sharing of private sector confidential information is an expression of confidence by each nation in the ability

---

[10] See Treaty between the Government of Canada and the Government of the US of America on Mutual Legal Assistance in Criminal Matters, 1990 Can TS No 19, 18 March 1985, entered into force 14 January 1990, 100th Cong., 2d Sess, Treaty Doc. 100–14; Exec. Rpt. 100–28; Exec. Rpt. 101–10; 24 ILM 1092–1099, July 1985, No. 4.

[11] See L. N. Freeman, 'US–Canadian Information Sharing and the International Antitrust Enforcement Assistance Act 1994' (1995) 84 *Georgetown Law Journal* 339.

[12] International Antitrust Enforcement Assistance Act 1994, Pub Law No. 103–438, 108 Stat 4597, 15 USC 6201–6212.

[13] IAEA Act ss. 8(a), 12(A).

of the competition authority of the other nation to maintain the confidentiality of that information. If a breach of confidentiality occurs, both nations must undertake remedial measures, including potential termination of the IAEAA. Accordingly, the confidentiality of corporate information remains sacrosanct.[14]

Furthermore, the IAEA Act requires *positive* comity provisions to be included within each IAEAA. These provisions enable a foreign competition authority to request the assistance of the US government or courts in relation to enforcement action in the US against the anti-competitive actions of US firms that harm its foreign markets. However, each request remains subject to the overriding consideration that the US public interest supports the provision of such assistance.

While the IAEA Act, with its mandates of reciprocity and confidentiality, provides a potent framework for the development of a network of Third Generation Agreements between the US and other nations, it has not yet proved effective in doing so. As at March 2006, only one IAEAA had been successfully negotiated, namely between the US and Australia in April 1999.[15] This is largely reflective of the strict confidentiality criteria set out within the IAEA Act as the IAEA Act sets a high threshold for negotiation of IAEAAs which most nations cannot yet meet. However, it also reflects the fact that most nations continue to guard their corporate information jealously, partly for fear of cross-border industrial espionage.

Third Generation Agreements Following the success of the innovative positive comity mechanism in the EU–US agreement and the support for positive comity embodied within the IAEA Act, some of the advanced industrialised nations sought to negotiate more extensive positive comity obligations into their bilateral competition law agreements. Furthermore, continued jurisdictional conflict between the EU and US in the context of the 1996 Boeing–McDonnell Douglas merger led the EU and US to seek a more comprehensive agreement in respect of positive comity issues. As a result, a number of Third Generation Agreements were negotiated, commencing with the US–Canada MLAT in 1995, and subsequently including a positive comity agreement between the US and EC in 1998,[16] the IAEAA

---

[14] See L. L. Laudati & T. J. Freidbacher, 'Trading Secrets: The International Antitrust Enforcement Assistance Act' (1996) 16 *Northwestern Journal International Law & Business* 478.
[15] See Agreement between the Government of the US of America and the Government of Australia on Mutual Antitrust Enforcement Assistance, Washington DC, 27 April 1999.
[16] See Agreement between the Government of the US of America and the European Communities on the Application of Positive Comity Principles in the Enforcement of their Competition Laws, Washington DC and Brussels, 4 June 1998.

Element	Description
Notification	Comprehensive notification requirements, similar to those in Second Generation Agreements, require each nation to notify the other of any significant information bought to its attention that could warrant enforcement activity by the other.
Information exchange	Comprehensive information exchange requirements, mandate the sharing of confidential and commercially-sensitive information relating to the activities of private sector entities. The IAEAAs, in particular, represent the greatest extent to which nations have agreed to share private sector confidential information and overcome confidentiality restrictions.
Co-operation	Full co-operation obligations, similar to those in Second Generation Agreements, require each competition authority to assist its foreign counterpart to the fullest extent consistent with its laws, important interests and available resources.
Consultation	Comprehensive consultation procedures exist, beyond those in Second Generation Agreements, and also contemplate the conclusion of bilateral agreements at an inter-agency level rather than an inter-governmental level.
Negative comity	The full 'negative comity' obligations mitigate over-regulation by requiring an enforcing nation to consider any adverse affects of enforcement on the interests of affected nations. However, they also include an implied commitment for the affected nation not to act unilaterally, via extra-territorial application of competition laws, until all enforcement options in the enforcing nation have been exhausted.
Positive comity	Full 'positive comity' obligations seek to mitigate under-regulation by requiring an enforcing nation to consider any requests for enforcement by an affected nation. Again, they include an implied commitment for the affected nation not to act unilaterally, via extra-territorial application of competition laws, until all enforcement options in the enforcing nation have been exhausted. In the case of the EU–US positive comity agreement, so-called 'who goes first' provisions prioritise which nation should investigate particular anti-competitive conduct.

Figure 21: *Six principal elements of the Third Generation Agreements*

between the US and Australia in 1999, and an agreement between the EC and Canada in October 1999.[17] The six principal elements of these Third Generation Agreements are identified in Figure 21.

Importantly, a number of procedural provisions are built into Third Generation Agreements that bolster the principle of positive comity, relative to the more limited form of positive comity incorporated within Second Generation Agreements. In the EC–US agreement, for example, a requested nation must report back to the requesting nation outlining whether or not it intends to take enforcement action.[18] After consultation, the requesting nation may accept the requested nation's conclusions, seek to modify them, or pursue its own extraterritorial enforcement action. In addition, the EC–US Agreement distinguishes between 'co-operative' positive comity, in which the requesting nation may assist with enforcement action, and 'allocative' positive comity in which the requesting nation may defer all enforcement action to the requested nation.

The positive comity provisions in Third Generation Agreements enable a ratifying nation to request enforcement action by the second nation against anti-competitive conduct that the first nation cannot otherwise remedy. This approach promotes more efficient cross-border enforcement as the competition authority undertaking enforcement action would be the authority with the greatest ability to gather necessary evidence.[19] Furthermore, there is a reduced need for the cross-border sharing of information given that the competition authority with the best access to information will usually undertake the enforcement action. Such positive comity provisions seek to mitigate the negative externality associated with under-regulation identified in Chapter 3 of this book.

Importantly, positive comity does not resolve the existence of the underlying negative economic externalities identified in Chapter 3 of this book, although it provides a mechanism to address them partly. The positive comity mechanism does have its limitations. In order for positive comity to be successful, the conduct must be illegal in the second nation as well as the first nation, hence the second nation must have in existence a strong competition law that is similar in nature to that of its counterpart. Moreover, the first nation must have sufficient confidence and trust in

---

[17] See Agreement between the European Communities and the Government of Canada Regarding the Application of their Competition Laws, Brussels, 7 October 1999.
[18] The success of the US–EU Agreement is illustrated by the successful co-ordination of numerous cross-border merger investigations since 1998.
[19] See OECD, 'International Options to Improve the Coherence between Trade and Competition Policies', COM/TD/DAFFE/CLP(99)102/ FINAL, Paris, 11 February 2000, p. 4.

the abilities of its counterpart to enforce the relevant conduct effectively. Finally, as positive comity procedures remain voluntary, there is no obligation on the second nation to respond to any request.

Again, these limitations to positive comity reinforce the fact that Third Generation Agreements are predicated on the similarity of the competition laws of each jurisdiction and mutual confidence by each nation in the enforcement activities of the other. Without sufficient similarities of competition laws, and mutual trust and confidence, Third Generation Agreements would be difficult to negotiate and sustain. These strict pre-conditions mean that Third Generation Agreements are not yet common in the international community. These strict pre-conditions also mean that Third Generation Agreements are unlikely to be concluded between nations with significantly different incentives towards the regulation of anti-competitive conduct.

5.1.4 Fourth generation bilateral competition agreements

A further step beyond Third Generation Agreements are Fourth Generation Agreements. These agreements contemplate a form of reciprocal extension of jurisdiction on an extraterritorial basis. These agreements also contemplate the adoption of substantive cross-border competition law provisions. Fourth Generation Agreements are currently rare and are usually confined to circumstances where two jurisdictions maintain a high degree of economic integration. A notable Fourth Generation Agreement is provided by a memorandum of understanding between Australia and New Zealand in 1988 ('ANZ Agreement'), accompanied by a series of legislative provisions giving effect to that understanding.[20]

The ANZ Agreement required both Australia and New Zealand to extend their legislative prohibitions against abuses of market power to regulate an aggregate market embracing both jurisdictions ('trans-Tasman provisions').[21] In order to permit the trans-Tasman provisions to

---

[20] See Memorandum of Understanding Between the Government of New Zealand and the Government of Australia on the Harmonisation of Business Laws, CER, 1988. This formed part of the Australia-New Zealand Protocol on the Acceleration of Free Trade in Goods, (Australia) Department of Foreign Affairs and Trade Treaty Series: No. 18 of 1988; entry into force 18 August 1988; which in turn was part of the Australia-New Zealand Closer Economic Relations Trade Agreement, concluded 28 March 1983, commenced 1 January 1984 (1983) 22 ILM 948.

[21] See Australia's Trade Practices Act 1974 (Cth) s. 46A and New Zealand's Commerce Act 1986 s. 36A. Note also that government entities in Australia may not claim immunity from the application of these trans-Tasman provisions under New Zealand law, and vice versa.

Procedural issue	Description
Evidence	Each nation's competition authority is permitted to obtain evidence from the other's jurisdiction by way of an enforceable statutory notice. Similarly, evidence obtained under the legal rules and processes of one jurisdiction is recognised under the laws of evidence of the other, including proof of documents.
Subpoenas	The court of each jurisdiction is permitted to issue subpoenas that can be served and enforced against persons located in the other jurisdiction, requiring attendance in the court of the serving jurisdiction.
Submissions	Submissions are permitted to be made in the courts of each jurisdiction by way of video link, telephone or other electronic means from the other jurisdiction. If appropriate, each court is authorised to continue physically or conduct its proceedings in the other jurisdiction.
Enforcement	Final judgments and orders, including injunctions, made by a court of one jurisdiction are deemed enforceable merely by registration in the other jurisdiction.
Investigations	The Australian and New Zealand enforcement authorities have entered into co-operation arrangements, whereby one authority may commence preliminary investigations and hearings on behalf of the other and both authorities can jointly investigate a complaint.

Figure 22: *Procedural issues addressed by the ANZ Agreement*

operate effectively, both nations have extended their jurisdiction by mutual consent on a limited extraterritorial basis into the territory of the other. However, such an extension required a number of procedural issues to be resolved in the civil jurisdiction of both nations. Accordingly, innovative procedures were adopted in which both nations sought to ensure that any trans-Tasman litigation could be conducted efficiently and effectively. These provisions are summarised in Figure 22 and demonstrate that the resolution of procedural issues between jurisdictions is likely to remain one of the most difficult aspects of introducing substantive cross-border competition laws.

The extent of the ANZ Agreement is unique in the international community and the question arises why such an extension of jurisdiction was possible between Australia and New Zealand. In this respect:

- New Zealand and Australia share similar legal systems and share a common legal heritage in the form of English common law. The close proximity, culture and development of both nations mean there has been a natural tendency for both nations to look to each other for legislative models. Accordingly, the differences between the Australian and New Zealand legal systems have remained minimal when compared with the differences between other nations.
- The competition laws of both nations retain a high degree of harmonisation. New Zealand and Australian courts also frequently look to each other for interpretative guidance on competition issues, with the precedents of each other's courts considered highly persuasive.
- The ANZ Agreement constituted part of a far-reaching initiative towards greater economic integration and harmonisation of business laws and regulatory practices between the two nations. As part of that integration process, anti-dumping laws were repealed between the two nations, as discussed in Chapter 9 of this book. The trans-Tasman competition provisions were intended to provide a safeguard for each nation against anti-competitive conduct by firms in the other nation following the repeal of anti-dumping laws.

Accordingly, while the ANZ Agreement, as a Fourth Generation Agreement, extends well beyond the parameters of other bilateral agreements concluded to date, the pre-conditions leading to its negotiation are significant. However, the ANZ Agreement does indicate what may be achievable between nations with closely integrated economies, an existing extensive bilateral trade and economic relationship, similar competition laws, similar cultures and similar legal systems.

5.1.5 *Limitations of bilateral agreements*

When taken to its limits, the bilateral model proposes that a network of bilateral agreements could exist between the nations of the world to establish a cross-border competition law and ensure effective cross-border law enforcement. However, there remain a number of obvious difficulties with this approach, not least of which are the potential transaction costs involved in negotiating agreements between each nation and the scope for widely different results in each case. Furthermore, given that approximately 90 nations now have competition laws, such an approach would require a network of over 4,000 bilateral agreements.[22] If, say, 120 of the world's nations were to possess competition laws (as is eventually likely given the trend towards the adoption of competition laws), a network of over 7,000 bilateral agreements would be required.[23] In such circumstances there are clear benefits in adopting a plurilateral or multilateral approach.

Importantly, there also remain significant other difficulties impeding the negotiation of advanced bilateral competition law agreements:

- Differences in procedural rules make jurisdictional co-ordination between nations difficult where nations have different legal systems.
- Each nation's competition laws are intended to deal with those practices that harm its own markets. These laws are poorly designed to prevent harm to foreign markets, particularly where the concept of harm and anti-competitive conduct are perceived and characterised differently across different jurisdictions.
- As discussed in Chapter 3, each nation applies its competition laws in a manner consistent with its own national interests. A nation is unlikely to undertake competition law enforcement if such enforcement is detrimental to its national interest, notwithstanding concepts of positive comity or that such enforcement could be highly beneficial to the interests of consumers in foreign nations.
- Exchanges of private sector confidential information between competition authorities remain heavily circumscribed. Nations do not yet have sufficient confidence in the processes and procedures of each other's institutions to permit the cross-border sharing of confidential information, notwithstanding that much progress has been made by Second and Third Generation Agreements. Indeed, laws preventing the cross-border sharing of confidential information remain the greatest procedural obstacle to increased enforcement co-operation.

These difficulties explain why the number of bilateral agreements existing today in the international community remains limited, not even close to the 4,000 required to form a complete bilateral network. These difficulties also suggest that the most important limitations on the future development of bilateral agreements concern the extent of remaining differences

---

[22] The relevant mathematical formula is $N = (n \times (n-1))/2$, where N is the number of bilateral agreements required and n is the number of countries with competition laws existing at a given time.

[23] Underlining this point further, if all 200 of the world's nations were to adopt competition laws, a network of approximately 20,000 bilateral agreements would be required.

between the competition laws of nations, the perverse incentives created by economic externalities, and the degree of confidence by each nation in the institutions and enforcement activities of other nations. Without further convergence of laws, wider acceptance of comity principles, possible transfer payments (to coax nations to undertake enforcement action contrary to their national self-interest), and the relaxation of procedural safeguards for confidential information, the development of a network of bilateral agreements is likely to remain slow. This creates a clear role for plurilateral and multilateral initiatives to promote greater convergence of competition laws, and wider acceptance of comity and information exchange principles, so as to accelerate the negotiation of bilateral agreements.

However, notwithstanding these limitations, bilateral agreements have proved valuable in lessening the differences between nations in the application of their competition laws while creating an environment conducive to cross-border competition law co-operation. Bilateral agreements may also be perceived as a positive mechanism for increasing confidence and reducing regulatory anomalies between nations while to some extent mitigating the negative economic externalities identified in Chapter 3 of this book via positive and negative comity provisions to address under-regulation and over-regulation, respectively. As such, each bilateral arrangement represents an incremental step towards the negotiation of more sophisticated bilateral, plurilateral or multilateral competition law agreements.

5.2 The current momentum towards plurilateral agreement

A number of plurilateral initiatives have been instigated over the past few decades to address cross-border competition law issues. The most significant of these plurilateral initiatives have been launched within the context of:

- APEC, in relation to the nations of the Asia-Pacific region;
- the EU, in relation to the nations of Western Europe; and
- the Organisation of American States in relation to the nations of the American continent within the context of the Free Trade Agreement for the Americas.

All three initiatives envisage different degrees of economic integration and differ significantly in their consideration of competition policy issues. In particular:

(a) the APEC initiative envisages a low to moderate degree of economic integration and the adoption of common competition policies and greater bilateral co-operation; and
(b) the EU initiative envisages a very high degree of economic integration and involves a competition law with supranational character enforced by supranational institutions.

The APEC and EU approaches are considered further below.

5.2.1 APEC – common competition policies and greater bilateral co-operation

The promotion of competition law and policy within APEC was previously discussed in Chapter 4 of this book and remains one of the most important and ambitious of the current plurilateral initiatives towards the development of a cross-border competition law.

Historically, in a series of reports from 1993 to 1995, an advisory panel known as the APEC Eminent Person Group ('EPG') outlined a vision and strategic plan for APEC. Each of these reports recommended that APEC should initiate regional co-operation on competition law and policy. In Osaka in 1995, the EPG's vision was implemented via an 'Osaka Action Agenda' in which the APEC nations initiated a competition law and policy work programme with the assistance of the Pacific Economic Co-operation Council.[24] In Manila in 1996, the APEC nations detailed their individual and collective action plans on competition policy within a 'Manila Action Plan'.[25] Three years later, in Auckland in 1999, the APEC nations agreed on a framework of common principles for an APEC-wide competition policy ('APEC Competition Principles').[26] Accordingly, competition law and policy has gradually escalated in importance within APEC, culminating with the adoption and implementation of the APEC Competition Principles.

Importantly, as mentioned in Chapter 4 of this book, harmonisation of competition laws is not a current objective of APEC. Indeed, the experiences within the ANZ Agreement (as outlined above) and the EU (as outlined below), suggest that full harmonisation is unlikely to be practical

---

[24] See APEC, 'The Osaka Action Agenda: APEC Leaders' Declaration', Osaka, 19 November 1995.
[25] See APEC, 'The Manila Action Plan: APEC Leaders' Declaration', Manila, 25 November 1996.
[26] See APEC, 'The Auckland Challenge: APEC Leaders' Declaration', Auckland, 13 September 1999.

except where nations have a high degree of economic integration. It is also true that most of the benefits of an international competition law could be realised without full harmonisation, as discussed in Chapter 11 of this book. The APEC Competition Principles therefore seek only to promote greater convergence of APEC competition policies.

In particular, the APEC Competition Principles promote four overriding core principles of non-discrimination, comprehensiveness, transparency and accountability. These core principles must be implemented via ten 'best efforts' implementation procedures. Relevantly, each APEC nation must:[27]

- address anti-competitive behaviour by implementing 'competition policy to protect the competitive process';
- foster confidence and build capability in the application of competition policy by building expertise in its competition authorities and adequately resourcing these authorities; and
- develop effective means of co-operation between APEC competition authorities while ensuring these authorities are adequately resourced.

Accordingly, the essence of APEC's initiative over the past decade has been to promote greater bilateral co-operation and convergence of competition policy as a mechanism for plurilateral agreement. The success of this approach is graphically illustrated by the diagram in Figure 23, which shows that the degree of bilateral co-operation on competition law matters between APEC nations remains very high by world standards.

The APEC experience suggests that where nations exhibit considerable diversity and a low to moderate degree of economic integration, an appropriate strategy may be to promote convergence of competition policy and greater co-operation in enforcement activity, rather than harmonisation of competition laws. The APEC Competition Principles also recognise the need to emphasise institution building in conjunction with the development of effective competition laws to ensure such laws are effectively enforced and implemented. In addition, the APEC initiative demonstrates that agreement on competition principles is significantly easier to achieve at the plurilateral level, rather than at the multilateral level, as the interests of a smaller numbers of nations must be accommodated.

---

[27] See 'APEC Principles to Enhance Competition and Regulatory Reform: Open and Competitive Markets are the Key Drivers of Economic Efficiency and Consumer Welfare', as an attachment to the Auckland Declaration, above n. 26.

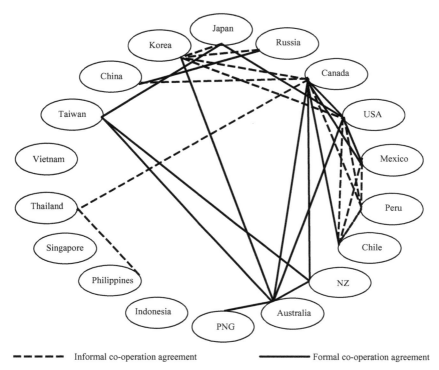

----- Informal co-operation agreement ———— Formal co-operation agreement

Figure 23: *Competition co-operation agreements within APEC*

5.2.2 The European Union – supranational competition law within a customs union

The competition laws of the EU (previously known as the EEC and then the EC)[28] represent the furthest that any group of nations have progressed in adopting a comprehensive cross-border competition framework. In contrast to APEC's emphasis on co-operation and convergence, the most significant feature of EU competition law is that it has a supranational status in the form of a 'higher law' that overrides national competition laws.[29] This supranational status has proved critical to the success of EU

---

[28] To avoid confusion, the term 'European Union' (EU) will also be used to describe the European Economic Community (EEC) and the European Community (EC).
[29] See discussion in J. T. Barnes, 'Competition Policy in the EU' in J. T. Barnes (ed.), *The Enlarged European Union* (Longman, London, 1995), ch. 11.

competition law and is a direct consequence of the substantive form of the EU institutional arrangement.

The EU (at that time known as the EEC) was established via the Treaty of Rome in 1957, which had the express constitutional objective of creating a unified European single common market with common external policies and free internal movement of goods, services, labour and capital.[30] The methodology for realising this objective primarily involved removing internal barriers to trade but was heavily influenced by the historical experiences of the member states, including their extensive exposure to cartels and trade restrictions in the preceding decades.

Accordingly, the member states incorporated a set of competition provisions into the Treaty of Rome that were intended to assist the realisation of a unified market by outlawing anti-competitive conduct that hindered trade between member states. For this reason, an important objective of EU competition policy has remained as market unification and EU competition laws have sought to prevent anti-competitive practices so that goods and services can be traded freely between EU member nations in conditions of undistorted competition.

In addition, the Treaty of Rome sought to replace protectionist national trade laws between the EU member states with a common EU external tariff *vis-à-vis* the rest of the world. However, in order to do so, the member states sought alternative protection against unfair business conduct that could occur between member states in the absence of trade remedies. The competition provisions of the Treaty of Rome were intended to provide such protection and are currently set out in Articles 81 and 82 as follows:[31]

- Article 81 prohibits as incompatible with the common market any agreements, decisions by associations and concerted practices which affect trade between EC member states and which have as their common object or effect the prevention, restriction or distortion of competition within the common market.
- Article 82 prohibits any abuse of a dominant position within the common market in so far as it affects trade between member states.

These competition provisions have remained fundamental to EU policy and have been entrenched in the subsequent drives towards a single

---

[30] Treaty for the Establishment of the European Economic Community, signed in Rome, 25 March 1957, 298 UNTS 3.
[31] As consolidated by Treaty of Amsterdam of the European Community, signed in Amsterdam, 2 October 1997.

HAVE EXISTING INITIATIVES PROVED SUFFICIENT? 127

European market, monetary union and greater economic integration. These provisions have also been supplemented by a variety of European Council and European Commission Regulations, which together establish a comprehensive EU competition law. Most importantly, Articles 81 and 82 were supplemented by the EC Merger Regulation in 1989, which sought to regulate large transactions that led to the acquisition or strengthening of dominance in any EU market where these transactions had a Community dimension.[32] Where this merger regime applies, it pre-empts merger laws of member states and requires approval by the European Commission before a transaction occurs.

The competition provisions of the Treaty of Rome have been incorporated into the national law of each EU member state and are therefore directly enforceable by each national court. In this manner, the Treaty of Rome has created a supra-national competition law that overrides national competition laws and creates rights and obligations between individuals, as well as between individuals and governmental authorities, within the EU. This supra-national competition law was historically enforced on a supra-national basis by the European Commission, which remains accountable to the European Council and the European Court of Justice. However, in recent years greater enforcement powers have been devolved to national competition authorities.

An important condition precedent for membership of the EU has been the implementation of EU-style competition rules, hence as other nations have sought to join the EU, so the supranational competition law of the EU has progressively expanded. For example, the EU established bilateral agreements between itself and various Central and Eastern European Countries ('CEECs') to enable those CEECs to progress towards full membership of the EU. Under these agreements, the CEECs committed to applying EU case law to matters affecting trade between each CEEC and the EU. In this manner, the sphere of geographic influence of EU competition law has expanded and is likely to continue to do so as further nations join the EU or seek the benefits of EU membership. The European Experts Group on Competition Policy has referred to this as a 'domino effect'.

In summary, the EU articulates a broader conception of a unified supra-national cross-border competition law, centrally enforced by a

---

[32] Council Regulation 4064/89/EEC of 21 December 1989 on the control of concentrations between undertakings, OJ 1985 No. L395, 30 December 1989, OJ 1990 No. L257, 21 September 1990) with amendments introduced by Council Regulation 1310/97/EC of 30 June 1997, OJ 1997 No. L180, 9 July 1997.

supra-national law enforcement authority. However, the extent to which this model is relevant to the internationally community is questionable given the unique degree of market integration and subordination of sovereignty on which it is premised. The EU model suggests that where a very high degree of legal and economic integration exists between nations, innovative steps towards the development of a cross-border supra-national competition law become possible. In such circumstances it may be possible to eliminate completely the effects of the economic externality identified in Chapter 3 by binding nations to act in the collective interest, as has been possible in the EU. This suggests that, as a general presumption, the greater the extent of legal and economic integration between nations, the greater the potential for a cross-border competition law.

5.2.3 Limitations of plurilateral agreements

While controversial, an important theoretical justification for the existence of regional *trade* agreements is that such regional agreements act as 'building blocks' towards multilateral free trade.[33] In this manner, initiatives at the regional level can become models for later incorporation into a multilateral system and may create sufficient momentum to sustain negotiation of a multilateral agreement. This justification for regional trade arrangements is widely known in international trade literature as the 'building block theory' and assists in explaining why regional trade agreements are tolerated by the WTO notwithstanding their trade diverting effects.[34]

The building block theory is one manifestation of the broader concept of political consensus-building in public choice theory. Under this model, smaller consensual clusters eventually merge into a large consensual group via a process of negotiation, trade-offs and political logrolling. Such political consensus-building is unavoidable in the negotiation of multilateral treaties due to the need for multipartisan support and this suggests that a 'building block' approach, involving the use of plurilateral competition

---

[33] The controversy arises because the removal of trade barriers among groups of countries may make it harder rather than easier to remove barriers in relation to other countries if much of the political support that could have been harnessed to remove barriers against outsiders has already been dissipated in the process of the bilateral or regional liberalisation.
[34] See, for example, J. J. Schott, *More Free Trade Areas?* (Institute for International Economics, Washington DC, 1989). See also J. Viner, *The Customs Union Issue* (Carnegie Press, New York, 1950), ch. 4.

initiatives, is consistent with the optimal strategy for the negotiation of an multilateral competition agreement.[35]

Regional initiatives to promote the convergence and enforcement of competition law across national boundaries may be viewed in this light. Such plurilateral initiatives provide a foundation for political consensus-building towards the ultimate objective of a multilateral competition law agreement. In particular, regional initiatives enable the continued evolution of successful models for a truly international competition law while gradually harmonising and reducing differences between nations.[36]

5.3 Current initiatives towards the realisation of multilateral agreement

At the multilateral level, the most significant initiatives towards the development of international competition law have been launched under the auspices of:

- the United Nations Conference on Trade and Development ('UNCTAD'), via the UNCTAD Inter-governmental Group of Experts on Competition Law and Policy;
- the Organisation for Economic Co-operation and Development ('OECD'), via the OECD Committee on Competition Law and Policy; and
- the WTO, via the WTO Working Group on the Interaction between Trade and Competition Policy.

Each of these multilateral initiatives has promoted the evolution of cross-border competition laws. In recent years, these initiatives have each sought to combine their efforts, leading to the possibility of a unified strategy for achieving a single multilateral competition agreement. Each of these initiatives are discussed further below.

---

[35] See P. Nicolaides, 'For a World Competition Authority: The Role of Competition Policy in Economic Integration and the Role of Regional Blocs in Internationalising Competition Policy' (1996) 30 *Journal of World Trade* 131.

[36] The process of trading-off various policies also provides a mechanism for welfare transfers between nations and thus may assist in encouraging nations to enter into an international competition agreement where they may not otherwise have incentives to do so.

5.3.1 UNCTAD and the Code on Restrictive Business Practices

UNCTAD was established in 1964 as a permanent inter-governmental body and a principal organ of the United Nations ('UN') General Assembly in the field of trade and development. UNCTAD now forms an important part of the UN secretariat and provides a focal point within the UN for the integrated treatment of development, trade, finance, technology and investment issues.

The principal objective of UNCTAD has been to maximise the trade, investment and development opportunities of less developed and developing countries ('LDCs') and to assist the integration of LDCs into the global economy on an equitable basis. Historically, UNCTAD has pursued these objectives by undertaking research and policy analysis, fostering inter-governmental deliberations, promoting technical co-operation, and by interacting with business and non-governmental organisations. UNCTAD has also maintained a close working relationship with the WTO.

Competition law concepts initially arose before UNCTAD during the 1970s as part of the drive by LDCs for a 'new international economic order'. LDCs perceived international competition rules as a mechanism for redistributing international welfare and sought international endorsement of their view that multinational corporations were exploiting LDCs, retarding their development, and transferring wealth to industrialised nations. Accordingly, the LDCs sought a binding code that would declare certain conduct by multinational corporations to be anti-competitive. As a result, the formulation of an international competition code was placed on the UNCTAD agenda.[37]

During a decade of negotiations throughout the 1970s, the industrialised nations sought to assuage LDC concerns while steering the UNCTAD competition code towards more conventional notions of competition regulation and away from the more radical views of some LDCs. The resulting code reflected more conventional views of competition policy but was still governed by the objective of protecting LDCs from the restrictive business practices of multinational corporations. Furthermore, some elements were never agreed, for example, LDCs sought to prohibit export cartels while Western states sought only to prohibit international cartels,

---

[37] See D. Thompson, 'UNCTAD: Model Law on Restrictive Business Practices' (1980) 14 *Journal of World Trade* 444. See also S. E. Bensen, 'The UN Code on Restrictive Business Practices: An International Antitrust Code is Born' (1981) 30(4) *American University Law Review* 1031.

meaning that no provision on export cartels was ever concluded.[38] Eventually, notwithstanding such difficulties, the UNCTAD Code on Restrictive Business Practices ('UNCTAD Code') was unanimously adopted by the UN General Assembly on 5 December 1980.[39]

Importantly, the UNCTAD Code remains the only multilateral instrument in existence today that comprehensively addresses competition law and policy.

The UNCTAD Code lacks a mechanism for effective dispute settlement, contrary to the wishes of LDCs who desired that the Secretary-General of the United Nations should be vested with a power to convene consultations.[40] The industrialised nations agreed, instead, on a non-binding consultative mechanism that urges member states to 'give full consideration to requests for consultation' and to conduct all consultations in good faith.[41] The importance accorded to a dispute resolution mechanism during negotiation of the UNCTAD Code recognises that an effective dispute resolution procedure will be critical to the success of any multilateral competition agreement, as discussed in Chapter 12 of this book.[42]

Contrary to the desire of LDCs to make the UNCTAD Code binding on all nations, the legal status of the UNCTAD Code remains, at best, recommendatory. The UNCTAD Code contains a set of guiding aspirations in the form of voluntary guidelines, rather than a set of legally binding precepts of international law.[43] Indeed, the UNCTAD Code was deliberately drafted in non-mandatory terms so as *not* to create legally binding obligations and any argument that particular provisions may have crystallised into customary international law is therefore tenuous. As a result

---

[38] See 'UNCTAD: Restrictive Business Practices Conference' (1980) 14 *Journal of World Trade* 172.
[39] See UNCTAD, *The Set of Multilaterally Agreed Principles and Rules for the Control of Restrictive Business Practices*, (1980) UN Doc TD/RBP/CONF/10, Annexe, adopted by UN General Assembly, Res 35/63, 35th Session, 5 December 1980, reprinted in (1980) 19 ILM 813.
[40] Petersmann notes that when preparing for the Uruguay Round, proposals by less developed countries to include restrictive business practices on the agenda were resisted by developed nations, notably the US. See E. U. Petersmann, 'International Competition Rules for the GATT and World Trading System' (1994) 28(4) *Journal of World Trade* 35, 40.
[41] UNCTAD Code, Part IV, Section F, see above n. 39.
[42] See C. Schede, 'The Strengthening of the Multilateral System: Article 23 of the WTO Dispute Settlement Understanding – Dismantling Unilateral Retaliation Under Section 301 of the 1974 Trade Act' (1996) 20 *World Competition* 109.
[43] Acceptance of these principles and rules is voluntary for both firms and governments. However, the fact that the Code was approved by the UN General Assembly without dissent means that it carries considerable authoritative weight.

of this non-binding status, the impact of the UNCTAD Code has remained limited and even its existence is not widely known. However, this non-binding status has not prevented a number of LDCs from adopting the principles of the UNCTAD Code into their national laws.

Nevertheless, notwithstanding its non-binding nature, and radical background, the UNCTAD Code has received increasing support over the last two decades as nations have sought to generate momentum towards realisation of a multilateral agreement on cross-border competition law. The UNCTAD Code has also had a significant 'soft law' influence, as discussed in Chapter 11 of this book. Moreover, the legitimacy of the UNCTAD Code has been reaffirmed unanimously by three United Nations conferences, most recently in September 2000.[44] The 2000 conference recommended that all UN nations should implement the provisions of the UNCTAD Code and that UNCTAD should develop a similar code to apply on a regional basis, particularly for smaller and developing nations.

A significant factor behind the growing support for the UNCTAD Code, particularly by industrialised nations, could be that such nations recognise its tactical value as a mechanism for soliciting vital support from LDCs for any multilateral competition law agreement. The LDCs have already expressed concern that any international competition agreement may not reflect their concerns or recognise the 'development dimension'. Accordingly, the UNCTAD Code has both symbolic and political importance and could have significant strategic value in any multilateral negotiations on a cross-border competition agreement given that it already addresses this development dimension.

UNCTAD, as the organisation dedicated to promoting development issues in trade policy, will also have a critical role in promoting international consensus for a similar reason. UNCTAD has political clout given that it is effectively the de facto agent for the interests of the LDCs. Furthermore, given the complexity of the issues likely to arise in negotiation of any multilateral competition agreement, UNCTAD's role will be critical in assisting and resourcing LDCs and providing an alternative forum for the discussion of competition and development issues. This was expressly recognised and endorsed by the 2000 conference, which noted that the creation of effective competition law structures requires the development of sophisticated legal instruments and analytical capabilities by LDCs.

---

[44] See UNCTAD, 'Review of All Aspects of the Set of Multilaterally Agreed Equitable Principles for the Control of Restrictive Business Practices', Resolution adopted 29 September 2000, UNCTAD, TD/RBP/CONF.5/15, Geneva, 4 October 2000.

In conclusion, the UNCTAD Code provides a useful conceptual framework, which will influence the content of any future international competition agreement. However, UNCTAD does not itself provide an appropriate institutional framework for such an agreement, particularly given its express orientation towards LDCs and its lack of a strong dispute resolution framework. The UNCTAD Code does not expressly address the types of issues identified in Chapter 3 of this book, although it has proved useful in encouraging developing nations to adopt competition laws. However, UNCTAD's involvement will be important in ensuring that any international competition agreement sufficiently addresses the 'development dimension' and therefore receives support from LDCs. UNCTAD's high level of involvement to date in international competition issues also provides a clear basis for UNCTAD's future involvement in any negotiations on a multilateral competition agreement, notwithstanding that such negotiations could occur in an alternative forum such as the WTO.

5.3.2 The OECD Competition Law and Policy Committee

While UNCTAD represents the interests of LDCs, the OECD may be perceived as representing the interests of advanced industrialised nations. The OECD was originally established to facilitate the post-World War II distribution of economic aid in Europe pursuant to the Marshall Plan, but was subsequently reorganised to promote the discussion and development of international economic and social policy among advanced industrialised nations. Today the OECD is an international organisation with thirty member nations and an annual budget of around US$200 million. The OECD comprises twelve policy directorates, supporting around 200 specialised policy committees, working groups and expert groups, comprising representatives of the member nations.

The OECD Competition Law and Policy Committee ('OECD Committee') was formed by the OECD member nations in 1967 to investigate issues of competition law and policy.[45] Over the past thirty-five years, it has actively facilitated the convergence of competition law and policies between OECD member nations and has promoted international co-operation among competition authorities. In particular, it has promulgated an important series of non-binding recommendations that have proved highly persuasive in urging OECD member nations to adopt

---

[45] The OECD Committee of Experts on Restrictive Business Practices was renamed the Committee on Competition Law and Policy on 18 September 1987.

certain competition policies. The three most important recommendations to date have been the 'Co-operative Recommendation',[46] the 'Conflict Recommendation',[47] and the 'Cartel Recommendation':[48]

- *Co-operation Recommendation*   The Co-operation Recommendation was initially promulgated in 1967, but was subsequently revised in 1973 and 1986 and, most recently, in 1995. The 1967 and 1973 Recommendations set out a series of policy principles that were intended to co-ordinate competition law enforcement activities to reduce the costs of inter-jurisdictional conflict, thereby promoting the development of First Generation Agreements. The 1995 Recommendation established a series of principles that facilitated the development of Second Generation Agreements, including the principles of positive and negative comity. OECD nations were urged to co-operate in the investigation of international restrictive business practices and to create a network of bilateral 'mutual assistance' treaties to facilitate the exchange of confidential information.
- *Conflict Recommendation*   The Conflict Recommendation of 1986 urged OECD nations to evaluate continually the international competition and trade implications of their domestic trade and competition policies. OECD nations were urged to adopt domestic policies that minimised the potential for inter-jurisdictional competition law conflict and conflicts between trade law and competition law. The Recommendation also encouraged substantive changes to the laws of OECD nations to increase convergence and reduce the scope for jurisdictional conflict.
- *Cartel Recommendation*   The Cartel Recommendation of 1998 urged OECD nations to enact domestic competition laws against collusive price fixing, collusive tendering, collusive output restrictions and collusive market division. The Recommendation also urged member nations to co-operate with each other to eliminate such activities. A noticeable feature of the Recommendation is that it advocated substantive

---

[46] See OECD, 'Revised Recommendation of the Council Concerning Co-operation Between Member Countries on Restrictive Business Practices Affecting International Trade', C(86)44(Final), 21 May 1986, (1986) 25 ILM 1629; C(95)130/Final, 28 July 1995.

[47] See OECD, 'Recommendation of the Council Concerning Co-operation Between Member Countries on Potential Conflict between Competition and Trade Policies', C(86)65(Final), 23 October 1986.

[48] See OECD, 'Recommendation of the OECD Council Concerning Effective Action Against Hard Core Cartels', C(98)35/Final, 30 March 1998. See also OECD, 'Hard Core Cartels', OECD Press Release, 30 March 1998.

competition laws, rather than mere co-operation. As such, it was more ambitious than its predecessors and actively facilitated selective convergence of particular aspects of domestic competition laws.

These three OECD recommendations, while non-binding, have proved important in promoting the convergence of international opinion. As such, they are likely to continue to play a vital role in consensus-building towards realising a multilateral competition agreement. Interestingly, each successive recommendation has pioneered the widespread international adoption of the principles it has espoused, illustrating the important role of the OECD in promoting and reinforcing international consensus on competition policy.

The OECD itself does not provide an appropriate institutional vehicle for an international competition agreement given its emphasis on policy development rather than substantive law and given its limited membership of advanced industrialised nations. However, as with UNCTAD, the continued involvement of the OECD will remain important in sustaining momentum towards negotiation of any international competition agreement. In this regard, the OECD is currently seeking to co-ordinate the development of international policy on cross-border competition issues.

5.3.3 The WTO Working Group on Competition Law and Policy

As discussed in detail later in this book, the WTO remains the preferred vehicle for a multilateral competition agreement. With this in mind, the issue arises as to what efforts, if any, the international community has undertaken at present to introduce competition law into the WTO. In this regard, during the preparatory work for the Uruguay Round negotiations in the early 1980s, LDCs formally proposed that restrictive business practices should be included on the agenda for the Uruguay Round, building on the UNCTAD Code. This proposal was resisted by industrialised nations, most notably by the US, on the basis that insufficient international consensus existed to permit meaningful negotiations on competition policies at that time.

Close to the conclusion of the Uruguay Round, in February 1992, the President of the European Commission, Sir Leon Brittan, formally called for the negotiation of competition rules within the WTO. He proposed that the next WTO round of multilateral trade negotiations should address restrictive business practices, particularly cartels, and that preliminary work should be undertaken with this in mind.[49]

Partly in response to these views, a clause was negotiated into Article 9 of the WTO Agreement on Trade-Related Investment Measures ('TRIMS'), which provided:

> Not later than five years after the date of review of entry into force of the WTO Agreement, the Council for Trade in Goods shall review the operation of [the TRIMS] agreement... In the course of this review, the Council for Trade in Goods shall consider whether [the TRIMS] agreement should be complemented with provisions on... competition policy.

In December 1996, the EU formally proposed to a WTO Ministerial Conference held in Singapore that a WTO Working Group on the Interaction between Trade and Competition Policy ('WTO Working Group') should be created in accordance with Article 9 of TRIMS. The resulting Singapore Ministerial Declaration of December 1996 established the WTO Working Group with a mandate to study issues raised by WTO members relating to the interaction between trade and competition policy.

The objective of the WTO Working Group was set as identifying any areas of competition policy that may merit further consideration in the WTO framework. These areas were intended to provide the basis for future multilateral negotiations among members of the WTO. In this manner, the WTO Working Group's mandate was expressly analytical and explanatory and it was not permitted to propose new rules or commitments, although it could recommend further work on such issues if necessary.

Reflecting its mandate, the WTO Working Group has issued several annual reports summarising the extensive submissions it has received, but has deliberately not set out any conclusions or recommendations on substantive policy issues within these reports. Rather, the reports contemplate each WTO nation forming its own views on the extent to which competition law should be incorporated into the WTO. The issues addressed by the WTO Working Group reports to date are summarised in Figure 24.

The WTO Working Group has therefore provided a forum for the analysis of cross-border competition issues to support potential WTO multilateral negotiations. More recent developments regarding the introduction of competition law into the WTO are discussed in detail in Chapter 13 of this book.

---

[49] See Rt Hon Sir Leon Brittan, QC, 'A Framework for International Competition', Address to the World Competition Forum, Davos, 3 February 1992. See also Rt Hon Sir Leon Brittan, QC, 'Competition Policy and International Relations', Address to the Centre for European Policy Studies, 17 March 1992.

Year	Issue
1997[50]	The relationship between the objectives, principles, concepts, scope and instruments of trade and competition policy, including their relationship to economic growth.
	The appropriateness of existing instruments, standards and activities regarding trade and competition policy, particularly national competition policies, laws and instruments as they relate to trade, the existing WTO provisions, and existing agreements and initiatives.
1998[51]	The interaction between trade and competition policy, the impact of anti-competitive practices on trade, the impact of state monopolies and regulatory policies on competition and trade, the relationship between intellectual property rights and competition policy, the relationship between investment and competition policy, and the impact of trade policy on competition.
1999–2001[52]	The relevance of fundamental WTO principles such as national treatment, transparency, and most favoured nation treatment to competition policy and vice versa.
	The best approaches to promoting co-operation and communication among WTO Members, including in the field of technical co-operation.
	The likely contribution of competition policy towards achieving the objectives of the WTO, including the promotion of international trade.
2002[53]	Clarification of core principles, including transparency, non-discrimination and procedural fairness, and provisions on hard core cartels.
	Clarification of modalities for voluntary co-operation.
	Clarification of support for progressive reinforcement of competition institutions in developing countries through capacity-building.
2003[54]	The nature and scope for compliance mechanisms that might be applicable under a multilateral framework on competition policy.
	Possible elements of progressivity and flexibility that might be included in a multilateral framework on competition policy.

Figure 24: *Competition issues addressed by the WTO Working Group*

---

[50] See also 'Report (1997) of the Working Group on the Interaction of Trade and Competition Policy to the General Council', WTO, WT/WGTCP/1, 29 November 1997.

[51] See also 'Report (1998) of the Working Group on the Interaction of Trade and Competition Policy to the General Council', WTO, WT/WGTCP/2, 8 December 1998.

[52] See 'Report (1999) of the Working Group on the Interaction of Trade and Competition Policy to the General Council', WTO, WT/WGTCP/3, 11 October 1999. See also 'Report (2000) of the Working Group on the Interaction of Trade and Competition Policy to the General Council', WTO, WT/WGTCP/4, 18 October 2000. See also 'Report (2001) of the Working Group on the Interaction of Trade and Competition Policy to the General Council', WTO, WT/WGTCP/5, 8 October 2001.

[53] See 'Report (2002) of the Working Group on the Interaction of Trade and Competition Policy to the General Council', WTO, WT/WGTCP/6, 9 December 2002.

[54] See 'Report (2003) of the Working Group on the Interaction of Trade and Competition Policy to the General Council', WTO, WT/WGTCP/7, 17 July 2003.

5.3.4 Limitations to multilateral initiatives

The issue arises why a bilateral or plurilateral approach to negotiation of a cross-border competition law may be preferable to a multilateral approach. In this regard it is true that a multilateral agreement remains the optimal international competition law instrument as it promises uniform cross-border competition rules applying between all nations, provided agreement can be obtained. However, for the same reasons that such a multilateral agreement offers the greatest potential rewards, it also presents the greatest obstacles. With so many diverse national interests to be taken into consideration, any multilateral negotiations would be slow, cumbersome, expensive and uncertain, frequently achieving lowest common denominator results.

The principal cause of these difficulties in multilateral treaty negotiations is the rule of unanimous consent. This rule is embodied within Article 11 of the Vienna Convention on the Law of Treaties and provides that nation states cannot be bound by international treaties without their consent: *pacta tertiisnec nocent nec prosunt.*[55] This rule adds a difficult dynamic to multilateral negotiations, as a single nation can veto the development of a common position allowing it to exert a disproportionate influence over multilateral negotiations, frequently leading to the adoption of lowest common denominator results. Similarly, larger nations can use their increased bargaining power to sway the course of multilateral negotiations to favour their own domestic political interests, thereby imposing their own political agenda on weaker states. Accordingly, multilateral negotiations are necessarily susceptible to power politics, hidden political agendas, and vested national interests. Multilateral negotiations therefore require extensive, time-consuming and often costly multilateral diplomacy.[56]

Similarly, the rule of unanimous consent creates a situation analogous to a shipping convoy, in which the speed of the convoy moving towards the conclusion of a multilateral agreement is limited by the speed of the slowest ship. In such circumstances, frustration and impatience with the slow pace of multilateral progress may blunt enthusiasm and slow overall momentum. When these factors combine to prevent progress towards an international agreement at an acceptable pace, bilateral and regional

---

[55] Vienna Convention on the Law of Treaties, Arts. 11 and 35 to 37, concluded at Vienna, 23 May 1969, entered into force, 27 January 1988, 1155 UNTS 331.

[56] See B. Spector & G. Sjostedt, *Negotiating International Regimes: Lessons from UNCED* (Graham & Trotman, New York, 1994).

arrangements can offer a pragmatic alternative, enabling nations with common interests to conclude agreements rapidly between themselves. Such an approach is often an improvement over creeping progress, or no progress at all, in a multilateral forum.[57]

5.4 Insights into an international competition agreement

The analysis set out in this chapter provides a range of insights into the appropriate approach for any international competition agreement. These insights are summarised below and are revisited in Part III of this book.

Bilateral agreements are the easiest form of agreement to conclude and enable two nations to reach agreement in circumstances where differences between all nations remain great. Current agreements embody important concepts that could have plurilateral or multilateral application, including notification, consultation, and negative comity and positive comity procedures. The concept of co-operation embodied in such agreements has provided an important mechanism to ameliorate the adverse effects of extraterritoriality. However, such flexibility is a double-edged sword due to the heterogeneity it creates. As the European Commission Group of Experts on Competition Law noted in 1995, it is 'difficult to imagine the emergence of a level playing field if this were to be founded only on a group of inevitably heterogenous bilateral agreements'.[58]

Yet it is also true that bilateral agreements necessarily align the interests of each party and thereby incrementally promote a convergence of interests between nations. As the interests of groups of nations converge, so the expansion and deepening of bilateral agreements may facilitate the development of a plurilateral competition framework. A plurilateral framework could involve the aggregation of a pre-existing network of bilateral agreements.

Plurilateral agreements in turn create momentum towards greater convergence of competition laws by emphasising the collective interests of nations. This is demonstrated by the evolution of competition law and policy within APEC. This approach is also supported by the expansion of EU competition law on a supranational basis into Central and Eastern Europe. In both instances, plurilateral initiatives are geographically and

---

[57] See G. Palmer, 'New Ways to Make International Environmental Law' (1992) 86 *American Journal International Law* 259.
[58] See European Group of Experts on Competition Law, 'Competition Policy in the New Trade Order: Strengthening International Co-operation and Rules, European Community', Brussels, July 1995.

substantively expanding, thereby deepening and broadening the extent of co-operation and convergence between nations.

Strategies at the plurilateral level can also be transposed to the multilateral level. Multilateral initiatives within UNCTAD, OECD and the WTO, in particular, have assisted in identifying and resolving differences between nations, increasing confidence, and promoting bilateral and plurilateral solutions to cross-border competition issues. The OECD recommendations, for example, have facilitated the further deepening and broadening of bilateral co-operation and led to the widespread adoption of concepts of positive and negative comity. In this manner, bilateral, plurilateral and multilateral initiatives each assist each other in a form of cumulative causation. This was perhaps recognised by the UNCTAD Code with its promotion of simultaneous initiatives at each of the national, regional and international levels.

However, there remain a number of significant obstacles to the development of cross-border competition laws. Most important are:

- confidence by each nation in the enforcement procedures of other nations;
- abnormalities and significant differences between the competition law of different nations, indicating the likely benefits of further convergence;
- procedural restrictions on the sharing of confidential information;
- issues of sovereignty and jurisdiction; and
- the incentive effects of the externalities identified in Chapter 3.

If each of these issues could be targeted and overcome, the chances of realising an international competition law agreement would be significantly greater.

Given the existence of substantive differences between nations, a uniform supranational competition law does not seem realistic at this time. Rather, the approach of APEC seems more pragmatic, in which agreement is achieved notwithstanding substantive differences in national competition laws by emphasising the importance of underlying core principles based on common standards and approaches. Such core principles could provide a basis for selective harmonisation and convergence of competition laws while providing a foundation for future development of more detailed competition provisions. Core principles could be included in any multilateral competition agreement, for example, to address such issues as non-discrimination, transparency and accountability. The draft competition agreement set out in Chapter 14 of this book adopts this approach.

Furthermore, given that initiatives at a number of levels are complementary, a mixed architecture of tiered multilateral, plurilateral and bilateral initiatives could co-exist to address cross-border competition laws. A number of permutations are possible, for example:

- A *multilateral* instrument could establish core principles to be adopted by all nations, thereby ensuring nations had broadly consistent objectives and ensured a degree of standardisation in the approach taken by different nations to competition law and policy issues. A multilateral instrument could also provide agreed procedures for resolving bilateral disputes and could foster negotiation of bilateral agreements.
- *Plurilateral* instruments could translate broad principles at the international level into more specific laws and policies at the domestic level. Plurilateral instruments could also ensure enforcement was co-ordinated at a regional level via more advanced comity and jurisdictional mechanisms.
- *Bilateral* instruments could provide for clear rights and obligations between parties to ensure effective cross-border law enforcement and to prevent jurisdictional disputes. There is also no rule that bilateral agreements should remain bilateral, so such agreements could be extended to form trilateral or limited plurilateral agreements, as exemplified by a tripartite co-operation agreement between the competition authorities of Canada, New Zealand and Australia concluded on 26 October 2000.

Following this theme, plurilateral instruments need not be regional in application, and could be based, for example, on common interests between like nations (such as an instrument between LDCs alone, as now contemplated by UNCTAD). Similarly, any multilateral instrument need not be comprehensive and could selectively regulate particular sectors or markets within the international economy, as has occurred with telecommunications and shipping. In industries more prone to competition issues, for example, there may be perceived to be a greater need for a cross-border competition law (although there remains the danger of a fragmented approach to the development of an international competition agreement). Given such flexibility, substantive progress could be made sooner rather than later.

Importantly, it also remains true that only roughly half of the nations in the world have enacted competition laws. Of this group, most have had only brief experience with competition laws and they are still developing the expertise and political support necessary for sound and effective enforcement. Most of the nations without competition laws are LDCs, with some notable exceptions. The UNCTAD experience suggests that concessions for developing nations will be essential in realising LDC support.

5.5 Conclusion: existing initiatives towards the regulation of cross-border conduct have clear limitations that could be overcome by an international competition agreement

In summary, a number of initiatives have been undertaken in recent years at the bilateral, plurilateral and multilateral levels to regulate cross-border anti-competitive conduct. Each of these initiatives has clear limitations and has therefore achieved only qualified success. Given these limitations, these existing initiatives would not be sufficient in themselves to realise the benefits identified in Chapter 3 of this book. In particular:

- Bilateral initiatives have progressively increased in sophistication in recent decades. They have largely been confined to date to circumstances in which two jurisdictions with similar competition laws and similar views on competition law have found it expedient to co-operate. The pre-conditions for more complex bilateral agreements are stringent, as evidenced by the UC–EU agreement and the Australia–New Zealand agreement. While bilateral agreements are the easiest form of agreement to conclude, they are heterogeneous. Furthermore, a network of bilateral agreements would be highly inefficient given that roughly 7,000 agreements would be required between the world's 120 nations currently possessing competition laws.
- Existing plurilateral initiatives within the context of APEC and the EU have proved successful although both initiatives have limitations. While the APEC initiative has, to date, focused on competition policy rather than competition law, it does illustrate the extent to which agreement on broad competition principles may contribute towards the co-ordination of competition policy. The EU approach represents the furthest any group of nations have travelled to date in adopting a comprehensive cross-border competition law, although the EU approach is premised on the existence of a customs union between nations with a very high degree of legal and economic integration.
- Existing multilateral initiatives have also faced clear limitations. Of these, the UNCTAD Code was the most ambitious, but it met with significant political opposition from industrialised nations given the perception that it unduly favoured the interests of developing nations.

The OECD proved relatively successful in influencing the development of cross-border co-operation on competition issues, but its limited membership of advanced industrialised countries discouraged support from developing nations. The WTO competition initiative has gathered momentum over the last decade and may provide the most appropriate vehicle for an international competition agreement, particularly as it may provide a means to bridge the 'North–South' divide.

An international competition agreement would overcome many of the limitations of the existing initiatives. Such an agreement would be necessary if the benefits identified in Chapter 3 were to be realised. However, such an agreement would be unlikely to be of itself sufficient, rather it would need to complement and build upon the existing initiatives. The combination of existing initiatives with an international competition agreement would provide a sufficient framework for the regulation of cross-border anti-competitive conduct in order to realise the benefits identified in Chapter 3.

In conclusion, Chapters 2 and 3 of this book have identified that such an agreement would be welfare enhancing and would address externalities in the cross-border regulation of competition. Chapter 4 has identified that there is a sufficient basis for such an agreement. Chapter 5 has concluded that existing initiatives towards the regulation of cross-border anti-competitive conduct have clear limitations that could be overcome by such an agreement.

Part I of this book has therefore reached the conclusion that an international competition agreement is desirable.

PART II

The WTO Would Provide a Suitable Institutional Vehicle

6

Would the WTO provide a suitable institutional vehicle for an international competition agreement?

> The WTO is sometimes described as a 'free trade' institution, but that is not entirely accurate. The system does allow tariffs and, in limited circumstances, other forms of protection. More accurately, it is a system of rules dedicated to open, fair and undistorted competition.
>
> (World Trade Organisation Secretariat, 1999)[1]

Part II of this book, commencing with Chapter 6, considers whether the WTO would provide a suitable institutional vehicle for an international competition agreement.

Importantly, Chapter 6 of this book does not consider whether the WTO would provide the *optimal* institutional framework for an international competition agreement. An analysis of whether the WTO would provide the optimal institutional framework is deferred to Chapter 10. Rather, Chapter 6 only considers, the extent to which it would be *feasible* to incorporate an international competition agreement into the WTO and the likely benefits of doing so.

Chapter 6 has three principal sections:

- Section 6.1 identifies the limited historical inclusion of competition law within the GATT, the evolution of the WTO, and various historical initiatives to include competition law within the GATT and the WTO. Section 6.1 identifies aspects of competition law incorporated into the WTO by the Uruguay Round.
- Section 6.2 considers the theoretical relationship between international competition law and trade law and establishes the context for assessing proposals to integrate the two disciplines.

---

[1] See World Trade Organisation, *Trading into the Future* (World Trade Organisation, Geneva, 1999), p. 7.

- Section 6.3 identifies areas of convergence between international competition law and international trade law and proposes a theoretical means to reconcile both laws, based on the concept of market contestability.

Chapter 6 concludes that the WTO could provide a suitable institutional vehicle for an international competition agreement provided that the relationship between competition law and trade law were suitably reconciled. At a theoretical level, Chapter 6 argues that both disciplines could be reconciled via the concept of market contestability. However, the practical issues associated with any such reconciliation would need careful examination. Chapters 7 to 9 of this book subsequently undertake that examination.

6.1 Historical relationship between trade law and competition law

In order to determine whether the WTO would provide a suitable institutional vehicle for an international competition agreement, it is useful to examine the historical relationship between competition law and trade law and to identify the extent to which competition law is already addressed by the various WTO agreements.

6.1.1 Early proposals for the regulation of cross-border anti-competitive conduct

Anti-competitive activity has long been recognised as requiring co-ordinated regulatory attention at the international level. The earliest recorded proposals for regulating international anti-competitive conduct date back as far as a World Economic Forum hosted by the League of Nations in 1927. During that Forum, William Oualid, a professor of economics, presented a paper to the Industrial Committee of the International Economic Conference titled 'The Social Effects of International Industrial Agreements' which observed that regulatory co-ordination at the international level would be required to address effectively the adverse effects of international cartels.[2] Given that competition laws only existed in a small handful of nations at that time, Oualid's proposal was both

---

[2] See W. Oualid, 'The Social Effects of International Industrial Agreements', Paper Presented to the Industrial Committee of the International Economic Conference, World Economic Forum, 1927.

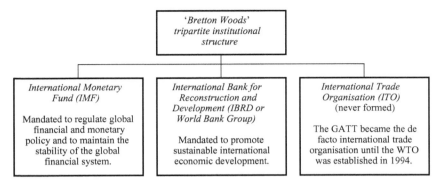

Figure 25: *Institutional structure for the world economy proposed at Bretton Woods (1947)*

radical and premature.[3] Following discussion at that time, the Committee determined that national attitudes on such issues were too diverse to support any international regulatory regime, ironically voicing the same concerns that are still expressed today, some seventy-five years later.

During World War II, a paradigm shift in international thought occurred in which the adverse political consequences of industrial cartelisation were clearly recognised, as were the adverse welfare effects of excessive concentration of economic power. The Allied nations utilised the period of post-war economic reconstruction as an opportunity to promote their ambitious objective of institutionalising international economic relations, liberalising world trade, and establishing an open and stable international economic system.

As discussed in depth in the literature, the foundation for modern international economic law was laid in that period. Commencing in Bretton Woods in 1945 the Allied nations sought to establish a post-war international economic order supported by a tripartite institutional structure, as illustrated by Figure 25, comprising:[4]

---

[3] However, as Portnoy has commented, Oualid's proposal was remarkable in that its general form has been followed by almost all subsequent proposals for an international competition regime. See B. Portnoy, 'Building the Missing Pillar? Multilateralism, Extraterritoriality and Cooperation in International Antitrust', Paper presented to CASPIC MacArthur Scholars' Conference, Wilder House, University of Chicago, 1 May 1999.

[4] Each of these three institutions was intended to be a specialised agency that would bolster the United Nations system, in respect of international economic and social co-operation, as contemplated by the UN Charter, Art. 57. See Charter of the United Nations; concluded at San Francisco, 26 June 1945; entered into force, 29 December 1945; 1 UNTS xvi; (1976) YBUN 1043; 59 Stat 1031; TS 933.

- an International Monetary Fund (IMF), to assist the formulation and implementation of world financial and monetary policy;
- an International Bank for Reconstruction and Development (IBRD), now known as the World Bank Group, to finance and promote economic development projects in both war-devastated nations and the Third World; and
- an International Trade Organisation (ITO), to govern all aspects of global trade.

Reflecting the emphasis of the Allied nations, the ITO's trade mandate was to be complemented by a mandate to regulate and promote cross-border international competition.

The background to the proposed role of the ITO in relation to competition is important. In 1945, the US and the UK had jointly published a comprehensive policy paper entitled, 'Proposal for Expansion of World Trade and Employment'.[5] This paper proposed that anti-competitive behaviour should be viewed as a barrier to world trade and should be subject to international regulation, consistent with the conclusions of the Oualid paper some two decades earlier. Following this paper, the US State Department proposed a draft charter for the ITO ('Draft Charter'), which included a range of provisions mandating the multilateral regulation and surveillance of international anti-competitive behaviour.[6] As has been noted, this Draft Charter contained some of the most ambitious proposals yet devised for curbing international anti-competitive behaviour.[7]

The Draft Charter advocated strict controls on international restrictive business practices, including a rebuttable presumption that certain conduct was anti-competitive, including price fixing, market division, collective boycotts and abuses of intellectual property rights.[8] This presumption was complemented by a sweeping trade-related prohibition, which prohibited any business practices that restrained competition, restricted access to markets, or fostered monopolistic control in international

---

[5] See 'Suggested Charter for an International Trade Organisation of the United Nations', Department of State Publication No. 2598, (1946) 93 *Commercial Policy Series* 1 ('Draft Charter').
[6] See 'Proposal for Expansion of World Trade and Employment', Department of State Publication No. 2411, (1945) 79 *Commercial Policy Series* 1.
[7] See E. M. Fox, 'Competition Law & the Agenda for the WTO: Forging the Links of Competition and Trade' (1995) 4(1) *Pacific Rim Law & Policy Journal* 1.
[8] Draft Charter, above n. 5, Art. 34(2).

trade.[9] The Draft Charter contemplated that the ITO would regulate and co-ordinate international competition policy. Remarkably, private parties and ratifying nations alike would be empowered to petition the ITO to undertake investigatory action.[10] If the ITO concluded that a breach of the Draft Charter had occurred, then the ITO could direct ratifying nations to 'take action' to rectify any business practices the ITO considered harmful.[11]

Such conferral of standing to private parties was a radical proposition, particularly as such standing is rarely granted by international treaties even today. In combination with the ability of the ITO to issue legally binding directions, and strict presumptions that certain conduct was anti-competitive, such standing would have provided a potent mechanism for private parties to influence governmental conduct.

6.1.2 The Havana Charter for the ITO – from cradle to early grave

Given the radical nature of the Draft Charter proposed by the US, it is not surprising that it was widely opposed, including by Britain and the Benelux nations. Most nations, for example, advocated that the ITO should only have a recommendatory role and should not have the power legally to bind ratifying nations. At an international conference convened in Havana in 1947, the US reluctantly agreed to soften various provisions of the Draft Charter.[12] Following intense negotiations, a revised charter for the ITO was tabled by the United States in 1948, which subsequently became known as the 'Havana Charter'.[13]

The Havana Charter retained the Draft Charter's general structure, involving a general trade-related prohibition supplemented by a number of specific prohibitions against anti-competitive conduct. Where conduct was specifically prohibited, a 'rule of reason' approach was applied, by reference to the effect of the conduct on international trade.[14] Only ratifying nations could petition the ITO for investigatory action.[15] If the ITO determined that a breach of the Havana Charter had occurred, then the ITO could request each relevant ratifying nation to take 'every possible

---

[9] Ibid., Art. 34(1). [10] Ibid., Art. 35(2). [11] Ibid., Art. 37(5).
[12] See discussion in J. H. Jackson, *The World Trading System: Law and Policy of International Economic Relations* (2nd edn, MIT Press, Cambridge, 1997), pp. 34–9.
[13] See Havana Charter for an International Trade Organisation, Department of State Publication No. 3117, (1947) 93 *Commercial Policy Series* 1. Competition law issues were addressed within Ch. IV (Commercial Policy) and Ch. V (Restrictive Business Practices).
[14] Ibid., Art. 46(3)(a)–(f). [15] Ibid., Art. 48(3).

remedial action'.[16] Each ratifying nation was obliged to 'take full account' of any ITO requests and to take any action they considered appropriate having regard to their obligations under the Havana Charter.[17] Unlike under the Draft Charter, the ITO decisions and requests were recommendatory in nature, rather than being legally binding.

The Havana Charter contained further procedural requirements for international consultation, investigations and decision-making. Ratifying nations were required to provide information to the ITO on request and the ITO was required to conduct hearings and publish its findings. Certain procedural requirements were intended to dilute the powers of the ITO further. For example, a two-thirds vote of the ratifying nations was required before the ITO could adjudicate that a business practice in a specific instance was a 'restrictive business practice'. This two-thirds voting procedure gave the ratifying nations a high element of political control over the potential enforcement activities of the ITO.

Most importantly, the Havana Charter required ratifying nations to enact various competition laws to ensure that private and public enterprises within their jurisdiction did not engage in certain anti-competitive practices. Article 50(1) of the Havana Charter required each ratifying nation to:

> [T]ake all possible measures by legislation or otherwise, in accordance with its constitution or system of law or economic organisation, to ensure, within its jurisdiction, that private and public commercial enterprises do not engage in practices which are as specified in paragraphs 2 and 3 of Article 46.

The Havana Charter therefore, in effect, sought to establish a minimum competition law among ratifying nations as well as a supranational enforcement body with recommendatory powers. While the Havana Charter was not as ambitious as the Draft Charter, the Havana Charter was still radical for its time and was nearly successful in its attempt to impose an over-arching international system for the regulation of international trade and competition.

In 1950, the Havana Charter was abandoned by the international community, notwithstanding that over fifty nations had ratified it by that time. Ironically, the abandonment of the Havana Charter was engineered

---

[16] *Ibid.*, Art. 48(7).   [17] *Ibid.*, Art. 50(4).

principally by the US, the nation that had most enthusiastically championed the establishment of the ITO.[18] The US State Department viewed the Havana Charter as a threat to stricter US competition laws, while the US Congress viewed it as an unwarranted threat to US economic hegemony and domestic political sovereignty in the post-war era. Following extensive hearings and several unsuccessful attempts, the US State Department did not submit the Havana Charter for ratification.[19]

Accordingly, while the first two institutions of the tripartite world trading system proposed in 1947 were established and remain in existence today (namely the IMF and the World Bank Group), the third institution, the ITO, foundered. An alternative to the ITO was therefore developed at the international level. This alternative did not contemplate international competition law or policy. This alternative was limited to trade and commercial policy and did not extend to international regulation of competition.

6.1.3 Historical initiatives to incorporate competition law into the GATT

As a result of delays in negotiating the Havana Charter in 1947, a group of twenty-three nations decided to agree various trade liberalising measures among themselves ahead of the formation of the ITO. These nations agreed a stand-alone treaty, known as the General Agreement on Tariffs and Trade ('GATT'), which established a sophisticated mechanism for the progressive reduction of tariffs and quantitative restraints.[20] As the GATT was intended as an interim measure, it was deliberately less comprehensive in scope than the Havana Charter. Importantly, the GATT contained no provisions addressing anti-competitive trade practices and did not contemplate any direct or indirect linkage between competition law and trade law. Once the ratification of the Havana Charter ultimately failed in 1950, the GATT increased in importance in the resulting vacuum, becoming the de facto international instrument regulating international trade.

---

[18] See G. Diebold, *The End of the ITO: Essays in International Finance No. 16* (Princeton University, Princeton, 1952), para. 2.5.

[19] See *Hearings on HRJ Resolution 236 before the House Committee on Foreign Affairs*, 81st Cong. 2d Sess. (1950).

[20] General Agreement on Tariffs and Trade, 30 October 1947, 61 Stat (5), (6) TIAS No. 1700, 55 UNTS 194.

The GATT was established with the fundamental objective of liberalising trade, thereby enhancing the welfare of all nations.[21] To achieve this objective, the GATT was subsequently amended to create a framework for the progressive reduction of trade barriers and the non-discriminatory treatment of imported goods. Importantly, the GATT incorporated two key overriding principles of non-discrimination:

- The GATT principle of 'most favoured nation treatment' which was set out in Article I of the GATT. Article I obliged each contracting party to extend to every other contracting party the same favourable treatment that it had accorded to any other individual GATT contracting party.
- The GATT principle of 'national treatment' which was set out in Article III of the GATT. Article III obliged each GATT contracting party to treat all imported goods no less favourably than domestically produced goods once the imported goods had passed through customs checkpoints and entered the stream of commerce of the GATT contracting party.

The initial approach of the GATT required the GATT contracting parties to negotiate 'tariff bindings'. These tariff bindings set out maximum permissible tariff rates for each imported good in comprehensive product lists. Successive tariff bindings, agreed in successive rounds of multilateral trade negotiations, had an incremental ratchet effect towards free trade. In the period following World War II, this GATT mechanism proved highly successful in reducing tariffs and thereby freeing the flow of international trade between the GATT contracting parties.

In addition, while the original GATT dealt principally with direct barriers to trade, namely tariffs and quantitative restrictions, it also had modest provisions to address indirect 'non-tariff' barriers, such as discriminatory customs valuation procedures, government procurement practices, and subsidies. The scope of the GATT was subsequently expanded in the Kennedy Round (1967) and Tokyo Round (1979) to address such 'non-tariff' barriers further. In this manner, modern public international trade law evolved as a complicated set of international agreements, instruments and institutions coalescing around the GATT.[22]

---

[21] Refer to the recitals to the GATT, above n. 19.
[22] Many of the original GATT obligations were supplemented by separately negotiated treaty instruments known as 'GATT Codes'. See J. H. Jackson, 'National Treatment Obligations & Non-tariff Barriers' (1989) 10 *Michigan Journal of International Law* 207, 208.

Notwithstanding the expansion of the GATT, the GATT continued in substantially the same form as it had been drafted in 1947 until the conclusion of the Uruguay Round of multilateral trade negotiations in 1994. However, due to the historical relationship between competition policy and trade policy, a number of initiatives were made by the GATT contracting parties to incorporate competition law into the GATT over that forty-seven-year period.

Of particular importance were seventeen meetings of the contracting parties held between 1954 and 1960, which considered the introduction of competition principles into the GATT. Similarly, attempts were made to incorporate competition policy into the United Nations system as a regulatory alternative to the GATT:

- *1953* In 1953, the United States, Canada and others, acting via the Economic and Social Council of the United Nations ('ECOSOC'), prepared a draft agreement envisaging the formation of an international co-ordinating agency that would receive complaints, investigate and recommend remedial action relating to anti-competitive behaviour in international trade. This initiative was intended to redress the failure of the GATT to reflect the competition law provisions of the Havana Charter by establishing a competition agency under the auspices of the United Nations.[23]

    Simultaneously, a GATT working party was formed to consider competition policy within the GATT.[24] Ironically, both initiatives backfired when ECOSOC and the GATT working party each absolved itself of responsibility and concluded that the other was better placed to deal with any international competition law initiatives.[25]

- *1956* In a 1956 session of the GATT contracting parties, a GATT committee was formed to consider again the extent to which the GATT should address competition law issues. This committee established a commission of competition law experts who reported back to the GATT committee in 1959 and 1960.

---

[23] See G. N. Addy, 'International Co-ordination of Competition Policies' in E. Kantzenbach, H. E. Scharrer & L. Waverman (eds.), *Competition Policy in an Interdependent World Economy* (Nomos Verlagsgesellschaft, Baden-Baden, 1993), p. 292.

[24] Norway, Sweden and Denmark proposed simply inserting the ECOSOC draft text into the GATT.

[25] See comments in B. Furnish, 'A Transnational Approach to Restrictive Business Practices' (1970) 4 *International Lawyer* 317, 328.

The minority of the experts concluded that the GATT should address competition policy under the GATT's Article XXV collective decision-making powers and, by majority vote of the contracting parties, should agree to bring surveillance or dispute resolution under Article XXIII. In this manner, the contracting parties would agree to apply the Article XXIII nullification or impairment breach provisions of the GATT to trade-related completion issues. However, the majority of the experts recommended, in relation to Article XXV, that:[26]

> [R]egardless of the question whether Article XXIII could legally be applied . . . no action [should be taken to introduce competition laws] under this Article. Such action would involve the grave risk of retaliatory measures under . . . paragraph 2 of that Article.

The reference to paragraph 2 of Article XXIII is important. Paragraph 2 enables the GATT contracting parties to authorise retaliatory enforcement action in circumstances where a nullification or impairment of a GATT obligation has not been resolved. The concern of the majority of the experts was that most competition issues would be likely to fall into this category and would frequently require the GATT contracting parties to authorise retaliatory enforcement action. Presumably an underlying concern of the majority of the experts was that trade measures used to enforce competition provisions could adversely affect pre-existing WTO trade concessions, as discussed in Chapter 12 of this book.

The expert commission unanimously concluded that it was unrealistic for international competition law to be introduced into the GATT at that time, as insufficient international consensus existed on competition law issues. The expert commission did recommend, however, that voluntary consultations should be held under Article XXII of the GATT whenever a GATT contracting party considered that it had been harmed by the anti-competitive behaviour of the residents of any other GATT contracting party.[27] However, Article XXII consultations may be futile where significant differences of opinion remain between the relevant GATT contracting parties that are incapable of resolution by bilateral negotiation, as are likely in competition law disputes.

---

[26] See 'Report of the Expert Group on Restrictive Business Practices' (1961) BISD 9S/170.
[27] The GATT, Art. XXII sets out a procedure for consultation between any GATT contracting parties involved in a trade dispute, with the aim of achieving a bilateral negotiated outcome.

- *1960* In 1960, the GATT contracting parties adopted the unanimous recommendation of the expert commission and determined that Article XXII would form the basis for a new GATT resolution against private restrictive business practices. However, the subsequent GATT resolution of 18 November 1960 ('1960 Resolution') had little legal weight.[28] The 1960 Resolution simply recommended that each GATT contracting party should, at the request of any other affected GATT contracting party, enter into bilateral negotiations on the harmful effects of any private restrictive business practices to which its residents were a party. The 1960 Resolution provided:[29]

> The party addressed should accord sympathetic consideration to and should afford adequate opportunity for consultations with the requesting party, with a view to reaching mutually satisfactory conclusions, and if it agrees that such harmful effects are present it should take such measures as it deems appropriate to eliminate these effects, and decide that:
>
> (a) if the requesting party and the party addressed are able to reach a mutually satisfactory conclusion, they should jointly advise the secretariat of the nature of the complaint and the conclusions reached;
>
> (b) if the requesting party and the party addressed are unable to reach a mutually satisfactory conclusion, they should advise the secretariat of the nature of the complaint and the fact that a mutually satisfactory conclusion cannot be reached; and
>
> (c) the secretariat shall convey the information referred to under (a) and (b) to the Contracting Parties.

The usefulness of this consultative mechanism is therefore questionable. The mechanism is devoid of any objective way to define restrictive business practices and any investigative means to determine or analyse the applicable facts. The 1960 Resolution does not provide any scope for conflict resolution if the parties cannot reach agreement. Under the 1960 Resolution, the GATT contracting parties simply agreed that they will co-operate between themselves to eliminate restrictive business practices where such practices have the effect of hampering 'the expansion of world trade and economic development in individual countries'.[30]

---

[28] See 'Restrictive Business Practices: Arrangements for Consultations' (1961) BISD 9S/28.
[29] *Ibid.*, p. 29.   [30] *Ibid.*, p. 29.

However, on the other hand the Resolution does represent the first multilateral commitment reached among the world's nations to combat international anti-competitive behaviour. It also has an important 'soft law' quality as will be discussed in Chapter 11 of this book. The consultative mechanism therefore represents a first step towards realising an international competition agreement.

In conclusion, while the Havana Charter expressly addressed anti-competitive behaviour and established an important historical precedent, the GATT hesitated to do so. Differences in national competition laws and most nations' inexperience in competition law, proved insurmountable in the period between 1947 and 1994. The end result of a number of initiatives during this period was the weak GATT consultative protocol set out in the Resolution above applying to international anti-competitive behaviour.

Meanwhile, the GATT contracting parties made efforts progressively to supplement, expand and strengthen the provisions of the original GATT, principally via eight rounds of multilateral trade negotiations. Of these, the Uruguay Round of GATT multilateral trade negotiations proved to be the most revolutionary round of them all and led to renewed efforts to introduce competition law within the world trading framework.

6.1.4 The Uruguay Round and competition provisions introduced into the WTO

On 15 December 1993, the Uruguay Round was concluded after a marathon seven years of difficult negotiations. Many significant changes to the GATT resulted that further extended and altered the regulation of international commerce and reshaped the framework of the global multilateral trading system.[31]

Most importantly, the GATT itself was incorporated within a new umbrella international trading organisation known as the World Trade

---

[31] The GATT was supplemented by additional agreements for trade in services, trade-related intellectual property and trade-related investment measures, and a new set of procedures for international trade dispute resolution. See E. U. Petersmann, 'The Transformation of the World Trading System through the 1994 Agreement Establishing the World Trade Organisation' (1994) 21 *European Journal International Law* 161.

Organisation ('WTO').[32] This new institutional system was intended to be the modern day equivalent of the ITO, as contemplated by the Havana Charter in 1947. The Uruguay Round agreements also created a skeletal framework of general principles and rules, upon which specific commitments could be fleshed out.[33]

Unlike the Havana Charter, the Uruguay Round agreements did not contemplate the regulation of international anti-competitive conduct except in a very isolated manner, as discussed below. While international anti-competitive conduct was briefly considered during Uruguay Round negotiations, the GATT nations concluded that insufficient international consensus existed at the time to make any significant progress, ironically reflecting the same reservations expressed some sixty-five years earlier. Furthermore, the relationship between international trade law and competition law was recognised as highly complex and the GATT nations considered that further investigative work was required. Accordingly, as discussed in Chapter 5 of this book, a review provision was included within the Uruguay Round's Agreement on Trade Related Investment Measures (TRIMS).[34] Partly as a result of initiatives flowing from this review provision, competition law and policy still remains on the WTO agenda.[35]

The Uruguay Round successfully introduced a number of limited competition provisions into WTO law. These competition provisions supplemented several existing GATT provisions that had been interpreted by WTO jurisprudence as regulating, in a specific manner, certain anti-competitive conduct. The competition law provisions existing in the WTO agreements as at March 2005 are summarised in Figure 26.[36]

---

[32] Final Act and Agreement Establishing the World Trade Organisation, General Agreement on Tariffs and Trade, Uruguay Round, Marrakesh, Morocco, 15 April 1994 and The Results of the Uruguay Round of Multilateral Trade Negotiations: The Legal Texts (GATT Secretariat, Geneva, 1994).

[33] See, for example, detailed discussion on the Uruguay Round in J. Schott, *The Uruguay Round: An Assessment* (Institute of International Economics, Washington DC, 1994).

[34] Agreement on Trade-Related Investment Measures, Art. 9, Annexe 1A: Multilateral Agreement on Trade in Goods, Final Act.

[35] See A. Hoda, 'WTO: Working Group on Trade and Competition Policy' (1997) 25(11) *International Business Lawyer* 449. See also World Trade Organisation, *Report (1998) of the Working Group on the Interaction between Trade and Competition Policy to the Generic Council*, WT/WGTCP/2, Doc No. 98–4914, 8 December 1998.

[36] See, for example, discussion in OECD, 'Competition Elements in International Trade Agreements: A Post-Uruguay Round Overview of WTO Agreements', OECD Joint Group on Trade and Competition, COM/TD/DAFFE/CLP(98)26/FINAL, 28 January 1999.

WTO agreement	Article	Nature of competition obligation
GATT 1947	II:4, XVII	If a party maintains an import monopoly, that monopoly must not afford protection greater on average than agreed in the schedules. Similarly, non-discrimination obligations for state-owned enterprises may be applied against monopolies.
GATT 1947	III	GATT Panels have interpreted the national treatment obligation as requiring equality of competitive conditions between domestic and imported products.
GATT 1947	XI and XX(d)	The provisions against quantitative restraints have occasionally been used to target import monopolies that are not justifiable under Article XX.
GATT 1947	XVII	State trading enterprises must act in a manner consistent with the principles of non-discriminatory treatment. State trading enterprises must also make purchases or sales in accordance with commercial considerations and allow enterprises from other members the opportunity to compete.
GATT 1947	XXIII: 1(b)	A WTO Panel has reasoned that industrial policies that upset the competitive conditions of a market could be actionable as a non-violation complaint.[37]
Interpretation of Article XVII[38]	1	State-trading enterprises with exclusive or special privileges must be subjected to greater surveillance, potentially including competition privileges.
Anti-dumping Agreement[39]	3.5	'Trade-restrictive practices and competition between foreign and domestic producers' are factors for determining injury caused by private injurious dumping.
TRIMS	9	A WTO working party must consider whether the TRIMS agreement should be complemented by provisions on competition policy, as noted above.

Figure 26: *Existing competition law provisions in the WTO agreements*

[37] See the *Kodak-Fuji* case discussed in Chapter 7 of this book.
[38] Understanding on the Interpretation of Article XVII of the General Agreement on Tariffs and Trade 1944, Annexe 1A, Final Act.
[39] Agreement on the Implementation of Article VI of the General Agreement on Tariffs and Trade 1944, Annexe 1A, Final Act.

WTO agreement	Article	Nature of competition obligation
Pre-shipment Inspection[40]	2, 6	Governments must prohibit certain activities of private pre-shipment inspection entities, some of which may have anti-competitive effects.
Technical Barriers to Trade[41]	3, 4, 8	The preparation, adoption and application of technical regulations and standards by non-governmental bodies must be no more trade-restrictive than is necessary.
Subsidies[42]	6, 15.5	'Trade-restrictive practices and competition' and 'price undercutting' are deemed as relevant factors for determining injury caused by certain subsidies.
Safeguards	11.1(b)	VERs, orderly marketing arrangements and compulsory import cartels are prohibited. Governments must not support enterprises involved in such conduct.
GATS	VII, IX	Governments must ensure that 'monopolies and exclusive service suppliers' do not undermine GATS commitments. Anti-competitive practices of third parties are recognised as constraining trade in services. Many governments have also pre-committed themselves to curbing abuses of dominance, particularly in the telecommunications sector, by way of binding commitments.
GATS	XVII:1 and 3	Each member must accord to services and service suppliers of any other member, in respect of all measures affecting the supply of services, treatment no less favourable than that it accords to its own like services and service suppliers. Formally identical or formally different treatment is considered less favourable if it modifies the conditions of competition in favour of services or service suppliers of the member compared to like services or service suppliers of any other member.
Financial Services[43]	1, 10	Existing monopoly rights must be identified. Members must endeavour to remove or limit certain measures, potentially including measures that may encourage anti-competitive conduct.

Figure 26: (cont.)

[40] Agreement on Pre-shipment Inspection, Annexe 1A, Final Act.
[41] Agreement on Technical Barriers to Trade, Annexe 1A, Final Act.
[42] Agreement on Subsidies and Countervailing Measures, Annexe 1A, Final Act.
[43] Decision on Financial Services, Annexe 4, Final Act.

WTO agreement	Article	Nature of competition obligation
Basic Telecoms	Ref. Paper	The Reference Paper to the GATS telecommunications annexe contains a general commitment for members to prevent certain anti-competitive practices, as discussed in Chapter 7 of this book.
TRIPS [44]	17, 22, 39, 31.	Unfair trade rules relating to intellectual property must be obeyed, such as a prohibition on restraint of trade. Intellectual property rights must not be abused in a manner that restricts competition.
TRIPS	8, 39, 40.	The WTO must agree on appropriate measures to prevent the abuse of intellectual property rights and to prohibit practices, which unreasonably restrain trade or unfairly restrain competition.
Government Procurement [45]	X, XV	Government tendering procedures must optimise international competition, while collusive tendering is prohibited.

Figure 26: (cont.)

Importantly, these competition law provisions are largely intended to prevent governments avoiding reciprocal tariff concessions by disguised means. The provisions are relatively ad hoc in application and limited in nature. Half of the provisions are procedural and mandate competition law as a relevant consideration when exercising certain administrative discretions.[46] The remaining provisions are directed at the most severe forms of anti-competitive behaviour, such as monopolies and cartels.[47] The majority of the provisions are isolated to particular sectors (such as telecommunications, shipping, and intellectual property) and

---

[44] Agreement on Trade-Related Aspects of Intellectual Property Rights, Annexe 1C, Final Act ('TRIPS').

[45] Agreement on Government Procurement, Annexe 4: Plurilateral Trade Agreements, Final Act.

[46] See, for example, Agreement on Implementation of Article VI, Art. 3.5; Agreement on Pre-shipment Inspection, Arts. 2, 6; Agreement on Technical Barriers to Trade, Arts. 3, 4, 8; Agreement on Subsidies and Countervailing Measures, Arts. 6, 15.5; and Agreement on Government Procurement, Arts. X, XV.

[47] See, for example, the GATT, Arts. II:4, XVII; Agreement on Safeguards and Countervailing Measures, Art. 11.1(b); and the GATS, Arts. 7–9, 14.

are therefore of limited application.[48] In each case, trade policy is given pre-eminence but is tempered by competition law where anti-competitive consequences arise that could hinder trade objectives. There is no generic obligation regulating cross-border anti-competitive conduct.

While the selective inclusion of competition law into the WTO is meritworthy, competition policy is therefore currently addressed in an ad hoc, highly localised and inconsistent manner by the WTO agreements without any attempt to create an overall unified approach. Furthermore, the fundamental relationship between trade law and competition law is not satisfactorily addressed by these provisions. This is not conducive to the effective regulation of cross-border anti-competitive conduct and tends to reflect a strongly trade-oriented view of competition issues without recognising the wider benefits of a competition-oriented approach. As proposed later in this book, a better integrated and coherent approach should ideally be adopted to best address the issues identified in this book. However, as discussed later in this chapter, any such approach would need to resolve carefully the complex issues associated with the relationship between competition law and international trade law.

6.2 Are international trade law and international competition law complementary?

In order to determine whether the WTO is a suitable institutional vehicle for an international competition agreement, it is necessary to identify whether international competition law and policy would complement international trade law and policy and the extent of any conflict or inconsistency. Adopting a systematic approach, it is useful to start at a high level of generality by identifying the theoretical rationale for the WTO and whether the inclusion of competition law and policy into the WTO would remain consistent with that theoretical rationale. From this starting point, the level of detail can be increased by comparing the objectives, theoretical basis and methodology of international competition law and policy and international trade law and policy. Finally, conclusions can be drawn as to whether both disciplines are complementary and, if so, to what extent.

---

[48] See, for example, Agreement on Financial Services, Arts. 1, 10; various provisions in the Reference Paper on Basic Telecommunications; TRIPS, Arts. 8, 17, 22, 31, 39, 40.

6.2.1 What is the theoretical rationale for the WTO?

Key insights into the theoretical rationale for the WTO are provided by three relevant modern schools of thought, namely liberal constitutional theory, law and economics theory, and public choice theory. Each of these theories indicate that a key rationale for the WTO is to promote welfare maximising trade policies by domestic governments in an international trade context. Each of these three schools of thought are considered below and provide insights into the incorporation of competition law into the WTO. These three schools of thought form part of a body of knowledge known as 'international relations theory' which constitutes a massive literature that is beyond the scope of this book.

Liberal constitutional theory   Liberal constitutional theory views public international agreements as constitutive as they bind sovereign states, establish the parameters for acceptable governmental conduct, and entrench internationally-accepted norms and values. International agreements, for example, impose important constraints on governmental action by preventing abuses of power, thereby preserving fundamental human rights and economic freedoms.[49] Liberal constitutional theory views international agreements as important for the maintenance of harmonious international relations, fundamental democratic values and the Rule of Law.

When applied to the WTO, liberal constitutional theory views the WTO as preserving the rights of firms to engage in international trade without adverse governmental interference.[50] Liberal constitutional theory recognises the high degree of discretion available to governments when exercising their trade policy powers, and reasons that the WTO places restraints on such discretions by ensuring governments act reasonably and fairly and do not, for example, discriminate between domestic and foreign entities.

If competition law and policy were incorporated into the WTO, it would reinforce this 'liberal constitutional' rationale for the WTO. Competition policy is inherently deregulatory and seeks to reduce governmental

---

[49] See, for example, discussion in E. U. Petersmann, *Constitutional Functions of Public International Economic Law: International and Domestic Foreign Trade Law and Foreign Trade Policy in the United States, the European Community and Switzerland* (Fribourg University Press, Zurich, 1991).

[50] See E. U. Petersmann, 'The Transformation of the World Trading System Through the 1994 Agreement Establishing the WTO' (1995) 6(2) *European Journal of International Law* 161, 163.

interference in markets. Competition policy also recognises the importance of maintaining institutions and preserving fundamental economic rights (such as property rights) to ensure markets operate effectively. Competition law is then viewed by competition policy as the minimum necessary government interference in markets consistent with the correction of market failures arising from the concentration of market power, so is consistent with a minimalist approach. Accordingly, competition law and policy would broadly complement the theoretical rationale for the WTO viewed from a liberal constitutional theory perspective.

Law and economics theory   While liberal constitutional theory views law as a means of preserving fundamental rights, law and economics theory views law as a means to promote increased social welfare via greater economic efficiency. Law and economics theory regards each nation as acting rationally in its own self-interest to maximise its national welfare, regardless of benefits or detriments to other nations.[51] Law and economics theory thus identifies the existence of economic 'externalities' in which one nation's (or government's) self-interested policies can have significant negative spillover effects for other nations and for international society as a whole, as identified in Chapter 3 of this book. Law and economics theory recognises that international agreements may correct such externalities by requiring governments to formulate their own domestic policies with regard to the collective interests of international society rather than in their individual self-interest.[52]

When applied to the WTO, law and economics theory recognises the existence of externalities arising from each nation's (or government's) desire to erect trade barriers in its national (or political) self-interest. Accordingly, the theory identifies the need for international regulatory intervention to correct such market failures and views the WTO as a policy instrument achieving this.[53] In this manner, the theory suggests that the WTO is premised on the existence of mutual gains from

---

[51] Law and economics theory recognises the benefits of agreements as mechanisms for the mutually beneficial exchanges of resources between economic agents, thereby creating economic value.

[52] See discussion in J. Dunoff & J. P. Trachtman, 'The Law and Economics of International Law' (1999) 24 *Yale Journal of International Law* 1. See also J. P. Trachtman, 'The International Economic Law Revolution' (1996) 17 *University of Pennsylvania Journal of International Economic Law* 33.

[53] See discussion in J. P. Trachtman, 'Externalities and Extraterritoriality: The Law and Economics of Prescriptive Jurisdiction' in A. Sykes & J. Bhandari (eds.), *Economic Dimensions in International Law* (Cambridge University Press, New York, 1997), ch. 17.

co-operative activity relative to a non-co-operative approach.[54] Such co-operative activity is enforced by penalties for self-interested defection in the form of trade sanctions.

As discussed previously, competition law and policy is heavily grounded in economic theory, so would reinforce this law and economics rationale for the WTO. The precise interaction between international trade theory and international competition theory is complex and is analysed in detail later in this chapter. However, the discussion later in this chapter suggests that competition law and policy would broadly complement the theoretical rationale for the WTO viewed from a law and economics perspective.

Public choice theory While law and economics theory explains instances of 'market failure', public choice theory explains instances of 'government failure'.[55] Public choice theory not only identifies the potential for governments to act in their national self-interest at the expense of international society, but also recognises that such self-interest incentives are typically a function of internal domestic processes within each nation. Public choice theory views governments as subject to political capture by national interest groups engaged in rent-seeking activities. Similarly, public choice theory reasons that domestic constitutive rules can be subverted by rent-seeking and hidden political interests. International agreements are viewed as counterbalancing such domestic interests so as to influence the behaviour of governments in a manner beneficial to the public good.

When applied to the WTO, public choice theory identifies that domestic trade policy formation is susceptible to political capture, particularly by producer interests. Small groups representing concentrated domestic producer interests, for example, are easier to organise and more effective at influencing the political process than large groups reflecting dispersed consumer interests. Trade bureaucracies may also perpetuate particular policies in their own self-interest, influencing the formation of domestic

---

[54] See W. Poundstone, *Prisoner's Dilemma* (OUP, Oxford, 1992). See also discussion in S. P. Hargreaves-Heap, M. Hollis, B. R. Lyons, R. Sugden & A. P. Weale, *The Theory of Choice* (Basil Blackwell, London, 1992). See also, for example, K. Bagwell, 'The Theory of the WTO', Paper presented to the First World Congress of the Game Theory Society, 24 July 2000, Bilbao, Spain.

[55] The seminal work on public choice theory is J. M. Buchanan & G. Tullock, *The Calculus of Consent: Logical Foundations of a Constitutional Democracy* (University of Michigan Press, Ann Arbor, 1962). James Buchanan subsequently won a Nobel Prize in economics for his work on public choice theory.

trade policy. By requiring nations to commit to certain policies, the WTO reduces the scope for domestic rent-seeking and reinforces domestic governmental accountability and transparency, thereby reducing 'government failure'.

Again, the introduction of competition law and policy into the WTO would reinforce this public choice theory rationale for the WTO. Competition law, for example, is generally less susceptible to rent-seeking than trade law, and more resilient to political intervention, due to the generic approach of competition law and the heavy grounding of competition law in objective microeconomic theory. Similarly, competition policy promotes greater transparency of governmental regulation and reduces the scope for detrimental governmental regulation by adopting a deregulatory approach. The precise effects of competition law and policy on governmental behaviour were discussed in detail in Chapter 2 of this book, supporting the conclusion that competition law and policy would reinforce the theoretical rationale for the WTO viewed from a public choice theory perspective.

In summary, competition law and policy is broadly consistent with the theoretical objectives of the WTO as assessed under the three relevant modern schools of thought identified above, namely liberal constitutional theory, law and economics theory, and public choice theory.

6.2.2 Objectives of international competition and international trade law and policy

The next issue arising when determining whether competition law and policy could be incorporated into the WTO, is to identify the similarities and differences between international competition law and policy and international trade law and policy. These similarities and differences can initially be identified by analysing their respective objectives.

A comparison between the objectives of international trade law and policy and international competition law and policy is set out in the matrix in Figure 27. Consistent with the discussion in Chapter 2 of this book, the ultimate objectives of both disciplines are identical, namely to increase economic efficiency and thereby increase global and national welfare via a KHE improvement (as defined in Chapter 2).

More controversially, some incidental welfare redistributing objectives may also be incorporated into international competition policy and international trade policy. The efficiency objective of international

Objectives		International trade policy	International competition policy
Efficiency objective	Objective	Improved *level* of global and national welfare	Improved *level* of global and national welfare
	Causal mechanism	Trade liberalisation to achieve 'liberalised trade' (colloquially known as 'free trade')	Market deregulation and behavioural regulation to achieve 'workable competition'
Distributional objective	Objective	Improved *distribution* of global and national welfare	Improved *distribution* of global and national welfare
	Causal mechanism	A variety of causal mechanisms may be adopted to achieve 'fair trade'	A variety of causal mechanisms may be adopted to achieve 'fair competition'

Figure 27: *Matrix illustrating objectives of international trade policy and international competition policy*

competition policy and international trade policy is, in both cases, given primary importance relative to any distributional objectives, reflecting an emphasis by both disciplines on increasing welfare rather than redistributing it.

Efficiency objective At the broadest level, the efficiency objectives of international trade law and policy and international competition law and policy are entirely consistent, namely to improve total economic welfare in absolute terms.[56] In order to realise these objectives, both disciplines seek to promote greater economic efficiency. However, while international trade law and policy promotes trade liberalisation as a means to increase economic efficiency, competition law and policy promotes market deregulation and behavioural regulation. In this manner, each discipline follows a different causal mechanism, as illustrated by the matrix in Figure 27. The causal mechanisms and their relationship are analysed in detail later in this chapter.

[56] See World Bank, *Competition Policy in a Global Economy: An Interpretative Summary* (World Bank, Washington DC, 1998), ch. 2.

Distributional objectives International trade law and policy and international competition law and policy may also be subject to a range of distributional objectives intended to improve the distribution of welfare on a national and global basis:

- The causal mechanisms by which international trade law and policy may seek to redistribute global welfare fall under the rubric of 'fair trade'.[57] Fair trade, for example, may encompass such diverse objectives as environmental protection, preservation of human rights, prevention of labour exploitation, and transfer of welfare to third world nations. Generally, fair trade considerations involve an exception from, or a less strict application of, one or more WTO obligations.[58] A degree of welfare redistribution from developed nations to developing nations, for example, is achieved via the WTO concept of 'special and differential treatment' for developing nations. Considerable debate continues regarding the extent to which 'fair trade' considerations should be reflected within the WTO.
- International competition law and policy is similarly susceptible to distributional influences.[59] The causal mechanism by which international competition policy may seek to redistribute global welfare is known as 'fair competition'. The various distributional influences on competition law and policy were identified in Chapter 2 of this book.

The causal mechanisms used by international trade law and policy and international competition law and policy to achieve any distributional objectives are illustrated by the matrix in Figure 27.

Importantly, any distributional objectives of international trade policy and international competition policy remain controversial. Distributional objectives are inherently subjective and determined by the particular normative perceptions of social justice and distributional fairness of international society at the time. For this reason, this chapter does not consider distributional issues in further detail.

---

[57] See R. Howse & M. J. Trebilcock, 'The Fair Trade–Free Trade Debate: Trade, Labour and the Environment' (1996) 16 *International Review of Law & Economics* 61. See also general discussion in J. N. Bhagwati & H. T. Patrick (eds.), *Fair Trade and Harmonisation: Prerequisites for Free Trade?* (MIT Press, Cambridge MA, 1996).
[58] This is illustrated, for example, by the GATT, Art. XX, which provides a general exception to the GATT for measures necessary, for example, to protect animal life.
[59] See M. J. Trebilcock, 'Competition Policy and Trade Policy: Mediating the Interface' (1996) 31 *Journal of World Trade* 71.

6.2.3 Comparison between international competition and international trade law and policy

The relationship between international trade law and policy and international competition law and policy is notoriously complex. The complexity of the relationship is exacerbated by apparent general similarities in policy approach, but substantial differences in particular legal application.

To simplify the comparison of the two disciplines, this chapter first compares three fundamental elements constitutive of international competition *policy* and international trade *policy:*

- the *efficiency objective*, which was already identified above so is not further analysed;
- the *underlying theory*, namely the underlying economic theory describing how economic efficiency is achieved; and
- the *causal mechanism*, namely the mechanism by which practical effect is given to that underlying theory so as to increase economic efficiency via a KHE improvement (as defined in Chapter 2 of this book).

This chapter then compares three fundamental elements constitutive of international competition *law* and international trade *law:*

- the *regulatory subject*, namely the particular subject matter of regulation to give effect to the causal mechanism identified above;
- the *regulatory methodology*, namely the particular means (consistent with the causal mechanism) by which regulation of the particular subject matter can achieve the desired regulatory effect; and
- the *international regulatory justification*, namely the reason why international legal obligations are required to give effect to that causal mechanism, rather than relying simply on domestic law and policy in each nation.

Each of these elements is addressed in turn below and the elements are summarised in the table in Figure 28.

Underlying theory The economic theories underlying international trade policy and international competition policy are different but interrelated:

- *International trade policy* The causal theory underlying international trade law and policy is the Ricardian Theory of Comparative

Analytical category		International trade	International competition
Policy	Efficiency objective	Improved level of global and national welfare	Improved level of global and national welfare
	Underlying theory	Ricardian Theory of Comparative Advantage	First Fundamental Theorem of Welfare Economics
	Causal mechanism	Trade liberalisation and regulation occurs to achieve and maintain 'liberalised trade' (colloquially known as 'free trade')	Market deregulation and behavioural regulation occur to achieve and maintain 'workable competition'
Law	Regulatory subject	International trade laws regulate market structure, namely governmental barriers to trade	International competition laws regulate market behaviour, namely private anti-competitive conduct
	Regulatory methodology	International trade laws regulate governmental conduct and thereby directly regulate governmental barriers to trade	International competition laws regulate governmental conduct and thereby indirectly regulate private anti-competitive conduct
	International regulatory justification	Nation A may impose a barrier to trade with adverse effects on itself and spillover/externality effects on Nation B	Nation A may under- or over-regulate anti-competitive conduct with adverse spillover/externality effects on Nation B

Figure 28: *Comparison between international trade law and policy and international competition law and policy*

Advantage.[60] Ricardian Theory reasons that if each nation specialises production in its area of comparative advantage then freely trades the resulting products, this process of specialisation and exchange will

---

[60] The theory of comparative advantage was published by David Ricardo in 1817. This theory provides that even if a nation has an absolute disadvantage or is less efficient in the production of commodities, there is still a basis for mutually beneficial trade if the less efficient nation specialises in the production of, and exports, the commodity of its smallest absolute disadvantage (comparative advantage) and trades part of its output for other commodities. See D. Ricardo, *The Principles of Political Economy and Taxation* (reprint, Irwin, Homewood, 1963).

realise net welfare gains.[61] Net improvements in productive efficiency can be realised from specialisation and exchange, via mechanisms such as division of labour, even if an economy is less efficient in absolute terms (relative to other economies) in its area of comparative advantage.

- *International competition policy* The causal theory underlying international competition policy was outlined in detail in Chapter 2 of this book by reference to the First Fundamental Theorem of Welfare Economics. The First Fundamental Theorem reasons that perfect competition will always lead to Pareto efficiency if various assumptions hold.

These two underlying theories are interrelated because the First Fundamental Theorem of Welfare Economics assumes that producers will behave rationally in a competitive environment to maximise profits by minimising production costs. Such cost-minimising behaviour in the presence of competition should motive the type of specialisation identified in the Ricardian Theory of Comparative Advantage.

Causal mechanism The causal mechanisms underlying international trade policy international competition policy are similarly interrelated:

- *International trade policy* The causal mechanism for international trade law and policy is 'trade liberalisation' with the intent of achieving liberalised trade. Liberalised trade refers to maximum practical trade, rather than the utopian concept of perfectly free trade, but is often known colloquially as 'free trade'. The causal mechanism identifies that barriers to trade hinder a nation's ability to engage in international trade and distort specialisation incentives, reducing efficiency gains from specialisation and exchange.

    International trade policy views regulatory intervention as necessary to remove governmental impediments to trade, via a process of trade liberalisation, so as to achieve liberalised trade.

- *International competition policy* The causal mechanism for international competition law and policy is 'market deregulation' and associated 'behavioural regulation' with the intent of achieving workable competition. Workable competition refers to maximum practical competition, rather than perfect competition. The causal mechanism identifies that excessive market power arising from reduced competition may

[61] Productive efficiency would increase because producers could acquire the particular goods and services they require at lower prices. Allocative efficiency would increase as a greater diversity of goods and services would be available to consumers for consumption. See discussion in P. K. Krugman & M. Obstfeld, *International Economics: Theory & Practice* (3rd edn, Harper Collins, New York, 1994), p. 228.

lead to allocative, productive and dynamic inefficiency, as outlined in Chapter 2 of this book.

International competition policy views regulatory intervention via market deregulation as necessary to remove governmental structural impediments to competition so as to achieve workable competition. Regulatory intervention, via competition law, is also viewed as a necessary behavioural safeguard to prevent the aggregation of excessive market power in a deregulated market environment.

These causal mechanisms are interrelated because trade liberalisation is usually a subset of market deregulation. International trade policy and international competition policy coincide to the extent a barrier to trade is also an impediment to competition. Given that barriers to trade impede competitive market access, it is usually the case that trade liberalisation simultaneously promotes market deregulation. Furthermore, as trade liberalisation achieves a degree of market deregulation, competition law may act as a behavioural safeguard in an environment of liberalised trade, as discussed in further detail below.

Regulatory subject   Against this policy backdrop, legal obligations have been formulated that apply to a particular regulatory subject. The differences in the regulatory subject indicate a key point of divergence between international trade law and international competition law.

- *International trade law*   The regulatory subject of international trade law is governmental 'barriers to trade', essentially domestic governmental cross-border trade regulation. International trade law seeks to remove discriminatory impediments to cross-border trade, bind governments to their multilateral tariff commitments and prevent governments utilising various types of non-tariff barriers to trade to circumvent tariff commitments. International trade law may therefore be viewed as regulating one facet of market structure under the SCP paradigm (as identified in Chapter 4 of this book).
- *International competition law*   The regulatory subject of international competition law is private anti-competitive conduct. Essentially, international competition law would seek to promote the adoption of appropriate competition laws that reduce the scope for cross-border private anti-competitive conduct. International competition law may therefore be viewed as regulating market behaviour under the SCP paradigm.

In this manner, international trade law is intended to regulate governmental (or 'public') conduct and market structure, whereas international competition law is intended to regulate private conduct and market behaviour.

Regulatory methodology   Given that public international trade law only regulates governmental conduct, rather than private conduct, the 'public versus private' distinction has important implications for the regulatory methodology adopted by the two disciplines in the context of any public international law treaty obligations:

- *International trade law*   In order to regulate governmental barriers to trade, international trade law applies legal obligations directly to governments to achieve its regulatory effect. The application of international trade law to governmental, rather than private, conduct is discussed in detail in Chapter 7 of this book.
- *International competition law*   In order to regulate private anti-competitive conduct, international competition law applies legal obligations to governments that, in turn, require those governments to take certain steps to regulate private conduct. The application of international competition law to private anti-competitive conduct is therefore necessarily indirect. The application of international competition law to governmental conduct in order to regulate private conduct is discussed in detail in Chapter 8 of this book.

In this manner, while international trade law achieves its regulatory effect *directly*, international competition can only *indirectly* achieve its regulatory effect. In order to be consistent with the current approach of the WTO and public international law, any international competition obligations would need to be formulated in such a way that they applied only to governments, not directly to private entities. The proper formulation of such obligations is outlined in Chapter 11 of this book.

International regulatory justification   The justification for regulation of trade and competition at the international, rather than domestic, level has close similarities between the two disciplines:

- *International trade law*   As identified earlier in this chapter, international trade law is justified on the basis that if nations (or governments) were left to act in their own self-interest (or political interest), the optimal result would rarely be achieved – both from the perspective of the particular nation and the global community. International trade law therefore enables individual countries to overcome political obstacles to the adoption of trade policies that ultimately increase net domestic welfare. International trade law also seeks to prevent barriers to trade being erected by a government acting in its own domestic political self-interest which may result in significant adverse spillover effect for other nations seeking to export goods and services into that nation, usually via discriminatory over-regulation.[62]

An international regulatory approach is therefore justified on the basis that domestic regulation is not sufficient to maximise domestic and global welfare given each government's desire to act in its own political self-interest to the detriment of national and global welfare.

- *International competition law*   As identified in Chapter 3 of this book, international competition law is similarly justified on the basis that if nations (or governments) were left to act in their own self-interest (or political interest), the optimal result would rarely be achieved. Chapter 3 identified that governments may over-regulate or under-regulate cross-border anti-competitive conduct relative to the globally optimal level (due to the interaction of negative and positive externalities in underlying conduct with negative externalities in regulatory decision-making), thereby creating adverse spillover effects for other nations. Chapter 3 also identified that the current solution to under-regulation of cross-border anti-competitive conduct, namely the extra-territorial application of competition laws, can be highly destabilising to harmonious international relations.

Importantly, while international trade law is focused on both national and global welfare, international competition law is focused principally on global welfare. This means that international trade obligations are typically adopted where every nation gains via some form of welfare improvement (i.e. a Pareto improvement, as discussed in Chapter 2). However, international competition obligations tend to be more focused on the net global welfare effects, so may result in some nations suffering a net welfare loss, while others suffer a net welfare gain (i.e. a KHE improvement, as discussed in Chapter 2). This may mean that the political achievability of an international competition agreement will be dependent on the ability of the net welfare-gaining nations to compensate the net welfare-losing nations adequately, as discussed in detail in Chapters 10 and 13 of this book.

As summarised in the matrix in Figure 28, the previous analysis indicates that while international trade policy and international competition policy have a number of similarities, international trade law and international competition law have several fundamental differences. Whereas

---

[62] See OECD, 'Strengthening the Coherence between Trade and Competition Policies: Joint Report by the Trade Committee and the Committee on Competition Law and Policy' (1996) OECD Documents, OCDE/GD(96), 90.

international trade law directly regulates market structure by regulating governmental barriers to trade, international competition law indirectly regulates market behaviour by regulating governmental laws that, in turn, regulate private anti-competitive conduct. The consequences of these fundamental differences in approach are analysed in detail in Chapters 7 and 8 of this book.

However, it is also true that both disciplines exhibit synergies in their respective regulatory approaches.

- First, both international trade law and policy and international competition law and policy have the effect of increasing domestic competition. International trade law and policy, for example, promotes market access by removing trade barriers, thus enabling foreign firms to enter the domestic market to increase competition.
- Secondly, both international trade law and policy and international competition law and policy have the effect of promoting opportunities for increased international trade. International competition policy, for example, promotes market access by reducing governmental structural impediments to competition, irrespective of whether such impediments have cross-border application. International competition law, for example, promotes market access by reducing the scope for anti-competitive behaviour, irrespective of whether such behaviour is discriminatory against foreign market entry or not.

To this extent, international trade law and policy and international competition law and policy are broadly complementary, as discussed in greater detail below.

In summary, the analysis set out above indicates that while there are significant differences between international competition law and international trade law, they are broadly complementary. The issue therefore arises whether the two disciplines can be reconciled. A first step is to consider whether the two disciplines can be reconciled at the theoretical level.

6.3 Can international trade theory and international competition theory be reconciled?

6.3.1 Cross-perspectives between international competition law and international trade law

In order to consider a means to reconcile international trade theory with international competition theory, it is necessary to consider the cross-perspectives between the two disciplines (i.e. how each discipline views the other). This is summarised by Figure 29.

Cross-perspectives	Trade perspective on competition	Competition perspective on trade
Consistency	By preventing private anti-competitive conduct, international competition law reduces a particular private barrier to international trade and thereby promotes greater opportunity for market access.	By reducing trade barriers, international trade law reduces a particular structural barrier to market entry and thereby increases market competition via greater opportunity for entry by foreign firms.
Inconsistency	Certain trade measures that may be permitted by international trade law may be prohibited under international competition law.	By permitting certain trade measures that prevent market entry by foreign firms, international trade law may reduce market competition.

Figure 29: *Cross-perspectives between international trade law and international competition law*

Competition perspective on trade   Competition theory views a 'barrier to trade' as a form of structural barrier to market entry created by government border regulation. If trade barriers are significant in respect of a particular domestic market, foreign firms will have a reduced ability to enter that domestic market to compete with domestic firms, reducing competition. Conversely, if such trade barriers are reduced, foreign firms can more readily enter domestic markets to increase competition. To the extent that international trade law reduces such trade barriers, it is complementary to competition law as it facilitates competition by promoting greater market entry.

Furthermore, competition law is focused principally on the regulation of market conduct as discussed in Chapters 2 and 4 of this book although it may indirectly affect market structure. Other forms of regulation are usually required to complement competition laws and regulate market structure. International trade law provides one of these other forms of regulation by directly regulating market structure.[63] International trade law removes structural barriers to market entry created by excessive governmental barriers to trade. Competition theory therefore

[63] In New Zealand, for example, the structural separation of electricity line companies from electricity retail companies was achieved by way of industry-specific competition law in the form of New Zealand's Electricity Industry Reform Act 1998.

recognises that international trade law facilitates the removal of certain governmental structural measures that would otherwise facilitate anti-competitive behaviour by private enterprises and that would otherwise fail to be addressed by competition law alone.

Trade perspective on competition International trade law only applies to barriers to trade that are governmental in character, so does not effectively regulate barriers to trade that may be private in origin. Such private barriers to trade may be caused by anti-competitive conduct of firms in the domestic market, including by such measures as exclusive dealing and exclusionary arrangements. International competition law provides a means to regulate such private anti-competitive activity.

Accordingly, international competition law is viewed by trade theory as a key mechanism regulating a particular form of trade barrier, namely private trade barriers associated with private anti-competitive activity.[64] Competition law may assist trade regulators to achieve more effective market access. From the perspective of international trade theory, international competition law therefore provides an important mechanism for promoting greater market access for foreign firms. International competition law also provides a mechanism for preventing private anti-competitive activity from impeding the degree of trade liberalisation achieved in trade negotiations.

In particular, private anti-competitive conduct is viewed by international trade theory as a 'non-tariff barrier' to international trade or a 'private barrier to trade'. Such non-tariff barriers have increased in relative importance in recent decades given the effectiveness of the GATT and WTO in reducing more formal barriers to international trade, such as tariffs. In essence, as these overt formal impediments to trade have gradually declined, so more subtle and covert impediments have been revealed in the form of non-tariff barriers. Jackson's metaphor is well known, in which: 'the receding waters of tariffs and other forms of overt protection inevitably uncover the rocks and shoals of non-tariff barriers'.[65] Non-tariff barriers are being increasingly targeted for WTO regulatory attention on the basis that they are preventing the further realisation of gains from international trade.

Yet trade theory also recognises clear limitations to the effectiveness of international competition law in promoting market access. International

---

[64] Relevant private trade barriers include, for example, domestic cartels, exclusive dealing and other exclusionary arrangements.
[65] See J. H. Jackson, *The World Trading System: Law and Policy of International Economic Relations* (MIT, Boston, 1989), p. 63.

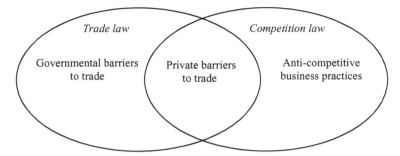

Figure 30: *Potential overlap between trade law and competition law*

competition law does not address private barriers to market access that are not associated with anti-competitive conduct. In the context of the Japan–US trade disputes, for example, while certain private Japanese business practices were alleged to discriminate against US firms in the Japanese domestic market, these private Japanese business practices were neither 'anti-competitive' nor inconsistent with competition law objectives.

In conclusion, and as illustrated in Figure 30, while international trade law and international competition law are broadly complementary, their potential overlap is not perfect.[66] The synergies between international trade law and international competition law may provide a means to reconcile both disciplines, enabling the more effective inclusion of international competition law into the WTO, as discussed in detail below.

6.3.2 Contestability theory as a means to reconcile trade and competition law

As indicated above, synergies between international trade laws and competition laws arise because of an overlap between the concepts of:

- barriers to *market entry* in competition law (also known as 'barriers to entry'); and
- barriers to *market access* in international trade law (also known as 'barriers to trade' or 'trade barriers').

[66] Importantly, to the extent that trade laws are *liberating*, they are consistent with competition law, as they enable structural barriers to entry to be reduced. However, to the extent that trade laws enable protectionistic conduct, they are anathema to competition law. As a general rule, competition law is therefore inconsistent with protectionistic trade measures, but is complementary to liberal trade policies.

While the overlap of these concepts is imperfect, this overlap does suggest a means for reconciling international competition theory with international trade theory, namely through the 'theory of contestable markets'.[67] The concept of a contestable market is considered below and refers to a market with no barriers to *market entry* and therefore no barriers to *market access*.

The concept of a 'barrier to market entry' is fundamental to modern competition analysis as barriers to market entry are considered a critical structural determinant of the extent of potential competition in a market. In particular, barriers to market entry determine the speed and ease by which new market entrants may enter the market to compete with incumbent firms. Where barriers to market entry are relatively high, the threat of potential competition from such market entrants is commensurately lower and therefore the market power of incumbent firms is greater.

The definition of barriers to entry has been controversial in economic theory.[68] Several schools of thought have evolved over the last four decades since Bain published his seminal work entitled *Barriers to New Competition* in 1956. Modern competition theory now recognises that governmental barriers to trade, such as tariffs and quotas, can act as a significant barrier to market entry by impeding foreign firms from exporting their competitive goods and services into domestic markets. Indeed, a 'barrier to trade' is a trade-specific concept referring to any impediment that prevents a foreign firm selling its goods or services into, or otherwise entering, a foreign market. In this manner, competition theory views barriers to trade as a subset of the broader concept of barriers to market entry, as illustrated by Figure 31.

As noted above, a potential means of reconciling international trade law with international competition law is suggested by the concept of 'market contestability'. The theory of contestable markets was advanced by Baumol in 1982.[69] Baumol reasoned that a theoretical condition for realising perfect competition is a perfectly 'contestable' market. Baumol defined a 'contestable' market as a market that has no barriers to market entry such that entry and exit by competitors can occur effortlessly and

---

[67] See T. J. Schoenbaum, 'The Theory of Contestable Markets in International Trade: A Rationale for Justifiable Unilateralism to Combat Restrictive Business Practices?' (1996) 30 *Journal of World Trade* 160, 165.

[68] See P. A. Geroski, R. J. Gilbert & A. Jacquemin, *Barriers to Entry and Strategic Competition* (Harwood, Zurich, 1990).

[69] See W. J. Baumol, 'Contestable Markets: An Uprising in the Theory of Industry Structure' (1982) 7 *American Economic Review* 1.

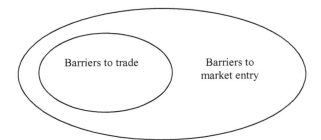

Figure 31: *Venn diagram of relationship between barriers to trade and barriers to market entry*

without any associated cost. Baumol reasoned that such a market would be characterised by 'hit and run' market entry by competitors that could quickly enter the market when circumstances were profitable and leave the market when circumstances were not profitable. While a perfectly contestable market could never be achieved in practice, it nevertheless provided an important policy goal.[70]

In this manner, the mere threat of market entry by such competitors acted as an important constraint on the ability of incumbent firms within the market to exercise any market power they may have. If such firms were to raise their prices to recover supernormal profits, other firms would quickly enter the market and undercut such firms, so competition would reduce the market price to minimum sustainable levels. Given the risk of attracting market entry, firms would be unwilling to increase their prices.[71] As a consequence, the threat of market entry reduced effective market power. The central idea of market contestability is therefore that, although a market may be highly concentrated and exhibit limited actual competition, if barriers to market entry are sufficiently low the mere threat of market entry may act as an effective constraint on market power.

---

[70] See W. J. Baumol, J. C. Panzar & R. D. Willig, *Contestable Markets and the Theory of Industry Structure* (Harcourt Price & Jovanovich, New York, 1982). If a market is contestable, then welfare will not be enhanced by attempting to change the structure of the market to align it more closely with the 'perfectly competitive' model.

[71] A market is said to be 'contestable' if barriers to market entry, are set sufficiently low that suppliers to the market must set their prices equal to minimum average cost. This means that firms within a contestable market are unable to make monopoly profits, but are constrained in their pricing by competitive forces. Contestability implies that the prices in the market would be those that would prevail were the market characterised by long-run perfect competition.

Contestability theory is consistent with both competition theory and international trade theory:

- From a trade perspective, contestability theory promotes maximum market access. A perfectly contestable market necessarily contemplates no barriers to trade and therefore no impediments to foreign firms accessing a market to compete with domestic firms. Importantly, a perfectly contestable market also contemplates no restrictive business practices within the market that may prevent market access (given that such behaviour can itself constitute a barrier to entry). In this manner, contestability theory contemplates the removal of both governmental *and* private barriers to market access.
- From a competition perspective, contestability theory promotes maximum competition. A perfectly contestable market implies no barriers to entry and thus maximum potential competition. While contestability theory principally relates to issues of market structure and mandates reduced barriers to entry, contestability theory also contemplates the elimination of any anti-competitive business practices that reduce the ability of competitors to enter a market quickly and compete.

Accordingly, contestability theory is broadly consistent with both competition theory and international trade theory. As such, market contestability provides an important common policy objective for both international competition law and international trade law. In particular, both disciplines could seek to achieve the same objective safe in the knowledge that their respective regulatory methodologies would be unlikely to conflict.[72]

Market contestability, for example, enables trade law to operate at the structural level, to reduce trade barriers and governmental barriers to entry; but also enables competition law to operate at the behavioural level, to impose behavioural constraints on firms. In this manner, contestability theory emphasises the mutual interdependence of international competition law and international trade law. Contestability theory directly highlights the synergies between both disciplines and recognises that each discipline would better realise its objectives with the support of the other.

In this manner, contestability theory may provide important future guidance to governments in implementing international trade and

---

[72] See A. Zampetti & P. Suavé, 'Onwards to Singapore: The International Contestability of Markets and the New Trade Agenda' (1996) 19(3) *The World Economy* 333.

competition policies.[73] Contestability theory may provide a means to strengthen and deepen the existing WTO framework, while extending the WTO to encompass competition law. Indeed, the use of the contestability theory within international trade law would require a reconsideration of the degree of openness that is sought from domestic markets. Yet once these issues are worked through, contestability theory may provide an important vision for achieving greater and more effective international economic integration in the coming decades.

6.4 Conclusion: the WTO could provide a suitable institutional vehicle for an international competition agreement

In summary, there is a clear historical precedent for introducing competition law into the WTO. The Havana Charter of 1947, for example, expressly contemplated that competition law would form part of the world trading system. During the 1950s and 1960s, several initiatives to introduce competition law into the GATT failed, partly due to the weaker and less effective institutional structure of the GATT, but also due to insufficient international consensus and inexperience in competition law and policy. With the revitalisation of the world trading system in 1994, the potential for introducing competition law provisions at the international level was boosted considerably. The Uruguay Round incorporated a number of provisions into the WTO addressing various competition issues in a very limited and issue-specific manner, establishing a further precedent. A number of provisions in the WTO agreements now have a competition law flavour.

However, if competition law is to be more fully incorporated into the WTO, the relationship between international trade law and policy and international competition law and policy would need to be suitably reconciled. While both disciplines are to some extent complementary, they are not fully complementary and there is scope for conflict. For example, WTO trade measures may adversely affect competition, while the regulation of anti-competitive behaviour may permit conduct that is perceived as unfair from a trade policy perspective.

In this respect, both international competition policy and international trade policy have the same ultimate efficiency outcome of

---

[73] See R. Z. Lawrence, T. Ito & A. Bressand, 'Towards Globally Contestable Markets' in OECD, *Market Access After the Uruguay Round: Investment, Competition and Technology Perspectives* (OECD, Paris, 1986).

increasing the level of global welfare and rely on interrelated causal mechanisms to achieve this. However, international competition law and international trade law adopt a different regulatory approach. Whereas international trade law directly regulates market structure by regulating governmental barriers to trade, international competition law indirectly regulates market behaviour by regulating governmental laws that, in turn, regulate private anti-competitive conduct.

Yet competition laws and trade laws do overlap to the extent that both seek to promote greater market contestability. Contestability theory may therefore provide a theoretical means to reconcile international trade law and policy, with international competition law and policy, given that it represents a point of overlap between the two disciplines.

In conclusion, the WTO could provide a suitable institutional vehicle for an international competition agreement, provided that the relationship between trade and competition were suitably reconciled. This chapter has identified a means to reconcile both disciplines in theory, Chapters 7 to 9 of this book next identify the practical issues arising in relation to any such reconciliation.

7

Would a WTO competition agreement promote international trade?

> The relationship between trade and competition policy has been and remains an analytic quagmire.
>
> (Portnoy, 1991)[1]

Chapter 6 of this book concluded that international trade law and international competition law could be reconciled at a *theoretical* level via the concept of 'market contestability'. Chapters 7 and 8 now consider the appropriate reconciliation of both disciplines at a practical level by applying the concept of 'market contestability' to examples of under-regulation.

The analysis of *under*-regulation in Chapters 7 and 8 can be contrasted with the analysis of *over*-regulation in Chapter 4 of this book. Chapter 4 identified the blocking of international mergers and the extra-territorial enforcement of competition laws as examples of over-regulation. Chapters 7 and 8 now consider examples of 'under-regulation' involving anti-competitive conduct and problematic trade measures from the respective perspectives of international trade law and international competition law. In particular:

- Chapter 7 considers anti-competitive behaviour from the perspective of international trade. Chapter 7 identifies various private anti-competitive practices impeding international trade that are not effectively regulated either by existing international trade law or domestic competition law. These examples evidence 'under-regulation' in the application, enforcement and substantive content of *domestic competition laws*.
- Chapter 8 adopts the opposite perspective and considers international trade measures from the perspective of international competition. Chapter 8 identifies various trade measures that are not regulated

---

[1] See B Portnoy, 'Building the Missing Pillar? Multilateralism, Extraterritoriality, and Cooperation in International Antitrust', Paper presented to CASPIC MacArthur Scholars' Conference, University of Chicago, 1 May 1999, p. 39.

by existing international trade law, but that adversely affect international competition. These examples evidence 'under-regulation' in the application, enforcement and substantive content of *international trade law*.

In both cases, Chapters 7 and 8 identify how an international competition agreement could be used to correct such under-regulation and thereby prevent conduct that would otherwise reduce market contestability and global welfare.

Consistent with this approach, Chapter 7 first considers anti-competitive behaviour from the perspective of international trade and has six principal sections:

- Section 7.1 considers the impact of anti-competitive practices on cross-border trade flows and market access. Section 7.1 identifies how certain private anti-competitive conduct with an adverse effect on international trade may pass through a 'loophole' in the trade–competition regulatory matrix, leading to under-regulation.
- Section 7.2 explores the existence of under-regulation by identifying the inherent limitations of existing WTO law in addressing private anti-competitive conduct. The WTO *Fuji-Kodak Film* case of April 1998 clearly illustrates these limitations.

The remaining sections consider how this under-regulation arises in practice. In particular, why certain anti-competitive conduct is not regulated by WTO law and why such conduct is not otherwise prevented by the domestic competition laws of the nations concerned (including as a result of the negative externalities identified in Chapter 3 of this book):

- Sections 7.3 and 7.4 consider examples of anti-competitive conduct arising in the *domestic market* that has the effect of denying market access to foreign firms (i.e. 'Domestic Conduct'). Sections 7.3 and 7.4 analyse various historical allegations of under-regulation made by the US against Japan as practical case studies.
- Section 7.5 considers examples of anti-competitive conduct arising in *international markets* that has adverse effects on international trade (i.e. 'International Conduct'). Section 7.5 analyses historical attempts by the US to regulate the OPEC oil cartel.
- Section 7.6 analyses the WTO Agreement on Basic Telecommunications as a specific example where WTO law has sought to regulate anti-competitive conduct effectively, consistent with a globally optimal result.

Chapter 7 concludes that an international competition agreement could correct particular instances of under-regulation with a beneficial impact on international trade and international competition. In particular, an international competition agreement could regulate private anti-competitive conduct which is adversely affecting international trade and which is not effectively regulated by existing international trade law or domestic competition law.

7.1 The effects of anti-competitive practices on international trade

7.1.1 A useful analytical framework

For the purposes of this chapter, there are two relevant categories of anti-competitive conduct that may adversely affect international trade:

- First, domestic consumers in Nation A may be prevented from acquiring goods or services from firms associated with Nation B due to the domestic anti-competitive conduct of firms operating in Nation A ('Domestic Conduct').
- Secondly, domestic consumers in Nation A may be prevented from acquiring goods or services from firms associated with Nation B due to the anti-competitive conduct of firms operating in Nation B and/or the international anti-competitive conduct of firms operating in any number of third party jurisdictions ('International Conduct').

Each type of conduct is summarised below.

- *Domestic Conduct*   Private anti-competitive conduct by incumbent firms in the domestic market (i.e. 'Domestic Conduct') may act as a private 'non-tariff' barrier to international trade by denying foreign firms access to domestic markets, or by impeding foreign firms selling goods and services, or otherwise entering, domestic markets. The range of anti-competitive techniques that could lead to such a denial of market access includes, for example, foreclosure, exclusive dealing, tying, forcing, bundling, predatory behaviour, boycotts, and refusals to supply.

  A denial of market access directly prevents international trade and thereby prevents each nation from specialising in its areas of comparative advantage, undermining the potential welfare gains to global society contemplated by Ricardian trade theory.
  - *Example*   Domestic producers may engage in joint boycotts of domestic distributors that purchase foreign imports.

- *Example* A domestic cartel may coerce domestic customers into exclusive purchase agreements by threats of adverse allocation in times of shortage.
- *Example* Domestic producers may enter into exclusive dealing arrangements with domestic distributors that foreclose foreign firms from distributing competing products.[2]
- *International Conduct* International Conduct (including anti-competitive conduct across a number of jurisdictions or in international markets), can distort the flow of international trade between nations. Such distortions again reduce global welfare by preventing nations from specialising in their areas of comparative advantage, thus undermining Ricardian trade theory:
  - *Example* An international cartel can raise prices and impose territorial restraints on its members to enforce country-based price discrimination.
  - *Example* A supplier with significant market power in an international market could act in the same manner as a firm with such power in a domestic market (including by raising prices and engaging in price discrimination).

The question arises whether such Domestic Conduct and International Conduct can be prevented by existing domestic and international regulation.

Trade-competition regulatory matrix In this regard, there are two principal relevant tiers of regulation that may restrain anti-competitive conduct that harms international trade, namely international trade law and domestic competition law. These two tiers of regulation may be viewed, conceptually, as comprising a 'trade–competition regulatory matrix'.

The critical issue from an international trade perspective is to identify the particular circumstances in which both international trade law and domestic competition law fail to prevent Domestic Conduct and International Conduct. In such circumstances, such anti-competitive conduct would slip through a 'loophole' in the trade–competition regulatory matrix and thereby escape effective regulation, as illustrated by Figure 32. This 'loophole' evidences 'under-regulation', consistent with the conclusions identified in Chapter 3 of this book.

---

[2] See T. Boudin, 'American Anti-Trust Abroad: The Problem of Foreign Private Restraints on U.S. Exports' in Boudin (ed.), *Private Investments Abroad: Problems and Solutions for International Business in 1990* (Mathew Bender, New York, 1991).

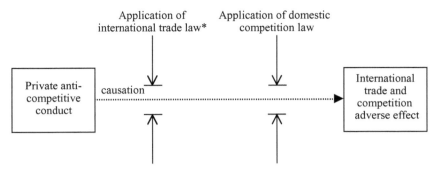

Figure 32: *Trade-competition regulatory matrix, showing regulatory 'loopholes'*
NOTES: Certain private anti-competitive conduct is not effectively regulated either by international trade law or domestic competition law (i.e. regulatory 'loopholes' exist, evidencing 'under-regulation'). Such private anti-competitive conduct may cause adverse effects on international trade and competition.
* The application of international trade law to private anti-competitive conduct is indirect as international trade law usually regulates governmental, not private, measures.

An international competition agreement could then be drafted to correct such under-regulation specifically. Such an agreement could, for example, require governments to take appropriate steps to regulate the relevant anti-competitive conduct with a view to increasing market contestability and global welfare, consistent with the conclusions in Chapter 6 of this book. The manner in which the obligations in such an international competition agreement could be drafted are identified later in Chapter 11 of this book.

With this approach in mind, there are two critical issues in identifying such under-regulation:

(a) the extent to which the WTO currently seeks to prevent particular private anti-competitive conduct that adversely affects international trade (i.e. by imposing international obligations on governments to prevent such conduct); and
(b) where such conduct is not prevented by the WTO, the extent to which such conduct escapes effective regulation under existing domestic competition laws (i.e. evidencing 'under-regulation' by domestic competition laws relative to the globally optimal result).

The analysis in the remainder of this chapter therefore first considers the extent to which the WTO currently regulates anti-competitive conduct.

The analysis then considers reasons why domestic competition law does not regulate such conduct, leading to under-regulation, as illustrated by various examples. These examples focus on the trading relationship between the US and Japan given the extent of frictions between these nations in the past two decades and the significance of their trading relationship as a percentage of overall global trade.[3]

7.1.2 To what extent does the WTO currently prevent private anti-competitive conduct?

As treaties concluded between sovereign states, the WTO agreements are instruments of public international law and their obligations apply, on the basis of *pacta sunt servanda*, between contracting nations. Importantly, this means that the WTO obligations apply only as between governments. The WTO obligations do not apply directly to private entities unless the relevant governments have enacted domestic legislation mandating such direct application. In its present formulation, the WTO does not contain any provisions that purport to regulate the anti-competitive conduct of private entities directly. Rather, the existing provisions in the WTO that apply to anti-competitive conduct (as identified in Chapter 6), apply to governments alone.

The particular character of these existing obligations is important. As discussed in Chapter 6, there are no general provisions in the WTO that impose a positive obligation on governments to enact or enforce generic competition legislation. Creative arguments that the WTO imposes a positive obligation on governments to enact legislation to eliminate discriminatory private anti-competitive practices have been regarded by commentators as 'highly untenable'.[4] While some of the existing competition provisions in the WTO do contemplate a positive obligation on governments to take action against certain anti-competitive practices, such obligations are in each case limited in nature and sector-specific. Such obligations include, for example, requirements to prevent certain anti-competitive practices in the telecommunications sector (as discussed later in this chapter) and obligations relating to the prevention of abuses of intellectual property rights.

---

[3] The US has frequently threatened trade sanctions against Japan as a means to address perceived anti-competitive behaviour, creating significant 'system frictions'.
[4] See, for example, W. Fikentscher, 'Competition Rules for Private Agents in the GATT/WTO' (1994) 49 *Aussenwirtschaft* 281.

Furthermore, *positive* regulatory obligations in WTO law requiring governments to *promulgate* regulation remain uncommon. The traditional approach of the WTO has been to impose positive obligations on governments only in relation to the *elimination* of regulation. Furthermore, the majority of WTO law comprises *negative* obligations that seek to restrain governments from taking certain actions, consistent with the general approach of international regulation to date. Given such existing limitations to WTO law, various creative arguments have been made over the years (including under the GATT prior to 1994), regarding the application of the WTO to private anti-competitive conduct.[5]

The most important example, to date, of an attempt to regulate anti-competitive conduct via existing generic WTO law was the *Kodak-Fuji Film* case of April 1998.[6] That case involved, in effect, an attempt to read competition obligations into the generic GATT obligations against non-discrimination. Given that these GATT obligations are negative in character and prohibit certain governmental measures, it was necessary in that case to link causally the particular private anti-competitive conduct to particular governmental measures that breached GATT negative obligations. The failure by the US to establish its claim against Japan in the *Kodak-Fuji Film* case illustrates that the successful establishment of such a causal link will, in most cases, be exceptionally difficult (as identified in detail below).[7] To the extent that private anti-competitive conduct cannot be attributed in some way to a particular governmental measure, such conduct will usually fall outside the current ambit of WTO law.

7.2 The *Kodak-Fuji Film* case – application of WTO law to anti-competitive conduct

The *Kodak-Fuji Film* case involved a claim for WTO dispute settlement brought against the Japanese government by the US Government Office of the Trade Representative ('USTR') at the petition of the Eastman Kodak

---

[5] Arguments include authorisation for countermeasures to address nullification or impairment caused by anti-competitive conduct. See also J. F. Rill, 'Statement on Japanese Competition Policies and the US Response before the Senate Judiciary Committee, 29 July 1992' (1992) 16(1) *World Competition* 143.

[6] *See Japan – Measures Affecting Consumer Photographic Film and Paper*, WT/DS44, WTO Panel Report adopted 6 December 1998.

[7] Technically, there is no concept of *stare decisis* in WTO law. However, in practice, WTO Panel Reports often serve as authoritative precedents for subsequent decisions. See R. Bhala, 'Precedent Setters: De Facto Stare Decisis in WTO Adjudication' (1999) 9 *Journal of Trade Law & Policy* 1.

Company of the United States ('Kodak'). Kodak alleged that certain measures taken by the Japanese government enabled the Fuji Photo Film Company of Japan ('Fuji') to impede access by Kodak to the Japanese distribution system for photographic film and paper.

The *Kodak-Fuji Film* case represents the furthest extent to date to which any nation has sought to challenge private anti-competitive activity within the context of *generic* WTO obligations. However, other challenges have been made within the context of *sectoral* WTO obligations, as discussed later in this chapter.

Before the US lodged its case in the WTO, it had first exhausted any Japanese domestic competition law remedies. Kodak had initially petitioned the USTR under section 301 of the United States Trade Act of 1974 alleging that Fuji, with the support of the Japanese government, was engaging in anti-competitive practices that restricted access by Kodak to the Japanese market.[8] Following bilateral negotiations, the Japanese and US governments agreed that Kodak should lodge a complaint directly with the Japanese Fair Trade Commission ('JFTC'). The JFTC subsequently investigated Fuji's conduct and concluded that it was not in breach of the Japanese Antimonopoly Act 1947.[9]

Given that the claim involved effects in the Japanese market, and not the US domestic market, neither Kodak nor the USTR could invoke US antitrust law on an extraterritorial basis. Accordingly, the US lodged a claim for formal dispute settlement before the WTO.[10]

While the *Kodak-Fuji Film* case was factually complex, and the final WTO Panel Report runs to over 500 pages, the US, in essence, made three distinct factual allegations. These three factual allegations each adopted the causal stance that the Japanese government had directly or indirectly introduced various measures that effectively prevented Kodak from entering the Japanese market, as follows:

- During the 1960s and 1970s, the Japanese government had restructured the Japanese distribution system for photographic film and paper

---

[8] See F. J. Schweitzer, 'Flash of the Titans: A Picture of Section 301 in the Dispute Resolution Between Kodak and Fuji and a View Towards Anticompetitive Practices in the Japanese Distribution System' (1996) 11 *American Journal of International Law & Policy* 847.
[9] See Japan Fair Trade Commission, *Survey of Transactions Among Firms Regarding Photographic Color Film for General Use*, 23 July 1997.
[10] See *Japan – Measures Affecting Consumer Photographic Film and Paper*, Request for Consultations by the US (21 June 1996), WT/DS44/1, G/L/87. See also *Japan – Measures Affecting Distribution Services*, Request for Consultations by the US (20 June 1996), WT/DS45/1, S/L/22.

via measures that created an exclusive system oriented towards domestic manufacturers ('Distribution Countermeasures'). In particular, the Japanese government had engineered greater vertical integration by promoting vertically-oriented standardised procedures and by imposing pricing that encouraged greater vertical integration.
- From 1974, the Japanese government had enacted legislation that restricted the development of larger retail stores ('Large Retail Store Laws'). Such larger stores would have been more likely to stock foreign film, or enter into direct supply arrangements, than smaller stores due to their greater economies of scope and scale and thus could have provided alternative channels for the distribution and sale of foreign film in Japan.
- From the late 1960s, the Japanese government had promulgated a number of ordinances that limited the use of advertising and premium offers ('Promotion Countermeasures'). The Promotion Countermeasures, in turn, impeded the sales promotion of foreign film in Japan.

The US then based its claim for dispute settlement by the WTO on three distinct legal grounds:

- First, the US claimed that Japan had not published all its governmental regulations that affected the sale and distribution of film within Japan, constituting a direct violation of Article X.1 of the GATT. This claim was unique to Japan and its concept of 'administrative guidance' and is not relevant to competition law issues, so is not addressed further.[11]
- Secondly, the US claimed a failure by Japan to provide national treatment to imported products, in that US (Kodak) film had been treated less favourably than Japanese (Fuji) film, constituting a direct violation of Article III.4 (National Treatment) of the GATT ('Violation Complaint').
- Thirdly, the US claimed that Japan had 'nullified or impaired' a WTO tariff concession under Article XXIII.1(b) of the GATT ('Non-Violation Complaint').

The second and third of these three claims are considered in greater detail below.

Importantly, the US did not expressly allege anti-competitive behaviour by Fuji given the express finding of the JFTC that no anti-competitive behaviour had occurred and given that no WTO obligations existed

[11] See M. Dean, 'Administrative Guidance in Japanese Law: A Threat to the Rule of Law?' [1991] *Journal of Business Law* 52, 55.

prohibiting such behaviour. However, allegations of anti-competitive exclusive dealing and vertical foreclosure by Fuji were implicit within the US' claims for WTO dispute settlement.

7.2.1 Violation complaint under Article III (National Treatment) of the GATT

Article III (National Treatment) of the GATT constitutes one of the fundamental WTO principles of non-discrimination and obliges a WTO contracting party to treat all imported goods no less favourably than 'like' domestically produced goods once they have passed through customs checkpoints and entered its stream of domestic commerce.[12] Article III.4 provides:

> The products of the territory of any contracting party imported into the territory of any other contracting party shall be accorded treatment no less favourable than that accorded to like products of national origin in respect of all laws, regulation and requirements affecting their internal sale, offering for sale, purchase, transport or use.

Article III.4 is routinely interpreted in WTO jurisprudence as a requirement to 'provide equality of competitive conditions for imported products in relation to domestic products'.[13]

The US claimed that Japan had directly violated Article III.4 as the individual and collective effect of each of the Distribution Countermeasures, Large Retail Store Laws and Promotion Countermeasures was to lock in a distribution system more favourable to Fuji than to foreign entrants. In considering this claim, the WTO Panel in the *Fuji-Kodak case* reasoned that three elements are required to establish a violation of Article III:4, consistent with previous WTO and GATT Panel decisions, as follows:[14]

- *First, whether the domestic and imported products at issue were 'like products'* The 'likeness' of Fuji and Kodak film and photographic paper was effectively conceded by Japan and was thus not in dispute.[15]

---

[12] See *Italy – Discrimination Against Imported Agricultural Machinery (1958)*, GATT Panel Report, adopted 23 October 1958, BISD 76/90, para. 13.
[13] See WTO Panel Report on Film Case, above n. 6, para. 10.370.
[14] This approach was affirmed by the WTO Appellate Body in *Korea – Measures Affecting Imports of Fresh, Chilled and Frozen Beef*, WTO Appellate Body Report, AB-2000-8 WT/DS161, 169/AB/R (00–5347), adopted 10 January 2001, para. 133.
[15] In *European Communities – Measures Affecting Asbestos and Asbestos-Containing Products*, WTO Appellate Body Report, AB-2000-11 WT/DS135/AB/R (00–1157), adopted 5 April

- *Second, whether the measure at issue was a 'law, regulation or requirement affecting . . . internal sale . . . or use'* The WTO Panel followed previous Panel Reports and gave the words 'law, regulation or requirement' a broad construction to include 'action by private parties that may be assimilated to government action'.[16] The WTO Panel reasoned, in particular, that 'past GATT cases demonstrate that the fact that an action is taken by private parties does not rule out the possibility that it may be deemed to be governmental if there is sufficient government involvement with it'.[17]

  The WTO Panel reasoned that the second element was satisfied by the Distribution Countermeasures, Large Retail Store Laws and Promotion Countermeasures as 'it is clear that non-binding actions, which include sufficient incentives or disincentives for private parties to act in a particular manner, can potentially have adverse effects on competitive conditions of market access'.[18]

- *Third, whether the imported products were accorded 'less favourable' treatment than that accorded to like domestic products* The WTO Panel reasoned that the US had failed to demonstrate that the relevant measures accorded less favourable treatment to imported products (i.e. Kodak film) relative to the like domestic products (i.e. Fuji film). The WTO Panel concluded that the relevant measures did not, on the face of it, discriminate against foreign film, hence were not de jure discriminatory.[19]

  However, the WTO Panel reasoned that:[20]

  > Even in the absence of *de jure* discrimination (measures which on their face discriminate as to origin), it may be possible for the United States to show *de facto* discrimination (measures which have a disparate impact on imports). However, in such circumstances, the complaining party is

---

2001, para. 99, the WTO Appellate Body confirmed that an expansive interpretation of 'likeness' is appropriate under Article III:4 and the relevant test is 'fundamentally, a determination about the nature and extent of a competitive relationship between and among products'.

[16] See WTO Panel Report on the Film Case, above n. 6, paras. 10.373 to 10.376.
[17] *Ibid.*, para. 10.56.
[18] *Ibid.*, para. 10.49. This followed *Japan – Semi-conductors*, GATT Panel Report, BISD 35S/116, para. 109 in which the GATT Panel reasoned that non-mandatory requests could still be regarded as governmental measures if: ' First, there were reasonable grounds to believe that sufficient incentives or disincentives existed for non-mandatory measures to take effect. Second, the operation of the measures . . . was essentially dependent on Government action or intervention.'
[19] *Ibid.*, paras. 10.380 to 10.381.   [20] *Ibid.*, paras. 10.84 to 10.86.

called upon to make a detailed showing of any claimed disproportionate impact on imports resulting from the origin-neutral measure. And, the burden of demonstrating such impact may be significantly more difficult where the relationship between the measure and the product is questionable.

The WTO Panel reasoned that, for the US to prove de facto discrimination, it would at least need to prove that the governmental measures adversely modified the conditions of competition between domestic and imported film in a manner that had a disproportionate effect on foreign competition.[21] However, as the US had not proved such a disproportionate effect, no breach of Article III.4 had occurred.

Accordingly, while the US failed in its attempt to establish a violation of Article III.4, the WTO Panel Report does provide a basis on which future claims under Article III.4 could succeed, namely if governmental measures promote anti-competitive conduct and such measures are either de jure discriminatory or applied in a manner which constitutes de facto discrimination.

In summary, the *Kodak-Fuji* case indicates that there are significant difficulties in challenging private anti-competitive behaviour under Article III:4:

- The private behaviour will need to be sufficiently linked to a governmental measure. In this regard, the *Japan – Semi-Conductors* case establishes two criteria to determine when a government is responsible for non-mandatory measures undertaken by a private entity:[22]

    First, there were reasonable grounds to believe that sufficient incentives or disincentives existed for non-mandatory measures to take effect. Second, the operation of the measures . . . was essentially dependent on Government action or intervention.

---

[21] In the subsequent WTO Appellate Body Report on the *Korean Beef* case, para. 149, the WTO Appellate Body has clarified the test for discrimination in the context of Article III:4 in the following terms: 'A formal difference in treatment between imported and like domestic products is thus neither necessary, nor sufficient, to show a violation of Article III:4. Whether or not imported products are treated "less favourably" than like domestic products should be assessed instead by examining whether a measure modifies the conditions of competition in the relevant market to the detriment of imported products.'

[22] See *Japan – Trade in Semi-Conductors*, GATT Panel Report adopted 4 May 1988, BISD 35S/116, para. 109.

This two-stage test has been successfully applied in subsequent WTO decisions.[23] In this manner, while it would usually be exceptionally difficult to establish the requisite link, it remains possible with the right set of facts.

The careful avoidance of any express allegations of anti-competitive conduct by the US in the *Kodak-Fuji Film* case suggests that any WTO case would need to be pleaded carefully with an emphasis on underlying governmental measures, rather than private anti-competitive conduct. Typically, the government would need to be actively encouraging particular private anti-competitive conduct for a claim to succeed.

- Even if a governmental measure exists, the issue arises whether that measure is discriminatory. If the measure is not discriminatory on its face, the issue will arise whether there is de facto discrimination on the basis that the measure modifies the conditions of competition in the relevant market to the detriment of imported products. Professor John Jackson, an eminent authority on GATT and WTO law, has described this de facto discrimination issue as 'one of the most difficult conceptual problems of the GATT':[24]

> One of the most difficult conceptual problems of the GATT is the application of the national treatment obligation in the context of a national regulation which *on its face* appears to be non-discriminatory, but because of various circumstances of the market, has the effect of tilting the scales against imported products.

The outcome of the *Kodak-Fuji Film* case therefore suggests that the prospect of successfully applying Article III:4 to private anti-competitive conduct is not great.

Similar difficulties arise in the application of other WTO provisions to private anti-competitive conduct, as evidenced by the consideration of Article XXIII.1(b) of the GATT in the *Kodak-Fuji* case.

7.2.2 Non-violation complaint under Article XXIII.1(b) of the GATT

In addition to the Article III.4 claim, the US alleged in the *Kodak-Fuji Film* case that Japan had 'nullified or impaired' WTO tariff concessions

---

[23] See *Canada – Certain Measures Concerning Periodicals*, WTO Panel Report adopted 14 March 1997, WT/DS31/R, para. 5.36.

[24] See J. H. Jackson, 'National Treatment Obligations and Non-tariff Barriers' (1989) 10 *Michigan Journal of International Law* 207.

in breach of Article XXIII.1(b) of the GATT. Such 'non-violation' complaints are rare in international law.[25] An understanding of such complaints requires an understanding of the operation of the WTO dispute settlement system.

The WTO dispute settlement system is premised on Article XXIII.1 of the GATT, which provides as follows:

> If any contracting party considers that any benefit accruing to it directly or indirectly under the GATT is being nullified or impaired or the attainment of any objective of the GATT is being impeded as the result of:
>
> (a) the failure of another contracting party to carry out its obligations under the GATT; or
> (b) the application by another contracting party of any measure; or
> (c) the existence of any other situation,
>
> the contracting party may, with a view to the satisfactory adjustment of the matter, make written representations or proposals to the other contracting parties which it considers to be concerned...

Article XXIII.1, as affirmed by the WTO Dispute Settlement Understanding of 1995, therefore gives complaining parties a choice of three different alternative routes for WTO dispute resolution:

(a) *violation complaints*, arising from 'the failure of another contracting party to carry out its obligations under the GATT';
(b) *non-violation complaints*, arising from 'the application by another contracting party of any measure' whether or not it conflicts with the provisions of the GATT; and
(c) *situation complaints*, involving 'the existence of any other situation'.

At least one of these three routes must result in either of the following:

(d) the nullification or impairment of a benefit accruing to a member directly or indirectly under the WTO Agreement; or
(e) the impeding of the attainment of any objective of the WTO Agreement.

Accordingly, there are usually six possible permutations for WTO dispute settlement.

---

[25] See B. Williams, 'Non-Violation Complaints in the WTO System' in P. Mengozzi (ed.), *International Trade Law on the 50th Anniversary of the Multilateral Trade System* (Dott. A. Giuffrè Editore, 1999), p. 667.

Importantly, each of the three alternative routes has a different burden of proof and different procedural consequences:

- *Violation complaint*   A violation complaint under Article XXIII.1(a) requires the complaining nation to prove that the offending nation has failed to perform a WTO obligation, triggering a presumption of nullification and impairment. Unless the offending state can rebut this presumption, the validity of the complaint is affirmed. The US allegation of breach of Article III.4 by Japan in the *Kodak-Fuji Film* case (as discussed in detail above) was a violation complaint.
- *Non-violation complaint*   A non-violation complaint under Article XXIII.1(b) does not require the complaining nation to prove a failure to perform a WTO obligation. Instead, it must prove that a 'measure' of the offending nation has nullified or impaired a WTO benefit, which would have otherwise accrued to another member. Such non-violation complaints are subject to more onerous evidential requirements, including that the complaining nation must present a 'detailed justification' to support any complaint. If the WTO finds against the offending nation, then the offending nation is not obliged to withdraw the offending measure, but may simply compensate the complaining nation.
- *Situation complaint*   A situation complaint under Article XXIII.1(c) is similar to a non-violation complaint, but requires proof of 'any other situation' rather than proof of a 'measure'. This broader scope of situation complaints is offset by severe procedural consequences. Situation complaints may not exploit the streamlined WTO Panel Report adoption procedures that were introduced by the Uruguay Round in 1994. Rather, an offending nation retains an ability to veto the adoption of a WTO Panel Report. This proved a major hurdle to effective dispute settlement under the GATT prior to 1994 as an offending nation could veto the adoption of any Panel Report contrary to its interests.[26]

As Brett Williams notes, the potential scope of non-violation complaints is 'staggering'. On a literal interpretation of Article XXIII.1(b), such complaints could, for example, potentially apply to domestic competition laws as the 'absence of competition law in one country may adversely affect the market access that may be gained by another country's exporters'.[27] However, the *Kodak-Fuji Film* case indicates that even with such potentially

---

[26] See discussion in P. T. B. Kohona, 'Dispute Resolution Under the World Trade Organisation: An Overview' (1994) 28(5) *Journal of World Trade* 23.
[27] See Williams, above n. 25, p. 704.

broad application, the likelihood of any nation successfully establishing a non-violation complaint in a competition law context remains low.

In the *Kodak-Fuji Film case*, the US made a non-violation complaint against Japan under Article XXIII.1(b) of the GATT alleging that Japan had adopted measures that nullified or impaired previous tariff concessions Japan had made to the US. The US alleged that the individual and collective effect of the Distribution Countermeasures, Large Retail Store Laws and Promotion Countermeasures was to offset tariff concessions for imported film provided by Japan to the US during the Kennedy, Tokyo and Uruguay Rounds of GATT multilateral negotiations.

In considering the non-violation complaint, the WTO Panel considered the *Oilseeds* case and the seven other instances where non-violation complaints had previously been considered by GATT and WTO panels.[28] Consistent with these previous decisions, the WTO Panel reasoned that the US was required to establish three elements to make a cognisable claim under Article XXIII:1(b):

(a) the application of a measure by the Japanese government;
(b) a benefit accruing under a WTO agreement, as legitimately expected by the US (requiring, in turn, that the application of the measure by Japan was not reasonably anticipated by the US); and
(c) nullification or impairment of the benefit as the result of the application of the measure by the Japanese government.

In relation to the first element, the WTO Panel decided that a 'measure' existed consistent with the reasoning in relation to the 'law, regulation or requirement' in Article III:4 above.

In relation to the second element, the WTO Panel considered that a benefit had accrued to the US in the form of tariff concessions by Japan during the Kennedy, Tokyo and Uruguay Rounds. However, to the extent that certain of the measures already existed prior to the commencement of these Rounds, the US was presumed to be aware of these measures and had not rebutted that presumption. As the US should have known of the Japanese measures in place at that time, it could not have legitimately expected the relevant benefits given the likelihood of the offsetting effects of the Japanese measures in existence at that time.

---

[28] See, for example, *EEC – Payments and Subsidies Paid to Processors and Producers of Oilseeds and Related Animal-feed Proteins* (L/6627), GATT BISD 37S/86, GATT Panel Report, adopted on 25 January 1990.

In relation to the third element, the WTO Panel equated the concept of 'nullification or impairment' with 'upsetting the competitive relationship established between domestic and imported products as a result of tariff concessions', consistent with the reasoning in the *Oilseeds* case.[29] The WTO Panel reasoned that this contemplated both de jure and de facto discrimination. Consistent with the WTO Panel's reasoning in relation to Article III:4, the WTO Panel found that no de jure or de facto discrimination had occurred.

In summary, in order for a non-violation complaint to succeed, a complainant would need to establish the existence of a governmental measure that adversely modified the conditions of competition between domestic and imported products leading to nullification or impairment. The *Kodak-Fuji* case suggests that, in most cases, this would be difficult to establish.

Furthermore, any such challenge could usually only successfully occur in relation to governmental measures that were not reasonably anticipated at the time the relevant benefit was provided. A complaining party would face a high burden of proof and would need to provide a detailed justification to uphold its complaint. Even if the complaint succeeded, there would be no guarantee that the relevant government measure would be withdrawn.

In conclusion, the *Kodak-Fuji Film* case illustrates that the potential for successful WTO claims against private anti-competitive practices remains limited. If private anti-competitive practices have a detrimental effect on international trade, but are not prevented by domestic competition laws, then it is unlikely international trade law would prevent these practices. Such conduct may thus escape regulation entirely, leading to 'underregulation'.

7.3 To what extent do domestic competition laws otherwise prevent such conduct?

Given that international trade law does not usually prevent private anti-competitive conduct (i.e. Domestic Conduct and International Conduct, as defined earlier), the issue arises as to the circumstances in which such conduct is not otherwise prevented by domestic competition laws so escapes regulation altogether.

---

[29] See *Ibid.*

Chapter 3 of this book identified a key reason why certain anti-competitive conduct may not be effectively regulated by domestic competition laws. Namely, each nation is usually concerned only with effects on its own domestic markets and not the markets of other nations, leading to a negative externality in regulatory decision-making. In turn, this leads to 'under-regulation' and 'over-regulation'.

This chapter now illustrates that these negative externalities in regulatory decision-making can be manifested in three distinct ways:

- *Exemption*   A nation may expressly exempt certain anti-competitive conduct from its domestic competition laws.
  - *Example*   Chapter 7 identifies exemptions provided to import cartels.
- *Ineffective enforcement*   A nation may not enforce its existing domestic competition laws sufficiently or effectively.
  - *Example*   Chapter 7 considers '*dango*' bid-rigging in Japan as an example of historic insufficient enforcement.
- *Inadequate laws*   A nation may have inadequate national competition laws (including competition laws that are weaker in some respects than the international norm).
  - *Example*   Chapter 7 considers historical allegations of ineffective enforcement by Japan against '*keiretsu*' business practices.

Each of these evidence 'under-regulation' and are considered in greater detail below by reference to specific examples of Domestic Conduct and International Conduct. In relation to each of these examples, four critical questions are considered:

- What is the relevant anti-competitive conduct?
- Why is the relevant anti-competitive conduct detrimental to international trade?
- Why isn't the relevant anti-competitive conduct subject to effective regulation under WTO law? (Usually, this is due to insufficient governmental involvement, consistent with the analysis above.)
- Why isn't the relevant anti-competitive conduct subject to effective regulation under domestic competition law? (Usually, this is due to exemption, ineffective enforcement and/or inadequate laws, as identified above.)

Later in this chapter, a number of suggestions are proposed as to how anti-competitive conduct that is not effectively regulated either by WTO law or domestic competition law could be addressed by an international competition agreement (thereby promoting greater market contestability consistent with the conclusions in Chapter 6 of this book).

7.3.1 Domestic Conduct (horizontal concerted) – import cartels

Domestic Conduct has most frequently been problematic to international trade in the context of concerted conduct by firms in a domestic market. As discussed in Chapter 4, concerted conduct is typically considered anti-competitive where it has collusive or exclusive effects that substantially lessen competition in a relevant market, although certain forms of concerted conduct may be considered sufficiently culpable that they are deemed 'per se' anti-competitive. Concerted conduct may be characterised as 'horizontal' or 'vertical'.

As identified in Chapter 3 of this book, the existence of negative economic externalities in regulatory decision-making means that governments are likely to permit Domestic Conduct that has a net positive effect on domestic welfare, notwithstanding that it may have negative spillover effects on foreign nations and a net adverse effect on global welfare. Domestic Conduct may be expressly exempted from domestic competition laws on the basis of minimal domestic effects, for example, even though that conduct has a substantial adverse impact on international trade. Historically, this has most commonly occurred in the context of exemptions from domestic competition laws given to domestic import cartels.

- *What are import cartels and how do they operate?* Import cartels are usually horizontal arrangements between purchasers of a good or service in a single nation for the purpose of co-ordinating the importation of a good or service into the domestic market of that nation.
  - *Example* The US Department of Justice investigated eight Japanese fishing and trading companies in 1982 that had allegedly formed an import cartel to drive down the price they would pay the Alaskan processors of a particular kind of crab destined for the Japanese domestic market.[30]
- *Why are import cartels detrimental to international trade?* Adverse effects in international markets may arise where the members of the import cartel exercise their collective market power to take actions that

---

[30] *United States v. C Itoh & Co et al*, No. C-82-810 (WD Wash, 1982).

impede foreign products entering the domestic market.[31] Such market power effects may be exacerbated if the import cartel members control strategically important barriers to entry, such as exclusive import licences, distribution systems, and infrastructure bottlenecks.[32] However, as governmental measures are susceptible to challenge under the WTO, import cartels have increasingly been structured in a manner that avoids direct governmental involvement.

Such market power effects may also be exacerbated if the cartel members collectively have substantial market power as purchasers in the international market (i.e. 'oligopsony' power). The import cartel may exercise its oligopsony market power to drive down the purchase price for products at the expense of exporters in foreign countries. However, the circumstances in which an import cartel in a *single nation* would hold monopsony power are rare as the nation would need to dominate international consumption of the relevant product (as in the crab example above).

- *Why aren't import cartels subject to effective regulation under the WTO?* To the extent that import cartels can be linked to governmental measures, action could be taken under the WTO. However, the *Kodak-Fuji Film* case suggests WTO action would be unsuccessful unless the cartel were premised on a governmental measure.
- *Why aren't import cartels subject to effective regulation under domestic competition laws?* In most nations, import cartels are potentially subject to domestic competition laws. However, there are two related circumstances in which domestic competition laws do not apply to import cartels:
  - *Authorisations (i.e. by regulatory decision)* Domestic competition laws are usually concerned only with the effect of the import cartel on domestic competition, and therefore any wider international trade effects typically escape scrutiny. Competition authorities may authorise import cartels on the basis of efficiency benefits exceeding any anti-competitive effects in the domestic market, with no consideration given to wider effects on international trade or markets in other jurisdictions.

---

[31] See I. W. Tsai & C. G. H. Yang, 'Taiwan's GATT Accession and the Changing Environment for Competition and Antitrust Enforcement' in C. J. Cheng, L. Liu & C. K. Wang (eds.), *International Harmonisation of Competition Laws* (Martinus Nijihoff, Dordrecht, 1995), p. 297.

[32] Infrastructure bottlenecks typically arise where the import cartel controls particular infrastructure that is vital to the supply of the import on competitive terms, but that is uneconomical for competing firms to duplicate. See, for example, S. Gorinson, 'Essential Facilities and Regulation' (1989) 58 *Antitrust Law Journal* 871.

Import cartels are often authorised by domestic governments, for example, on the basis that they realise significant productive efficiencies, including by enabling firms to reduce transactions costs and obtain pecuniary economies of scale by way of bulk discounts and rebates.

- *Exemptions (i.e. specified in legislation)* In addition to the reasons identified above, domestic competition laws may expressly exempt specified import cartels if they countervail the market power of foreign suppliers on the basis of net benefits to domestic consumers, particularly if the foreign suppliers also operate as a cartel.

  A principal concern with authorising or exempting import cartels is that once a cartel has been authorised or exempted, competition law has reduced ability (other than as provided within the express terms of the authorisation or exemption) to prevent the cartel members from abusing their market power.

- *Example* The US Department of Justice originally granted an authorisation to US oil companies in 1971 to enable them to countervail the market power of the OPEC oil cartel.[33] However, this authorisation was subsequently withdrawn due to alleged anti-competitive effects on the domestic market by US oil importers arising from their ability to enter into collective import arrangements.[34]

In summary, import cartels may have adverse effects on international trade and may fail to be adequately regulated under domestic competition law due to express authorisations or exemptions. Accordingly, import cartels (and other such measures exempted from domestic competition laws) may escape both international and domestic regulation. Such 'under-regulation' could be addressed by an international competition agreement by ensuring authorisations or exemptions are not given which have net adverse effects on global welfare.

7.3.2 Domestic Conduct (horizontal concerted) – 'dango' bid-rigging

Domestic cartel conduct that adversely impacts on international trade may also escape effective regulation where domestic competition laws are not effectively enforced. Again, ineffective enforcement may arise because

---

[33] This authorisation was set out in a series of Business Review Letters by which companies are advised of the likely reaction of authorities to any of their practices.

[34] See OECD, 'Strengthening the Coherence Between Trade and Competition Policies: Joint Report by the Trade Committee and the Committee on Competition Law and Policy' OECD, Paris, OCDE/GD(96)90, 1996.

a nation does not appropriately recognise the effects of anti-competitive conduct on market entrants from foreign nations. An example is illustrated by the allegations of '*dango*' bid-rigging made by the US against Japan.

- *What was* dango *bid-rigging and how did it operate?* The Japanese government historically utilised a licensing system to regulate bidders for Japanese public works construction projects. Only licensed general contractors were authorised to bid for these construction projects. However, the Japanese licensing regime involved a 'Catch 22' mechanism that had the effect of excluding foreign competitors. One of the key criteria for granting licences to general contractors was significant previous experience in Japanese public works construction projects. However, such previous experience could only be obtained by licensed general contractors.[35]

  The bottleneck effect of this regulatory environment created the conditions for an alleged cartel among the licensed Japanese general contractors, known in Japan as '*dango*'.[36] The *dango* allegedly involved a form of bid-rigging in which the licensed general contractors determined which firm would bid on any given project and at what price. Corrupt public officials were alleged to provide the *dango* contractors with inside information concerning the minimum price for each public works contract.[37] This practice was estimated to cost the Japanese government approximately 50% more than under a sealed bid system.

- *Why was* dango *bid-rigging detrimental to international trade?* The detriment caused to international trade by the *dango* practice is illustrated by the frequent trade disputes between Japan and the United States during the 1980s regarding access by United States firms to the estimated AU$500 billion Japanese construction market.[38] These trade disputes caused significant 'system frictions' (as defined in Chapter 3 of this book).

---

[35] See J. MacMillan, 'Dango: Japan's Price-Fixing Conspiracies' (1991) 3 *Economics & Politics* 201. See also M. Nihashi, T. Saijo & M. Une, 'The Outsider and Sunk Cost Effects on "Dango" in Public Procurement Bidding: An Experimental Analysis', Research Paper No. 514, Osaka Institute of Social and Economic Research, Osaka, 1995.

[36] See J. J. Schott, 'The Law of United States–Japan Trade Relations' (1990) 24(2) *Journal of World Trade* 37.

[37] See M. W. Punke, 'Structural Impediments to United States–Japan Trade: The Collision of Culture and Law' (1990) 23 *Cornell International Law Journal* 55, 59.

[38] See J. H. Jackson, 'Statement on Competition and Trade Policy before the U.S. Senate Committee on Judiciary', 18 June 1992; reprinted in (1992) 26 *Journal of World Trade* 111.

- *Example* In 1987, Senator F. Murkowsi in the US instigated legislation that barred Japanese firms from the US market if they did not grant reciprocal access. In 1988, this legislation was applied against Kiewet Construction and Kajima Engineering in relation to a Washington, DC subway project. Simultaneously, the US government took steps to impose unilateral trade sanctions under 'Super 301' of the United States Trade Act of 1974. Eventually, the Japanese government succumbed to this pressure and encouraged the *dango* contractors to enter into a 'Major Projects Agreement' to increase the transparency of bidding procedures.[39] *Dango* practices now appear to have been eliminated and the JFTC is now actively undertaking enforcement.
- *Why wasn't* dango *bid-rigging subject to effective regulation under the WTO? Dango* practices could probably be challenged if they recurred today under *Kodak-Fuji Film* principles given their governmental basis. There are now also specific provisions in the plurilateral WTO Agreement on Government Procurement that would prevent such practices, including express prohibitions against certain procurement conduct that adversely affects competition (although not every WTO member is a signatory to that plurilateral agreement). However, *dango* practices are an exception to the norm. Most private cartel conduct would not have a governmental basis so would not be effectively regulated by the WTO.
- *Why wasn't* dango *bid-rigging subject to effective regulation under domestic competition laws?* Technically, the *dango* practice was illegal under Japanese competition law. However, insufficient enforcement occurred. The *dango* example illustrates that even where domestic competition laws exist, these laws may not necessarily be effectively enforced, resulting in the persistence of private anti-competitive conduct that may harm international trade.
  - *Example* In 1993, the former Japanese Liberal Democratic Party Minister of Construction, Kishiro Nakamura, was convicted of receiving AU$200,000 for blocking criminal accusations against the Japanese construction company, Kajima Incorporated during an independent governmental inquiry into the rigging of a major construction project bid.

As identified in Chapter 3, a nation is less likely to take enforcement action against conduct which does not adversely affect the domestic

---

[39] See A. Y. Seita, 'US Japan Antitrust Co-operation' (1993) 23 *Law & Policy in International Business* 1081.

market (or which benefits vested interests in the domestic market), even though such conduct may have significant adverse effects on global welfare. Without international pressures for effective competition law enforcement, such conduct may escape regulation. Again, such 'under-regulation' could be addressed by an international competition agreement by ensuring enforcement action is taken where there are net adverse effects on global welfare.

7.3.3 Domestic Conduct (vertical concerted) – 'keiretsu' business practices

Vertical agreements involve agreements between firms at different levels of the product supply chain, usually between firms competing in different functional markets. Of particular concern to international trade are vertical agreements in domestic markets that prevent a foreign firm from accessing a domestic distribution system (i.e. vertical foreclosure). Allegations of vertical foreclosure triggered a number of serious trade conflicts between the US and Japan in the 1980s and early 1990s, including in the context of the *Kodak-Fuji Film* case. In several notable instances, these practices led to threats of unilateral trade sanctions by the US against Japan under section 301 and 'Super 301' of the United States Trade Act of 1974.

Of those trade conflicts, the series of trade disputes between the US and Japan over automobiles (1980–1995) were particularly severe.[40] The principal allegation made by the United States over this fifteen-year period was that the vertical '*keiretsu*' relationships of Japanese car manufacturers foreclosed US car manufacturers and component suppliers from competing in the Japanese car market.[41] The destabilising nature of these trade disputes led many international commentators to advocate the introduction of competition principles into the WTO.

---

[40] See M. W. Lochmann, 'The Japanese Voluntary Restraint on Automobile Exports: An Abandonment of the Free Trade Principles of the GATT and the Free Market Principles of the United States Antitrust Law' (1996) 27 *Harvard International Law Journal* 99.

[41] *Keiretsu* originated after World War II when the state-promoted industrial conglomerates, known as *zaibatsu*, were disbanded by the US Military Government in Occupation under tough competition laws. During the 1950s and 1960s, the Japanese government relaxed these competition laws and established *keiretsu* practices as a key component of Japanese industrial policy. The companies of the former *zaibatsu* acquired large volumes of stock in each other and sought to confine their business relations to other firms within the original structure. See J. Davidow, 'Application of U.S. Antitrust Laws to Keiretsu Practices' (1994) 18 *World Competition* 5. See also J. Davidow, 'Keiretsu and US Antitrust' (1993) 24 *Law & Policy in International Business* 1035.

- *What are* keiretsu *and how do they operate?* The term '*keiretsu*' is used to describe extensive vertical and horizontal integration by Japanese firms by way of cross-shareholdings and long-term quasi-contractual relationships.[42] The *keiretsu* are Japanese business conglomerates, typically assembled around a major bank or cash-rich trading company that provides low cost capital on a preferential basis to other members of the *keiretsu* group. Such organisational structures range from small affiliations to extensive multi-national corporate networks. In 1990, the JFTC estimated that 90% of all domestic business transactions within Japan were among parties involved in long-standing relations in the nature of *keiretsu*.[43]

  In the Japanese automotive industry, the *keiretsu* business structure was alleged by the US government to foreclose upstream and downstream markets via 'closed supply pyramids' and 'preferential distribution networks'. The US alleged these involved long-term vertical restraints of the following nature:
  - Vertically-integrated pyramids of hundreds of suppliers and component manufacturers supplied all the requirements of principal car manufacturers, effectively closing out foreign suppliers.
  - Preferential distribution networks regulated the flow of products from the manufacturer to the consumer in the form of franchises in which Japanese car dealers agreed to sell only selected brands of cars.

  The US alleged that cheap financing arrangements, and preferential treatment as a reward for loyalty, had encouraged the development of long-term arrangements that were, in effect, exclusive.[44] Dore summarised the US foreclosure allegations in the following terms: 'imports penetrate into markets, but where there are no markets, only a network of established "supply relationships", it is hard for them to make any headway'.[45]

- *Why are* keiretsu *business practices detrimental to international trade?* As with the *dango* practices, the adverse effect of *keiretsu* business practices on international trade is illustrated by the frequent trade

---

[42] See A. Helou, 'The Nature and Competitiveness of Japan's Keiretsu' (1993) 27(2) *Journal of World Trade* 99. See also S. Zenichi, 'A Texan Raid on a Japanese Company' (1989) 16(4) *Japan Echo* 61, 65. See also O. Nariai, *History of the Modern Japanese Economy* (Foreign Press Centre, Tokyo, 1994), p. 32.

[43] See J. F. Rill, 'Statement of Japanese Competition Policies and United States Response Before the US Senate Judiciary Committee, 29 July 1992' (1992) 16(1) *World Competition* 143.

[44] See I. Ken'ichi, 'The Legitimacy of Japan's Corporate Groups' (1990) 17(3) *Japan Echo* 23.

[45] See R. Dore & I. Masamichi, 'Japan and the United States: Reviewing the Structure of Japan–US Relations' (1992) 19(1) *Japan Echo* 37, 40.

disputes and 'system frictions' between the US and Japan. Of these disputes, a particular dispute in June 1995 involving the Japanese car distribution network was particularly severe ('Auto Trade Dispute').

The Auto Trade Dispute involved allegations by the US that the *keiretsu* business practices identified above were foreclosing the Japanese car distribution system and preventing US car manufacturers from marketing their cars to Japanese consumers. US Deputy Trade Representative, C. Barshevsky, alleged in June 1995, for example:[46]

> The Big Three [US car manufacturers] have invested over US $140 billion in the last five years alone to penetrate the Japanese market . . . After months of trying, Ford only managed to secure seven out of thousands of Japanese dealerships . . . We seek an end to the *keiretsu* system which so disadvantages Japanese consumers and stifles competition.

Japan responded that US car manufacturers were not sufficiently customising their products to the unique demands of the Japanese car market.[47] Japanese Minister, R. Hashimoto, commented, for example:[48]

> A country that has a significant trade imbalance with another . . . will often accuse its trading partner of unfair trade practices and of maintaining closed markets . . . last year, the 'Big Three' United States auto manufacturers did not offer a single model in the '2000cc or under' category, which represents some 80% of the Japanese car market – and offered only two models with right-hand drive . . . clearly, the poor presence of United States auto-makers is due to the fact that they do not make enough of an effort.

The US threatened to take legal action against Japan in the WTO and also threatened unilateral trade sanctions against Japan under the 'Super 301' provisions of the United States Trade Act of 1974. The Auto Trade Dispute culminated on 28 June 1995 with the US imposing a deadline for the imposition of 100% punitive tariffs on nearly US $6 billion worth of Japanese luxury cars. These tariffs were calculated to price these cars out of the US domestic market by doubling their retail price.

---

[46] See 'Trade Sanctions Could Hit Japanese Autos', *Asian Wall Street Journal*, Hong Kong, 17 May 1995.
[47] See D. Audet & M. Harbour, 'Market Access in Automobile Distribution' (1996) 12 *The OECD Observer* 11.
[48] See 'Japanese Luxury Car Makers Face Dilemma Due to United States Tariff', *Asian Wall Street Journal*, Hong Kong, 18 May 1995.

At the eleventh hour in Geneva on 28 May 1995, negotiations between the US and Japan reached an accord. In the subsequent US-Japan Automotive Trade Agreement, Japan agreed to increase the number of Japanese dealers selling US cars from 200 to 1,200 within five years.[49] Japan agreed to ensure that Japanese companies purchased US$12 billion of US components over a period of three years. Japan also pledged to manufacture 500,000 new cars in the US by 1998, an increase of 25%.[50]

- *Why aren't* keiretsu *business practices subject to effective regulation under the WTO?* The *Fuji-Kodak Film* case directly illustrates the difficulties experienced in taking claims against vertical private anti-competitive conduct under WTO law. Even where governmental measures are found to exist, there is likely to be insufficient evidence of de jure or de facto discrimination.
- *Why aren't* keiretsu *business practices subject to effective regulation under domestic competition laws?* In the Auto Trade Dispute, the US alleged ineffective enforcement and inadequate laws. The US complained that Japanese competition law was deficient in not regulating certain *keiretsu* practices. The US also alleged that the JFTC was not properly enforcing existing provisions in the Japanese Antimonopoly Act 1947.

The reduction of 'system frictions' was discussed in detail in Chapter 3 of this book in the context of the extra-territorial application of competition laws. However, as illustrated by the *dango* and *keiretsu* business practices above, such 'system frictions' can also arise in other circumstances. Trade sanctions can be imposed by a nation in direct response to perceived anti-competitive conduct in foreign markets so as to coerce effective competition regulation. Given its superpower status, the US has most commonly taken such action.

The Auto Trade Dispute, in particular, illustrates that rather crude retaliatory measures may be adopted by more powerful governments to coerce less powerful governments to alter their domestic laws and policies.[51] While such coercion was successful in the case of the Auto Trade Dispute,

---

[49] See United States – Japan Automotive Agreement and Supporting Document, 23 August 1995, reprinted in (1995) 34 *ILM* 1482.

[50] See 'Japan Transport Chief Stops Traffic at Auto Trade Talks', *Asian Wall Street Journal*, Hong Kong, 30 May 1995, 1.

[51] See discussion in M. W. Lochmann, 'The Japanese Voluntary Restraint on Automobile Exports: An Abandonment of the Free Trade Principles of the GATT and the Free Market Principles of the United States Antitrust Law' (1996) 27 *Harvard International Law Journal* 99.

such coercion is anathema to harmonious international relations.[52] Unilateral trade sanctions violate the most-favoured nation principle of Article I of the GATT and invariably other WTO provisions as well. In the Auto Trade Dispute, Japan threatened WTO action against the US if unilateral trade sanctions were applied.

The continued potential for such unilateral trade measures, notwithstanding WTO illegality, is clearly of concern to the continued stability of the international trading system. Such an approach is inherently damaging to international relations and undermines the WTO multilateral system. The use of an international competition agreement to address such issues is preferable as it would further encourage the application of any trade sanctions on a more objective and principled basis under WTO procedures.

7.4 International Conduct

While the previous examples illustrate the harm caused to international trade by Domestic Conduct, it is also clear that International Conduct (as defined above) can harm international trade. Such International Conduct may arise, for example, where an international cartel or conglomerate has significant market power in an international market, enabling it to manipulate the flow of international trade by reducing supply and raising prices.

Such practices would usually be subject to the extra-territorial application of domestic competition laws given that such conduct may satisfy various forms of the 'effects test'. However, a variety of reasons exist why such extra-territorial application may be ineffective, including by:

(a) government involvement, as illustrated by the OPEC oil cartel; and
(b) structuring of business activities to reduce the risk competition law enforcement.

7.4.1 International Conduct (concerted) – OPEC oil cartel

Historically, international cartels have been pervasive within international commerce.[53] The WTO Working Group on Trade and Competition Policy

---

[52] See W. J. Pengilley, 'Extraterritorial Effects of US Commercial and Antitrust Legislation: A View from Down Under' (1993) 16(4) *Vanderbilt Journal of Transnational Law* 833.
[53] See R. T. Griffiths, *International Cartel History Site*: http://www.let.leidenuniv.nl/history/rtg/cartels/

has also commented that a large number of current international cartels had been identified by various competition authorities.[54]

- *What are international cartels and how do they operate?* International cartels are horizontal agreements between a number of firms from different countries operating in the international market, typically involving arrangements for the reduction of output, the increasing of prices and/or the division of particular markets.

  The most famous international cartel is the Organisation of the Petroleum Exporting Countries ('OPEC') oil cartel. OPEC is a permanent inter-governmental organisation, formed on 14 September 1960, comprising nations that are substantial net exporters of oil. OPEC's stated objective is to co-ordinate and unify petroleum policies among its eleven member nations.[55] To further this objective, the oil and energy ministers of the OPEC nations meet in ordinary session twice each year to co-ordinate their oil production policies. An important feature of OPEC is its governmental character, with the OPEC governments determining the oil production levels of state-controlled oil companies.

- *Why are international cartels detrimental to international trade?* International cartels may prove particularly harmful to international trade where they operate in important service sectors, such as maritime shipping, energy and financial services.

  In relation to the OPEC cartel, for example, the OPEC nations collectively produce around 60% of the oil traded internationally and possess around 78% of the world's total proven crude oil reserves. OPEC has therefore dominated the international oil trade. The OPEC nations have used this considerable collective market power to reduce oil production and increase the international market price for oil. Given that oil is, to some extent, the lifeblood of the modern international economy, OPEC has wielded considerable political and economic power.[56] In October 1973, for example, the Arab members of OPEC deliberately restricted the supply of oil to protest against the support by the United States for Israel during the Arab-Israeli war. Within a few months, the oil price

---

[54] See *Report (1998) of the Working Group on the Interaction Between Trade and Competition Policy to the General Council*, World Trade Organisation, WT/WGTCP/2 33, 8 December 1998, para. 87, p. 30.
[55] Algeria, Indonesia, Iran, Iraq, Kuwait, Libya, Nigeria, Qatar, Saudi Arabia, UAE and Venezuela.
[56] See A. Hamilton (ed.), *Oil: The Price of Power* (Rainbird, London, 1986). See also J. M. Griffin & D. J. Teece (ed.), *OPEC Countries' Behaviour and World Oil Prices* (Allen & Unwin, London, 1982).

quadrupled to unprecedented price levels leading to a global energy crisis known as the 'First Oil Shock' and triggering economic recession in oil-importing nations.
- *Why aren't international cartels subject to effective regulation under the WTO?* International cartels are not usually addressed by the WTO given that such cartels typically involve the actions of private enterprises and not the actions of government. Furthermore, international cartels do not usually impede market access or give rise to a form of discrimination that is regulated by the WTO, so circumstances of de facto discrimination by governments would be rare. For this reason, it is not usually possible to take WTO action against international cartels.

  In the case of OPEC, which does involve governmental conduct, some members of OPEC are not yet members of the WTO. However, those OPEC members that are bound by WTO obligations have a number of potential arguments why their policies would not breach WTO obligations, including:[57]
  - there are no quantitative export restrictions that breach Article XI of the GATT as OPEC utilises non-discriminatory production quotas;
  - Article XI:2(b) of the GATT permits quantitative restrictions deemed necessary to the marketing of commodities in international trade; and
  - Article XX(h) of the GATT provides an exemption for measures undertaken in pursuance of obligations under any intergovernmental commodity agreement which conforms to criteria submitted to the WTO contracting parties and is not disapproved or which is itself so submitted and not disapproved.

  However, OPEC is an exception. To the extent international cartel conduct has a governmental character, there is a high likelihood it will be regulated by the WTO.
- *Why aren't international cartels subject to effective regulation under domestic competition laws?* International cartels may not be subject to effective regulation due to exemptions, ineffective enforcement and inadequate laws, as identified previously. In the case of OPEC, the government of an OPEC member country would have no desire to apply its own domestic competition laws (if any) to prohibit its own conduct. The governmental character of OPEC has also thwarted its effective regulation under the domestic competition laws of other nations as the OPEC nations enjoy a number of jurisdictional and substantive defences

---

[57] See UNCTAD, *Trade Agreements, Petroleum and Energy Policies* (UNCTAD, Geneva, 2000), UNCTAD/ITCD/TSB/9.

that are not available to private companies.[58] This is evidenced by the various attempts by US plaintiffs to apply US antitrust laws on an extraterritorial basis to the OPEC oil cartel.

In the case, *International Association of Machinists (IAM)* v. *OPEC*,[59] a union in the US sued OPEC under the extraterritorial 'effects doctrine' of US antitrust law alleging oil price fixing with adverse effects on US markets. Both a federal District Court and, on appeal, the US Court of Appeal, declined to apply US antitrust laws against OPEC.

The District Court held that OPEC was protected by the sovereign immunity doctrine, which provides that each sovereign nation is beyond the jurisdiction of national courts. The US Congress codified this doctrine in the Foreign Sovereign Immunities Act of 1976.[60] While that Act considered a foreign nation to be deemed to have waived its immunity when it engaged in 'commercial activity', the District Court held that OPEC did not involve commercial activity as OPEC involved sovereign nations' decisions, how their natural resources would be exploited. Under this reasoning, a challenge to a foreign government cartel would rarely succeed in the US.

The Court of Appeal reached the same conclusion but with different reasoning. It relied on the 'act of state' doctrine, which declares that a US court will not adjudicate a politically sensitive dispute, which would require the court to judge the legality of the sovereign act of a foreign state. This doctrine is not jurisdictional, but prudential, as it deems a judicial remedy inappropriate due to international comity and non-justiciability. The court reasoned:[61]

> When the courts engage in piecemeal adjudication of the legality of the sovereign acts of states, they risk disruption of our country's international diplomacy. The executive may utilize protocol, economic sanction, compromise, delay, and persuasion to achieve international objectives. Ill-timed judicial decisions challenging the acts of foreign states could nullify these tools and embarrass the US in the eyes of the world.

In 2001, a class action was lodged against OPEC in Alabama by Prewitt Enterprises, a small-time petroleum products seller, again alleging the

---

[58] See US Department of Justice and Federal Trade Commission, *Antitrust Enforcement Guidelines for International Operations* (5 April 1995), reprinted at 4 Trade Reg Rep (CCH) 13,107, at § 3.31 (Foreign Sovereign Immunity) and § 3.33 (Acts of State).
[59] 477 F Supp 553 (CD Cal 1979), aff'd, 649 F 2d 1354 (9th Cir 1981), cert denied, 454 US 1163 (1982).
[60] 28 USC § 1330 *et seq.* [61] 649 F 2d at 1358.

extraterritorial application of US antitrust laws. Distinguishing *International Association of Machinists*, a US District Judge held that OPEC was in violation of US antitrust laws and issued an injunction purporting to order OPEC to refrain from further oil production cuts. OPEC lawyers subsequently succeeded in overturning this decision on the basis that OPEC had not been properly served with the law suit (because OPEC resides in Austria, and Austrian law prohibits service without OPEC's consent, the complaint was dismissed for lack of jurisdiction).[62] The dismissal was upheld on appeal.[63]

As well as court challenges, legislative challenges have also been made against OPEC in the US. On 24 June 2000, a number of US senators introduced anti-OPEC legislation into the House of Representatives, known as the No Oil Producing and Exporting Cartels Bill. This Bill sought to exempt OPEC nations from the provisions of the US Foreign Sovereign Immunities Act of 1976 to the extent OPEC engaged in anti-competitive behaviour with regard to petroleum products.[64] The Bill also authorised lawsuits against OPEC nations by US enforcement authorities and mandated courts to authorise the seizure of OPEC government assets. While this Bill was clearly politically motivated, and sought to make OPEC a presidential election issue, it does illustrate a mechanism by which such cartels could be subjected to extraterritorial competition law enforcement.

However, any possible enforcement action raises practical questions as to whether jurisdiction would be recognised, how a factual investigation could be conducted with respect to documents and witnesses located in foreign nations, and the nature and enforceability of any remedy. More importantly, any enforcement action would raise complex issues related to international jurisdiction, sovereignty and diplomatic relations. Any action would constitute an unwarranted interference in the sovereignty of nation states with very considerable adverse political fallout. For this reason, any such enforcement action would be anathema to harmonious relations in the international community and would certainly be politically untenable at this time, resulting in very significant 'system frictions'.

---

[62] See S. W. Waller, 'Suing OPEC' (2002) 64 *University of Pittsburgh Law Review* 105.
[63] *Prewitt Enterprises Inc* v. *Organisation of Petroleum Exporting Countries*, US Court of Appeals (11th Cir), Appeal from the US District Court for the Northern District of Alabama, 18 December 2003.
[64] The Bill was approved by a Senate subcommittee on 27 July 2000, but never became law.

Importantly, the OPEC oil cartel is unique and it is not suggested that an international competition agreement would seek to regulate OPEC. However, the principle identified above in relation to International Conduct is the same as identified for Domestic Conduct, namely the need for an international competition agreement to mitigate instances of exemption, ineffective enforcement and inadequate laws that may enable international cartels to escape effective regulation.

7.5 Existing WTO provisions regulating Domestic Conduct and International Conduct

The examples set out above illustrate that anti-competitive behaviour that is harmful to international trade will usually be prevented by domestic competition laws, unless:

(a) exemptions exist from domestic competition laws;
(b) domestic competition laws are not effectively enforced; or
(c) domestic competition laws are somehow substantially deficient or inadequate.

In the context of International Conduct, there is also considerable scope for entities to arrange their affairs in a manner that exploits such exemptions, ineffective enforcement and inadequate laws, further exaggerating their effect.

The challenge for any international competition agreement is to address these issues (i.e. to close these 'loopholes' in the trade–competition regulatory matrix). However, it is notable that the WTO nations have already agreed several competition provisions in the WTO with this in mind, as identified in Chapter 6 of this book. The General Agreement on Trade in Services ('GATS'), for example, includes several provisions addressing anti-competitive behaviour, including:

- Article VIII (Monopolies and Exclusive Service Suppliers), which requires member nations to ensure monopoly and exclusive service suppliers do not act in a manner inconsistent with the member's Article II non-discrimination obligations and specific GATS commitments; and
- Article IX (Business Practices), which recognises that certain business practices can restrain competition and thereby restrict trade in services, so requires consultation between member nations on request with a view to eliminating such practices.

Many governments have also committed to curbing anti-competitive behaviour in particular service sectors by way of binding GATS specific sectoral commitments. The GATS sectoral commitments in relation to basic telecommunications, in particular, represent the furthest extent of any competition obligations included in the WTO to date. These telecommunications sectoral obligations are considered in detail below and provide a useful precedent for an international competition agreement.

7.5.1 WTO Agreement on Basic Telecommunications

The potential for anti-competitive conduct in the context of the telecommunications sector is well recognised. Incumbent infrastructure owners have considerable market power by virtue of their control over access to essential infrastructure to which market entrants must interconnect if they are to compete effectively. Such market power effects are exacerbated given the need for market entrants to ensure any-to-any connectivity for their telephony customers and the natural monopoly characteristics of the industry, which prevents replication of the relevant facilities, by market entrants. In an international trade context, a major concern during the negotiation of the GATS was the extent to which such private sector conduct could negate negotiated market access commitments.

While GATS included a specific Telecommunications Annexe with a view to addressing such issues, a group of around 70 WTO nations considered this Annexe insufficient to address these concerns. Accordingly, these nations negotiated further GATS commitments relating to basic telecommunications within the context of a WTO Agreement on Basic Telecommunications, which came into effect from February 1998 ('WTO Basic Telecoms Agreement').[65] Under the WTO Basic Telecoms Agreement each nation is bound by its own individual schedule which describes the manner and extent to which that nation will ensure national treatment and market access with respect to specific modes of supply for particular basic telecommunications services.

Most of the signatories to the WTO Basic Telecoms Agreement included in their individual schedules a commitment to some or all features of a negotiated regulatory 'Reference Paper,' which set out principles for the establishment and maintenance of a competitive market.[66] In this

---

[65] See GATS Agreement on Basic Telecommunications, Annexe 1B, Final Act.
[66] See Reference Paper on Basic Telecommunications as incorporated by various nations into their respective Schedules of Specific Commitments forming part of the Fourth Protocol to the General Agreement on Trade in Services (adopted 30 April 1996; entry into force 5 February 1998).

manner, the WTO Basic Telecoms Agreement established an international minimum standard for the regulation of anti-competitive practices in the telecommunications industry of those nations. This Reference Paper included a number of competition law and policy commitments including, for example:

- adoption of safeguards to protect against anti-competitive behaviour; and
- establishment of terms and conditions for non-discriminatory interconnection.

In the decision *Mexico – Measures Affecting Telecommunications Services*, the WTO Panel explained the rationale behind the Reference Paper in the following terms:[67]

> ... Members recognised that the telecommunications sector, in many cases, was characterised by monopolies or market dominance. Removing market access and national treatment barriers was not deemed sufficient to ensure the effective realisation of market access commitments in basic telecommunications services. Accordingly, many Members agreed to additional commitments to implement a pro-competitive regulatory framework desired to prevent continued monopoly behaviour, particularly by former monopoly operators, and abuse of dominance by these or any other major suppliers. Members wished to ensure that market access and national treatment commitments would not be undermined by anti-competitive behaviour by monopolies or dominant suppliers, which are particularly prevalent in the telecommunications sector ...

Importantly, Section 1.1 of the Reference Paper, for example, effectively required that domestic competition laws should be adopted in the following terms:

> Appropriate measures shall be maintained for the purpose of preventing suppliers who, alone or together, are a major supplier from engaging in or continuing anti-competitive practices.

The obligations in the Reference Paper were tested in the April 2004 decision *Mexico – Measures Affecting Telecommunications Services* quoted above. In that dispute, the US accused Mexico of breaching Mexico's commitments under the WTO Basic Telecoms Agreement in relation to cost-based interconnection and the adoption of appropriate measures to prevent the incumbent telecommunications carrier (Telmex)

---

[67] See *Mexico – Measures Affecting Telecommunications Services*, WT/DS204/R, Report of the WTO Panel, 2 April 2004, para. 7.237.

engaging in anti-competitive practices. The decision is important as it identifies a number of fundamental competition concepts in the context of interpreting the WTO Basic Telecoms Agreement and its associated instruments.

Of particular importance were the WTO Panel's comments on Section 1.1 of the Reference Paper (set out above). The Panel reasoned:

- On its own, the concept of an 'anti-competitive practice' is broad in scope, suggesting actions that lessen rivalry or competition in the market. However, its meaning is then informed by whether the practice is condemned in the domestic competition legislation of most WTO members and the provisions of key international instruments that address competition policy, including the 1948 Havana Charter, the UNCTAD Code, and the OECD Recommendations (as identified in Chapters 5 and 6 of this book).
- If a law requires an anti-competitive practice to be engaged in, such a law would result in a member nation not meeting its obligation to maintain appropriate measures. However, the obligation to maintain appropriate measures may also require a member nation to amend or terminate regulatory measures that lead to anti-competitive practices, including immunities granted from the application of domestic competition laws. The concept of 'appropriate measures' otherwise reserves a degree of flexibility and regulatory autonomy for member nations in meeting their regulatory commitment under the Reference Paper.

This reasoning emphasises the importance of determining whether conduct is anti-competitive by reference to principles that are widely accepted in the international community, as evidenced by the majority of competition laws and key international instruments. This reasoning also emphasises that an obligation to maintain appropriate measures to prevent anti-competitive practices does require a member nation to take proactive steps to ensure its laws do not require or facilitate those anti-competitive practices. These concepts are important to the appropriate approach of any WTO competition agreement and are considered in further detail in Chapter 11 of this book.

In summary, as identified in Chapter 6 of this book, the WTO has already sought to regulate certain anti-competitive conduct, consistent with a globally optimal result. The WTO has done so in an indirect manner by regulating governmental measures that may permit private anti-competitive conduct that may, in turn, negate market access commitments.

The Reference Paper represents the furthest extent of such obligations to date and the decision *Mexico – Measures Affecting Telecommunications Services* represents the greatest extent of their application. Importantly, such provisions remain limited in scope and sectoral in nature.

7.6 Conclusion: an international competition agreement would promote international trade

In conclusion, there are a number of 'loopholes' (deliberate or not) that arise in the international regulatory matrix due to the failure of both international trade law and domestic competition law to apply to particular anti-competitive conduct that may have an adverse impact on international trade. Such 'loopholes' could potentially be addressed by an international competition agreement, promoting greater market contestability.

The analysis in this chapter indicates that international trade law will rarely address Domestic Conduct and International Conduct (as defined earlier) in the absence of governmental involvement. The *Kodak-Fuji Film* case illustrates that for WTO law to prevent private anti-competitive conduct, it would need to be sufficiently linked to an underlying government measure. This government measure would also need to be de jure or de facto discriminatory by permitting the adverse modification of the conditions of competition between domestic and imported products.

While a number of specific competition provisions have now been introduced into the WTO to address private anti-competitive conduct, the scope of these provisions remains limited. However, the decision *Mexico – Measures Affecting Telecommunications Services* does indicate that such provisions would usually be interpreted broadly and in a manner consistent with international best practice in competition regulation.

In the absence of regulation of private anti-competitive conduct by WTO law, the regulation of such conduct will therefore be critically dependent on the effectiveness of the relevant domestic competition law. However, domestic competition laws may fail to address anti-competitive conduct for a number of reasons, namely:

- *Exemption* Certain anti-competitive conduct may be exempted from the application of national competition laws due to domestic policy considerations or benefits to the national economy, without regard to wider cross-border effects (e.g. exemptions for import cartels).

- *Ineffective enforcement* National competition laws may address anti-competitive conduct, but may be inadequately enforced (e.g. *dango* bid-rigging in Japan). Inadequate enforcement may occur for a number of different reasons, including corrupt or inept enforcement agencies, poorly resourced enforcement agencies, or due to differences in enforcement practices between nations.
- *Ineffective laws* National competition laws may fail to address certain forms of anti-competitive conduct relative to the globally optimal level of regulation (e.g. *keiretsu* business practices in Japan).

Finally, International Conduct can be arranged by firms to take advantage of such exemptions, ineffective enforcement and inadequate laws.

Given these issues, a number of preliminary recommendations can be made for the content of any international competition agreement based on the need to address the issues of exemption, ineffective enforcement and inadequate laws identified in this chapter. In particular, an international competition agreement should:

- seek to limit the scope for exemptions from domestic competition laws where these exemptions have wider adverse effects on international trade and competition, perhaps by requiring each nation to consider the international implications of domestic exemptions;
- promote greater international co-operation on competition law enforcement, particularly in respect of evidential and procedural issues, including international recognition of subpoenas and international enforcement of judgments (subject to considerations of comity and sovereignty);
- encourage nations to undertake greater consultation with a view to co-ordinating international competition law investigations and enforcement actions, based on principles of comity;
- seek to ensure that existing competition laws are adequately enforced, by ensuring greater accountability and transparency by governmental agencies, and by promoting greater resourcing of these agencies (including technical assistance from industrialised nations to assist law enforcement by developing nations);
- render any obligations on international competition law issues subject to adjudication under an appropriate dispute settlement body, which should ideally be the WTO dispute settlement body so that international trade sanctions could be mandated if necessary;
- promote commonly accepted international principles regarding the content of domestic competition laws, perhaps by promoting a

minimum standard for competition laws for different types of nations (e.g. large industrialised, small industrialised, developing and less developed); and
- seek to restrain nations from applying unilateral trade sanctions, or undertaking extraterritorial law enforcement, where alternative action exists (including WTO dispute settlement).

These recommendations are considered in greater detail in Chapter 14 of this book. They would promote market contestability and thereby give practical effect to the theoretical basis for reconciling international trade law and international competition law identified in Chapter 6 of this book. These recommendations would also address the types of 'under-regulation' identified in this chapter. In this manner, these recommendations would ensure that the application, enforcement and substantive content of domestic competition laws remained consistent with a globally optimal result.

8

Would competition regulation of trade measures promote competition?

Chapter 8 continues the examination commenced by Chapter 7 into the relationship between international competition law and international trade law. Chapter 8 now considers international trade measures from a competition perspective, adopting the converse but complementary view to Chapter 7.

The distinction between the analysis set out in Chapters 7 and 8 of this book is a subtle but crucial one:

- Chapter 7 adopted an international trade perspective on anti-competitive conduct. Chapter 7 considered the extent to which *private anti-competitive conduct* is not effectively regulated by either international trade law or domestic competition law, with resulting adverse affects on *international trade*. Given that private anti-competitive conduct is not usually directly regulated by international trade law (as evidenced by the *Kodak-Fuji* case[1]), Chapter 7 focused primarily on under-regulation in the application, enforcement and substantive content of *domestic competition laws*. Chapter 7 concluded that such under-regulation could be addressed by an international competition agreement.
- Chapter 8 now adopts an international competition perspective on international trade measures. Chapter 8 therefore considers the extent to which *governmental trade measures* are not effectively regulated by either international trade law or domestic competition law, with resulting adverse affects on *international competition*. Given that governmental trade measures are not usually directly regulated by domestic competition laws, Chapter 8 focuses primarily on under-regulation in the application, enforcement and substantive content of *international trade*

---

[1] See *Japan – Measures Affecting Consumer Photographic Film and Paper*, Panel Report (1998) adopted on 6 December 1998, WT/DS44, WTO.

law. Chapter 8 similarly considers how such under-regulation could be addressed by an international competition agreement.

Chapter 8 has four principal sections:

- Consistent with the analysis in Chapter 7, section 8.1 identifies that certain governmental trade measures with an adverse effect on international competition may slip through a 'loophole' in the trade-competition regulatory matrix and thereby escape effective regulation. Section 8.1 identifies the principal reasons why certain governmental trade measures are not effectively regulated by international trade law and why private anti-competitive conduct resulting from these trade measures is not effectively regulated by domestic competition law.
- Section 8.2 considers certain governmental trade measures with *domestic* application that facilitate domestic anti-competitive conduct, with particular reference to export cartels and trade-oriented industrial policies (i.e. 'Domestic Measures'). Section 8.3 considers certain governmental trade measures with *international* application that facilitate foreign anti-competitive behaviour, with particular reference to voluntary export restraints and voluntary import expansions (i.e. 'International Measures').

  Both sections analyse the adverse effect of such trade measures on international competition and also identify why such trade measures, and anti-competitive conduct resulting from such measures, are not effectively regulated by either international trade law or domestic competition law.
- Section 8.4 considers certain commercial activities of governments that have a significant trade-policy component, with particular reference to government procurement and state trading enterprises (i.e. 'Governmental Commercial Activities'). Section 8.4 analyses the adverse effect of such activities on international competition and why such activities are not effectively regulated by domestic competition laws and international trade laws.

Chapter 8 concludes that a WTO competition agreement should restrict the use of certain governmental trade measures to circumstances consistent with greater international competition. On this basis, Chapter 8 provides a number of recommendations for the content of any international competition agreement that would prevent under-regulation and thereby facilitate greater international competition and market contestability.

8.1 The effects of trade measures on international competition

8.1.1 A useful analytical framework

For the purposes of this chapter, the governmental trade measures that raise significant international competition concerns can be broadly divided into three categories:

- First, certain government trade measures with *domestic* application may facilitate anti-competitive behaviour by domestic firms ('Domestic Measures').
  - *Example* Domestic Measures include export cartel policies and certain trade-oriented industrial policies, as detailed in section 8.2 of this chapter.
- Secondly, certain government trade measures with *international* application may facilitate anti-competitive behaviour by foreign firms ('International Measures').
  - *Example* International Measures include voluntary export restraints and voluntary import expansions, as detailed in section 8.3 of this chapter.
- Thirdly, certain commercial activities by governments that have a significant trade policy component may adversely affect international competition ('Governmental Commercial Activities').
  - *Example* Governmental Commercial Activities include state trading and government procurement policies, as detailed in section 8.4 of this chapter.

The conceptual 'trade–competition regulatory matrix' identified in Chapter 7 of this book can be applied to the regulation of such governmental trade measures. This matrix indicated that there are two relevant tiers of regulation for the purposes of this book:

- international trade law (which regulates governmental trade measures); and
- domestic competition law (which regulates private anti-competitive practices).

Chapter 8 considers two critical issues in the application of this 'trade–competition regulatory matrix' to Domestic Measures and International Measures:

(a) first, the extent to which governmental trade measures which facilitate private anti-competitive conduct are not effectively regulated by international trade law; and

WOULD A WTO AGREEMENT PROMOTE COMPETITION? 227

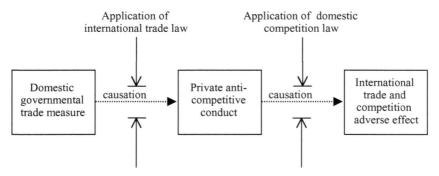

Figure 33: *Diagram illustrating analysis undertaken in Chapter 8*
NOTES: First, certain governmental trade measures which facilitate private anti-competitive conduct are not effectively regulated by international trade law. Secondly, private anti-competitive practices arising from these governmental trade practices are not effectively regulated by domestic competition law, in turn resulting in adverse effects on international trade and competition

(b) secondly, the secondary question as to the extent to which anti-competitive conduct arising from these governmental trade measures is not effectively regulated by domestic competition law, with resulting adverse effects on international competition.

These issues are illustrated by the diagram in Figure 33, which can be contrasted with the diagram in Figure 32 in Chapter 7.

In the case of Governmental Commercial Activities, the analysis is slightly different as Governmental Commercial Activities may themselves be anti-competitive. In such circumstances, the relevant issues are:

(a) first, the extent to which Governmental Commercial Activities are not effectively regulated by international trade law; and
(b) secondly, the extent to which those Governmental Commercial Activities are not effectively regulated by domestic competition law, with resulting adverse effects on international competition.

8.1.2 *To what extent are trade measures not effectively regulated by international trade law?*

The first issue identified above is the extent to which certain governmental trade measures which facilitate private anti-competitive conduct (i.e. Domestic Measures and International Measures) or which are themselves anti-competitive (i.e. Governmental Commercial Activities) are not effectively regulated by international trade law. In this respect, given that the relevant trade measures by definition have a governmental character, one would expect the WTO to apply prima facie. Governmental trade measures clearly fall within the purview of possible WTO regulation.

However, there are a number of circumstances in which the WTO does not effectively regulate certain trade measures that facilitate private anti-competitive conduct, as follows:

- *Incomplete coverage* While the WTO seeks to regulate international trade comprehensively, the coverage of the WTO is not complete. Certain aspects of international trade still remain outside the scope of current WTO law or are subject to a less severe application of WTO obligations. Typically, such unregulated aspects of international trade benefit from differential WTO treatment or have not yet been subjected to specific WTO obligations.
    - *Example* At present there are very few specific commitments by WTO members under the GATS in relation to energy services. In several negotiating proposals on energy services, reference has been made to the need to negotiate a multilateral instrument, similar to the Reference Paper on Basic Telecommunications (as discussed in Chapter 7), to ensure fair conditions of competition.[2]
- *No inconsistency* The WTO is currently focused on regulating international trade, particularly failures in governmental decision-making that may impede international trade. The WTO is not currently focused on international competition or failures in government decision-making that may impede competition in international markets, except to the extent that such decisions may also impede international trade commitments. Therefore, to the extent that any governmental trade measure remains consistent with WTO obligations it will be permitted by the WTO, even if it facilitates anti-competitive conduct.
    - *Example* Governmental trade measures permitting the operation of export cartels may not be inconsistent with WTO obligations but they may result in effects that are anti-competitive.
- *No breach* While certain governmental trade measures may appear inconsistent with fundamental WTO *principles*, they may not breach

---

[2] See S. Zarili, 'WTO Doha Declaration and Trade in Energy Goods and Services' (2003) 1(1) *Oil, Gas & Energy Law Intelligence* 1; available at http://www.gasandoil.com/ogel/samples/freearticles/roundup_14.htm.

actual WTO *obligations* due to the narrow or ambiguous drafting of these obligations or due to express exemptions. While the WTO does permit enforcement based on the 'nullification or impairment' of a WTO principle, there are limits to such enforcement as discussed in Chapter 7 of this book.
- *Example* Anti-dumping laws are arguably inconsistent with the objectives of the WTO in the 'elimination of discriminatory treatment in international commerce',[3] but are permitted under the express exemption set out in Article VI of the GATT, as discussed in Chapter 9 of this book.
- *No enforcement* Certain governmental trade measures may breach WTO obligations but may escape effective enforcement for a number of other reasons, including diplomatic restraint, insufficient evidence, insufficient legal standing, or lack of incentives for parties to seek WTO enforcement.
- *Example* Voluntary export restraints ('VERs') are technically in breach of WTO obligations but have historically tended to escape effective enforcement given that the two nations involved in the VER have no incentive to undertake enforcement action.

8.1.3 To what extent is anti-competitive conduct arising from such trade measures not effectively regulated by domestic competition law?

The fact that the WTO does not effectively regulate certain governmental trade measures which facilitate private anti-competitive conduct should be a matter of concern for international competition policy. In the absence of effective regulation by WTO law, nations are critically reliant on domestic competition law to regulate anti-competitive conduct that may be facilitated by such governmental trade measures.

This raises the secondary issue identified above, namely the extent to which certain private anti-competitive conduct arising from governmental trade measures (or associated with the trade measures themselves) is not effectively regulated by domestic competition law. This issue is almost identical to the issue concerning the application of domestic competition law considered in Chapter 7 of this book. The same three reasons identified in Chapter 7 for the non-application of domestic competition laws continue to apply, namely:

---

[3] Refer to the Preamble to the GATT 1947.

- *Exemption* Certain private conduct that would usually be considered anti-competitive may fall within express exemptions from national competition laws.
- *Ineffective enforcement* Existing national competition laws may be subject to insufficient or ineffective enforcement.
- *Inadequate laws* Existing competition laws may be inadequate, including competition laws that are weaker in some respects than the international norm.

8.1.4 Domestic Conduct, International Conduct and Governmental Commercial Activities

The remainder of this chapter applies the analytical framework identified above to various examples of governmental trade measures within the categories of Domestic Conduct, International Conduct and Governmental Commercial Activities identified previously. Two examples are considered for each of these three categories (i.e. six examples), as illustrated by the tabulated summary of this analysis in Figure 34.

In relation to each of these six examples, four key questions are considered, consistent with the analysis in Chapter 7 of this book:

- What is the relevant governmental trade measure and how does it operate?
- Why is the governmental trade measure detrimental to international competition?
- Why isn't the governmental trade measure subject to effective regulation under WTO law?[4]
- Why isn't the private anti-competitive conduct facilitated by the governmental trade measure (or the governmental trade measure itself) subject to effective regulation under domestic competition law?[5]

In relation to each of these six examples, this chapter also considers how the relevant governmental trade measure, or any private anti-competitive conduct resulting from that governmental trade measure, could be regulated by an international competition agreement.

---

[4] Usually, this is due to incomplete coverage, no inconsistency, no breach and/or no enforcement, as identified above.
[5] Usually, this is due to exemption, ineffective enforcement and/or inadequate laws, as identified above.

	Reasons for non-application of relevant laws						
	International trade law					Domestic competition law	
Governmental trade measure	Incomplete coverage	No inconsistency	No breach	No enforcement	Exemption	Ineffective enforcement	Inadequate laws
Domestic Measures:							
• export cartel policies	×						
• trade-oriented industrial policies		×	×		×		
International Measures:							
• Voluntary export restraints (VERs)				×	×	×	
• Voluntary import expansions (VIEs)				×	×	×	
Governmental Commercial Activities:							
• government procurement		×			×		
• state-trading enterprises (STEs)		×			×		

Figure 34: *Governmental trade measures considered in Chapter 8*

8.2 Domestic Measures

The two most notable examples of Domestic Measures are:

(a) export cartel policies; and
(b) trade-oriented industrial policies.

Both are considered in detail below.

8.2.1 Export cartel policies

Export cartel policies may escape regulation under the WTO if they remain consistent with WTO principles. Anti-competitive conduct flowing from export cartels may escape regulation under domestic competition laws due to express exemptions from domestic competition laws for public policy reasons. Alternatively, export cartel conduct may be immune from competition prosecution due to the high level of government involvement and the application of the 'act of state' and 'government compulsion' defences.[6]

- *What are export cartel policies and how do they operate?* Export cartels are the converse of the import cartel discussed in Chapter 7 of this book and usually constitute co-operative arrangements among firms in one country exporting their goods and services into foreign markets.[7] Export cartels enable exporters to increase their market power by colluding to increase prices and reduce output, allocate production and foreclose markets, thereby extracting greater rents from foreign purchasers. The scope for such rents is greatest if the cartel members possess significant international market power, usually by controlling a significant percentage of world production.[8]

Following World War II, an estimated 40% of international trade was undertaken through export cartels, although this percentage has subsequently declined significantly. Today, export cartels remain common to

---

[6] See H. C. Pitney, 'Sovereign Compulsion and International Antitrust: Conflicting Laws and Separating Powers' (1987) 25 *Columbia Journal of Transnational Law* 403. See also F. Achebe, 'The Act of State Doctrine and Foreign Sovereign Immunities Act of 1976: Can They Coexist?' (1989) 13 *Maryland Journal of International Law* 247, 300.

[7] See J. Davidow, 'Cartels, Competition Law and the Regulation of International Trade' (1983) 15 *New York University Journal of International Law & Politics* 351.

[8] See, for example, discussion in W. Ehrlich & P. Sharma, 'Competition Policy Convergence: The Case of Export Cartels', Policy Staff Paper No. 94/03, Canadian Department of Foreign Affairs and International Trade, April 1994.

most trading nations, including the US, Japan and the European Union, and assume a number of different guises.[9]

Export cartel policies are usually intended by governments to encourage export cartels involving domestic producers from that nation where the cartel is directed exclusively at supply into foreign markets. Such export cartels are perceived as enabling domestic firms to realise productive efficiencies from economies of scale, including by pooling resources and spreading risks, thereby assisting small and medium-sized firms to engage in export trade. Export cartels may also be encouraged to offset the market power of overseas purchasers, particularly where these purchasers have themselves formed import cartels.

- *Why are export cartel policies detrimental to international competition?* There are three main criticisms of export cartels which illustrate their adverse effect on international trade and competition. In addition, many of the criticisms of import cartels set out in Chapter 7 of this book apply equally to export cartels:
  - Export cartels enable producers in the exporting nation to profit at the expense of consumers in importing nations, resulting in welfare transfers to the exporting nation (and an associated deadweight loss) in the manner identified in Chapter 3 of this book.
  - Export cartels undermine effective competition policy. Collusion within an export cartel may spill over into the domestic market, particularly if any exemption from national competition laws is framed too broadly.[10]
  - Export cartels may generate significant trade friction and may trigger retaliatory action from trading partners. Such retaliatory action may include, for example, reciprocal import cartels or even the extraterritorial application of domestic competition laws.

Importantly, retaliatory action against export cartels may, in turn, trigger jurisdictional and political conflict (i.e. 'system frictions' as defined in Chapter 2 of this book).

- *Example* The *Daishowa* case involved a group of US wood pulp exporters who had formed an US export cartel, as permitted by

[9] In the US, for example, export cartels are exempted from the antitrust laws under the Webb-Pomerene Act 1918, and Title III of the Export Trading Company Act 1982. The intent of the laws was partly to permit small domestic firms to penetrate foreign markets more effectively and to secure economies of scale through co-ordinated marketing, and partly to alter the terms of trade and enhance payments balances by allowing domestic producers to exploit whatever power over export prices they might collectively possess.
[10] See A. Dick, 'The Competitive Consequence of Japan's Export Cartel Associations' (1992) *Journal of Japanese and International Economies* 275.

exemptions from US domestic antitrust laws.[11] In retaliation, a group of Japanese wood pulp importers formed an import cartel in Japan to boycott US wood pulp production. Simultaneously, the Japanese wood pulp importers challenged the validity of the US export cartel under US antitrust laws, alleging price fixing and a refusal to supply.

The US exporters counter-sued the Japanese importers via the extraterritorial application of US antitrust law to the import cartel in Japan. A US federal district court in San Francisco held that under US domestic law, the US export cartel was exempted from US antitrust law, but the Japanese import cartel was not. The court awarded damages to the US exporters. This judgment was perceived as highly unfair by the Japanese and triggered a diplomatic incident.[12]

- *Why aren't export cartel policies subject to effective regulation under the WTO?* Given such criticisms, the question arises why export cartel policies are permitted by the WTO. There are two related reasons:
  - First, the principal emphasis of the WTO is on non-discriminatory market access by *imports* (with WTO obligations tending to target government measures which discriminate between imports, or which impede entry of imports into domestic markets). As a result, the provisions of the WTO which regulate *exports* are not as extensive and not all aspects of export cartel conduct that impede international trade are addressed by the WTO.
  - Secondly, there are difficulties in applying those WTO provisions that do regulate exports; relevantly Article XI:1 of the GATT which prohibits quantitative restrictions on exports. Article XI:1 of the GATT provides:

    > No prohibition or *other restrictions other than duties, taxes or other charges*, whether made effective through quotas, import or export licenses or other measures, shall be instituted or maintained by any contracting party on the importation of any product of any other contracting party or *on the exportation or sale for export of any product destined for the territory of any other contracting party*. [emphasis added]

---

[11] *Daishowa International* v. *North Coast Export Co* 1982–3 Trade Reg Rep (CCH) 64,774, at 71,785 (ND Cal, 1982).

[12] See discussion in A. Fels, 'Trade and Competition in the Asia Pacific Region', Speech by the Chairman of the Australian Trade Practices Commission, Adelaide, 28 September 1995.

In the *Canadian Salmon* cases, a WTO Panel reasoned that Article XI:1 applies to export restrictions as broadly as it applies to import restrictions, so all governmental measures which impose quantitative restrictions on exports are regulated, including both internal and border measures.[13] However, the relevant trade instrument that gives effect to export cartels is typically legislation which exempts export cartels from domestic competition laws.

In this manner, the government's role is permissive rather than proactive, and any restriction imposed on exports by colluding firms arguably occurs at their own behest, although it would be possible to construct an argument using the reasoning identified in Chapter 7 if the government's role were greater. Furthermore, to the extent that export cartel conduct does not involve quantitative restrictions, such as price fixing activities, it will usually fall outside the potential ambit of Article XI:1.

- *Why isn't anti-competitive conduct facilitated by export cartel policies subject to effective regulation under domestic competition laws?* Without an exemption from domestic competition laws, export cartels would typically violate fundamental anti-cartel obligations. An exemption from domestic competition laws for export cartels is therefore common and is usually based on public policy considerations, in which the perceived increased trade and productive efficiency benefits to the domestic economy of permitting export cartels are considered to outweigh any domestic anti-competitive detriments and efficiency losses.[14]

  However, a clear difficulty with such exemptions is that they usually consider only domestic effects and do not consider spillover effects upon foreign markets or wider detrimental effects on international competition, as identified in Chapter 3 of this book.
  - *Example* Export cartels were an important instrument of Japanese industrial policy during the 1950s to 1980s.[15] In Japan, certain export cartels are exempted from the Japanese Antimonopoly Law by the Japanese Export and Import Transaction Law, provided that they are notified to the government and do not use or encourage 'unfair

---

[13] See *Canada – Measures Affecting Exports of Unprocessed Herring and Salmon*, Report of the Panel adopted on 22 March 1988 (BISD L/6268 – 35S/98). See also *In the Matter of Canada's Landing Requirement for Pacific Coast Salmon and Herring*, Final Report of the Panel, 16 October 1989, 17.

[14] See D. A. Larson, 'An Economic Analysis of the Webb-Pomerene Act' (1970) 6 *Journal of International Law & Economics* 497.

[15] See G. R. Saxonhouse, 'What Does Japanese Trade Structure Tell Us About Japanese Trade Policy?' (1993) 7(3) *Journal of Economic Perspectives* 21.

business practices'.[16] However, Japanese export cartels have typically had adverse effects on foreign markets, leading to trade tensions between Japan and the US in the 1980s and 1990s. Following pressure from the US in the late 1990s, Japan abolished most of its key export cartels, although a number still remain.[17]

In summary, export cartel policies are not subject to effective WTO regulation as they generally remain consistent with WTO principles. Anticompetitive conduct flowing from export cartel policies escapes regulation under domestic competition laws principally due to express exemptions from domestic competition laws. As export cartel policies have potentially significant adverse effects on international competition, under-regulation thus exists which could be addressed by an international competition agreement.

While an international competition agreement could adopt a number of mechanisms to regulate export cartels, there are two mechanisms that are worthy of serious consideration:

- First, export cartels may be beneficial to nations in certain circumstances, particularly as they may assist the development of export industries. Ideally, any international competition agreement should continue to enable the exemption of export cartels from domestic competition laws by way of an authorisation procedure. However, this authorisation procedure should require governments to consider the wider spillover effects of export cartels on international competition and foreign markets as well as any net welfare detriments to the home market. Where an export cartel has net adverse international anti-competitive effects, authorisation should not be granted.
- Secondly, any international competition agreement should require that exemptions from domestic competition laws should remain strictly limited in scope. Similarly, authorised export cartels should be subject to ongoing monitoring. In this manner authorised export cartels would be given heavily qualified, rather than unqualified, immunity from domestic competition laws. Authorisations should be revoked if net adverse effects on international competition result.

---

[16] The Japanese government retains a power to regulate prices and output and to disband the cartel if it no longer serves the national interest. See Export and Import Transaction Act of Japan, Law No. 299 of 1952.
[17] See World Trade Organisation, *Trade Policy Review: Japan*, WTO Trade Policy Review, 16 November 2000.

8.2.2 Trade-oriented industrial policies

Trade-oriented industrial policies may be inconsistent with WTO principles, but escape WTO regulation as they may be designed in a manner that exploits exemptions from, ambiguities in, and ineffective enforcement of, WTO obligations.[18] Anti-competitive conduct flowing from such policies may escape regulation under domestic competition laws due to express exemptions for public policy reasons. Alternatively, anti-competitive conduct may be immune from prosecution due to the high level of government involvement and the application of 'act of state' and 'government compulsion' defences.[19]

- *What are trade-oriented industrial policies and how do they operate?* Industrial policies generally involve government intervention in markets with the aim of altering industry structures so as to increase the productivity of particular industries (usually selected manufacturing industries) to stimulate economic growth and development.[20] Industrial policies may also have a range of other policy objectives, including the promotion of research and development, the nurturing of small enterprises, the revitalisation of structurally depressed industries, assisting regional development, countering foreign protectionism, and promoting export trade.[21]

  While some industrial policies are more interventionist than others, they each typically involve attempts by government to correct perceived market failures, usually by channelling additional resources into selected industries.
  - *Example* 'Import substitution policies' typically seek to assist domestic industry to become internationally competitive by erecting trade barriers to protect 'infant industry' against foreign competition until such time as it can survive such competition. Import

---

[18] See S. Laird, 'WTO Rules and Good Practice on Export Policy', World Trade Organisation, Staff Working Paper, TPRD9701, 1997.
[19] See H. C. Pitney, 'Sovereign Compulsion and International Antitrust: Conflicting Laws and Separating Powers' (1987) 25 *Columbia Journal of Transnational Law* 403.
[20] The World Bank has defined industrial policy as 'government efforts to alter industrial structure to promote productivity based growth'. See World Bank, *The East Asian Miracle: Economic Growth & Public Policy – A World Bank Policy Research Report* (OUP, New York 1993), p. 293.
[21] See J. Pinder, T. Hosomi & W. Diebold, *Industrial Policy and the International Economy: The Triangle Papers #19* (The Trilateral Commission, New York, 1979), p. 62.

substitution policies are inherently protectionistic and have remained controversial in economic theory.[22]

- *Example* 'Export promotion policies' adopt the converse approach and seek to increase exports, rather than restrict imports. The successful industrial policies implemented by Japan, Korea and Taiwan in the period 1950 to 1990 each involved a significant element of export promotion, utilising government financial assistance and special regulatory concessions.[23] These policies may also involve state-mandated mergers of exporting firms to increase industry concentration and realise economies of scope and scale.

- *Why are trade-oriented industrial policies detrimental to international competition?* While some modern industrial policies are consistent with competition policy, many industrial policies have historically had adverse effects on international trade and competition. Industrial policies have often permitted collusive arrangements in domestic markets and enabled exporters to increase their market power, sometimes via the formation of export cartels. Industrial policies have frequently proved inherently discriminatory as they have sought to provide certain domestic firms with preferential treatment relative to foreign firms.[24]

  - *Example* Industrial policies in Korea enabled the formation of the *chaebol* by increasing domestic market concentration and reducing import competition, thereby engineering the development of highly concentrated industries and domestic enterprises with substantial market power.[25]

- *Why aren't trade-oriented industrial policies subject to effective regulation under the WTO?* The WTO does not intend to prohibit nations from engaging in industrial policies. Rather, the WTO seeks to guide nations away from adopting industrial policies that involve trade restrictive

---

[22] See A. O. Krueger, 'Import Substitution Versus Export Promotion' [1985] *Finance & Development* 20. See also R. E. Baldwin, 'The Case Against Infant Industry Protection' (1969) 77 *Journal of Political Economy* 295. See H. J. Bruton, 'A Reconsideration of Import Substitution' (1998) 36 *Journal of Economic Literature* 903.

[23] See Y. Kawai, 'Competition Policy and Industrial Policy in Japan' in C. J. Cheng, L. Liu & C. K. Wang (eds.), *International Harmonisation of Competition Laws* (Martinus Nijihoff, Dordrecht, 1995), p. 47. See also K. Sakoh, 'Japanese Industrial Success: Industrial Policy or Free Market?' (1984) 3(2) *Cato Journal* 521.

[24] See A. N. Campbell & W. Rowley, *Industrial Policy, Efficiencies and the Public Interest – The Prospects for Harmonisation of International Merger Rules* (McMillan Binch, Toronto, 1993).

[25] See G. R. Ungson, *The Chaebol: Korea's New Industrial Might* (OUP, New York, 1989).

instruments inconsistent with the WTO.[26] A number of WTO provisions may therefore apply to the extent industrial policies affect export or import trade.

Industrial policies have been successfully challenged in the WTO on this basis.

- *Example* In 1998 the European Community, Japan and the US successfully challenged an Indonesian industrial policy that promoted the Indonesian car manufacturing industry.[27] In that case, a WTO Panel held that Indonesia had violated several WTO obligations, including the fundamental GATT most favoured nation and national treatment non-discrimination obligations, and restrictions on subsidies set out in the WTO Agreement on Subsidies and Countervailing Measures.

    As WTO obligations have strengthened over time, so the instruments of industrial policy have altered, resulting in a clear trend away from the use of tariffs and other regulated trade instruments. More novel instruments used by industrial policies now include financial and investment incentives, export processing zones, anti-dumping actions, safeguard measures, local content policies, non-actionable subsidies, and instruments consistent with WTO balance of payments exemptions.[28]

- *Why isn't anti-competitive conduct facilitated by trade-oriented industrial policies subject to effective regulation under domestic competition laws?* Anti-competitive conduct may be tolerated by a nation as a 'necessary evil' and may even be encouraged in some circumstances. For example, certain industries may be permitted to merge to increase market concentration, notwithstanding significant adverse effects on domestic and international competition. Exemptions for anti-competitive conduct from domestic competition laws are a common feature of industrial policies, often to increase domestic market concentration deliberately, although the exact nature of the exemption varies widely.[29]

---

[26] See P. J. Lloyd, B. Bora & M. Pangetsu, 'Industrial Policy and the WTO', UNCTAD/ITCD/TAB/7, Policy Issues in International Trade and Commodities: Study Series No. 6, UNCTAD, Geneva, 2000.

[27] See *Indonesia – Certain Measures Affecting the Automobile Industry*, Report of the WTO Panel adopted on 7 December 1998, WT/DS54/15, WT/DS55/14, WT/DS59/13, WT/DS64/12.

[28] See discussion in B. Bora, P. J. Lloyd & M. Pangetsu, 'Industrial Policy and the WTO', Paper prepared for the WTO/World Bank Conference on Developing Countries in a Millennium Round, Geneva, 13 September 1999.

[29] See M. Itoh, *Economic Analysis of Industrial Policy* (Academic Press, New York, 1991).

In summary, trade-oriented industrial policies can be formulated to avoid breaching WTO obligations, including by taking advantage of exemptions and ambiguities. Anti-competitive practices facilitated by industrial policies often escape regulation due to exemptions from domestic competition laws. However, as trade-oriented industrial policies have potentially significant adverse effects on international competition, under-regulation may exist which could be addressed by an international competition agreement.

Many industrial policies have valid objectives and may be vitally important to national economic development. However, where industrial policies are adopted they should be formulated in a manner consistent with greater international competition.[30] The formulation of guidelines that restricted or discouraged the use of certain industrial policies considered particularly harmful to international competition would assist in this regard. Such guidelines could be incorporated within an international competition agreement and could include requirements such as the following:

- Industrial policies should be intended to correct market failures and supplement market mechanisms in a manner consistent with the promotion of greater competition.[31]
- Governments should refrain from encouraging anti-competitive market structures and should not promote measures with an adverse impact on international competition.
- Foreign enterprises should be permitted to participate where possible or feasible (including, for example, in research and development ventures) to avoid discrimination between domestic and foreign firms.
- Where industrial policies are introduced to address short-term effects, the policies themselves should be temporary in nature and phased out within a defined time frame.

These guidelines suggest there would be a role for an international competition agreement to promote principles of international competition *policy*, as attempted in the context of APEC (as discussed in Chapter 4 of this book).

---

[30] See H. J. Chang, *The Political Economy of Industrial Policy* (St. Martins Press, New York, 1994).

[31] This necessarily raises the issue as to how any 'market failure' would be defined given the different schools of thought on the concept of 'market failure' as discussed in Chapter 2 of this book.

8.3 International Measures

The two most notable examples of International Measures are:

(a) voluntary export restraints ('VERs'); and
(b) voluntary import expansions ('VIEs').

Both are considered in detail below.

8.3.1 Voluntary export restraints (VERs)

VERs have historically escaped regulation under the WTO due to insufficient incentives for any nations to take enforcement action. Anti-competitive conduct flowing from VERs has typically escaped regulation under domestic competition laws due to express exemptions from domestic competition laws for public policy reasons. Alternatively, such anti-competitive conduct may be immune from prosecution due to the high level of government involvement and the application of the 'act of state' and 'government compulsion' defences.[32]

- *What are VERs and how do they operate?* A VER is a restriction imposed by an exporting firm, at the request of the importing country, on the quantity of goods that are exported into the importing country during a specified period of time, as illustrated by Figure 35.[33] VERs result from ad hoc agreements negotiated bilaterally between governments, or between government and foreign industry, or both. VERs have an effect similar to a protectionistic quantitative restriction as VERs protect domestic production in the importing nation against foreign competition from the exporting nation.[34]

A critical feature of VERs is that they are characterised by both parties as 'voluntary'. However, the word 'voluntary' is misleading as VERs are generally agreed by firms in weaker exporting nations under threat of trade or economic sanctions from powerful importing nations.[35]

---
[32] See, for example, *WS Kirkpatrick & Co* v. *Environmental Tectonics Corp* 493 US 400, 110 S Ct 701, 107 L Ed 2d 816 (1990) in which the US Supreme Court affirmed the act of state defence in the US.
[33] Orderly marketing arrangements are frequently a variant of the VER and constitute a formal bilateral VER, which is enforceable under US domestic law by way of automatic trade sanctions.
[34] See M. Itoh & S. Nagaoka, 'VERS, VIEs and Global Competition' in E. M. Graham & J. D. Richardson (eds.), *Global Competition Policy* (Institute for International Economics, Washington DC, 1997), ch. 15, p. 475.
[35] See H. G. Preusse, 'Voluntary Export Restraints – An Effective Means Against a Spread of Neo-Protectionism?' (1993) 27(1) *Journal of World Trade* 5.

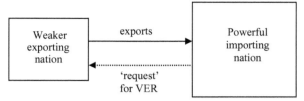

Figure 35: *Application of a VER*
NOTES: Exports entering the powerful importing nation may harm domestic industry in that nation, leading it to 'request' (i.e., coerce) firms in the weaker exporting nation to agree a VER which restricts exports.

Typically, a VER arises only because of such coercion, so it can only be characterised as 'voluntary' in the sense that the exporting country prefers it relative to the alternative of trade sanctions. Similarly, VERs may be agreed by the exporting nation to avert alternative, more damaging, trade barriers that are threatened by the importing nation.

VERs have been used since the 1930s, largely by the US government, in a protectionistic attempt to reduce the quantity of particular imports.[36] As VERs avoided GATT scrutiny until relatively recently, their appeal increased as GATT obligations were strengthened, particularly during the 1980s.[37] Under the Reagan administration in the 1980s, for example, the US deployed VERs most frequently against Japan and South Korea in relation to a number of products, including textiles, footwear, steel, machine tools and automobiles.[38]

- *Why are VERs detrimental to international competition?* VERs may have considerable adverse effects on international trade and competition. VERs tend to distort the operation of international markets, limit and restrict competition by their selective nature, result in discrimination between exporters and encourage the cartelisation of export trade. VERs lessen competitive pressures on domestic producers and may encourage abuses of market power in already concentrated foreign

---

[36] US President Lyndon B. Johnson was the first to implement a VER programme. This programme was implemented in response to increased foreign steel imports into the US.
[37] See K. C. Kennedy, 'Voluntary Restraint Agreements: A Threat to Representative Democracy' (1987) 11 *Hastings International & Comparative Law Review* 1. See also E. C. Emerson, 'Voluntary Restraint Agreements and Democratic Decision-Making' (1991) 31 *Virginia Journal of International Law* 281.
[38] According to the GATT secretariat, 12.5% of Japanese exports were subject to VERs in 1989.

markets, enabling both domestic and foreign producers to raise prices jointly at the expense of consumers in the domestic nation.[39] VERs also lead exporting firms to seek to circumvent the VER by increasing quality, so as to raise prices, while domestic firms are encouraged to over-invest to substitute domestic products for foreign products.

The inefficiencies, distortions and welfare losses associated with VERs are illustrated both by the steel VERs of 1984–1989 and the Japanese car VER of 1981–1992:

- *Example – steel VERs*   The steel VERs were negotiated by the US with twenty-eight countries in 1984 to protect the US steel industry from foreign competition.[40] The steel VERs covered 80% of steel imported into the US, thereby constituting some of the broadest protection ever awarded to American industry.[41] However, the steel VERs enabled foreign producers to collude to increase prices at the expense of US steel consumers. Between January 1988 and March 1989, the VERs caused the price of steel within the US to escalate dramatically by over 20%, causing steep cost escalations for steel-dependent industries, reducing their competitiveness and causing unintended shutdowns, lay-offs and cancellations of export sales.[42]
- *Example – automobile VER*   The Japanese automobile VER was initially negotiated between US and Japanese manufacturers in 1981 following the second OPEC oil shock and a surge in US demand for small Japanese fuel-efficient cars. Under coercion from the US, Japanese manufacturers agreed to cap exports of passenger cars to the US under a VER which was renewed regularly until 1992.[43] This VER had several unintended effects including incentives for Japanese manufacturers to increase prices, emphasise luxury models, and assemble cars in the US, Taiwan and South Korea.

---

[39] See M. O. Moore & S. M. Suranovic, 'Optimal Choice Between VERs and Tariffs Under the GATT' (1993) 26(2) *Canadian Journal of Economics* 447.
[40] See, for example, discussion in G. C. Hufbauer & E. Wada, 'Steel Quotas: A Rigged Lottery', International Economics Policy Briefs No. 99–5, Institute for International Economics, Washington DC, June 1999.
[41] See, for example, C. P. Seebald, 'Life After Voluntary Restraint Agreements: The Future of the Steel Industry' (1992) 25 *George Washington Journal of International Law & Economics* 875.
[42] See T. Fillinger, 'The Anatomy of Protectionism: The Voluntary Restraint Agreements on Steel Imports' (1988) 35 *UCLA Law Review* 953.
[43] See M. W. Lochmann, 'The Japanese Voluntary Restraint on Automobile Exports: An Abandonment of the Free Trade Principles of the GATT and the Free Market Principles of the US Antitrust Law' (1996) 27 *Harvard International Law Journal* 99.

Over the period 1986–1990, the automobile VER caused the prices of Japanese cars sold in the US to increase by an average of 14%.[44] While US car manufacturers were able to sell more cars, increasing their profits by about US$4 billion per year (an increase of over 8%), US consumers suffered an estimated loss of US$25 billion.[45] The US economy also suffered net welfare losses totalling some US$8.5 billion. A Brookings Institution Report calculated an annual consumer cost of US$300,000 for each job preserved in US industry by the VER during that period.[46]

- *Why aren't VERs subject to effective regulation under the WTO?* The recognised harmful effect of VERs led the WTO members to reach agreement not to implement any new VERs and to phase out any existing VERs as part of the WTO Agreement on Safeguards concluded as part of the Uruguay Round negotiations in 1994 ('WTO Safeguards Agreement').[47] The WTO Safeguards Agreement in Article 11:1(b) requires WTO members 'not to seek, take or maintain any voluntary export restraints, orderly marketing arrangements or any other similar measures on the export or import side'.[48] VERs were required either to conform to the WTO Safeguards Agreement or be phased out by 1999.

The WTO Safeguards Agreement now restricts the use of VERs to emergency 'safeguard' actions. A WTO member may temporarily restrict imports of a product only if its domestic industry is seriously injured or threatened with serious injury caused by an surge in imports. Such safeguard action must occur only after completion of a public and transparent government investigation, which must follow clearly defined rules and procedures, including considering arguments whether the safeguard action is in the public interest. Any safeguard measure must not last more than four years and compensation must be given to

---

[44] See D. E. Dekieffer, 'Antitrust and the Japanese Auto Quotas' (1982) 8 *Brooklyn Journal International Law* 59; and (1991) 50 *Antitrust Law Journal* 417. See also A. Dixit, 'Optimal Trade and Industrial Policy for the U.S. Automobile Industry' in R. Feenstra (ed.), *Empirical Methods for Industrial Trade* (Cambridge, MIT Press, 1988).

[45] All figures have been inflation adjusted to 2006 dollars. See D. K. Benjamin, 'Voluntary Export Restraints on Automobiles' (1999) 17(4) *PERC Reports* 5.

[46] See R. W. Crandall, 'Import Quotas and the Automobile Industry: The Costs of Protectionism' [1984] 3 *The Brookings Review* 16.

[47] See Agreement on Safeguards, Annexe 1A: Multilateral Agreements on Trade in Goods of Final Act and Agreement Establishing the World Trade Organisation, General Agreement on Tariffs and Trade, Uruguay Round, Marrakesh, Morocco, 15 April 1994.

[48] *Ibid.*, Art. 11:1(b).

the nation subject to the safeguard measure (or else retaliatory action can be taken).

However, VERs have historically rarely been the subject of WTO enforcement action as few nations have had any incentive to take such action.[49] The importing nation receives protection for its domestic industry, while the exporting nation averts potential trade sanctions or barriers against its exporters.[50] The artificial restriction in supply caused by the VER may enable exporters to increase the price of goods sold into the importing nation, so the exporting nation is effectively bribed with 'tariff-equivalent' revenue.[51] Third party nations are rarely adversely affected by a VER so have little incentive to take enforcement action. In most cases, third party nations can sell into the importing nation at higher prices due to excess demand, while purchasing products from the exporting nation at lower prices due to excess supply.[52]

- *Why isn't anti-competitive conduct facilities by VERs subject to effective regulation under domestic competition law?* The anti-competitive effects of VERs may escape regulation under domestic competition law. The government of the exporting nation, for example, may provide exemptions from domestic competition laws to enable its exporters to restrict exports to the importing nation via an export cartel. Exporting nations therefore face a dilemma between the benefits of resolving trade disputes with other nations via VERs, and the detriments of permitting domestic enterprises to engage in anti-competitive conduct.

Where a government has imposed a VER on domestic industry, firms implementing a VER have relied on the defence of government compulsion to defend against liability resulting from the extra-territorial application of the competition laws of other nations. This defence applies where a firm can show that it has been compelled by a domestic or foreign government to engage in anti-competitive activity.[53]

---

[49] VERs essentially constitute a bilateral agreement in which both nations receive a benefit, so neither nation is likely to take enforcement action.
[50] While consumers in the importing nation clearly suffer, typically VERs arise where the government gives greater weight to the concerns of domestic industry than the concerns of domestic consumers.
[51] See H. Schoegel, 'Trade and Competition Policy Aspects of VERs: A Comment' in E. U. Petersmann & M. Hilf (eds.), *The New GATT Round of Multilateral Negotiations: Legal and Economic Problems* (Kluwer Publications, Boston, 1991).
[52] See K. Jones, 'The Political Economy of Voluntary Export Restraint Agreements' (1984) 37(1) *Kyklos* 82.
[53] See E. M. Hizon, 'The Safeguard Measure/VER Dilemma: The Jekyll & Hyde of Trade Protection' (1994) 15 *Northwestern Journal of International Law & Business* 105.

- *Example* The Japanese government can direct Japanese exporters to restrict exports to certain nations.[54] To avoid potential US extraterritorial antitrust liability of Japanese car manufacturers to American consumers in relation to the automobile VER, the Japanese government allegedly administered the VER and mandated the division of market shares so that Japanese manufacturers could avail themselves of the government compulsion defence.[55]

In summary, VERs are not subject to effective WTO regulation as they have traditionally escaped WTO regulation due to a reluctance of WTO members to take enforcement action and for diplomatic and strategic reasons. Since 1994, VERs are permitted only under a limited WTO exemption for safeguard measures.[56] Anti-competitive conduct resulting from VERs has typically escaped regulation under domestic competition laws due to express government exemptions from domestic competition laws and due to the defence of government compulsion. However, as VERs have potentially significant adverse effects on international competition, this suggests under-regulation exists which could be addressed by an international competition agreement.

Given that VERs are now directly addressed by the WTO Safeguards Agreement, the need for an international competition agreement to regulate VERs is less pressing. However, an international competition agreement could require that safeguards introduced under the WTO Safeguards Agreement (including VIEs) should be implemented in a manner least restrictive to international competition.

Given that VERs are also frequently implemented by way of export cartels, the same considerations discussed previously in relation to export cartels also apply. Any international competition agreement could seek to reinforce existing WTO obligations while introducing guiding principles with a competition policy orientation.

8.3.2 Voluntary import expansions (VIEs)

As with VERs, VIEs have historically escaped regulation under the WTO due to insufficient incentives for any nations to take enforcement action.

---

[54] See Foreign Exchange and Foreign Trade Control Law and the Export and Imports Transactions Law. See also M. Matsushita, 'Export Control and Export Cartels in Japan' (1979) 20 *Harvard International Law Journal* 103.

[55] The involvement of the Japanese government would now be capable of challenge under the WTO.

[56] See Art. XIX of the GATT.

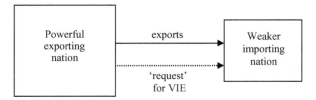

Figure 36: *Application of a VIE*
NOTES: The powerful exporting nation may consider that the weaker importing nation is preventing exports from entering its markets, leading the powerful exporting nation to 'request' (i.e. coerce) the weaker importing nation to agree a VIE which increases the market share of the exports from the powerful exporting nation.

However, even where nations have commenced enforcement action, deliberate ambiguity in the drafting of the WTO has tended to thwart successful enforcement.[57]

As with VERs, anti-competitive conduct flowing from VIEs has typically escaped regulation under domestic competition laws due to express exemptions from domestic competition laws for public policy reasons. Alternatively, such anti-competitive conduct may be immune from prosecution due to the high level of government involvement and the application of the 'act of state' and 'government compulsion' defences.[58]

- *What are VIEs and how do they operate?* VIEs are a novel and reverse form of VER, as illustrated by Figure 36. A VIE essentially comprises a pledge by a weaker importing nation (under threat of trade sanctions) to assist a powerful exporting nation's exporters to realise a defined market share, or defined volume, of the importing nation's domestic market.[59]

VIEs have, to date, been invoked where the exporters of a powerful exporting nation (again, usually the US) encounter barriers to entry

---

[57] See C. S. Kaufman, 'The US–Japan Semiconductor Agreement: Chipping Away at Free Trade' (1994) 12 *Pacific Basin Law Review* 307. See also K. Ohe, 'A Case Study of the US–Japan Semiconductor Agreement' (1989) 17 *Australian Business Law Review* 126.
[58] See, for example, *WS Kirkpatrick & Co v. Environmental Tectonics Corp* 493 US 400, 110 S Ct 701, 107 L Ed. 2d 816 (1990) in which the US Supreme Court affirmed the act of state defence in the US. See also the extensive discussion in E. M. Fox, 'Competition Law & the Agenda for the WTO: Forging the Links of Competition and Trade' (1995) 4(1) *Pacific Rim Law & Policy Journal* 1, 21.
[59] See C. MacDonagh-Dumler, 'Implementing Market Access through Threats of Administrative Relief: VIEs via ARMs', Brookings Institution Paper, 1996.

when exporting into a weaker importing nation.[60] In such circumstances, the powerful exporting nation may coerce the weaker importing nation to enter into a 'voluntary' agreement, known as a VIE, in which that weaker importing nation must purchase a certain volume of the exporting nation's products.[61]

Metaphorically, while VERs act as a protectionistic 'shield' to prevent competing imports entering the domestic market, VIEs operate as a 'sword' to allow domestic exports to penetrate closed foreign markets.

VIEs were first developed in the late 1980s by the US as a way of expanding US exports into Japanese markets. Under the assumption that Japan maintained barriers to trade that restricted the entry of US exports, Japan was coerced to increase its volume of imports on specified products including semiconductors, automobiles, auto parts, medical equipment and flat glass.[62] The intention was that VIEs would force a pattern of trade that more closely replicated the free trade level.

- *Example – semiconductor VIE* The Japan–US semiconductor VIE of 1986–1991 arose in the context of allegations by the US that Japanese manufacturers were dumping semiconductors in Japan and Asia to the detriment of US semiconductor exporters.[63] Japan was coerced by the US to enter into a 'Semiconductor Agreement', which comprised a VIE coupled with a VER. Under the VIE, Japanese firms 'voluntarily' agreed to purchase at least 20% of their domestic semiconductor requirements from the US.[64]
- *Example – auto parts VIE* In 1995, the US sought to compel the Japanese government to accept a VIE in cars and auto parts, leading to a major crisis in US–Japanese relations as discussed in Chapter 7 of this book.

---

[60] See T. M. Greaney, 'Import Now! An Analysis of Market-share Voluntary Import Expansions (VIEs)' (1996) 40 *Journal of International Economics* 149.

[61] See P. Krishna, 'On the Choice of Instrument: Voluntary Import Expansions (VIEs) vs Voluntary Export Restraints (VERs)', Working Paper 96–6, Brown University, Department of Economics.

[62] See S. Nakato, 'U.S. Trade Strategy Toward Japan Under the Clinton Administration: Implications of VIEs (Voluntary Import Expansions) and Numerical Targets' (1998) 8(2) *Ritsumeikan Journal of International Studies* 57.

[63] See D. A. Irwin, 'Trade Politics and the Semiconductor Industry' in A. O. Krueger (ed.), *The Political Economy of American Trade Policy* (Chicago University Press, Chicago, 1996), p. 11. See also L. Tyson, *Who's Bashing Whom?: Trade Conflict in High–Technology Industries* (Institute for International Economics, Washington DC, 1992).

[64] See K. Flamm, *Mismanaged Trade?: Strategic Policy and the Semiconductor Industry* (Brookings Institution, Washington DC, 1996), p. 49.

- *Why are VIEs detrimental to international competition?* While VIEs and VERs are different in application, VIEs and VERs both distort resource allocation and have significant detrimental effects:[65]
  - VIEs are inherently discriminatory and require domestic firms to prefer and purchase products from a particular nation, leading to an anti-competitive reallocation of market resources and potentially significant welfare losses.
  - As exporting firms have a guaranteed market share in the importing market, they have also little incentive to reduce prices and improve product quality, and they may even seek to raise prices to exploit their guaranteed market position.[66] Existing firms in the importing market are likely to behave less competitively towards the exporting firms given that these existing firms are required to comply with the VIE to ensure that the exporting firms achieve their mandated market share.
  - VIEs are also detrimental to international trade and competition given that they constitute a form of 'managed trade' in which the importing government must force firms in the importing nation to prefer certain imports. VIEs may require some form of government intervention to facilitate the successful penetration of imports from the exporting nation.[67]
  - VIEs may also require co-operation between firms in the importing market to ensure that they do not undercut the foreign imports, enabling the relevant market share to be achieved. The risks of inducing cartel behaviour are therefore significantly increased.

  Following a detailed analysis, the Institute of International Economics concluded in 1998 that VIEs are almost always harmful to international trade and competition.[68]
- *Why aren't VIEs subject to effective regulation under the WTO?* As with VERs, VIEs may breach WTO obligations, including GATT Articles I, XI, XIII and XIX to the extent there is sufficient government involvement. VIEs are also more likely to be challenged than VERs given that

---

[65] See J. Bhagwati, 'Quid Pro Quo DFI and VIEs: Political-Economy-Theoretic Analyses' (1987) 1 *International Economic Journal* 1.

[66] See D. A. Irwin, *Managed Trade: The Case Against Import Targets* (American Enterprise Institute, Washington DC, 1994).

[67] See L. D. Tyson, 'Managed and Mismanaged Trade: Policy Lessons for the 1990s' (Institute for International Economics, Washington DC, 1990).

[68] See M. Itoh & S. Nagoaka, 'VERS, VIEs and Global Competition' in E. M. Graham & J. D. Richardson (eds.), *Global Competition Policy* (Institute for International Economics, Washington DC, 1997), ch. 15, p. 475.

VIEs more clearly discriminate against third countries by giving particular nations more favourable domestic treatment.

However, even where VIEs have been challenged, ambiguities in WTO law and evidential issues have so far precluded effective enforcement action. The most notable challenge to VIEs to date involved a challenge by the European Community to the Semiconductor VIE, alleging that Japan had given the US preferential treatment.[69] However, that action was ultimately unsuccessful due to the ambiguity of WTO law in this area and a lack of causal evidence.

As with VERs, VIEs are subject to the WTO Safeguards Agreement's prohibition on voluntary export restraints, orderly marketing arrangements and 'any other similar measures on the export or import side'.[70] Accordingly, VIEs are now arguably outlawed by the WTO except in circumstances where they are used as 'safeguard measures', as discussed previously in relation to VERs.

- *Why isn't anti-competitive conduct facilitated by VIEs subject to effective regulation under domestic competition laws?* As with VERs, VIEs may involve collusion between domestic firms whereby the firms agree to purchase products from a particular nation even though those products may not necessarily provide the best value for money. VIEs may involve a quota agreed between firms to 'share the pain' of doing so. Express exemptions from domestic competition laws in the nation introducing the VIE are therefore common.

In summary, VIEs are not subject to effective WTO or domestic competition law regulation for the same reasons as VERs. As VIEs have potentially significant adverse effects on international competition, under-regulation again exists which could be addressed by an international competition agreement.

As with VERs, VIEs have now been directly addressed by the WTO Safeguards Agreement (as identified above) so the need for an international competition agreement to address VIEs, is less pressing. However, as with VERs, an international competition agreement could require that safeguards introduced under the WTO Safeguards Agreement should remain consistent with key competition principles and, if VIEs are used, they

---

[69] See *Japan–Trade in Semiconductors*, GATT Panel Report adopted June 1995, (1989) 35 BISD 155.
[70] Article 11.1(b), WTO Safeguards Agreement. See also Y. Lee, 'Critical Issues in the Application of the WTO Rules on Safeguards in the Light of the Recent Panel Reports and the Appellate Body Decisions' (2000) 34(2) *Journal of World Trade* 131.

should be designed in a way that reduces the potential for anti-competitive effects. Given that VIEs are frequently implemented by way of import cartels, the same considerations discussed previously in relation to import cartels also apply. For the purpose of an international competition agreement, VERs and VIEs could be treated similarly.

8.4 Governmental Commercial Activities

Governments may affect international competition not only by implementing trade measures (as discussed above), but also by directly engaging in commercial activities. The two most notable examples of Governmental Commercial Activities that may adversely affect international competition are:

(a) government procurement activities; and
(b) state trading enterprises.

Both are considered in detail below.

8.4.1 Government procurement

Government procurement activities are still subject to a number of WTO exemptions, although these exemptions were tightened significantly following the conclusion of the Uruguay Round in 1992. Anti-competitive conduct associated with government procurement activities frequently escapes regulation under domestic competition laws due to express exemptions from domestic competition laws for public policy reasons. Alternatively, such anti-competitive conduct may be immune from prosecution due to the high level of government involvement and the application of the 'act of state' defence.

- *What is government procurement and how does it operate?* Government procurement is the term used for the purchasing activities of governmental authorities by way of written contract for the supply of goods and the provision of services, including construction services, telecommunications equipment, ship building and consulting services. At present, national government expenditures of OECD member countries accounts for approximately 25% to 50% of their GDP. In most OECD nations, government procurement usually accounts for approximately 15% of GDP.

- *Why is government procurement detrimental to international competition?* As governments may have significant market power as purchasers in domestic or even international markets, they can use this market power to influence competition. Frequently, government procurement policies seek to use this market power to achieve domestic policy goals, including the promotion of local industrial sectors or business groups.[71] Government procurement policies can, for example, discriminate in favour of selected domestic industries by requiring that a specified percentage of purchases by government entities be made from certain domestic firms.

  Government procurement policies can also be designed to restrict international trade via a variety of other devices including, for example, purchasing prohibitions, preference margins, set-asides and offsets, and discriminatory tendering requirements. To the extent that government procurement policies impose conditions more favourable to domestic firms, they place foreign suppliers at an unfair disadvantage and thus operate as a hidden barrier to international trade.[72] Such favourable treatment provided by government to certain industries has a significant impact on international competition and may result in sizeable welfare losses on an international basis.[73]

- *Why isn't government procurement subject to effective regulation under the WTO?* Government procurement is specifically exempted from the GATT by Article III:8, and from the GATS by Article XIII:1, so key WTO obligations, such as the obligation of national treatment, do not apply.

  In recognition of the importance of government procurement, the GATT nations negotiated an agreement on government procurement during the Tokyo Round of GATT multilateral negotiations.[74] While the GATT agreement contained 'national treatment' obligations, it had important limitations, including a threshold value, and exemptions for

---

[71] See R. McAfee, R. Preston & J. McMillan, 'Government Procurement and International Trade' (1989) 26 *Journal of International Economics* 291.
[72] See F. Naegelen & M. Mougeot, 'Discriminatory Public Procurement Policy and Cost Reduction Incentives' (1998) 67 *Journal of Public Economics* 349.
[73] See 'Annual Report on Discrimination in Foreign Government Procurement', Office of the US Trade Representative, Washington DC, 30 April 1996.
[74] See Agreement on Government Procurement, concluded in Tokyo in 1979, entered into force in 1981, as amended in 1987, GATT Secretariat, Geneva, 1988.

national security, public order and safety.[75] The GATT agreement covered only a relatively small proportion of government procurement.

In an effort to address these issues, the WTO members negotiated a procurement agreement during the Uruguay Round negotiations which entered into force in 1996.[76] The WTO Procurement Agreement is significantly broader in scope than the GATT agreement and emphasises procedures for increasing transparency. However, the WTO Procurement Agreement is plurilateral in nature and currently binds only twenty-eight WTO members, so its impact remains limited.

- *Why isn't anti-competitive behaviour within the context of government procurement subject to effective regulation under domestic competition laws?* Government procurement activities may be subject to express exemptions from domestic competition laws in many nations. In this manner, arrangements which have a significant adverse effect on competition may escape regulation.

    Furthermore, given the direct involvement of government, the extraterritorial application of competition laws may also be thwarted by such defences as 'act of state' to the extent they are available in particular jurisdictions.

In summary, government procurement policies are not subject to effective WTO regulation due to the current incomplete coverage of WTO law. Anti-competitive conduct associated with government procurement policies has typically escaped regulation under domestic competition laws due to express exemptions. However, as government procurement activities have potentially significant adverse effects on international competition, under-regulation exists which could be addressed by an international competition agreement.

Ideally, any international competition agreement should encourage WTO members to become signatories of the existing WTO Procurement Agreement. In this manner, important limitations would be placed on the ability of governments to use government procurement policies to impede international competition. For non-signatories, any international

---

[75] See discussion in B. M. Hoekman & P. C. Mavroidis (eds.), *Law and Policy in Public Purchasing: The WTO Agreement on Government Procurement* (University of Michigan Press, Ann Arbor, 1997).

[76] See Agreement on Government Procurement, Annexe 4(b) of Annexe 4 (Plurilateral Trade Agreements), of Final Act and Agreement Establishing the World Trade Organisation, General Agreement on Tariffs and Trade, Uruguay Round, Marrakesh, Morocco, 15 April 1994.

competition agreement could set out key principles to ensure that government procurement activities were conducted in a manner least detrimental to international competition.[77] Ideally, domestic competition laws should be applied to government procurement activities.

8.4.2 State trading enterprises

State trading enterprises ('STEs') are arguably now effectively regulated by WTO law. Anti-competitive conduct associated with state trading enterprises frequently escapes regulation under domestic competition laws due to express exemptions from domestic competition laws for public policy reasons. Alternatively, such anti-competitive conduct may be immune from prosecution due to the high level of government involvement and the application of the 'act of state' defence.

- *What are state trading enterprises and how do they operate?* STEs are generally enterprises that are authorised to engage in trade and are owned, sanctioned or otherwise supported by government.[78] The nature of such authorisation is typically statutory or constitutional and grants STEs special rights or privileges which they can use to influence the purchase, sale or distribution of selected imports or exports.[79]

  STEs typically act as sole agents for production, imports and exports in particular sectors of the economy and are often supported by production levies, export or import licensing, or direct government funding.[80] In many nations, STEs have a considerable influence over trade in primary products.[81]

---

[77] See, for example, S. Arrowsmith, 'Towards A Multilateral Agreement on Transparency in Government Procurement' (1998) 47 *International Comparative Law Quarterly* 793.

[78] See World Trade Organisation, 'Operations of State Trading Enterprises as they Relate to International Trade', Background Paper by the WTO Secretariat, World Trade G/STR/2, 26 October 1995.

[79] See V. L. Sorenson, 'The Economic and Institutional Dimensions of State Trading' in *State Trading in International Dimensions and Select Cases* (International Policy Council on Agriculture and Trade, Washington, 1991).

[80] See K. Ackerman, P. Dixit & M. Simone, 'STEs: Their Role in World Markets' [1997] *Agricultural Outlook*, ERS, USDA, 11–17.

[81] See M. M. Kostecki, 'State Trading in Agricultural Products by the Advanced Countries' in M. M. Kostecki (ed.), *State Trading in International Markets* (London, The Macmillan Press, 1982), p. 308.

- *Examples* STEs include marketing boards, fiscal monopolies, producer boards, nationalised industries and central desk selling arrangements.[82]
- *Why are state trading enterprises detrimental to international competition?* STEs can have a significant impact on international trade and competition, particularly where an STE possesses a monopoly on certain imports or exports.[83] Anti-competitive effects may arise in markets where exclusive rights or privileges are exercised as well as associated upstream or downstream markets.[84]

The domestic market power conferred by the government on a monopoly can, for example, create an unfair advantage when it enters into trade agreements with suppliers of services operating in competitive markets by enabling it to leverage its market power across markets.[85] These anti-competitive effects are exacerbated in the limited circumstances where an STE has market power in international markets.

STEs also provide opportunities for governments to create disguised import tariffs or hidden import quotas (as illustrated by the *Korean Beef* case).[86] STEs also provide opportunities for governments to provide disguised export subsidies (as illustrated by the *Canadian Dairy* case).[87] Indeed, STEs frequently benefit from competitive advantages resulting from various forms of government support. Issues typically arise in the equality of treatment accorded to STEs and private enterprises.[88]

---

[82] See World Trade Organisation, 'Illustrative List of the Relationships Between Governments and State Trading Enterprises and the Kinds of Activities Engaged in by these Enterprises', Discussion Paper by the WTO Working Party on State Trading Enterprises, G/STR/4, 30 July 1999.

[83] See, for example, US General Accounting Office, 'Report to Congressional Requesters: Canada, Australia and New Zealand, Potential Ability of Agricultural STEs to Distort Trade', GAO/NSIAD-96-94, June 1996.

[84] See H. Matejka, 'Trade Policy Instruments, State Trading and First-Best Intervention' in M. M. Kostecki (ed.), *State Trading in International Markets* – The Macmillan Press, London, 1982), p. 161.

[85] See H. A. Love & E. Murningtyas, 'Measuring the Degree of Market Power Exerted by Government Trade Agencies' (1992) 74 *American Journal of Agricultural Economics* 546.

[86] See *Korea – Measures Affecting Imports of Fresh, Chilled and Frozen Beef*, WTO Panel Report, WT/DS161/R, 10 January 2001.

[87] See *Canada – Measures Affecting the Importation of Milk and the Exportation of Dairy Products*, WTO Panel Report, WT/DS103/RW, 11 July 2001.

[88] A government, as shareholder and/or financier of an STE, and possessing a dual role as market regulator and market participant, may give the STE certain financial or regulatory advantages to improve its competitive position. See P. J. Lloyd, 'State Trading and the Theory of International Trade' in M. M. Kostecki (ed.), *State Trading in International Markets* (The Macmillan Press, London, 1982), pp. 107–14.

- *Why aren't state trading enterprises subject to effective regulation under the WTO?* Given governmental involvement, WTO obligations apply directly to the anti-competitive conduct of STEs, as illustrated by the *Korean Beef* case and the *Canadian Dairy* case. STEs are generally subject to WTO disciplines, notably via GATT Article XVII. Article XVII establishes a number of guidelines and requirements with respect to the activities of STEs and the obligations of WTO members, including that:
  - STEs must act in a manner consistent with the principles of non-discriminatory treatment.
  - STEs must make any purchases or sales in accordance with commercial considerations and must allow enterprises from other WTO members the opportunity to compete.
  - WTO members must provide certain information to the WTO secretariat about STE activities, subject to commercial confidentiality and the public interest, to ensure greater transparency in the operation of STEs.

Problems with interpreting Article XVII and chronic non-compliance with the reporting requirements of Article XVII, led to the agreement of an Understanding on the Interpretation of Article XVII of the GATT 1994 during the Uruguay Round.[89] The Article XVII Understanding addresses procedural weaknesses in Article XVII by improving the process for obtaining and reviewing information, and it gives WTO members the opportunity to question information provided by other WTO members and to raise any issues before the WTO Council on Trade in Goods. The Article XVII Understanding also established a WTO working party on STEs, which has reviewed and commented on the accuracy of STE notifications.

Arguably, STEs are now effectively regulated under the WTO.

- *Why aren't state trading enterprises subject to effective regulation under domestic competition laws?* Domestic competition laws often provide express exemptions for STEs, particularly where they hold state-mandated monopolies in particular industries, although a number of countries have been progressively phasing out such exemptions.[90]

---

[89] See Understanding on the Interpretation of Article XVII of the General Agreement on Tariffs and Trade, Annexe 1A: Multilateral Agreements on Trade in Goods of Final Act and Agreement Establishing the World Trade Organisation, General Agreement on Tariffs and Trade, Uruguay Round, Marrakesh, Morocco, 15 April 1994, MTN/FA II-AIA-1(b).

[90] See W. D. Dobson, 'The New Zealand Dairy Board: Will the Boards Exporting Privilege Survive?' [1998] 1 *Choices* 8.

Again, the extra-territorial application of competition laws is usually prevented by the defence of 'state action'.

In summary, WTO regulation has improved in recent years to the extent that it may be argued that no further regulation is necessary. Anti-competitive conduct associated with STEs has typically escaped regulation under domestic competition laws due to express government exemptions from domestic competition laws. However, as STE activities have potentially significant adverse effects on international competition (particularly if they have international market power), under-regulation exists which could be addressed by an international competition agreement.

While the Article XVII Understanding has significantly improved the application of the WTO to STEs, there is still room for further improvement. An international competition agreement could, for example, promote competitive neutrality in the treatment of STEs by government. An international competition agreement could also seek greater transparency relating to the government's role in commercial activity to ensure greater accountability. Ideally, domestic competition laws should apply equally to private and public sector enterprises.

8.5 Conclusion: competition regulation of trade measures would promote competition

In conclusion, there are a number of loopholes that arise in the international regulatory matrix due to the failure of international trade law and domestic competition law to regulate particular governmental trade measures that cause anti-competitive conduct. Again, such loopholes could be addressed by an international competition agreement with a view to promoting greater market contestability.

The analysis in this chapter indicates that there are a number of issues which may prevent international trade law from effectively regulating governmental trade measures that, in turn, facilitate anti-competitive conduct (or are themselves anti-competitive):

- *Incomplete coverage* While the WTO seeks to regulate international trade comprehensively, the coverage of the WTO is not complete (e.g. the WTO Procurement Agreement is only plurilateral in nature).
- *No inconsistency* To the extent that any governmental trade measure remains consistent with WTO obligations it will be permitted by the WTO, even if it facilitates anti-competitive conduct (e.g. export cartel policies).

- *No breach* While certain governmental trade measures may appear inconsistent with fundamental WTO *principles*, they may not breach actual WTO *obligations* (e.g. certain trade-oriented industrial policies).
- *No enforcement* Certain governmental trade measures may breach WTO obligations but may escape effective enforcement for a number of other reasons (e.g. VERs and VIEs).

Relevantly, the failure of international trade law to address certain trade measures partly arises due to WTO's emphasis on trade rather than competition, hence an international competition agreement could assist by adding a competition dimension into the WTO. Such an approach would assist in correcting the 'under-regulation' identified in this chapter.

Again, in the absence of regulation of governmental trade measures by WTO law, the only remaining potential form of regulation is domestic competition law. However, domestic competition laws frequently fail to address anti-competitive conduct arising in the context of governmental trade measures due to governmental involvement and associated exemptions or defences. This is clearly illustrated by the analysis of Domestic Conduct, International Conduct and Governmental Commercial Activities set out in this chapter.

Given these issues, a number of recommendations can be made for the content of any international competition agreement in addition to the recommendations set out in Chapter 7. In particular, an international competition agreement should:

- seek to restrict the use of trade measures to circumstances consistent with greater international competition;
- include a set of competition policy principles to encourage domestic trade measures to be formulated in a manner least detrimental to international competition and in a manner not conducive to anti-competitive conduct;
- encourage those nations that do introduce domestic trade measures that have adverse effects on international competition to justify such measures and to ensure that such measures are short-term in nature and no more detrimental to international competition than necessary to achieve their intended result;
- reinforce the broad range of existing WTO obligations that promote principles of non-discrimination and competitive neutrality, including more recent WTO agreements such as the WTO Safeguards Agreement, the WTO Procurement Agreement and the Article XVII Understanding;

- ensure that domestic competition laws apply on a non-discriminatory basis both between domestic and foreign firms and between public and private sector conduct;
- encourage nations to consider the spillover effects of domestic policies on international competition and to restrict exemptions from domestic competition laws to circumstances in which any impact on international competition is minimised; and
- ensure that exemptions from domestic competition laws are limited in nature and subject to continued monitoring.

These recommendations are considered in greater detail in Chapter 14 of this book. As with Chapter 7, they would promote market contestability and thereby give practical effect to the theoretical basis for reconciling international trade law and international competition law identified in Chapter 6 of this book. These recommendations would address the types of 'under-regulation' identified in this chapter. In this manner, these recommendations would ensure that the substantive content and enforcement of international trade laws remained broadly consistent with the optimal regulation of international competition.

9

Should competition principles be introduced into anti-dumping law?

Anti-dumping laws are an issue at the forefront of any consideration of incorporation of competition laws into the WTO. This is because anti-dumping laws are the most obvious example of governmental trade measures that are permitted by WTO law, but that have significant potential adverse effects on international competition. In this manner, there is a potential *direct conflict* between existing international trade law and any international competition agreement. A chapter of this book has therefore been devoted to an analysis of anti-dumping laws, illustrating the benefits of amending the WTO anti-dumping provisions to incorporate a competition law approach.

In particular, Chapter 9 considers whether anti-dumping laws could be replaced or supplemented by competition laws in certain circumstances to mitigate the adverse effects of anti-dumping laws on international competition. Chapter 9 has two principal sections:

- Section 9.1 considers the evolution of anti-dumping law and analyses its objectives in terms of economic efficiency and distributional equity. Section 9.1 identifies a number of procedural criticisms of anti-dumping law and recognises that in certain circumstances anti-dumping measures may reduce competition.
- Section 9.2 considers international competition law as an alternative to anti-dumping law. In particular, Section 9.2 considers the replacement of anti-dumping law with competition law between Australia and New Zealand. Section 9.2 considers whether competition principles should be introduced into the Anti-dumping Agreement to ensure that anti-dumping measures do not adversely affect international competition.

Chapter 9 concludes that while there are clear advantages in replacing anti-dumping law with competition law, the pre-conditions for doing so are significant. However, material benefits could be realised by the progressive introduction of competition principles into anti-dumping law to discourage the application of anti-dumping measures where they are inconsistent with market contestability and greater international competition.

9.1 The basis and purpose of modern anti-dumping law

Dumping traditionally refers to the sale of a good in an export market at a price lower than the same good is sold in the domestic market by the exporting firm. Anti-dumping law addresses dumping and has been controversial in international trade. Recent critics of anti-dumping law have proposed that competition law should now replace anti-dumping law at the international level.[1] The question arises, is such replacement worthy of serious consideration?

9.1.1 The origins of anti-dumping law and its inclusion within the world trading system

As is well known, the earliest anti-dumping laws date from the turn of the century, with Canada enacting the first anti-dumping law in 1904.[2] New Zealand and Australia quickly followed, enacting their own anti-dumping laws in 1905 and 1906, respectively. All three nations enacted anti-dumping laws principally to combat the perceived predatory conduct of powerful firms in the US. Canada, for example, enacted anti-dumping legislation to protect its fledgling steel industry against predatory behaviour by powerful US steel makers.[3] During World War I, the US itself enacted a criminal anti-dumping law, ostensibly to protect itself from predatory conduct by industrial cartels in Germany.[4] The US later corrected procedural difficulties with this legislation and gave it civil application. The UK and several other countries enacted anti-dumping legislation in the inter-war era, following the lead of the US.

---

[1] See, for example, P. Nicolaides, 'Does the International Trade System Need Anti-dumping Rules?' (1990) 14 *World Competition* 1.

[2] Canadian Antidumping Act of 1904, An Act to Amend the Customs Tariff 1897, SC 1904. However, the concept of 'dumping' dates back as far as 1791. See G. Marceau, 'Economic, Legal and Strategic Considerations in Dumping Practices' in *Antidumping and Antitrust Issues in Free Trade Areas* (Clarendon Press, Oxford, 1994).

[3] See J. Jackson, 'Dumping in International Trade: Its Meaning and Context' in J. Jackson & E. Vermulst (eds.), *Antidumping Law and Practice: A Comparative Study* (University of Michigan Press, Ann Arbor, 1989).

[4] United States Revenue Act of 1916 (also referred to as the Antidumping Duty Act of 1916), ch. 463, 800–801, Stat 798 (codified at 15 USC 712).

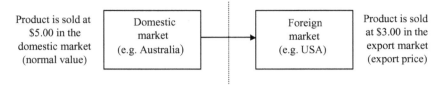

Figure 37: *Dumping occurs where the export price is less than normal value*

These historical origins of anti-dumping law provide insights into its underlying objectives. Anti-dumping legislation enabled governments to combat perceived unfair trade and anti-competitive behaviour by powerful foreign industrial conglomerates. Accordingly, anti-dumping law was initially motivated less by economic efficiency and more by considerations of equity and fairness. Such early anti-dumping legislation was unashamedly nationalistic in character and sought to protect domestic industries, while retaliating against the perceived unfair conduct of foreign firms.

The earliest anti-dumping legislation was therefore both offensive and defensive, metaphorically it equipped governments with both a sword and a shield to combat foreign firms engaging in unfair trade.

After World War II, anti-dumping law achieved widespread international tolerance following its inclusion within the GATT. Such inclusion largely arose because the nations negotiating the GATT 1947 were not prepared to surrender their anti-dumping laws at that time. Article VI of the GATT therefore sets out the GATT's condemnation of dumping and was modelled on the early US anti-dumping legislation. Article VI condemns dumping where it causes or threatens material injury to an established or developing domestic industry of a GATT contracting party.[5] Article VI permits the GATT contracting party to combat such dumping with anti-dumping duties imposed on the firm engaging in the dumping. Following World War II, a number of nations incorporated anti-dumping provisions into their domestic legislation within the limits permitted by Article VI of the GATT.

As illustrated by Figure 37, Article VI of the GATT requires that before a nation can impose anti-dumping duties on a foreign firm, the nation must establish 'dumping' by that firm. Dumping occurs under Article VI

[5] The GATT 1947 condemns dumping without prohibiting it. Instead, the GATT 1947 allows GATT contracting parties to take appropriate measures against dumping along the lines set out in the GATT 1947.

where the firm's export price for a product ('export price') is *less than* the price at which the firm normally sells the product within its own domestic market ('normal value'). Article VI then requires the nation to establish that this dumping threatens or has caused 'material injury' to an established or developing industry within the nation. After establishing dumping and material injury, the GATT permits the nation to impose an anti-dumping duty against the foreign firm no greater than the 'margin of dumping' and no greater than necessary to protect against material injury.

The drafting of Article VI contained a number of ambiguities that caused much consternation among the GATT contracting parties. Accordingly, in 1967, an agreement on the implementation of Article VI was concluded ('GATT Anti-dumping Code').[6] Relevantly, the GATT Anti-dumping Code clarified various definitions set out within Article VI while providing a procedural framework for nations to undertake anti-dumping investigations. The GATT Anti-dumping Code was further improved during the Tokyo Round (1973–1979) of GATT multilateral trade negotiations. However, even with the GATT Anti-dumping Code, difficulties in implementing Article VI remained.[7] Consequently, the GATT contracting parties reconsidered the application of Article VI during the Uruguay Round (1986–1993) of GATT multilateral trade negotiations.

While the Uruguay Round led to many significant changes to the GATT, the Uruguay Round's response to anti-dumping law was comparatively less ambitious. The Uruguay Round concluded a new agreement on the implementation of Article VI ('Anti-dumping Agreement'),[8] which formed part of the agreements creating the WTO.

The Anti-dumping Agreement improved the implementation of Article VI and addressed a significant number of criticisms. However, the Anti-dumping Agreement did not resolve the inherent arbitrariness of many anti-dumping rules and introduced further procedural complexity.[9] Notwithstanding the Anti-dumping Agreement, and subsequent WTO Panel Reports interpreting and applying the Anti-dumping Agreement,

---

[6] See Agreement on the Implementation of Article VI of the General Agreement on Tariffs and Trade, concluded on 30 June 1967, GATT, VI, 61 Stat A-11, 55 UNTS 194.
[7] See C. Morgan, 'Competition Policy and Anti-dumping: Is it Time for a Reality Check?' (1996) 30 *Journal of World Trade* 61, 69.
[8] See Agreement on Implementation of Article VI of the General Agreement on Tariffs and Trade 1994, Annexe 1A, WTO Agreements.
[9] See J. Schott, 'Antidumping' in J. Schott (ed.), *The Uruguay Round: An Assessment* (Institute for International Economics, Washington DC, 1994).

significant difficulties remain with modern anti-dumping law and this has led critics to challenge its continued role in the modern global economy.

9.1.2 Anti-dumping law and economic efficiency

As with most international economic laws, anti-dumping law may be analysed in terms of two objectives, namely economic efficiency and distributional fairness, as discussed in Chapter 2 of this book. As illustrated by the historical origins of anti-dumping law, it is heavily biased towards achieving distributional fairness and is less concerned with economic efficiency. The reduced role of economic efficiency in anti-dumping law is also illustrated by the modern economic analysis of anti-dumping law.

The modern economic analysis of anti-dumping law recognises two fundamental forms of dumping:[10]

(a) dumping by international price discrimination; and
(b) dumping by pricing below cost.

International price discrimination The concept of *international price discrimination* refers to the ability of a firm to sell the same product at different prices in different national markets. Such different pricing across national markets is possible due to different levels of competitiveness in these national markets. In a less competitive market, a firm will have greater market power and may thus set its prices at a higher level than in more competitive markets. By price discriminating in this manner, the firm will maximise its profits and will realise greater profits in less competitive markets.

Dumping by international price discrimination typically occurs where an incumbent firm has market power in its less competitive domestic market (and thus charges high domestic prices), but the firm exports into a more competitive export market (and thus reduces its export prices to competitive levels). Accordingly, the firm will set its export price below normal value. By prohibiting such dumping, anti-dumping law encourages a firm to decrease its domestic market price while increasing its export market price, thereby achieving price equalisation. However, as

---

[10] See A. Deardorff, 'Economic Perspectives on Anti-dumping Law' in J. Jackson & E. Vermulst (eds.), *Antidumping Law and Practice: A Comparative Study* (University of Michigan Press, Ann Arbor, 1989). These two forms of dumping reflect differing interpretations of 'normal value'. International price discrimination determines the normal value by the home market price. Pricing below cost determines the normal value on the basis of the home market cost.

these price movements are in different directions, the net welfare consequences of prohibiting dumping by international price discrimination are ambiguous. Accordingly, most economists are reluctant to draw policy conclusions as to the merits of prohibiting dumping by international price discrimination.

Pricing below cost By comparison, dumping by *pricing below cost* refers to a firm selling a product in an export market at a price less than the firm's domestic cost of producing the product. By pricing below cost the firm necessarily sustains a loss. Economic theory concludes that no rational firm would deliberately price below average variable cost in the long run unless it was seeking to drive competitors out of the market.[11] Economic theory reasons that all other rational instances of below cost pricing may be justified on other grounds (although the relevant measure of cost, and the duration of any pricing below cost, has a material bearing on the ability of the firm to sustain the loss and remains controversial).

Economic theory concludes that dumping by pricing below cost reduces global welfare only in the narrow range of circumstances where a firm deliberately prices below marginal cost on a long-term basis to drive out competitors and subsequently increases its prices (recouping the costs of such conduct while increasing net profits).[12] This is viewed as 'predatory dumping'. Most economists conclude that anti-dumping law is unambiguously welfare enhancing only in the narrow range of circumstances where it prevents predatory dumping.

Unfortunately this economic justification for anti-dumping law is not supported by empirical evidence. There are few, if any, documented examples of successful predatory dumping.[13] As there is thus no practical justification for anti-dumping law, many economists remain sceptical of any need for it. Furthermore, anti-dumping law may *reduce* economic efficiency in certain circumstances. For example, anti-dumping laws may be invoked for protectionistic reasons or to impose additional costs on foreign competitors. Such instances of abuse of anti-dumping law are empirically common in international trade law.[14]

---

[11] See G. Yarrow, 'Economic Aspects of Anti-dumping Policies' (1987) 3(1) *Oxford Review of Economic Policy* 66.
[12] See S. Davies & A. McGuiness, 'Dumping at Less than Marginal Cost' (1982) *Journal of International Economics* 169.
[13] See *The Economic Effects of Anti-Dumping*, United States International Trade Commission, Washington DC, 1995.
[14] See, for example, R. Bhala, 'Rethinking Anti-dumping Law' (1995) 29 *George Washington Journal International of Law & Economics* 1.

Accordingly, many economists perceive anti-dumping law as an unsatisfactory policy instrument and consider that anti-dumping law may cause more harm than good from an economic efficiency perspective. Some economists have proposed that the particular circumstances where anti-dumping law is efficiency enhancing may be better addressed by more appropriate and better focused policy instruments, such as competition law.[15]

This conclusion underscores the reality that anti-dumping laws are not principally motivated by a desire to increase economic efficiency. Rather, anti-dumping laws are principally concerned with distributional fairness. This is further confirmed by the earlier historical analysis in which anti-dumping law was initially enacted as an 'unfair trade' law to address perceived imbalances of power between nations, particularly where industrial conglomerates of larger nations exported into nations with vulnerable smaller industries.[16]

9.1.3 Anti-dumping law and distributional fairness

As discussed previously in Chapters 3 and 6 of this book, distributional fairness is a highly subjective concept that is heavily influenced by underlying social values and beliefs. Accordingly, the concept is culturally nuanced and nationally distinctive. Different societal perceptions of fairness have enabled the evolution of slightly different domestic anti-dumping regimes within each nation. Domestic anti-dumping legislation may justify the prohibition of dumping on a wide variety of social grounds, some of which may have only a very indirect causal relationship to the dumping itself, such as, for example, adverse affects on unskilled workers.

The redistributional objectives of anti-dumping law are usually associated with perceived international power imbalances between the firms of different nations. These power imbalances are relevant to trade law as when a firm takes advantage of these power imbalances, trade-distorting effects may arise. Anti-dumping law is therefore justified as *offsetting* such trade-distorting effects by enabling governments to impose an anti-dumping duty against a foreign firm that is perceived as abusing its market

---

[15] See P. Nicolaides, 'The Competition Effects of Dumping' (1995) 29 *Journal of World Trade* 115, 121.
[16] See J. R. Morris, 'International Trade and Antitrust: Comments' (1993) 61 *University of Cincinnati Law Review* 945, 947.

power.[17] Accordingly, anti-dumping law may be perceived as a legislative instrument whereby one nation may counteract and offset the market power of firms from another nation.

Proponents of anti-dumping law have also argued that anti-dumping law has wider *structural* effects that justify its existence. In particular, proponents argue that anti-dumping law promotes the removal and reform of those barriers to entry (e.g. tariffs) that contribute to the market power of a firm engaging in dumping.[18] However, the causal mechanism for such structural reform is questionable. Proponents of anti-dumping law have suggested that an incumbent firm subjected to an anti-dumping duty would seek to lobby its own government for structural reform to its home market. Yet why would any rational incumbent firm engage in such lobbying given that such structural reform would involve the lowering of barriers to entry and therefore greater competition in its home market? Such reform would be contrary to the incumbent firm's interests as it would undermine its market power and ability to realise high domestic profits.[19] Accordingly, the argument that anti-dumping law has wider structural effects is open to challenge.

Anti-dumping law thus appears limited in the extent to which it may correct the underlying structural causes of dumping. Instead, anti-dumping law simply offsets any distorting effects on trade of particular dumping conduct. Anti-dumping law is therefore potentially inferior to other policy instruments that do address the underlying structural causes of dumping. For example, the WTO already contains a means to address the underlying structural causes of dumping via its mechanism for reducing tariffs. In causal terms, a reduction in tariffs would promote greater competition in national markets by increasing import competition, hence less competitive markets would become more competitive and resulting price equalisation would reduce the scope for dumping.

Given that anti-dumping law is essentially a means to offset harmful trade effects, rather than correcting these effects, the question arises why anti-dumping law was included in the GATT. Furthermore, anti-dumping law is inherently discriminatory as it enables a nation to impose

---

[17] See P. K. Krugman & M. Obstfeld, *International Economics: Theory & Practice* (3rd edn, Harper Collins, New York, 1994), p. 228.
[18] See B. M. Hoekman, & P. C. Mauroidis, 'Dumping, Antidumping and Antitrust' (1996) 30(1) *Journal of World Trade* 27, 29.
[19] Structural reform would reduce barriers to entry into the home market, enabling more competitors to enter the market, thereby promoting greater competition. This would reduce prices and thus profits.

sanctions selectively against the firms of particular countries. Accordingly, anti-dumping law directly contradicts the overriding principle of non-discrimination set out in Article I of the GATT. In this manner, Article VI of the GATT, by permitting the imposition of anti-dumping duties, constitutes an exception to Article I. Why was anti-dumping law considered so important that it was exempted from the application of Article I?

The WTO has itself explained that Article VI was originally intended as a *remedial* mechanism within the GATT. Article VI was viewed as necessary to provide GATT contracting parties with a form of immediate protection from particular instances of unfair trading conduct by powerful foreign firms. Without such protection, many nations indicated they would not ratify the GATT. However, the remedial character of Article VI suggests it was intended to have limited application. In this manner, the narrow and case-specific concept of distributional fairness associated with anti-dumping law would not unduly interfere with the broad principle of non-discrimination set out in Article I of the GATT.

The question then arises whether modern anti-dumping law is consistent with this remedial philosophy behind Article VI of the GATT. If modern anti-dumping law in fact promotes the narrow and case-specific concept of distributional fairness mandated by Article VI, then one could hypothesise that the circumstances in which anti-dumping law is usually applied should be consistent with such distributional fairness. For example, one would expect anti-dumping law to be invoked most frequently against powerful international conglomerates by small and more vulnerable, less developed nations. Yet empirical evidence does not support this hypothesis.

Ironically, anti-dumping law has been most frequently applied by the most advanced industrialised nations and often to protect some of the world's most powerful firms. In many cases, anti-dumping laws have been invoked against Third World firms at the request of powerful First World industrial conglomerates that are dominant in their domestic markets.[20] This counter-intuitive result suggests that anti-dumping law tends to promote a form of distributional 'fairness' that is heavily biased towards producers and national interests. This, in turn, suggests that domestic anti-dumping law is heavily susceptible to influence by those with vested interests, notwithstanding the distributional objectives of Article VI of the GATT.

---

[20] See R. W. McGee, 'The Case to Repeal the Anti-dumping Laws' (1993) 13 *Journal of International Business* 491, 542.

Conceptually this is not surprising. Anti-dumping law is less heavily grounded in objective economic theory than competition law, so is less principled in its approach. Accordingly, anti-dumping law is more susceptible to national and parochial influences and may be more readily captured or influenced by those with political muscle and vested interests. In economic terms, anti-dumping law is highly susceptible to rent seeking.[21] One would therefore expect anti-dumping laws to favour producer interests, as the empirical evidence confirms. Accordingly, while anti-dumping law is intended to achieve redistributional outcomes, it has proved relatively ineffective in doing so. Further, the empirical evidence suggests that anti-dumping law has frequently been captured by those with vested interests.

9.1.4 Procedural criticisms of anti-dumping law

Not only are anti-dumping laws susceptible to rent-seeking, but producers in most nations are sufficiently concentrated and have sufficient vested interests and resources to lobby government successfully for favourable anti-dumping policies. Such lobbying has a high chance of success given that politically appealing arguments can be made for protection against 'unfair' foreign competition. On a global basis, the coalition of interests in favour of maintaining and strengthening anti-dumping laws has grown faster, and has more political power, than the reform and abolition coalition. This does not bode well for any attempts at reform. Anti-dumping law may reflect such vested interests directly and indirectly. First, legislators may enact anti-dumping laws that directly favour those with vested interests. Secondly, legislators may confer broad administrative discretions that enable administrative decision-makers to favour those with vested interests.

The criticisms of US anti-dumping law are illustrative and apply to many other nations:

- At the direct legislative level in the US most amendments to domestic anti-dumping law over the past twenty-five years have assisted US nationals to lodge anti-dumping petitions more easily against

---

[21] Economists use this term to describe situations where individuals or special interest groups seek special privileges or protection from government, forcing someone else to pay for their own benefits.

foreign firms.[22] Law reform has generally favoured US national interests.

Gary Haufbauer of the Institute for International Economics commented in August 1999, for example, that a coalition of lawyers, industrialists and bureaucrats with vested interests have historically captured the US domestic reform lobby and have tended to manipulate anti-dumping law reform in their favour.[23] Haufbauer also commented that this lobby continues to have disproportionate domestic and international influence. In particular, Haufbauer considered that this lobby was instrumental in persuading the US administration to oppose the inclusion of further anti-dumping law reform on the agenda for the Millennium Round of GATT multilateral trade negotiations.

- At the indirect administrative level in the US, for example, administrative authorities have historically had significant discretion in implementing anti-dumping procedures. Such discretion has enabled these authorities to favour those with vested interests notwithstanding constraints imposed by administrative law.

McGee, for example, extensively documented administrative abuses of US anti-dumping procedures over the period 1986–1993.[24] These abuses included wholly inadequate due process and natural justice for foreign firms, such as unreasonably tight time frames for the preparation of submissions and unreasonable information requests. Other examples included bias in the calculation of anti-dumping margins and the arbitrary application of critical anti-dumping definitions.[25]

Computational inconsistencies in the application of anti-dumping laws were also empirically common.[26] Inconsistencies arose in the calculation of comparative home and foreign market prices, including failing to recognise unique features of foreign markets, comparing prices at different levels of the marketing chain (e.g. wholesale against retail), disregarding volume discounts, and using discriminatory price averaging

---

[22] See 'Antidumping Law: A Look at the United States Experience – Lessons for Indonesia', Speech by G. C. Haufbauer, Institute of International Economics, Washington DC, for the Ministry of Industry & Trade, Republic of Indonesia, 20 August 1999.
[23] See ibid., p. 3.
[24] See R. W. McGee, 'The Case to Repeal the Anti-dumping Laws' (1993) 13 Journal of International Business 491, 542.
[25] See B. M. Streen, 'Economically Meaningful Markets: An Alternative Approach to Defining "Like Product" and "Domestic Industry" Under the Trade Agreements Act of 1979' (1987) 73 Vanderbilt Law Review 1459.
[26] See C. M. Barbuto, 'Towards the Convergence of Antitrust and Trade Law: An International Trade Analogue to Robinson-Patman' (1994) 62 Fordham Law Review 2047, 2075.

techniques.[27] Inconsistencies also arose in the calculation of dumping duties, including in the application of exchange rates and costs of production.

While the Anti-dumping Agreement sought to prevent such abuses of anti-dumping law, the Anti-dumping Agreement still leaves administrative decision-makers with considerable discretion. The criteria for determining the margin of dumping and material injury, for example, remain imprecise, leaving scope for abuse. Likewise, there are no specific criteria for determining the relevant market and there is no generally accepted mechanism for examining the causal relationship between the dumped imports and any material injury.

Accordingly, modern anti-dumping law continues to have a number of significant failings and there are significant political barriers to further reform. While any proposal to replace anti-dumping law with competition law remains worthy of consideration, any such proposal must address the vested interests and lobbying power of producer groups in many nations.

9.2 International competition law as an alternative to anti-dumping law

As with anti-dumping law, competition law seeks to balance the twin objectives of economic efficiency and distributional fairness, as discussed in Chapter 2 of this book. Unlike anti-dumping law, competition law gives pre-eminence to considerations of economic efficiency. Competition law seeks to enhance economic efficiency via the causal mechanism of promoting greater market competition. Competition is viewed as a means of disciplining firms, reducing their market power, and thus ensuring that the market forces of supply and demand operate more effectively and efficiently in allocating global resources. Competition law is grounded, fundamentally, in modern microeconomic theory and is heavily disciplined by economic rationality so is more resilient to political pressures.

However, this does not mean that competition law avoids distributional issues. Competition law seeks to lessen power imbalances between firms to ensure that all firms have an equal opportunity to compete on their merits. Competition law also prevents producers from using certain business practices to capture additional wealth from consumers,

---

[27] McGee refers, for example to the US dumping investigation of New Zealand kiwifruit. See *Fresh Kiwifruit from New Zealand*, US ITC Pub 2510 at A-4 (May 1992); 56 Fed Reg 13695 (1992). See McGee, above n. 24.

with associated distributional consequences. Indeed, competition laws are commonly drafted so as to favour the interests of end consumers over the interests of producers.

As discussed in Chapter 4, competition law is usually applied on a generic basis to all legal entities within the economy and regulates the behaviour of these entities across all markets. The methodology followed by competition law to achieve these objectives involves the regulation of market structure and market conduct, although competition law is, traditionally, heavily oriented towards the prohibition of anti-competitive market conduct. Competition law usually involves a 'rule-of-reason' analysis in which conduct is assessed, and prohibited, on the basis of any significant anti-competitive effects.

A fundamental difference between competition law and anti-dumping law is that while anti-dumping law seeks to protect competitors, competition law seeks to protect the competitive process itself. Accordingly, while anti-dumping law focuses on material injury to individual firms, competition law is concerned only with the extent to which the relevant conduct harms the competitive process by reducing the level of competition. This means that the methodologies of anti-dumping laws and competition laws may conflict. Anti-dumping law typically seeks to maintain the profitability of domestic firms by reducing the effectiveness of international competition, while competition law promotes greater competition and thus reduced profitability. To the extent that anti-dumping law excludes foreign competition from the domestic market, it may be viewed as anti-competitive.

Notwithstanding such differences, competition law appears an ideal substitute for anti-dumping law for several reasons. Competition laws redirect government policies away from the protection of domestic firms and towards the enhancement of consumer and producer welfare via greater economic efficiency. Competition laws have a strong grounding in microeconomic theory so are less susceptible to influence by those with vested interests. Competition law enforcement authorities have significantly less discretion than anti-dumping law authorities in implementing their respective laws. Competition laws are more selective in their application and are more effective at distinguishing between 'fair' and 'unfair' trade practices.[28] Furthermore, both competition law and anti-dumping law are concerned to prevent predatory conduct.

---

[28] See H. M. Applebaum & D. R. Grace, 'US Antitrust Law and Anti-Dumping Actions Under Title VII of the Trade Agreements Act of 1979' (1987) 56 *Antitrust Law Journal* 497.

Given the perceived advantages of competition law over anti-dumping law, policy-makers in some nations have advocated the reform of anti-dumping law and its abolition and replacement with cross-border competition law. Such reform has been successfully implemented in several instances, notably within the context of the European Union, the Australia–New Zealand trade agreement, and the recent Canada–Chile trade agreement.[29] The Australia–New Zealand experience, in particular, provides important insights into the relationship between competition law and anti-dumping law.

9.2.1 The Australia–New Zealand Closer Economic Relations Trade Agreement

The Australia–New Zealand Closer Economic Relations Trade Agreement ('CER') came into operation on 1 January 1984.[30] The CER sought to promote closer economic relations between Australia and New Zealand via the mutually beneficial expansion of free trade. The CER mandated comprehensive bilateral free trade in goods in accordance with an agreed timetable.

Relevantly, Article 12(1)(a) of the CER obliged both Australia and New Zealand to 'examine the scope for taking action to harmonise requirements relating to ... restrictive trade practices'. The New Zealand parliament responded to this directive by enacting the Commerce Act 1986 which largely adopted the approach of Australia's competition legislation. The Commerce Act contained New Zealand's competition law and was central to New Zealand's programme of extensive microeconomic reform at the time. Over the following years, both Australia and New Zealand took further steps to harmonise their respective competition laws.

A review of the CER was undertaken in 1988 that extended the coverage of the CER and accelerated its implementation.[31] As part of this review, Australia and New Zealand entered into a memorandum of understanding

---

[29] See Canada-Chile Free Trade Agreement, commenced 5 July 1997. Chapter M-01 provides for the non-application of anti-dumping laws between Canada and Chile from 1 January 2003. Chapter J-01 provides for minimum competition laws and enforcement co-operation between Canada and Chile.
[30] See Australia–New Zealand Closer Economic Relations Trade Agreement, concluded 28 March 1983, commenced 1 January 1984, (1983) 22 *ILM* 948.
[31] See Australia–New Zealand Protocol on the Acceleration of Free Trade in Goods, (Australia) Department of Foreign Affairs and Trade Treaty Series: No. 18 of 1988; entry into force 18 August 1988.

relating to the further harmonisation of their business laws.[32] Both nations enacted exemptions from their anti-dumping laws in respect of goods originating in the jurisdiction of their counterpart. Yet both nations still considered that some controls over unfair trade practices were required, so Australia and New Zealand simultaneously amended their misuse of market power provisions to have bilateral application.

These reciprocal competition law amendments have permitted the extra-territorial application of the relevant competition laws of one nation to the other.[33] In each nation, no corporation with a substantial degree of market power in a trans-Tasman market may take advantage of that power for an anti-competitive purpose.

To ensure that this bilateral, or 'trans-Tasman',[34] jurisdiction would operate effectively, both nations enacted ancillary amendments to their respective statutes to address evidence, judicial procedure and the enforcement of foreign judgments.[35] These amendments effectively prevented Australian and New Zealand firms from claiming they were outside the jurisdiction of the relevant court or regulatory authority of the other nation. These laws also enabled the courts of Australia and New Zealand to sit in each other's jurisdictions in respect of competition law cases. Yet the bilateral competition law provisions remained limited in their scope. A comprehensive bilateral competition law was not an objective of the CER and was not considered necessary in the context of replacing anti-dumping law. Only the prohibitions against misuse of market power were considered necessary for addressing the mischief that anti-dumping laws had previously addressed. There has been little subsequent pressure to expand the trans-Tasman competition provisions to cover other areas of competition law.

Under the competition law provisions, any price discrimination between Australian and New Zealand markets must be shown to be predatory before any action may be taken. A necessary condition for a finding of predation is that a significant degree of market power (or dominance)

[32] See Memorandum of Understanding Between the Government of New Zealand and the Government of Australia on the Harmonisation of Business Laws, CER, 1998.
[33] See Trade Practices Act 1974 (Cth), s. 46A and Commerce Act 1986 (NZ) s. 36A.
[34] The term 'trans-Tasman' refers to matters pertaining to both Australia and New Zealand. The Tasman Sea is the body of water separating the two countries.
[35] In New Zealand, the Law Reform (Miscellaneous Provisions) Act 1990 amended New Zealand's Judicature Act 1908, Reciprocal Enforcement of Judgments Act 1934 and Evidence Act 1908. In Australia, the Trade Practices (Misuse of Trans-Tasman Market Power) Act 1990 amended the Federal Court of Australia Act 1976 and the Commonwealth Evidence Act 1905.

exists in the market of either nation, or the combined trans-Tasman market. This predation must constitute a deliberate use of market power for the purpose of eliminating competitors or reducing competition. Accordingly, the thresholds to establish a breach of the trans-Tasman competition provisions are significantly higher than was previously the case under the respective anti-dumping laws of both New Zealand and Australia.

In implementing the transition from anti-dumping law to bilateral competition law, New Zealand and Australia moved their policy emphasis from trans-Tasman dumping to the concept of 'misuse of market power'. Central to this change in emphasis was the concept of predatory pricing. Furthermore, the traditional trade policy language of 'fairness' and 'market access' was replaced with the competition law language of 'competition', 'efficiency' and 'consumer welfare'. These concepts are important in determining the effectiveness of the change in policy emphasis and are considered in greater detail below.

Over the decade since their inception, the bilateral competition law provisions have been invoked only once, in respect of an unsuccessful interlocutory injunction application by an Australian company.[36] However, in the previous decade, sixteen anti-dumping actions were brought in Australia against New Zealand exports, and ten anti-dumping actions were brought in New Zealand against Australian exports.[37] Several reasons have been proposed why this may be the case, including that the competition law thresholds are higher than the anti-dumping law thresholds, as further explained below. One important theory is that the CER has promoted the equalisation of prices and costs between Australia and New Zealand so the conditions necessary for dumping no longer apply.

The issue arises whether the Australia–New Zealand experience is transferable to other nations. Australia and New Zealand's substitution of competition law for anti-dumping law appears to have been predicated on the existing high degree of convergence in business practices and legal systems between the two nations, as well as close similarities in competition legislation.[38] Australia and New Zealand also have similar social, economic and cultural backgrounds and have a tradition of trans-Tasman

---

[36] Under the Trade Practices Act 1974 (Cth), s. 46A. See *Berlaz Pty Ltd v. Fine Leather Care Products Ltd* (1991) ATPR 41–118.
[37] See R. Ahdar, 'The Role of Antitrust Policy in the Development of Australia–New Zealand Free Trade' (1991) 12 *Northwestern Journal of International Law & Business* 317.
[38] See R. P. Kewalram, 'The Australia–New Zealand Closer Economic Relations Trade Agreement: An Experiment with the Replacement of Anti-Dumping Law with Trade Practices Legislation' (1993) 27 *Journal of World Trade* 111.

inter-governmental dialogue. Further, each nation maintains a high degree of confidence in the competition agency of its counterpart. These unique circumstances suggest that the Australia–New Zealand precedent may not be readily transferable to other nations.

Furthermore, the anti-dumping law amendments were controversial in both Australia and New Zealand and provoked considerable opposition. Manufacturers were the most vocal lobby group and protested that the amendments caused a net reduction in producer protection.[39] A necessary condition for the reform of anti-dumping laws in the Australia–New Zealand context was that these vested interests could be successfully overcome. When following the Australia–New Zealand approach, other nations with more powerful industrial lobbies may face much greater domestic producer opposition.

9.2.2 Criticisms of a competition law approach

The previous analysis suggests that critical issues in the replacement of anti-dumping law with competition law are therefore:

(a) whether competition law can effectively address the same type of welfare-reducing conduct as anti-dumping law, namely predatory dumping; and
(b) whether competition law can achieve the same redistributional outcomes as anti-dumping law, namely to address power imbalances between the firms of different nations.

For competition law to be viewed as the preferred international policy instrument relative to anti-dumping law, competition law must address these economic efficiency and distributional fairness issues more effectively than anti-dumping law and with less risk of capture by those with vested interests. While the evidence suggests that competition law addresses efficiency issues more effectively and is less susceptible to political capture, competition law is less effective in achieving the same redistributional outcomes as anti-dumping law. Accordingly, competition law is a policy instrument of limited application in a dumping context.

There is no concept of 'dumping' in competition law. Rather, competition law addresses dumping conduct via its prohibition against predatory

---

[39] See J. Farmer, 'Towards a Single Trans-Tasman Market: A Lawyer's Perspective' (1992) 12(1) *World Competition* 39.

pricing.[40] The concept of predatory pricing has two inter-twined elements, namely price discrimination and sales below cost. As discussed previously, these same elements exist in anti-dumping law, so there is a degree of conceptual overlap between competition law and anti-dumping law. However, the methodology used to assess predatory pricing in competition law is significantly different from the methodology used to assess dumping in anti-dumping law. These different methodologies result in an imperfect overlap between anti-dumping law and competition law.

Competition law views predatory pricing as a particular type of abuse of market power.[41] Predatory pricing is usually defined as deliberate price-cutting in the short run by a firm with market power with a view to driving competitors out of the market. By doing so, the firm may then raise prices in the long run, in the absence of competition, and thus recoup any losses while realising greater profits.[42] Predatory pricing may also be motivated by other strategic considerations, but always involves a calculated trade-off between short-term losses and long-term gains. Accordingly, the prohibition against predatory pricing in competition law would also tend to prohibit dumping by pricing below cost. However, there are a number of critical differences between the competition prohibition and anti-dumping law, three of which are particularly important.

- *Market power threshold* Predatory pricing is usually viewed by competition law as a misuse of market power. Accordingly, in the anti-dumping context, domestic firms suffering injury would be required to establish that the foreign firm undertaking the dumping had the requisite degree of market power in its home market. While the relevant thresholds of market power are different between nations, the existence of any such threshold is fundamentally different from anti-dumping law which has no such threshold. Accordingly, competition law would not apply to dumping by any firm without market power and this means that such firms could engage in dumping by international price discrimination or pricing below cost without fear of sanction.

---

[40] While the US enacted specific competition laws against price discrimination via the Clayton Act 1914 and the Robinson-Patman Act 1936, these laws were subsequently interpreted by reference to predatory pricing. The US Supreme Court implicitly affirmed this predatory pricing standard within the landmark case *Matsushita Electric Industrial Co v. Zenith Radio Corporation* 475 US 574 (1986).
[41] Also known as 'monopolisation'. See *AA Poultry Farms Inc v. Rose Acre Farms Inc* 881 F 2d 1396 (7th Cir 1989), 1401.
[42] See OECD, *Predatory Pricing* (OECD, Paris, 1989), p. 81.

- *Requisite purpose or intent* The competition laws of many nations require that, for predatory pricing to occur, a firm with market power must have used its market power with the requisite purpose or intent. Prohibitions against any misuse of market power based solely on anti-competitive effects are less common. Accordingly, in the dumping context, firms would usually be prohibited from predatory pricing by competition law only to the extent that they were proved to have the requisite purpose or intent. Evidence of any such purpose may be difficult to obtain given that the firm would be located in a foreign jurisdiction and successful international discovery of documents is notoriously difficult.[43] This contrasts with anti-dumping law which does not require purpose, but instead simply requires evidence of price differences and consequential injurious effects.
- *Pricing threshold* The principal focus of predatory pricing in competition law is on below-cost sales. Sales below cost are viewed as prima facie evidence of predatory intent and thus an anti-competitive purpose. Predatory pricing is less concerned with price discrimination as such conduct has a number of innocent explanations so does not establish any inference of predatory intent. However, anti-dumping law has traditionally focused on the lower threshold of price discrimination, rather than the higher threshold of sales below cost, as the trigger for remedial action.

    Similarly, when courts consider predatory pricing cases they typically have difficulty distinguishing between inefficient and unfair 'predatory behaviour', and efficient and fair 'fierce competition'.[44] One is to be condemned, the other is to be endorsed. Given the difficulty in distinguishing between these two types of conduct, there is an understandable reluctance on the part of courts to conclude that predatory pricing has occurred. Successful predatory pricing actions are therefore extremely rare in competition law unless there is clear evidence of pricing below cost. No such difficulties arise in anti-dumping actions.

As these three differences suggest, the prohibition against predatory pricing involves significantly different tests and higher thresholds than the prohibition against dumping. While competition law addresses the same

---

[43] See P. E. Areeda, & D. Turner, 'Predatory Pricing and Related Practices under section 2 of the Sherman Act' (1975) 88 *Harvard Law Review* 697. Later incorporated into P. E. Areeda & H. Hovenkamp, *Antitrust Law* (3rd edn, Little Brown, Boston, 1989).

[44] See R. Merkin, 'Predatory Pricing or Competitive Pricing: Establishing the Truth in English in EEC Law' (1987) 7(2) *Oxford Journal of Economic Studies* 182.

type of predatory conduct that anti-dumping law addresses, competition law tends to be much narrower in its application and targets a particular subset of conduct that would be prohibited by anti-dumping law.[45] Competition law is less concerned with distributional considerations of 'fairness'. The particular subset of anti-dumping conduct that competition law addresses is conduct that would reduce economic efficiency. Accordingly, the wider distributional outcomes of anti-dumping law are not effectively addressed by competition law.

Further, the domestic difficulties in bringing successful predatory pricing actions under competition law are exacerbated at the international level due to cross-border evidential difficulties, exchange rate complications and fundamental differences in business practices and market structure.[46] Competition law actions are therefore less likely to be successful than anti-dumping law actions at the international level.

9.2.3 Could competition principles be introduced into the Anti-dumping Agreement?

The issue further arises whether it would be politically expedient to replace anti-dumping law with competition law at the international level. The politics of doing so suggest not. International reform of anti-dumping laws would not be politically expedient without strong bipartisan support, particularly from the European Union and the US. Anti-dumping laws are deeply entrenched within the laws of many of the world's nations, particularly the US.[47] As discussed previously, such laws will most likely be heavily defended by those with vested interests. The repeal of international dumping laws on an international basis therefore seems unlikely in the foreseeable future.

Abolition of anti-dumping laws has, so far, only been achieved at a regional level as an integral part of customs unions, or free trade areas. This can be traced back to the inability of competition laws to address 'unfair trade' distributional issues fully, such as price discrimination. By illustration, customs unions and free trade areas promote the reduction of

---

[45] See D. J. Gifford, 'Rethinking the Relationship Between Antidumping and Antitrust Rules' (1991) 6 *American Journal of International Law & Policy* 277.
[46] See N. H. Barcelo, 'The Antidumping Law: Repeal It or Revise It' (1979) 1 *Michigan Yearbook of International Legal Studies* 53.
[47] See P. A. Messerlin, 'Competition Policy and Antidumping Reform: An Exercise in Transition' in J. J. Schott (ed.), *The World Trading System: Challenges Ahead* (Institute for International Economics, Washington DC, 1996).

border controls and thus lead to a reduction in barriers to entry between national markets. This, in turn, permits less scope for international price discrimination by promoting the equalisation of prices across markets and by reducing the market power of incumbent firms.

With such price equalisation, dumping by international price discrimination is less likely to occur, so nations may consider that the broad prohibitions of anti-dumping law are no longer necessary while the narrower prohibitions of competition law are more appropriate. In essence, customs unions and free trade areas create less scope for cross-border distributional unfairness and therefore an emphasis on economic efficiency is more appropriate by adopting competition law rather than anti-dumping law. The corollary of this analysis is that any substitution of anti-dumping law by competition law is unlikely to occur where the potential for significant international price discrimination remains.[48]

Accordingly, the international abolition of anti-dumping laws appears to be an unlikely international policy objective at this time.[49] This does not, however, mean that competition law cannot complement or reinforce anti-dumping law. A more realistic policy objective may be to implement gradual reform of anti-dumping laws, principally via the integration of competition principles into anti-dumping legislation. This could commence, for example, with the greater inclusion of competition principles within the Anti-dumping Agreement. Five key recommendations are set out below, any combination of which could be adopted:

> The Anti-dumping Agreement should require the use of a market power threshold whereby firms with significant market power cannot use anti-dumping law to reduce competition

Similarly, economic principles should be imported into anti-dumping law so that anti-dumping duties are not applied in circumstances where they preserve the high profitability or high inefficiency of domestic firms.[50] Firms with significant market power should not be permitted to benefit from anti-dumping law where this may have the effect of strengthening or perpetuating their market power.

---

[48] See E. U. Petersmann, 'International Competition Rules for Governments and Private Business: The Case for Linking Future WTO Negotiations on Investment, Competition and Environmental Rules to Reforms of Anti-dumping Laws' (1996) 30 *Journal of World Trade* 5, 33.

[49] See M. Morkre & K. Kelly, 'Perspectives Concerning the Effects of Unfair Imports on Domestic Industries' (1993) 61 *University of Cincinnati Law Review* 919.

[50] See R. Botuck & S. Kaplan, 'Conflicting Entitlements: Can Antidumping and Antitrust Regulation be Reconciled?' (1993) 61 *University of Cincinnati Law Review* 903.

One means to achieve this effect, consistent with greater international competition, may be to permit anti-dumping action to be taken only against firms with significant market power either:

(a) on behalf of firms without significant market power; or
(b) on behalf of firms with significant market power provided that this would have net benefits for global competition.

This would also ensure that anti-dumping law is applied in a manner consistent with the original remedial intention for including it within Article VI in the GATT.

The Anti-dumping Agreement should require the use of a public interest or competition test before anti-dumping duties may be imposed

Anti-dumping duties should only be imposed where there is a 'public interest' in doing so in the same manner as in the WTO Safeguards Agreement. This public interest should take into consideration the efficiency and distributional implications of imposing any anti-dumping duty in the particular circumstances of each case, particularly in respect of price impacts on end consumers. Alternatively, a determination of material injury should only be permitted where there are proven anti-competitive effects. This would require that any injury would be assessed on the basis of general anti-competitive effects and harm to the process of competition, rather than on the basis of harm to particular domestic producers. In essence, this approach would be akin to a 'rule-of-reason' and 'effects based' competition test.

Such an approach may also mean that the responsibility for investigating and enforcing anti-dumping laws could be passed to competition authorities. While the Anti-dumping Agreement already provides for very limited consideration of such matters by giving consumers an opportunity to make their views known to anti-dumping authorities, this provision is extremely limited in its scope and arguably ineffectual.[51]

The Anti-dumping Agreement should mandate a competition law investigation that should precede or complement any anti-dumping investigation

Any anti-dumping investigation should be preceded or complemented by competition law investigations in both the exporting and the importing

---

[51] Article 6.11(iii) of the Anti-dumping Agreement.

nations to determine whether any anti-competitive conduct has occurred. In many cases it may be possible to co-ordinate such investigations between the respective competition authorities of each nation. Such investigations may assist in determining the underlying structural causes of the dumping and may enable any action to be commenced and resolved within a competition law context, if appropriate. Any competition law investigation would recognise that certain anti-dumping conduct can be addressed within a competition law fora.

The Anti-dumping Agreement should promote more effective market definition

The relevant market for any anti-dumping analysis should be determined with greater reference to the competition law principles of market definition, rather than the trade law principles of 'like product'. Competition law has a sophisticated process of market definition heavily grounded in microeconomic theory. In contrast, the approach of trade law is arbitrary and typically highly subjective. A competition law approach may enable a more rational and consistent approach and thus a greater likelihood of a proper 'apples with apples' comparison between products.

The Anti-dumping Agreement should require that administrative discretions given to anti-dumping authorities should be subjected to greater judicial scrutiny

Anti-dumping laws should be subjected to greater judicial scrutiny. Greater opportunity should be provided for a review of decisions by anti-dumping authorities either on a *de novo* basis or on the basis of a failure to meet fundamental standards of procedural fairness. In some jurisdictions, for example, it could be possible to appeal the decisions of an anti-dumping authority to a competition authority, therefore ensuring greater opportunity. In other jurisdictions, greater procedural fairness could be introduced into anti-dumping procedures. Generally, the greater the opportunity for review and appeal of anti-dumping decisions, the greater the accountability of anti-dumping authorities and the less scope for administrative abuses in the application of anti-dumping laws.

The introduction of such competition principles into anti-dumping law would provide significantly less scope for anti-dumping law to be influenced by those with vested interests. Clarisse Morgan, an economic affairs officer at the WTO, has argued that many of the amendments to anti-dumping law introduced by the Uruguay Round (as set out in the Anti-dumping Agreement) were, at least in part, intended to make anti-dumping laws more 'pro-competitive'. This suggests that the precedent for introducing competition principles into the Anti-dumping Agreement is already well established.

9.3 Conclusion: competition principles should be introduced into anti-dumping law

Many criticisms of anti-dumping law assume that economic efficiency should be the policy objective of anti-dumping law. As previously discussed, the economic rationale for anti-dumping law is limited and anti-dumping laws frequently retard economic efficiency. From an efficiency perspective, competition laws are clearly preferable. However, this assumption as to the proper objective of anti-dumping law is not necessarily correct. Anti-dumping laws were developed, historically, as 'unfair trade' laws and were intended to redress imbalances of power between powerful foreign conglomerates and vulnerable domestic firms. The principal policy objectives of anti-dumping law are therefore redistributional.

When assessing whether competition law should replace anti-dumping law, it is necessary to consider these distributional objectives. Anti-dumping laws initially evolved to fulfil a distributional purpose. The risk of unfair trading issues, as well as lingering protectionism, led Article VI to be included as a remedial mechanism in the GATT. While competition law would achieve greater economic efficiency, the greater procedural constraints inherent in competition law (particularly the high thresholds associated with establishing predatory pricing), suggest that competition law would have only limited application to such unfair trade issues. Competition law therefore does not appear as well suited to achieving the distributional objectives of anti-dumping law.

However, there are clearly procedural advantages in replacing anti-dumping law with competition law as competition law is less susceptible to capture or influence by those with vested interests. This is illustrated by the many documented examples of administrative abuses of anti-dumping laws, usually to enable domestic firms to fend off international competition. Competition law is highly resistant to political pressures due to its heavier reliance on objective economic concepts and its solid grounding in economic rationality.

Notwithstanding these procedural advantages, any replacement of anti-dumping law with competition law would have clear limitations. Given that competition law does not effectively address 'unfair' trade issues, nations have only considered replacement in circumstances where unfair trade issues are less likely to arise, such as customs unions and free trade areas. Accordingly, important prerequisites for the replacement of anti-dumping laws by competition laws include harmonised competition laws, few market access barriers and a reasonable degree of economic integration. Furthermore, little political will exists at this time to substitute anti-dumping law with competition law on an international basis. There are extensive vested interests against any such initiative, particularly in the US, whose support for any reform initiative would be critical.

Some form of pragmatic balance is therefore desirable to build upon the strengths of both competition law and anti-dumping law. A realistic and valuable policy objective may be to implement gradual reform of anti-dumping laws by the progressive integration of competition principles into anti-dumping legislation. It may be useful as outlined previously, for example, to enable preliminary competition investigations, promote better market definition, require the use of competition tests and market power thresholds, and provide greater scope for judicial review of anti-dumping law decisions.

The progressive introduction of competition principles into anti-dumping law may provide an important future objective for international trade and competition policy-makers alike. Such an approach will enable the distributional benefits of anti-dumping laws to be retained, while ensuring that such laws remain consistent with efficiency theory and are not captured by those with vested interests. Such an approach may provide an important vision for achieving greater and more effective international economic integration in the coming decades.

In summary, anti-dumping law is a particular trade measure permitted by the WTO law which has been subjected to significant international criticism due to its potential adverse effects on international competition. However, such criticisms fail to recognise adequately that anti-dumping law has evolved to fulfil a particular distributional purpose. Accordingly, it is not simply the case that competition law could supplant existing trade measures of this nature, rather the original policy basis for each trade measure would need to be carefully examined. Yet it is also clear that material benefits could be realised by the progressive introduction of competition principles into such trade measures as anti-dumping law to discourage the application of such measures where they are inconsistent with market contestability and greater international competition.

Summarising the conclusions from Chapters 7 to 9 of this book, a variety of practical trade and competition policy measures can be adopted that would reconcile the relationship between international trade law and international competition law, consistent with the concept of market contestability identified in Chapter 6. In turn, this would realise substantive benefits both to international trade and to international competition.

PART III

The Optimal Form for a WTO
Competition Agreement

10

What are the optimal objectives and principles for a WTO competition agreement?

Parts II and III of this book reached a number of conclusions regarding the desirability and theoretical and practical scope for any WTO competition agreement. However, this book has not yet considered whether the WTO would provide the *optimal* institutional vehicle for any international competition agreement. Part III of this book therefore identifies the optimal form for an international competition agreement.

Chapter 10 of this book has four main sections:

- Section 10.1 considers whether the WTO would provide the optimal institutional vehicle for an international competition agreement relative to the most likely alternative institutional vehicles.
- Section 10.2 analyses three previous proposals for the incorporation of competition law into the WTO and identifies the respective merits and shortcomings of these proposals. Section 10.2 identifies how the previous shortcomings could be avoided.
- Sections 10.3 and 10.4 identify the key objectives and core principles that should guide any WTO competition agreement and the extent to which these would correlate with pre-existing WTO objectives and core principles.

Chapter 10 concludes that the WTO would provide the optimal institutional vehicle for an international competition agreement.

10.1 What would be the optimal institutional vehicle for an international competition agreement?

In order to identify whether the WTO would provide the optimal institutional vehicle for an international competition agreement, it is necessary to compare the WTO with the other most likely alternative institutional vehicles. With this in mind, Chapter 10 considers the following four potential institutional vehicles:

- *WTO Agreement* An international competition agreement could be negotiated as a multilateral or plurilateral agreement under the WTO framework in the same manner as TRIMS, TRIPS, or the Agreement on Government Procurement.[1]
- *UN Treaty* An international competition agreement could be negotiated as a multilateral or plurilateral treaty under the auspices of the United Nations, relying on pre-existing United Nations institutions such as UNCTAD.[2] Such an approach was attempted in relation to the UNCTAD Code discussed in Chapter 5 of this book. However, unlike the UNCTAD Code, such an international competition agreement would have legally binding status in international law.
- *Stand-Alone Treaty* An international competition agreement could be negotiated as a stand-alone multilateral or plurilateral treaty with its own unique international institutions and secretariat.[3] A number of stand-alone international environmental treaties, for example, adopt such an approach.[4]
- *OECD Treaty* An international competition agreement could be negotiated as a plurilateral treaty within the context of the OECD. Such an approach was attempted in relation to the unsuccessful Multilateral Agreement on Investment which was negotiated among OECD member nations between 1995 and 1998.[5]

In order to evaluate the suitability of these four alternative institutional structures as a vehicle for an international competition agreement, it is necessary to identify the relevant evaluation criteria.[6] This chapter utilises four principal evaluation criteria as follows:

---

[1] See Agreement on Trade-Related Investment Measures ('TRIMS'), Agreement on Trade-Related Aspects of Intellectual Property Rights ('TRIPS') and Agreement on Government Procurement within the Final Act and Agreement Establishing the World Trade Organisation, Marrakesh, Morocco, 15 April 1994.

[2] See http://www.unctad.org.

[3] See B. Hindley, 'Competition Law and the WTO: Alternative Structures for Agreement' in J. Bhagwati & R. Hudec (eds.), *Fair Trade and Harmonisation Prerequisites for Free Trade?* (1996, OUP, New York).

[4] An example is provided by the 1973 Convention on International Trade in Endangered Species of Wild Fauna and Flora (CITES).

[5] The negotiating text for the Multilateral Agreement on Investment is available from the OECD website at: http://www.oecd.org/dataoecd/46/40/1895712.pdf. See also OECD, 'The Multilateral Agreement on Investment: Draft Consolidated Test', DAFFE/MAI(98)7/REV1, OECD, Paris, 22 April 1998.

[6] See, generally, V. Rittberger (ed.), *Regime Theory in International Relations* (Harper, Boston, 1995). See also L. Martin & B. Simmons, 'Theories and Empirical Studies of International Institutions' (1998) 52 *Industrial Organisation* 729.

- *'effectiveness'*, namely the ability of the relevant institutional structure to provide policy instruments that address the 'under-regulation' and 'over-regulation' identified in Chapter 3 of this book;
- *'scope'*, namely the potential geographic, functional and sectoral coverage of each institutional structure;
- *'context'*, namely the likely synergies and conflicts associated with the incorporation of an international competition agreement into each institutional structure; and
- *'achievability'*, namely the likely political support, existing preferences and negotiation costs associated with the incorporation of an international competition agreement into each institutional structure.

Each of these four evaluation criteria can then be applied to the four institutional vehicles identified above (i.e. WTO Agreement, UN Treaty, Stand-Alone Treaty, and OECD Treaty) to determine the optimal institutional vehicle in the manner set out below.

Effectiveness The first of the four evaluation criteria identified above is 'effectiveness'. This measures the ability of the relevant institutional structure to match policy instruments, such as treaty obligations, to achieve the desired policy objectives. For the purposes of this chapter, the greater the ability of any institutional structure to correct the 'under-regulation' and 'over-regulation' identified in Chapter 3, the greater the extent to which that institutional structure should be viewed as 'more effective' than others.

Each of the four institutional structures identified above could, *in theory*, provide policy instruments to address the 'under-regulation' or 'over-regulation' identified in Chapter 3.[7] However, *in practice*, the extent to which such obligations could be incorporated into any such agreement would be determined by issues of 'achievability'. In this manner, effectiveness is qualified by what obligations are practically achievable within the context of the particular institutional structure.

Bearing this in mind, Figure 38 suggests that a WTO Agreement should be regarded as more effective than the other three institutional structures.[8]

---

[7] Namely via treaty obligations that facilitate positive and negative comity, improve co-operation and impose restraints on extraterritoriality.

[8] See, for example, discussion in J. M. Finger, 'The GATT as an International Discipline Over Trade Restrictions: A Public-Choice Approach' in Vaubel & Willet (eds.), *The Political Economy of International Organisation: A Public-Choice Approach* (Westview Press, Boulder, 1992), p. 125. See also discussion in K. W. Abbott, 'International Law and International Relations Theory: Building Bridges' (1992) 86 *American Society of International Law Proceedings* 167.

Institutional structure	Effectiveness rating	Explanation for effectiveness rating (ordered from most effective to least effective)
WTO Agreement	High	The WTO Agreement has a proven track record of effectively influencing and disciplining governmental behaviour. WTO enforcement has proved highly effective in promoting compliance with WTO obligations at the international level.
Stand-Alone Treaty	High to medium	The effectiveness of the Stand-Alone Treaty would depend on the obligations that could actually be achieved. A Stand-Alone Treaty is less likely to be achieved in a form as effective as the WTO, meaning that it should be viewed as less effective than the WTO Agreement.
UN Treaty	Medium	The UNCTAD Code was incorporated into the UN system in the early 1980s and has only proved moderately effective in influencing governmental behaviour. The reasons for the ineffectiveness of the UNCTAD Code were identified in Chapter 5 of this book.
OECD Treaty	Low	The OECD has traditionally been an institution for the development of international policy. The OECD Treaty would thus tend to emphasise non-binding policy principles and policy development. Hence, while the OECD Treaty may prove influential, it would not usually have the binding authoritative force of the other models.

Figure 38: *Effectiveness of each institutional structure*

Scope The second of the four evaluation criteria identified above is 'scope', which complements the 'effectiveness' criteria. Generally, the greater the geographic coverage,[9] functional coverage,[10] and sectoral coverage[11] of any institutional structure, the more effective any policy instruments within that structure are likely to be in comprehensively addressing the 'under-regulation' and 'over-regulation' identified in Chapter 3 of this book.

[9] Geographic coverage can be assessed in terms of international membership.
[10] Functional coverage can be assessed in terms of particular functions included.
[11] Sectoral coverage can be assessed in terms of the number of regulated industry sectors.

Institutional structure	Scope ranking	Explanation for scope ranking (ordered from greatest scope to narrowest scope)
UN Treaty	High	The UN Treaty would tend to have the greatest geographic scope given that the membership of the United Nations comprises almost all nations in the international community.
WTO Agreement	High	The WTO Agreement would address roughly 80% of the world's 193 nations, including the principal trading nations. WTO membership stands at 150 in March 2006 and is continuing to expand via WTO accessions.
Stand-Alone Treaty	Medium	The geographic scope of the Stand-Alone Treaty would depend upon the number of nations entering into such an agreement. Generally, this would involve fewer nations than the WTO Agreement, but potentially more nations than the OECD Treaty.
OECD Treaty	Low	The OECD Treaty would tend to be targeted at OECD member nations, so may exclude the majority of the international community. In any event, non-member nations are likely to be less accepting of a structure evolving from an OECD initiative.

Figure 39: *Scope of each institutional structure*

The four institutional models identified above all have a very similar potential sectoral and functional scope, so the analysis can focus on the significant differences in geographic scope. The analysis in Figure 39 suggests that the UN Treaty and the WTO Agreement should be preferred above the other two institutional structures given that they would involve a potentially greater geographic scope.

Context The third of the four evaluation criteria identified above is 'context'. In general, the greater the policy synergies that could be realised by a particular institutional structure and the lower the potential for policy conflicts, the greater the likely effectiveness of any competition agreement and the greater the resulting welfare benefits both for individual nations and the international community.

The WTO Agreement appears to realise the greatest policy synergies from the four institutional structures and has the lowest potential for policy conflicts. This is largely because of the synergies between international competition law and international trade law identified in Chapter 6 of this book. The WTO Agreement enables synergies in underlying theory and synergies in policy co-ordination to be realised, as follows:

- *Synergies in underlying theory*   As discussed in Chapter 6 of this book, the underlying causal theories, objectives and approaches of competition law and international trade law are complementary. Chapter 6 indicated that it would be possible to realise a number of synergies by reconciling international trade law and competition law theory via the concept of market contestability. The inclusion of competition rules within the WTO would also enable these rules to be grounded in the fundamental WTO principles of transparency and non-discrimination, as identified later in this chapter.
- *Synergies in policy co-ordination*   The inclusion of international competition policies within the WTO would enable the greater co-ordination of international competition policy with other economic policies already embodied in WTO agreements and would reduce the risk of policy conflict. The WTO has now become the key international forum for economics-based rules and the leading institution focused on global trade and commerce.[12] On a subject matter and policy inter-linkage basis, the WTO would appear to be the most appropriate multilateral forum for addressing international competition law issues.[13]

Bearing this in mind, Figure 40 suggests that the WTO Agreement should be preferred above the other three institutional structures.

Achievability   The last of the four evaluation criteria identified above is 'achievability'. This criteria is the most critical of the four evaluation

---

[12] The WTO, for example, now includes rules on intellectual property, subsidies, investment and state enterprises, which each cross-impact upon international competition law. See D. Palmeter & P. C. Mavroidis, 'The WTO Legal System: Sources of Law' (1998) 92 *American Journal of International Law* 398. See also E. Vermulst, P. C. Mavroidis & P. Waer, 'The Functioning of the Appellate Body After Four Years – Towards Rule Integrity' (1999) 33(2) *Journal of World Trade* 1. See also R. Behboodi, 'Legal Reasoning and the International Law of Trade – The First Steps of the Appellate Body of the WTO' (1998) 32(4) *Journal of World Trade* 55.

[13] The WTO has adopted a deeper 'integrated approach' recognising the increasing globalisation of international commerce and subject inter-linkages. See M. J. Trebilcock, 'Competition Policy and Trade Policy: Mediating the Interface' (1996) 31 *Journal of World Trade* 71. See also WTO Press Release, 'Growing Complexity in International Economic Relations Demands Broadening and Deepening of Multilateral Trading System: WTO Director General', 16 October 1995. See also M. Matsushita, 'Co-ordinating International Trade with Competition Policies' (1988) 5 *Studies in Transnational Economic Law* 395, and E. U. Petersmann & M. Hilf, *The New GATT Round of Multilateral Trade Negotiations* (Kluwer Publications, Boston, 1991).

Institutional structure	Context ranking	Explanation for context ranking (ordered from best context to worst context)
WTO Agreement	High	The analysis above suggests that the WTO Agreement would prove most effective in achieving synergies in underlying theory and synergies in policy co-ordination.
OECD Treaty	Medium	The OECD Treaty may provide a basis for realising synergies in policy co-ordination and some synergies in underlying theory, but would be unlikely to be as effective as the WTO Agreement.
UN Treaty	Medium to Low	The UN Treaty may similarly provide a basis for realising some synergies, particularly if undertaken within the context of UNCTAD, although the scope for this is less certain.
Stand-Alone Treaty	Low	The Stand-Alone Treaty would tend to address competition issues in an isolated manner so would be less likely to be conducive to the realisation of synergies in underlying theory and synergies in policy co-ordination.

Figure 40: *Context for each institutional structure*

criteria given that it determines the extent to which the other criteria could practically be achieved.

There are a number of factors which support the conclusion that the WTO Agreement would be the most achievable of the four institutional structures, as detailed below:

- *Existing international support* The WTO is one of the few international economic organisations outside the United Nations which has the confidence of the vast majority of the international community.[14] This is a key determinant of its international acceptability:
  - The *processes* of the WTO are supported by a broad constituency of developed and developing nations, comprising most of the international community.[15] The WTO processes function through consensus and negotiation which, although slow, enables a thorough discussion

---

[14] See W. Fikentscher, 'Competition Rules for Private Agents in the GATT/WTO' (1994) 49 *Aussenwirtschaft* 281.

[15] See H. Hauser & E. U. Petersmann (eds.), 'International Competition Rules in the GATT/WTO System' (1994) *Swiss Review of International Economic Relations (Aussenwirtschaft)*, Special Issue 169. See also, generally, E. M. Graham & J. D. Richardson, *Global Competition Policy* (Institute for International Economics, Washington DC, 1995).

of potential new rules and prevents the outvoting of minority members.[16] By utilising such processes, the WTO has adopted a balanced and pragmatic approach to the regulation of international trade and commerce that has resulted in meaningful, internationally-accepted rule systems.[17]

- The *institutions* of the WTO are widely respected and have the confidence of the international community. The WTO institutions are perceived as relatively neutral, independent and well-resourced.[18] The WTO institutions are also perceived as credible, with the ability to address and resolve the views of disparate groups in a relatively impartial manner.[19]

- *Historical precedent* As discussed in Chapter 6 of this book, there is a clear historical precedent for incorporation of competition law into the WTO. Competition law was included within the initial Havana Charter of 1946, from which the GATT was derived. Several initiatives were made in subsequent decades to incorporate competition law into the GATT. Upon the completion of the Uruguay Round in 1994, a number of competition law provisions were incorporated into several sector-specific WTO agreements. Any international competition agreement could build upon and develop these embryo competition provisions. In addition, where international competition law has been addressed by international agreements to date, it has been addressed most frequently within the context of existing trade agreements further emphasising the inter-linkages between trade and competition and establishing a precedent for considering both disciplines together.[20]

---

[16] Thereby empowering those nations with less economic and political power. See J. Croome, *Reshaping the World Trading System: A History of the Uruguay Round* (2nd edn, OUP, New York, 1999). See also B. M. Hoekman & M. M. Kostecki, *The Political Economy of the World Trading System: from GATT to the WTO* (Wiley, New York, 1995).

[17] See A. D. Melamed, 'International Antitrust in an Age of International Deregulation', Address delivered before the George Mason Law Review Symposium: Antitrust in the Global Economy, Washington, DC, 10 October 1997.

[18] See Japanese Delegation to the WTO, 'Non-Paper on Trade and Competition by the Japanese Delegation to the WTO' (1996) 24(10) *International Business Lawyer* 463.

[19] Any stand-alone international institution created outside the scope of the WTO would not benefit from this goodwill and this would tend to reduce its authority and credibility relative to the WTO Agreement. See S. P. Croley & J. H. Jackson, 'WTO Dispute Procedures, Standard of Review, and Deference to National Governments' (1996) 90 *American Journal of International Law* 193.

[20] See C. A. Jones, 'Toward Global Competition Policy – The Expanding Dialogue on Multilateralism' (2000) 23(2) *World Competition* 95.

- *Relevance of existing institutions* The WTO incorporates an existing suite of agreements and institutions which could address competition law issues with relatively little modification.[21] The WTO has pre-existing procedures for rule-of-law adjudication, including a WTO Dispute Settlement Body, which have proved highly successful in resolving inter-governmental disputes associated with international trade and commerce.[22] The WTO also incorporates a form of international enforcement via political pressure, remedial measures and trade sanctions.[23] A reliance on these existing WTO agreements and institutions would reduce the complexity and duration of negotiations for any international competition agreement, thereby increasing the likelihood of realising international consensus.
- *Benefit of comprehensive negotiations* As noted in Chapter 3 of this book, as an international competition law may result in net welfare transfers between different nations in the international community, it may be necessary to compensate nations by way of welfare transfers. In the international community, such welfare transfers tend to be agreed within the context of international treaty negotiations in which particular policies are traded off against each other so as to ensure all nations receive some benefit from a particular agreement. International negotiations canvassing a greater range of issues provide greater scope for all nations to be compensated, so are more likely to result in international agreement. WTO rounds of multilateral negotiations provide the greatest opportunity to realise an international competition agreement given that they address the greatest range of issues and permit the greatest range of trade-offs.
- *Existing international preferences* The WTO is one of the few existing international institutions with an existing awareness of competition law and policy. There is also a broad international consensus that if any international competition agreement is to be negotiated, it should be negotiated within the context of the WTO.[24] As discussed in Chapter 5

---

[21] See P. C. Mavroidis & S. J. Siclen, 'The Application of the GATT/WTO Dispute Resolution System to Competition Issues' (1997) 31(5) *Journal of World Trade* 5.
[22] See discussion in P. T. B. Kohona, 'Dispute Resolution Under the World Trade Organisation: An Overview' (1994) 28(5) *Journal of World Trade* 23. See also E. Rowbotham, 'The Changing Nature of Dispute Settlement Under the GATT' (1995) 5 *Global Environmental Change* 71.
[23] See C. M. Valles & B. P. McGivern, 'The Rights to Retaliate under the WTO Agreement – The Sequencing Problem' (2000) 24(2) *Journal of World Trade* 63.
[24] See WTO, 'Singapore Ministerial Declaration', WT/MIN(96)/DEC, 18 December 1996, para. 20. See also WTO Press Release, 'Competition Policies: Work Programme for

of this book, the WTO nations established a Working Group at the first WTO Ministerial Conference in Singapore in December 1995 to consider the incorporation of competition law into the WTO. This Working Group has made substantive progress in identifying a range of issues associated with the interface between trade and competition policy.

Based on the analysis set out above, the ranking of the different institutional structures under the 'achievability' criteria is set out in Figure 41.

In summary, based on the evaluation criteria set out in Figures 38, 39, 40 and 41 above, the WTO is the most suitable of the four most likely institutional vehicles for an international competition agreement. This is graphically illustrated by the aggregated ranking in the table in Figure 42 in which the WTO emerges fairly conclusively as the optimal institutional vehicle for any international competition agreement. This ranking also suggests that, of the other alternatives, a UN Treaty should be preferred above a Stand-Alone Treaty and that the OECD Treaty is the least suitable institutional vehicle.

10.2 Existing proposals for a WTO competition agreement

Given the conclusion above that the WTO would provide the optimal institutional vehicle for an international competition agreement, the issue arises as to what the substantive content of any WTO competition agreement should be. As a first step in identifying such content, it is useful to consider previous proposals to include competition law in the WTO.

10.2.1 Previous proposals for introducing competition law into the WTO

At least three significant proposals have been made over the past decade for the introduction of an international competition agreement into the WTO:

- In 1995, a 'Group of Experts in Competition Law', appointed by EC Competition Commissioner Karel Van Miert to consider mechanisms

Ministerial Conference in Singapore', November 1996. See also WTO, 'Singapore Ministerial Declaration' (1997) 36 *International Legal Materials* 218.

Institutional structure	Achievability ranking	Explanation for achievability ranking (ordered from most achievable to least achievable)
WTO Agreement	High	As identified above, the WTO Agreement exhibits: existing international support; historical precedent; relevant existing institutions; benefits from comprehensive negotiations; and existing preferences.
UN Treaty	Medium	The UN Treaty exhibits historical precedent (via the UNCTAD Code) and exhibits relevant existing institutions. The UN Treaty may also enable trade-off benefits from comprehensive negotiations. However, UNCTAD is perceived by developed nations as partisan to the views of developing nations, suggesting a UN Treaty utilising UNCTAD would not receive full international support.
Stand-Alone Treaty	Medium to Low	The Stand-Alone Treaty provides the greatest flexibility as it is not confined to existing institutions. However, this may inhibit achievability given that the subject matter to be covered during negotiations would be necessarily more extensive as a result. There would also be less scope to provide trade-offs to nations suffering net welfare losses.
OECD Treaty	Low	There is little precedent for the negotiation of an international competition agreement within the context of the OECD. Rather, OECD initiatives to date have been undertaken at the policy level. In addition, the OECD is arguably not sufficiently representative of the entire international community to facilitate the negotiation of an international competition agreement.

Figure 41: *Achievability of each institutional structure*

for strengthening international co-operation on competition law matters, proposed a WTO competition agreement ('EC Proposal').[25]
- In 1995, Professor Frederic Scherer of the United States proposed a WTO competition agreement within his Brookings Institution report

[25] See European Community Commission Group of Experts, *Competition Policy in the New Trade Order: Strengthening International Co-operation and Rules* (EC Commission, Brussels, 1995).

Ranking by evaluation criteria (low number indicates more preferable)	WTO Agreement	UN Model	Stand-alone	OECD Treaty
Effectiveness	1	3	2	4
Scope	2	1	3	4
Context	1	3	4	2
Achievability	1	2	3	4
TOTALS	5	9	12	14

Figure 42: *Ranking to identify most suitable institutional vehicle for an international competition agreement*

entitled *Competition Policies for an Integrated World Economy* ('Scherer Proposal').[26]
- Most importantly, on 10 July 1993, a private group of twelve leading competition and trade law academics and practitioners who referred to themselves as the International Antitrust Code Working Group ('Munich Group') formally proposed a draft competition code to the Uruguay Round negotiators ('Munich Code').[27]

These three proposals differ in their approach but may be classified onto a continuum on the basis of the extent to which they would require modification of the existing WTO rules and institutions, as illustrated by Figure 43. Each of these proposals is summarised below:

- *EC Working Group Proposal* The EC Working Group proposed that substantive international competition rules could be incorporated into a plurilateral WTO agreement without establishing any new WTO institutions. Each ratifying nation would commit itself to adopting these substantive competition rules and to implementing an effective enforcement structure. These adopted competition rules would then be enforceable by national competition authorities under domestic laws within each ratifying nation. Each ratifying nation would agree to enter into positive comity co-operation agreements with the national

[26] See F. M. Scherer, *Competition Policies for an Integrated World Economy* (The Brookings Institution, Washington DC, 1994).
[27] See International Antitrust Code Working Group (Munich Group), 'Draft International Antitrust Code as a GATT-MTO Plurilateral Trade Agreement' (1993) 65(1628) *Antitrust & Trade Reg Rep* (BNA), Special Supplement, 19 August 1993, S-5.

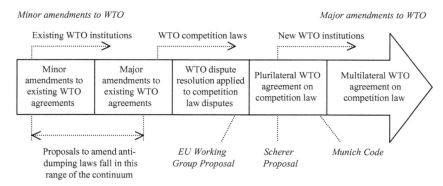

Figure 43: *Continuum indicating the extent to which the WTO could be amended to incorporate competition rules*

competition authorities of other ratifying nations. In the event that any national competition authority failed to take appropriate enforcement action, WTO dispute resolution could be sought by an aggrieved national competition authority, or another ratifying nation, using the existing dispute resolution mechanism of the WTO.

- *Scherer Proposal* The Scherer Proposal was more ambitious as it contemplated an International Competition Office under the auspices of the WTO that would enforce agreed WTO core competition standards. Scherer proposed that these core competition standards would relate only to serious anti-competitive conduct that offset international trade and investment. Scherer's International Competition Office would have jurisdiction to investigate any conduct that affected international markets or where complaints were made regarding cross-border anti-competitive practices. However, the International Competition Office would be required to respect national sovereignty and to use national competition authorities where possible to assist its investigations and implement corrective action. WTO enforcement mechanisms would only be employed in cases of national intransigence.[28]

- *Munich Code* The Munich Code of July 1993 pre-dated both the Scherer and the EC Working Group Proposals and was formed as part of a study by the Max Planck Institute for Foreign and International Patent,

[28] See F. M. Scherer, 'Competition Policy Convergence: Where Next?' (1996) 24(10) *International Business Lawyer* 485.

Copyright and Competition Law of Munich into the development of an international competition agreement.[29] The Munich Code contemplated the establishment of an International Antitrust Authority which would enforce a set of harmonised and substantive competition rules as part of the then-proposed WTO.[30] The International Antitrust Authority would have the power to request domestic competition authorities to commence competition investigations. Any investigation could subsequently be challenged before an International Antitrust Panel by an aggrieved contracting party.

Various elements of these three proposals for introducing an international competition agreement into the WTO are considered in greater detail in Chapter 11 of this book with a view to identifying the workable content and structure for a WTO Competition Agreement. However, before doing so, it is useful to analyse the Munich Code in greater detail, given that it is the most sophisticated and ambitious proposal to date for the incorporation of an international competition agreement into the WTO.

10.2.2 The Munich Group's Draft International Antitrust Code

The Munich Code has been the most serious and comprehensive initiative undertaken to date to resolve inconsistencies between trade and competition laws and to establish a set of enforceable international competition standards. While the Munich Code was, in many respects utopian, it subsequently became a key part of the international dialogue on the need for international competition rules.

The Munich Group drafted the Munich Code between 1991 and 1993, in the closing stages of the Uruguay Round, in recognition that many GATT nations at that stage were seriously considering the extent to which competition principles should be adopted into the proposed World Trade Organisation.[31] The Munich Code was intended to guide and promote

---

[29] See also International Antitrust Working Group, *Draft International Antitrust Code as a GATT–MTO Plurilateral Trade Agreement* (Max Planck Institute, Munich, 1993). See also H. Hauser & E. U. Petersmann, 'Draft International Antitrust Code' (1994) *Swiss Review of International Economic Relations (Aussenwirtschaft)*, Special Issue 310.

[30] See International Antitrust Working Group, 'Draft International Antitrust Code, (DIAC)' (1995) 5 *World Trade Materials* 126.

[31] See E. U. Petersmann, 'International Competition Rules for Governments and for Private Business: The Case for Linking Future WTO Negotiations on Investment, Competition and Environmental Rules to Reforms of Anti-Dumping Laws' (1996) 30 *Journal of World Trade* 5.

discussion on the development of an international competition law within the WTO and to provide an initial basis for international agreement. As such, the Munich Group sought to anchor the Munich Code into the WTO by deliberately reflecting a number of competition concepts initially set out within the Havana Charter of 1944 that were historically intended for inclusion within the proposed 'International Trade Organisation'.

The Munich Group proposed that the Munich Code would be adopted as a new plurilateral trade agreement under Annexe 4 of the WTO Agreement. Plurilateral agreements can be incorporated into the WTO by consensus, but do not require all WTO Members to be signatories. Instead, plurilateral agreements may have a more limited membership.[32] In this manner, a plurilateral approach is beneficial as it avoids the need for unanimity on all issues addressed by it. By adopting the plurilateral approach, the Munich Group recognised that many GATT nations were, at that time, unwilling to accede to a substantive international competition agreement and/or did not have sufficient domestic institutions and legislation in place to comply with any such agreement.

Importantly, the Munich Code did not purport to override domestic competition laws directly. Such an approach was considered unrealistic given that nations would be unlikely to agree to such an affront to their sovereignty. However, the Munich Code still sought to establish overriding principles and minimum substantive standards for domestic and international competition laws.[33] Once a nation became a signatory, that nation would be obliged to enact whatever domestic legislative measures were necessary to implement its obligations under the Munich Code including, for example, by upgrading existing competition laws, establishing an independent national competition authority and by removing exemptions from competition laws to the extent necessary. Not surprisingly, this approach was still unpalatable to most nations given that it was perceived by these nations as unnecessarily fettering their sovereign right to determine their own domestic competition laws and institutions.[34]

---

[32] See Article X:9 of the Final Act and Agreement Establishing the WTO, General Agreement on Tariffs and Trade, Uruguay Round (including GATT 1994), Marrakesh, 15 April 1994.
[33] See E. U. Petersmann, 'The International Competition Policy of the EC and the Need for an EC Initiative for a "Plurilateral Agreement on Competition and Trade" in the WTO' in F. Snyder (ed.), *Constitutional Dimensions of European Integration* (Kluwer Law International, London, 1996).
[34] See 'International Antitrust Code will be Studied by GATT Members' (1993) 65(1628) *Antitrust & Trade Regulation Reports* 259. See also J. R. Atwood, 'An International Antitrust Challenge: The Role of National Antitrust Laws in the Protection of International

In recognition of these political difficulties, the Munich Group was itself split on the appropriate substantive content of the Munich Code. The majority of the Munich Group proposed a comprehensive, detailed and more interventionist code with twenty articles divided into eight key parts.[35] In contrast, the minority of the Munich Group favoured a minimalist and less interventionist approach promoting the adoption of fifteen fundamental principles to guide the development of international competition rules. These fifteen principles were intended to promote greater consistency in the application of domestic competition law at the international level. The majority and minority approaches are considered in turn below.

The majority of the Munich Group drafted the Munich Code to reflect five core principles:

- *Minimum domestic standards*   Domestic competition laws were to be amended and enforced by ratifying nations to an agreed minimum standard based on the three key tenets of modern competition law (i.e. regulation of concerted conduct, prohibition of abuses of market power, and regulation of business concentration).
- *A principle of national treatment*   All ratifying nations were to observe a principle of equality and non-discrimination in the treatment of foreign and domestic entities when adopting and enforcing these minimum domestic standards.
- *Substantive international standards*   All ratifying nations were to enforce substantive international standards for the regulation of cross-border anti-competitive conduct via the domestic or extraterritorial application of their minimum domestic standards.
- *A principle of international procedural initiatives*   All ratifying nations were to adopt sufficient institutional arrangements and procedures to ensure effective enforcement of these domestic and international standards both at the international level by a supra-national international institution, and at the domestic level, by national competition agencies.

Competition' (1989) 10 *Journal of International Law & Business* 89. See also T. Man, 'National Legal Restructuring in Accordance with International Norms' (1997) 4 *International Journal of Global Legal Studies* 471.

[35] These parts addressed: general provisions and basic principles; horizontal and vertical restraints; control of concentration and restructuring; abuses of a dominant position; remedies; public undertakings and state authorisation; institutional provisions; and future development of the Munich Code.

- *A principle of exclusivity* The Munich Code would apply only to *cross-border* anti-competitive behaviour, rather than anti-competitive behaviour solely within the borders of a particular nation.

The majority of the Munich Group proposed a detailed institutional and substantive framework to give effect to these five core principles. The institutional framework involved the establishment of an International Antitrust Authority (IAA) under the WTO to be headed by a president, appointed for a six-year term, backed by a twenty-member 'International Antitrust Council'. This institutional structure paralleled that of the WTO with its President and Ministerial Council. The IAA was mandated to supervise the effective enforcement of the minimum domestic and international standards set out in the Munich Code as follows:

- *Enforcement of domestic standards* The IAA would be empowered to investigate complaints and initiate enforcement action before domestic competition authorities and courts. The IAA would be permitted to take action itself against national competition authorities in national courts if the relevant authority refused to take appropriate measures against anti-competitive conduct.

  In this manner, the minimum standards set out in the Munich Code would not be directly enforceable by the IAA against private entities. Rather, the IAA could only enforce the minimum standards indirectly, by requiring the relevant national competition authority to take appropriate enforcement action. However, the IAA would still be granted sufficient legal standing in national courts by ratifying nations to enable the IAA to obtain injunctions directly against private persons and to appeal decisions of a national authority or court (even as a non-party).
- *Enforcement of international standards* The IAA would have the ability to undertake international dispute settlement proceedings before a permanent International Antitrust Panel. The International Antitrust Panel would be a permanent dispute resolution body, functioning subject to the same rules and procedures as the WTO Dispute Settlement Body, including powers to interpret the Munich Code and to resolve disputes between ratifying nations. The IAA would have the ability to seek dispute settlement itself against a ratifying nation, before the International Antitrust Panel, where that nation breached any of its obligations under the Munich Code. Controversially, the Munich Code proposed that decisions of the International Antitrust Panel would be legally binding in the domestic law of member nations, overriding domestic courts and the decisions of national authorities.

Importantly, the powers of the proposed IAA extended well beyond the powers granted to many similar existing institutions at the international level, including the WTO Dispute Settlement Body. The concept of a supra-national enforcement agency and panel overriding national courts was a notion clearly of concern to most nations. This institutional framework was a significant factor contributing to the scepticism with which the Munich Code was treated by the international community, as discussed below.[36]

To complement these international institutions, the majority of the Munich Group proposed substantive rules for the Munich Code that would act as minimum standards for national and international competition rules. While international treaty obligations are not binding in domestic law until they have been incorporated into domestic law in most nations, the Munich Group proposed to overcome this hurdle by requiring ratifying nations to enact domestic laws of at least the same standard and content as that of the Munich Code. In this manner, the Munich Code would become the minimum standard for all domestic competition laws on an international basis.

Importantly, a number of these minimum standards were prescriptive and relatively detailed. On aspects of competition law subject to international disagreement, these standards tended to adopt a philosophical view of competition law that was EU-oriented and relatively interventionist. This EU-orientation no doubt reflected the composition of the Munich Group, which was comprised predominantly of EU scholars.[37] Given this perceived EU-orientation, it is probably not surprising that the Munich Code was rejected by the US, its strongest critic.[38]

In contrast to the majority approach, the *minority* of the Munich Group proposed fifteen draft principles that were intended to respect the existence of international diversity in competition law by avoiding prescriptive international standards. The minority proposed that differences in national competition laws should be tolerated and that any international

---

[36] See, for example, C. S. Stark, 'Enhancing Market Access Through Trade and Antitrust Law', Address Before the Section of International Law and Practice of the American Bar Association, 8 August 1995.

[37] See D. J. Gifford, 'The Draft International Antitrust Code Proposed at Munich: Good Intentions Gone Awry' (1996) 6 *Minnesota Journal of Global Trade* 1.

[38] See, for example, J. I. Klein, 'Anticipating the Millennium: International Antitrust Enforcement at the End of the Twentieth Century', Address Before the Fordham Corporate Law Institution, 16 October 1997. See also J. I. Klein, 'A Note of Caution with Respect to a WTO Agenda on Competition Policy', Address Presented at the Royal Institute of International Affairs, 18 November 1996.

agreement should instead set out a few clear and strong framework principles. While an IAA would still exist, its powers would be limited and its primary function would be to provide advice and assistance, while acting as an arbiter of international jurisdictional disputes. The IAA would also promote the convergence of national competition laws and the adoption of internationally-standardised procedures for such matters as merger notifications.

Under the minority approach, each nation would be required to have regard to the foreign effects of its enforcement activities, essentially imposing an obligation of positive comity. Substantive standards would only be proposed for the worst anti-competitive conduct, such as hard core cartels. Ratifying nations would be encouraged to minimise exceptions from domestic competition laws and to reduce existing defences, such as the defence of foreign sovereign compulsion. Ratifying nations would also be required to seek to harmonise key competition and trade laws, such as laws against predatory pricing and anti-dumping.

10.2.3 Criticisms of the Munich Code: why was it never adopted?

The Munich Code was an important proposal that captured the imagination of many academics and practitioners. The Munich Code also provided a number of insights into a specific path for integrating competition policy within the WTO and thus acted as an important catalyst for international debate on the need for international competition rules. However, the Munich Code was treated with considerable scepticism by the governments of most nations.[39] The OECD, comprising most of the nations with advanced competition laws in the international community, rejected the Munich Code.[40] In addition, the US (one of the key nations whose support was needed to progress WTO negotiations), proved to be one of the strongest critics of the Munich Code.[41] As a result, the Munich

---

[39] See D. P. Wood, 'Antitrust: A Remedy for Trade Barriers?', Address by the Deputy Assistant Attorney-General, Antitrust Division, US Department of Justice, before the Asian Law Programme, Japan Information Access Project, Washington DC, 24 March 1995. See also W. Fikentscher & U. Immenga (eds.), *Draft International Antitrust Code* (Nomos Verlag, Baden-Baden, 1995).

[40] See 'OECD Committee Lacks Enthusiasm for Draft International Antitrust Code' (1993) 65(1644) *Antitrust & Trade Regulation Reports* 771.

[41] See, for example, J. I. Klein, 'No Monopoly on Antitrust: It Would be Premature for the WTO to Seek to Enforce Global Competition Rules', *Financial Times*, 13 February 1998, p. 20.

Code initiative faded. The issue arises, why was the Munich Code treated with such scepticism by the international community?

In hindsight, the essential problem with the Munich Code was that it was too ambitious. The Munich Code was premature in its advocacy of particular institutional structures and binding competition law principles. The particular form of these institutional structures and substantive rules proposed by the Munich Code was also inappropriate. While criticisms of the Munich Code by most nations were never clearly articulated, they appeared to be directed primarily at the 'strong' form of internationalisation and more interventionist approach promoted by the Munich Code. In the case of the US, for example, the idea of a substantive and detailed rule-based framework, coupled with a supra-national dispute resolution authority, was considered contrary to US national interests and was viewed as interfering with well-established US antitrust laws and principles.[42]

The criticisms of the Munich Code by the international community therefore appeared to concern two distinct points of contention, both of which are discussed in further detail below:

- First, the institutions and supra-national procedures set out in the Munich Code unnecessarily infringed on national sovereignty ('Institutional Concerns').
- Secondly, the substantive rules of the Munich Code were unnecessarily detailed and did not respect legitimate national differences ('Substantive Concerns').

Even the EU, an initial proponent of the Munich Code, recognised the validity of these concerns.

Institutional Concerns The first contention identified above was that the Munich Code was considered unacceptable to most governments because its institutions and supra-national procedures were perceived as unnecessarily infringing on national sovereignty. The Munich Code created a significant international competition law enforcement bureaucracy with supra-national powers.[43] The concept of such an authority having binding authority over both national courts and national competition authorities was anathema to most nations, particularly those nations that

---

[42] See S. W. Waller, 'An International Common Law of Antitrust' (1999) 34 *New England Law Review* 1.
[43] See B. J. Phillips, 'Comments on the Draft International Antitrust Code' (1994) 49 *Swiss Review of International Economic Relations (Aussenwirtschaft)* 327. See also D. J. Gifford, 'Antitrust and Trade Issues: Similarities, Differences and Relationships' (1995) 44 *DePaul Law Review* 1049.

traditionally emphasised the preservation of individual rights vis-à-vis the state, such as the US.[44] Similarly, the Munich Code advocated a centralised, European-style, supra-national model of competition law enforcement, rather than a decentralised enforcement regime that promoted enforcement by individual competition authorities and self-interested market participants.[45]

Accordingly, the supra-national enforcement mechanism proposed by the Munich Code appears to have been inappropriate for the modern international community, in which each nation continues to guard jealously its own territorial sovereignty. The Munich Code also failed to recognise the interests of nations with competition law regimes premised on private enforcement action.[46]

The Munich Group recognised that direct supra-national enforcement of domestic law by the IAA against private entities was inappropriate, particularly where effective national competition enforcement agencies already existed for this task. The Munich Group instead contemplated indirect supra-national oversight by the IAA to ensure that national enforcement authorities undertook effective domestic enforcement against private sector conduct. The IAA was thus empowered to undertake enforcement action by obtaining injunctions in national courts, appealing judicial and administrative decisions, and undertaking supra-national enforcement action against domestic competition authorities where the domestic enforcement action of these institutions was inadequate.

Yet, even under this indirect approach, there are dangers in a supra-national agency effectively 'second-guessing' the decisions of national competition agencies in this manner:

- First, most nations already seek to ensure the accountability of their national competition agencies via an administrative or judicial appellate process. A further right of appeal would potentially conflict with

---

[44] See, 'Antitrust Division Official Predicts Scant Prospect of International Code' (1994) 66(1650) *Antitrust & Trade Regulation Reports* 181. See also J. Davidow & L. Chiles, 'The United States and the Issue of the Binding or Voluntary Nature of International Codes of Conduct Regarding Restrictive Business Practices' (1978) 72(2) *American Journal of International Law* 247.

[45] See 'World Competition Regulation' (1994) 1 *Business Law Brief* 36. See also R. E. Hudec, 'GATT/WTO Constraints on National Regulation: Requiem for an Aim and Effects Test' (1998) 32 *International Lawyer* 619.

[46] See E. U. Petersmann, 'International Competition Rules for the GATT – MTO World Trade and Legal System' (1993) 27(6) *Journal of World Trade* 35.

existing appellate processes and may trigger jurisdictional conflicts.[47] Accountability to an international administrative agency, rather than domestic judicial agencies, also tends to undermine the separation of powers between the judiciary and the executive so may have constitutional ramifications in many nations.
- Secondly, such a supra-national oversight role would have necessarily required the IAA to undertake complex competition analyses itself.[48] Yet competition cases tend to be highly complex and fact-intensive and involve nuances specific to particular national markets and domestic legislation.[49] It is therefore questionable whether the decisions of the IAA would be qualitatively as good as those of national competition agencies and courts.[50]

Given these issues, the Munich Code should have adopted an appropriate international institutional structure that ensured effective enforcement of competition laws by national competition agencies, but *without* unduly infringing on national sovereignty. The Munich Code should have avoided interfering in the pre-existing appellate processes of each nation or 'second-guessing' enforcement decisions. The Munich Code could have achieved this by adopting a more 'decentralised' approach, as follows:

- National enforcement authorities could have been empowered to undertake all necessary enforcement action without interference by the IAA. Each national enforcement agency would have been accountable only to the governments and courts of its own nation. The relevant government would, in turn, have been accountable for meeting its international obligations under the Munich Code.
- In circumstances where a nation believed that another nation had not complied with the Munich Code, the aggrieved nation could have been required to lodge an international dispute with the International Antitrust Panel. The International Antitrust Panel would have adjudicated the dispute based on the application of the international law set out in the Munich Code.

---

[47] See N. Covelli, 'Public International Law and Third Party Participation in WTO Panel Proceedings' (1999) 33 *Journal of World Trade* 125.
[48] For example, to assess whether national competition agencies had met their obligations under the Munich Code.
[49] The length and complexity of the *Kodak Fuji* case illustrates, for example, the likely evidential difficulties associated with the adjudication of private anti-competitive conduct, even indirectly, by the WTO.
[50] See also Y. Jung, 'Modelling a WTO Dispute Settlement Mechanism in an International Antitrust Agreement – An Impossible Dream?' (2000) 34(1) *Journal of World Trade* 89.

- In circumstances where a domestic court interpreted domestic law in a manner inconsistent with the international agreement, the onus could have been on the relevant government to enact legislation to remedy the inconsistency to avoid breaching the Munich Code and facing trade sanctions.[51]

Conceptually, this alternative approach would have avoided the need for a 'pro-active' supra-national administrative agency, such as the IAA, with inquisitorial powers to undertake enforcement activities directly against private entities. Rather, this approach would have relied on a 'reactive' quasi-judicial agency, such as the WTO Dispute Settlement Body.[52] Such an approach would have better addressed the concerns of nations regarding territorial jurisdiction and sovereignty and would have avoided the 'strong' form of internationalisation that alarmed most nations. More importantly, this reliance on adjudication-based enforcement would have been entirely consistent with the current approach of the WTO, which relies on trade sanctions authorised by the WTO Dispute Settlement Body. This approach would also have been in keeping with the approach most commonly adopted for the application of international public law within multilateral agreements of this nature.

However, notwithstanding this principal reliance on an adjudicatory body for enforcement action, an important co-ordinating role for an international competition agency would have remained. Consistent with the proposal by the minority of the Munich Group, an international competition agency could have still retained an important role in facilitating cross-border competition investigations and promoting a consistent and harmonised approach to international enforcement activities.

Substantive Concerns   The second contention identified above was that the substantive rules of the Munich Code were unnecessarily detailed, too interventionist and did not respect legitimate national differences. The mandatory international harmonisation of competition law proposed by the Munich Code was considered by many nations to be politically unpalatable. Many nations considered that the adoption of the Munich Code would have forced a level of standardisation that would

---

[51] See, for example, discussion in J. H. Jackson, 'The WTO, Dispute Settlement Understanding – Misunderstandings on the Nature of Legal Obligation' (1997) 91 *American Journal of International Law* 60.

[52] See WTO, 'Rules of Conduct for the Understanding on Rules and Procedures Concerning Settlement of Disputes' (1997) 36 ILM 477.

undermine their political preferences and economic policies.[53] Similarly, other nations considered that such standardisation could impede the future development and evolution of their domestic competition laws and could prevent nations tailoring their domestic competition laws to reflect legitimate national concerns.[54]

Examples of circumstances where domestic laws legitimately differed from the Munich Code, but would have been forced to have been amended by the Munich Code, were as follows:

- certain horizontal restraints (e.g. customer division) and vertical restraints were defined as per se illegal by the Munich Code, but are not defined as such in many jurisdictions;[55]
- qualitatively lower thresholds than the Munich Code apply in a number of jurisdictions, particularly in relation to the assessment of business concentration;
- different levels of relative importance are attached to infringements of certain competition rules by many jurisdictions (e.g. US jurisprudence adopts a more relaxed view of vertical restraints than the Munich Code);
- a number of industries in many jurisdictions were subject to exemptions which are inconsistent with the requirements set out in the Munich Code;
- competition authorities of different jurisdictions are required to take into account non-competition considerations, such as the national interest, with such considerations not necessarily consistent with the Munich Code; and
- certain acts of state are exempted entirely by the competition laws of many jurisdictions, such exemptions being inconsistent with the Munich Code.

In light of such issues, it is not surprising that the Munich Code was viewed as subjecting domestic competition law to a level of standardisation that was unacceptable.

---

[53] See Y. P. Chu, 'Towards the Establishment of an Order of Competition for the International Economy: With References to the Draft International Antitrust Code, the Parallel Imports Problem, and the Experience of Taiwan' in C. J. Cheng, L. Liu & C. K. Wang (eds.), *International Harmonisation of Competition Laws* (Martinus Nijihoff, Dordrecht, 1995), p. 453.

[54] See, for example, discussion in A. D. Melamed, 'International Antitrust in an Age of International Deregulation' (1998) 6 *George Mason Law Review* 437, 444.

[55] See W. S. Comanor & P. Rey, 'Competition Policy Toward Vertical Restraints in Europe and the United States', Paper Presented at Conference 'Global Issues on Competition Policy', Vienna, 20 June 1996.

Furthermore, the Munich Code drew heavily on the European model of a harmonised substantive competition law. As discussed in Chapter 5 of this book, the European model is best suited to nations with similar competition policy and a pre-existing high degree of economic and legal integration. Such pre-conditions do not yet exist within the wider international community. Sir Leon Brittan, the EU Commissioner, himself subsequently acknowledged that it was unrealistic to extend the harmonisation principle of EU competition policy on an international basis at this stage. It also remains questionable whether a high level of standardisation is even desirable, as discussed in Chapter 12 of this book.[56]

Given the pre-existing diversity of domestic competition laws, the level of detail of the substantive competition provisions of the Munich Code was important. Generally, the greater the level of detail of any international agreement, the greater the differences encountered between nations, and the more difficult it is to realise international consensus. The Munich Code sought to avoid unnecessary detail by phrasing its substantive competition rules at a high level of generality, thereby glossing over a number of significant international differences between the competition laws of different nations. However, in some cases the Munich Code prescribed relatively detailed and prescriptive competition standards on aspects of competition law subject to international disagreement. Furthermore, in such circumstances, the Munich Code tended to adopt a particular philosophical view and wording of competition law that was EU-oriented and fairly interventionist. To some extent, as noted above, this EU bias was possibly inevitable given the composition of the Munich Group. In essence, a failure of the Munich Code was too much detail.

A lesson from the Munich Code is therefore that, to the extent any WTO competition agreement prescribes detailed rules and procedures, it will encounter difficulties in satisfying the different standards and expectations of the international community. If the Munich Code had

[56] There remain significant differences in the principles, objectives and substantive provisions of the domestic competition laws of the nations that have currently adopted competition laws in the international community. These differences reflect not only different economic trade-offs between producer and consumer welfare, but also divergent political views about the appropriate role of government in market economies, as well as different political traditions and power relationships. There exist several different schools of economic thought that often lead to different recommendations on competition policy, such as the relative importance of market contestability. Even among the members of the OECD, which represents most of the world's developed countries, there exist considerable differences between members in their approach to competition law. See, for example, OECD, *Merger Cases in the Real World: A Study of Merger Control Procedures* (OECD, Paris, 1994).

been more selective in its approach, it could have avoided such difficulties by applying substantive competition standards only to aspects of competition law on which broad international consensus had been achieved, such as the prohibition of 'hard-core' cartels. The remaining aspects could have been either subject to a consensus-building procedure or could have been addressed at a higher level of abstraction sufficient to gloss over international differences. Under such an approach, the Munich Code would have continued to promote the convergence of competition concepts and principles via broad standards while seeking to entrench only internationally-accepted substantive standards at any great level of detail.

Finally, the Munich Code did not address many of the interface problems associated with the relationship between competition law and international trade law. Rather, it focused on the introduction of stand-alone competition principles into the WTO and avoided the potential need to redraft certain WTO rules on state monopolies and anti-dumping to ensure greater consistency with a competition-oriented approach. The Munich Code could, for example, have taken the opportunity to promote a deeper and better integrated approach to competition policy at the international level.[57]

Notwithstanding such criticisms, the Munich Code was a conceptually well-developed proposal that enabled nations to identify elements of an international competition agreement that they considered were acceptable, and elements that were clearly unacceptable. The Munich Code galvanised US resistance to the concept of a supra-national enforcement agency with detailed international competition rules.[58] The Munich Code also assisted the subsequent EC initiative to adopt competition rules within the WTO.[59] In this manner, the Munich Code enabled nations to articulate better their particular preferences, enabling a potential compromise to be identified.

---

[57] This approach would have been consistent with the approach of the Uruguay Round negotiations at the time. See E. M. Fox, 'Competition Law and the Agenda for the WTO: Forging the Links of Competition and Trade' (1995) 4 *Pacific Rim Law & Policy Journal* 1.

[58] See 'US Trade Official Cannot Foresee Prospect of International Antitrust' (1994) 66(1663) *Antitrust & Trade Regulation Report* 548.

[59] See 'European Commission will Urge WTO to Spearhead World Antitrust Battle' (1996) 70 *Antitrust & Trade Regulation Report* 1767.

10.3 The objectives for a WTO competition agreement

The previous proposals for incorporating competition law into the WTO therefore provide a number of insights (as identified above). The remainder of this chapter, and Chapters 11 and 12, seek to identify the optimal content for a WTO competition agreement building on these insights. A draft WTO Competition Agreement giving effect to the conclusions from these chapters is set out in the Appendix to this book with an accompanying commentary.

In considering the optimal content of a WTO competition agreement it is useful to start with the general (i.e. the objectives and core principles) and work towards the specific (i.e. substantive legal standards).

At the most fundamental level all nations agree that competition law and policy is intended to increase social welfare. All nations also agree, in accordance with internationally accepted principles of microeconomic theory, that competition law and policy is primarily intended to increase social welfare by promoting or maintaining competition, thereby encouraging the more efficient use of society's resources. In 1999, for example, the World Bank and OECD identified a convergence of international opinion that the principal objective of competition law is to 'maintain and encourage competition in order to promote economic efficiency and total economic welfare'.[60] Similarly, in a 1998 study, the WTO Secretariat identified an international consensus that the most basic objective of competition law and policy is to maintain 'a healthy degree of rivalry among firms in markets for goods and services'.[61] This is consistent with the analysis of the 'efficiency' objective of competition law identified in Chapter 6 of this book.

However, differences between nations arise when distributional objectives are factored into the equation. These distributional objectives may take myriad different forms under the rubric of the 'public interest'.[62] In the 1998 study mentioned above, the WTO Secretariat identified at least ten distributional objectives which were common in domestic

---

[60] See World Bank/OECD, *A Framework for the Design and Implementation of Competition Law and Policy* (World Bank, Washington DC, 1999).
[61] See WTO Secretariat, 'Synthesis Paper on the Relationship of Trade and Competition Policy to Development and Economic Growth', Working Group on the Interaction between Trade and Competition Policy, WT/WGTCP/W/80, 18 September 1998.
[62] Distributional objectives may include, for example, the promotion of consumer interests, employment, pluralism, regional development, or the diffusion of economic power via the protection of smaller enterprises.

competition legislation, in varying permutations. These multiple objectives may require nations to engage in difficult balancing exercises between a range of often conflicting social, political and economic concerns.

These distributional objectives may also complement or even contradict the economic efficiency objective of competition law and are weighted differently by different nations, often reflecting the political preferences of the government of the day. China, for example, has formulated its competition laws to give greater weight to social considerations and distributional fairness.[63] In contrast, US antitrust laws give pre-eminence to considerations of economic efficiency. There is no obvious global trend towards either extreme with different nations tending towards greater economic efficiency (e.g. New Zealand, Italy) or greater distributional fairness (e.g. France, India).[64]

Given such issues, the objectives of domestic competition legislation can be notoriously inconsistent between nations.[65] Legislation may identify a single objective in a few words, typically where the legislation focuses only on economic efficiency.[66] Legislation may specify a mix of efficiency and distributional objectives, as in Canada's Competition Act 1986. Legislation may even fail to mention objectives at all, as in the United States, which leaves competition authorities and the courts to construe any objectives from the language of the legislation and extrinsic evidence.

The question arises, given such diversity, what objectives should be drafted into a WTO Competition Agreement?

If one assumes that an international treaty can only document principles on which there is international consensus, this suggests that any

---

[63] See L. S. Liu, 'Efficiency, Fairness, Adversary and Moralsuasion: A Tale of Two Chinese Competition Laws' in C. J. Cheng, L. Liu & C. K. Wang (eds.), *International Harmonisation of Competition Laws* (Martinus Nijhoff, Dordrecht, 1995), p. 361.

[64] See discussion in 'The Evaluation of Past Activities and Proposal for Future Work in the WGTCP', Communication from the Republic of Korea, Working Group on the Interaction between Trade and Competition Policy, WT/WGTCP/W/154, 9 March 2001.

[65] The concept of 'fairness' is internationally nuanced and culturally distinctive and is inherently moulded to fit a particular society. The challenge is to identify and distil broad concepts of fairness that are common to competition law and trade law and that may provide a basis for reconciling concepts of distributional equity between both laws. Refer, for example, to Art. 7 of the Universal Declaration of Human Rights, Adopted by the UN General Assembly, 10 December 1948, GA Res 217A, UN GAOR, 3rd Sess, Part 1, Resolutions, at 71 UN Doc A810 (1948).

[66] See, for example, Art. 2 of the Mexican Federal Law of Economic Co-operation, which states as its objective: '... the purpose of this law is to protect the process of competition and free market participation ...'.

international agreement should adopt a two-tiered approach, separating efficiency objectives from distributional objectives, as follows:

- *Efficiency objectives* A WTO competition agreement could identify, as its primary objective, the maintenance of workable competition in international markets and domestic markets, via effective competition laws, so as to promote economic efficiency and increased aggregate domestic and global welfare.[67] If economic efficiency were promoted as the principal objective of domestic competition laws, this may support a more consistent application of domestic competition laws, as discussed in Chapter 6 of this book, and would be supported by most nations.
- *Distributional objectives* However, the issue arises, to what extent should any WTO competition agreement seek to shape or determine distributional objectives? Some level of regulation is clearly desirable, otherwise distributional objectives could be used as a loophole to subvert the overriding efficiency objective. Clearly this is a potentially controversial and politically contentious issue.

Many economists would argue, for example, that competition laws should not have a distributional objective at all. Such an approach would be consistent with the 'instrumentation principle' underpinning the drafting of many WTO obligations.[68] This principle maintains that any market failure should be corrected by the policy instrument directed closest to the source of the market failure.[69] Under this principle, distributional issues would be better addressed by other policy instruments directed at the particular distributional concerns (e.g. welfare subsidies).

A solution to this issue is to consider competition law objectives within the context of *competition policy*. A competition policy approach would require that any distributional objectives are not inconsistent with greater market competition. A useful precedent for such an

---

[67] While each nation may only enter into an international agreement if it were to provide net welfare gains to that nation, some nations may suffer net welfare losses as a result of entering into an international competition agreement, requiring trade concessions as a mechanism for compensating welfare losses.

[68] See discussion in B. Williams, 'The Influence and Lack of Influence of Principles in the Negotiation for China's Accession to the World Trade Organisation' (2001) 33 *George Washington International Law Review* 791, 819. See also discussion in E. Petersmann, 'National Constitutions, Foreign Trade Policy and European Community Law' (1993) 2 *European Journal of International Law* 1, 32.

[69] Competition law is viewed as a policy instrument directly targeting market failures associated with the excessive concentration of market power, but only indirectly addresses redistributional issues.

approach is provided by the APEC Competition Principles identified earlier in this book. Adopting a competition policy approach, a WTO competition agreement could contain two principles to guide the adoption of distributional objectives for domestic competition laws:

- First, distributional objectives should be minimised, even discouraged, consistent with the 'instrumentation principle' of the WTO.
- Secondly, where distributional objectives of domestic competition law are retained, they are not implemented in ways that are inconsistent with the maintenance of workable competition in domestic and international markets.

A suggested formulation for an Article in a WTO competition agreement to give effect to this two-tiered approach is set out in Article 4 of the draft WTO Competition Agreement in the Appendix to this book.

10.4 Core principles for a WTO competition agreement

Ranking below objectives in level of generality are the core principles upon which a WTO competition agreement could be based. While objectives are not legally enforceable and hence have only interpretative effect, principles may be enforceable in certain circumstances, depending on the degree of specificity with which they are expressed. The principle of non-discrimination in the GATT, for example, is directly enforceable against nations and is one of the key obligations of WTO law.

In determining the core principles for a WTO competition agreement it is useful to consider relevant pre-existing WTO principles and the extent to which these principles could be supplemented by principles unique to international competition law. By framing the principles for a WTO competition agreement in an expansive manner, it is possible to encompass related concepts within a single principle, thereby integrating international competition law principles with existing WTO principles. For example, accountability is a function of transparency and is related to procedural fairness so is superfluous as a stand-alone principle. Competitive neutrality is a form of non-discrimination.

Based on the analysis set out later in this chapter, five core principles could be articulated by a WTO competition agreement:[70]

---

[70] As noted earlier in this chapter, the 'instrumentation principle' of the WTO is also relevant in influencing the appropriate objectives for a WTO competition agreement. This principle

- a principle of international co-operation;
- a principle of non-discrimination;
- a principle of comprehensiveness;
- a principle of transparency; and
- a principle of procedural fairness.

Given the extent to which these five core principles are consistent with existing WTO jurisprudence (as identified below), agreement on these principles would better integrate any WTO competition agreement into the WTO while providing a strong foundation for international agreement on substantive competition rules.

However, the issue arises, what should be the appropriate nature and character of each of these principles within an international competition context? More importantly, how could they be drafted into a WTO competition agreement? These issues are addressed below.

10.4.1 A principle of international co-operation

The principle of co-operation is a fundamental principle of international law and is enshrined in such constitutive international law documents as the United Nations Charter and the Friendly Relations Declaration of 1970.[71] The Friendly Relations Declaration, for example, confirms that each nation has a specific duty in international law to co-operate with every other nation in accordance with the United Nations Charter.[72]

The principle of international co-operation already underpins the drafting of a number of WTO obligations, including in relation to the regulation of anti-competitive behaviour. As discussed in Chapter 6 of this book, a resolution of the GATT council introduced a consultative procedure relating to restrictive business practices into GATT law in 1960.

---

maintains that any market failure should be corrected by the policy instrument directed closest to the source of the market failure. Rather than expressing this as a sixth core principle, the instrumentation principle can be viewed as implicit within the subordination of distributional objectives to efficiency objectives.

[71] Indeed, one of the fundamental objectives of the United Nations itself, as set out in Art. 1:3 of the United Nations Charter, is to promote 'international co-operation in solving international problems of an economic . . . character'.

[72] While a key basis for this duty is to promote the rule of law among nations and to maintain international peace and security, the duty also encompasses co-operation to achieve such matters as international economic stability and the general economic welfare of nations. The principle of co-operation is also closely correlated with the obligation of every nation not to intervene in the affairs of any other nation and to resort to the settlement of international disputes by peaceful means.

Building on this procedure, an obligation to co-operate in relation to anti-competitive behaviour was expressly incorporated into the WTO at its inception in 1994 via Article IX of GATS,[73] and Article 40 of TRIPS.[74] In each case, a WTO nation must enter into consultations on request from another WTO nation with a view to eliminating business practices that may restrain competition.[75]

In an international competition law context, as discussed in Chapter 5, the obligation to co-operate has to date been expressed in two types of international instruments:

- *OECD recommendations* The OECD's Co-operation Recommendation, discussed in Chapter 5 of this book, already contemplates a principle of co-operation at the international level.[76] The Co-operation Recommendation urged OECD nations to co-operate in the investigation of international restrictive business practices and to create a network of bilateral 'mutual assistance' treaties to facilitate the exchange of confidential information.[77] As discussed in Chapter 5, the Co-operation Recommendation has catalysed the convergence of international opinion. Many of the procedures contemplated by the Co-operation Recommendation are now recognised as international best practice.
- *Bilateral co-operation agreements* Bilateral competition agreements (both on an inter-governmental and inter-agency basis) have become progressively more sophisticated, evolving from first generation agreements to fourth generation agreements. Most importantly, the co-operation-based concepts of positive and negative comity have now been recognised as essential to the effective enforcement of competition

---

[73] Article IX of GATS requires each WTO nation, on request from another WTO nation, to enter into consultations with a view to eliminating such business practices of service suppliers that may restrain competition and restrict trade in services.

[74] Article 40 of TRIPS addresses licensing practices or conditions pertaining to intellectual property, which restrain competition and have adverse effects on trade or technology transfer. Where a WTO nation believes that an intellectual property right owner of another WTO nation is undertaking practices in contravention of that other WTO nation's competition laws, the first WTO nation may request consultations.

[75] The requested nation must also supply publicly available non-confidential information of relevance to the matter in question and may supply confidential information (subject to its domestic laws and the conclusion of satisfactory confidentiality arrangements).

[76] See OECD, 'Revised Recommendation of the Council Concerning Co-operation Between Member Countries on Restrictive Business Practices Affecting International Trade' (1986) C(86)44(Final), 21 May 1986, (1986) 25 ILM 1629; 28 July 1995, C(95)130/Final.

[77] In addition to procedures for negative and positive comity, the Co-operation Recommendation set out procedures for international notification, exchange of information and co-ordination of international enforcement action.

law on an international basis and have been incorporated into a number of bilateral competition law agreements.

The concepts of 'negative comity' and 'positive comity' are fundamental to addressing the issues of 'under-regulation' and 'over-regulation' identified in Chapter 3 of this book. Accordingly, the principle of co-operation is fundamental in rectifying the economic externalities identified in Chapter 3. A principle of co-operation that could be incorporated into a WTO competition agreement is set out in Article 8 of the draft WTO Competition Agreement in the Appendix to this book.

10.4.2 A principle of non-discrimination

The WTO principle of non-discrimination is the *sine qua non* of the multilateral trading system. The principle of non-discrimination is heavily entrenched within existing WTO jurisprudence and has a distinct, internationally-accepted, form and function.[78] Some academics have even argued that the principle of non-discrimination is close to becoming a principle of customary international law.[79]

Within modern WTO law, the principle of non-discrimination assumes two distinct forms, both of which are intended to prevent discrimination on the basis of nationality:

- *Most favoured Nation Treatment ('MFN')* MFN essentially requires that any WTO member must not discriminate between the goods or services of different WTO members. The MFN principle is drafted into Article I of the GATT, Article II of the GATS and Article 4 of TRIPS. In the GATT, the MFN principle ensures that any trade concession given to any nation must benefit all other GATT ratifying nations. In the GATS, the MFN principle involves 'no less favourable treatment' which is breached if a particular governmental measure modifies the conditions of competition to favour services from particular nations, above those from others.
- *National Treatment ('NT')* NT essentially requires that any WTO member must not discriminate against the goods or services of another

---

[78] See, 'The Fundamental WTO Principles of National Treatment, Most-Favoured-National Treatment and Transparency', Background Note by the WTO Secretariat, Working Group on the Interaction between Trade and Competition Policy, WT/WGTCP/W/114, 14 April 1999.

[79] See K. M. Meessen, 'Antitrust Jurisdiction and Customary International Law' (1984) 78 *American Journal of International Law* 783.

WTO member vis-à-vis its own goods or services. The NT principle is drafted into Article III of the GATT, Article XVII of the GATS and Article 3 of TRIPS. While the NT principle has a slightly different formulation in each of these three WTO agreements, the common theme of these formulations is that they each impose a 'no less favourable treatment' standard of non-discrimination based on nationality.[80] This standard has been interpreted as requiring equality of competitive opportunities between domestic and foreign goods, services and firms, as discussed in Chapter 7.[81] The standard is breached if a particular governmental measure modifies the conditions of competition in favour of domestic goods, services or entities.[82]

Hence while the MFN principle ensures a level playing field between foreign competitors from different nations, the NT principle ensures a level playing field between foreign and domestic competitors.[83] Clearly, this is consistent with the objective of competition law and policy in ensuring that each firm has an opportunity to compete on its own merits.

The application of the twin WTO principles of non-discrimination when translated into the context of competition law and policy could require an international competition agreement to impose an obligation on nations not to discriminate formally against firms on the basis of their corporate nationality:

- Adopting an NT approach, a foreign firm entering a market should not be subject to higher competition standards than domestic firms by reason of corporate nationality alone.
- Adopting an MFN approach, one foreign firm should not be subjected to a higher competition standard in a domestic market than another foreign firm by reason of corporate nationality alone.

---

[80] See J. H. Jackson, 'National Treatment Obligations and Non-tariff Barriers' (1989) 10 *Michigan Journal of International Law* 207.
[81] See *United States – Section 337 of the Tariff Act of 1930*, GATT Panel Report, BISD 36S/345, L/6439, adopted on 7 November 1989, para. 5.10. See also *United States – Taxes on Petroleum and Certain Other Imported Substances*, GATT Panel Report, BISD 34S/136, L/6175, adopted on 17 June 1987, para. 5.1.9.
[82] See *Italian Discrimination against Imported Agricultural Machinery*, GATT Panel Report, BISD 7S/60, L/833, adopted on 23 October 1958 para. 12. See also *EC – Regime for the Importation, Sale and Distribution of Bananas*, WTO Panel Report, WT/DS27/R, adopted on 22 May 1997, para. 7.175.
[83] The NT principle is the flip side of the MFN principle. See *European Communities – Regime for the Importation, Sale and Distribution of Bananas*, WTO Appellate Body Report, WT/DS27/AB/R, adopted on 9 September 1997.

Such a broad obligation of non-discrimination (encompassing both NT and MFN) is entirely consistent with the objectives of competition policy in ensuring that each firm has an opportunity to compete on its own merits.

Furthermore, given that a fundamental principle of competition law and policy is to encourage equality of competitive conditions, and thus a level playing field, it is possible to give the principle of non-discrimination much broader application within a competition law context. The principle can also be applied across *all* markets, whether for goods or services. The different and limited formulations of NT and MFN in the existing WTO agreements mean that such a broad competition-oriented obligation is not clearly imposed in a uniform manner across all markets at the present time.[84]

The question then arises, why limit the non-discrimination obligation only to corporate nationality? There is also scope for a significantly broader application of the principle of non-discrimination within a competition law and policy context to address such matters as discrimination between public sector and private sector enterprises. The APEC Competition Principles, for example, contain a broad concept of non-discrimination based on 'competitive neutrality' which essentially requires that regulation must be applied in a manner that does not discriminate between economic entities in like circumstances regardless of nationality.[85] Yet this broader approach extends beyond the traditional approach of WTO law and is therefore less likely to be internationally acceptable, particularly as it tends to prescribe matters within the territorial jurisdiction of nations.[86] While this approach may be appropriate as a broad non-binding principle to influence government policy formulation, it is less likely to be palatable as a binding obligation set out within a WTO agreement.

The next significant issue when drafting a principle of non-discrimination into a WTO competition agreement, is to identify the

---

[84] See A. K. Abu-Akeel, 'The MFN as it Applies to Service Trade – New Problems for an Old Concept' (1999) 33 *Journal of World Trade* 103.

[85] See 'Principles to Enhance Competition and Regulatory Reform' as Attachment to APEC, 'The APEC Challenge', APEC Economic Leaders' Declaration, Auckland, 13 September 1999. See also K. M. Vautier, 'The PECC Competition Principles', PECC Trade Policy Forum, Auckland, 3 June 1999. See also Pacific Economic Co-operation Council, 'PECC Competition Principles: PECC Principles for Guiding the Development of a Competition-Driven Policy Framework for APEC Economies', Singapore, 1999.

[86] See, for example, J. P. Trachtman, 'International Regulatory Competition, Externalisation, and Jurisdiction' (1993) 34 *Harvard International Law Journal* 47.

types of discriminatory treatment that any non-discrimination obligation should discipline. In particular, whether such a principle should apply to de facto discrimination (i.e. discrimination occurring in the application of this domestic law to particular factual situations) as well as de jure discrimination (i.e. discrimination embodied within particular formulations of domestic competition law). In this regard, discriminatory treatment could potentially occur within the following scenarios:

- De jure *discrimination* (i.e. discrimination in formulation of the law itself) could occur, for example, in relation to:
  (a) the formulation of competition law legislation; and
  (b) the formulation of guidelines for its application and enforcement.
  A prohibition against de jure discrimination would require ratifying nations to ensure that their domestic competition laws and associated guidelines were framed in a manner that did not discriminate between firms (or their goods or services) on the basis of corporate nationality.

  It would be rare to find such de jure discrimination in most existing domestic competition laws, given that such discrimination undermines the rationale of competition law. However, such an obligation would be useful as it would prevent ratifying nations from amending their competition laws to effect discriminatory treatment at a later point in time.
- De facto *discrimination* (i.e. discrimination in the application of the law to the facts) could occur, for example, in relation to:
  (a) the decision by the competition regulator to initiate enforcement action;
  (b) the procedures in decision-making by the competition regulator; and
  (c) the substantive regulatory decisions themselves.
  A prohibition against de facto discrimination would apply to specific regulatory decisions and would prevent discrimination in the application of competition laws to particular factual situations.

  The WTO Anti-dumping Agreement provides a useful precedent and indicates that it would be possible to regulate discrimination in relation to decisions to take regulatory action and discrimination in the procedures employed by regulators. However, it would not usually be practical to regulate discrimination occurring in the context of the substantive regulatory decisions themselves. The latter approach would be more consistent with the supra-national enforcement regime that was anathema to most nations in the context of the Munich Group proposal, as discussed above.

This analysis suggests that any WTO competition agreement should adopt a binding non-discrimination principle which absolutely prohibits de jure discrimination. This binding non-discrimination principle should also prohibit certain types of de facto discrimination (namely discrimination in decisions to initiate enforcement actions and discrimination in the application of regulatory procedures). However, the remaining types of de facto discrimination (namely the substantive regulatory decisions themselves) should simply be discouraged by a non-binding principle.

Given the conclusion that a non-discrimination principle should be given binding effect in relation to de jure discrimination and only certain types of de facto discrimination, an important issue arises as to the nature and extent of exemptions from this principle. The principle of non-discrimination has several significant exceptions under WTO law which could also apply to a WTO competition agreement. Most important of these are the 'general exceptions' which address measures necessary to protect public morals, maintain public order, protect life or health, and secure compliance with laws or regulations not inconsistent with the provisions of the WTO.[87] These exemptions could continue to apply in the context of a WTO competition agreement and would ensure that competition laws could be formulated in a manner which discriminates on the basis of corporate nationality *only* where such discrimination is justifiable for legitimate public policy reasons.[88]

Based on the above analysis, a possible principle of non-discrimination that could be incorporated into a WTO competition agreement is set out in Article 5 of the draft WTO Competition Agreement in the Appendix to this book.

---

[87] These general exceptions are subject to the requirement that measures taken pursuant to them are applied in a manner which would not constitute a means of arbitrary or unjustifiable discrimination between countries where like conditions prevail or where they would assume the form of a disguised restriction on international trade. See Art. XX of GATT and Art. XIV of GATS. See W. Schwartz & A. O. Sykes, 'Toward a Positive Theory of the Most Favoured Nation Obligation and Its Exceptions in the WTO/GATT System' (1996) 16 *International Review of Law and Economics* 27.

[88] Other exceptions are included in the WTO for such matters as national security, government procurement, regional trading arrangements and less developed nations. See Art. III:8(a) of the GATT and Art. XIII of the GATS for the exception for government procurement. See Art. XXI of the GATT and Art. XIV*bis* of the GATS for the exceptions for national security. See Art. XXIV of the GATT for the exemption from the MFN obligation for free trade agreements and customs unions. See Decision of 28 November 1979 on 'Differential and More Favourable Treatment, Reciprocity and Fuller Participation of Developing Countries', GATT Document L/4903, 28 November 1979, BISD 26S/203 for the exceptions for developing countries.

10.4.3 A principle of comprehensiveness

Unlike the principles of non-discrimination and transparency discussed above, a principle of comprehensiveness is not articulated by pre-existing WTO obligations. Rather, such a principle is arguably implicit within the objectives of the WTO in liberalising trade on a comprehensive basis across all trade sectors.

However, notwithstanding the progressive expansion of the WTO in successive rounds of multilateral negotiations, the coverage of the WTO continues to be incomplete and numerous exemptions exist from the application of WTO law. The WTO obligations are themselves framed in a manner which differentiates between sectors and industries including, for example, the broad distinction between trade in goods and trade in services and the differential treatment of service sectors. An express principle of comprehensiveness could seek to address such issues by informing future rounds of WTO multilateral negotiations and promoting a broader and more integrated approach to the development and application of WTO law.[89]

In a competition law context, the principle of comprehensiveness is fundamental. Competition laws are usually drafted in a generic and all-encompassing manner to apply to all markets (whether for goods or services) and all modes of supply. In this manner, competition law ensures that all firms are treated on an equivalent basis and market distortions are minimised. Under the deregulatory approach of competition policy, competition law is perceived as the minimum necessary regulation of competition consistent with the maximisation of economic efficiency, so is necessarily uniformly minimal in its approach. While additional industry-specific regimes may be applied to address particular instances of market failure or anti-competitive behaviour, such additional regulation is typically limited to network industries, financial markets and international shipping.[90]

In the context of a WTO competition agreement, a principle of comprehensiveness would ensure that the WTO competition agreement applied

---

[89] See OECD, *Antitrust and Market Access: The Scope and Coverage of Competition Laws and Implications for Trade* (OECD, Paris, 1996). See also OECD, 'Complementarities between Trade and Competition Policies', OECD, COM/TD/DAFFE/CLP(98)98/FINAL, Paris, 1998. See also OECD, 'Consistencies and Inconsistencies between Trade and Competition Policies', OECD, COM/TD/DAFFE/CLP(98)25/FINAL, Paris, 1998.

[90] See, for example, discussion in World Bank, *Bureaucrats in Business: The Economics and Politics of Government Ownership* (World Bank, Washington DC, 1997).

to all ratifying nations, all markets (including financial markets), all modes of supply, and to both private and public sector entities engaged in commercial economic activity. Exemptions for firms or sectors from the application of competition law could ideally be kept to a minimum. However, under many existing domestic competition laws, certain economic sectors are totally or partially excluded from the application of competition law, as discussed in Chapter 4.[91] Such broad sectoral exclusions may enable domestic firms to deny market access to foreign competitors. Ideally, any exemptions from the application of domestic competition laws should therefore be no greater than necessary in the circumstances and should be based on legitimate public policy reasons and sound economic principles. A WTO competition agreement could provide the means to achieve this.

Based on the above analysis, a possible principle of comprehensiveness that could be incorporated into a WTO competition agreement is set out in Article 8 of the draft WTO competition agreement in the Appendix to this book.

10.4.4 A principle of transparency

As with the principle of non-discrimination, the principle of transparency is fundamental to WTO jurisprudence. Transparency obligations assume two distinct forms:[92]

- *Obligations to publish* WTO nations are subject to broad obligations to make publicly available all relevant laws, regulations and administrative decisions. Such 'obligations to publish' are set out in broad terms in the three key WTO agreements, principally in Article X of the GATT, Article III of GATS and Article 63 of TRIPS. These obligations are framed expansively in each agreement and are usually comprehensive, applying, for example, to laws, regulations, judicial decisions and administrative decisions of general application.

---

[91] The World Bank has identified, for example, more common exemptions from domestic competition laws as including: collective bargaining activity to negotiate terms and conditions of employment; co-operation between insurance companies to underwrite risk collectively; and co-operation between trade associations for the purposes of disseminating information and developing product standards.

[92] See European Commission, 'A Multilateral Framework Agreement on Competition Policy', Communication from the European Community and its Member States, Working Group on the Interaction between Trade and Competition Policy, WT/WGTCP/W/152, 25 September 2000.

- *Obligations to notify* WTO nations are also subject to specific obligations to notify various forms of governmental action to other WTO members in particular circumstances. These 'obligations to notify' tend to be more specific in application, but are correspondingly more numerous and diverse within the WTO agreements. A Working Group during the Uruguay Round identified 165 different notification obligations within the GATT-related agreements alone, each obligation tailored to its particular context. Generally, notification requirements are employed where GATT obligations are framed broadly, because the scope for discretionary governmental measures is large in such circumstances and the need for external transparency is therefore greater.

These two types of transparency obligations have several objectives within WTO law:

(a) to create a rules-based environment more conducive to the Rule of Law by ensuring greater regulatory certainty and predictability, increased confidence and reduced market risk;[93]
(b) to disseminate information to economic actors, thereby more effectively influencing their future behaviour; and
(c) to facilitate effective monitoring and compliance, thereby promoting accountability.[94]

Importantly, these transparency obligations reinforce other WTO obligations by ensuring that any breach of a WTO obligation is more readily identifiable, ensuring greater accountability and stricter compliance.[95]

The WTO principle of transparency is entirely consistent with a competition law approach. Transparency of competition law is critical to

---

[93] See P. Clark & P. Morrison, 'Key Procedural Issues: Transparency' (1998) 32 *International Lawyer* 851. See T. Wälde, 'Treaty and Regulatory Risk in Infrastructure Investment: The Effectiveness of International Law Disciplines versus Sanctions by Global Markets in Reducing the Political and Regulatory Risk for Private Infrastructure Investment' (2000) 34(2) *Journal of World Trade* 1. See S. Arrowsmith, 'Towards A Multilateral Agreement on Transparency in Government Procurement' (1998) 47 *International and Comparative Law Quarterly* 793.

[94] In one of the foundation cases for establishing the rule of law, *Entick* v. *Carrington* (1765) 19 St Tr 1030 (Court of Common Pleas), for example, Lord Camden CJ stated: 'If it is law, it will be found in our books. If it is not to be found there, it is not law'. As a juristic principle, the rule of law requires that any encroachment by government on the liberties of the citizen be clearly stated in advance, thereby holding government accountable for its actions.

[95] See G. Marceau & P. N. Pedersen, 'Is the WTO Open and Transparent?' (1999) 33(1) *Journal of World Trade* 5. See D. J. Gervais, 'The TRIPS Agreement' (1999) 21 *European Intellectual Property Review* 156.

ensure firms operating in the market can readily determine the legality of their conduct. Transparency also assists firms to notify domestic competition authorities (or seek redress in the courts) against anti-competitive behaviour by other firms. Transparency requirements are also critical in promoting the accountability of domestic competition authorities.[96]

A WTO competition agreement could incorporate a broad 'obligation to publish', coupled with specific 'obligations to notify' in circumstances where greater accountability is desired:

- A broad *obligation to publish* could not only prescribe publication of the relevant legislative framework and relevant competition laws and regulations of each nation, but could also require the publication of guidelines and communications setting out how these laws and regulations are applied.[97]
- Specific *obligations to notify* could arise in respect of the identification of sectoral exclusions and exemptions. Specific notification obligations could also arise in the context of positive and negative comity processes, as contemplated by Chapter 5 of this book and mentioned above.[98]

As with the principle of non-discrimination, the principle of transparency is subject to a number of exceptions in WTO law. WTO members are not required to disclose confidential information that would impede law enforcement or otherwise be contrary to the public interest, or which would prejudice the legitimate commercial interests of particular enterprises, whether public or private. In a competition law context, such exceptions would address the issues raised in Chapter 5 of this book, whereby many nations are averse to sharing commercially sensitive corporate information with other nations. Accordingly, the principle of transparency is

---

[96] The World Bank, for example, in a 1998 study, recommended that all national competition authorities should be subject to requirements of transparency and accountability. See World Bank, *Competition Policy in a Global Economy: An Interpretive Summary* (World Bank, Washington DC, 1998).

[97] This approach, for example, has been taken by the European Commission, which has recognised that the broad phraseology of competition provisions alone is often insufficient for firms to assess the legality of their actions accurately. See discussion in European Commission, 'Submission from the EC and its Member States to the Working Group on the Interaction Between Trade and Competition Policy: The Relevance of Fundamental WTO principles of National Treatment, Transparency and Most Favoured Nation Treatment to Competition Policy and Vice Versa', WTO Working Paper, WTO/WGTCP/W/117, 29 March 1999.

[98] See 'Response to Key Questions', Communication from the European Community and its Member States, Working Group on the Interaction between Trade and Competition Policy, WT/WGTCP/W/160, 14 March 2001.

essential for a WTO competition law agreement as is the need to identify confidentiality exceptions from it.

Based on the above analysis, a draft principle of transparency is set out in Article 6 of the draft WTO competition agreement in the Appendix to this book.

10.4.5 A principle of procedural fairness

While the principles of non-discrimination and transparency are fundamental to WTO law there is another principle that is fundamental to the Rule of Law itself, namely the principle of procedural fairness. The principle of procedural fairness is a fundamental principle shared universally by all nations that uphold the Rule of Law in its true democratic spirit.[99] Procedural fairness may be interpreted as a requirement to ensure that powers are not exercised arbitrarily and that governmental entities with powers are held accountable for their actions. Procedural fairness also ensures that circumstances do not exist that may encourage unfairness, such as bias or pre-determination. In the context of administrative law, procedural fairness ensures, for example, that decision-makers act within the scope of their powers, both reasonably and fairly.[100]

The concept of procedural fairness underlies the careful drafting of the WTO agreements, and the safeguards, checks and balances built into WTO law.[101] The WTO agreements on product standards, government procurement and intellectual property, for example, contain detailed procedural and 'due process' requirements that are intended to ensure that policies are transparent and substantive rules are not easily circumvented (thereby maintaining the effectiveness of negotiated trade concessions). TRIPS, for example, sets out specific procedural guarantees applicable to the enforcement of intellectual property rights through administrative and

---

[99] The concept of the Rule of Law is an idea extending back at least as far as Plato with his ideal of a government of laws, rather than a government of individuals where there is risk of abuse of government powers. For a discussion on the Rule of Law, see A. V. Dicey, 'The Rule of Law: Its Nature and General Applications' in A.V. Dicey, *Introduction to the Study of the Law of the Constitution* (10th edn, OUP, Oxford, 1959). See also T. R. S. Allan, 'Legislative Supremacy and the Rule of Law – Democracy and Constitutionalism' (1985) 44 *Cambridge Law Journal* 111. See also G. Q. Walker, *The Rule of Law – Foundation for Constitutional Democracy* (McGraw, New York, 1988).

[100] See, generally, H. W. R. Wade, *Administrative Law* (6th edn, Clarendon Press, London, 1988). See also discussion in G. Palmer & M. Chen, *Public Law in New Zealand: Cases, Materials, Commentary & Questions* (OUP, Melbourne, 1993), ch. 31.

[101] See D. Palmeter, 'The Need for Due Process in WTO Proceedings' (1997) 31(1) *Journal of World Trade* 51.

judicial proceedings.[102] TRIPS also imposes specific obligations regarding the use of evidence, availability of particular remedies, including provisional relief, and other procedural guarantees.

Another example of the principle of procedural fairness within WTO jurisprudence is provided by the judicial interpretation of Article X:3(a) and (b) of the GATT which provides, in part:

> ... Each Member shall administer in a uniform, impartial and reasonable manner all its laws, regulations, decisions and rulings of the kind described in paragraph 1 of this Article ...
>
> ... Each Member shall maintain, or institute as soon as practicable, judicial, arbitral or administrative tribunals or procedures for the purpose, inter alia, of the prompt review and correction of administrative action relating to customs matters ...

In the *Shrimp/Turtle* decision of 1999, on appeal from a WTO Panel Decision, the WTO Appellate Body reasoned that 'Article X:3 of the GATT 1994 establishes certain minimum standards for transparency and procedural fairness in the administration of trade regulations'.[103] The *Shrimp/Turtle* decision was controversial as it read into a provision intended to have comparative application (i.e. to prevent discrimination between nations), an absolute standard of due process not based upon comparative treatment. However, notwithstanding an apparent lack of clarity regarding the legal basis for its reasoning, the Appellate Body's decision arguably established that due process is an important requirement of WTO law.[104]

The principle of procedural fairness could be usefully and expressly articulated within a competition law context. In doing so, such a principle would not only guide the application of competition law at the international level, but could also influence the future development of the WTO

---

[102] TRIPS requires procedures which permit 'effective action', grant expeditious remedies sufficient to deter infringement and are 'fair and equitable'. See Agreement on Trade-Related Aspects of Intellectual Property Rights (1994) 33 *International Legal Materials* 81. See also, for example, E. M. Fox, 'Trade, Competition and Intellectual Property: TRIPS and its Antitrust Counterparts' (1996) *Vanderbilt Journal of Transnational Law* 481.

[103] See *United States – Import Prohibition of Certain Shrimp and Shrimp Products*, WTO Appellate Body Report, WT/DS58/AB/R, 12 October 1998; on appeal from *United States – Import Prohibition of Certain Shrimp and Shrimp Products*, WTO Panel Report, WT/DS58/R, 15 May 1998.

[104] The Appellate Body based its reasoning on the references to impartiality and reasonableness set out in Art. X:3, references to unjustified and arbitrary discrimination set out in Art. XX of the GATT, and 'general principles of international law'. See discussion in G. Búrca & J. Scott, 'The Impact of the WTO on EU Decision-making', Harvard Law School, Jean Monnet Papers, No. 6/00.

and, potentially, the future interpretation and application of other WTO agreements. As evidenced by the reasoning in the *Shrimp/Turtle* decision and the WTO agreements identified above, there is clearly scope for an express principle of procedural fairness to be incorporated into WTO law.[105]

In the context of a WTO competition agreement, a principle of procedural fairness would contemplate both procedural and structural safeguards in relation to the administration and enforcement of domestic competition law by national competition authorities.[106] These safeguards could take a number of different forms and could be expressed at differing levels of generality. Ideally, any principle of procedural fairness would ensure the following:

- national competition agencies should be independent, insulated from political and budgetary interference and capture by interest groups;
- national competition agencies should nonetheless be held accountable for their activities (e.g. via parliamentary oversight and the potential for judicial review);
- competition legislation should ideally separate the activities of investigation, prosecution and adjudication;
- entities should have access to competition authorities, including a basic right to petition national competition authorities;
- there should be due process in the conduct of competition investigations, including rights to be heard and basic standards for the protection of confidential information;
- the processes of investigation, prosecution and adjudication should have built-in checks and balances including, for example, rights of appeal, reviews of decisions and transparent administrative procedures;
- proceedings and case resolutions should be expeditious to avoid unnecessary transactions costs; and
- the enforcement of competition laws, and remedial action and penalties, should be proportionate although intended to have a deterrent effect.

However, the concept of procedural fairness is relatively amorphous and ill-defined, having a different meaning in different contexts. Even among developed nations, there are differing common law and civil law concepts

---

[105] See, for example, discussion in P. C. Mavroidos, 'Trade and Environment after the Shrimps-Turtles Litigation' (2000) 34(1) *Journal of World Trade* 73.

[106] See 'Creating a Culture of Competition: Issues Involved in Establishing an Effective Antitrust Agency', Communication from the United States, Working Group on the Interaction between Trade and Competition Policy, WT/WGTCP/W/142, 3 August 2000.

of procedural fairness.[107] Similarly, different nations have different legal traditions and place a different emphasis on judicial and administrative agencies. Furthermore, there are important and valuable differences among domestic competition law regimes and administrative and judicial systems.

For this reason, any obligations relating to procedural fairness would need to be expressed at a fairly high level of abstraction to avoid adopting an unnecessary prescriptive approach. It is unlikely that consensus could be realised on anything other than high-level principles within a WTO competition agreement. Any such obligations would similarly need to avoid any attempt to harmonise competition law enforcement procedures among nations.[108] Yet procedural fairness requirements would ensure that competition authorities remained accountable for their actions, hence some degree of obligation would be desirable.

Based on the above analysis, a possible principle of procedural fairness that could be incorporated into a WTO competition agreement would have the following elements, which have necessarily been framed broadly at a high level of abstraction:

- national competition authorities should be required to respect all human, civil and procedural rights in accordance with the Rule of Law in the particular nation and in accordance with internationally applicable standards;
- the national competition authority should act within the scope of the power and discretion conferred on it, both reasonably and fairly, when making regulatory decisions or otherwise exercising its regulatory powers;
- the national competition authority should not act capriciously and should not amend or alter regulatory requirements without due consultation with affected parties;
- the decisions and procedures of the national competition authority should be impartial and should not have any bias; and
- interested parties should be provided with a fair and reasonable opportunity to appraise the national competition authority of their views and

[107] See discussion in Canadian Competition Bureau, 'Options for the Internationalisation of Competition Policy: Defining Canadian Interests', Canadian Government, Ottawa, 1999, p. 9. See also Canadian Bar Association, 'Submission on The Internationalisation of Competition Policy', National Competition Law and International Law Sections of the Canadian Bar Association, 12 August 1992.
[108] See P. Marsden, 'A WTO "Rule of Reason"?' (1998) 19 *European Common Law Review* 530.

the national competition authority should give full and reasonable consideration to all submissions it receives and should clearly explain the reasoning for its decisions.

Each of these elements (except the first element) should not be an absolute obligation given that different nations have different legal traditions and institutions. Rather, each ratifying nation should use reasonable endeavours to give effect to these elements. However, the first element could be given direct legal effect. Various structural obligations could also be incorporated into the WTO competition agreement to ensure that institutions remain accountable for their actions. Most importantly, national competition authorities could be held accountable for their actions and decisions by requiring nations to adopt an appropriate appellate procedure.

A draft principle of procedural fairness based on these elements is set out in Articles 7 and 21 of the draft WTO competition agreement in the Appendix to this book.

10.5 Conclusion: the WTO is the optimal vehicle for an international competition agreement

In summary, while a number of potential institutional vehicles exist into which an international competition agreement could be incorporated, the WTO emerges fairly conclusively as the optimal institutional vehicle for any international competition agreement relative to such potential alternatives. The WTO is the most effective and achievable of the various institutional vehicles considered in this book.[109] The institutions of the WTO are widely respected and have the confidence of the international community. Incorporation of competition law into the WTO would also reflect historical precedent, and would realise synergies in underlying theory and synergies in policy co-ordination. It would also utilise existing WTO institutions which are ideally suited to competition issues and it would recognise existing international support for an international competition agreement in the context of the WTO.

When considering previous precedent, at least three proposals have been made for incorporating a WTO competition agreement into the WTO, although these previous proposals have not received international acceptance. The Munich Code was the most ambitious of these proposals but was rejected for two key reasons, namely that its institutions and

---

[109] For example, the processes of the WTO are supported by a broad constituency of developed and developing nations, comprising most of the international community.

supra-national approach unnecessarily infringed against national sovereignty, and that its substantive rules were unnecessarily detailed and did not respect legitimate national differences. There is a clear scope for the introduction of an international competition agreement into the WTO which addresses the issues raised in Chapters 3 to 9 of this book, but which avoids the pitfalls of such previous proposals.

Bearing this precedent in mind, Chapter 10 sought to identify the objectives and core principles for a WTO competition agreement. There is a general consensus regarding the principal objective of competition law, namely to maintain and encourage competition in order to promote economic efficiency and total economic welfare. However, there is a considerable divergence of opinion between nations regarding the appropriate distributional objectives for competition laws (and good arguments why competition laws should not have distributional objectives at all). Any WTO competition agreement would need to endorse this commonly accepted efficiency objective while permitting nations to adopt alternative distributional objectives as long as such objectives were not inconsistent with the promotion of economic efficiency via increased competition.

In addition to this objective, this chapter identified five core principles that should be adopted by a WTO competition agreement, namely principles of international co-operation, non-discrimination, comprehensiveness, transparency, and procedural fairness. Provisions to give effect to these five core principles are set out in the draft WTO competition agreement in the Appendix to this book.

11

What is the optimal content for a WTO competition agreement?

Following from the analysis in Chapter 10, Chapter 11 now considers the optimal *substantive content* of a WTO competition agreement.

Chapter 4 of this book analysed similarities between the competition laws of the APEC nations and identified the substantive elements of competition law that could be regulated by a WTO competition agreement. Chapter 4 also identified a number of principles and obligations that could be appropriately incorporated into a WTO competition agreement. However, in order to apply the conclusions from Chapter 4, it is necessary to identify the appropriate level of abstraction, and particular legal character, that should be accorded to such principles and obligations when they are drafted into a WTO competition agreement.

In undertaking this analysis, the following four questions are fundamental:

- To what extent should any WTO competition agreement seek to achieve harmonisation of domestic competition laws?
- To what extent should any WTO competition agreement seek to prescribe minimum international standards?
- To what extent should the provisions of a WTO competition agreement be legally enforceable as binding precepts of international law?
- To what extent should any WTO competition agreement seek to modify existing WTO rules and jurisprudence?

Chapter 11 considers each of these four questions in turn below. These four issues are fundamental to the negotiation of a WTO competition agreement as they determine the level of agreement that will be required between nations on any substantive competition obligations.

Chapter 11 concludes that any WTO competition agreement should promote selective convergence of domestic competition laws in those areas likely to realise the greatest benefits. Any competition obligations should ideally be negotiated within the context of a 'co-regulatory' approach that blends international 'hard law' obligations with 'soft law' principles. By adopting such a strategy, the level of agreement required between nations on substantive competition obligations could be reduced while still realising significant benefits.

11.1 To what extent should any WTO competition agreement seek to achieve harmonisation of domestic competition laws?

International harmonisation of laws usually refers to a process whereby nations negotiate and agree on uniform, or nearly uniform, substantive standards for their domestic laws.[1] International harmonisation of laws typically requires each nation to amend its domestic laws to adopt an internationally-agreed 'ideal' standard. A WTO competition agreement could act as a catalyst for international harmonisation of domestic competition laws by prescribing an agreed ideal standard and establishing a time frame for ratifying nations to adopt that standard by amending their domestic competition laws accordingly.[2]

However, the important question arises whether such harmonisation of domestic competition laws is desirable. In particular, to what extent *should* any WTO competition agreement seek to achieve harmonisation of domestic competition laws? Insights into this question may be provided by analysing the costs and benefits of harmonisation.

Importantly, 'harmonisation' is a concept which must be carefully defined when undertaking any analysis of costs and benefits. Harmonisation has been used in the literature to contemplate any number of states of partial or full harmonisation ranging from considerable similarity of legal structure through to identical wording, enforcement and legal interpretation. Before undertaking an analysis of the costs and benefits of harmonisation, it is therefore necessary to clarify the concept of 'harmonisation' and the appropriate use of terminology.

For the purposes of this chapter, the following terminology is used, as illustrated by the 'convergence-harmonisation continuum' in Figure 44:

---

[1] See, for example, discussion in E. M. Fox, 'Harmonisation of Law and Procedures in a Stabilised World: Why, What and How?' (1991) 60(2) *Antitrust Law Journal* 593. See also general discussion in C. Cheng, L. S. Liu & C. Wang (eds.), *International Harmonisation of Competition Laws* (Martinus Nijhoff, New York, 1995).

[2] See, for example, discussion in M. R. Joelson, 'An Antitrust Challenge: Harmonisation – A Doctrine for the Next Decade' (1989) 10 *Journal of International Law & Business* 133.

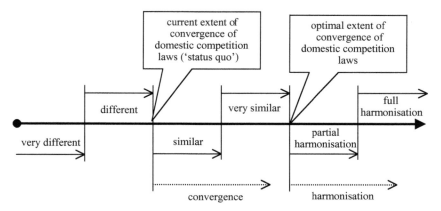

Figure 44: *Convergence-harmonisation continuum illustrating terminology*

- 'Full harmonisation' is taken to refer to a range of points at the extreme end of the convergence-harmonisation continuum within which two or more nations exhibit near uniformity of their substantive competition obligations and procedures for more than 80% of their respective competition laws.[3]
- 'Partial harmonisation' is taken to refer to a range of points on the convergence-harmonisation continuum within which two or more nations exhibit near uniformity of substantive competition obligations and procedures in respect of between 60% and 80% of their respective competition laws.
- 'Convergence' is taken to refer to a state less than partial harmonisation within which two or more nations achieve a reasonable degree of similarity in their domestic competition laws but continue to retain different standards and approaches. Convergence can be described by the adjectives 'similar' and 'very similar' as illustrated by Figure 44.
- Where no or very little convergence of domestic competition laws has occurred, this state of the world can be described by the adjectives 'very different' and 'different'.

The existing level of international convergence of domestic competition laws (referred to as the 'status quo') can be perceived on this continuum as bordering between 'different' and 'similar', as depicted by

---

[3] The 80% figure is arbitrary. The quantification is intended to demonstrate the contrast between full and partial harmonisation.

Figure 44. Existing domestic competition laws exhibit some degree of structural similarity between nations, and some similarities in standards and approaches, but considerable differences remain and little pre-existing convergence or harmonisation has occurred.

Bearing this terminology in mind, in order to assess the costs and benefits of harmonisation properly, it is next necessary to undertake a 'cost-benefit analysis' in which the costs and benefits of achieving greater convergence, partial harmonisation or full harmonisation of domestic competition laws are each assessed relative to the 'status quo'. Ideally, a WTO competition agreement should seek to achieve that state of convergence or harmonisation of domestic competition laws which realises the greatest *net* benefits to international society.[4]

One method of approaching such a cost-benefit analysis is to assess how the costs and benefits change as one proceeds along the convergence-harmonisation continuum from the status quo towards a state of full harmonisation. Adopting concepts from microeconomic theory, such an analysis can be undertaken in 'marginal terms' to determine the optimal level of convergence or harmonisation. Such a marginal analysis requires an assessment whether the additional (marginal) benefits of moving from one state of convergence or harmonisation, to the next state, exceeds the additional (marginal) costs associated with that move. Ideally, successive moves should be made along the continuum until one reaches the point at which the marginal costs of any further move exceed the marginal benefits, such point being the optimal level of convergence or harmonisation, as explained in greater detail below.

While it is extremely difficult to quantify the magnitude of such costs and benefits given the absence of relevant historical data, a non-quantitative analysis can provide a rough approximation of the likely nature of these costs and benefits.[5] By applying economic reasoning, the relative behaviour of these costs and benefits can indicate in broad terms the likely optimal extent of harmonisation or convergence for domestic competition laws.

---

[4] Note that no nation is likely to enter into an international treaty that does not give it a net benefit. Given that some nations may be net losers from an international competition agreement, this will require those nations to be compensated by way of some other negotiated trade concessions.

[5] See, for example, UNCTAD, 'Empirical Evidence of the Benefits from Applying Competition Law and Policy Principles to Economic Development in Order to Attain Greater Efficiency in International Trade and Development', UNCTAD, TD/B/COM.2/EM/10/Rev.1, 25 May 1998, para. 11.

11.1.1 The benefits of harmonisation

A useful starting point for the cost-benefit analysis is to identify the *absolute* benefits and the *absolute* costs of achieving *full* harmonisation relative to the status quo.

In this regard, Chapter 3 of this book identified that an international competition agreement could provide a means to address underlying economic externalities causing 'under-regulation' and 'over-regulation' by aligning national decision-making with the collective interest of the international community. By harmonising domestic competition laws, a WTO competition agreement would address under-regulation and over-regulation by aligning domestic competition laws with the globally optimal level of regulation. In this manner, national decision-making would be more likely to be aligned with the collective interest of the international community as each nation's competition laws would treat the same conduct in the same way.[6]

When deconstructing this *absolute* analysis into *marginal* terms for the purposes of the cost-benefit analysis of harmonisation, it is necessary to identify the extent to which such benefits are contingent on full harmonisation, rather than mere convergence. This question is essentially a causal one.[7] In this respect, it is likely that many of the benefits associated with full harmonisation could be achieved simply by greater convergence.

In particular, greater convergence of domestic laws would lead nations to treat the same conduct in a similar manner, thereby reducing the extent to which under-regulation and over-regulation would occur. Furthermore, transactions costs and system frictions would be reduced accordingly.[8] While full harmonisation would realise the greatest absolute benefits, the additional (marginal) benefits from full harmonisation are likely to be considerably lower than the significant benefits already gained by convergence relative to the status quo. This suggests that the marginal benefit gained by each successive step towards full harmonisation is

---

[6] In a fully harmonised environment, each nation's individual discretion could also be curtailed by harmonised procedures and guidelines.

[7] The *marginal* costs and benefits can be identified by asking the question whether such benefits and costs would still have occurred if the relevant state less than full harmonisation had been achieved. This can be expressed in terms of a 'but for' causation test (i.e. 'but for' full or partial harmonisation, what benefits, if any, could not be achieved?).

[8] See, for example, discussion in S. Picciotto, 'The Regulatory Criss-Cross: Interaction between Jurisdictions and the Construction of Global Regulatory Networks' in W. Bratton (ed.), *International Regulatory Competition and Coordination: Perspectives in Economic Regulation in Europe and the US* (OUP, New York, 1996).

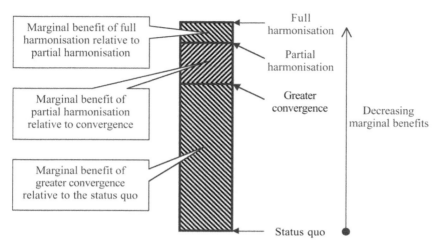

Figure 45: *Illustration of marginal benefits in cost-benefit assessment*

decreasing, even though the absolute benefit continues to increase.[9] In economic terms, harmonisation exhibits 'decreasing marginal benefits'. This is illustrated by the decreasing size of the shaded rectangles in Figure 45.

If the benefits from harmonisation were portrayed as a function of increasing harmonisation, one would expect to see large initial benefits from greater convergence, but progressively lower benefits towards full harmonisation. Mathematically, this is illustrated by the curve 'MB' (Marginal Benefits) in Figure 47.

11.1.2 The costs of harmonisation

In order to identify the *absolute costs* of achieving full harmonisation, the realisation of fully harmonised domestic competition laws can be perceived in terms of the adoption of an 'ideal' competition law by all nations. Necessarily, the identification of that 'ideal' is a normative process

---

[9] This result arises due to likely sequencing. Under the approaches of greater convergence and partial harmonisation, the elements of competition law that would be most likely to benefit from greater harmonisation would be harmonised first. As harmonisation proceeded, the elements of competition law that would benefit less from harmonisation would in turn be harmonised. Inevitably a point would be reached at which certain elements were harmonised, even when there was no zero benefit. This 'zero benefit' point would only be reached under a full harmonisation approach.

fraught with difficulty, as each nation will have its own subjective perception as to exactly what that 'ideal' should be.[10] Each nation's 'ideal' competition law will be a function of its economic, cultural, societal and institutional structure, its competition objectives and the relative importance of competition policy to that nation. The difficulties in determining and adopting such an 'ideal' competition law have four important cost consequences:

- First, where differences between nations are significant (as in the case of competition law), the likelihood of nations making concessions during multilateral negotiations to accommodate the ideals of other nations is relatively low.[11] As a rule of thumb, the greater the differences between nations and the greater the number of nations involved in multilateral negotiations, the greater the range of issues upon which agreement will be required, the more ambitious the harmonisation effort required (including associated time and costs), and the less likelihood there would be of ever reaching multilateral agreement. Furthermore, given the absence of a pre-existing consensus on many competition law and policy issues, the possibility of achieving agreement on an 'ideal' competition law remains remote. Accordingly, the costs in realising full harmonisation of competition laws, if such harmonisation is even possible, are likely to be exceedingly high.[12]
- Secondly, an 'ideal' competition law necessarily assumes that one size fits all. This may not be the case. The existence of diversity between nations may be beneficial. Full harmonisation of competition laws fails to recognise that differences between the competition laws of different nations may be based on legitimate differences between the economies,

---

[10] See E. M. Fox, 'Antitrust & Regulatory Federalism: Races Up, Down and Sideways' (2000) 75 *New York University Law Review* 1780.

[11] See, for example, P. Nicolaides, 'Towards Multilateral Rules on Competition: The Problems of Mutual Recognition of National Rules' (1994) 17(3) *World Competition* 5.

[12] Harmonisation of laws and policies on a multilateral basis is a notoriously difficult exercise. Harmonisation requires costly and time-consuming negotiations among nations to determine a mutually acceptable 'ideal'. Harmonisation also requires nations to take positive steps to amend or reshape their domestic laws, customs and procedures to bring them into line with the 'ideal'. Yet even within a group of a dozen nations, harmonisation of laws and policies may be difficult to achieve, as illustrated by the experience of the European Community and other nations. See Commission of the European Community, *Completing the Internal Market: White Paper from the Commission of the European Community* (June 1985), European Commission, The Hague, pp. 19, 22.

markets and policies of different nations and their different distributional objectives. For example, smaller nations with more concentrated markets may favour higher market power thresholds than larger nations with less concentrated markets.[13] Similarly, as recognised by the EC, an 'ideal' competition law may be insufficiently flexible to cater for new developments.[14] The US has expressed concern, for example, that a prescriptive international competition law could create a rigid and static set of rules that could not be adapted to address rapidly changing circumstances in the global market or future developments in economic theory.[15]

- Thirdly, full harmonisation assumes that any 'ideal' competition law will also be an 'optimal' international competition law that is consistent with the maximisation of international welfare. Again, this is by no means the case. An 'ideal' competition law would be the product of extensive multilateral negotiations. However, the interplay of domestic strategies and stances within multilateral negotiations is not necessarily consistent with the realisation of an optimal law. Multilateral negotiations are inevitably influenced by those with greater economic and political power.[16] Stronger nations have the ability to influence negotiations in a manner favourable to their domestic interests, at the expense of nations with less economic and political power.[17] Accordingly, a single harmonised competition law may disenfranchise less powerful nations and may well be sub-optimal from an international perspective.

---

[13] See, for example, discussion in M. Gal, *Competition Policy for Small Market Economies* (Harvard University Press, Cambridge, 2003).

[14] See discussion in European Commission, 'A Multilateral Framework Agreement on Competition Policy', Communication from the European Community and its Member States, Working Group on the Interaction between Trade and Competition Policy, WT/WGTCP/W/152, 25 September 2000.

[15] See, for example, discussion in A.W. Wolff, 'Unanswered Questions: The Place of Trade and Competition Policy in the Seattle Round', Paper delivered at the OECD Conference on Trade and Competition, Paris, 30 June 1999.

[16] See L. J. Schoppa, 'The Social Context in Coercive International Bargaining' (1999) 53 *International Organisation* 307. See also discussion in B. I. Spector, G. Sjosted, and I. W. Zartman (eds.), *Negotiating International Regimes* (Kluwer, London, 1994). See also I. W. Zartman, *International, Multilateral Negotiations: Approaches to the Management of Complexity* (Jossey-Bass, San Francisco, 1994).

[17] See K. Bagwell and R. W. Staiger, 'Multilateral Trade Negotiations, Bilateral Opportunism and the Rules of GATT', Internet working paper, www.ssrn.com, March 2000. See also B. Specter & G. Sjostedt, *Negotiating International Regimes: Lessons from UNCED* (Graham & Trotman, New York, 1994).

- Finally, the requirement to achieve unanimity in multilateral negotiations creates pressures towards the 'lowest common denominator', so that the interests of all nations can be met.[18] In this manner, the resulting competition law may prescribe enforcement thresholds that are lower than they ideally should be.[19] One of the concerns of the US, for example, has been that any international competition agreement would require the US to amend its competition laws to comply with it.[20] Given that the US arguably has some of the toughest competition laws in the world, an international competition agreement based on an averaging of existing competition laws among nations would set lower standards than are set by existing US laws. US compliance with a weaker harmonised international standard would therefore impact upon the normatively desirable pro-consumer/efficiency stance of US competition law that has evolved over the decades by way of statute and case law.[21]

Importantly, each of these costs is likely to escalate disproportionately the further one proceeds towards full harmonisation given the progressively greater harmonisation effort required. Accordingly, the *marginal* costs of achieving full harmonisation, relative to achieving greater convergence, are likely to be considerably higher. In economic terms, harmonisation exhibits 'increasing marginal costs'. This is illustrated by the increasing size of the shaded rectangles in Figure 46, which can be contrasted with Figure 45.

If the costs of harmonisation were portrayed as a function of increasing harmonisation, one would expect to see low initial costs from greater convergence, but progressively higher costs towards full harmonisation. Mathematically, this is illustrated by the curve 'MC' (Marginal Costs) in Figure 47.[22]

---

[18] See, for example, discussion in G. Palmer, 'New Ways to Make International Environmental Law' (1992) 85 *American Journal of International Law* 259.

[19] See J. McMillan, 'A Game-Theoretic View of International Trade Negotiations: Implications for the Developing Countries,' in J. Whalley (ed.), *Developing Countries and the Global Trading System* (University of Michigan Press, Ann Arbor, 1989), vol. I, p. 26.

[20] See, for example, J. I. Klein, 'Anticipating the Millennium: International Antitrust Enforcement at the End of the Twentieth Century', Address Before the Fordham Corporate Law Institution, 16 October 1997.

[21] See comments in A. D. Melamed, 'International Antitrust in an Age of International Deregulation' (1998) 6 *George Mason Law Review* 427.

[22] Note that the curved shape of the marginal benefit (MB) and marginal cost (MC) reflects decreasing marginal benefits and increasing marginal costs towards full harmonisation, respectively. The basis for these assumptions has already been identified previously in the main text.

OPTIMAL CONTENT FOR A WTO AGREEMENT   345

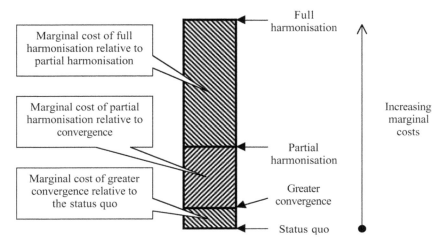

Figure 46: *Illustration of marginal costs in cost-benefit assessment*

11.1.3 The optimal level of convergence or harmonisation of domestic competition laws

Based on this analysis, the marginal benefits of harmonisation (MB) are decreasing towards full harmonisation, while the marginal costs of harmonisation (MC) are increasing. The likely mathematical shape of these marginal benefit and marginal cost functions is illustrated by Figure 47. Consistent with the concept of optimisation in microeconomic theory, a point will be reached when proceeding along the convergence-harmonisation continuum at which marginal costs are equivalent to marginal benefits (MC = MB).[23] This point will be the optimal extent of harmonisation and is the point at the apex of the 'total net benefit' (TNB) parabola in Figure 47. The non-quantitative analysis set out above suggests that this optimal point could lie somewhere in the range between 'convergence' and 'partial harmonisation' of competition laws.

If this cost-benefit analysis is correct, then the objective of full harmonisation of competition laws should be discounted. Instead, any international competition agreement should focus on achieving greater convergence and selective harmonisation. Indeed, the above analysis suggests that a preoccupation with full harmonisation may do more harm than

---

[23] See W. J. Baumol & A. S. Blinder, *Economics: Principles & Policy* (3rd edn, Harcourt, New York, 1985), ch. 24 for a discussion regarding principles of optimisation in economics and the concepts of marginal costs and marginal benefits.

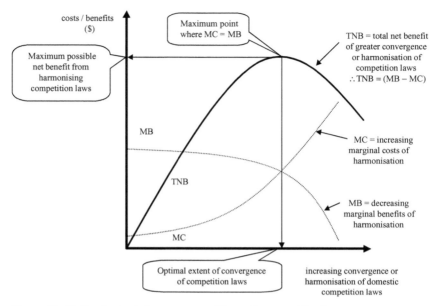

Figure 47: *Optimal extent of convergence of domestic competition laws*

good as the costs of achieving full harmonisation are likely to exceed the resulting benefits.[24]

As a corollary to the above cost-benefit analysis, the additional point must be made that the costs and benefits of achieving greater convergence or harmonisation are not necessarily uniform across all aspects of competition law. There will be some elements of competition law, for example, that will realise considerably greater benefits from convergence and partial harmonisation than other elements. Ideally, any WTO competition agreement should seek to cherry-pick those elements of competition law that would benefit from greater convergence or partial harmonisation, and target those elements for greater regulatory attention. Such a selective approach would maximise the benefits possible from any WTO competition agreement.[25]

---

[24] See A. Sykes, 'Regulatory Competition or Regulatory Harmonisation? A Silly Question' (2000) 3(2) *Journal of International Economic Law* 257. See also A. Sykes, 'The (Limited) Role of Regulatory Harmonisation in International Goods and Services Markets' (1999) 2(1) *Journal of International Economic Law* 24.

[25] See also E. M. Fox, 'Competition Law and the Agenda for the WTO: Forging the Links of Competition and Trade' in J. O. Haley & H. Iyori (eds.), *Antitrust: A New International Trade Remedy* (Pacific Rim Law & Policy Association, Seattle, 1995).

The difficulty arising from such a selective approach is to identify those elements of competition law that would benefit most from greater convergence or partial harmonisation. Necessarily, this would require a careful analysis to identify critical differences between the competition laws of nations and the costs and benefits associated with removing those differences. A number of comparative competition law surveys have assisted in this respect and could inform this analysis.[26] Chapter 4 of this book also undertook a basic comparative analysis of the competition laws of the APEC nations.

Most relevantly, in 1995, Graham and Richardson, edited and coauthored a book entitled *Global Competition Policy* for the Institute for International Economics (IIE). Within the book the authors sought to identify the benefits of greater convergence for various domestic competition law elements ('IIE Survey').[27] The IIE Survey was not an in-depth empirical survey, so its results should be treated with caution. However, the results of the IIE Survey do indicate that the four key elements of competition law most likely to benefit from selective convergence are:

(a) laws prohibiting price fixing;
(b) anti-cartel laws;
(c) laws regulating horizontal restraints (other than cartels); and
(d) merger and acquisition laws.

Furthermore, four key trade policy areas also emerge as most likely to benefit from selective convergence:

(a) modification of anti-dumping laws;
(b) prohibition of Voluntary Export Restraints ('VERs');
(c) adoption of a national treatment principle (as proposed in Chapter 10 of this book); and
(d) prohibition of Voluntary Import Expansions ('VIEs').

---

[26] In 1999, for example, the American Bar Association very broadly identified certain key differences between domestic competition laws on an international basis, namely their coverage, degree of government intervention, objectives, assumptions, procedures, enforcement and jurisdiction. See also, for example, G. B. Doern & S. Wilks, *Comparative Competition Policy* (Clarendon Press, Oxford, 1996). See also, for example, A. N. Campbell & M. J. Trebilcock, 'A Comparative Analysis of Merger Law: Canada, the United States, and the European Community' (1995) 15(3) *World Competition* 5.
[27] See E. M. Graham & J. D. Richardson, *Global Competition Policy* (Institute for International Economics, Washington DC, 1995), ch. 17, pp. 553–8.

11.2 To what extent should any WTO competition agreement seek to prescribe minimum international standards?

Given the conclusion above that selective convergence of certain elements of domestic competition law is desirable, the issue arises how such selective convergence could be achieved. In this respect, there are several potential mechanisms by which a WTO competition agreement could specifically target such elements for greater convergence. Four mechanisms are considered in detail in this chapter, namely:

(a) by prescribing binding minimum standards;[28]
(b) by prescribing binding standards set at the 'optimal' level;
(c) by prescribing non-binding principles set at the 'optimal' level; or
(d) by 'co-regulation', being a combination of binding standards and non-binding principles.[29]

Each of these mechanisms has its own advantages and disadvantages, as discussed below.

Importantly, the decision as to which of these mechanisms should be preferred requires an analysis of the following issues:

- the extent to which any WTO competition agreement should prescribe binding minimum standards for domestic competition laws; and
- the extent to which any 'ideal' standards set out in an international competition agreement should be legally binding.

These two issues are, to some extent, inter-related and are addressed below.

11.2.1 Minimum standards for domestic competition laws

Mathematically, it is likely that the international differences between domestic competition laws assume a particular distribution around a statistical mean. For the purposes of this book, that statistical distribution is assumed to be a 'normal distribution', as represented by Figure 48.[30]

---

[28] See discussion in E. U. Petersmann, 'The International Competition Policy of the EC and the Need for an EC Initiative for a "Plurilateral Agreement on Competition and Trade" in the WTO' in F. Snyder (ed.), *Constitutional Dimensions of European Integration* (Kluwer Law International, London, 1996).
[29] See K. Nicolaïdis, 'Co-regulation: Beyond Traditional Standardisation' in A. Sykes (ed.), *Products Standards for Internationally Integrated Goods Markets* (Brookings Institution, Washington DC, 1995).
[30] The vertical axis of the standard distribution curve indicates the number of competition laws. The horizontal axis of the standard distribution curve indicates the relative 'strength'

OPTIMAL CONTENT FOR A WTO AGREEMENT 349

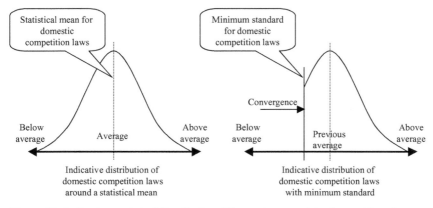

Figure 48: *Indicative statistical distribution of domestic competition laws with and without a minimum standard*

The competition laws of the US, for example, will fall above the statistical mean given that US competition laws are among the strictest in the world.[31] Conversely, the competition laws of China, for example, will fall below this mean given that Chinese competition law contains relatively weak substantive standards, omits significant competition law elements, and is not yet effectively enforced.

The challenge for a WTO competition agreement is to strengthen those competition laws falling below the statistical mean so that they converge towards the mean, but without weakening those competition laws that lie above the statistical mean. Not surprisingly, therefore, previous proposals for a WTO competition agreement, such as the Munich Code, have sought to prescribe substantive binding *minimum* legal standards for domestic competition laws.

As identified in Chapter 10 of this book, under the Munich Code each ratifying nation would have been required to ensure that its domestic competition laws contained standards that were not qualitatively lower than

---

of each competition law, as assessed relative to the concept of 'under-regulation' and 'over-regulation' identified in Chapter 3 of this book. The diagram is indicative only. In practice, that distribution is likely to be skewed by certain commonly-accepted competition law models such as the European model or US model.

[31] See J. S. Kingdom, 'Recent Anti-trust Developments in the United States' in J. Maitland-Walker (ed.), *International Antitrust Law: Towards 1992 – The Development of International Antitrust* (ESC Publishing, Oxford, 1989), p. 120.

the minimum standards set out in the Munich Code.[32] The Munich Code enabled nations to adopt standards for their competition laws that were higher than those set out in the Munich Code. The impact of this binding minimum standard on the normal distribution of competition laws is illustrated by the truncated standard distribution curve in Figure 48.

In theory, minimum international competition standards serve a useful purpose. Minimum international standards are a safeguard against nations amending their domestic competition laws in the future in a manner that weakens these laws (below the agreed minimum standard). Minimum international standards are also intended to promote the enactment of minimum competition standards into domestic law by those nations without existing competition legislation. Essentially minimum international standards are perceived as creating a minimum standard of conduct in international competition. This minimum standard of conduct is perceived as more desirable than the current situation of ad hoc, or no discernible, standards for regulating international competition.

11.2.2 Criticisms of minimum standards

Yet while minimum standards are desirable in theory, the practice is somewhat different. A key difficulty with establishing a minimum standard is that it is first necessary to identify exactly what that minimum standard should be. In the context of the Munich Code, for example, the minimum international standards were intended as standards that codified the existing international consensus on an appropriate competition law standard.[33] The resulting criticisms of the Munich Code highlight the difficulties with such an approach:

- First, criticism of the Munich Code was directed at whether the standards were realistic 'minimum standards' given that the standards were set at a high level.[34]

---

[32] See International Antitrust Code Working Group (Munich Group), 'Draft International Antitrust Code as a GATT-MTO Plurilateral Trade Agreement' (1993) 65(1628) *Antitrust & Trade Regulation Reports (BNA)*, Special Supplement, 19 August 1993, S-5. See also International Antitrust Working Group, *Draft International Antitrust Code as a GATT-MTO Plurilateral Trade Agreement* (Max Planck Institute, Munich, 1993).

[33] See discussion in E. U. Petersmann, 'International Competition Rules for the GATT – MTO World Trade and Legal System' (1993) 27(6) *Journal of World Trade* 35.

[34] See 'Antitrust Division Official Predicts Scant Prospect of International Code' (1994) 66(1650) *Antitrust & Trade Regulation Reports* 181.

- Secondly, conversely, the Munich Code's attempt to codify the international consensus and set minimum standards was criticised as prescribing minimum standards rather than appropriate standards, suggesting that the minimum standards were perceived by many nations as being set too low. [35]
- Thirdly, the Munich Group tended to adopt a Euro-centric approach to certain issues which would have required nations to amend their competition laws to bring them into line with EU standards.[36]

These issues together suggest that a key difficulty in deriving a minimum standard is therefore to identify sufficient consensus on that standard.

Another inter-related key difficulty with establishing a binding minimum standard is that it must be an internationally agreed standard to which nations are willing to bind themselves. This creates a potentially problematic dynamic. Any binding multilateral competition agreement will necessarily require consensus among WTO ratifying nations. Accordingly, any nation can thwart the realisation of a multilateral agreement by refusing to give its consent to such an agreement (i.e. each nation has a 'veto' power). Furthermore, a nation will not usually be willing to bind itself to minimum standards that it does not meet unless that nation receives compensation for the cost of complying with the higher standard. In the absence of compensation, that nation will typically veto any proposed minimum standard with which it does not already comply.

As a result, it is difficult to include in any multilateral agreement any minimum standard set at a level that any nation cannot meet (unless non-compliant nations are given concessions that offset their costs of meeting the higher standard). The usual result is therefore that any minimum standard is necessarily a 'lowest common denominator' standard or very close to it. While this analysis is simplistic, the dynamic it identifies is a real one and there are clear pressures on nations during multilateral negotiations continually to reduce any minimum standards to enable a greater number of nations, if not all, to comply with them.

This issue of a 'lowest common denominator' standard is an important one. The ultimate objective is greater convergence of competition laws.

---

[35] The US, for example, advocated ideal standards rather than minimum standards.
[36] For example, Australia would have been required to implement mandatory pre-notification of mergers and acquisitions rather than retaining its voluntary pre-notification approach. The Australian Trade Practices Act 1974 provides for voluntary pre-notification of mergers. See also discussion in W. Fikentscher, 'The Draft International Antitrust Code in the Context of International Technological Integration' (1996) 72 *Chicago-Kent Law Review* 533.

However, if a standard is set at a level that all nations already comply with, that standard will not create any pressures on nations to amend their competition laws to achieve greater convergence. Accordingly, the extent to which minimum standards would promote any useful degree of convergence on the key elements of competition law identified previously is questionable. This therefore raises an important criticism of any minimum international standards negotiated in a multilateral context. As such standards are susceptible to 'lowest common denominator' pressures, so are likely to be meaningless in a convergence context, the question is simply – why bother?[37]

Furthermore, this is not the only difficulty identified with minimum standards. One of the principal concerns of the US with any WTO competition agreement that attempted to set a minimum standard is that any such minimum standard would have an impact not only on laws below that standard, but also on laws above that standard. This has been one of the main reasons given historically by the US for opposing any attempt to include competition law within the WTO, as illustrated by the US criticisms of the Munich Code noted above.[38] Joel Klein, Assistant Attorney-General of the US Department of Justice, for example, commented in a speech in 1996 that:[39]

> Doubts were expressed as to whether the inclusion of competition policy in the WTO would be of any significant value since large multilateral agreements involving many parties have a tendency to be watered down to the 'lowest common denominator'. . . we must guard against a lowest-common-denominator outcome in the development of competition rules by the WTO. That is, efforts to achieve a 'minimum' set of competition principles or to identify common substantive standards could end up legitimating weak and ineffective rules, which certainly would not serve the goals of trade liberalisation. As we all know, minimum standards often become the maximum.

---

[37] See, for example, comments by A. Fels of the Australian Competition & Consumer Commission quoted in M. Maiden, 'Fels Backs Global Race But Toils to Keep Pace', *The Age*, Melbourne, 8 July 1999.

[38] See A. D. Melamed, 'International Cooperation in Competition Law and Policy: What Can Be Achieved at the Bilateral, Regional, and Multilateral Levels' (1999) 2(3) *Journal of International Economic Law* 472. See also D. L. Roll, 'The Globalisation of Competition Law: Impact of U.S. Initiatives on the Asia Pacific Region', Paper presented at the Lex Mundi 1999 Regional Meeting, Tokyo, 9 April 1999.

[39] See J. I. Klein, 'A Note of Caution with Respect to a WTO Agenda on Competition Policy', Address by the Acting Assistant Attorney-General, US Department of Justice, to the Royal Institute of International Affairs, Chatham House, London, 18 November 1996.

A year later, Douglas Melamed, Principal Deputy Assistant Attorney-General of the US Department of Justice also commented: 'any WTO rules would be lowest-common-denominator rules that would merely serve to justify weak national antitrust enforcement'.[40] Subsequent comments from the US have been similar.

Accordingly, the concern of the US is that the adoption of a minimum standard within a WTO competition agreement, would undermine the incentives on nations to establish competition laws set at a standard higher than that minimum standard. Meanwhile, nations with competition laws already set at a level higher than that standard could decide to amend their competition laws down to that low standard (although this ignores their reasons for initially adopting a higher standard). In this manner, the fear of the US is that any minimum standard would act as a point of convergence for all competition laws, and that point of convergence would be an inappropriately low one.[41]

On the other hand, the nation with the strictest competition law often has the most impact on the structure of an international transaction. In international mergers, for example, a merger is constrained by the highest threshold of the nations it affects, so is constrained by the highest common denominator. This means that there may be some benefit in creating pressures towards an 'ideal' law even where this may result in the weakening of some competition laws, given that some competition laws may be unnecessarily strict and may 'over-regulate' international conduct (as discussed earlier).[42] However, a balance would need to be struck.

There are several possible solutions to this 'lowest common denominator' issue that could be adopted in the context of the negotiation of a WTO competition agreement:

---

[40] See A. D. Melamed, 'International Antitrust in an Age of International Deregulation', Address by the Deputy Assistant Attorney-General of the Antitrust Division US Department of Justice to the George Mason Law Review Symposium: Antitrust in the Global Economy, Washington DC, 10 October 1997.

[41] This argument may be over-stated given that it assumes that there would be successful internal lobbying by industry within each nation to weaken that nation's domestic competition laws to reflect lower international standards in circumstances where that nation has adopted laws tougher than the international standard. It is by no means obvious that such lobbying would occur. Even if it did, it remains questionable whether such lobbying would be successful.

[42] See, for example, discussion in A. N. Campbell & W. Rowley, *Industrial Policy, Efficiencies and the Public Interest – The Prospects for Harmonisation of International Merger Rules* (McMillan Binch, Toronto, 1993).

- First, any multilateral agreement could establish differential standards for different groups of nations. For example, nations with strong competition laws could agree to be bound by higher standards than nations with weak competition laws. However, the difficulty with this approach is that it would tend to entrench the status quo and would reduce incentives on nations to move towards a state of greater convergence.
- Secondly, rather than negotiating a multilateral agreement, a group of nations could negotiate a plurilateral agreement within the context of the WTO. In this manner, nations with weaker competition laws would not need to be involved in negotiations as such nations would not ultimately be bound by the resulting agreement. Rather, the only nations involved in negotiations would be those nations with preexisting stronger competition laws. However, the difficulty with this approach is that nations with weaker competition laws are not involved in negotiations, hence it defeats the purpose of the exercise, as such nations would have little incentive to adopt stronger competition laws and convergence will not occur in respect of those nations.
- Thirdly, rather than adopting detailed substantive obligations, those obligations could be expressed in a more abstract manner that glossed over the obligation sufficiently so that all nations complied with it. However, yet again the issue arises that if nations already comply with the obligation, they will have no incentive to amend their competition laws to achieve greater convergence.
- Finally, any obligations could be expressed in non-binding terms, such as non-binding principles. In this manner, the lowest common denominator dynamics would be avoided and nations could instead concentrate on identifying the relevant minimum principle. Thus, while a nation would not necessarily comply with the principle, the existence of the principle within an international competition agreement would be sufficient to crystallise that principle as a point of international convergence for domestic competition laws. However, this then begs the question: why should the principle be a *minimum* principle? Would it not be better simply to articulate an 'optimal' non-binding principle that would become the appropriate point of convergence for international competition law?

The last point provides an important insight into the relevance of minimum standards to a WTO competition agreement. Rather than seeking to adopt proscriptive minimum standards, the better solution may be simply to promote non-binding 'ideals'. This necessarily requires an analysis of how such 'ideals' should be drafted and whether such ideals should be legally binding.

11.3 To what extent should the provisions of a WTO competition agreement be legally enforceable as binding precepts of international law?

11.3.1 How should 'ideal' competition obligations be drafted?

It is a fundamental principle of international law that, as firms and individuals do not have international legal personality, they are not directly bound by international treaties. Similarly, international treaties cannot usually directly affect the rights and duties of firms and individuals within most nations until they have been incorporated into the domestic law of that nation, either generally (such as via the constitution of a country) or specifically (such as via adopting legislation).[43] While the specific detail of this requirement may differ between jurisdictions, the general principle remains the same.

The critical issue for a WTO competition agreement is therefore how competition obligations should be drafted so as to impose binding legal obligations on nation states that:

- directly affect the behaviour of the nation state to prevent over-regulation and under-regulation; and
- by directly affecting the behaviour of the nation state, indirectly affect the behaviour of firms and individuals under the jurisdiction of that nation state.[44]

In this respect, there are a number of possible options that a WTO competition agreement could adopt, although four options are most significant:

- *Option One (negative obligations)* A WTO competition agreement could set out various negative obligations that directly prohibit nations from taking certain actions, such as a prohibition against discriminatory treatment.

---

[43] See I. Brownlie, *Principles of Public International Law* (5th edn, Oxford, London, 1998), Part II; noting the differences between 'monist' and 'dualist' legal systems.
[44] See P. Eeckhout, 'The Domestic Legal Status of the WTO Agreement: Interconnecting Legal Systems' (1997) 34 *Common Market Law Review* 11. See also M. Hilf, 'The Role of National Courts in International Trade Relations' (1997) 18 *Michigan Journal of International Law* 321.

Option One reflects the historical approach of GATT law, which relied on negative obligations to prevent governments undertaking certain conduct that would harm or impede international trade.[45] This approach was adopted largely because negative obligations were easier to negotiate and enforce on a multilateral basis. The use of negative obligations avoided any need to define an 'ideal' standard that nations should adopt and avoided the need to address issues of convergence to an agreed international norm.

However, given the conclusion above that a WTO competition agreement should seek to promote selective convergence of competition laws, and given that Option One would not promote convergence to any great extent, the utility of Option One to a WTO competition agreement is relatively limited.

- *Option Two (positive obligations with cross-border application)* A WTO competition agreement could set out various positive obligations requiring governments, in effect, to amend their competition laws towards an agreed international norm, but only in so far as those laws applied to cross-border conduct.

Option Two reflects the contemporary approach of WTO law which is to rely on positive, as well as negative, obligations. This approach was first introduced into the WTO by the TRIPS Agreement which set out a number of positive obligations on governments to incorporate minimum requirements for the protection of intellectual property into their domestic laws.[46] TRIPS relied on a WTO adjudication procedure, backed by trade sanctions, to enforce these commitments.[47]

However, Option Two would only apply competition laws to cross-border conduct. Any such approach therefore risks creating differential competition laws, as rules relating to international conduct would be subject to the requirements of the WTO competition agreement, while rules relating to domestic conduct would not usually be subject to those requirements. This potential differential treatment of competition laws

---

[45] See R. E. Hudec, 'A WTO Perspective on Private Anti-competitive Behaviour in World Markets' [1999] 34(1) *New England Law Review* 79.

[46] See discussion in E. M. Fox, 'Trade, Competition and Intellectual Property: TRIPS and its Antitrust Counterparts' (1996) *Vanderbilt Journal of Transnational Law* 481.

[47] See D. J. Gervais, 'The TRIPS Agreement' (1999) 21 *European Intellectual Property Review* 156. See also discussion in J. Schmidt-Szalewski, 'The International Protection of Trademarks After the TRIPS Agreement' (1998) 9 *Duke Journal of Comparative & International Law* 189. See also L. Ferrera, 'First WTO Decision on TRIPs' (1998) 20 *European Intellectual Property Review* 69.

is problematic as it risks creating market distortions and treating domestic and international competitors differently.
- *Option Three (positive obligations with both cross-border and domestic application)* A WTO competition agreement could set out various positive obligations requiring governments, in effect, to take steps to amend their competition laws towards an agreed international norm, regardless of whether those laws applied to cross-border conduct.

  Option Three extends beyond Option Two by applying to competition laws both on a cross-border basis and a domestic basis. A difficulty with Option Three is that it raises potential sovereignty concerns given that it affects each nation's application of its own competition laws in matters solely within its exclusive territorial jurisdiction. However, given a choice between Option Two and Option Three, the disadvantages associated with Option Two seem more significant, so Option Three would be the preferred option.
- *Option Four (full domestic incorporation)* A WTO competition agreement could set out various positive obligations requiring governments to incorporate certain provisions of the WTO competition agreement directly into their domestic laws via appropriate domestic legislation, thereby enabling provisions of the treaty to be directly enforceable in domestic courts against firms and individuals.

  Option Four is, in essence, a more prescriptive version of Option Three.

In addition, it is certainly possible to have a combination of Options One to Four. For example, certain provisions of a WTO competition agreement could have pure cross-border application, such as international co-operation arrangements. Other provisions of a WTO competition agreement could set out standards for domestic competition laws. Other provisions of a WTO competition agreement could prescribe certain rules and procedures that should be incorporated into domestic law to be given direct legal effect.[48] Indeed, a combination of these different elements may result in a creative and optimal solution to the appropriate content of a WTO competition agreement.

---

[48] See, for example, discussion in E. U. Petersmann, 'Proposals for Negotiating International Competition Rules of the GATT–WTO World Trade and Legal System' (1994) 49 *Swiss Review of International Economic Relations (Aussenwirtschaft)* 231. See also E. M. Fox, 'Competition Law and the Next Agenda for the WTO' in OECD, *New Dimensions of Market Access in a Globalising World Economy* (OECD, Paris, 1995), p. 169.

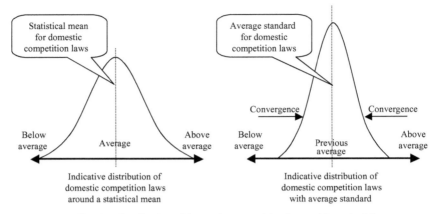

Figure 49: *Indicative distribution of domestic competition laws with and without convergence to a minimum standard*

Assuming, based on the conclusions above, that a combination of Options One to Four is the most desirable option and that minimum legal standards alone are unlikely to be satisfactory within a multilateral context, the issue arises as to how these options would actually promote convergence of domestic competition laws to the agreed international 'ideal'.

In this respect, the normal distribution diagram referred to in Figure 48 is again useful. Ideally, a WTO competition agreement would not wish to prescribe a precise standard with which all nations must comply, for reasons discussed above (namely that a lowest common denominator standard would result). Rather, a WTO competition agreement would wish to create sufficient pressures to narrow the distribution of laws around the mean and accelerate convergence as illustrated by Figure 49. Accordingly, an obligation could be phrased in reasonably broad terms that continued to permit the existence of differences between nations but which still influenced their behaviour.

Interestingly, this approach has been adopted by the 1997 WTO Agreement on Basic Communications, being the Fourth Protocol to the GATS ('WTO Basic Telecoms Agreement').[49] As identified in Chapter 7 of this

---

[49] See General Agreement on Trade in Services, Annexe B of the Agreement Establishing the World Trade Organisation, done at Marrakesh on 15 April 1994, (1994) 33 *International Legal Materials* 1167. GATS Annexe on Telecommunications (1994) 33 *International Legal Materials* 1192.

book, most of the signatories to the WTO Basic Telecoms Agreement included in their individual commitment schedules some or all features of a negotiated regulatory 'Reference Paper', which set out principles for the establishment and maintenance of competition in national telecommunications markets.[50]

The drafting of the Reference Paper provides two important insights:

- First, the Reference Paper avoids prescribing substantive legal standards by phrasing any obligations in broad terms, such as commitments to preventing major suppliers from 'engaging in or continuing anti-competitive practices'.[51] As identified in Chapter 7, the decision *Mexico – Measures Affecting Telecommunications Services* indicates that WTO Panels would assess the concept of an 'anti-competitive practice' by reference to principles that are widely accepted in the international community, as evidenced by the majority of competition laws and key international instruments.[52] In essence, this approach identifies an 'average' point consistent with Figure 49.

- Secondly, the Reference Paper seeks to avoid any infringement of sovereignty by deliberately not specifying the particular regulatory regimes or institutional structures that should be adopted.[53] Rather, nations have discretion, for example, to maintain 'appropriate measures . . . for the purpose of preventing' the anti-competitive practices.[54] In the decision *Mexico – Measures Affecting Telecommunications Services*, the WTO Panel reasoned that the use of the word 'appropriate' required it to assess whether the relevant governmental measures were 'suitable for achieving their purpose'.[55] The WTO Panel indicated that such ambiguity was intended to reserve for WTO members a degree of flexibility in meeting their commitments to avoid infringing the regulatory autonomy of WTO members. In essence, this approach indicates that a lot of judicial tolerance would be exercised in determining consistency with the 'average' point identified above.

Importantly, in the decision *Mexico – Measures Affecting Telecommunications Services*, the WTO Panel was not required to consider the

---

[50] See Reference Paper (1997) 36 *International Legal Materials* 367.
[51] *Ibid.*, s. 1.1.
[52] See *Mexico – Measures Affecting Telecommunications Services*, WT/DS204/R, Report of the WTO Panel, 2 April 2004, para. 7.266.
[53] See discussion in P. I. Spector, 'The World Trade Organisation Agreement on Telecommunications' (1998) 32 *International Lawyer* 217.
[54] Section 1.1 of the Reference Paper; see above n. 50.
[55] See *Mexico – Measures Affecting Telecommunications Services*, above n. 52, para. 7.266.

appropriateness of Mexico's competition laws. Rather, the WTO Panel considered the appropriateness of laws that required anti-competitive practices. However, the comments by the WTO Panel suggest that competition laws could be subject to direct scrutiny if they contain provisions not suitable for achieving their purpose of preventing major suppliers from engaging in or continuing anti-competitive practices, as measured against principles that are widely accepted in the international community.[56]

The WTO Basic Telecoms Agreement therefore provides an important insight into a particular technique for incorporating competition law obligations into an international agreement, namely to articulate those obligations at different levels of abstraction and binding character.

This raises a further important issue, as identified earlier in this chapter: to what extent should the provisions of a WTO competition agreement be legally enforceable as binding precepts of international law?

11.3.2 International 'soft law' and co-regulation

The most commonly cited statement of the formal sources of international law is Article 38 of the Statute of the International Court of Justice. There is then much debate whether the sources of international law could also include more controversial and informal types of international commitments, including instruments short of a formal international treaty such as non-binding treaties, joint declarations and memoranda of understanding. The latter forms of commitments are typically referred to by the concept of international 'soft law' which is perceived as a type of international commitment falling short of the 'hard law' of treaties and custom.[57] In addition, the term 'soft law' may be used to describe rules that are included in an international treaty, but are imprecise or weak, so are theoretically unenforceable.[58]

---

[56] *Ibid.*, para. 7.267.
[57] See, for example, D. Wellens & R. Borchardt, 'Soft Law in European Community Law' (1989) 14 *European Law Review* 267. See also P. Handl, 'A Hard Look at Soft Law' (1988) 82 *American Society of International Law Proceedings* 371. See also P. Gruchalla-Wesierski, 'A Framework for Understanding Soft Law' (1984) 30 *McGill Law Journal* 37.
[58] See J. Hildenberg, 'A Fresh Look at Soft Law' (1999) 10(3) *European Journal of International Law* 35. See also C. M. Chinkin, 'The Challenge of Soft Law: Development and Change in International Law' (1989) 38 *International & Comparative Law Quarterly* 850.

The concept of international 'soft law' remains controversial and there is much confusion as to its precise legal character, if any.[59] Is international 'soft law' legally binding? In this respect, Weil comments that: it would seem better to reserve the term 'soft law' for rules that are imprecise and not really compelling, since sub-legal obligations are neither 'soft law' not 'hard law': they are simply not law at all.[60] Guzman also comments that the general presumption appears to be that 'soft law' is somehow 'less binding' than the formal sources of international law and, as a consequence, nations are less likely to comply with it.[61]

Summarising the current academic literature, it is likely that soft law has two distinct forms:

(a) soft law which is created by non-treaty instruments which, by definition, are not intended to be legally binding; and
(b) soft law which is created by unenforceable provisions in otherwise binding treaties, which cannot be legally binding as such provisions are, in a legal sense, 'void and inapplicable on account of uncertainty and unresolved discrepancy' (or provisions that are expressed not to be legally binding).[62]

Strictly speaking, soft law is not legally binding in both circumstances. Yet notwithstanding the lack of academic consensus on the precise legal character of international 'soft law', it clearly has a considerable impact upon the behaviour of nations.[63] This is best illustrated, for example, by the importance accorded by the international community to soft law instruments such as the Basle Accord in international banking and

---

[59] See, for example, discussion in O. Schachter, 'The Twilight Existence of Non-binding International Agreements' (1977) 71 *American Journal of International Law* 300. See also D. Aust, 'The Theory and Practice of Informal International Instruments' (1986) 35 *International Comparative Law Quarterly* 787.

[60] See P. Weil, 'Toward Relative Normativity in International Law' (1983) 77 *American Journal of International Law* 413, 414.

[61] See A. T. Guzman, 'International Law: A Compliance Based Theory', UC Berkeley School of Law, Public Law and Legal Theory Working Paper No. 47, April 2001.

[62] *Ibid.*

[63] See H. Székely, 'Non-binding Commitments: A Commentary on the Softening of International Law Evidenced in the Environmental Field' in *International Law on the Eve of the 21st Century – Views from the International Law Commission* (AUP, New York, 1997). See also Palmer, above n. 18. See also Hildenberg, above n. 58. See also D. Shelton (ed.), *Commitment and Compliance: The Role of Non-binding Norms in the International Legal System* (OUP, New York, 2000).

finance law, and the Rio Declaration in international environmental law.[64]

Bearing this in mind, a useful analogy to soft law is the distinction between laws and morals, which is a distinction associated with the consequences of not meeting the commitment they entail. While laws are enforceable with legally mandated sanctions, morals are not legally enforceable but their breach may result in social censure. Similarly, a breach of international 'hard law' results in the potential application of a range of legally mandated sanctions, including the international law concepts of state responsibility, compensation and reprisals. However, a breach of international 'soft law' simply results in international censure and potential adverse political repercussions. This means that while 'soft law' is not legally binding, and does not avail itself of legally mandated sanctions, international 'soft law' can still articulate agreed 'moral' understandings and principles and can create pressures for nations to comply with these understandings and principles.[65]

Indeed, the concept of international 'soft law' has proved important to the development of international law. The existence of an intermediate step between 'no agreement' and 'binding agreement' has proved particularly useful where differences between nations are significant and there is little chance of sufficient consensus to realise a binding bilateral or multilateral treaty.[66] International 'soft law' has therefore enabled governments to be perceived as achieving progress, via an 'in principle' agreement, without the need to fetter their legislative sovereignty and amend their domestic laws. In this manner, 'soft law' techniques may facilitate rapid consensus building, thereby permitting the eventual introduction of hard law instruments.[67] Similarly, 'soft law' techniques have enabled political momentum to be sustained in the face of protracted international negotiations over difficult and complex issues.

---

[64] See *Rio Declaration on Environment & Development*, adopted by the UN Conference on Environment & Development (UNCED) at Rio de Janeiro, 13 June 1992; UN Doc A/Conf 151/26 (Vol. 1) (1992) 31 *International Legal Materials* 874.

[65] See W. H. Reinicke, *Norms in the International Legal System* (OUP, Oxford, 2000).

[66] See W. H. Reinicke, 'Interdependence, Globalisation, and Sovereignty: The Role of Non-Binding International Legal Accords' in Shelton, above no. 63. See also Palmer, above n. 18.

[67] Such consensus building is illustrated by international environmental law in which international soft law instruments such as the non-binding Rio Declaration, and the non-binding Helsinki Declaration on the Protection of the Ozone Layer provided the foundation for subsequent hard law binding treaties.

Furthermore, international 'soft law' has avoided the need to express matters in black and white terms and has therefore remained consistent with the approach of international diplomacy and its myriad nuances and shades of grey. 'Soft law' techniques have achieved this effect partly via the use of 'studied ambiguity', which is the use of deliberate ambiguity to gloss over differences between nations when expressing international agreement. Such studied ambiguity enables international issues to be expressed in terms of agreement, rather than disagreement, thereby promoting international comity and co-operation.

However, the considerable discretion often drafted into soft law instruments as a result of studied ambiguity and other similar techniques typically prevents any meaningful third-party adjudication. In many instances the principles themselves are discretionary. Frequently soft law instruments simply express a series of aspirations in the form of agreed political statements or values.

'Soft law' techniques could, however be applied within a WTO competition agreement to achieve greater convergence of domestic competition laws. Studied ambiguity could be utilised to express competition law obligations in broad and discretionary terms, consistent with the approach adopted by the Reference Paper. These competition law obligations would be non-enforceable due to their high discretionary character. However, these competition law obligations could be pitched at a level which accorded with any international 'ideal', even if this 'ideal' was itself required to be expressed in broad terms due to insufficient international consensus. As discussed above, while this would not create legally binding pressures towards convergence, it would create political and moral pressures.[68] Governments would also be able to commit to these ideals as appropriate standards for their competition laws and would not need to reject these ideals by reason of current non-compliance.

This means that while a WTO competition agreement would be binding, certain elements of it could be not legally binding. The binding components of the agreement could contemplate matters which are accepted by almost all of the international community, such as requirements of non-discriminatory treatment. The non-binding elements of the agreement could address areas where a higher level of abstraction is desirable given continued disagreement on particular details. Those elements of

---

[68] See J. G. Ruggie, 'International Regimes, Transactions, and Change: Embedded Liberalism in the Postwar Economic Order' (1982) 36 *International Organisation* 195.

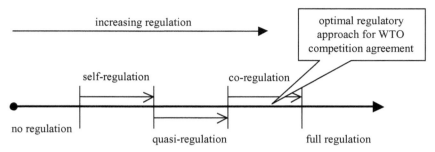

Figure 50: *Continuum of regulatory approaches*

competition law where greater convergence would be more beneficial could be expressed at a greater level of detail and could be given a binding legal character. Nations should also be given the ability to set out binding commitments in schedules to the agreement in which they agreed to maintain their competition laws to a particular minimum standard.

Importantly, the concept of 'co-regulation' can be applied in this context.[69] Co-regulation is a concept increasingly used in industries such as telecommunications to describe a regulatory regime premised both on mandated government regulation and voluntary by the self-regulation industry.[70] More generally, the concept of 'co-regulation' has been taken to refer to a blend of regulatory measures which involve both binding and non-binding elements.[71]

On a continuum of regulatory approaches from no regulation through to fully-binding government-mandated regulation, co-regulation lies towards the middle of the continuum, as illustrated by Figure 50.

In a domestic context, co-regulation contemplates that a government will set detailed and binding regulatory obligations for particular areas

---

[69] See J. Black, 'Constitutionalising Self-Regulation' (1996) 59 *Modern Law Review* 25, 27 for different descriptions of models of self-regulation. See also J. Black, *Rules and Regulators* (Oxford, Clarendon Press, 1997). See also J. Black, 'Talking About Regulation' [1997] *Public Law* 77–105. See also J. Black, 'Which Arrow: Rule Type and Regulatory Policy' [1995] *Public Law* 94–117.

[70] See J. Plante, 'Telecommunications Co-regulation: The Australian Experience', OFTEL Stakeholder Workshop on Industry Self-regulation, June 2000. See also P. Grabosky and J. Braithwaite, *Of Manners Gentle: Enforcement Strategies of Australian Business Regulatory Agencies* (Oxford University Press, Melbourne, 1986), p. 83.

[71] See K. Gordon, 'Rules for the Global Economy: Synergies between Voluntary and Binding Approaches', OECD Working Paper on International Investment, No. 1999/3, November 1999.

of concern, but will avoid binding regulation in other areas.[72] Rather, the government will establish a broad framework for industry self-regulation and will set out key policy principles. Within this broad framework, the industry itself is expected to undertake self-regulation to give effect to the policy principles.[73] In an international competition context, a co-regulatory approach would involve a WTO competition agreement adopting 'soft law' in some areas (thereby leaving competition regulation to domestic governments), but 'hard law' in others (thereby setting an international standard with which domestic governments would be required to abide). A co-regulatory approach would therefore seem to be the optimal approach for any WTO competition agreement and would be consistent with the conclusions identified earlier in this chapter.

In summary, a 'co-regulatory' approach would involve a mixture of binding international law obligations with non-binding international 'soft law' principles. A non-binding 'soft law' approach could be adopted for issues where further convergence is required but there is an existing divergence of international approach. Where there is already a pre-existing level of convergence on fundamental aspects of competition law (e.g. prohibition of hard core cartels), such obligations could be expressed as binding international 'hard law' obligations.

11.4 Amendments to existing WTO trade rules

The final issue raised at the commencement of this chapter was the extent to which any WTO competition agreement should seek to modify existing WTO rules and jurisprudence. As discussed in Chapter 6 of this book, the different approaches and methodologies of trade and competition law may result in conflicts between the two disciplines. However, ultimately there is a common unifying theme between international trade law and international competition law which means both laws are broadly complementary. Namely, both laws seek to ensure market contestability (i.e. reduced barriers to market entry).

Given the complementary nature of competition law, it may be worth considering whether an additional objective should be introduced into

---

[72] See discussion in A. Page, 'Financial Services: the Self-Regulatory Alternative?' in R. Baldwin & C. McCrudden (eds.), *Regulation and Public Law* (OUP, London, 1987), 298–322. See also C. Graham, 'Self Regulation' in H. Genn & G. Richardson, *Administrative Law and Government Action* (Clarendon, Chicago, 1993).
[73] See A. Opus, 'Rethinking Self-Regulation' (1995) 15 *Oxford Journal of Legal Studies* 97. See also N. Gunningham & J. Rees, 'Self-Regulation' (1997) 19(4) *Law and Policy* 58.

the WTO – namely the objective of ensuring market contestability. In particular, negotiators should consider whether the use of 'market access' in a WTO context should be supplemented with the competition-based concept of ensuring 'market contestability' and whether the concept of 'market contestability' should inform the application of WTO law and the negotiation of new WTO agreements.[74] Existing WTO obligations could be assessed to ensure they are not inconsistent with the principles set out in the WTO competition agreement once it is incorporated within the WTO framework.

A WTO competition agreement could also:

- establish a soft law principle that trade measures should be avoided where their use would not be consistent with market contestability and greater international competition in markets where a nation has already given a tariff binding or similar scheduled commitment;
- establish a set of soft law competition policy principles to encourage domestic trade measures to be formulated in a manner least detrimental to international competition and in a manner not conducive to anti-competitive conduct and to encourage nations to consider the spillover effects of their domestic policies on international competition;
- encourage, via soft law principles, those nations that do introduce domestic trade measures that have adverse effects on international competition to justify such measures and to ensure that such measures are short-term in nature and no more detrimental to international competition than necessary to achieve their intended result; and
- clarify the extent to which the WTO prohibits de facto discrimination in a competition policy context via non-binding principles of interpretation of the existing WTO national treatment obligations.

Importantly, each of these approaches contemplates the use of non-binding soft law to influence the conduct of nations, without forcing

---

[74] See, for example, discussion in E. M. Fox, 'Toward World Antitrust and Market Access' (1997) 91 *American Journal of International Law* 1. See also discussion in E. M. Graham, & R. L. Lawrence, 'Measuring the International Contestability of Markets: A Conceptual Approach' (1996) 30 *Journal of World Trade* 5. See also discussion in R. Z. Lawrence, T. Ito & A. Bressand, 'Towards Globally Contestable Markets' in OECD, *Market Access After the Uruguay Round: Investment, Competition and Technology Perspectives* (OECD, Paris, 1986). See also discussion in A. Zampetti & P. Suavé, *Onwards to Singapore: The International Contestability of Markets and the New Trade Agenda* (1996) 19(3) *The World Economy* 333. See also discussion in T. J. Schoenbaum, 'The Theory of Contestable Markets in International Trade: A Rationale for "Justifiable" Unilateralism to Combat Restrictive Trade Practices?' (1996) 30 *Journal of World Trade* 1.

OPTIMAL CONTENT FOR A WTO AGREEMENT 367

them to amend their conduct. Any binding substantive approach beyond this would most likely prove too politically controversial and ambitious to have any degree of success at present within a multilateral context.

Yet this does not imply that certain minimal substantive amendments to existing WTO laws could not be attempted to ensure such laws were not inconsistent with greater international competition. The IIE Survey, for example, demonstrates that at least four specific elements of international trade law would benefit from greater regulatory attention within a competition law context, namely:

(a) modification of anti-dumping laws;
(b) prohibition of VERs;
(c) adoption of a national treatment principles; and
(d) prohibition of VIEs.

Elements (a), (b) and (d) are considered below in the light of the discussion undertaken in previous chapters in this book. Element (c), the adoption of a national treatment principle, was already considered in Chapter 10. In each case, it is likely that any amendments to existing WTO law and procedures could be minimal and thus politically palatable.

11.4.1 Modification of anti-dumping laws

Chapter 9 of this book considered in detail the issue whether competition law could replace anti-dumping law within the context of the WTO. Chapter 9 outlined that while there would be procedural advantages in replacing anti-dumping law with competition law, there were also prerequisites for any successful replacement that were unlikely to be met in most cases. As an alternative, Chapter 9 therefore suggested that anti-dumping laws should be subjected to gradual reform via the progressive integration of competition principles.

In particular, Chapter 9 made five key recommendations for modifying anti-dumping laws within the context of the WTO. The WTO Anti-dumping Code should:

- mandate a competition investigation that should precede or complement any anti-dumping investigation;
- promote more effective market definition;
- require the use of a public interest or competition test before anti-dumping duties may be imposed;

- require the use of a market power threshold whereby firms with significant market power cannot use anti-dumping law to reduce competition; and
- require that administrative discretions given to anti-dumping authorities should be subjected to greater judicial scrutiny.

Importantly, the implementation of these five recommendations would remove many of the inconsistencies between modern anti-dumping law and the promotion of greater international competition. Accordingly, the adoption of these five recommendations would proceed a long way to achieving greater convergence of anti-dumping law within a competition law context.

11.4.2 Prohibition of VERs and VIEs

Chapter 8 of this book considered the application of existing WTO law to VERs and VIEs. Chapter 8 identified that while the WTO Safeguards Agreement had created an additional obligation intended to restrict the use of VIEs and VERs, there remains further scope for regulation.

Given that the IIE Survey specifically identified VIEs and VERs as existing trade practices that would benefit from greater WTO regulation within a competition law context, the question arises as to what further amendments could be made to WTO law to regulate VIEs and VERs effectively:

- In this regard, Chapter 8 identified that the WTO Safeguards Agreement could be amended to require that safeguards introduced under it were implemented in a manner least restrictive to international competition.
- Chapter 8 also acknowledged that the application of a WTO competition agreement to export cartels and import cartels would assist in regulating VIEs and VERs, given that export cartels and import cartels are frequently the principal means used to give effect to VIEs and VERs.

11.5 Conclusions on optimal content and approach for a WTO competition agreement

The conclusions of this chapter can be summarised succinctly. A WTO competition agreement should not seek to achieve full harmonisation of national competition laws given that the costs of achieving this (if such full harmonisation is even possible) would exceed any benefits. Rather, a WTO competition agreement should seek to achieve selective convergence of domestic competition laws in those areas that would realise the greatest benefits. The IIE Survey suggests that such areas would most likely include regulation of price fixing, cartelisation, horizontal restraints, and merger and acquisition laws. Certain WTO trade measures may also benefit from such an approach, including reform of anti-dumping laws, prohibition of VERs and VIEs, and greater adoption of the national treatment principle. This chapter recommends that the WTO Working Group should undertake further research into these issues.

Given that a minimum standard for domestic competition laws would create 'lowest common denominator' issues, a 'soft law' or 'co-regulatory' approach is clearly preferable. In this manner, where insufficient international consensus exists on particular issues, those issues could be expressed at a high level of generality as non-binding 'soft law' principles. Where sufficient international consensus exists, matters could be expressed in greater detail as binding 'hard law' obligations. This chapter notes that while international 'soft law' remains controversial, it does have a recognised positive effect on international conduct. It is this positive effect which should be targeted by a WTO competition agreement.

Given such conclusions, this chapter recommends that the WTO should seek to promote a 'selective convergence' and 'co-regulatory' strategy. By adopting such a strategy, the level of agreement required between nations on substantive competition obligations would be reduced and the likelihood of realising a WTO competition agreement would be considerably improved.

12

What is the optimal structure for a WTO competition agreement?

Following from the analysis in Chapters 10 and 11, and in light of the conclusions in Chapters 2 to 9 of this book, Chapter 12 identifies an appropriate institutional structure for a WTO competition agreement.

Chapter 12 assumes that the institutional arrangements supporting a WTO competition agreement would largely be determined by three critical functions:

(a) a *secretariat* function, involving the general administration of the agreement;
(b) a *compliance* function, promoting effective compliance with the agreement; and
(c) a *dispute settlement* function, involving the mitigation and resolution of disputes.

Of these three functions, the secretariat function could be carried out by the existing WTO secretariat, so few issues arise.[1] However, the second and third functions identified above both raise further issues, as follows:

- What would be the most appropriate institutional basis for a WTO competition agreement to promote effective compliance with its substantive obligations?
- What would be the most appropriate institutional basis for a WTO competition agreement to *mitigate* potential international competition disputes?
- What would be the most appropriate institutional basis for a WTO competition agreement to *resolve* international competition disputes?
- Would suspension of trade concessions be an appropriate sanction for a failure to comply with a WTO competition agreement, including any failure to adopt a dispute settlement decision?

---

[1] The WTO secretariat would need additional resourcing to enable it to bolster its competition expertise.

Each of these four key questions are considered in detail in this chapter. Based on the answers to these four questions, this chapter makes a number of recommendations for the optimal institutional structure of a WTO competition agreement.

12.1 What would be the most appropriate institutional basis for a WTO competition agreement to promote effective compliance with its substantive obligations?

The international legal system does not have omni-powerful *executive* authorities that can take enforcement action, similar to those that exist in domestic legal systems.[2] Rather, the international system that has existed since the Peace of Westphalia in 1648 and continued into the modern era following the creation of the United Nations, emphasises the sovereign equality of nations. As a consequence, international treaties are reliant on other institutional mechanisms to promote effective compliance. As identified below, these mechanisms may involve either coercive or non-coercive techniques.

12.1.1 Coercive techniques to promote effective compliance

As illustrated by Figure 51, there are six potential coercive relationships that could promote effective compliance in relation to a WTO competition agreement. Each of these six coercive relationships are briefly examined in turn below.

- *Option One (supra-national entity supervises governments)* As indicated by the arrows 'S→X' and 'S→Y' in Figure 51, a supra-national authority could coerce national governments to promote compliance with a WTO competition agreement.

  As indicated above, a fundamental tenet of public international law is that one nation cannot be subjected to the rules, processes or

---

[2] Domestic law enforcement is based on a clear power hierarchy in which omni-powerful executive or judicial authorities may impose sanctions to compel compliance with domestic legal obligations, such as pecuniary penalties, forfeiture of assets, loss of certain legal rights, or restrictions on freedom. If a party breaches a contract, for example, the other party would have rights to enforce the contract in court and obtain a judicial order for damages which could then be enforced against the breaching party as necessary. See P. Allott, 'The Concept of International Law' (1999) 10 *European Journal of International Law* 31.

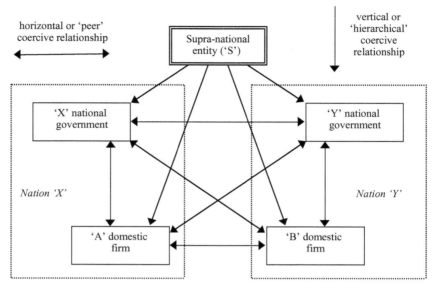

Figure 51: *Potential coercive relationships*

enforcement powers of another without its consent.[3] This tenet precludes a hierarchy in which coercive sanctions are imposed on nations by supra-national entities to promote compliance, *unless* such a hierarchy is created by a multilateral treaty ratified by that nation.[4]

Most nations are averse to supra-national executive enforcement given the consequential loss of national sovereignty. This was one of the main concerns leading to the widespread rejection of the Munich Code and its 'strong form' of internationalisation, as discussed in Chapter 10 of this book. Yet weaker forms of supra-national enforcement may be acceptable. A supra-national entity could, for example, be empowered to implement non-binding compliance measures.[5]

---

[3] See J. C. Barker, 'State Immunity, Diplomatic Immunity and Act of State: A Triple Protection against Legal Action?' (1998) 47 *International & Comparative Law Quarterly* 950. See also the range of obligations set out in the Charter of the United Nations; concluded at San Francisco, 26 June 1945; entered into force, 29 December 1945; 1 UNTS xvi; (1976) YBUN 1043: 59 Stat 1031, TS 933, including Arts. 1 and 2.

[4] Chapter VII of the UN Charter enables the UN Security Council to pass resolutions authorising the use of trade sanctions and, in some cases, military operations. However, this is limited to the worst instances of threats to international peace, breaches of peace and acts of international aggression. See discussion in I. Brownlie, *Principles of Public International Law* (5th edn, Oxford, London, 1998). See also J. G. Starke, *Introduction to International Law* (10th edn, Butterworths, London, 1989).

[5] The minority of the Munich Group advocated such an approach.

Nations more commonly submit themselves to adjudication by international *judicial* or *quasi-judicial* entities. The WTO agreements, for example, create the WTO Dispute Settlement Body ('WTO DSB') which has the ability to make adjudicatory decisions, and authorise sanctions by WTO members against other WTO members pursuant to the terms of the WTO agreements. As a quasi-judicial entity, the WTO DSB does not have the power to initiate its own enforcement proceedings.

The United Nations Charter also establishes the International Court of Justice ('ICJ') in the Hague as a permanent international judicial body for the settlement of disputes between nations.[6] Where the ICJ has jurisdiction to adjudicate an international dispute, its decisions are legally binding on the relevant nations that are parties to that conflict.[7] Yet the ICJ only has jurisdiction where nations *consent* to its jurisdiction, providing an effective right by any nation to veto ICJ adjudication. The ICJ therefore only has a weak supranational character.[8] In addition, the ICJ would most likely decline to hear actions for breaches of WTO agreements given existing WTO obligations to submit disputes to WTO panels.[9]

In summary, any supranational enforcement of a strong form is unlikely to be acceptable within the context of a WTO competition agreement. However, the WTO already has a weak supra-national quasi-judicial entity in the form of the WTO DSB which is likely to be acceptable. The potential relevance of the WTO DSB is considered in detail later in this chapter.

- *Option Two (supra-national entity supervises firms)* As indicated by the arrows 'S→A' and 'S→B' in Figure 51, a supra-national authority could coerce domestic firms so as to promote compliance with a WTO competition agreement.

Private firms are not entities subject to public international law. Rather, public international law applies only to nation states. Some form of incorporation of international law into domestic law would

---

[6] See Statute of the International Court of Justice, concluded at San Francisco, 26 June 1945; entered into force 24 October 1945; (1976) YBUN 1052, 59 Stat 1031, TS No 993.
[7] Article 94(1) of the UN Charter.
[8] A nation is not able to veto ICJ jurisdiction if that nation has consented unconditionally to the jurisdiction of the ICJ. See Art. 36(2) of the ICJ Statute. While the UN Security Council may theoretically enforce judgments of the ICJ, such enforcement has been rare in practice and nations have frequently boycotted ICJ proceedings or failed to comply with ICJ judgments. ICJ adjudication therefore remains of only limited utility. See Art. 94(2) of the UN Charter.
[9] Article 23(2) of the WTO Dispute Settlement Understanding. However, there is no judicial precedent on how ICJ jurisdiction relates to WTO dispute settlement.

therefore usually be required in each jurisdiction before supra-national enforcement action could be taken by any supra-national entity directly against domestic firms.[10]

As discussed in detail in Chapter 10, supra-national enforcement is generally unsuitable in a competition law context given the existence of adequate domestic enforcement authorities in most jurisdictions. Such an approach risks significant jurisdictional conflict by second-guessing the decisions of domestic judicial and administrative bodies. Chapter 10 also indicated that it was doubtful whether a supra-national enforcement authority would have the resourcing and local knowledge to make decisions as efficiently and accurately as a domestic enforcement agency.[11]

- *Option Three (governments supervise governments)* As indicated by the arrows 'X→Y' and 'Y→X' in Figure 51, governments could coerce each other so as to promote compliance with a WTO competition agreement.

In the absence of omni-powerful supra-national entities, the international community relies heavily on inter-governmental 'peer' mechanisms to promote compliance with international law. Each state encourages every other state to comply with international law by imposing consequences for non-compliance.[12] In this manner, the enforcement relationship in international law is based on the mutual threat of retaliation between nations. Such retaliation is formalised in international law via such concepts as 'retorsion',[13] 'reprisal',[14] and 'collective sanctions'.[15]

However, as such sanctions are inherently coercive in character, their application does run the risk of souring international relations between nations. Nations therefore frequently resort to less coercive mechanisms to promote compliance with international obligations, such as political pressure and diplomatic dialogue. In addition, many multilateral

---

[10] See P. Eeckhout, 'The Domestic Legal Status of the WTO Agreement: Interconnecting Legal Systems' (1997) 34 *Common Market Law Review* 11.

[11] For example, competition cases are fact intensive yet nations remain averse to requiring their domestic firms to disclose confidential information to foreign agencies.

[12] See F. L. Kirgis, 'Enforcing International Law', ASIL *Insight* No.1, 1998. See also discussion in A.W. Samman, 'Enforcement of International Environmental Treaties: An Analysis' (1993) 5 *Fordham Environmental Law Journal* 261.

[13] 'Retorsion' is a legal act by a wronged nation that is intended to injure the wrongdoing nation, such as by terminating economic aid or severing diplomatic relations.

[14] 'Reprisal' is an act that is otherwise illegal, but which is justified as a response to a prior illegal act of the wrongdoing nation, such as certain economic countermeasures.

[15] 'Collective sanctions' are a collective form of retorsion or reprisal in which a group of nations may respond even though only one nation may have been affected by the wrongdoing nation.

treaties establish specific mechanisms to improve the effectiveness of inter-governmental 'peer' mechanisms. The WTO, for example, utilises a Trade Policy Review Mechanism, as discussed later in this chapter. The WTO also permits nations to initiate dispute settlement against other nations before the WTO DSB, as mentioned above.

- *Option Four (governments supervise firms)*   As indicated by the arrows 'X→A', 'X→B', 'Y→A' and 'Y→B' in Figure 51, governments could coerce firms so as to promote compliance with a WTO competition agreement.

    Multilateral treaties rarely establish institutional arrangements to support domestic enforcement relationships. Such arrangements are usually viewed as properly within the jurisdiction of national governments. Rather, a WTO competition agreement could *indirectly* influence domestic enforcement by imposing obligations on national governments to take appropriate domestic enforcement action.[16]

    Extraterritorial coercion may also occur, involving enforcement action by a government in one nation against anti-competitive activity in another nation. However, Chapter 3 recommended against extraterritoriality in the context of international competition issues given the significant difficulties it creates.

- *Option Five (firms supervise governments)*   As indicated by the arrows 'A→X', 'B→X', 'A→Y' and 'B→Y' in Figure 51, firms could coerce governments so as to promote compliance with a WTO competition agreement.

    Private firms would not usually have standing to enforce public international law against governments unless they were conferred standing by an international treaty to enforce particular provisions of that treaty against a government. Such conferral of standing remains rare, currently limited largely to cross-border investment treaties that provide standing to private parties to sue a government for compensation in the event of expropriation of assets.[17] It is unlikely any government would be willing to subject itself to private enforcement in relation to competition issues.

- *Option Six (firms supervise firms)*   As indicated by the arrows 'A→B' and 'B→A' in Figure 51, firms could coerce other firms so as to promote compliance with a WTO competition agreement.

---

[16] In that manner, a WTO competition agreement could, for example, ensure that effective enforcement of domestic competition laws occurred and that national competition authorities were held accountable for their domestic enforcement actions.

[17] See Convention on the Settlement of Investment Disputes Between States and Nations of Other States, concluded at Washington DC, 18 March 1965; entered into force 14 October 1966.

Again, private firms would not usually have standing to enforce international law unless international laws were incorporated in some form into domestic law. Private enforcement of domestic competition law is a feature of some jurisdictions. However, given that private enforcement is not widespread, it is questionable whether it could be promoted by any WTO international agreement.

In conclusion, of the coercive techniques to promote compliance identified above, the most appropriate for a WTO competition agreement would involve weak supra-national quasi-judicial institutions, coupled with inter-governmental peer enforcement.

Importantly, the WTO agreements already create a supra-national quasi-judicial institution namely the WTO DSB, as identified in greater detail later in this chapter.

12.1.2 Non-coercive techniques to promote compliance

Coercive techniques to promote compliance with international obligations are frequently inappropriate, particularly where continued harmonious relations are desired.[18] Given that a WTO competition agreement will regulate a diplomatically sensitive area, alternative non-coercive techniques to promote compliance are highly desirable. Noteworthy in this regard are the concepts of 'positive compliance' and 'mobilisation of shame', both of which are already adopted by the WTO agreements:

- *'Positive compliance'* recognises that in certain circumstances, a breach of an international agreement may derive from a nation possessing insufficient technical capability. Rather than applying coercive techniques, compliance in such circumstances could be better promoted via inter-governmental technical assistance.

    In the WTO context, the WTO secretariat and WTO nations may already provide technical assistance on a case-by-case basis as the circumstances require.[19] This existing institutional mechanism could readily be applied to competition issues.

- *'Mobilisation of shame'* refers to a process by which nations are required to report publicly on compliance with their international obligations.

---

[18] Retorsion, reprisal and international sanctions would not be appropriate for soft law given the absence of any underlying legally binding international obligation to which they could attach.

[19] The extent of any technical assistance provided depends on budgetary constraints, the co-operation of WTO nations and the needs of the particular nation requiring assistance.

This mechanism increases transparency while providing other governments and independent third parties with the ability to exert peer pressure for greater compliance via international scrutiny and criticism.[20]

The WTO includes a 'mobilisation of shame' procedure known as the Trade Policy Review Mechanism ('TPRM').[21] The TPRM was established in December 1988 during the Uruguay Round multilateral negotiations and was designed to improve adherence by WTO members to their commitments under the various WTO agreements.[22]

The TPRM review process involves the Trade Policies Review Division of the WTO secretariat compiling a detailed written report critiquing the trade policies and institutions of the relevant nation from the perspective of compliance with WTO obligations and objectives.[23] Each report is tabled publicly before the Trade Policy Review Body, comprising the full membership of the WTO Council operating under special rules and procedures. Following debate, the elected Chairperson of the Body may make a public press release outlining the conclusions of the Body. The press release represents, in essence, a peer group assessment of the performance of the relevant nation in meeting its WTO commitments and may embarrass the relevant government into taking remedial action to rectify any WTO non-compliance.[24]

The TPRM process could be expanded to encompass WTO competition obligations.[25] However, given compliance concerns, WTO members are likely to ensure that any competition that the TPRM initially reviews remains restricted in scope, such as considering only the trade effects of key competition policies.

---

[20] The 'mobilisation of shame' procedure is common in the human rights field.
[21] See P. Mavroidis 'Surveillance Schemes: The GATT's New Trade Policy Review Mechanism' (1992) 13:2 *Michigan Journal of International Law* 374. See also JS Mah 'Reflections of the Trade Policy Review Mechanism in the World Trade Organisation' (1997) 31:5 *Journal of World Trade* 49.
[22] Annexe III of the WTO Agreement. The TPRM sought to achieve this by increasing the transparency of the trade policies of WTO nations via a formal review process. See, for example, R. Abbot, 'GATT and the Trade Policy Review Mechanism: Further Reflections on Earlier Reflections' (1993) 27(3) *Journal of World Trade* 117. See also V. C. Price, 'GATT's New Trade Policy Review Mechanism' (1991) 14(2) *The World Economy* 227.
[23] Under the TPRM review process, the four contracting parties with the greatest share of world trade (currently the EU, US, Japan and Canada) are subject to a formal review every two years, the next sixteen contracting parties are reviewed every four years, and the remainder are reviewed every six years (although least developed nations may be subject to a longer review period).
[24] See, for example, A. H. Qureshi, 'The New GATT Trade Policy Review Mechanism: An Exercise in Transparency or "Enforcement"?' (1990) 24(2) *Journal of World Trade* 142.
[25] The WTO nations would be required to consent to such expansion.

12.2 What would be the most appropriate institutional basis for a WTO competition agreement to *mitigate* potential international competition disputes?

The likelihood for international conflict remains high in a competition law context as the differences between nations remain considerable and important national interests may be at stake. Mechanisms to *mitigate* international competition disputes are therefore as important as mechanisms to *resolve* such disputes once they arise.

12.2.1 Nature of international competition disputes

In order to identify appropriate institutional mechanisms to mitigate international competition disputes, it is helpful to identify the key types of disputes that are likely to arise in a competition law context. In this respect, there are three principal types of international disputes that could arise in an international competition context. The different characteristics of these disputes are identified below and summarised in the matrix in Figure 52:

- *Jurisdictional disputes* Jurisdictional disputes relate to overlapping claims of jurisdiction by two or more nations. Such overlapping claims may arise if a nation applies its competition law on an extraterritorial basis to conduct which has occurred in another jurisdiction, or where the relevant conduct has occurred in multiple jurisdictions so is subject to multiple domestic competition laws. Jurisdictional disputes occur when different legal consequences arise under the domestic competition laws of different nations. In such circumstances, one nation may seek to assert its jurisdiction as superior to that of another nation. The dispute will therefore involve determination of which law and legal consequences should apply to the particular conduct. The relevant adjudicating bodies will be the courts of the different jurisdictions. Each court will apply its own domestic law in an attempt to resolve the dispute.
- *Procedural disputes* Procedural disputes relate to differences between the evidential and procedural rules of different nations. Conflict may arise where the courts of one nation may be unwilling to recognise the evidential and procedural rules of another nation. Hence, a nation may undertake enforcement action in its jurisdiction, but remain unable to obtain evidence, enforce court orders, or enforce judgments against

	Jurisdictional disputes	Procedural disputes	Substantive disputes
Subject matter of dispute	Assertion of jurisdiction	Evidential and procedural rules	WTO obligations
Source of conflict	Different jurisdictions apply different substantive competition rules	Different jurisdictions apply different evidential and procedural rules	Nation is breaching its substantive WTO obligations
Issue to be resolved	Whether domestic competition laws of nation A or nation B should apply	Whether evidential and procedural rules of nation A should be recognised by nation B	Whether nation A has complied with its WTO obligations
Adjudicating body	Courts of two different jurisdictions	Court of foreign country	WTO dispute settlement panel
Mechanism to resolve dispute	Law of domestic court in which case is heard	Law of domestic court in which case is heard	WTO law

Figure 52: *Characteristics of the three principal types of competition disputes*

firms in another jurisdiction. In such circumstances, the critical issue will be whether the evidential and procedural rules of one nation should be recognised by the courts of the other. The relevant adjudicating body would be the court of the foreign jurisdiction.

- *Substantive disputes* Substantive disputes relate to the application of substantive WTO obligations to the conduct of the government of a particular nation. International obligations would not usually have direct application to private firms given private firms are not usually subject to public international law. A substantive dispute may arise if a nation is bound by WTO law, but does not comply with its WTO obligations. Conflict will arise because the nation will be potentially in breach of its WTO obligations and another nation may suffer harm as a result. The issue to be resolved would be whether the nation has in fact breached its WTO obligations. The adjudicating body would most likely be the WTO DSB which would apply WTO law, as discussed below.

12.2.2 Mechanisms for mitigating competition disputes

The question then arises as to how these three types of competition disputes could be mitigated by institutional mechanisms set out within a WTO competition agreement:

- *Mitigating jurisdictional disputes*   Jurisdictional disputes could be mitigated in three key ways:
  - *Restrictions on extraterritoriality*   One means to avoid jurisdictional disputes over the extraterritorial application of domestic competition laws would be to restrict extraterritorial enforcement.[26] However, significant restrictions on extraterritorial enforcement are unlikely to be palatable to the international community at the present time.

    Yet it may be possible to introduce a general principle that nations should *avoid* extraterritorial enforcement of competition laws. This principle would apply where there already exist adequate mechanisms in place to ensure the effective domestic enforcement of domestic competition laws against the relevant anti-competitive conduct. In essence, extraterritorial enforcement should be subject to comity considerations as discussed in detail later in this chapter.
  - *Positive and negative comity*   Similarly, to the extent jurisdictional disputes arise from multiple national enforcement against anti-competitive conduct that extends over jurisdictional boundaries, such disputes could be mitigated by international co-operation in respect of such enforcement activity.[27] Again, this could occur, for example, if nations were expressly required to have regard to the interests of other nations when making enforcement decisions. Obligations of negative and positive comity to give effect to this requirement were discussed in detail in Chapter 5 of this book.
  - *Rules of jurisdictional precedence*   It may also be possible to pre-determine which jurisdiction should have precedence in the event

---

[26] See S. K. Mehra, 'Extraterritorial Antitrust Enforcement and the Myth of International Consensus' (1999) 10(1) *Duke Journal of Comparative and International Law* 191. See also R. P. Alford, 'The Extraterritorial Application of Antitrust Laws: The United States and European Community Approaches' (1992) 33(1) *Virginia Journal of International Law* 1, 16.

[27] See also P. Clark & P. Morrison, 'Key Procedural Issues: Transparency Comments' (1998) 32 *International Lawyer* 851. See also M. D. Kresic, 'The Inconvenient Forum and International Comity in Private Antitrust Actions' (1983) 52 *Fordham Law Review* 399.

of jurisdictional conflict.[28] This issue is discussed in greater detail later in this chapter.
- *Mitigating procedural disputes* Procedural disputes could be mitigated if nations co-operated with each other to a greater extent in respect of cross-border enforcement activity. In addition, if greater convergence or mutual recognition of evidential rules and procedures occurred on an international basis in relation to competition law enforcement, the scope for procedural conflict would be correspondingly reduced.[29]

With this in mind, there are two mechanisms that could assist in achieving greater convergence of evidential and procedural rules in competition law enforcement, as follows:
- *Procedural mutual recognition* A nation could recognise the evidential and procedural rules of another nation solely in respect of competition law cases. Some advanced bilateral competition law co-operation agreements already contain provisions facilitating limited cross-border recognition of evidential and procedural rules. Australia and New Zealand, for example, permit certain evidential rules and legal procedures to be recognised in each other's domestic courts for certain competition actions.

  However, as discussed in Chapter 5, the Australia–New Zealand situation is based on the high degree of similarity of institutions and legal procedures between the two jurisdictions and the high degree of confidence of each nation in the courts and legal system of the other. Given the absence of such pre-conditions within the wider international community, the likely furthest extent of any obligation in a WTO competition agreement relating to procedural mutual recognition at the present time, would be a discretionary or 'soft law' principle.[30] This soft law principle could encourage nations to enter into bilateral agreements relating to mutual recognition of certain rules of evidence and procedure in competition law cases, but would not require them to do so.

---

[28] See, for example, S. W. Chang, 'Extraterritorial Application of U.S. Antitrust Laws to Other Pacific Countries: Proposed Bilateral Agreements for Resolving International Conflicts Within the Pacific Community' (1993) 16 *Hastings International & Comparative Law Review* 295.

[29] See D. M. Rosenzweig, 'Enforcement of Foreign Judgments' (1999) 33 *International Lawyer* 437.

[30] See C. M. Chinkin, 'The Challenge of Soft Law: Development and Change in International Law' (1989) 38 *International & Comparative Law Quarterly* 850. See also P. Handl, 'A Hard Look at Soft Law' (1988) 82 *American Society of International Law Proceedings* 371.

- *Procedural convergence* Nations could also seek greater convergence of certain procedures specific to competition law. Merger review procedures, for example, would benefit from greater convergence between nations, particularly in relation to notification requirements. However, procedures specific to competition law are not usually the source of procedural disputes; rather it is broader rules of evidence and procedure that are the main source of conflict. Accordingly, it is questionable the extent to which competition-specific procedural convergence would assist in mitigating procedural disputes.
- *Mitigating substantive disputes* Substantive disputes could be mitigated by greater convergence of competition laws between nations and via the use of comity procedures. These issues were discussed in detail in Chapters 11 and 5 of this book, respectively.

However, a formal consultative process may also assist in mitigating substantive disputes before they proceeded to full WTO dispute resolution. As discussed in Chapter 6 of this book, a limited consultative procedure specific to competition law was introduced into the WTO in November 1960.[31] The consultative procedure has rarely been invoked, although it was invoked in the context of the *Fuji-Kodak Film* dispute discussed in Chapter 7 of this book. An international competition agreement could build upon this pre-existing consultative procedure. Indeed, as discussed in Chapter 10 of this book, both GATS and TRIPS have incorporated elements of this consultative procedure into their respective competition obligations.

The WTO consultative procedure could, for example, be mandated prior to lodgement of a dispute before the WTO Dispute Settlement Body on any international competition issues.[32] The WTO already requires the parties to have attempted to resolve a dispute via consultation before a dispute is submitted to a WTO panel, hence a mandatory consultative procedure would dovetail with existing WTO dispute settlement procedures.[33] Such a strengthening of the consultative procedure would complement the principle of co-operation discussed in Chapter 10 of this book.

---

[31] See Resolution of 18 November 1960, (1961) BISD 9S/28, as discussed in Chapter 6 of this book.

[32] See, for example, discussion in H. Graham & J. D. Richardson, *Global Competition Policy* (Institute for International Economics, Washington DC, 1995).

[33] The consultations could be bilateral or multilateral, as the circumstances dictated, although bilateral consultations would usually be the norm. There would be no requirement to resolve the dispute via the consultation procedure, although an obligation to negotiate in good faith would apply. See G. N. Horlick, 'The Consultation Phase of WTO Dispute Resolution – A Private Practitioner's View' (1998) 32 *International Lawyer* 685.

In summary, there are a number of appropriate procedural and institutional mechanisms that could be incorporated into a WTO competition agreement to mitigate the scope for potential competition disputes, as identified above.

12.3 What would be the most appropriate institutional basis for a WTO competition agreement to *resolve* international competition disputes?

Given that the WTO already contains an existing institution to promote effective dispute settlement, namely the WTO Dispute Settlement Body ('WTO DSB'), the key issue is whether the WTO DSB is the most appropriate institution for resolving international competition disputes (and, if not, what modifications could be made or alternatives adopted).

12.3.1 The WTO Dispute Settlement Body

Prior to 1994, the GATT dispute resolution procedure was harshly criticised by legal practitioners and academics alike.[34] Many examples were cited of lengthy hearings before GATT dispute resolution panels, only to have the final reports of these panels blocked by an effective veto of the offending party at the critical adoption stage. Upon the completion of the Uruguay Round in 1994 the GATT dispute resolution procedure was significantly improved.[35] Time constraints were imposed to speed up hearings and the infamous veto was largely eliminated. As a result, the WTO now incorporates a comprehensive, streamlined and successful rules-based dispute settlement procedure that wields substantive legal power. Vermulst commented in 1996, for example:[36]

> The consistent trend over the past decade has been to introduce more formal rules into GATT Dispute Settlement and, hence, further legalise dispute settlement in international trade law. Against this background of slow change, the Dispute Settlement Understanding has taken a great leap forward. The Dispute Settlement Understanding creates a system of rules

---

[34] See, for example, W. J. Davey, 'Dispute Settlement in the GATT' (1987) *Fordham International Law Journal* 51, 63.

[35] See P. T. B. Kohona, 'Dispute Resolution Under the World Trade Organisation: An Overview' (1994) 28(5) *Journal of World Trade* 23.

[36] See E. A. Vermulst, 'An Overview of the WTO Dispute Settlement System and its Relationship with the Uruguay Round: Nice on Paper But Too Much Stress for the System?' (1995) 29(2) *Journal of World Trade* 131.

that are not only more comprehensive than the body of law in force in GATT Dispute Settlement, but which ... is almost exemplary compared with dispute settlement in other fields of public international law.

Indeed, the WTO dispute settlement system is now frequently viewed as one of the cornerstones of the modern multilateral trade order.

As discussed in Chapter 7, WTO dispute settlement is premised on Article XXIII:1 of the GATT, as affirmed by the WTO Dispute Settlement Understanding of 1995. Article XXIII:1 gives complaining parties a range of different procedural alternatives for WTO adjudication. Each of these alternatives has a different burden of proof and different consequences, as outlined in detail in Chapter 7. The WTO dispute settlement procedure currently operates in the following manner:

- *Consultations* The WTO dispute settlement process usually commences with a request by a WTO nation for bilateral consultations with another WTO nation.[37] If the dispute is not settled within 60 days, the complaining party may request the establishment of a WTO dispute panel (usually three experts).[38]
- *Panel review* The parties have a reasonable degree of flexibility to agree the terms of reference, composition of panellists, and principles to be adhered to by WTO panels.[39] Panels normally complete their work within six months and refer their reports to the WTO DSB.[40] Panel reports must be adopted by the WTO DSB within sixty days unless the WTO DSB decides otherwise by consensus or a party notifies the DSB of its intention to appeal.
- *Appellate review* Decisions of the WTO panel may be appealed to an Appellate Body which is more formalised and adjudicatory in its approach. The Appellate Body comprises seven permanent members, of whom three will sit on any case. An appeal is limited to issues of law covered in the panel report and legal interpretations developed by

---

[37] Bilateral consultations must occur within 30 days of the request. See Art. 5 of the WTO DSU.
[38] If the parties do not agree to follow an alternative form of dispute resolution voluntarily, a WTO panel will be established within strict time frames. Standard terms of reference will apply unless the parties agree to special terms within twenty days of the panel's establishment.
[39] Where the parties do not agree on the composition of the panel, this can be determined by the Director-General of the WTO.
[40] WTO Panel Reports are usually referred to the WTO DSB for adoption twenty days after they are issued to members.

the WTO panel. The appeal proceeding must not take more than sixty days and the resulting report must be adopted by the WTO DSB within thirty days of its issuance, unless the WTO DSB decides by consensus otherwise.
- *Implementation* Once the WTO Panel report or WTO Appellate Body report is adopted, the party concerned must notify the WTO DSB of its intentions with respect to the implementation of the relevant recommendations. The WTO DSB will monitor the implementation of the recommendations and, if not implemented, the parties may negotiate compensation. If these negotiations are unsuccessful within a defined time frame, the WTO DSB has the power to authorise the WTO member having invoked the dispute settlement process to suspend concessions or other obligations owed to the WTO member concerned.[41] WTO nations must not unilaterally suspend concessions until they have followed through the dispute settlement procedure and received the approval of the WTO DSB.

12.3.2 Resolution of substantive disputes and procedural disputes

With this background in mind, analysis reveals that the WTO DSB could be readily applied to substantive disputes and procedural disputes, for the following reasons:[42]

- *Substantive disputes* There are a number of points which indicate that the WTO DSB is already capable of adjudicating substantive competition law disputes:[43]
  (a) A significant number of the disputes brought before the DSB to date have already involved a competition or unfair trade component.[44]

---

[41] Disagreements over the proposed level of suspension may be referred to arbitration within a strict time frame. Generally, the concessions will be suspended in the relevant areas of concern, but in unusual circumstances may be suspended in other circumstances and under other WTO agreements.

[42] See Y. Jung, 'Modelling a WTO Dispute Settlement Mechanism in an International Antitrust Agreement – An Impossible Dream?' (2000) 34(1) *Journal of World Trade* 89. See also W. Davey, 'Supporting the World Trade Organisation Dispute Settlement System' (2000) 34(1) *Journal of World Trade* 167.

[43] See P. C. Mavroidis & S. J. V. Siclen, 'The Application of the GATT/WTO Dispute Resolution System to Competition Issues' (1997) 31(5) *Journal of World Trade* 5.

[44] These cases have related to such matters as tax discrimination, monopoly practices (e.g. Canadian and US liquor boards), domestic and export subsidies, countervailing duties and anti-dumping measures.

(b) The WTO contains a number of substantive competition obligations, particularly the WTO Basic Telecoms Agreement. Any disputes arising in respect of these competition obligations will necessarily have to be adjudicated upon by the WTO DSB.[45]

(c) As noted in Chapter 7 of this book, a number of existing WTO obligations have been interpreted in the context of effects on competition.[46]

However, consistent with the conclusions in Chapter 10 of this book, domestic competition law cases should not be second-guessed by the WTO DSB, hence limits on WTO DSB decision-making are required.[47] Domestic competition cases are notoriously fact-intensive and are best suited to adjudication by domestic institutions. Similarly, the WTO DSB should not have the ability to undertake enforcement action against domestic firms. Rather, the WTO DSB should be confined to resolving disputes between governments regarding compliance with WTO obligations, consistent with its existing role under the WTO.[48]

- *Procedural disputes* There is no precedent for the adjudication of procedural disputes by the WTO DSB. Existing WTO law obligations do not require nations to recognise the rules of evidence and procedure of other nations. Rather, procedural disputes have usually been determined at the domestic level via a refusal by a nation or its courts to recognise the evidential and procedural rules of another nation.

  In order for the WTO DSB to adjudicate procedural disputes, the WTO competition agreement would be required to set out various obligations relating to mutual recognition of rules of evidence and procedure. Such obligations could, for example, require the government of a

---

[45] See C. C. Parlin, 'WTO Dispute Settlement: Are Sufficient Resources Being Devoted to Enable the System to Function Effectively?' (1998) 32 *International Lawyer* 863.

[46] For example, the concept of discrimination in the context of Article III of the GATT is routinely assessed against whether the relevant measure would adversely affect the conditions of competition in respect of the relevant imported product. See J. I. Charney, 'The Implications of Expanding International Dispute Settlement Systems' (1996) 90 *American Journal of International Law* 69.

[47] See I. Shapiro, S. B. Wilson & D. G. Waddell, 'National Perspectives on the WTO Dispute Settlement System' (1998) 32 *International Lawyer* 811.

[48] A related issue is whether private sector entities should have the ability to seek WTO dispute settlement. At present, private individuals do not have standing before WTO dispute settlement panels and only government entities have a right to petition the WTO DSB. Any expansion of the WTO to provide standing to private applicants would be controversial and unlikely to receive support from WTO members. See N. Covelli, 'Public International Law and Third Party Participation in WTO Panel Proceedings' (1999) 33 *Journal of World Trade* 125.

WTO nation to enact legislation to recognise the rules of evidence and procedure of another nation. The relevant procedural dispute could then involve the relatively straightforward issue as to whether the relevant WTO obligation had been complied with and, if not, what consequences should arise for the breaching party. However, it is unlikely at this time that nations would be willing to agree to such obligations given sovereignty and constitutional concerns and given insufficient confidence in each other's institutions.

In summary, the WTO DSB would be ideally placed to resolve *substantive* disputes and has already proved itself capable of adjudicating substantive competition issues.[49] The WTO DSB could also adjudicate *procedural* disputes if procedural obligations were incorporated into a WTO competition agreement, although it seems unlikely nations would agree to such procedural obligations at this time.

12.3.3 Resolution of jurisdictional disputes

Again, there is no precedent for the adjudication of jurisdictional disputes by the WTO DSB. Existing WTO law does not purport to delineate the jurisdiction of different nations. Rather, disputes over jurisdictional competence have historically been subject to ICJ adjudication. This raises two issues:

(a) whether there is a risk of conflict between the ICJ and WTO DSB; and
(b) whether the WTO DSB is the appropriate forum for determining jurisdictional issues.

In relation to the first issue, potential issues of conflict between the WTO DSB and the ICJ could be addressed by a clause in a WTO competition agreement which required parties to have recourse only to the WTO DSB.[50] In relation to the second issue, there would appear to be no difficulty in principle with enabling the WTO DSB to determine a matter of jurisdiction provided that jurisdictional issues were the subject of substantive WTO obligations. However, as with procedural disputes, it remains highly unlikely that WTO members would be willing to agree to such obligations.

---

[49] See, for example, comments in T. P. Stewart & M. M. Burr, 'The WTO Panel Process: An Evaluation of the First Three Years' (1998) 32 *International Lawyer* 709.
[50] See J. B. Mus, 'Conflict between Treaties in International Law' (1998) 45 *Netherlands Law Review* 208.

If nations were willing to permit the WTO DSB to adjudicate on matters of jurisdiction, clear principles could be set out in a WTO competition agreement to assist such adjudication. Such jurisdictional rules could pre-determine jurisdictional priority and guide the exercise of concurrent jurisdiction in relation to competition law issues. If two or more states asserted jurisdiction over the same subject matter, such rules could delineate which nation would have jurisdiction and would regulate the exercise of any concurrent jurisdiction.[51]

The application of such jurisdictional rules would necessarily involve restrictions on extraterritorial jurisdiction. Each WTO nation would enact legislation to fetter the jurisdiction of its national courts and require its courts to follow the WTO jurisdictional rules and procedures in the event of inter-jurisdictional conflict. Alternatively, governments could enact legislation to give effect to jurisdictional rulings of the WTO DSB. In many nations such legislation may raise constitutional issues and may face significant opposition.[52]

However, pre-determination of jurisdictional rules seems unlikely to be palatable to WTO Members at this time. Accordingly, WTO members may instead prefer to adopt an overriding non-binding 'soft law' principle to regulate extraterritoriality. The *obiter dictum* of Judge Fitzmaurice of the ICJ in the *Barcelona Traction* case may be of guidance in this regard. Judge Fitzmaurice reasoned:[53]

> It is true that, under present conditions, international law does not impose hard and fast rules on States delimiting spheres of national jurisdiction in such matters ... but leaves to States a wide discretion in the matter. It does however:
>
> (a) postulate the existence of limits though in any given case it may be for the tribunal to indicate what these are for the purposes of that case; and
>
> (b) involve for every State an *obligation to exercise moderation and restraint as to the exercise of the jurisdiction assumed by its courts in cases having a*

---

[51] Necessarily, therefore, such rules would have the effect of preventing national courts from asserting jurisdiction in certain circumstances. See comments in R. E. Price, 'Foreign Blocking Statutes and the GATT: State Sovereignty and the Enforcement of US Economic Laws Abroad' (1995) 28 *George Washington Journal of International Law & Economics* 315.

[52] Precedents do exist for such a procedure. Similar mechanisms were established for the resolution of investment disputes via the Convention establishing the International Centre for Settlement of Investment Disputes. See also Convention on the Settlement of Investment Disputes between States and Nationals of Other States, entered into force 14 October 1966.

[53] See Judge Fitzmaurice's separate opinion in *Barcelona Traction* [1970] ICJ Reports 4.

> *foreign element, and to avoid undue encroachment on a jurisdiction more properly appertaining to or more appropriately exercisable by, another State.*
>
> (emphasis added)

This requirement to exercise moderation and restraint has been recognised in the domestic law of the US and the law of the EU, being the two entities which have applied their competition laws on an extraterritorial basis most frequently.[54] A general principle that nations should exercise moderation and restraint in the extraterritorial application of competition laws could usefully be included in a WTO competition agreement, given that such a principle would remain consistent with the ICJ judicial precedent and the domestic laws of most key nations.[55]

In summary, WTO jurisdictional rules are unlikely to be palatable to the international community in an international competition law context at this time. However, a non-binding 'soft law' principle could be included in a WTO competition agreement that required each nation to exercise moderation and restraint in the exercise of extraterritorial jurisdiction to avoid undue encroachment on the jurisdiction of any other nation, consistent with the principle expounded in the *Barcelona Traction* case.[56] As a 'soft law' principle, it would not be subject to WTO DSB adjudication.

12.4 Would the suspension of trade concessions be an appropriate sanction for a failure to comply with a WTO competition agreement?

Assuming international competition obligations were incorporated into the WTO and subject to dispute settlement by the WTO DSB, the issue arises whether the existing WTO sanctions should apply to any breach of these international competition obligations.

At present, as identified above, if a WTO member fails to implement the recommendations of the WTO DSB, the parties are required to negotiate

---

[54] See R. D. Alford, 'The Extraterritorial Application of Antitrust Laws: The United States and European Community Approaches' (1992) 33 *Virginia Journal of International Law* 1. See also though D. J. Gerber, 'The Extraterritorial Application of the German Antitrust Laws (1983) 77 *American Journal of International Law* 756.
[55] See, for example, *United States* v. *Aluminium Co of America (Alcoa)* 148 F 2d 416 (2nd Cir, 1945). See also *A. Ahlstrom Osakeytio* v. *Commission* (1988) 4 CMLR 901 ('*Woodpulp* case').
[56] See *Barcelona Traction Case* [1970] ICJ Reports 4.

compensation voluntarily.[57] Accordingly, the WTO places primary emphasis on compensation for any breaches of WTO obligations rather than encouraging retaliation in the form of trade sanctions. However, the WTO DSB does have the power to authorise suspension of WTO concessions (i.e. impose trade sanctions) if negotiations on compensation fail.[58]

This raises a fundamentally important issue in the context of a WTO competition agreement: *is suspension of trade concessions an appropriate sanction for a failure to comply with a WTO competition agreement* (and, if not, what alternative should apply)?

A number of commentators, particularly Bhagwati, have argued that extended use of trade sanctions under the WTO to address other subject areas is *not* appropriate.[59] This view is closely related to the vexed issue of 'linkages' under the WTO, namely the extent to which the ambit of the WTO should be extended to address issues such as competition policy, investment, environmental standards, labour standards and human rights. These commentators highlight that the WTO is intended as a vehicle for liberalising trade, not a vehicle for promoting the wider regulation of the international economic system or a vehicle for the more general imposition of moral and social standards.[60]

As identified by Charnovitz, a key concern of these commentators is 'sanction envy'.[61] Because the WTO has such an effective dispute settlement system, a wide array of regulatory interest groups may seek to link their particular regulatory interests into the WTO so as to benefit from the use of trade sanctions.[62] Leebron, for example, makes the following insightful comment:[63]

[57] Compensation in this context usually means action by the defendant government to reduce trade barriers, rather than financial compensation (although that outcome is not precluded). See S. Charnovitz, 'Rethinking WTO Trade Sanctions' (2001) 95(4) *American Journal of International Law* 792.
[58] See discussion in R. E. Hudec, 'The New WTO Dispute Settlement Procedure: An Overview of the First Three Years' (1999) 8 *Minnesota Journal of Global Trade* 1. See also discussion in J. C. Spierer, 'Dispute Settlement Understanding: Developing a Firm Foundation for Implementation of the World Trade Organization' (1998) 22 *Suffolk Transnational Law Review* 63.
[59] See J. Bhagwati, 'Afterword: The Question of Linkage' (2002) 96 *American Journal of International Law* 126, 127.
[60] The key 'moral exception' in existing WTO law is provided by Art. XX of the GATT. Significant policy debate continues as to whether the scope of Art. XX should be expanded.
[61] See S. Charnovitz, 'The Moral Exception in Trade Policy' (1998) 38 *Virginia Journal of International Law* 689.
[62] In this manner, if a nation does not achieve a particular regulatory standard, it would risk losing its trade privileges under the WTO.
[63] See D. Leebron, 'Linkages – Symposium: The Boundaries of the WTO' (2002) 96 *American Journal of International Law* 5, 14.

Claims for sanction linkage do not necessarily depend on any substantive relationship between the issue areas. Sanction linkage may be sought even though it affects neither the negotiating positions in the linked regime nor the distribution of benefits in either regime. Rather, the sanction claim for linkage is a specific example of a more general type of linkage benefit, namely regime borrowing. That is, linkage may be sought to obtain the institutional and procedural benefits of an existing regime, when similar arrangements cannot be independently negotiated for the issues seeking to be linked.

Such use of trade sanctions undermines negotiated trade commitments, constitutes an exception to the WTO's principles of non-discrimination and, in effect, may provide an excuse for trade barriers to be re-erected. In this manner, the objective of the WTO in liberalising international trade may be impeded by the simultaneous use of the WTO as a vehicle for the imposition of trade sanctions within a broader international regulatory system. Overuse of trade sanctions would, ultimately, weaken the WTO's ability to realise its liberalised trade objectives.

Bearing these concerns in mind, it is clear that the key concern relating to the extended use of trade sanctions relates to the potential weakening of the WTO's ability to achieve and maintain liberalised trade (assuming cross-retaliation notwithstanding use of a plurilateral WTO agreement). In order to prevent such weakening, a number of commentators have sought to identify objective criteria that can be applied in order to screen whether it is appropriate for particular issues to be addressed by the WTO.[64] Importantly, commentators, including Bhagwati, have recognised that competition policy issues have a stronger claim for inclusion in the WTO under such criteria than issues such as labour standards. Bhagwati explains, for example, that competition policy linkages have a clearly accepted rationale namely: 'opening markets will lead to increased trade, but this increase can be frustrated by public and private business practices that proximately nullify the effects of the enhanced openness; as a result, we may negotiate mutually acceptable rules (under the rubric of "competition policy") in regard thereto at the WTO'.[65]

Many of these commentators are therefore, in effect, implicitly applying a 'cost-benefit' analysis to assess whether an extension of the WTO is appropriate. In the terminology discussed in Chapter 2 of this book,

---

[64] See, for example, J. P. Trachtman, 'Institutional Linkage: Transcending Trade and . . .' (2002) 96 *American Journal of International Law* 77.

[65] See Bhagwati, above n. 59.

these commentators are identifying whether a 'KHE improvement' would occur. Where a particular linkage is consistent with existing WTO law and policy (such as competition policy), the net benefits of including that linkage are likely to be considerable. However, where a particular linkage constitutes, in effect, an exception to existing WTO principles (such as labour standards and environmental standards), the benefits may be few while the costs may be considerable. Furthermore, where a linkage is principally intended to redistribute welfare, rather than increase welfare, there is unlikely to be a KHE improvement overall.

Such economic reasoning can be applied to the specific issue whether the WTO should permit trade sanctions to be imposed for any breach of a WTO competition agreement, as a sub-set of the more general issue whether competition policy should be included in the WTO. The relevant test for this specific issue is whether the benefits of increasing the scope of the WTO to include enforceable competition obligations are outweighed by the costs in permitting trade sanctions for breaches of these obligations. Under this analysis, trade sanctions should be permitted if the aggregate costs from trade sanctions (including costs associated with impeding WTO trade liberalisation objectives) are outweighed by the aggregate benefits of ensuring compliance with WTO competition obligations:

- *Aggregate benefits*   Chapters 2 and 3 of this book indicated that a WTO competition agreement is likely to be welfare enhancing. While it is beyond the scope of this book to quantify precisely the magnitude of the likely welfare gains from a WTO competition agreement, this book did indicate that the net welfare benefits of an international competition agreement would be material and probably substantial. The threat of sanctions is likely to be necessary to ensure compliance with any competition obligations, hence the existence of a right to impose sanctions is, arguably, determinative of these benefits.
- *Aggregate costs*   Each nation that has trade sanctions imposed against it is likely to suffer direct economic costs. The precise nature and magnitude of those costs would depend on the frequency, nature, scope and duration of the particular trade sanctions imposed. Furthermore, indirect costs may arise for other parties, as follows:
    (a) sanctions do not necessarily work and no relief is necessarily provided to the relevant injured private economic actors;
    (b) trade sanctions may harm the country imposing the sanction and may harm innocent consumers in both nations;

(c) third party nations may also suffer from the imposition of trade sanctions due to distortions in trade flows and associated spillover effects; and

(d) sanctions undermine the WTO and its objective of liberalised trade, and may encourage discrimination and protectionism.

Yet it is also important to note that the aggregate costs of trade sanctions in a competition law context are likely to be relatively low. When they are applied, sanctions usually have an isolated effect on a particular trade sector of a particular nation. In addition, trade sanctions are a 'last resort' option in the WTO that have rarely been applied in practice and are similarly likely to be rarely applied in a competition law context.[66]

On this basis, the aggregate costs of trade sanctions are likely to be significantly outweighed by the benefits of a WTO competition agreement. This indicates that there may be significant net benefits in utilising trade sanctions to enforce a WTO competition agreement. Clearly, this conclusion would need to be tested as part of any quantification of the aggregate costs and benefits. However, this conclusion seems reasonably robust for the purposes of this book given that long-term material benefits to the global community as a whole are being contrasted with a handful of isolated detriments to particular nations.

Yet this analysis highlights that it is important to reduce unnecessary costs when applying trade sanctions. Hence trade should be proportionate in nature and directed at the particular obligation breached so as to reduce unnecessary costs. A causal nexus between the sanction and the breach would greatly assist in achieving this. Such an approach could be articulated in a WTO competition agreement to maximise net benefits by minimising costs.

12.5 Conclusions on optimal institutional structure for a WTO competition agreement

In summary, a WTO competition agreement could best promote effective compliance with its substantive obligations via a supra-national, quasi-judicial institution, coupled with inter-governmental peer enforcement.

---

[66] Charnovitz notes that of sixty-five WTO cases that have gone to final judgment, only six have resulted in the authorisation of suspension of concessions or other obligations. Of these six authorised cases, only three have actually resulted in the application of trade sanctions. See discussion in S. Charnovitz, 'The WTO's Problematic Last Resort Against Compliance' (2002) 57 *Aussenwirtschaft* 409, 413.

The WTO DSB has already been developed with such a role in mind. The WTO also contains mechanisms to promote compliance via non-coercive techniques, including the TPRM and technical assistance, both of which could be applied in a competition law context.

International competition disputes are likely to comprise three distinct types, namely jurisdictional disputes, procedural disputes and substantive disputes. A variety of mechanisms could be adopted to mitigate the likelihood of such disputes arising including, for example, greater use of consultative procedures, greater co-operation and comity and restrictions on extraterritoriality. However, to the extent such disputes do arise, any WTO competition agreement could continue to use the WTO DSB as the principal forum for the resolution of such disputes. While the use of trade sanctions to enforce international competition obligations may be controversial, the benefits of applying trade sanctions would appear greatly to outweigh any detriments.

In conclusion, based on the brief analysis undertaken in this chapter, the optimal institutional structure for a WTO competition agreement would involve the use of the existing WTO institutions, particularly the WTO secretariat and the existing WTO DSB.

The discussion in Chapters 10 to 12 of this book, when combined with the earlier conclusions in this book (particularly Chapter 4), indicates that the optimal content, approach and structure for a WTO competition agreement can be clearly ascertained.

13

Would a WTO competition agreement be politically achievable?

> The WTO will likely suffer from slow and cumbersome policy-making and management – an organisation with more than 120 member countries cannot be run by a 'committee of the whole'. Mass management simply does not lend itself to operational efficiency or serious policy discussion.
>
> (Jeffrey Schott, Institute for International Economics, 2000)

Chapter 13 of this book considers whether a WTO competition agreement would be politically achievable. Chapter 13 has three sections.

- Section 13.1 identifies the procedure for incorporating a WTO competition agreement into the WTO and considers whether the public stances of key WTO nations would enable this readily to occur.
- Section 13.2 considers likely concessions that could be made to recognise the interests of developing nations given their critical role in determining achievability.
- Section 13.3 identifies a four-point incremental strategy for incorporating competition law into the WTO based on the insights identified in this book.

Chapter 13 concludes that a multilateral WTO competition agreement would *not* be politically achievable at the present time. However, a plurilateral competition agreement may be achievable if the four-point incremental strategy identified in this chapter were adopted.

13.1 The negotiation of a WTO competition agreement

13.1.1 The procedure for incorporating a competition agreement into the WTO

In order for a competition agreement to be incorporated into WTO law, it must be incorporated into the Agreement Establishing the WTO ('WTO

Agreement') which is the formal compilation of all WTO agreements.[1] The procedure for amending the WTO Agreement is set out in Article X. Article X contemplates two relevant alternatives:

(a) a competition agreement could be incorporated into the WTO as a plurilateral agreement in Annexe 4 of the WTO Agreement, with the intention that it would apply only to a subset of WTO nations ('Plurilateral Option');[2] or
(b) a competition agreement could be incorporated into the WTO as a multilateral agreement in Annexe 1 of the WTO Agreement, with the intention that it would apply to all WTO nations ('Multilateral Option').[3]

A consensus decision by the Ministerial Conference would be required to incorporate the text of the WTO competition agreement either as a plurilateral agreement into Annexe 4 of the WTO Agreement or a multilateral agreement into Annexe 1.[4] A 'consensus decision' requires all WTO nations at least to acquiesce to the decision so that no formal objection is made by any nation. However, if such a consensus decision were not made within ninety days of the proposal to the Ministerial Conference, WTO nations could vote to incorporate the agreement into the WTO by a formal two-thirds majority vote. Once incorporated into the WTO, the agreement would be presented to WTO nations for formal ratification.

- The procedures set out in the *plurilateral* agreement would govern when it entered into force to bind those WTO nations that ratified it.
- The extent of ratification required before the multilateral agreement takes effect is determined by the significance of amendments to the WTO Agreement, but generally requires either consensus agreement or at least two-thirds positive support. However, the Ministerial Conference would rarely seek to incorporate a multilateral agreement into the WTO if it were not accepted by a consensus decision.[5]

---

[1] See Final Act and Agreement Establishing the World Trade Organisation, General Agreement on Tariffs and Trade, Uruguay Round, Marrakesh, Morocco, 15 April 1994.
[2] Plurilateral agreements are set out in Annexe 4 of the WTO Agreement. An example of a plurilateral agreement is the Agreement on Government Procurement.
[3] Multilateral agreements are set out in Annexe 1 of the WTO Agreement. Examples of multilateral agreements include GATT, GATS, TRIMS and TRIPS.
[4] Article X:1, WTO Agreement. The Ministerial Conference is the plenary body of the WTO and comprises all WTO nations which may each exercise one vote.
[5] Article X:3, WTO Agreement. The Ministerial Conference could under Article X:1 and X:4, by a three-quarters vote, coerce nations opposed to a WTO competition agreement

In practice, the consensus decision of the Ministerial Conference would represent the culmination of extensive prior multilateral negotiations and consensus-building.[6] Such negotiations have historically assumed three different forms:

(a) sectoral negotiations, such as the WTO negotiations on basic telecommunications;
(b) issue-based negotiations, involving the grouping of clusters of inter-linking multiple-sector issues for negotiation, such as the WTO negotiations on government procurement; and
(c) an integrated 'Round' of WTO negotiations, in which a comprehensive range of inter-linking issues and sectors would be considered, such as the Uruguay Round of WTO multilateral negotiations.

The decision as to the appropriate form of negotiations and the agenda for these negotiations would usually be determined by the Ministerial Conference, again by consensus.

This means three distinct procedural steps must be followed to enable the incorporation of a competition agreement into WTO law:

- *Agenda negotiations* Competition policy must be placed on the agenda for WTO multilateral negotiations by a consensus decision of the Ministerial Conference, requiring agreement on that agenda via negotiation and consensus-building prior to the Ministerial Conference.[7]
- *Substantive negotiations* WTO nations must reach consensus agreement on the text of the competition agreement to enable a consensus decision of the Ministerial Council to incorporate it into the WTO Agreement.
- *Ratification* The competition agreement must be ratified by WTO nations, with such ratification procedure dependent upon whether the Multilateral Option or Plurilateral Option is followed. As discussed in Chapter 10, the most likely alternative for incorporating a competition

---

to ratify it under threat of expulsion from the WTO. However, in practice, such enforced ratification would only be contemplated as a last resort mechanism if a nation reneged on its negotiated commitment to ratify a WTO agreement.

[6] See J. J. Schott & J. Watal, 'Decision-Making in the WTO', *International Economics Policy Briefs Number 00–2*, Institute for International Economics, Washington, DC, 2000. A consensus decision by the Ministerial Conference represents the end product of WTO negotiations. Before an agreement was presented to the Ministerial Conference, extensive multilateral negotiations would usually be required to enable WTO nations to resolve their differences and reach a compromise.

[7] 'Negotiation' in this context is intended to describe a structured discussion of difficult issues, rather than the process of reaching a formal, binding agreement.

agreement in the WTO would be the Plurilateral Option, as this would enable nations to 'opt out' from the provisions of the agreement, increasing flexibility. Accordingly, the provisions of the plurilateral WTO competition agreement would determine when it entered into force.

As the agenda negotiations determine the agenda for the subsequent substantive negotiations which, in turn, determine the text of the WTO competition agreement, the agenda negotiations are critically important to the incorporation of a competition agreement into the WTO. Historic agenda negotiations involving competition policy, in the context of the Singapore, Geneva, Seattle, Doha and Cancún Ministerials, are therefore considered in greater detail below. The history of these negotiations provides a number of key insights into a likely strategy for realising a WTO competition agreement.

13.1.2 Singapore Ministerial (1996) – a competition work programme commences

The first WTO Ministerial Conference was held in Singapore between 9 and 13 December 1996 ('Singapore Ministerial').[8] While the Singapore Ministerial focused on the implementation of the Uruguay Round agreements, it also introduced a number of new issues into the WTO for further consideration, namely competition policy, government procurement, environmental policy and labour policy.[9] Importantly, as discussed in Chapter 5 of this book, the Singapore Ministerial adopted the Singapore Ministerial Declaration which mandated the establishment of a Working Group to study issues raised by WTO members relating to the interaction between trade and competition policy.[10]

The international politics behind the Singapore Ministerial are important:

- The inclusion of competition policy in the WTO was advocated principally by the EU, which sought to establish a mandate for the Working Group to consider WTO competition rules.

---

[8] See WTO, 'Report of the Ministerial Council to the Ministerial Conference: Singapore 9–13 December 1996', WT/MIN(96)/2, Vols. I and II, 26 November 1996.
[9] See V. A. Leary, 'The WTO and the Social Clause: Post-Singapore' (1997) 8 *European Journal of International Law* 11.
[10] See WTO, 'Singapore Ministerial Declaration' (1997) 36 *International Legal Materials* 218.

- The US supported the EU but also sought to protect US domestic producer interests by keeping anti-dumping law reforms off the WTO agenda.[11]
- Japan, South Korea and Hong Kong sought a more comprehensive mandate for the Working Group, including anti-dumping, subsidies, safeguard measures and investment issues.
- The developing nations, led by India, sought to characterise WTO competition rules in terms of the regulation of restrictive business practices of multinational corporations, reflecting the development-oriented approach of the UNCTAD Code, as discussed in Chapter 5 of this book.[12]

The EU proposed that this WTO Working Group should explore a framework of rules for competition in the WTO.[13] Under this proposed framework, all WTO nations would eventually adopt and enforce their own competition rules along common agreed principles.[14] This framework would develop gradually, commencing with the establishment of common domestic competition structures and proceeding to the identification of common principles of competition policy, beginning with hard-core cartel conduct. In addition, WTO nations would identify what procedural and substantive elements could be made subject to the WTO dispute settlement mechanisms.[15]

This proposal proved too ambitious for most nations, including the US, which advocated a more conservative approach of careful study and consensus building.[16] In particular, the US resisted the EU proposal on four grounds:

---

[11] See J. I. Klein, 'A Note of Caution with Respect to a WTO Agenda on Competition Policy', Speech by Acting Assistant Attorney-General, US Department of Justice, Presented at The Royal Institute of International Affairs, Chatham House, London, 18 November 1996.
[12] See M. Khor, 'Competing Views on Competition Policy in WTO', *South-North Development Monitor- SUNS No. 3895*, 7 April 1996.
[13] In support of the EU, the Japanese government tabled a paper that called for a thorough examination of the links between trade and competition policy. However, the Japanese paper suggested confining the scope of WTO deliberations on trade and competition to government measures, since WTO rules were intended to discipline states rather than private individuals. See 'Non-Paper on Trade and Competition by the Japanese Delegation to the WTO' reprinted in (1996) 26(11) *International Business Lawyer* 463.
[14] See 'The New Round: EC Approach to Trade and Competition', European Commission, April 2000, http://europa.eu.int/comm/trade/2000_round/seacomp.htm.
[15] See K. Van Miert, 'The WTO and Competition Policy: the Need to Consider Negotiations', Address before Ambassadors to the WTO, Geneva, 21 April 1998.
[16] See A. Hoda, 'WTO: Working Group on Trade and Competition Policy' (1997) 25(11) *International Business Lawyer* 449.

- the interests of WTO members are too diverse to enable the adoption of a common approach to competition policy;
- any negotiations could lead to lowest common denominator results that would weaken existing initiatives towards cross-border competition laws;
- an agreement on competition law in a trade context could permit the misuse of confidential information by governments for trade law measures;
- WTO dispute resolution mechanisms are inappropriate to review domestic competition law decisions due to sovereignty and confidentiality issues.[17]

The carefully worded Singapore Declaration was intended to balance these competing interests.[18] The Working Group established by the Singapore Declaration was expressly required to consider the development dimension and to have regard to the work of UNCTAD, thereby reflecting the concerns of developing countries. The Working Group was also mandated to consider any issues raised by WTO nations, enabling it to consider anti-dumping law issues raised by Japan, South Korea and Hong Kong.

Yet by clearly stating that an explicit consensus would be required before any multilateral negotiations were undertaken on competition issues, the Singapore Declaration protected US interests by enabling the US to continue to veto the inclusion of anti-dumping law reforms on the WTO agenda.[19] In this manner, while the Singapore Declaration initiated a work programme on competition policy, a number of important international differences in opinion remained unresolved.[20]

13.1.3 Geneva Ministerial (1998) – the competition work programme continues

The second WTO Ministerial Conference was held in Geneva, Switzerland between 18 and 20 May 1998 ('Geneva Ministerial') and adopted two

---

[17] See US Department of Justice, 'A Note of Caution with respect to a World Trade Organisation Agenda on Competition Policy', Speech by J. I. Klein to the Royal Institute of International Affairs, Chatham House, London, 18 November 1996.

[18] See WTO Declaration, above n. 10.

[19] See Council of Economic Advisers, *America's Interest in the World Trade Organization* (CEA, Washington, DC, 1999). See D. T. Griswold, 'WTO Report Card: America's Economic Stake in Open Trade' *Cato Trade Briefing Paper* No. 9, Washington DC, 3 April 2000.

[20] See C. Raghavan, 'Competition Group Has Work Programme of Sorts' *Third World Economics* No. 166, 22 August 1997. See also C. Raghavan, 'More Level Playing Fields for TNCs?' *Third World Economics* No. 166, 15 August 1997.

Ministerial Declarations.[21] The more important of these two Geneva Declarations was intended to enable the WTO General Council to commence preparations for the launch of a new round of WTO multilateral negotiations at the Seattle Ministerial in 1999.[22] While competition policy was not expressly mentioned, the Geneva Declarations did contemplate that the WTO General Council would make 'recommendations concerning other possible future work on the basis of the work programme initiated at Singapore'.[23]

During the Geneva Ministerial, the positions of different nations on the inclusion of competition policy in the WTO became clearly discernible.[24] These positions may be loosely categorised into four distinct views relating to the incorporation of a competition agreement into the WTO:

- *EU view* The EU considered that WTO rules should require each nation to enact domestic competition laws that ensured firms of foreign nations were granted market access on a non-discriminatory basis without anti-competitive impediments. However, the EU opposed reforms to anti-dumping laws, presumably seeking to safeguard its recourse to domestic retaliatory trade remedies. The EU view was supported by Canada, Australia and New Zealand as well as a number of nations within the EU sphere of influence such as Norway and Switzerland.[25]
- *US view* The US was less supportive of WTO competition rules.[26] The US strongly opposed any reforms to existing retaliatory trade remedies such as anti-dumping laws and insisted that any WTO competition rules should only be addressed at private anti-competitive practices

---

[21] See http://www.wto.org/english/thewto_e/minist_e/min98_e/min98_e.htm. The Geneva Ministerial adopted two Declarations, one dealing with the preparations for the Third Ministerial Conference and the other with electronic commerce. See also WT/MIN(98) series in WTO online document database.

[22] See http://www.wto.org/english/thewto_e/minist_e/min98_e/mindec_e.htm.

[23] See World Trade Organisation, 'Ministerial Declaration at the Geneva WTO Ministerial 1998', WTO Ministerial Conference, World Trade Organisation, Geneva, adopted on 20 May 1998, para. 9(b).

[24] Such entrenchment is evident in the oral presentations and papers submitted by various delegations to the Working Group. See WT/WGTCP/W/ series in WTO online document database.

[25] See 'Trade and Competition: Preparations for the 1999 Ministerial', Communication from Norway to the World Trade Organisation General Council, WT/GC/W/310, 7 September 1999.

[26] See P. Morci, 'US Goals for WTO Negotiations', Economic Strategy Institute, Washington, DC, 2000.

that impeded market access.[27] This approach most likely reflected the US reliance on extraterritorial and retaliatory measures to protect its national interests.[28]

- *Japanese view* Japan and South Korea sought a comprehensive approach to consideration of WTO competition issues, including consideration of reforms to existing competition-inconsistent trade measures such as anti-dumping laws.[29] The Japanese view presumably reflected the export-orientation of these nations and their desire to realise greater market and investment opportunities. The Japanese view presumably also reflected its desire to limit the retaliatory trade measures frequently used by import-oriented nations (such as the US and the members of the EU) against it.[30]

- *LDC view* The developing countries, led by India, Malaysia and Kenya, sought to characterise WTO competition rules as protecting the smaller enterprises of developing countries from predatory conduct by powerful multinational firms. Developing countries were also concerned to eliminate export and import cartels in international markets, as they considered such cartels were impeding their ability to obtain access to the markets of developed nations on equitable terms.[31]

These four distinct views became further entrenched in the period after the Geneva Ministerial leading to significant divergences in approach at the third WTO Ministerial Conference in Seattle.

---

[27] See A. Zampetti & P. Suavé, 'Onwards to Singapore: The International Contestability of Markets and the New Trade Agenda' (1996) 19(3) *The World Economy* 333.

[28] See 'Federal Register Notice: Public Comments on Preparations for the Fourth Ministerial Conference of the World Trade Organization', Memorandum to Trade Advisory Committees from C. Sevilla, Acting Assistant US Trade Representative for Intergovernmental Affairs and Public Liaison, Washington, DC, 10 April 2001.

[29] See 'World Trade Organization: Informal Meeting in Frankfurt (Overview and Evaluation)', Paper by the International Organizations Division, Ministry of Foreign Affairs of Japan, Tokyo, 24 January 2001. See also Japanese Delegation to the WTO, 'Non-Paper on Trade and Competition by the Japanese Delegation to the WTO' (1996) 24(10) *International Business Lawyer* 463.

[30] See 'Trade and Competition: Preparations for the 1999 Ministerial', Communication from Japan to the World Trade Organisation General Council, WT/GC/W/308, 25 August 1999.

[31] See 'The Interaction Between Trade and Competition Policy: Preparations for the 1999 Ministerial', Communication from Kenya on behalf of the African Group to the WTO General Council, WT/GC/W/300, 6 August 1999. See also C. Raghavan, 'South's Focus on Development, TNCs in Competition Policy' *Third World Economics* No. 166, 15 August 1997.

13.1.4 Seattle Ministerial (1999) – competition becomes a bargaining chip against agriculture

The third WTO Ministerial Conference was held in Seattle, US between 30 November and 3 December 1999 ('Seattle Ministerial').[32] The Seattle Ministerial was envisaged as providing a forum for the launch of a new 'Millennium Round' of WTO multilateral trade negotiations.[33] This Millennium Round was intended to contemplate core sector-specific negotiations on agriculture and key services as part of the WTO mandatory 'built-in agenda'.[34] These core negotiations were to be supplemented by issue-specific negotiations on Uruguay Round implementation issues, mechanisms to increase WTO transparency and mechanisms to assist developing countries.[35] Given that such negotiations were to be characterised as a formal WTO 'round', they were also intended to provide an opportunity for consideration of the various new issues raised in the Singapore Ministerial, including competition policy.[36]

However, the Seattle Ministerial proved both controversial and acrimonious, dramatically failing in its attempt to launch a Millennium Round.[37] A number of analyses have been made of the Seattle Ministerial to identify the causes of the impasse in WTO agenda negotiations.[38] These analyses highlight that the Seattle Ministerial was both premature and overambitious in its attempt to launch a Millennium Round.[39] Three causes of the Seattle impasse frequently identified by these analyses are:

---

[32] See http://www.wto.org/english/thewto_e/minist_e/min99_e/min99_e.htm.
[33] See OECD, 'Focus-Millennium Trade Round' (Special Section) (1999) 219 *OECD Observer* 34. See also D. K. Tarullo, 'Seattle Light' (1999) 13(6) *The International Economy* 43.
[34] See US General Accounting Office, 'Seattle Ministerial: Outcomes and Lessons Learned', Testimony Before the Subcommittee on Trade, Committee on Ways and Means, House of Representatives, Washington, DC, 8 February 2000.
[35] See D. L. Aaron, 'The New Round', Speech to the Institute for International Economics, Washington, DC, 26 October 1999.
[36] See B. Lindsey, D. T. Griswold, M. A. Groombridge & A. Lukas, 'Seattle and Beyond: A WTO Agenda for the New Millennium' *CATO Trade Policy Analysis*, No. 8, 4 November 1999.
[37] Insufficient consensus existed even to adopt a limited Ministerial Declaration. While a draft Ministerial Declaration was negotiated at Seattle, this draft was never agreed and therefore has no status.
[38] See, for example, J. J. Schott, *The WTO After Seattle* (Institute for International Economics, Washington, DC, 2000). See also US General Accounting Office, Testimony, above n. 34.
[39] See US General Accounting Office, Testimony, above n. 34.

(a) the range of substantive issues remaining unresolved immediately prior to the Seattle Ministerial;[40]
(b) deep divisions between developed nations and developing countries on various substantive trade policy issues;[41] and
(c) a lack of confidence expressed by developing countries in the underlying WTO negotiation procedures.[42]

However, the failure of the EU, Japan and the US to reach agreement themselves on various substantive trade policy issues was also identified as a cause of the failures in Seattle, particularly as these constituted the three most influential WTO delegations.[43] The EU and Japan sought a broad round of WTO multilateral negotiations, while the US favoured sector-specific negotiations targeted principally at agriculture and key services.[44]

As a compromise, the US offered to support a broader initiative (including competition policy) if the EU and Japan supported reforms to agricultural trade.[45] Importantly, given the vested interests of Cairns Group agricultural nations (such as Canada, Australia, New Zealand and Brazil) in such agricultural reforms, these nations followed the US position, thereby subordinating their desire for a WTO competition agreement

---

[40] The draft Seattle Ministerial Declaration was over thirty-two pages long and contained nearly 400 unresolved bracketed items, indicating considerable disagreement among WTO nations.

[41] This involved significant disagreement between developed and developing nations on a number of substantive trade policy issues, including competition policy and the implementation of Uruguay Round agreements. Developing nations expressed concern that disproportionately more of the economic benefits from the Uruguay Round agreements had flowed to developed nations and demanded that the Uruguay Round agreements should be renegotiated as a matter of priority to correct this imbalance. Accordingly, the developing nations favoured issue-specific WTO negotiations on trade and development issues, and opposed the launch of a Millennium Round.

[42] Developing nations expressed concerns with the transparency of consensus-building negotiations prior to the Seattle Ministerial.

[43] See R. Ruggerio, 'Reflections from Seattle' in J. J. Schott (ed.), *The WTO After Seattle* (Institute for International Economics, Washington, DC, 2000). See 'Seattle Draft Declaration', 3 December 1999, Inside US Trade Special Report, 10 December 1999.

[44] See 'The EU Approach to the Millennium Round Proposal for Decisions to Be Taken by The Council at the WTO's Third Ministerial Conference', Communication from the Commission to the Council and to the European Parliament, Seattle, 30 November 1999. See also 'The Real Losers', *The Economist*, London, 11 December 1999, p. 15.

[45] See J. Kahn & D. E. Sanger, 'Seattle Talks on Trade End With Stinging Blow to US', *New York Times*, 5 December 1999. See also G. C. Hufbauer, 'World Trade After Seattle: Implications for the United States', *International Economics Policy Briefs* No. 99–10, Institute for International Economics, Washington, DC, December 1999.

to their greater desire for agricultural reforms. In this manner, competition policy became a bargaining chip within the wider international trade agenda.[46]

13.1.5 Doha Ministerial (2001) – negotiations on competition issues are contemplated

The fourth WTO Ministerial Conference was held in Doha, Qatar between 9 and 13 November 2001 ('Doha Ministerial'). The Doha Ministerial was intended to repair the damage caused by the Seattle Ministerial by initiating the new round of WTO multilateral negotiations initially intended for launch at Seattle. Importantly, the Doha Ministerial was successful and launched a new round of multilateral negotiations with a comprehensive agenda and goals. Reflecting the significant influence of developing nations over the WTO, this new round became known as the 'Doha Development Round'. This new round was characterised as principally intended to address the concerns of developing countries.

In the lead-up to the Doha Ministerial, the EU actively lobbied nations for the commencement of negotiations on competition issues in the WTO. The EU adopted two new tactics, recognising the level of opposition from developing countries to competition issues in Seattle:

- The EU proposed that competition issues should only be addressed within the context of a plurilateral agreement. In this manner, developing countries would not need to sign the resulting agreement. This was treated with considerable suspicion by many developing nations who viewed the EU as seeking a stricter multilateral agreement by backdoor means. Other nations voiced a philosophical objection to a plurilateral approach on the basis that it would undermine the multilateral system.
- Alternatively, the EU proposed that competition issues should be structured in the form of a 'positive list' as adopted by the GATS. In this manner, nations would agree to stricter competition obligations on a voluntary basis as their competition laws matured. Again, this was treated with considerable suspicion by developing nations and similar concerns were expressed.

---

[46] See A. Kay, 'Towards a Theory of the Reform of the Common Agricultural Policy' (2000) 4 *EIP* 9. See also W. A. Kerr, 'The Next Step will be Harder: Issues for the New Round of Agriculture Negotiations at the World Trade Organisation' (2000) 34(1) *Journal of World Trade* 123. See 'WTO Negotiations-State of Play', Speech by Pascal Lamy, European Commissioner for Trade, to the Transatlantic Business Dialogue Dinner, Brussels, 23 May 2000.

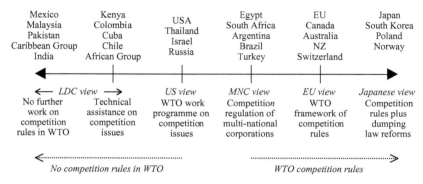

Figure 53: *Negotiating positions of nations at the Doha Ministerial*

The US indicated that it would only support negotiations for a more limited, non-binding WTO competition agreement based on core WTO principles and transparency. The US indicated that this should provide a set of principles that could only be referred to in the context of a peer review mechanism. The US also favoured continued investigation of competition issues by the WTO Working Group.

Prior to the Doha Ministerial Conference, the positions of the nations that publicly indicated their stance on WTO competition rules are summarised in Figure 53.[47]

Following consultation and negotiations, two alternatives were proposed in the first draft of the Doha Ministerial Declaration reflecting a roughly 50:50 split among WTO members as to whether negotiations on competition issues should be commenced:

(a) to start negotiations on competition policy (with a number of elements for negotiation identified in the draft Declaration); or
(b) to continue with the study process already being undertaken by the WTO Working Group.

---

[47] See M. Moore, 'The WTO: What is at Stake?', WTO News, Speech by M. Moore to the 6th John Payne Memorial Lecture, Director-General WTO, London, 12 March 2001. See also M. P. Carl, 'Towards Basic Rules on Trade-related Competition Policy', Speech by M. P. Carl, Director-General, DG TRADE, Brussels, 2 March 2001. See also M. Clough, 'Prospects for a New WTO Round' (2001) 29(4) *International Business Lawyer* 146. See also 'Competition Policy and Globalisation: The EU Views on Global Competition Forum', Speech by M. Monti, European Commissioner for Competition Policy to the ABA meetings, Washington, 29 March 2001.

However, negotiations during the Doha Ministerial were characterised by considerable opposition by most developing countries to the commencement of negotiations on competition issues in the WTO. Eventually, language was agreed which sought to address the concerns of developing countries by requiring that they would receive greater flexibility, technical support and capacity building. In return, the developing countries agreed to wording that competition negotiations could be commenced once an 'explicit consensus' was achieved. This wording, in effect, simply stated the obvious – that negotiations would proceed once all nations unanimously agreed to the commencement of those negotiations.

Ultimately, the Doha Ministerial Declaration therefore contained the following elements, clearly reflecting the different negotiating positions of the various WTO interest groups:[48]

- Negotiations on competition policy were agreed as commencing after the Cancún Ministerial in 2003 on the basis of a decision to be taken, by explicit consensus, at Cancún on 'modalities of negotiations'.
- Developing countries were expressly recognised as requiring enhanced support for technical assistance and capacity building in relation to competition policy. Full account would also be taken of the needs of developing countries and appropriate flexibility provided to address them.
- The WTO Working Group on the Interaction between Trade and Competition Policy would continue with its study process, now focusing on the clarification of:
  (a) core principles, including transparency, non-discrimination and procedural fairness, and provisions on hard-core cartels;
  (b) modalities for voluntary co-operation; and
  (c) support for progressive reinforcement of competition institutions in developing countries through capacity building.

13.1.6 Cancún Ministerial (2003) – competition issues again treated as a bargaining chip

The fifth WTO Ministerial Conference was held in Cancún, Mexico between 10 and 14 September 2003 ('Cancún Ministerial'). The Cancún Ministerial was intended to stocktake progress with the 'Doha

---

[48] See 'Ministerial Declaration of the WTO Ministerial Conference Fourth Session at Doha, 9–14 November 2001, Adopted on 14 November 2001' in *Doha Declarations: Doha Development Agenda* (World Trade Organisation, Geneva, 2001).

Development Round' while expanding its scope to include such issues as the 'Singapore issues' and agricultural policy. However, the Cancún Ministerial failed dramatically – resulting in a damaging impasse.

The Cancún Ministerial was heavily focused on agricultural trade and the concerns of developing countries. In the lead-up to the Cancún Ministerial, the US and EU released a joint proposal for liberalisation of agricultural trade. Shortly after, a group of developing countries issued a paper rejecting the US–EU joint proposal on the basis that it permitted the US and EU to avoid liberalisation of the most protected areas and that it required disproportionate liberalisation from developing countries. This group of developing countries crystallised into a new negotiating bloc known as the 'G20', led by India and Brazil. The G20 has subsequently exerted significant influence over all aspects of the Doha Development Round, including negotiations in relation to competition policy.

In relation to competition policy, it became clear in negotiations leading to the Cancún Ministerial that the negotiating positions identified in Seattle and Doha had not significantly changed. The EU and Japan both proposed draft texts for the inclusion of competition policy within the Doha Development Round under an ambitious timetable. However, both were unable to secure widespread support for these proposals given strong opposition from the G20. The US indicated it would only support negotiations relating to a non-binding 'soft agreement' on competition issues.

In the draft Ministerial Declaration released prior to the Cancún Ministerial, the Director-General of the WTO indicated that 'that there are still considerable differences among Members' and 'consultations in Geneva have not enabled us to make proposals on possible modalities that could attract the explicit consensus of Ministers'.[49] The draft Cancún Ministerial Declaration therefore proposed two options relating to competition issues:

(a) commencement of negotiations on the basis of modalities set out in Annexe E to the draft Declaration; or

---

[49] See Draft Cancún Ministerial Text prepared by WTO General Council chairperson, Carlos Pérez del Castillo and WTO Director-General, Supachai Panitchpakdi, 31 August 2003: http://www.wto.org/english/ thewto_e/minist_e/min03_e/draft_decl_e.htm. See also the covering letter: http://www.wto.org/english/thewto_e/minist_e/min03_e/draft_decl_covletter_e.htm.

(b) referral of competition issues back to the WTO Working Group as part of a continued work programme to assist in agreeing such modalities.

The modalities identified in Annexe E of the draft Cancún Ministerial Declaration are set out in Figure 54.

During the Doha Ministerial Conference, it became clear that the G20 were not willing to agree to the commencement of negotiations on WTO competition issues, hence no 'explicit consensus' would be achievable.[50] The EU indicated that it would only drop its request for the 'Singapore issues' (particularly competition and investment issues) being included in the Doha Development Round if the G20 dropped its opposition to the joint EU–US proposal on agriculture. The US supported the EU position. The G20 refused to agree to this linkage and complained at the EU and US tactics, resulting in an impasse.[51] A redrafted Ministerial Declaration was proposed which identified that further work was required by the WTO Working Group to identify possible modalities for competition negotiations.[52] However, ultimately even this redraft failed.

Eventually, the Cancún Ministerial Conference ended on 14 September after its chairperson, Mexican Foreign Minister Derbez, concluded that despite considerable movement in consultations, members remained entrenched, particularly on the 'Singapore' issues. A short Cancún Ministerial Declaration was agreed which commented that officials would 'continue working on outstanding issues with a renewed sense of urgency and purpose and taking fully into account all the views we have expressed in this Conference'.[53]

---

[50] See M. Khor, 'Cancún Draft Text Flawed, Imbalanced, say Developing Countries', *South-North Development Monitor- SUNS No. 5405*, 26 August 2003. See C. Raghavan, 'Cancún – Part of Journey, Impasse or Breakdown?', *South-North Development Monitor- SUNS No. 5436*, 8 October 2003. See also J. J. Schott, 'Unlocking the Benefits of World Trade' in special report by *The Economist*, 1 November 2003.

[51] See C. Raghavan, 'Self-serving Post-Cancún Versions Add to Distrust', *South-North Development Monitor- SUNS No. 5422*, 18 September 2003.

[52] See Draft Cancún Ministerial Text (Second Revision), also known as the 'Derbez Text', 13 September 2003: http://www.wto.org/english/ thewto_e/minist_e/min03_e/draft_decl_rev2_e.htm.

[53] See World Trade Organisation, 'Ministerial Statement', Fifth Session Cancún, 10–14 September 2003, Adopted 14 September 2003, WT/MIN(03)/20, 23 September 2003: http://www.wto.org/english/thewto_e/minist_e/min03_e/min03_20_e.doc.

Modality	Proposed agreement
Objective of negotiations	Establish an agreement to secure better and more equitable conditions for international trade by: • facilitating effective voluntary co-operation on anti-competitive practices which adversely affect international trade, in particular hard-core cartels which have an impact on developing and least-developed countries' economies, and • assisting WTO Members in the establishment, implementation and enforcement of competition rules within their respective jurisdictions.
Elements of negotiations	The elements identified in the Doha Declaration and identified by the WTO Working Group.
Application to national authorities	Individual decisions of national competition authorities would not be subject to challenge or recommendations under the WTO dispute settlement system.
Application to competition policies	The negotiations would not deal with state-to-state arrangements that limit competition or with practices implemented pursuant to such arrangements.
Obligations for non-discrimination	A principle of non-discrimination would apply to laws, regulations and guidelines of general application.
Obligations for procedural fairness	A principle of procedural fairness would apply to the legal and judicial systems of each WTO member.
Inclusion of peer review mechanism	Consideration would be given to the inclusion of a possible peer review mechanism.
Scope of general exceptions	A right to implement exceptions from the application of national competition laws on the basis of transparent domestic legal processes would be safeguarded.
Scope of developing country exceptions	Full account would be taken of the industrial policy, social policy and other needs of developing countries and appropriate flexibility provided.
Use of transitional periods	Transition periods for implementation of the agreement by developing countries would apply.
Extent of technical assistance	WTO nations would continue to work towards providing adequate technical assistance and capacity building to developing countries.

Figure 54: *Proposed modalities set out in draft Cancún Declaration*

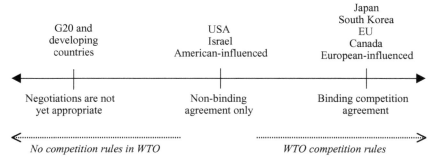

Figure 55: *Negotiating positions of nations after the Cancún Ministerial*

A summary of the negotiating positions of nations after the Cancún Ministerial are summarised in Figure 55, and this indicates that the negotiating positions can now be consolidated into three distinct views.

13.1.7 Insights from WTO negotiations to date

The agenda negotiations in the context of the Singapore, Geneva, Seattle, Doha and Cancún Ministerial Conferences, as discussed above, provide a number of important insights into issues likely to arise in the context of negotiations regarding a WTO competition agreement. Six key insights are particularly instructive:

- Competition policy is perceived by most WTO nations as lower in priority than a number of other international trade concerns (including agriculture and developing country 'implementation issues'). As a result, competition policy is increasingly being treated as a bargaining chip within the wider international trade agenda – most recently in the context of agricultural concessions.[54]
- Competition policy is not considered of sufficient importance at present to support its own issue-specific WTO negotiations.[55] Competition policy is only likely to be negotiated into the WTO at this stage as part of a formal round of WTO multilateral negotiations.

---

[54] This is illustrated by the US desire to trade competition policy for Japanese and EU agricultural reforms at Seattle
[55] See A. Mattoo & A. Subramanian, 'Multilateral Rules on Competition Policy – A Possible Way Forward' (1997) 31(5) *Journal of World Trade* 95.

- A significant number of nations, including the US, would prefer to undertake further work, and obtain greater understanding on competition policy issues before they are incorporated into the WTO agenda for multilateral negotiations.[56] Such deferral would be the likely default position in the absence of any consensus decision by the Ministerial Council to include competition policy on the WTO agenda for multilateral negotiations.
- The support of developing countries will be critical to the successful inclusion of competition policy on the agenda for WTO trade negotiations.[57] However, developing countries are only likely to support a WTO competition agreement if it addressed their concerns regarding anti-competitive behaviour by multinational firms and provided them with suitable concessions. Accordingly, any WTO agenda including a competition agreement would necessarily need expressly to consider the views of developing countries and the need to treat developing countries differently.[58] Concessions for developing countries are considered further below.
- The reform of competition-inconsistent trade remedies remains a point of considerable contention between developed nations, particularly between Japan and the US. A creative solution may be required to accommodate Japanese requests for reform while recognising the desire of the US to protect its domestic interests. The most likely outcome would be for such reforms to trade measures to be distinguished from the negotiation of a WTO competition agreement and subjected to further analysis by the Working Group.
- Similarly, there remains a philosophical difference between Japan, the EU and the US as to whether any WTO competition law should be targeted as facilitating market access or should adopt a wider approach targeted at promoting global competition. The US continues to advocate a non-binding WTO competition agreement.

---

[56] See 'Fact Sheet: White House on Benefits of Trade, Objectives in WTO', *The Washington File*, Washington, DC, 10 November 1999.

[57] See C. Michalopoulos, 'Developing Countries' Participation in the World Trade Organization', World Bank Policy Research Working Paper, No. 1906, The World Bank, Washington, DC, March 1998.

[58] See C. Michalopoulos, 'Developing Country Strategies for the Millennium Round' (1999) 33(5) *Journal of World Trade* 1. See also N. Mukherjee, 'GATS and the Millennium Round of Multilateral Negotiations – Selected Issues from the Perspective of the Developing Countries' (1999) 33 *Journal of World Trade* 87. See also C. Michalopoulos Working Paper, above no. 57.

13.2 Meeting the concerns of developing countries

The concept of a 'developing country' ('DC') is not defined in the WTO agreements.[59] Rather, it is for WTO nations themselves to announce whether they are DCs, subject to challenge by other WTO nations. At present, roughly three-quarters of the WTO's member nations have announced themselves as DCs.[60] Collectively, these DCs account for roughly one-third of world trade.[61]

As illustrated by the Seattle, Doha and Cancún Ministerials, DCs are not averse to exercising their collective power to oppose any proposal that is not in their collective economic interests.[62] Indeed, the concerns of DCs are now the most important determinant of the likelihood of realising a WTO competition agreement in the foreseeable future, particularly given the current need to secure an 'explicit consensus' on the modalities of any negotiations on competition issues.[63] The issue therefore arises, how could a WTO competition agreement address the concerns of DCs in a manner which solicited their support?[64]

The GATT has historically recognised the legitimacy of concerns expressed by DCs that international trade law disproportionately benefited developed nations.[65] Over the years, developed nations granted more favourable treatment to DCs to address concerns of distributive justice. WTO law now contains a diverse range of concessions to DCs which are commonly referred to as 'special and differential treatment' ('S&D'). S&D provisions currently comprise five main forms:

[59] See discussion in M. Pangestu, 'Special and Differential Treatment in the Millennium: Special for Whom and How Different?' (2000) 23(9) *The World Economy* 1285.
[60] I.e. about 100 of the WTO's 142 members have declared themselves to be developing countries.
[61] In addition, the WTO recognises the United Nations concept of 'least developed countries'. Currently one-quarter of the WTO's membership comprises least developed countries, giving them alone significant collective voting power.
[62] See T. L. Brewer & S. Young, 'WTO Disputes and Developing Countries' (1999) 33(5) *Journal of World Trade* 169.
[63] See N. Yacheistova, 'What May the Commonwealth of Independent States Expect from Multilateral Competition Rules?' (2000) 23 *World Competition* 51. See J. Sikhakhane, 'Developing Countries Do Want a Trade Round – In the Right Circumstances' (2000) 5(1) *Economic Perspectives* 59.
[64] A detailed analysis of this issue is set out in the article by H. Nottage, 'Trade and Competition in the WTO: Pondering the Applicability of Special and Differential Treatment' (2003) 6(1) *Journal of International Economic Law* 23–47.
[65] See T. N. Srinivasan, 'Developing Countries in the World Trading System: From GATT 1947 to the Third Ministerial Meeting of the WTO, 1999' (1989) 22(8) *The World Economy* 1047. See also Brandt Commission, *North-South: A Program for Survival* (The MIT Press, Cambridge, MA, 1979).

- *Provisions aimed at increasing trade opportunities* WTO law has formalised the concept of S&D in a variety of ways. Part IV of the GATT, for example, creates a principle of non-reciprocity for DCs so that they may benefit from trade concessions granted by WTO members without granting their own reciprocal concessions. The Decision on Differential and More Favourable Treatment, Reciprocity and Fuller Participation of Developing Countries of 1979 ('Enabling Clause') clarifies that WTO nations may grant S&D to DCs without breaching the non-discrimination obligations in the WTO.[66] This Enabling Clause provides the basis for the WTO's 'Generalised System of Preferences' in which developed nations may provide preferential treatment to products originating from DCs.
- *Provisions which require WTO nations to safeguard the interests of DCs* A number of provisions in the WTO agreements expressly require WTO nations to take into account the interests of DCs when formulating trade measures. The WTO Anti-dumping Agreement, for example, stipulates that constructive remedies provided for by the Anti-dumping Agreement must be explored before applying anti-dumping duties where they would affect the essential interests of DCs. Actions in favour of DCs may also be taken under 'waivers' from the WTO rules granted by the WTO General Council.
- *Provisions allowing flexibility to DCs in the use of policy instruments* Many WTO agreements provide DCs with greater flexibility when implementing their WTO commitments. Such provisions may, for example, permit DCs to continue using trade measures that have been outlawed for other WTO nations.[67] Such provisions may also enable DCs to set tariffs, for example, at levels significantly higher than other WTO nations.[68]
- *Provisions allowing longer transitional periods to DCs* Longer transitional periods for implementation of WTO commitments by DCs are incorporated in most WTO agreements. Such transitional time

---

[66] See Decision on Differential and More Favourable Treatment, Reciprocity and Fuller Participation of Developing Countries (1980) BISD, 26th Supplement 203.
[67] See, for example, UNCTAD Secretariat, *The TRIPs Agreement and Developing Countries* (UNCTAD/ITE/1, Geneva, 1997).
[68] See C. Ng'ong'ola, 'The World Trade Legal Order and Developing Countries: an Assessment of Important Concessions and Commitments, with Special Reference to Sub-Saharan Africa' (1999) 11 *African Journal of International Law* 14. See also South Centre, *The WTO Multilateral Trade Agenda and the South* (South Centre, Geneva, 1998).

periods are intended to address shortfalls in the institutional capability of DCs.[69]

- *Provisions facilitating technical assistance to DCs* A number of WTO agreements facilitate the provision of technical assistance from developed nations to DCs. In general, such technical assistance is intended to inform DC governments of the nature of their WTO rights and obligations while assisting them to build the capability to implement their obligations while actively participating in WTO discussions.[70]

The provision of similar concessions to DCs will be a necessary requirement to solicit their support for a WTO competition agreement, but this is unlikely to be sufficient.[71] Any WTO competition agreement would also need to address various additional concerns raised by DCs.[72] DCs have expressed specific reservations, for example, that a WTO competition agreement may impede their ability to pursue pro-development industrial policies and other similar development policies.

With this background in mind, the drafting of a WTO competition agreement may be palatable to DCs if it addresses their concerns in the following manner:

- *S&D in assessing anti-competitive conduct* WTO nations should be required to have specific regard to the interests of DCs when assessing the effects of anti-competitive conduct. Authorisations for export or import cartels given by developed nations should be discouraged, for example, where such activities would have a disproportionate impact on DCs. However, authorisations given by DCs should be permitted to have special regard to their development needs.
- *Greater flexibility in competition obligations* DCs should be given a higher degree of flexibility when meeting the obligations set out in a WTO competition agreement. DCs could, for example, be granted the

---

[69] See J. Whalley, 'Special and Differential Treatment in the Millennium Round' (1999) 22 *World Economy* 1065.
[70] See C. Michalopoulous, 'Developing Countries in the WTO' (1999) 22(1) *The World Economy* 117.
[71] See C. Raghavan, 'Egypt–South Africa Initiative for New Round, With Investment', *South-North Development Monitor- SUNS No. 4871*, 5 April 2001.
[72] DCs historically advocated international competition rules, as illustrated by the UNCTAD Code discussed earlier in this book. See 'UNCTAD: Restrictive Business Practices Conference' (1980) 14 *Journal of World Trade* 172. See 'UNCTAD: Restrictive Business Practices' (1982) 16 *Journal of World Trade* 174. See UNCTAD Secretariat, 'Collusive Tendering', TD/B/RBP/12, 23 September 1983.

ability to 'opt out' from any part of a WTO competition agreement or could be subjected to less onerous obligations. Such 'opt out' provisions would recognise that DCs tend to have less sophisticated competition laws and less well resourced institutions.[73] Indeed, many DCs have no competition laws at all.

Such 'opt out' provisions may also assuage the concerns of DCs that a WTO competition agreement could be used by developed nations as a means to force greater access to the markets of DCs. The EU, for example, has recognised such exemptions as 'another avenue through which governments could ensure that competition law did not adversely affect . . . development related objectives'.[74]

- *Transitional arrangements* Another similar approach may be to exclude DCs from the application of certain stricter competition obligations but permit them to 'opt in' on a voluntary basis when their laws are compliant. A plurilateral WTO competition agreement, for example, could adopt such an approach for the entire WTO competition agreement. Alternatively, DCs should be given a greater length of time for the implementation of any WTO competition obligations should they choose to adopt them.
- *Technical assistance* Capacity building through technical assistance is also crucial for DCs, as such nations are not as well resourced as developed nations. In this regard, UNCTAD, the OECD and the World Bank have each already played an important role in facilitating technical assistance to DCs on competition issues.

If such concessions to the interests of DCs were incorporated within a WTO competition agreement, DCs would be more likely to agree to a proposal for a WTO competition agreement.[75]

Suggested drafting that recognises the concerns of DCs is incorporated within the draft WTO competition agreement set out in the Appendix to this book.

---

[73] See A. Krueger, 'The Developing Countries and the Next Round of Multilateral Trade Negotiations' (1999) 22(7) *The World Economy* 99.
[74] See WTO Working Group on the Interaction Between Trade and Competition Policy, Report of the Meeting of 5–6 July 2001, Note by the Secretariat, 14 August 2001, WT/WGTCP/M/15, para. 13.
[75] See H. Handelman, 'The Political Economy of Third World Development' in H. Handelman, *The Challenge of Third World Development* (Prentice Hall, New Jersey, 2000).

13.3 Four-point incremental strategy for realising a WTO competition agreement

Bearing in mind the conclusions above and the insights identified earlier in this book, four elements appear particularly important to the success of any negotiations on a WTO competition agreement:

- *Building on bilaterals*   Any WTO competition agreement should build upon existing bilateral and plurilateral initiatives, as identified in Chapter 5 of this book.
- *Selective convergence*   Any WTO competition agreement should avoid full harmonisation and adopt an approach based on greater convergence and partial harmonisation, targeted at those areas of competition law that would reap the greatest benefits, as identified in Chapter 11 of this book.
- *Soft law principles*   Any WTO competition agreement should utilise non-binding 'soft law' principles, rather than relying purely on binding 'hard law' obligations, as identified in Chapter 11 of this book.
- *Recognition of differences*   Any WTO competition agreement should recognise the interests of different nations, particularly DCs, as identified in this chapter.

Each of these four points are considered in further detail below.

These four elements could provide the basis for a four-point strategy to realise a WTO competition agreement.

13.3.1 Building on bilaterals

Bilateral agreements are the easiest form of international agreement to conclude and provide greater flexibility to reach agreement between nations in circumstances where differences between nations remain great. Bilateral agreements have proved valuable in lessening the differences between nations in the application of their competition laws while creating an environment conducive to cross-border competition law co-operation.[76] Each bilateral agreement represents an incremental step

---

[76] Bilateral agreements may be perceived as a positive mechanism for increasing confidence and reducing regulatory anomalies between nations.

towards the negotiation of more sophisticated bilateral, plurilateral or multilateral competition law agreements.[77]

Chapter 5 of this book also identified that a variety of initiatives have been undertaken in recent years at the plurilateral and multilateral levels towards the realisation of an international competition law. Such plurilateral arrangements would provide a foundation for consensus-building in which smaller consensual clusters of nations could negotiate their own plurilateral competition agreements. Over time, these plurilateral agreements would gradually harmonise competition laws and reduce differences between nations.

Chapter 5 then identified initiatives at the multilateral level, including within the WTO. The increasing recent co-operation between these initiatives has created the possibility of a unified strategy for achieving a multilateral competition agreement that bridges the different approaches of different interest groups.[78] UNCTAD, for example, is heavily supported by DCs, so the involvement of UNCTAD in any WTO competition agreement may assist in realising their support.[79]

Chapter 5 identified that bilateral initiatives are complementary to plurilateral and multilateral initiatives and that each initiative can assist and accelerate progress with the other, so all three initiatives are mutually reinforcing. Chapter 5 therefore proposed a mixed architecture for a WTO competition agreement comprising tiered multilateral, plurilateral and bilateral initiatives.[80] In essence, a multilateral agreement would establish core principles and would ensure broadly consistent objectives and a reasonable degree of standardisation. Plurilateral instruments would supplement the broad principles with more specific laws and policies. Bilateral instruments could provide for clear rights and obligations as

---

[77] See T. Lampert, 'International Co-operation among Competition Authorities' (1999) 20 *European Competition Law Review* 214.

[78] The OECD, for example, has proved instrumental in influencing the views of the key developed nations, so the support of the OECD may be vital in fostering consensus among the key developed nations. See, for example, C. A. Jones, 'Toward Global Competition Policy – The Expanding Dialogue on Multilateralism' (2000) 23(2) *World Competition* 95. See also, for example, OECD, 'Council Revised Recommendation C(95)130/FINAL Concerning Co-operation Between Member Countries on Anticompetitive Practices Affecting International Trade' (1996) 35 *International Legal Materials* 1313.

[79] By ensuring that any international competition agreement sufficiently addresses the 'development dimension' and therefore receives support from developing nations

[80] This complementarity was recognised by the UNCTAD Code with its promotion of simultaneous initiatives at the national, regional and international levels.

between nations to ensure effective cross-border enforcement and to avoid jurisdictional disputes.[81]

In summary, the 'building on bilaterals' limb of the four-point strategy for realising a WTO competition agreement would seek to build upon the substantive content and approach of bilateral and plurilateral agreements while facilitating greater multilateral co-operation. Nations would be expressly encouraged to conclude bilateral and plurilateral agreements as an incremental step towards realisation of a multilateral competition agreement.

13.3.2 Selective convergence

Chapter 11 of this book considered the extent to which any WTO competition agreement should seek to achieve harmonisation or convergence of domestic competition laws. Chapter 11 highlighted that full harmonisation of competition laws on policies on a multilateral basis would be a difficult, if not impossible, exercise. The costs of achieving full harmonisation would significantly exceed the benefits. Such harmonisation would not recognise legitimate differences between nations and therefore may be sub-optimal. Chapter 11 identified that any WTO competition agreement could rather seek selectively to target those elements of competition law that would benefit most from greater convergence or partial harmonisation.

In summary, the 'selective convergence' limb of the four-point strategy for realising a WTO competition agreement would cherry-pick particular areas of competition law for greater convergence and partial harmonisation, while avoiding regulation in other areas.

13.3.3 Soft law principles

Chapter 11 of this book considered the extent to which any WTO competition agreement should seek to proscribe minimum international standards. However, Chapter 11 also noted a number of criticisms of minimum standards, including pressures towards the lowest common denominator. Chapter 11 considered a number of solutions to address these difficulties including the use of non-binding 'soft law' principles.

---

[81] See, for example, C. D. Ehlermann, 'The International Dimension of Competition Policy' (1994) 17 *Fordham Law Journal* 833.

Chapter 11 identified that certain components of a WTO competition agreement could be expressed as broad, non-binding 'soft law' principles that would introduce moral and political pressures towards compliance. The use of 'soft law' would thus potentially influence the conduct of nations without forcing them to amend their conduct and would be more likely to be palatable within international negotiations given its non-enforceability. Chapter 11 suggested that the concept of 'co-regulation' could be applied to a WTO competition agreement in which certain provisions would be expressed in broad, non-binding 'soft law' terms, but other elements would be expressed as binding legal obligations.

In summary, the 'soft law principles' limb of the four-point strategy for realising a WTO competition agreement would incorporate soft law principles into a WTO competition agreement. If nations were unable to agree on detailed obligations in the WTO competition agreement, the obligations could be expressed at a lower level of detail and/or given a soft law character.[82]

13.3.4 Recognition of differences

This chapter identified that DCs comprise roughly three-quarters of the WTO's member nations and therefore will have significant influence over both the adoption of a WTO competition agreement and the substantive content of that agreement. DCs would most likely oppose any proposal that was not in their collective economic interests. Without the support of DCs, any negotiations on a WTO competition agreement would fail.[83]

This chapter identified that DCs have historically been granted a diverse range of S&D concessions within WTO agreements. A WTO competition agreement could follow this precedent including, for example, a requirement for developed nations to have specific regard to the interests of DCs when developed nations apply their competition laws. This chapter also identified that such an agreement would also need to address other specific concerns raised by DCs, including, for example, via the use of 'opt out' and 'opt in' procedures.

In summary, the 'recognition of differences' limb of the four-point strategy for realising a WTO competition agreement would expressly

---

[82] In this manner, a WTO competition agreement would become easier to negotiate and could be amended further down the track to introduce binding commitments as necessary.
[83] See R. A. Blackhurst & J. F. Francois, 'The Uruguay Round and Market Access: Opportunities and Challenges for Developing Countries' in W. Martin & L. A. Winters (eds.), *The Uruguay Round and the Developing Countries* (Cambridge University Press, 1996).

recognise the interests of DCs in order to solicit their support for a WTO competition agreement.

13.4 Conclusion: a plurilateral WTO competition agreement is politically achievable

In summary, in order to incorporate an international competition agreement into the WTO, a consensus decision of the WTO members would be required. Such a decision would be required both to authorise the commencement of substantive negotiations on a WTO competition agreement, and also at the adoption stage following the conclusion of such negotiations. This consensus requirement has a critical impact on the likely content of any such WTO competition agreement.

Three distinct views have now emerged regarding the inclusion of an international competition agreement in the WTO. Most DCs remain opposed to the commencement of negotiations on an international competition agreement at this time. The US and nations under its influence would oppose any international competition agreement except an agreement that was non-binding in character. The EU and Japan and nations under their respective influence are supportive of immediate negotiations on a binding competition agreement whether multilateral or plurilateral in character.

Any WTO competition agreement would therefore clearly need to address the concerns of DCs given that their support is required to realise an 'explicit consensus' on the 'modalities' of negotiations in relation to an international competition agreement. The existing WTO agreements already contain significant concessions to DCs and such concessions should be reflected within a WTO competition agreement. For example, DCs should be given greater flexibility, greater technical assistance, special concessions and greater implementation periods. DCs should also be given an 'opt out' ability, given their need to build the necessary institutions and processes to enable the adoption of effective national competition laws.

Notwithstanding such concessions, it remains unlikely that DCs would support a multilateral WTO competition agreement at the present time. However, DCs may be more willing to support a plurilateral WTO agreement as long as it sufficiently addresses their particular needs. Given such support, a plurilateral agreement may be politically feasible.

With the above in mind, a four-point incremental strategy could be adopted for realising a WTO competition agreement. First, a WTO competition agreement should build upon existing initiatives at the bilateral, plurilateral and multilateral level. Secondly, a WTO competition agreement should avoid full harmonisation and instead promote selective convergence in key areas. Thirdly, a WTO competition agreement should utilise non-binding 'soft law' principles rather than relying entirely on binding 'hard law' obligations. Fourthly, a WTO competition agreement should recognise the different interests of different nations, particularly the interests of DCs.

The draft WTO plurilateral competition agreement set out in the Appendix to this book seeks to reflect this four-point strategy while giving practical effect to the conclusions reached in each chapter of this book.

14

Conclusion: a plurilateral competition agreement should be incorporated into the WTO

This book proposes that a plurilateral competition agreement should be incorporated into the WTO.

14.1 Summary

With this in mind, Part I of this book concluded that an international competition agreement is desirable. Part II of this book concluded that the WTO could provide a suitable institutional vehicle for an international competition agreement. Part III of this book concluded that the optimal form for such an international competition agreement at the present time would be a plurilateral WTO agreement in the form identified in the Appendix to this book.

Each of the chapters of this book contributed to these conclusions in the following manner.

14.1.1 An international competition agreement is desirable and would be welfare-enhancing relative to the status quo (Chapters 2 and 3)

Modern competition law is intended to promote and maintain workable competition in order to facilitate greater market efficiency. Such efficiency will, in turn, promote economic growth and increased social welfare. While direct empirical evidence of the benefits of competition law is difficult to obtain, the available evidence suggests such benefits are significant. Essentially, competition law deters and prevents anti-competitive conduct that may otherwise result in welfare losses to society.

Competition law is the principal instrument of competition policy and may create an environment conducive to the adoption of complementary competition policies, such as market deregulation. Such competition policies, in turn, may materially contribute to economic growth and increased social welfare. The benefits of such competition policies have been empirically quantified and are also significant.

Domestic competition law is inherently territorial in its approach, creating difficulties in an increasingly globalised world in which transactions subsume multiple territorial spaces. Anti-competitive conduct is currently regulated on an ineffective and inconsistent basis across jurisdictions using domestic laws. However, the application of domestic competition law in an international context is influenced by economic externalities which result in over-regulation and under-regulation. This situation has been exacerbated in recent decades by globalisation, greater economic integration and multinational corporate expansion, as illustrated by the Boeing/McDonnell Douglas merger and the GE/Honeywell merger.

While the extraterritorial application of domestic competition laws has provided a de facto mechanism for nations to regulate cross-border anti-competitive conduct in the absence of international competition laws, such an extraterritorial approach has clear deficiencies. Such extraterritoriality controversially impinges on state sovereignty and may trigger serious diplomatic disputes, as illustrated by the *Laker* litigation and *Uranium* litigation. Nations have also enacted blocking legislation to thwart such extraterritoriality, generating further system frictions. Extraterritoriality does not address the underlying negative externality and may in fact exacerbate over-regulation and system frictions by providing a mechanism for one nation to interfere in the domestic affairs of another.

While beyond the scope of this book, a number of economic models have concluded that greater international co-ordination of competition law would be welfare enhancing relative to a situation in which each nation enforces its competition laws on an extraterritorial basis in accordance with its national self-interest. Empirical evidence quantifying these benefits is difficult to obtain, but the conclusions from Chapter 2 regarding the welfare benefits arising from competition law and policy suggest that the welfare benefits of an international competition agreement would be significant.

14.1.2 There is a sufficient basis for an international competition agreement (Chapter 4)

There is sufficient commonality among the competition laws of different nations to support an international competition agreement. Commonality exists notwithstanding considerable diversity, as illustrated by a sample group of nations comprising those nations within the Asia-Pacific Economic Co-operation (APEC). An analysis of the competition laws of APEC nations indicates that commonly accepted principles and themes can be readily distilled. An international competition agreement could be based on these principles and themes. However, there also remain areas where considerable differences are apparent and where international consensus would be unlikely to be achieved at the present time.

Competition laws have similar efficiency objectives and a common structure. Competition laws are based on commonly accepted economic concepts of markets and market power. Competition laws typically adopt a tripartite structure involving merger laws, anti-monopoly laws and concerted conduct laws. However, the particular formulation and application of those laws may differ considerably. While many of the broad features of competition laws are similar across jurisdictions, the particular nuances and specific detail of competition laws in each jurisdiction differ widely, as does their particular factual application.

The APEC analysis suggests that any international competition agreement should not be overly ambitious and could simply establish broad principles to guide the appropriate content of national competition laws. A number of insights and common themes can be identified in relation to merger laws, anti-monopoly laws and concerted conduct laws that would enable a competition agreement to be adopted based on broad principles without proscribing specific formulations of law. Any such agreement should also recognise the institutional pre-conditions for competition laws and the need sufficiently to recognise legitimate diversity, resource limitations and competition law experience. With this in mind, a broad framework for an international competition agreement can be identified. There is therefore a sufficient basis for an international competition agreement.

14.1.3 Existing initiatives towards the regulation of cross-border anti-competitive conduct have clear limitations that could be overcome by an international competition agreement (Chapter 5)

A number of initiatives have been undertaken in recent years at the bilateral, plurilateral and multilateral levels to regulate cross-border anti-competitive conduct. Each of these initiatives has clear limitations and has therefore achieved only qualified success. Given these limitations, these existing initiatives would not be sufficient in themselves to realise the benefits identified in Chapter 3 of this book.

Bilateral initiatives have progressively increased in sophistication in recent decades. They have largely been confined to date to circumstances in which two jurisdictions with similar competition laws and similar views on competition law have found it expedient to co-operate. The pre-conditions for more complex bilateral agreements are stringent, as evidenced by the US–EU agreement and the Australia–New Zealand agreement. While bilateral agreements are the easiest form of agreement to conclude, they are inevitably heterogeneous and this restricts their collective benefit. Furthermore, a network of bilateral agreements would be highly inefficient given that roughly 7,000 agreements would be required between the world's 120 nations currently possessing competition laws.

Existing plurilateral initiatives within the context of APEC and the EU have proved relatively successful although both initiatives also have clear limitations. While the APEC initiative has, to date, focused on competition policy rather than competition law, it does illustrate the extent to which agreement on broad competition principles may contribute towards the co-ordination of competition policy. The EU approach represents the furthest any group of nations has travelled to date in adopting a comprehensive cross-border competition law, although the EU approach is premised on the existence of a customs union between nations with a very high degree of legal and economic integration.

Existing multilateral initiatives have also faced clear limitations. Of these, the UNCTAD Code was the most ambitious, but it met with significant political opposition from industrialised nations given the perception that it unduly favoured the interests of developing nations. The OECD proved relatively successful in influencing the development of cross-border co-operation on competition issues, but its limited membership of advanced industrialised countries discouraged support from developing nations. The WTO competition initiative has gathered momentum over the last decade and may provide the most appropriate vehicle for an international competition agreement, particularly as it may provide a means to bridge the 'north-south' divide.

An international competition agreement would overcome many of the limitations of the existing initiatives. Such an agreement would be necessary if the benefits identified in Chapter 3 were to be realised. However, such an agreement would be unlikely to be of itself sufficient, rather it would need to complement and build upon the existing initiatives. The combination of existing initiatives with an international competition agreement would provide a sufficient framework for the regulation of cross-border anti-competitive conduct in order to realise the benefits identified in Chapter 3.

14.1.4 The WTO could provide a suitable institutional vehicle for an international competition agreement, provided that the relationship between trade and competition were suitably reconciled (Chapter 6)

There is a clear historical precedent for introducing competition law into the WTO. The Havana Charter of 1947, for example, expressly contemplated that competition law would form part of the world trading system. During the 1950s and 1960s, several initiatives to introduce competition law into the GATT failed, partly due to the weaker and less effective institutional structure of the GATT, but also due to insufficient international consensus and inexperience in competition law and policy. With the revitalisation of the world trading system in 1994, the potential for introducing competition law provisions at the international level was boosted considerably. The Uruguay Round incorporated a number of provisions into the WTO addressing various competition issues in a very limited and issue-specific manner, establishing a further precedent. A number of provisions in the WTO agreements now have a competition law flavour.

However, if competition law is to be more fully incorporated into the WTO, the relationship between trade law and competition law would need to be suitably reconciled. While competition law and international trade law are to some extent complementary, they are not fully complementary and there is scope for conflict. For example, WTO trade measures may adversely affect competition, while the regulation of anti-competitive behaviour may permit conduct which is perceived as unfair from a trade policy perspective.

In this respect, both competition law and international trade law have the same ultimate outcome of increasing the level and distribution of global welfare and, to this extent, both disciplines are complementary. However, both disciplines have different causal objectives, theoretical foundations and regulatory methodologies. Yet competition laws and trade laws do overlap to the extent both seek to promote greater market contestability. Contestability theory may therefore provide a theoretical means to reconcile international trade theory with international competition theory given that it represents a point of overlap between the two disciplines.

In summary, the WTO could provide a suitable institutional vehicle for an international competition agreement, provided that the relationship between trade and competition were suitably reconciled. Such reconciliation could occur in theory via the concept of contestability.

14.1.5 The relationship between trade and competition law can be reconciled by appropriate measures, realising substantive benefits to international trade and international competition (Chapters 7, 8 and 9)

There are a number of loopholes that arise in the international regulatory matrix due to the failure of both international trade law and domestic competition law to apply to particular anti-competitive conduct that may have an adverse impact on international trade. On the one hand, the *Kodak Fuji Film* case, for example, illustrates the difficulty in applying WTO law to private anti-competitive conduct given that the WTO is intended to regulate governmental measures. On the other hand, various forms of anti-competitive behaviour may escape effective regulation by domestic competition law for various reasons, including exemptions, ineffective enforcement, and inadequate competition laws.

A WTO competition agreement could adopt a range of measures to address these issues, giving effect to the concept of contestability identified in Chapter 6 of this book. Measures could include, for example, limiting the scope for exemptions from domestic competition laws where such exemptions would have wider adverse effects on international trade. An international competition agreement could also, for example, promote greater co-operation between nations in relation to the investigation and enforcement of cross-border anti-competitive conduct with adverse effects on international trade. Such measures would address the 'under-regulation' identified in this book by ensuring the application, enforcement and substantive content of domestic competition laws remained consistent with a globally optimal result.

Certain governmental trade measures with an adverse impact on international competition may also slip through a 'loophole' in the trade–competition regulatory matrix and thereby escape effective regulation. On the one hand, such measures may escape effective regulation under WTO law due to WTO exemptions, consistency with WTO obligations, or due to ineffective WTO enforcement. On the other hand, such measures may escape effective regulation by domestic competition law due to exemptions, inadequate enforcement, insufficient or inadequate competition laws, or due to jurisdictional, evidential and procedural impediments. Again, a WTO competition agreement could adopt a number of measures to bolster WTO law and domestic competition law, consistent with greater market contestability, thereby closing such loopholes and facilitating greater international trade.

Similarly, a number of loopholes arise in the international regulatory matrix due to the failure of international trade law and domestic competition law to regulate particular governmental trade measures that cause anti-competitive conduct. Again, a WTO competition agreement could adopt a number of measures to bolster WTO law and domestic competition law, consistent with greater market contestability, thereby closing such loopholes and facilitating greater international competition. An international competition agreement could, for example, require nations to justify the use of trade measures where there were alternative trade measures that could be used that were more consistent with greater international competition. An international competition agreement could also, for example, encourage nations to consider the spillover effects of their domestic trade policies and measures on international competition.

Anti-dumping law is a particular trade measure permitted by the WTO law which has been subjected to significant international criticism due to its potential adverse effects on international competition. However, such criticisms fail to recognise adequately that anti-dumping law has evolved to fulfil a particular distributional purpose. Accordingly, it is not simply the case that competition law could supplant existing trade measures of this nature, rather the original policy basis for each trade measure would need to be carefully examined. Yet it is also clear that material benefits could be realised by the progressive introduction of competition principles into such trade measures as anti-dumping law to discourage the application of such measures in circumstances in which they were clearly inconsistent with greater international competition.

In summary, Chapters 7 to 9 demonstrated that a variety of practical trade and competition policy measures could be adopted that would reconcile the relationship between international trade law and international competition law, improving market contestability. In turn, this would realise substantive benefits both to international trade and to international competition.

14.1.6 *The WTO would provide the optimal institutional vehicle for an international competition agreement (Chapter 10)*

While a number of potential institutional vehicles exist into which an international competition agreement could be incorporated, the WTO emerges fairly conclusively as the optimal institutional vehicle for any international competition agreement relative to such potential alternatives.

In particular, the WTO is the most effective and achievable of the various institutional vehicles considered in this book. The institutions of the WTO are widely respected and have the confidence of the international community. Incorporation of competition law into the WTO would also reflect historical precedent, and would realise synergies in underlying theory and synergies in policy co-ordination. It would also utilise existing WTO institutions which are ideally suited to competition issues and it would recognise existing international support for an international competition agreement in the context of the WTO.

When considering previous precedent, at least three proposals have been made for incorporating a WTO competition agreement into the WTO, although these previous proposals have not received international acceptance. The Munich Code was the most ambitious of these proposals but was rejected for two key reasons, namely that its institutions and supranational approach unnecessarily infringed against national sovereignty, and that its substantive rules were unnecessarily detailed and did not respect legitimate national differences. There is a clear scope for the introduction of an international competition agreement into the WTO which addresses the issues raised in Chapters 3 to 9 of this book, but which avoids the pitfalls of such previous proposals.

14.1.7 The optimal content, approach and structure for a WTO competition agreement can be clearly ascertained (Chapters 10, 11 and 12)

There is a general consensus regarding the principal objective of competition law, namely to maintain and encourage competition in order to promote economic efficiency and total economic welfare. However, there is a considerable divergence of opinion between nations regarding the appropriate distributional objectives for competition laws (and good arguments why competition laws should not have distributional objectives at all). Any WTO competition agreement would need to endorse this commonly accepted efficiency objective while permitting nations to adopt alternative distributional objectives as long as such objectives were not inconsistent with the promotion of economic efficiency via increased competition.

Chapter 10 also identified five core principles that should be adopted by a WTO competition agreement, namely principles of international co-operation, non-discrimination, comprehensiveness, transparency and procedural fairness. Provisions to give effect to these five core principles are set out in the draft WTO competition agreement in the Appendix to this book.

A WTO competition agreement should not seek to achieve full harmonisation of national competition laws given that the costs of achieving this (if such full harmonisation is even possible) would exceed any benefits. Rather, a WTO competition agreement should seek to achieve selective convergence of domestic competition laws in those areas that would realise the greatest benefits. The IIE Survey suggests that such areas would most likely include regulation of price fixing, cartelisation, horizontal restraints, and merger and acquisition laws. Certain WTO trade measures may also benefit from such an approach, including reform of anti-dumping laws, prohibition of VERs and VIEs, and greater adoption of the national treatment principle. Chapter 11 recommended that the WTO Working Group should undertake further research into these issues.

Given that a minimum standard for domestic competition laws would create 'lowest common denominator' issues, a 'soft law' or 'co-regulatory' approach is preferable. In this manner, where insufficient international consensus exists on particular issues, those issues could be expressed at a high level of generality as non-binding 'soft law' principles. Where sufficient international consensus exists, matters could be expressed in greater detail as binding 'hard law' obligations. Chapter 11 noted that while international 'soft law' remains controversial, it does have a recognised positive effect on international conduct. It is this positive effect which should be targeted by a WTO competition agreement.

Given such conclusions, Chapter 11 recommended that the WTO should seek to promote a 'selective convergence' and 'co-regulatory' strategy. By adopting such a strategy, the level of agreement required between nations on substantive competition obligations would be reduced and the likelihood of realising a WTO competition agreement would be considerably improved.

A WTO competition agreement could best promote effective compliance with its substantive obligations via a supra-national, quasi-judicial institution, coupled with inter-governmental peer enforcement. The WTO DSB has already been developed with such a role in mind. The WTO also contains mechanisms to promote compliance via non-coercive techniques, including the TPRM and technical assistance, both of which could be applied in a competition law context.

International competition disputes are likely to comprise three distinct types, namely jurisdictional disputes, procedural disputes and substantive disputes. A variety of mechanisms could be adopted to mitigate the likelihood of such disputes arising including, for example, greater use of consultative procedures, greater co-operation and comity and restrictions on extra-territoriality. However, to the extent such disputes do arise, any WTO competition agreement could continue to use the WTO DSB as the principal forum for the resolution of such disputes. While the use of trade sanctions to enforce international competition obligations may be controversial, the benefits of applying trade sanctions would appear greatly to outweigh any detriments.

Based on the brief analysis undertaken in Chapter 12, the optimal institutional structure for a WTO competition agreement would involve the use of the existing WTO institutions, particularly the WTO secretariat and the existing WTO DSB.

In summary, the discussion in Chapters 10 to 12 of this book, when combined with the earlier conclusions in this book (particularly Chapter 4), indicates that the optimal content, approach and structure for a WTO competition agreement can be clearly ascertained.

14.1.8 A multilateral WTO competition agreement would not be politically achievable at the present time. However, a plurilateral WTO competition agreement would be politically achievable (Chapter 13)

In order to incorporate an international competition agreement into the WTO (including a plurilateral agreement), a consensus decision of the WTO members would be required. A consensus decision would be required to authorise the commencement of substantive negotiations on a WTO competition agreement. A consensus decision is also required at the adoption stage following the conclusion of such negotiations. This consensus requirement has a critical impact on the likely content of any such WTO competition agreement.

Three distinct views have now emerged regarding the inclusion of an international competition agreement in the WTO. Most developing countries ('DCs') remain opposed to the commencement of negotiations on an international competition agreement at this time. The US and nations under its influence would oppose any international competition agreement, except an agreement that is non-binding in character. The EU and Japan and nations under their respective influence are supportive of immediate negotiations on a binding competition agreement whether multilateral or plurilateral in character.

Any WTO competition agreement would clearly need to address the concerns of DCs given that their support is required to realise any 'explicit consensus' on the 'modalities' of negotiations in relation to an international competition agreement. The existing WTO agreements already contain significant concessions to DCs and such concessions should be reflected within a WTO competition agreement. For example, DCs should be given greater flexibility, greater technical assistance, special concessions and greater implementation periods. DCs should also be given an 'opt out' ability, given their need to build the necessary institutions and processes to enable the adoption of effective national competition laws.

Notwithstanding such concessions, it remains unlikely that DCs would support a multilateral WTO competition agreement at the present time. However, DCs may be more willing to support a plurilateral WTO agreement as long as it sufficiently addresses their particular needs. Given such potential support, a plurilateral WTO competition agreement may be politically feasible.

With the above in mind, a four-point incremental strategy could be adopted for realising a WTO competition agreement. First, a WTO competition agreement should build upon existing initiatives at the bilateral, plurilateral and multilateral level. Secondly, a WTO competition agreement should avoid full harmonisation and instead promote selective convergence in key areas. Thirdly, a WTO competition agreement should utilise non-binding 'soft law' principles rather than relying entirely on binding 'hard law' obligations. Fourthly, a WTO competition agreement should recognise the different interests of different nations, particularly the interests of DCs.

Bearing the above analysis in mind, a plurilateral agreement should be incorporated into the WTO in the form set out in the Appendix to this book.

The negotiating text for a draft plurilateral WTO competition agreement is set out in the Appendix to this book with associated commentary. This draft indicates, in detail, the manner in which a plurilateral WTO competition agreement could address the various issues raised in this book. The draft contains some innovative proposals to address a number of issues identified in this book. This draft also gives practical effect to the conclusions reached in each chapter of this book including the four-point strategy identified in Chapter 13. While there are issues that would require detailed negotiations, these issues do not appear insurmountable and the

Appendix proposes a range of creative ways in which such issues could be addressed.

14.2 Conclusion

An international competition agreement is clearly desirable. Such an agreement would be welfare enhancing and would address externalities in the cross-border regulation of competition. There is a sufficient basis for such an agreement. Existing initiatives towards the regulation of cross-border anti-competitive conduct have clear limitations that could be overcome by such an agreement.

The WTO would provide the optimal institutional vehicle for an international competition agreement. The relationship between international trade law and international competition law can be reconciled at a theoretical level by the concept of market contestability. At a practical level, an international competition agreement could address under-regulation and over-regulation in the trade–competition regulatory matrix, realising substantive benefits to international trade and competition.

However, a multilateral WTO competition agreement would not be politically achievable at this time. Rather, the current preferred form for an international competition agreement should be a plurilateral WTO competition agreement. This book has identified the appropriate content and structure for a plurilateral competition agreement and proposes a draft negotiating text with accompanying commentary.

This book concludes that a plurilateral competition agreement should be incorporated into the WTO in the form identified in the Appendix to this book.

Appendix

Draft negotiating text for a plurilateral WTO competition agreement

Following from the conclusions earlier in this book, particularly Chapters 10 to 13, this Appendix sets out a draft negotiating text for a plurilateral WTO competition agreement ('Agreement'). The Agreement is intended to provide the basis for substantive negotiations either alone or within the context of a formal WTO Round.

A commentary, that explains the intent of each provision of the Agreement and the manner in which it gives practical effect to the conclusions reached in this book, is set out in the footnotes.

Plurilateral Agreement on International Competition

Structure of the Agreement[1]

Preamble

Part One	General Provisions[2]	
	Article 1	Acceptance and accession
	Article 2	Implementation of the Agreement
	Article 3	Scope of application and jurisdiction
Part Two	Objectives and Core Principles[3]	
	Article 4	Objectives of the Agreement
	Article 5	Principle of non-discrimination
	Article 6	Principle of transparency
	Article 7	Principle of procedural fairness
	Article 8	Principle of comprehensive application
	Article 9	Principle of international co-operation

---

[1] The Agreement comprises eleven distinct parts, which adopt the general structure and approach of existing WTO agreements.
[2] Part One of the Agreement commences by identifying its application and implementation.
[3] Parts Two to Six proceed from the general to the specific, setting out objectives, principles and substantive obligations.

Part Three	**Universal Competition Principles**
	Article 10 Markets
	Article 11 Market contestability
Part Four	**Regulation of Unilateral Conduct**
	Article 12 Abuses of market power
Part Five	**Regulation of Concerted Conduct**
	Article 13 Horizontal restraints
	Article 14 Vertical restraints
	Article 15 Export, import and international cartels
Part Six	**Regulation of Market Concentration**
	Article 16 Business concentrations with an international dimension
	Article 17 Notification requirements
	Article 18 Excessive market concentration
Part Seven	**Enforcement**[4]
	Article 19 Territorial and extraterritorial enforcement
	Article 20 Remedies
Part Eight	**Institutional Provisions**[5]
	Article 21 National Competition Agencies
	Article 22 Competition Council
	Article 23 International Competition Agency
	Article 24 Relationship with existing institutions
	Article 25 Dispute resolution
Part Nine	**Developing and Least Developed Countries**[6]
	Article 26 Special and differential treatment
	Article 27 Technical assistance
Part Ten	**Development of the Agreement**[7]
	Article 28 Annual review and regular negotiations
	Article 29 Amendments
	Article 30 Consideration of competition policy in the WTO

---

[4] Part Seven sets out substantive obligations relating to domestic enforcement of competition laws by parties to the Agreement.
[5] Part Eight of the Agreement creates the institutional structure for the Agreement and delineates its relationship with existing WTO institutions, including provisions relating to dispute resolution.
[6] Part Nine creates a specific regime for developing and least developed countries.
[7] Part Ten addresses the future development of the Agreement and the general introduction of competition principles into existing WTO jurisprudence.

Part Eleven Final Provisions[8]
                 Article 31   Withdrawal and non-application
                 Article 32   Deposit and registration
                 Article 33   Miscellaneous

Schedule of Specific Commitments
Annexe on Non-Discrimination Exemptions[9]

Preamble[10]

The Parties to this Agreement (hereinafter referred to as 'Parties'),

Recognising the effectiveness of competition in ensuring markets operate efficiently when allocating scarce resources and recognising that increased efficiency, in turn, increases overall social welfare;

Recognising that anti-competitive conduct can distort the effective operation of markets, reduce efficiency, hinder cross-border trade and market access, and therefore reduce social welfare;[11]

Recognising similarly the need to ensure that anti-competitive behaviour does not negate the realisation of benefits that arise from the liberalisation of tariff and non-tariff barriers affecting international trade;

Recognising that competition laws can promote effective competition by deterring anti-competitive conduct and excessive market concentration;

Considering the consequential need for a sound and effective multilateral framework of rights and obligations with respect to the formulation and application of domestic competition laws, regulations, procedures and practices in the context of anti-competitive conduct that affects cross-border trade;[12]

---

[8] Part Eleven of the Agreement concludes with the usual final provisions common in WTO agreements of this nature.
[9] Importantly, the Agreement also contains a schedule of specific commitments for each party and an annexe setting out exemptions from the principle of non-discrimination outlined in Art. 5.
[10] The Preamble is intended to set out methodically the background to the Agreement and the underlying policy rationale behind it. The Preamble is not legally binding but is intended to assist the interpretation of the Agreement.
[11] The Preamble commences by identifying the importance of competition in increasing global welfare and the associated welfare reducing impact of anti-competitive behaviour, as discussed in Chapter 2 of this book. On this basis, the Preamble identifies the underlying policy justification for competition law.
[12] The Preamble justifies the existence of the Agreement in terms of creating a framework for application of domestic competition laws to anti-competitive conduct that affects cross-border trade. The issue was discussed in detail in Chapter 3 of this book.

Taking into account that each Party may have its own unique formulation of competition law which may be appropriate to the particular circumstances of that Party;[13]

Taking particular account of the development, financial and trade needs of developing countries, and the particular needs arising from the special economic situation of the least developed countries;[14]

Desiring to build upon existing bilateral, plurilateral and multilateral initiatives towards an international competition agreement, including initiatives within UNCTAD;[15]

Desiring to encourage the progressive acceptance of and accession to this Agreement by WTO members not initially party to it;[16]

Having undertaken further negotiations in pursuance of these objectives;

Hereby *agree* as follows:

Part One: General Provisions[17]

Article 1 Acceptance and accession [18]

Section 1 Acceptance

This Agreement shall be open for acceptance, by signature, by governments that are members of the WTO and by the European Community.

---

[13] The Preamble expressly recognises the diversity of existing competition laws between nations and implicitly recognises the futility of full harmonisation, as discussed in Chapter 11 of this book.

[14] The Preamble also expressly recognises the unique needs of developing and less developed countries, as discussed in Chapter 13 of this book.

[15] The Preamble expressly refers to the need to build upon existing bilateral, plurilateral and multilateral initiatives. The express reference to UNCTAD is intended to address further the interests of developing countries.

[16] The Preamble recognises that the Agreement is a plurilateral agreement and that a key objective is to expand the number of parties to the Agreement over time with a view to its eventual acceptance as a multilateral agreement in Annexe 1 of the WTO Final Act.

[17] Part One of the Agreement addresses a number of key procedural mechanisms intrinsic to the commencement of international treaties, namely entry into force, implementation, legal effect and application. Part One also establishes the procedural framework for the substantive obligations set out in Parts Two to Seven of the Agreement.

[18] The drafting provides that any WTO nation and the EU (as is usual) may accede to the Agreement on terms agreed with the Competition Council. Usually, the only requirement for accession would be to sign and subsequently ratify the Agreement. The requirement of Competition Council approval recognises that, in some cases, nations seeking to accede to the Agreement may not comply with it as from ratification; hence the existing parties may wish to resolve this compliance issue prior to the accession of that nation (e.g. via pre-conditions for accession).

Section 2 Entry into force [19]

This Agreement shall enter into force on [*DATE*] for those governments which have, by signature, accepted the Agreement, or have signed the Agreement subject to ratification and subsequently ratified the Agreement.

Section 3 Accession [20]

Any government which is a member of the WTO and which is not a Party to this Agreement may accede to this Agreement on terms to be agreed between that government and the Competition Council. Accession shall take place by deposit with the Director-General of the WTO of an instrument of accession which states the terms so agreed. The Agreement shall enter into force for an acceding government on the thirtieth day following the date of its accession to the Agreement.

Section 4 Reservations [21]

Reservations may not be entered in respect of any of the provisions of this Agreement without the prior written approval of the Competition Council.

Article 2 Implementation of the Agreement [22]

Section 1 National legislation

Subject to Section 2 of this Article, each government accepting or acceding to this Agreement shall ensure, no later than the date of entry into force of this Agreement for that government, the

---

[19] As a plurilateral agreement in Annexe 4 of the Final Act, the provisions of the Agreement itself determine when it enters into force. The drafting above provides for the Agreement to take legal effect on a particular agreed date and, from that date, immediately to bind those nations that ratify or accede to it.

[20] Once the Agreement enters into force, the Parties as at that date could influence the terms of accession of subsequent members. Nations that wish to avoid the need to obtain consent from the Parties (and have their laws and policies subject to greater scrutiny) would have an incentive to sign the Agreement before it enters into force. Consequently, the drafting of Art. 1 is intended to encourage maximum initial membership of the Agreement.

[21] The restrictions imposed on the use of reservations complement the requirement of Competition Council approval for accession and are intended to discourage nations from cherry-picking obligations with which they will comply, thereby reducing the effectiveness of the Agreement. The restriction also reflects the existence of a number of mechanisms in the Agreement that may be used as an alternative to a treaty reservation. The mechanisms in Art. 2 and Art. 24, for example, provide flexibility to enable parties to select by which of the obligations they will initially be bound.

[22] Article 2 differentiates the substantive competition obligations set out in Parts Three to Six of the Agreement from the remaining provisions of the Agreement. The remaining provisions of the Agreement are (mostly) legally binding immediately the relevant nation signs and ratifies the Agreement. The relevant nation must therefore ensure that its domestic

conformity of its laws and regulations, and associated administrative procedures and guidelines (including the rules and practices of its National Competition Agencies) with the provisions of this Agreement.

Section 2   Retention of legislative sovereignty

Parties may, but shall not be obliged to, implement in their domestic laws more extensive protection than is required by this Agreement, provided that such protection does not contravene the provisions of this Agreement. Parties are free to determine the appropriate method of implementing the provisions of this Agreement within their own legal system.

Section 3   Non-binding competitive safeguards[23]

Subject to Section 4 of this Article, the obligations set out in Parts Three to Six of this Agreement are not legally binding on any Party. However, each Party is encouraged to adopt appropriate measures to prevent persons within its territorial jurisdiction from undertaking the anti-competitive practices identified in Parts Three to Six of this Agreement, to the maximum extent possible in the circumstances consistent with the objectives and core principles of this Agreement, as if Parts Three to Six of this Agreement were legally binding on that Party.

Section 4   Binding competitive safeguards[24]

Where a Party considers that any of its laws and regulations, or associated procedures and guidelines, are consistent with Parts Three to

laws, regulations and procedures are consistent with those remaining provisions as from ratification, in accordance with Section 1.

[23] Parts Three to Six of the Agreement are not legally binding as from ratification, rather they only have effect as non-binding 'soft law' principles, as discussed in Chapter 10 of this book. The wording of Section 2 is intended to give these 'soft law' principles maximum moral persuasive force, reinforcing that such 'soft law' is still intended to influence the behaviour of nations, as discussed in Chapter 10 of this book, notwithstanding its unenforceable quality.

[24] Once a party considers that any part of its laws is compliant with Parts Three to Six, it has a discretion to notify the Competition Council that it will be legally bound in whole or in part by any obligations in respect of these parts of its laws. In this manner, a ratchet mechanism is created enabling a nation to enter into the Agreement even if its laws are non-compliant, but to agree to be bound by particular obligations once its laws become compliant with those obligations. This mechanism may discourage the use of initial treaty reservations while retaining maximum flexibility for nations, thereby encouraging greater membership. This mechanism will also provide a mechanism under which each party may adopt its own transitional provisions towards full compliance. The intention is that a party would only agree to be legally bound by the obligations set out in Parts Three to Six of the Agreement once its laws were compliant with those obligations.

Six of this Agreement, that Party may notify the Competition Council that it will be legally bound by the relevant obligations (in whole or in part) set out in Parts Three to Six of this Agreement in respect of those laws and regulations, and associated procedures and guidelines. From the date of notification, the Party will be legally bound by the notified obligations accordingly. The extent to which a Party is legally bound by those obligations will be recorded in its Schedule of Specific Commitments.

Section 5 Consistency with this Agreement[25]

Each Party must inform the Competition Council of the extent to which its laws and regulations, and associated procedures and guidelines, are consistent with Parts Three to Six of this Agreement on each anniversary of the date at which this Agreement enters into force. Where a Party considers its laws and regulations, and associated procedures and guidelines, are consistent with Parts Three to Six of this Agreement, and that Party has not given notice under Section 3 of this Article, that Party must identify the reasons why it has not given notice.

Section 6 Schedule of Specific Commitments[26]

Any Party, with the agreement of the Competition Council, may record in its Schedule of Specific Commitments, agreed obligations which are more stringent than, but consistent with, the obligations set out in this Agreement and its objectives and principles. Such agreed obligations shall be binding on that Party in accordance with their terms and may take incremental effect via a transitional

---

[25] Article 2 creates a reporting requirement whereby each party must inform the Competition Council of the extent to which its laws, regulations and procedures are consistent with Parts Three to Six of the Agreement. Where its laws are consistent, but the party has not agreed to be bound by the relevant obligations set out in Parts Three to Six, the party must provide a justification for its reasons for not agreeing to be bound. In this manner, the party's decision not to be bound remains transparent and can be subject to greater international scrutiny and comment, reinforcing international peer pressure in the manner discussed in Chapter 12 of this book.

[26] Section 6 creates a mechanism whereby parties may agree to be bound by additional obligations that are more stringent than the obligations set out in the Agreement. Such additional obligations will be recorded in the Schedule of Specific Commitments for each party, in the same manner as with the GATS. The Competition Council must agree the content of any party's Schedule and has maximum discretion to determine the nature and timing of any negotiations on such Specific Commitments. In this manner, the Agreement creates a framework for further international competition obligations, and negotiations on such obligations, further increasing flexibility and furthering the objectives of the Agreement. This approach also reflects the approach of the WTO itself, which creates a skeletal framework of rules and principles upon which specific commitments are fleshed out.

procedure. The Competition Council will determine the timing of periodic negotiations between the Parties to determine and update their Specific Commitments.

Article 3 Scope of application and jurisdiction[27]

Section 1 *Scope of application*[28]

This Agreement shall apply to all anti-competitive conduct in the sense of this Agreement which affects at least two Parties to this Agreement and therefore is deemed to have a 'cross-border dimension' for the purposes of this Agreement.

Section 2 *Effects principle and nationality principle*

A Party to the Agreement is 'affected' for the purposes of Section 1 whenever:

(a) there are economic effects in its territory or otherwise on its commerce arising from anti-competitive conduct; or

(b) private nationals of that Party, or legal entities domiciled in the territory of that Party, are the initiators or victims of anti-competitive conduct.

Section 3 *Territorial jurisdiction*[29]

Nothing in this Agreement is intended to prevent a Party taking action to prevent anti-competitive conduct occurring within its territory, whether or not that anti-competitive conduct affects other Parties. Each Party to this Agreement is encouraged to extend its laws, if its laws do not otherwise apply, to all anti-competitive conduct in the sense of this Agreement occurring within its territory.

---

[27] Article 3 clarifies that the Agreement is only intended to regulate cross-border activity (including domestic activity with a cross-border effect), rather than activity within each party's own domestic territorial jurisdiction that solely affects that jurisdiction. The concept of a 'cross-border dimension' is used as the relevant test for application of the Agreement and is defined widely via an effects-based test. The Agreement extends no further than necessary to address cross-border competition issues.

[28] In circumstances where there is no 'cross-border dimension', a party continues to retain its sovereign right to regulate competition as it pleases. However, given that each party remains subject to the non-discrimination obligation set out in Art. 5, it cannot impose competition laws on foreign legal entities that are stricter than it imposes on its own domestic legal entities.

[29] Section 3 confirms that each party retains its sovereign territorial right to regulate competition within its own borders and that nothing in the Agreement is intended to abrogate that right. Article 3 also encourages parties to ensure that their domestic laws apply to all anti-competitive conduct occurring within their territory so that they have sufficient ability to prevent such anti-competitive conduct.

Section 4 Extraterritorial jurisdiction[30]

A Party to this Agreement may regulate and apply its domestic laws to anti-competitive behaviour occurring outside its territory, with an adverse economic effect on its territory. However, in such circumstances, that Party is:

(a) encouraged to have regard to the principles of international cooperation set out in this Agreement and any obligations in this Agreement relating to the resolution of disputes;[31] and

(b) to exercise moderation and restraint as to the exercise of any such extraterritorial jurisdiction and to avoid undue encroachment on the territorial jurisdiction more properly appertaining to, or more appropriately exercisable by, another Party.

Part Two: Objectives and Core Principles[32]

Article 4 Objectives

Section 1 Objective of this Agreement[33]

The objective of this Agreement is to maintain workable competition in international markets, and in the domestic markets of any Party, via effective competition laws, so as to promote economic efficiency and increased domestic and global welfare.

---

[30] Section 4 continues to permit the extraterritorial application of competition law, recognising that, for example, the US and EU would not sign an Agreement that removed this ability at this time, as discussed in Chapter 13 of this book. However, Section 4 seeks to restrict the severity of such extraterritorial application by requiring each party to have regard to principles of comity, reflecting the obiter dictum of Judge Fitzmaurice in the *Barcelona Traction* case, as discussed in Chapter 3 of this book. The obligations in Section 4 are supplemented by the obligations in Section 2 of Art. 19 of the Agreement, which impose further obligations relating to extraterritorial enforcement, as discussed later.

[31] Importantly, Section 4(a) clarifies that the WTO Dispute Settlement Body, as referred to by Art. 25 of the Agreement, is given jurisdiction to adjudicate upon jurisdictional disputes arising in the context of the extraterritorial application of competition laws. However, as discussed in detail in Chapter 12 of this book, this concept would be unlikely to receive full international support so would most likely be removed during international negotiations.

[32] Part Two of the Agreement establishes the fundamental objectives of the Agreement and the core principles giving effect to those objectives. The fundamental objectives are not legally binding and only have 'soft law' effect while aiding interpretation. However, the core principles may impose binding legal obligations in some circumstances and therefore have a dual 'soft law' and 'hard law' character. As noted above, all legally binding obligations in Part Two are subject to an 'opt in' mechanism via each party's Schedule of Specific Commitments.

[33] The objective of the Agreement is to maintain 'workable competition' in international and domestic markets via effective competition laws. The concept of 'workable competition'

Section 2 Domestic objectives[34]

Each Party must ensure its domestic competition laws have, either expressly or implicitly, the objective of maintaining or promoting competition. Each Party may set out alternative domestic objectives for its competition laws, provided that such domestic objectives do not conflict with the objectives set out in Section 1 of this Article.

Section 3 Competition policy[35]

Consistent with Section 1 of this Article, each Party is encouraged, but is not required, to:[36]

(a) adopt domestic competition policies that are consistent with the promotion of competition in international and domestic markets;

(b) avoid the application of trade measures in circumstances where their application would not be consistent with market contestability and greater international competition in markets where a nation has already given a tariff binding or similar scheduled commitment;

---

was identified in Chapter 2 of this book and refers to the maximum practical competition achievable in the particular market circumstances. The objective of the Agreement addresses competition at both the domestic and international levels, correlating competition in international markets with increased global welfare, and competition in domestic markets with increased domestic welfare. In this manner, the objective implicitly requires a balance between the objective of maximising international welfare and the objective of maximising domestic welfare.

[34] The wording of Section 2 recognises that economic efficiency is not the sole objective of competition law, as discussed in Chapter 2 of this book, as domestic competition laws may frequently be given distributional objectives. Article 4 enables each party to maintain such alternative distributional objectives for its domestic competition laws as long as these objectives do not conflict with the ultimate objective of maintaining workable competition.

[35] Section 3 sets out five critical non-binding 'soft law' obligations associated with the interrelationship between international trade law and international competition law. In particular, Section 3 encourages parties to adopt domestic competition policies that are consistent with the promotion of domestic and international competition. The benefits of promoting competition policy as well as competition law were identified in Chapter 2 of this book.

[36] Section 3 also sets out several key non-binding 'soft law' obligations that are intended to influence the use of existing WTO trade measures to ensure consistency with the broad objectives of competition policy, as discussed in Chapter 7 of this book. In this manner, Section 3 takes an important step towards reconciling international trade law with the objectives of international competition law. Given that such obligations may be controversial, they are deliberately phrased in non-binding 'soft law' terms so as to have only moral influence. An alternative approach may be to express these obligations in binding terms, but to rely on an 'opt in' mechanism.

(c) formulate its domestic trade measures in a manner least detrimental to international competition and in a manner not conducive to anti-competitive conduct;

(d) reduce any adverse spillover effects of its domestic trade measures on international competition; and

(e) ensure that where domestic trade measures do adversely affect international competition, such measures are short-term in nature and no more detrimental to international competition than necessary to achieve their intended result.

Article 5 Principle of non-discrimination [37]

Section 1 De jure discrimination [38]

Parties must ensure that their competition laws and regulations, and associated procedures and guidelines, are formulated in a consistent manner that does not discriminate between or among legal entities on the basis of nationality.

Section 2 De facto discrimination [39]

Parties must ensure that decisions to initiate enforcement action and procedures in decision-making are undertaken in a consistent manner that does not discriminate between or among legal entities on the basis of nationality. Parties are encouraged to ensure that substantive regulatory decisions are consistent and do not discriminate between or among legal entities on the basis of nationality.

---

[37] The appropriate drafting of a principle of non-discrimination was discussed in detail in Chapter 10 of this book. The drafting set out in Article 5 is a hybrid of the principle of national treatment and the principle of most-favoured nation treatment, as discussed in detail in Chapter 10. The two limbs of Section 3 reflect these two principles.

[38] The principle of non-discrimination is phrased as a prohibition against non-discrimination on the basis of nationality, recognising the conventional approach of WTO law on discrimination as between nations. As discussed in Chapter 10, a broader wording of this obligation, such as an obligation to ensure competitive neutrality (including non-discrimination as between domestic firms), would extend beyond the conventional approach of the WTO and would most likely be politically unpalatable at the present time.

[39] As discussed in Chapter 10, Sections 1 and 2 deliberately differentiate between de jure discrimination (i.e. discrimination embodied within particular formulations of competition laws at the domestic level) and de facto discrimination (i.e. discrimination occurring in the application of this domestic law to particular factual situations). De jure discrimination and some elements of de facto discrimination are prohibited via a binding 'hard law' obligation, while the remaining elements of de facto discrimination are discouraged via a non-binding 'soft law' obligation. This approach reflects the conclusion in Chapter 10 of this book.

Section 3 Discrimination on the basis of nationality
Discrimination on the basis of nationality will occur if:
(a) foreign legal entities and their goods and services are treated less favourably than domestic legal entities and their goods and services in like competitive circumstances; or
(b) foreign legal entities and their goods and services are treated less favourably than foreign legal entities from different nations and their goods and services in like competitive circumstances.

Section 4 Permitted discrimination[40]
A Party may maintain competition laws and regulations, and associated procedures and guidelines, and make decisions, inconsistent with Section 1 provided that such competition laws and regulations, and associated procedures and guidelines are listed in, and meet the conditions of, and such decisions are made in accordance with, the Annexe on Non-Discrimination Exemptions annexed to this Agreement.

Article 6 Principle of transparency[41]

Section 1 Transparency of regulatory requirements[42]
Each Party must develop, apply, enforce and otherwise administer all competition laws and regulations, and associated procedures and guidelines, in a transparent manner. Each Party must take practical steps, where possible, to improve the transparency of its competition policy objectives and the manner in which its competition laws and regulations, and associated procedures and guidelines, are developed, applied, enforced and otherwise administered.

---

[40] Section 4 recognises that the principle of non-discrimination would need to be subject to a range of general and specific exceptions, as discussed in Chapter 10. This list would need to be negotiated between the parties and would address existing instances of justifiable discrimination plus the usual range of exceptions set out in the existing WTO agreements, to the extent applicable (e.g. Art. XIV of the GATS). Generally, parties would be required to justify existing instances of discrimination and consider phasing them out over a transitional period if they were not justifiable.

[41] The appropriate drafting of the principle of transparency was discussed in detail in Chapter 10 of this book. As discussed in Chapter 10, the principle has two elements, namely an obligation to publish and an obligation to notify. The obligation to publish is addressed by Art. 6 and is modelled on similar provisions set out in the existing WTO agreements.

[42] Section 1 sets out a general obligation of transparency that applies both to the development and administration of competition laws. This obligation contemplates, for example, that the process of formulating competition laws will be public, as will enforcement procedures and policies. Section 1 also imposes a positive obligation on parties to take practical steps to improve such transparency.

Section 2 *Obligation to publish*[43]
Each Party must publish promptly, or otherwise make publicly available, at the latest by the time of their entry into force (except in emergency situations), all relevant laws and regulations, and associated procedures and guidelines, administrative rulings and judicial decisions of general application which pertain to or affect the operation of this Agreement and its subject matter ('Relevant Information'). Such Relevant Information includes all international agreements entered into by that Party which affect the operation of this Agreement.

Section 3 *Notification of amendments*
Each Party must publish promptly, and promptly (and at least annually) inform the Competition Council and International Competition Agency, of the introduction of any new measures of a kind contemplated by Section 2, or any changes to the Relevant Information set out in Section 2, which materially affect its commitments under this Agreement or that relate to the regulation of competition.

Section 4 *Provision of requested information*[44]
Each Party must respond promptly to all reasonable requests by any other Party for Relevant Information within the meaning of Section 2. Each Party must also establish one or more enquiry points to enable such requested Relevant Information to be promptly provided to requesting Parties, upon request. Requests made by Parties to developing and least developed country Parties must recognise the reduced ability of those Parties to respond promptly to such requests.

---

[43] Section 2 sets out a specific obligation on parties to ensure all relevant laws are published by the time the party enters into the Agreement. This obligation could be met, for example, (at low cost for developing countries) simply by publishing such laws on the Internet website of the national competition agency. Section 3 sets out a corresponding obligation to ensure this published information is updated regularly.

[44] Section 4 sets out a requirement for parties to respond to requests from other parties for relevant information within the meaning of Section 2. Given that such information should already be publicly available, compliance with these requests should not be difficult. However, recognising the likely concerns of developing countries, Section 4 requires requests to developing and least-developed countries to take into account their reduced resourcing. The intention of the request procedure is to enable parties to determine readily the nature of each other party's competition laws and regulations, thereby enabling each party to determine more easily whether any anti-competitive conduct may have a Cross-Border Dimension.

448   INTERNATIONAL COMPETITION LAW

Section 5 *Confidential information*[45]
Nothing in this Agreement shall require any Party to provide confidential information, the disclosure of which is contrary to its laws or in breach of any binding legal obligation, or which would impede law enforcement, or otherwise be contrary to the public interest, or which would prejudice the legitimate commercial interests of particular enterprises, public or private.

Section 6 *Notification of non-compliance*[46]
Any Party may notify the Competition Council or International Competition Agency of any act, omission or measure, taken by any other Party, which it considers breaches the obligations of that Party under this Agreement.

Article 7 Principle of procedural fairness[47]

Section 1 *Rule of Law*[48]
Any National Competition Authority or any other governmental entity administering or enforcing competition laws and regulations, or associated procedures and guidelines ('Regulatory Agency') should respect all human, civil and procedural rights of legal entities affected by such administration or enforcement in accordance with the Rule of Law in the particular Party and applicable international agreements.

---

[45] Section 5 creates a specific exemption that parties are not required to disclose confidential information to other nations, as discussed in Chapters 5 and 10 of this book. Chapter 5 of this book noted, in particular, that confidentiality is a major issue affecting the cross-border sharing of information. Chapter 5 noted that such issues depended on mutual trust and confidence between the competition authorities of different nations, so are best addressed on a bilateral basis.

[46] Section 6 is an important provision in the Agreement which is intended to promote compliance, as discussed in Chapter 11. By enabling any party to notify breaches by any other party, a peer pressure mechanism is created to encourage greater compliance.

[47] The appropriate drafting of the principle of procedural fairness was discussed in detail in Chapter 10 of this book. As discussed in Chapter 10, given that competition law involves government intervention in the market, and given that such intervention can potentially adversely affect competition, it is necessary to ensure that such intervention is justifiable in the circumstances and is fair and reasonable. Accordingly, strict requirements of procedural fairness are necessary.

[48] Section 1 requires national competition authorities to respect the Rule of Law, both domestically and as set out in international agreements, establishing a broad principle of legal accountability.

Section 2 *Due process*[49]
   The Regulatory Agency should act within the scope of the power or discretion conferred on it, both reasonably and fairly, when making regulatory decisions or otherwise exercising its regulatory powers. The Regulatory Agency should not act capriciously and should not alter or amend its regulatory requirements without due consultation with affected legal entities.

Section 3 *Impartiality*
   The decisions of, and the procedures used by, Regulatory Agencies should be objective and impartial with respect to all affected legal entities. Regulatory Agencies and their personnel should not predetermine decisions, have any bias, or have any pecuniary interest in the outcome of a regulatory decision.

Section 4 *Natural justice*
   Where conduct is subject to enforcement or investigation by a Regulatory Agency, the Regulatory Agency should provide interested legal entities with a fair and reasonable opportunity to appraise the Regulatory Agency of their views. The Regulatory Agency should give full and reasonable consideration to all submissions it receives. Where feasible, the Regulatory Agency should clearly explain the reasoning for its decisions.

Section 5 *Recognition of different legal traditions*[50]
   Each Party should use reasonable endeavours to give effect to Sections 2 to 4 of this Article, with regard to the particular legal traditions and institutions of that Party, by ensuring its laws and regulations are not inconsistent with Sections 2 to 4.

---

[49] Sections 2 to 4 supplement that broad principle with specific obligations related to administrative fairness. Section 2 establishes that due process must be followed in all administrative actions and decisions. Sections 3 and 4 address particular aspects of the requirement of due process, namely impartiality and natural justice, both of which are discussed in detail in Chapter 10. Each of these elements is particularly important to the accurate application of competition laws and the accountability of administrative agencies.

[50] Section 5 recognises that the elements of administrative fairness set out in Sections 2 and 4 are subject to the particular legal traditions and institutions of each nation. With this in mind, Section 5 uses the wording 'are not inconsistent with' in relation to the obligations set out in Sections 2 to 4 so that they are expressed in non-binding 'soft-law' terms, rather than binding 'hard-law' terms, as discussed in Chapter 10.

Article 8 Principle of comprehensive application [51]

Section 1 Generic application [52]

Each Party should endeavour to give its domestic competition laws and regulations generic application to all markets within its territory and should minimise exceptions and exemptions from its domestic competition laws to the extent such exceptions and exemptions are not justifiable on the basis of public policy.

Section 2 Industry-specific regulation [53]

Nothing in this Agreement is intended to prevent a Party applying additional regulatory requirements to promote or maintain competition in particular markets or industries where those additional regulatory requirements are consistent with the core principles and objectives of this Agreement.

Section 3 Application to public sector

Each Party is encouraged to ensure that:

(a) its public undertakings, irrespective of their legal status, are subject to domestic competition laws as far as they engage in economic activities that could be carried out by private undertakings; and

---

[51] The appropriate drafting of the principle of comprehensive application was discussed in detail in Chapter 10 of this book. As discussed in Chapter 10, this principle does not expressly exist in any existing WTO agreements and is specific to competition law, reflecting the generic application of competition law to all markets. Accordingly, the wording of Art. 8 is unique to this Agreement.

[52] Section 1 sets out a non-binding 'soft law' principle that parties should endeavour to extend their domestic competition laws to cover all markets, which reinforces the obligation set out in Section 3 of Art. 3 relating to territorial jurisdiction. Section 1 further requires each party to minimise exemptions from its domestic competition laws, as discussed in detail in Chapter 10. Similarly, Section 3 sets out a non-binding 'soft law' principle that parties should endeavour to ensure that their domestic competition laws apply both to public sector entities involved in trade as well as private sector entities. In this manner, Art. 8 seeks to apply competition laws as widely as possible, reflecting the intention that they are given generic application to all markets within a particular nation.

[53] Section 2 confirms that each party remains free to apply additional regulatory requirements to promote or maintain competition. However, these additional requirements must be consistent with the Agreement. Additional regulatory requirements are necessary, for example, where generic competition law somehow proves ineffective in maintaining or promoting competition, which may occur in cases of severe market failure. Access to essential facilities (such as telecommunications networks and electricity grids) are situations where more heavy-handed regulation is frequently necessary to ensure effective competition, for example, as contemplated by the WTO Agreement on Basic Telecommunications.

(b) legal entities entrusted with the operation of services of general economic interest or having the character of a revenue-producing monopoly are subject to domestic competition laws in so far as the application of these laws does not obstruct the performance, in law or in fact, of the particular tasks assigned to them.

Section 4 *Defence of state authorisation* [54]

Each Party is encouraged to remove the defence of state authorisation in respect of anti-competitive conduct in its territory that has a direct adverse effect on economic activity within the territory of another Party.

Article 9 Principle of international co-operation [55]

Section 1 *Obligation to co-operate* [56]

Each Party must co-operate in good faith with every other Party in complying with its obligations under this Agreement and must co-operate with the Competition Council and International Competition Agency. Each Party must require its National Competition Agencies to co-operate with the National Competition Agencies of other Parties and the Competition Council and International Competition Agency.

Section 2 *Obligation to notify* [57]

Each Party must notify the National Competition Agency of any other affected Party if it becomes aware of:

---

[54] Section 4 sets out a non-binding 'soft law' principle that parties should seek to remove the defence of state authorisation to the extent that it permits anti-competitive activity with direct adverse effects on economic activity in other nations. This issue was discussed in detail in Chapter 10 and is also controversial, so may not survive international negotiations notwithstanding its non-binding character.

[55] The appropriate drafting of the principle of international co-operation was discussed in detail in Chapter 10 of this book. As discussed in Chapter 10, the principle of co-operation is fundamental to international law and is set out, for example, in the United Nations Charter and the existing WTO agreement in various guises. The principle of co-operation is also enshrined in a range of modern bilateral competition agreements and was the subject of OECD recommendations, as identified in Chapter 5 of this book.

[56] Section 1 sets out a general principle to co-operate, both as between parties and between their respective national competition agencies. This general principle is supplemented by a specific obligation to co-operate in relation to investigation and enforcement activities against anti-competitive conduct with a Cross-Border Dimension, as set out in Section 3.

[57] The obligation to notify, set out in Section 2, is intended to provide a mechanism for facilitating more effective law enforcement on an international basis by requiring competition

(a) any anti-competitive conduct within its territory that has a Cross-Border Dimension (as defined in Article 3) related to that other Party; or
(b) any anti-competitive conduct within the territory of that other Party that may warrant investigation and/or enforcement affecting that other Party.

Section 3 Cross-border investigations [58]

Each Party must ensure its National Competition Agencies use reasonable endeavours to co-operate with other National Competition Agencies, the Competition Council and the International Competition Agency with a view to avoiding jurisdictional conflict when undertaking investigations or enforcement proceedings against anti-competitive conduct with a Cross-Border Dimension.

Section 4 Limited positive comity [59]

Each Party must, at the request of any other Party:

(a) enter into consultations (supervised by the International Competition Agency, if necessary) with a view to eliminating anti-competitive conduct with a Cross-Border Dimension that is in breach of the requested Party's competition laws or regulations;
(b) accord full and sympathetic consideration to such a request and co-operate through the supply of publicly available non-confidential information of relevance to the anti-competitive conduct in question; and
(c) provide other available relevant information to the requesting Party, subject to confidentiality considerations (as set out in Section 5 of Article 6) and the conclusion of a mutually satisfactory agreement concerning the safeguarding of the confidentiality of any such information.

---

agencies to notify each other of anti-competitive conduct that they uncover which affects other nations.

[58] Together, Sections 3 to 5 establish a framework for international co-operation on competition law matters.

[59] Section 4 is based on provisions in existing WTO agreements as discussed in detail in Chapter 10. Section 4, in essence, creates a limited form of 'positive comity' as discussed in Chapter 6 of this book, in a non-binding 'soft law' form, via international consultations. Section 4 incorporates an associated requirement to share relevant information to assist enforcement activity, bolstering the obligations set out in Art. 6, but remaining subject to the exceptions for confidentiality set out in Section 5 of Art. 6. The comity obligation is critical in addressing the externalities identified in Chapter 3 of this book.

Section 5 Bilateral and plurilateral initiatives[60]

Parties should endeavour to enter into further agreements between themselves, whether bilateral or plurilateral, to facilitate improved co-operation in relation to the investigation and enforcement of anti-competitive conduct with a Cross-Border Dimension. On request by all Parties to such agreements, the Competition Council shall have regard to the appropriateness of incorporating obligations from such agreements in the Schedule of Specific Commitments for those nations with such obligations having limited application as between a subset of Parties.

Part Three: Universal Competition Principles[61]

Article 10 Markets[62]

Section 1 Dimensions of a market[63]

Each Party will maintain competition laws and regulations that are premised upon the economic concept of a market, as delineated by the dimensions of product, functional level, geography and

---

[60] Section 5 sets out a non-binding 'soft law' principle that parties should endeavour to conclude further agreements between themselves to facilitate more effective investigation and enforcement of anti-competitive conduct with a Cross-Border Dimension. Accordingly, Section 5 is intended to promote the increased use of bilateral and plurilateral agreements, reflecting the 'Building on Bilaterals' limb of the four-point strategy set out in Chapter 13 of this book. Importantly, Section 5 creates a mechanism to enable obligations from such agreements to be incorporated into the Agreement via each nation's Schedule of Specific Commitments. In this manner, the Agreement seeks to act as an umbrella or framework which can unify all international competition agreements.

[61] Part Three of the Agreement is intended to set out two fundamental underlying principles of international competition law, namely the concept of a 'market' and the concept of 'market contestability'. The concept of a 'market' is viewed as a fundamental concept which should underlie all competition laws, as discussed in Chapters 2 and 6 of this book. The concept of 'market contestability' is used as a mechanism to reconcile the interaction between international competition law and international trade law, as discussed in Chapter 6 of this book.

[62] As discussed in Chapter 4 of this book, the concept of a 'market' is fundamental to the application of competition law as it provides the framework for any competition assessment.

[63] Section 1 ensures that this concept of market is reflected in all competition laws. Section 1 also ensures that this concept is interpreted by reference to competition law concepts, rather than international trade law concepts. Section 1 therefore provides that a market should be viewed as having three or four dimensions (as appropriate) and that the concept of 'like product' in international trade law is not applicable, as discussed in Chapter 6 of this book.

(if considered necessary) time. The product dimension of a market should be determined by the economic concept of product substitutability rather than the GATT concept of 'like product'.

Section 2 *International dimension of markets* [64]

When considering anti-competitive behaviour that has a Cross-Border Dimension, each Party will endeavour to have due regard to any international dimension to the markets in which that anti-competitive behaviour occurs.

Section 3 *Limited negative comity* [65]

When administering or enforcing its competition laws, each Party will endeavour to have due regard to any anti-competitive behaviour within its territory that has a direct adverse effect on economic activity within the territory of another Party.

Article 11 Market contestability [66]

Section 1 *Market contestability* [67]

The Parties agree that international trade will be facilitated by the reduction of behavioural and structural barriers to market access, thereby promoting market contestability.

---

[64] Section 2 is fundamental to the international character of the Agreement in that it requires parties to recognise the international dimension of markets and to have regard to the effects of domestic anti-competitive conduct on the markets of other nations. In some instances, for example, markets should be considered as having an international dimension, particularly if trade barriers are low. Section 2 expressly recognises that as the WTO agreements reduce barriers to trade, so markets will become more integrated internationally.

[65] Section 3 establishes a form of limited negative comity, as discussed in Chapter 6 of this book, in which parties must have regard to the interests of other nations. Section 3 is expressed as a non-binding 'soft law' principle given that such an obligation of negative comity is likely to prove controversial. However, Sections 2 and 3 are critically important in creating a mechanism to address externalities as identified in Chapter 3 of this book.

[66] Chapter 6 of this book identified that the concept of market contestability was a key mechanism for reconciling international trade law with international competition law. Given that the Agreement will be a plurilateral agreement, it cannot override existing WTO multilateral agreements, hence if the Competition Council has insufficient jurisdiction to resolve an inconsistency it must be referred to the WTO Ministerial Conference for an interpretative determination. Article 11 assists the WTO Ministerial Conference in its interpretative role by clarifying the relationship between the objectives of the existing WTO multilateral trade agreements and the Agreement.

[67] Section 1 clarifies that international trade will be facilitated by market contestability via the reduction of behavioural and structural barriers to market access.

Section 2 Behavioural barriers [68]
> Parts Four and Five of this Agreement is intended to promote market contestability by reducing behavioural barriers to market access created by anti-competitive conduct. Part Six of this Agreement is intended to promote market contestability by reducing the structural potential for barriers to market access created by anti-competitive conduct.

Section 3 Structural barriers
> Section 3 of Article 4 of this Agreement is intended to promote market contestability by reducing structural barriers to market access created by existing governmental laws and regulations that are inconsistent with the objective of promoting and maintaining workable competition and that are not otherwise justifiable.

Section 4 Interpretation [69]
> In the event of any inconsistency between this Agreement and any provision in the existing WTO Agreements, such inconsistency is to be resolved to the extent possible by the Competition Council with regard to the objective of promoting market contestability as set out in Sections 1 to 3 of this Article. Otherwise, the inconsistency must be referred to the WTO Ministerial Council for determination.

Part Four: Regulation of Unilateral Conduct [70]

Article 12 Abuses of market power [71]

Section 1 Abuses of market power [72]
> Parties should prohibit anti-competitive abuses of market power by legal entities with threshold market power.

---

[68] Sections 2 and 3 link the key substantive obligations of the Agreement to the concept of market contestability. The behavioural-structural distinction was discussed in detail in Chapters 2 and 4 of this book.

[69] Section 4 utilises the concept of market contestability as a mechanism for reconciling inconsistencies between the WTO Competition Agreement and the existing WTO agreements.

[70] Part Four of the Agreement addresses the first of the three fundamental elements of competition law, as identified in Chapters 2 and 4 of this book, namely the regulation of unilateral conduct (also known as 'anti-monopoly law').

[71] Article 12 of this Agreement gives effect to the conclusions in Chapter 4 of this book regarding the regulation of unilateral conduct. These conclusions were based on an analysis of the key features of the competition laws of the APEC nations.

[72] Section 1 sets out the fundamental obligation of modern competition law that firms with threshold market power should not abuse that market power in an anti-competitive manner, as discussed in Chapters 2 and 4 of this book.

Section 2 *Threshold market power*[73]

The threshold market power should be determined by a Party by reference to its particular competition objectives and the existing concentration of its markets. The threshold market power should be set out in that Party's relevant competition laws. Common thresholds are 'market dominance', 'monopolisation' and 'significant market power'.

Section 3 *Purpose and effect*[74]

Anti-competitive abuses of market power may be determined by:

(a) purpose, relating to the extent to which the particular conduct by the legal entity with threshold market power was intended to have anti-competitive effects in any market; and/or

(b) effect, relating to the extent to which the particular conduct by the legal entity with threshold market power could reduce competition in any market.

Section 4 *International notification*[75]

Where a National Competition Agency of a Party becomes aware of conduct by an entity within its territory that:

(a) affects markets located in another Party or involves legal entities (or persons controlling legal entities) located or domiciled in another Party; and

(b) it believes that such conduct may constitute an anti-competitive abuse of market power under the laws or regulations of that other Party,

---

[73] Section 2 clarifies that the concept of threshold market power differs between parties, so each party should pick a threshold that addresses its particular objectives, as discussed in detail in Chapter 4. Section 2 identifies three common thresholds with this in mind. Section 2 also clarifies that the relevant threshold is typically determined by the extent of existing market concentration in the particular nation.

[74] Section 3 clarifies the concept of an abuse of market power and proposes that it may be assessed by reference to either purpose or effect, as discussed in detail in Chapter 4. A party may choose which of these approaches it prefers (including both approaches), although purpose is more common. Section 3 does not seek to prescribe particular purposes which may be considered anti-competitive, as each party will have its own unique approach, as discussed in Chapter 4.

[75] Section 4 reinforces the limited positive comity obligation set out in Art. 9 by specifically requiring each party to notify to any other party abuses of market power of which it becomes aware which may breach the competition laws of that other nation. In this manner, the Agreement promotes increased co-operation and more vigilant law enforcement on an international basis.

APPENDIX 457

the National Competition Agency should immediately notify the National Competition Agency of the other Party as well as the International Competition Agency.

Section 5 *No specific formulation* [76]
This Article is not intended to prescribe a particular formulation of domestic law. Rather, the domestic law of each Party should be consistent with the general principles set out in this Article.

Part Five: Regulation of Concerted Conduct [77]

Article 13   Horizontal restraints [78]

Section 1 *Anti-competitive horizontal restraints* [79]
Parties should prohibit agreements and understandings between or among actual or potential competitors to the extent that such agreements and understandings are anti-competitive.

Section 2 *Price-fixing is 'per se' anti-competitive* [80]
Agreements and understandings between or among competitors that fix prices are deemed to be anti-competitive.

---

[76] Section 5 ensures that the drafting of Art. 12 is more politically palatable by making certain that it does not prescribe a particular formulation of competition law, as discussed in Chapter 10 of this book. Section 5 also softens the impact of the obligations set out in Art. 12 by giving them binding legal effect only to the extent that a party does not have competition laws addressing abuses of market power, or to the extent that a party has competition laws which are clearly inconsistent with the principles set out in Art. 12. Again, a party may choose to bind itself via additional, more rigorous, Specific Commitments in the manner identified in Section 6 of Art. 2.

[77] Part Five of the Agreement addresses the second of the three fundamental elements of competition law, as identified in Chapters 2 and 4 of this book, namely the regulation of concerted conduct. This second fundamental element of competition is, in turn, split into two further elements, namely the regulation of horizontal restraints and the regulation of vertical restraints, as discussed in Chapters 2 and 4 of this book.

[78] Article 13 of this Agreement gives effect to the conclusions in Chapter 4 of this book regarding the regulation of concerted conduct with a horizontal dimension. These conclusions were based on an analysis of the key features of the competition laws of the APEC nations.

[79] Section 1 sets out the fundamental obligation of modern competition law that anti-competitive agreements between competitors should be prohibited, as discussed in Chapters 2 and 4 of this book.

[80] Section 2 recognises that most, if not all, parties consider that price fixing between competitors is anti-competitive. Accordingly, Section 2 acknowledges that this could be subject to a 'per se' test, where price-fixing is deemed anti-competitive. Section 3 recognises that all other forms of agreement between competitors must be assessed under a rule of reason

Section 3 Anti-competitive agreements[81]

Whether agreements or understandings are anti-competitive may be determined either by:

(a) purpose, relating to the extent to which the particular agreement or understanding was intended to have anti-competitive effects in any market; and/or

(b) effect, relating to the extent to which the particular agreement or understanding could reduce competition in any market.

Section 4 International notification[82]

Where a National Competition Agency of a Party becomes aware of an agreement or understanding between competitors that:

(a) affects markets located in another Party or involves undertakings (or persons controlling undertakings) located or domiciled in another Party; and

(b) it believes may be anti-competitive under the laws or regulations of that other Party,

the National Competition Agency should immediately notify the National Competition Agency of the other Party accordingly and the International Competition Agency.

Section 5 Authorisations and exemptions[83]

Agreements and understandings between or among competitors may not be anti-competitive if they are justifiable, or are exempted or authorised, on the basis of public policy considerations, including if

---

analysis, as discussed in Chapter 4 of this book. Section 2 therefore gives effect to the concept of 'Selective Convergence' as part of the four-point strategy identified in Chapter 13 of this book.

[81] Section 3 also clarifies that the rule of reason analysis may be assessed by reference to either purpose or effect. A party may choose which of these approaches it prefers and frequently both approaches are adopted. Section 3 does not seek to prescribe particular purposes which may be considered anti-competitive, as each party will have its own unique approach, as discussed in Chapter 4.

[82] Section 4 reinforces the limited positive comity obligation set out in Art. 9 by specifically requiring each party to notify any other party of horizontal restraints of which it becomes aware which may breach the competition laws of that other nation. In this manner, the Agreement promotes increased co-operation and more vigilant law enforcement on an international basis.

[83] Section 5 recognises that horizontal restraints may be authorised or exempted on a case-by-case basis on the basis of public policy considerations, as discussed in Chapter 5. Section 5 gives specific effect to the limited form of negative comity set out in Art. 10 by requiring parties to have regard to the effects of horizontal restraints on foreign markets when undertaking this authorisation or exemption process. Importantly, Sections 4 and 5 therefore expressly address the externalities identified in Chapter 3 of this book.

they have out-balancing pro-competitive effects. However, any public policy considerations should take into consideration the effects of the agreements or understandings on the markets of other Parties (including as notified by other Parties).

Section 6 *No specific formulation* [84]

This Article is not intended to prescribe a particular formulation of domestic law. Rather, the domestic law of each Party should be consistent with the general principles set out in this Article.

Article 14 Vertical restraints [85]

Section 1 *Anti-competitive vertical restraints* [86]

Parties should prohibit agreements and understandings between actual or potential suppliers and their actual or potential customers to the extent that such agreements and understandings are anti-competitive.

Section 2 *Anti-competitive agreements* [87]

Whether agreements or understandings are anti-competitive may be determined either by:

(a) purpose, relating to the extent to which the particular agreement or understanding was intended to have anti-competitive effects in any market; and/or

---

[84] Section 6 ensures that the drafting of Art. 13 is more politically palatable by ensuring it does not prescribe a particular formulation of competition law as discussed in Chapter 10 of this book. Section 6 also softens the impact of the obligations set out in Art. 13 by giving them binding legal effect only to the extent that a party does not have competition laws addressing horizontal restraints, or to the extent that a party has competition laws which are clearly inconsistent with the principles set out in Art. 13. Again, a party may choose to bind itself via additional, more rigorous, Specific Commitments in the manner identified in Section 6 of Art. 2.

[85] Article 14 of this Agreement gives effect to the conclusions in Chapter 4 of this Agreement regarding the regulation of concerted conduct with a vertical dimension. These conclusions were based on an analysis of the key features of the competition laws of the APEC nations.

[86] Section 1 sets out the fundamental obligation of modern competition law that anti-competitive agreements between suppliers and their customers should be prohibited, as discussed in Chapters 2 and 4 of this book.

[87] Section 2 recognises that all forms of vertical restraints should be assessed under a rule of reason analysis, as discussed in Chapter 4 of this book, given that there is no international consensus on 'per se' breaches in a vertical context. Section 2 also clarifies that the rule of reason analysis may be assessed by reference to either purpose or effect, as discussed in detail in Chapter 4. A party may choose which of these approaches it prefers and frequently both approaches are adopted. Section 2 does not seek to prescribe particular purposes which may be considered anti-competitive, as each party will have its own unique approach, as discussed in Chapter 4.

(b) effect, relating to the extent to which the particular agreement or understanding could reduce competition in any market.

Section 3 International notification[88]

Where a National Competition Agency of a Party becomes aware of an agreement or understanding between competitors that:

(a) affects markets located in another Party or involves undertakings (or persons controlling undertakings) located or domiciled in another Party; and

(b) it believes may be anti-competitive under the laws or regulations of that other Party,

the National Competition Agency should immediately notify the National Competition Agency of the other Party accordingly and the International Competition Agency.

Section 4 Authorisations and exceptions[89]

Agreements and understandings between actual or potential suppliers and their actual or potential customers may not be anti-competitive if they are justifiable, or are exempted or authorised, on the basis of public policy considerations, including if they have out-balancing pro-competitive effects. However, any public policy considerations should take into consideration the effects of the relevant agreement or understanding on the markets of other Parties (including as notified by other Parties).

Section 5 No specific formulation[90]

This Article is not intended to prescribe a particular formulation of domestic law. Rather, the domestic law of each Party should be consistent with the general principles set out in this Article.

---

[88] As with Art. 13, Section 3 reinforces the limited positive comity obligation set out in Art. 9 by specifically requiring each party to notify any other party of vertical restraints of which it becomes aware which may breach the competition laws of that other nation. In this manner, the Agreement promotes increased co-operation and more vigilant law enforcement on an international basis.

[89] As with Art. 13, Section 4 recognises that vertical restraints may be authorised or exempted on a case-by-case basis on the basis of public policy considerations. Section 4 gives specific effect to the limited form of negative comity set out in Art. 10 by requiring parties to have regard to the effects of vertical restraints on foreign markets when undertaking this authorisation or exemption process. Sections 3 and 4 expressly address the externalities identified in Chapter 3 of this book.

[90] As with Art. 13, Section 5 ensures that the drafting of Art. 14 is more politically palatable by ensuring it does not prescribe a particular formulation of competition law, as discussed in Chapter 10 of this book. Section 5 also softens the impact of the obligations set out in

Article 15 Export, import and international cartels [91]

Section 1 *Authorisation of export and import cartels* [92]

When exempting or authorising anti-competitive conduct under Articles 13 or 14 of this Agreement that is likely to have a Cross-Border Dimension, each Party must consult with each other affected Party (supervised by the International Competition Agency, if necessary) as to the likely consequences of such exemption or authorisation and provide a reasonable period of time for each consulted Party to respond with a written submission. Each Party must have due regard to the responses of the other Parties when making its exemption or authorisation decision.

Section 2 *Extent of authorisation* [93]

Any exemption or authorisation under Section 1 (including existing exemptions or authorisations of a Party as at the date this Agreement enters into force for that Party) must be no more competition-restrictive than necessary in the circumstances and must be reviewed, as if they were made afresh under Section 1, in the event of a material change in circumstances and at least every three years.

Section 3 *International cartels* [94]

Each Party will co-operate with every other Party (and the International Competition Agency) when investigating under Articles 13

Art. 14 by giving them binding legal effect only to the extent that a party does not have competition laws addressing vertical restraints, or to the extent that a party has competition laws which are clearly inconsistent with the principles set out in Art. 14. Again, a party may choose to bind itself via additional, more rigorous, Specific Commitments in the manner identified in Section 6 of Art. 2.

[91] Art. 15 is intended to address the specific issues associated with export, import and international cartels, identified in Chapter 7 of this book.

[92] Section 1 reinforces the limited negative comity obligations set out in Arts. 10, 13 and 14 by requiring each Party to consult with other affected Parties when authorising or exempting export and import cartels.

[93] Section 2 provides for such authorisations to be no more competition-restrictive than necessary in the circumstances and to be subject to periodic reviews. In this manner, the Agreement seeks to discourage the continued exemption of export and import cartels from competition laws where such exemptions are not justifiable or too broad in the circumstances, as discussed in Chapter 7 of this book.

[94] Section 3 creates a specific obligation of co-operation in relation to international investigations into international cartels, reinforcing the principle of co-operation set out in Art. 9. Section 3 also creates a specific mechanism for international enforcement activity against international cartels, although a party is not required to participate in any international enforcement activity that it believes is not reasonable or is unnecessary. Both issues were discussed in detail in Chapter 7 of this book.

or 14 of this Agreement anti-competitive conduct that has a Cross-Border Dimension and which involves legal entities domiciled or operating in two or more jurisdictions. Each Party will, on request, co-operate with every other Party in any multi-Party enforcement action which that requested Party agrees is reasonable or necessary as a result of any anti-competitive conduct with a Cross-Border Dimension that is discovered under any such investigation.

Part Six: Regulation of Market Concentration[95]

Article 16 Business concentrations with an international dimension[96]

Section 1 Business concentration
A business concentration arises where one or more legal entities (or other legal entities already controlling that legal entity, directly or indirectly) acquire, whether by purchase of securities or assets, by contract or by any other means, direct or indirect control of the whole or a substantial part of one or more other legal entities.

Section 2 International dimension[97]
A business concentration has an 'International Dimension' if it affects markets located in more than one Party, or involves legal entities (or persons controlling the legal entities involved in the transaction, either directly or indirectly) located or domiciled in more than one Party, or otherwise has a Cross-Border Dimension as defined in Article 3.

---

[95] Part Six of the Agreement addresses the third of the three fundamental elements of competition law, as identified in Chapters 2 and 4 of this book, namely the regulation of market concentration (also known as 'merger laws').

[96] As discussed in Chapter 4 of this book, a key element of any merger regime is that it defines when a relevant concentration occurs. Chapter 4 of this book identified that most, if not all, merger regimes define a concentration as occurring via either the acquisition of assets or the acquisition of shares, consistent with the two main legal mechanisms for assuming control of a business. Section 1 gives effect to that conclusion.

[97] Section 2 of this book contemplates that an international competition agreement should only apply to business concentrations with an international dimension. The concept of an 'International Dimension' in Section 2 is deliberately broader than the concept of a Cross-Border Dimension in Art. 3 so as to apply to controlling entities not directly involved in the relevant transaction that may be domiciled in other nations.

APPENDIX   463

Section 3   No specific formulation [98]
> This Article is not intended to prescribe a particular formulation of domestic law. Rather, the domestic law of each Party should be consistent with the general principles set out in this Article.

Article 17   Notification requirements [99]

Section 1   Mandatory or voluntary pre-notification [100]
> A Party may choose to require either mandatory or voluntary pre-notification to their National Competition Agency of business concentrations with an International Dimension. Parties are discouraged from relying only on post-notification.

Section 2   Notification requirements [101]
> Where a Party requires mandatory pre-notification of business concentrations with an International Dimension, the threshold requirements for such pre-notification should be set out clearly by that Party and should be publicly available.

Section 3   International notification [102]
> Where a National Competition Agency of a Party is notified of a business concentration that may have an International Dimension,

---

[98] Section 3 ensures that the drafting of Art. 16 is more politically palatable by not proscribing a particular formulation of competition law. Section 5 also softens the impact of the obligations set out in Art. 16 by giving them binding legal effect only to the extent that a party does not have merger laws, or to the extent that a party has competition laws which are clearly inconsistent with the principles set out in Art. 16. Again, a party may choose to bind itself via additional, more rigorous, Specific Commitments in the manner identified in Section 6 of Art. 2.

[99] As discussed in Chapter 4 of this book, merger regimes may differ significantly between nations. One key difference involves the distinction between mandatory and voluntary pre-notification, as discussed in Chapter 4.

[100] Section 1 discourages post-notification for the reasons discussed in Chapter 4. This should be non-controversial given that almost all nations use pre-notification rather than post-notification. Section 1 gives parties a discretion between mandatory or voluntary pre-notification.

[101] Section 2 requires that if mandatory pre-notification is selected, the threshold for notification should be clearly set out, reinforcing the Art. 6 principle of transparency.

[102] Section 3 reinforces the limited positive comity obligation set out in Art. 9, by specifically requiring any party that becomes aware of a business concentration with an International Dimension (as defined in Art. 17), to notify all other affected nations. This notification must contain sufficient information to enable these other parties to assess independently

that National Competition Agency should immediately notify the International Competition Agency and the National Competition Agency of any other Parties that it believes may be affected by that business concentration.

Section 4   *Notification to National Competition Agencies*
Subject to the confidentiality considerations set out in Section 5 of Article 6, a Party notifying another Party under Section 3 should:

(a) provide that Party with sufficient information to enable the notified Party to assess the nature of the transaction and itself approach the legal entities involved in the business concentration; and

(b) endeavour to provide any other information that it believes may be of assistance to the notified Party in the circumstances.

Section 5   *Notification to International Competition Agency*
When notifying the International Competition Agency, the Party must provide sufficient information to enable the International Competition Agency to determine whether any further Parties should be notified and to notify those other Parties in the manner contemplated by Section 4.

Article 18   Excessive market concentration [103]

Section 1   *Excessive market concentration* [104]
Parties should prohibit business concentrations with an International Dimension to the extent that such business concentrations are anti-competitive.

---

whether they need to undertake further investigations, subject to the confidentiality considerations set out in Art. 6. Where the International Competition Agency is notified, the notification must contain sufficient information to enable the International Competition Agency to check such notification and undertake its own notification if necessary.

[103] Article 18 gives effect to the conclusions in Chapter 4 of this book regarding the regulation of market concentration. These conclusions were based on an analysis of the key features of the competition laws of the APEC nations.

[104] Section 1 sets out the substantive merger regime threshold, as discussed in Chapter 4 of this book in which business concentrations with an international dimension that are anti-competitive are prohibited. The concepts of 'business concentration' and 'international dimension' are as defined in Art. 16.

Section 2 *Anti-competitive business concentrations*[105]

Whether a business concentration is anti-competitive should be determined by its:[106]

(a) purpose, relating to the extent to which the particular business concentration was intended to have anti-competitive effects in any market; and/or

(b) effect, relating to the extent to which the particular business concentration could reduce competition in any market.

Section 3 *Authorisations and exceptions*[107]

Business concentrations may not be anti-competitive if they are justifiable, or are exempted or authorised, on the basis of public policy considerations, including if they have out-balancing pro-competitive effects. However, any public policy considerations should take into account the effects of the business concentration on the markets of other Parties (including as notified by other Parties).

Section 4 *No specific formulation*[108]

This Article is not intended to prescribe a particular formulation of domestic law. Rather, the domestic law of each Party should be consistent with the general principles set out in this Article.

---

[105] The concept of 'anti-competitive' in the context of business concentrations is defined in Section 2. As discussed in detail in Chapters 2 and 4 of this book, the concept of anti-competitive conduct in the context of a merger regime is assessed indirectly, by reference to the potential for the merged entity to exercise greater market power than it was previously able to exercise. In turn, this is assessed by the likely reduction in market competition associated with the merger.

[106] Section 2 clarifies that anti-competitive conduct may be assessed by reference to either purpose or effect, as discussed in detail in Chapter 4. A party may choose which of these approaches it prefers, although the reference to effect is more common. Section 2 does not seek to prescribe particular purposes which may be considered anti-competitive, as each party will have its own unique approach, as discussed in Chapter 4.

[107] Section 3 recognises that business concentrations may be authorised or exempted on a case-by-case basis on the basis of public policy considerations, as discussed in Chapter 5. Section 4 gives specific effect to the limited form of negative comity set out in Art. 10 by requiring parties to have regard to the effects of business concentrations on foreign markets when undertaking this authorisation or exemption process. Sections 4 expressly addresses the externalities identified in Chapter 3 of this book.

[108] As with Art. 16, Section 4 ensures that the drafting of Art. 18 is more politically palatable by not prescribing a particular formulation of competition law. Section 4 also softens the impact of the obligations set out in Art. 18 by giving them binding legal effect only to the extent that a party does not have merger laws, or to the extent that a party has competition laws which are clearly inconsistent with the principles set out in Art. 18. Again, a party may choose to bind itself via additional, more rigorous, Specific Commitments in the manner identified in Section 6 of Art. 2.

Part Seven: Enforcement[109]

Article 19 Territorial and extra-territorial enforcement[110]

Section 1 *Territorial enforcement*[111]

Appropriate and proportionate sanctions should be imposed by a Party against any legal entity engaging in anti-competitive conduct in its territory within the meaning of this Agreement. Such sanctions should, where practicable, be of sufficient magnitude to deter future anti-competitive conduct, but should also be applied with regard to any mitigating factors.

Section 2 *Extraterritorial enforcement*[112]

Where a Party seeks to apply sanctions against a legal entity engaging in anti-competitive conduct in the territory of another Party, the first Party should take into account:

(a) the principles of international co-operation set out in Article 9 and should consult with the other Party with a view to determining whether the sanctions are appropriate;

(b) the need to exercise moderation and restraint as to the exercise of any such extraterritorial jurisdiction and to avoid undue encroachment on the territorial jurisdiction more properly appertaining to, or more appropriately exercisable by, the other Party; and

(c) any sanctions already imposed or likely to be imposed by the other Party.

---

[109] Part Seven of the Agreement addresses issues pertaining to the enforcement of domestic competition laws. Part Seven seeks to prescribe the appropriate manner in which domestic competition laws should be enforced, whether by governmental agencies or privately. Part Seven does not address the enforcement of the Agreement itself, which is addressed by Part Eight.

[110] Consistent with the conclusions reached in Chapter 4 of this book, Art. 19 establishes a principle that a party should apply appropriate and proportionate sanctions against anti-competitive conduct in its territory within the meaning of the Agreement.

[111] Section 1 establishes a principle that such sanctions should be of sufficient magnitude to deter future anti-competitive conduct. Section 1 also clarifies that mitigating factors should be considered when determining sanctions.

[112] Section 2 addresses situations where sanctions are imposed as a result of extraterritorial enforcement. Section 2 reinforces the approach of Art. 3 of the Agreement by again adopting of the wording from the *Barcelona Traction* case. Section 2 also specifically recognises the risk that any sanctions imposed may be inappropriate as between different jurisdictions. Accordingly, Section 2 creates an obligation to consult before imposing sanctions and also creates an obligation to avoid double jeopardy in criminal or quasi-criminal prosecutions.

Section 3 Private enforcement action [113]

Nothing in this Agreement is intended to preclude the right of a private legal entity to take enforcement action against another private legal entity by reason of that second private legal entity breaching the competition laws or regulations of any Party. However, where that enforcement action is extraterritorial in nature, Articles 3 and 19 of this Agreement may apply to require a government of a Party to enact legislation to regulate the proper exercise of extra-territorial jurisdiction in such circumstances, in accordance with Section 2, subject to domestic constitutional considerations.

Article 20 Remedies [114]

Each Party is encouraged to provide for the following remedies for anti-competitive conduct within the meaning of this Agreement, subject to the particular legal traditions and institutions of that Party:[115]

(a) injunctive relief;
(b) pecuniary penalties (whether or not including disgorgement or restitution of profits); and
(c) damages, to the extent enforcement action is possible by private legal entities under the competition laws and regulations of that Party.

---

[113] While Sections 1 and 2 address criminal and quasi-criminal administrative prosecutions by public entities, Section 3 addresses actions by private sector entities. Section 3 recognises that private sector enforcement may occur on an extraterritorial basis, leading to jurisdictional conflict. Section 3 therefore imposes an obligation on governments to enact legislation to regulate private extraterritorial enforcement in a manner consistent with Section 2. However, Section 3 also recognises that constitutional considerations in each nation may impose constraints.

[114] Consistent with the conclusions set out in Chapter 4 of this book, Art. 20 lists three key remedies that each party should provide to address anti-competitive conduct. Injunctive relief is necessary to seek the immediate cessation of the anti-competitive conduct. Pecuniary penalties are necessary to ensure that the anti-competitive conduct is penalised sufficiently that competition law acts as a deterrent to anti-competitive activity. Damages are necessary where private party enforcement is permitted in the relevant jurisdiction.

[115] However, recognising the difficulties identified with the Munich Code, as discussed in detail in Chapter 10 of this book, the list of remedies desired is considerably reduced. Furthermore, given that each jurisdiction has its own peculiarities, the requirement to provide for particular remedies is subject to the particular legal transitions and institutions of the relevant Party. As an additional qualification, recognising such peculiarities and differences, Art. 20 is expressed as a non-binding 'soft law' principle only.

Part Eight: Institutional Provisions[116]

Article 21 National Competition Agencies[117]

Section 1 *Establishment of a National Competition Agency*
Each Party to this Agreement must establish or operate at least one National Competition Agency for its territory. That National Competition Agency should comply with the principles of procedural fairness set out in Article 7 of this Agreement and should be sufficiently resourced to ensure it can give effect to the objectives of this Agreement.

Section 2 *Responsibilities of National Competition Agency*[118]
Each Party should assign clear responsibility for the application and enforcement of its domestic competition laws and regulations to its National Competition Agency. The objectives, powers and obligations of that National Competition Agency should be clearly and transparently defined and demarcated.

Section 3 *Investigative powers*
Each Party should ensure its National Competition Agency has sufficient powers to investigate anti-competitive conduct and initiate enforcement action, whether on request or at its own discretion. Such powers should include an ability to require legal entities under investigation to provide necessary evidence upon request, including appropriate sanctions for non-compliance with such a request.

---

[116] Part Eight of the Agreement sets out the institutional infrastructure supporting the Agreement. Part Eight sets out requirements both for appropriate domestic institutions in each nation and for appropriate international institutions. These institutions follow from the conclusions set out in Chapter 12 of this book.

[117] Consistent with the conclusions set out in Chapter 12 of this book, Art. 21 sets out a requirement for each Party to maintain one or more national competition agencies. This national competition agency should be sufficiently independent to meet the requirements of procedural fairness set out in Art. 7 and sufficiently resourced to promote the objectives of the Agreement. Both requirements were identified as particularly important in the discussion in Chapter 12 of this book.

[118] Sections 2 and 3 clarify that each national competition agency should be charged with the administration and enforcement of domestic competition laws in the territory of the relevant party and that it should have sufficient powers to enable it to fulfil these functions. To increase transparency and accountability, these powers should be clearly and transparently defined and demarcated. Section 3 ensures that such powers should include the ability to require persons to provide evidence on request, thereby enabling the competition agency to undertake its enforcement role effectively.

Section 4 Accountability[119]
>Each Party should maintain, or institute as soon as practicable, independent judicial, arbitral or administrative tribunals or procedures which ensure its National Competition Agency is held accountable for its decisions or actions. These processes or procedures should provide, at the request of any legal entity adversely affected by the decisions or actions of the National Competition Agency, for the prompt review of, and where justified, appropriate remedies for, administrative decisions affecting those legal entities. Where such procedures are not independent of the National Competition Agency, the Party should ensure that such procedures in fact provide for an objective and impartial review.

Section 5 Domestic constitutional issues
>The provisions of Section 4 shall not be construed to require a Party to institute tribunals or procedures where this would be inconsistent with its constitutional structure or the nature of its legal system.

Article 22 Competition Council[120]

Section 1 Competition Council
>In accordance with Article IV:8 of the Agreement Establishing the World Trade Organisation, the Council on International Competition (hereinafter referred to as the 'Competition Council') is hereby established as a body under this Plurilateral Trade Agreement. The Competition Council will operate within the institutional framework of the WTO and must keep the WTO General Council informed of its activities on a regular basis, including via annual reports.

---

[119] Section 4 sets out a requirement for each party to ensure that its competition agency is held accountable for its administrative decisions by an objective and impartial review procedure. The wording in Section 4 follows the similar wording in Art. VI:2 of the GATS. However, following the approach in Art. 20, Section 5 expressly recognises that each party may be precluded from adopting certain accountability mechanisms via its constitutional structure or the nature of its legal system.

[120] Article 22 establishes the first of the two key institutions necessary to enable the Agreement to operate effectively. The first institution is known as the Competition Council and comprises each of the parties to the Agreement. Section 1 clarifies the relationship of the Competition Council to the existing WTO institutions. Section 1 ensures that the Competition Council operates within the WTO framework and remains accountable to the WTO General Council and WTO Ministerial Conference.

470   INTERNATIONAL COMPETITION LAW

Section 2 Role of the Competition Council[121]
The Competition Council will carry out the functions assigned to it under this Agreement and will facilitate the implementation, administration and operation, and further the objectives, of this Agreement. In consultation with UNCTAD, the Council must seek to establish, within one year of its first meeting, appropriate arrangements for ongoing co-operation with UNCTAD.

Section 3 Structure of the Competition Council
The Competition Council comprises representatives of all Parties to this Agreement. It will meet as necessary, but not less than twice a year, for the purpose of affording Parties the opportunity to consult on any matters relating to this Agreement. The Council will elect its own Chairperson.

Section 4 Decision-making by the Competition Council[122]
Decisions must be made by consensus, or in the absence of consensus, by a 75% majority of the Parties (such majority including all of the initial Parties to the Agreement as at the date this Agreement enters into force). Each Party will have one vote. Where the European Communities exercise their right to vote, they shall have a number of votes equal to the number of their member States which are Members of the WTO.[123]

---

[121] Section 2 confirms that the role of the Competition Council is to further the objectives of the Agreement and oversee its operation, administration and implementation. Recognising the interests of developing countries, Section 2 requires the Competition Council to establish ongoing co-operative arrangements with UNCTAD, as discussed in Chapter 13. Section 3 clarifies the structure of the Competition Council. In particular, the Competition Council will elect its own chairperson and will meet at least twice a year.

[122] Section 4 sets out the procedures for decision-making by the Competition Council. Reflecting the tradition of consensus decision-making embodied in the WTO agreements, the preference is for decisions by the Competition Council to be made by consensus. However, recognising that the Competition Council will need to expedite decisions and the requirement for consensus could unnecessarily reduce the effectiveness of the Competition Council, an alternative voting mechanism is also utilised. Under this voting process, each party has one vote and decisions may be made by a 75% majority vote.

[123] Section 4 also requires that the 75% majority vote of the Competition Council must include affirmative votes from each of the parties to the Agreement as at the date it initially enters into force. In this manner, there are clear incentives created for as many nations as possible to become a party to this Agreement as from ratification, given that such nations will then have an effective veto over the decisions of the Competition Council. Nations that enter into the WTO Competition Agreement at a later stage will not be given this effective veto, although they will each have one vote.

Article 23 International Competition Agency[124]

Section 1   *International Competition Agency* [125]

The Competition Council must establish a subsidiary body, known as the International Competition Agency, to assist it to carry out its role and functions. The rules of procedure and terms of reference of the International Competition Agency must be agreed by the Competition Council. The International Competition Agency shall carry out such responsibilities as are assigned to it by the Competition Council.

Section 2   *Compliance role of the International Competition Agency* [126]

The International Competition Agency will monitor the operation of this Agreement and, in particular, the Parties' compliance with their obligations hereunder. The International Competition Agency may bring to the attention of the Competition Council any matter which in its opinion should be brought to the attention of the Competition Council, including any issues of non-compliance.

Section 3   *Structure and role of International Competition Agency* [127]

The International Competition Agency will be headed by a President, appointed by the Competition Council for a once-renewable term of three years. The President must be experienced in the field of international trade law and competition law. The responsibilities

---

[124] Article 23 establishes the second of the two key institutions necessary to enable the Agreement to operate effectively. The second institution is known as the International Competition Agency, being a division of the WTO Secretariat accountable directly to the Competition Council.

[125] Section 1 establishes the International Competition Agency as the operational arm of the Competition Council. The Competition Council will establish the rules and procedure and terms of reference of the International Competition Agency. As set out in Art. 24, the intention is that the International Competition Agency will comprise a division of the WTO Secretariat which is accountable to the Competition Council, given that the WTO Secretariat is charged with the responsibility for supervising all WTO agreements.

[126] Section 2 provides that the International Competition Agency is charged with the role of monitoring the operation of the Agreement and ensuring parties meet their respective obligations. The International Competition Agency may alert the Competition Council of any incidences of non-compliance, exerting greater peer pressure for greater compliance in the manner discussed in Chapter 11 of this book.

[127] Section 3 further details the structure and role of the International Competition Agency, clarifying that it is headed by a President, being a competition and trade expert, who will be appointed for a once-renewable term of three years. This potential six-year term ensures sufficient continuity of management, but the three-year renewal period ensures that the President remains accountable for his or her performance to the Competition Council.

of the President and of the staff of the International Competition Agency will be exclusively international in character. In the discharge of their duties, the President and staff of the International Competition Agency must not seek or accept instructions from any government but must remain accountable to the Competition Council and the WTO Secretariat.[128]

Section 4   *Powers and privileges of International Competition Agency*
The International Competition Agency and its staff will enjoy in the territory of each of the Parties such privileges and immunities as are necessary for the exercise of their functions. The International Competition Agency will have such legal capacity in the territory of each of the Parties as may be necessary for the exercise of its functions and fulfilment of its purposes. In carrying out its functions, the International Competition Agency may consult with and seek information from any source it deems appropriate.

Article 24   Relationship with existing institutions[129]

Section 1   *WTO Secretariat*[130]
This Agreement will be serviced by the WTO Secretariat with assistance from the Competition Council and the International Competition Agency. With the consent of the WTO Ministerial Conference, the International Competition Agency will comprise part of the WTO Secretariat and must work with the WTO Secretariat on the implementation of this Agreement.

Section 2   *Co-operation with UNCTAD and OECD*[131]
The International Competition Agency will make appropriate arrangements for consultation and co-operation with the United

---

[128] Section 3 also clarifies that the International Competition Agency is not accountable to any government, but is rather accountable to the Competition Council. Section 4 clarifies that the International Competition Agency has legal capacity in each nation that is party to the Agreement and that the President and staff of the International Competition Agency enjoy diplomatic immunities and privileges.

[129] Article 24 addresses a variety of issues associated with the relationship between the Competition Council and International Competition Agency and other existing international institutions.

[130] Section 1, for example, clarifies that the WTO Secretariat continues to have the primary obligation of servicing the Agreement, as required by the WTO Final Act, although it will be assisted by the International Competition Agency. The intention, as noted above, is that the International Competition Agency will comprise part of the WTO Secretariat.

[131] Section 2 imposes an express obligation on the International Competition Agency to consult and co-operate with UNCTAD and the OECD, reflecting the conclusions in

Nations and its specialised agencies (including UNCTAD) as well as any other appropriate inter-governmental organisations concerned with competition law and policy (including the OECD). Such consultation and co-operation will include the opportunity for such agencies and organisations to participate in the ongoing development of this Agreement and to assist in co-ordinating technical assistance contemplated by this Agreement.

Section 3 Trade Policy Review Mechanism[132]

The Parties will seek support from the WTO Ministerial Conference for the extension of the existing WTO Trade Policy Review Mechanism to encompass competition law and policy in respect of Parties to this Agreement. The Competition Council, via the International Competition Agency, will offer to assist the WTO Secretariat with any Trade Policy Review of any Party to the extent it addresses competition law and policy.

Article 25 Dispute resolution[133]

Section 1 Consultation and negotiation[134]

Each Party shall accord sympathetic consideration to, and shall afford adequate opportunity for, consultation regarding such representations as may be made by any other Party with respect to any matter affecting the operation of this Agreement. The provisions of Article XXII of GATT 1994, as elaborated and applied by the WTO Dispute Settlement Understanding, shall apply to such consultations under this Agreement.

Chapters 6 and 13 of this book. Section 2 also enables UNCTAD and the OECD to be given the opportunity to participate in the ongoing development of the Agreement and the co-ordination of technical assistance provided under it.

[132] Section 3 gives effect to the conclusions in Chapter 12 of this Agreement relating to the potential for the existing trade policy review mechanism in the WTO to be expanded to encompass competition policy. Section 3 clarifies that the International Competition Agency would assist the WTO Secretariat with its responsibilities in undertaking such a trade policy review to the extent it addressed issues of competition law and policy.

[133] Consistent with the conclusions set out in Chapter 12 of this book, Art. 23 enables all disputes arising under the Agreement to be resolved under the WTO's existing Dispute Settlement Understanding. As discussed in detail in Chapter 12, the WTO Dispute Settlement Body, as established by the Dispute Settlement Understanding, would be the optimal institutional structure for resolution of such disputes.

[134] Section 1 creates an obligation on the Parties to enter into consultation and negotiations before seeking dispute settlement before the Dispute Settlement Body. This consultation procedure is formalised by the WTO Dispute Settlement Understanding, hence Section 1 cross-references the Dispute Settlement Understanding.

Section 2 Good offices and mediation[135]

The WTO Dispute Settlement Body or the International Competition Agency may, at the request of a Party, consult with any Party or Parties in respect of any matter for which it has not been possible to find a satisfactory solution through consultation under Section 1. Each Party shall accord sympathetic consideration to, and shall afford adequate opportunity for, such consultation. The WTO Dispute Settlement Understanding shall apply to such consultations.

Section 3 Recourse to WTO Dispute Settlement Understanding[136]

If any Party should consider that any other Party has failed to carry out its obligations or specific commitments under this Agreement, it may, with a view to reaching a mutually satisfactory resolution of the matter, have recourse to the WTO Dispute Settlement Understanding.

Section 4 Enforcement[137]

If the WTO Dispute Settlement Body considers that the circumstances are serious enough to justify such action, it may authorise a Party or Parties to suspend the application to any other Party or Parties of obligations and Specific Commitments under this Agreement or any other WTO agreement in accordance with Article 22 of the WTO Dispute Settlement Understanding.

---

[135] Section 2 enables a Party to seek 'good offices' (i.e. informal intermediary mediation) by the WTO Dispute Settlement Body as necessary. Generally, this may be necessary if the parties sought assistance from a third party to break any deadlock. Sections 1 and 2 therefore give effect to the hierarchy of dispute settlement discussed in Chapter 12 of this book. The WTO Dispute Settlement Understanding itself also creates a clear hierarchy for the settlement of disputes which is cross-referenced by Sections 1 and 2.

[136] Section 3 applies whenever any party breaches its binding 'hard law' obligations under the WTO competition agreement. In such circumstances, Section 3 enables any other party to commence enforcement action before the WTO Dispute Settlement Body whether or not the enforcing party has suffered any damage or loss. A similar procedure, for example, is applied by the GATS and clarifies the scope for enforcement action in the event of a breach of the Agreement by supplementing the wording in Section 5 relating to nullification or impairment.

[137] Section 4 clarifies that, where a breach has occurred under Section 3, the WTO Dispute Settlement Body may impose sanctions in accordance with section 22 of the Dispute Settlement Understanding. Section 22 enables the compensation to be granted or the suspension of concessions as between nations, as discussed in detail in Chapter 12.

APPENDIX 475

Section 5 Nullification or impairment[138]

The provisions of Article XXIII of GATT 1994, as elaborated and applied by the WTO Dispute Settlement Understanding, shall apply to the settlement of disputes under this Agreement *mutatis mutandis* if any Party considers that any benefit accruing to it directly or indirectly under this Agreement (including any benefit that could reasonably have expected to accrue to that Party under a Specific Commitment of another Party) is being nullified or impaired or that the attainment of any objective of this Agreement is being impeded.

Section 6 Consequences of nullification or impairment[139]

If the WTO Dispute Settlement Body determines that a benefit has been nullified or impaired, or that the attainment of any objective of this Agreement is being impeded, then the Party affected shall be entitled to a mutually satisfactory adjustment, which may include the modification or withdrawal of the measure. In the event an agreement cannot be reached between the Parties concerned, Art. 22 of the WTO Dispute Settlement Understanding shall apply.

---

[138] Section 5 applies the traditional GATT concept of nullification or impairment to the WTO Competition Agreement, as discussed in detail in Chapter 12. This concept would enable a party to seek adjudication by the WTO Dispute Settlement Body if it has suffered the nullification or impairment of a benefit accruing to it under the Agreement, or if any other objective of the Agreement were being impeded. The tripartite application of the nullification and impairment procedure was discussed in detail in Chapter 12, together with a discussion of the different procedural consequences of each of these three distinct applications (i.e. violation complaints, non-violation complaints and situation complaints).

[139] As discussed in Chapter 12, a *violation complaint* refers to a party failing to carry out its obligations under the Agreement. A *non-violation complaint* refers to a party applying a measure, such as enacting legislation, which has the effect of nullifying or impairing any benefit of another nation, or impeding any objective of the Agreement. Non-violation complaints therefore create a broader range of enforcement activity, but have associated stricter evidential requirements. *Situation complaints* enable enforcement on the basis of the existence of any situation which nullifies or impairs a benefit or a party or which impedes any objective of the Agreement. Situation complaints therefore, in some circumstances, may enable enforcement action to be taken on the basis of a breach of a 'soft law' principle. However, as discussed in Chapter 12, such situation complaints are subject to a veto by any party of the relevant WTO Panel findings at the adoption stage. In this manner, a WTO Panel investigation would be likely to have only moral force.

Part Nine: Developing and Least Developed Countries[140]

Article 26 Special and differential treatment[141]

Section 1 Differential and more favourable treatment[142]

Each developed country Party shall provide differential and more favourable treatment to developing and least developed country Parties to this Agreement, through the following provisions of Part Nine of this Agreement. The Competition Council shall examine periodically the special and differential treatment granted to developing and least developed country Parties by this Agreement with a view to encouraging greater membership of, and compliance with, the provisions of this Agreement.

Section 2 Obligations on developed country Parties[143]

Parties should endeavour to give particular attention to the provisions of this Agreement concerning developing and least developed

---

[140] Part Nine of the Agreement sets out specific concessions for developing countries and least developed nations, consistent with the conclusions reached in Chapter 13 of this book. Such concessions would be necessary to solicit the support of developing and least developed countries to the WTO Competition Agreement given that the Agreement could only be adopted by a consensus decision of the WTO Ministerial Conference, as discussed in Chapter 13 (even though such nations may not seek to become members to the Agreement given that the Agreement would only have plurilateral application).

[141] In accordance with the conclusions in Chapter 13 of this book, Art. 26 sets out a range of specific concessions for developing and least developed countries. The intention of these concessions is to recognise the different circumstances of these nations and also encourage them to support and potentially enter into the Agreement. The support of developing and least developed countries would be critical to the success of the Agreement for reasons discussed in detail in Chapter 13.

[142] Section 1 sets out the principle that each developed nation must provide differential and more favourable treatment to developing and least developed countries in the Agreement in accordance with the provisions of Part Nine of the Agreement. The Competition Council will periodically review this special and differential treatment with a view to encouraging developing and least developed countries to enter into the Agreement and achieve compliance with it. Section 6 clarifies that least developed countries should be given special priority given their particular development needs.

[143] Section 2 sets out a substantive obligation that developed nations should take into account the needs of developing and least developed countries when developed nations implement the Agreement. Section 2 creates two particular 'soft law' non-binding obligations on developed nations. First, developed nations should have regard to the interests of developing and least developed countries when assessing the anti-competitive conduct with a Cross-Border Dimension or International Dimension. In this manner, this mechanism would assist developing and least developed countries to enforce their competition laws given that developed nations would be more likely to alert them to any anti-competitive conduct that was in breach of their competition laws. Secondly, developed

country Parties' rights and obligations and should endeavour to take into account the special development needs of developing and least developed country Parties in the implementation of this Agreement. In particular, Parties should endeavour to:

(a) have specific regard to the interests of developing and least developed country Parties when assessing the effects of anti-competitive conduct with a Cross-Border Dimension or International Dimension under Parts Four to Six of this Agreement; and

(b) minimise exemptions or authorisations for anti-competitive conduct under Parts Five and Six of this Agreement that would have a disproportionate adverse impact on developing or least developed country Parties.

Section 3 *Rights of developing and least developed country Parties*[144]

When providing exemptions or authorisations for anti-competitive conduct under Parts Five and Six of this Agreement, developing and least developed country Parties are permitted to have special regard to their particular development needs.

Section 4 *'Opt out' mechanism*[145]

Any developing or least-developed country Party may, with the consent of the Competition Council, choose not to be bound by the whole or any part of Articles 3 to 21 of this Agreement ('Opt Out'). When determining whether to give such consent the Competition Council shall have specific regard to the particular needs of

---

nations should seek to minimise authorisations or exemptions from their competition laws that would have a disproportionate adverse impact on developing or least developed countries.

[144] Section 3 creates an associated right of developing and least developed countries to provide authorisations or exemptions from their competition laws where such authorisations or exemptions are necessary given their particular development needs. Again, this is a key concession currently sought by developing and least developed countries in relation to the Agreement, as discussed in Chapter 13.

[145] Section 4 creates an 'opt out' mechanism for developing and least developed countries which would enable them, with the consent of the Competition Council, to opt out from certain substantive obligations in the Agreement. The intention is to provide greater flexibility for transitional provisions for developing countries, while encouraging such nations to enter into the Agreement by providing a means to address particular difficulties they may have achieving compliance with particular obligations. The Competition Council would have discretion to determine the appropriateness of the exemptions in each case, with particular regard to the particular needs of the relevant party and the significance of the particular obligation in question. These 'opt outs' would be recorded in the Schedule of Specific Commitments for the relevant nation.

the relevant Party and the significance of the particular Article in question. The Opt Out for any Party shall be recorded in that Party's Schedule of Specific Commitments.

Section 5   *Transitional provisions*[146]

The Competition Council should provide developing and least developed country Parties with an appropriate transitional period for the implementation of any obligations under this Agreement. Such transitional arrangements should take into consideration the special needs of developing and least developed country Parties with a view to providing such Parties with sufficient flexibility to address their particular development needs.

Section 6   *Special priority to least developed country Parties*

Special priority shall be given to least developed country Parties in the implementation of Article 24. Particular account shall be taken of the serious difficulty of least developed country Parties in implementing, administering and enforcing competition law and policy in view of their special economic situation and their special development, trade and financial needs.

Article 27   Technical assistance[147]

Section 1   *Co-ordination of technical assistance*[148]

General technical assistance to developing and least developed country Parties on competition law and policy will be provided on request,

---

[146] In conjunction with Section 4, Section 5 creates an obligation on the Competition Council to provide developing and least-developed countries with an appropriate transitional period for the implementation of the obligations of the Agreement. These transitional arrangements must take into consideration the particular needs of developing and least developed countries. The intention is that Section 5 would interact with Section 4 to enable the 'opt out' mechanism to be used as a basis for the transitional arrangements.

[147] Consistent with the conclusions in Chapter 13 of this book, Art. 26 creates a regime for the provision of technical assistance to developing and least developed countries. Such technical assistance is necessary to enable developing and least developed countries to build sufficient competition law expertise and capability to meet their obligations under the Agreement. Such technical assistance may encourage developing and least developed countries to enter into the Agreement.

[148] Section 1 confirms that such technical assistance will be co-ordinated at the multilateral level by the WTO Secretariat, assisted by the Competition Council and International Competition Agency. Section 4 confirms that in providing technical assistance, priority must be given to least developed countries, recognising their special needs.

and co-ordinated at the multilateral level by the WTO Secretariat, assisted by the Competition Council and International Competition Agency.

Section 2 *Role of developed country Parties* [149]

Developed country Parties to this Agreement (being Parties that are not developing or least developed countries) will assist the WTO Secretariat, Competition Council and International Competition Agency in providing the technical assistance contemplated by Section 1. In particular, developed country Parties will assist in devising and implementing programmes of technical assistance which may include, inter alia, training of personnel, assistance in preparing implementation measures, access to sources of information regarding competition law and policy, and advice on the application of the provisions of this Agreement.

Section 3 *Specific advice on request* [150]

Developed country Parties shall, if requested, advise developing and least developing country Parties, on:

(a) the preparation and implementation of domestic competition laws and regulations, and associated procedures and guidelines;
(b) the establishment of effective National Competition Agencies; and
(c) compliance with the obligations set out in this Agreement,

and shall encourage their National Competition Agencies to do likewise.

Section 4 *Priority to the needs of least developed countries*

In providing advice and technical assistance under Sections 1 to 3, the Competition Council, International Competition Agency and each Party shall give priority to the needs of the least developed country Parties.

---

[149] Section 2 creates a specific obligation on developed nations to assist in the provision of such technical assistance. In particular, developed country members must assist in devising and implementing technical assistance programmes.

[150] Section 3 creates an additional obligation on developed countries to provide certain specific forms of technical assistance on competition issues to developing and least developed countries on request. In both cases, these specific obligations are intended to facilitate greater technical assistance and hence the greater likelihood of compliance by developing and least developed countries with the provisions of the Agreement.

Part Ten: Development of the Agreement[151]

Article 28 Annual review and regular negotiations [152]

The Competition Council shall review annually the implementation and operation of this Agreement taking into account the objectives thereof and with a view to promoting the further development of this Agreement. Not later than the end of the third year from the entry into force of this Agreement and periodically thereafter, the Parties shall undertake further negotiations, with a view to broadening and improving this Agreement and its implementation and operation.

Article 29 Amendments [153]

The Parties may amend this Agreement having regard, inter alia, to the experience gained in its implementation. Any amendment to this Agreement, once the Parties have concurred in accordance with the procedures established by the Competition Council, shall not enter into force for any Party until it has been accepted by such Party.

Article 30 Consideration of competition policy in the WTO [154]

The Competition Council shall recommend to the WTO Ministerial Conference and/or WTO General Council on an annual basis any

---

[151] Part Ten sets out various requirements relating to the further development of the Agreement. Importantly, such further development includes the potential for suggesting amendments to other WTO agreements with a view to further reconciling international trade law with international competition law.

[152] Article 28 sets out a requirement for the parties to meet from time to time to review the implementation of the Agreement and to consider its further development. Art. 28 reflects the likely desire of the parties to the Agreement to ensure that the Agreement evolves over time to reflect developments in competition law and to include increasingly substantive and far-reaching obligations at the international level. Article 28 also creates an obligation after the third year for the parties to enter into negotiations relating to the broadening and improving of the Agreement, for similar reasons.

[153] Article 27 sets out the procedure for amending the Agreement. In accordance with usual practice, the consent of all parties would be required before the amendment takes effect. The Competition Council would determine the procedure to be followed for such amendments.

[154] Article 30 creates a specific obligation on the Competition Council to recommend to the WTO Ministerial Conference or WTO General Council any amendments necessary to other WTO agreements necessary to ensure greater consistency between those agreements

amendments necessary to other WTO agreements to ensure greater consistency between those other WTO agreements and the objectives and principles of this Agreement.[155]

Part Eleven: Final Provisions[156]

Article 31 Withdrawal and non-application[157]

Section 1 *Withdrawal from this Agreement*
Any Party may withdraw from this Agreement. Such withdrawal shall take effect upon the expiration of sixty days from the date on which written notice of such withdrawal is received by the Director-General of the WTO. Any Party may, upon receiving such notification, request an immediate meeting of the Competition Council.

Section 2 *Withdrawal from the WTO*
If a Party to this Agreement ceases to be a Member of the WTO, it shall cease to be a Party to this Agreement with effect from the same date.

Section 3 *Inter-Party non-application of this Agreement*
This Agreement shall not apply as between any two Parties if either of the Parties, at the time of accepting or accedeing to this Agreement, does not consent to such application.

---

and the objectives and principles of the WTO Competition Agreement. These recommendations must be made on an annual basis. Given that the WTO Ministerial Conference does not meet annually, the recommendation would be made to the WTO General Council in those years in which the WTO Ministerial Conference did not meet.

[155] Article 30 is intended to create a procedure for investigating further amendments to WTO agreements to ensure they became more consistent with the objectives of promoting international competition. Article 30 has no binding effect on the WTO Ministerial Conference, hence it is essentially a mechanism for stimulating greater debate at the international level regarding the appropriateness of the drafting of certain existing WTO provisions with regard to their adverse impact on international competition. Article 30 is intended to complement Art. 11 (market contestability) and Art. 4 (objectives).

[156] Part Eleven sets out miscellaneous provisions relating to the Agreement, including provisions relating to withdrawal and non-application, and provisions relating to deposit and registration.

[157] Article 31 sets out provisions relating to withdrawal from the Agreement and the consequences of a party not remaining a member of the WTO. These provisions are relatively standard within the various WTO agreements. Any party may call a meeting of the Competition Council to discuss the withdrawal of the party from the Agreement and any implications it may have for the future of the Agreement and the remaining parties, although such an impact would be unlikely to be significant in the context of the Agreement unless a large number of parties simultaneously withdrew.

Article 32 Deposit and registration[158]

Section 1 Deposit

This Agreement shall be deposited with the Director-General of the WTO, who shall promptly furnish to each Party a certified true copy of this Agreement and of each amendment thereto pursuant to Article 29, and a notification of each acceptance thereof or accession thereto pursuant to Article 1 and of each withdrawal pursuant to Article 31.

Section 2 Registration

This Agreement shall be registered in accordance with the provisions of Article 102 of the Charter of the United Nations.

Article 33 Miscellaneous

The Appendices and Annexes to this Agreement constitute an integral part thereof.

---

[158] Article 32 sets out standard procedures relating to the record-keeping role of the WTO Director-General. The requirement of registration under Article 102 of the United Nations Charter is necessary to enable the Agreement to be recognised by the United Nations and its entities. Article 33 and the Execution provisions are standard.

INDEX

act of state doctrine, 215, 241, 251, 254, 257
administration of competition, 100–2, 104
agricultural producer associations, 99
agriculture, 403–5, 408
Airbus, 51, 52, 53
allocative efficiency, 12, 18, 21
anti-competitive agreements
  APEC countries, 93–7
  collusion, 20, 93, 233
  EU legislation, 126
  evidence, 93
  exclusive effects, 94
  gentlemen's agreements, 93
  horizontal agreements, 94–5, 347
  international trade perspective, 178
  restraint of trade test, 95
  substantial lessening of competition, 95
  vertical agreements and restraints, 96–7, 208
anti-competitive behaviour
  APEC Principles, 124
  cross-border competition laws, 43–51, 201–12, 217
  cross-border inter-firm trade, 38–40
  cross-border intra-firm trade, 42
  cross-border strategic alliances, 42
  domestic conduct, 187–8, 203–12
  governmental trade measures. *See* domestic trade measures
  intellectual property, 190
  international conduct, 187, 188, 212–17
  international trade, effects on, 185, 187–91

Kodak-Fuji Film case, 191–201, 204, 211, 428
  private behaviour and WTO, 189–91, 196, 201, 217–21
  special and differential treatment, 415
  telecommunications, 190
Anti-dumping Agreement
  Anti-dumping Code, 263, 367–8
  and competition law investigations, 281–2
  and developing countries, 414
  discretion, 271, 282
  introduction of competition principles into, 279–83, 284
  market definition, 282
  market power thresholds, 280–1
  non-discrimination, 324
  origins, 263–4
  public interest test, 281
  reform proposals, 280–3
anti-dumping law
  See also Anti-dumping Agreement
  abuses, 270
  application, 268
  Australia–New Zealand CER, 273–6
  critique of competition law approach, 276
  discriminatory treatment, 229, 267–8
  and distributional fairness, 264, 266–9, 283
  and economic efficiency, 264–6
  GATT provisions, 229, 262–3, 267–8
  inconsistencies, 270–1
  or international competition law, 271–83

anti-dumping law (*cont.*)
  modification, 347, 367–8, 429
  origins, 261–4, 283
  procedural criticisms, 269–71
  remedial mechanism, 268
  structural effects, 267
  US position and practice, 269–71, 400
  vested interests, 269–70, 276
anti-monopoly laws
  APEC countries, 85, 89–92
  behavioural thresholds, 90
  common concept, 78
  conduct-oriented provisions, 91–2
  culpability-oriented provisions, 92
  EU legislation, 126
  market dominance test, 91
  meaning, 16
  mechanism, 16–19
  merger control, 88
  monopolisation test, 91
  result-oriented provisions, 92
  standardisation, 92
  structural thresholds, 90
  substantial degree of market power, 91
  threshold of dominance, 90–1
  and WTO, 162
Asia–Pacific Economic Community (APEC)
  anti-competitive agreements, 93–7
  anti-monopoly laws, 85, 89–92
  competition laws, 72–6
  Competition Principles, 123–4, 140, 318
  conduct-oriented approaches, 80
  development, 72
  differences in competition laws, 76, 424–5
  diversity, 72, 124–5
  enforcement agencies, 100–2
  enforcement of competition, 102–3
  exemptions from competition laws, 97–100
  institutional influences, 81
  macro issues, 76–9
  members, 71
  merger control, 84–9

  merger notifications, 85–7
  merger thresholds, 87–8
  methodology and structures of competition laws, 78–9
  micro issues, 79–84
  nations with competition laws, 74–6
  nations without competition laws, 73–4
  objectives of competition, 77
  origins, 72, 123
  plurilateral model, 72, 122–4, 426
  public interest cartels, 98–9
  remedies, 102–3
  result-oriented approaches, 80
  sectorial exemptions, 99
  similarities of competition laws, 75, 424–5
  state entity exemptions, 98
  vertical restraints, 96–7
Australia
  anti-competitive agreements, 95
  anti-dumping law, 261
  anti-monopoly laws, 91, 92
  ANZ Agreement 1988, 118–20
  Australia–New Zealand CER 1983, 273–6
  bilateral agreements, 109, 115, 117, 118–20
  blocking legislation, 58–9, 67
  conduct-oriented approach, 80
  co-operation agreements, 141
  cost of regulation, 31
  effects doctrine, 65
  extraterritorial jurisdiction, 64–5
  Geneva Ministerial, 401
  Hilmer reforms, 32
  merger control, 86, 87, 88, 89, 351
  recognition of New Zealand procedures, 381
  shipping exemptions, 99
  trans-Tasman provisions, 118–20, 274
  Uranium litigation, 56–7, 58–9
  vertical restraints, 97
Austria, 216
automobiles, 211, 243–4, 248

Bain, J., 180
Barshevsky, Charleen, 210

Basel Accord, 361
Baumol, William, 180–1
behavioural regulation, 16
Belgium, 65, 151
benefits of competition
 distributional fairness, 24
 economic efficiency, 271–83
 economic growth, 20–3
 economic welfare, 15–20
 empirical evidence, 31–3
 enhanced dynamic efficiency, 20–3
 enhanced static efficiency, 15–20
 generally, 7–33
 market efficiency, 8–15
 v other government policies, 28–33
Bhagwati, J., 391
bilateral agreements
 1st generation agreements, 107–10
 2nd generation agreements, 110–13
 3rd generation agreements, 113–18
 4th generation agreements, 118–20
 assessment, 139
 building on, 417–9
 comity principle, 110–12, 320–1
 and competition, 2
 and confidential information, 112–13, 114–15, 121–2
 co-operation, 320–1
 function, 141
 generally, 107–22
 limitations, 120–2
 mutual legal assistance treaties, 113–18
blocking statutes
 and Laker litigation, 59–61
 and Uranium litigation, 58–9
Boeing/McDonnell Douglas merger, 51–3, 115, 424
boycotts, 58, 97, 187, 233–4
Brazil, 110, 408
Bretton Woods order, 150
British Airways, 60
Brittan, Leon, 135, 313
Brunei, 73
building block theory, 128–9
bundling, 187
Bush, George W., 53

Cairns Group, 404
Canada
 anti-competitive agreements, 95
 anti-dumping law, 261
 anti-monopoly laws, 91, 92
 bilateral agreements, 109, 117, 273
 Canadian Dairy case, 255
 Canadian Salmon case, 235
 competition law, 75
 cost of regulation, 31
 effects doctrine, 65
 extraterritorial jurisdiction, 65
 GATT negotiations, 155
 Geneva Ministerial, 401
 merger control, 86, 87, 89
 MLAT with US, 114, 115
 objectives of competition, 316
 sport exemption, 99
 tripartite agreement, 141
 Uranium litigation, 57, 58–9
Cancún Ministerial 2003, 2, 407–11
capital accumulation, and competition, 21–3
capital markets, globalisation, 35
cartels
 cross-border trade
 depression cartels, 98
 and developing countries, 415
 export cartels, 98, 228, 232–6, 245, 246
 harmonisation of laws, 347
 import cartels, 98, 203–5
 ineffective enforcement of rules, 205–8
 international cartels, 212
 and merger control, 85
 OECD Recommendation, 134–5
 OPEC oil cartel, 62, 205, 212
 public interest cartels, 98–9
 rationalisation cartels, 98
 Uranium cartel, 56–9
 and voluntary import expansions, 249
 and WTO, 162
Caves, R. E., 20
CEEC countries, bilateral agreements, 127
chaebol, 238

Charnovitz, S., 390
Chicago School, 16
Chile, 85, 87, 92, 98, 273
China
   anti-monopoly laws, 91, 92
   competition agency, 102
   competition laws, 74, 349
   foreign ownership regulation, 42
   lack of merger control, 85
   objectives of competition, 316
Clinton, Bill, 52, 114–15
co-regulation, 364–5, 431
collective sanctions, 374
collusion, 20, 93, 233
comity
   bilateral agreements, 110–12, 320–1
   and extraterritorial jurisdiction, 63, 68
   mitigation of disputes, 380
   negative comity, 110
   positive comity, 112, 115, 117–18
comparative advantage theory, 170–1
competition. *See* benefits of competition; competition policies; domestic competition laws; international competition law
competition agencies, 100–2
competition policies
   deregulation, 29–30, 172, 326
   elements, 29–30
   empirical evidence, 31–3
   function, 28–33
   meaning, 28
compliance
   coercive techniques, 371–6
   domestic enforcement agencies, 100–2, 104
   firms supervised by firms, 375–6
   firms supervised by governments, 375
   firms supervised supra-nationally, 373–4
   governments supervised by firms, 375
   governments supervised supra-nationally, 371–3
   institutional basis, 371–7, 431

   inter-governmental coercion, 374–5
   mobilisation of shame, 376–7
   Munich Code, 305, 309–11, 372
   non-coercive techniques, 376–7
   positive compliance, 376
   retaliation, 156, 211–12, 233–4, 374–5
   trade sanctions, 211–12, 374–5, 389–93
comprehensiveness principle, 326–7
concerted conduct laws
   See also anti-competitive agreements
   APEC countries, 93–7
   common concept, 78
   exemptions, 203–5
   meaning, 16, 93
   mechanism, 19–20
   standardisation, 95
conduct-oriented approaches, 80
confidential information
   and bilateral agreements, 112–13, 114–15, 121–2
   and competition law, 329, 400
conflict of laws, and United States, 63
consensual approaches, 138–9, 295, 344, 396–8
consumer-consumer equity, 26
consumer surplus, 10, 11, 17, 21
consumers, and competition, 9–10
contestability theory, 79, 179–83, 185, 428
convergence of competition laws
   harmonisation-convergence continuum, 337–9
   meaning, 338–9
   optimal level, 345–7
   procedural convergence, 381–2
   selective convergence, 336–7, 369, 417, 419, 431
co-operation
   agreements, 141
   APEC countries, 124
   and competition, 19–20
   v extra-territoriality, 67
   non-co-operative approaches, 53–69
   OECD Recommendation, 134, 320

INDEX

principle of international
   competition law, 319–21
  procedural disputes, 381–2
cost-benefit analysis, 12
cumulative causation, 21–3
customary international law, 54, 131
customs unions, 279–80

Daishowa case, 233–4
'dango' bid-rigging, 205–8
Darcy v. *Allen*, 74
Darwinism, 21
Denmark, 58, 65
deregulation, and competition, 29–30, 172, 326
developing countries
  Cancún Ministerial, 408
  Doha Ministerial, 407
  fair trade, 169
  LDCs, 130–3, 135, 141, 402
  meaning, 413
  opt outs, 416
  recognition of diversity, 420–1
  special and differential treatment, 169, 413–15
  technical assistance, 415, 416
  transitional periods, 414–15, 416
  and WTO competition agreement, 412, 413–16
  and WTO process, 404, 408
discovery
  blocking statutes, 58
  extraterritorial application, 66–7
  global fishing expeditions, 67
dispute settlement
  DSB role, 383–9, 394, 431–2
  GATT, 383–4
  institutions, 383–9
  jurisdictional disputes, 378, 380–1, 387–9
  mitigation, institutions, 378–83
  mitigation mechanisms, 380–3
  nature of international competition disputes, 378–80
  procedural disputes, 378–9, 381–2, 386–7
  substantive disputes, 379–80, 382, 385–6

  and trade sanctions, 389–93
  UNCTAD Code, 131
  WTO. *See* WTO disputes
distributional fairness
  and anti-dumping, 264, 266–9, 283
  APEC policies, 77
  and competition, 271
  v economic efficiency, 316
  objective, 24, 168–9, 315–16, 317–18
diversity, recognition, 342–3, 417, 420–1
Doha Ministerial 2001, 2, 405–7
domestic competition laws
  See also over-regulation; under-regulation
  APEC, 72–6
  commonalities, 71–5, 105, 424–5
  and competition policies, 29
  compliance, APEC countries, 102–3
  conduct-oriented approaches, 80
  convergence. *See* convergence of competition laws
  cross-border effectiveness, 201–12, 217
  and 'dango' bid-rigging, 205–8
  distributional fairness objective, 24, 77, 271
  and domestic trade measures, 227, 229–30
  enforcement agencies, 104
  exemptions. *See* exemptions from competition laws
  and export cartels, 235–6
  extraterritoriality. *See* extraterritorial jurisdiction
  harmonisation. *See* harmonisation of domestic laws
  and Havana Charter, 152
  inadequate laws, 202, 208–12, 230
  ineffective enforcement, 202, 205–8, 230
  institutional conditions, 81, 103
  and international cartels, 214–17
  loopholes, 202, 429
  macro issues, 76–9
  methodology, 15–20, 78–9, 104
  micro issues, 79–84

488 INDEX

domestic competition laws (*cont.*)
  minimum standards approach, 348–55
  national self-interests, 44, 47–8, 121, 202
  objectives, 77, 104
  v other government policies, 28–33
  and public procurement, 253
  rationale, 8–24
  result-oriented approaches, 80
  scope, 226
  tensions between objectives, 26–8, 316
  and trade-oriented industrial policies, 239
  and voluntary export restraints, 245–6
  and voluntary import expansions, 250
domestic conduct, 187–8, 203–12
domestic trade measures
  categories, 226–7
  v domestic competition laws, 229–30, 235–6, 239, 245–6, 250
  domestic measures, 225, 226, 232–40
  effect on international competition, 224–5
  export cartels, 232–6, 245, 246
  export promotion policies, 238
  government procurement, 251–4
  governmental commercial activities, 225, 226, 227, 230, 251–7
  import substitution policies, 237–8
  and international competition law, 366
  international competition loopholes, 226–30, 428
  international measures, 225, 226, 241–51
  and international trade law, 227–9
  state trading enterprises, 254–7
  trade-oriented industrial policies, 237–40
  voluntary export restraints, 229, 241–6, 347, 367, 368
  voluntary import expansions, 246–51, 347, 367, 368
Dore, R., 209

due process, 330–4
dumping
  See also anti-dumping law
  and competition law, 276–9
  forms, 264
  international price discrimination, 264–5
  meaning, 261
  predatory dumping, 265
  predatory pricing, 277–9
  pricing below cost, 265
dynamic efficiency, 13, 20–3

economic efficiency
  allocative efficiency, 12, 18, 21
  and anti-dumping, 264–6
  and competition, 13–15, 271–83
  concept, 11–13
  v distributional fairness, 26–8, 316
  dynamic efficiency, 13, 20–3
  Kaldor-Hicks efficiency improvement, 12–15, 175, 392
  objective, 167–8, 317
  Pareto efficiency, 12, 172, 175
  productive efficiency, 13
  static efficiency, 15–20
effects doctrine, 61–4, 68, 212
energy, international regulation, 228
enforcement. *See* compliance
entry barriers, 79, 179–83
environmental protection, 169
equity
  and concerted conduct, 93
  consumer-consumer equity, 26
  distributional fairness. *See* distributional fairness
  fair trade, 169
  producer-consumer equity, 26
  producer-producer equity, 26
  social choice theory, 24–8
  social justice, 24–8
European Bank for Reconstruction and Development, 23
European Union
  approach to international competition, 412
  bilateral agreements, 110, 115–17, 127, 139

Boeing/McDonnell Douglas merger, 51–3, 115
Cancún Ministerial, 408, 409
competition law, 126–7
Doha Ministerial, 405
export cartels, 233
extraterritorial jurisdiction, 64, 389
GE/Honeywell merger, 53, 68
Geneva Ministerial, 401
harmonisation of competition law, 343
and Indonesian motor industry, 239
market integration, 128
and merger over-regulation, 51
objective, 126
plurilateral model, 122–3, 128, 426
proposal for WTO competition, 299, 300–1
Seattle Ministerial, 404
Singapore Ministerial, 398, 399–400
social equity considerations, 24
and Uruguay Round, 135–6
and voluntary import expansions, 250
exclusive dealing, 96, 97, 187, 188, 194
exclusive purchase agreements, 188
exemptions from competition laws
 APEC countries, 97–100
 discouraging, 104
 domestic trade measures, 229
 examples, 202
 export cartels, 235–6
 import cartels, 203–5
 issues, 100
 public policy, 97
 public procurement, 251, 253
 sectorial exemptions, 99, 327
 state trading enterprises, 98, 254, 256–7
 trade-oriented industrial policies, 237, 239–40
 voluntary export restraints, 245
exhaustion of domestic remedies, 192
export cartels, 98, 228, 232–6, 245, 246
export promotion policies, 238
export quotas, 234–5

externalities
 cross-border competition laws, 43–51
 extraterritoriality, 65
 international competition law, 175
 law and economics theory, 165–6
 manifestations, 202
 negative externalities, 44, 46, 65
 positive externalities, 44, 46
extraterritorial jurisdiction
 application, 53–6
 Australia, 64–5
 blocking statutes, 58–61
 and comity, 63, 68
 compliance mechanism, 375
 or co-operation, 67
 effects doctrine, 61–4, 68, 212
 European Union, 64
 ineffectiveness, 212–17
 Laker litigation example, 59–61
 limitations, 65–9
 non-co-operation, 53–69
 objective territoriality principle, 55
 and OPEC, 215–17
 and over-regulation, 61, 67–8
 requirements, 55
 restriction, 380
 soft law regulation, 388–9
 and sovereignty principle, 54
 system frictions, 2, 55–6, 68
 and under-regulation, 65–7
 United States, 54, 55, 61–4, 67
 universal jurisdiction, 54
 Uranium litigation example, 56–9

fair procedures, 330–4
Finland, 58, 65
forcing, 187
foreclosure, 187, 194
foreign direct investment, 35, 40, 41
foreign judgments, blocking statutes, 58
Fox, E. M., 150
France, 32, 58, 67, 109, 316

G-20, 408, 409
game theory, 79

GATS
  competition provisions, 218
  co-operation, 320
  most favoured nation treatment, 321
  public procurement, 252
  telecommunications, 218–21, 358–60
GATT
  Anti-dumping Code, 263, 367–8
  anti-dumping provisions, 262–3, 267–8
  and competition regulation, 153–8, 183
  and developing countries, 413
  dispute settlement, 383–4
  due process, 331–2
  incorporation into WTO, 158
  most favoured nation treatment, 154, 321
  national treatment principle, 154, 193, 194
  non-discrimination obligations, 191, 194
  non-tariff barriers, 154
  objective, 154
  public procurement, 252
  retaliation remedy, 156
  state trading enterprises, 256
  tariff bindings, 154
GE/Honeywell merger 2001, 51, 53, 68, 424
Geneva Ministerial 1998, 400–2
Germany, 32, 65, 109, 261
globalisation
  cross-border alliances, 36–43
  globalisation of competition, 35–53
  inter-firm commerce, 37
  international economy, 35–6
  intra-firm trade, 37
  rise of MNCs, 36–43
  terminology, 35–6
government compulsion defence, 241, 245
government procurement
  and competition, 251–4
  detrimental policies, 252
  and domestic competition laws, 251, 253

Japanese bid-rigging, 205–8
  operation, 251
  WTO Agreement, 207, 253, 397
  WTO exemption, 251, 252–3
Graham, Edward M., 347, 367, 369
Grand Utility Possibility Frontier, 24
Greece, 65
Guzman, A. T., 361

Hague Convention on Service of Process, 67
Hague Evidence Convention, 67
Harberger, A., 18
harmonisation of domestic laws
  benefits, 340–1
  benefits of diversity, 342–3
  convergence. *See* convergence of competition laws
  convergence-harmonisation continuum, 337–9
  cost-benefit analysis, 339
  costs, 341–4
  desirability, 336, 337–47
  full harmonisation, 338
  meaning, 337
  optimal level, 345–7, 431
  partial harmonisation, 338
Harvard School, 16
Hashimoto, R., 210
Haufbauer, Gary, 270
Havana Charter, 150–3, 155, 158, 159, 183, 220, 296, 303, 427
Hong Kong, 73, 399, 400
Hopkins, T. D., 31
horizontal agreements, 94–5, 347
human rights, 169

IAM v. OPEC, 215
IIE Survey, 347, 367, 369
IMF, creation, 149
immunities, sovereign immunity, 215
import cartels, 98, 203–5
import substitution policies, 237–8
India, 58, 86, 316, 399, 408
Indonesia, 90, 91
infant industries, 237
Institute for International Economics, 249, 270, 347

INDEX

institutions
  and APEC competition laws, 81
  and compliance, 371–7, 431
  criteria, 290–3
  dispute settlement, 383–9
  International Competition Agreement, 289–98, 370–1
  mitigation of disputes, 378–83
  pre-condition to competition law, 74, 81, 103
instrumentation principle, 317, 318
intellectual property, 42, 99, 162, 190
International Competition Agreement
  achievability, 291, 298, 395–422, 432–3
  and anti-competitive agreements, 95
  anti-monopoly laws, 92
  Article 4, 318
  Article 5, 325
  Article 6, 330
  Article 7, 334
  Article 8, 321, 327
  Article 21, 334
  binding precepts, 336, 355–65
  and cartels, 99, 236
  co-regulation, 364–5
  commonalities, 71–5, 105, 424–5
  compliance. *See* compliance
  comprehensiveness principle, 326–7
  co-operation principle, 319–21
  core principles, 140, 318–34, 430–1
  desirability, 34–70, 423–4
  and developing countries, 412, 413–16
  disputes. *See* dispute settlement
  distributional objective, 317–18
  and domestic trade measures, 366
  draft text, 433–4
  drafting obligations, 355–60
  efficiency objective, 316, 317
  EU initiative, 299, 300–1
  exemptions, 100, 104, 236, 327
  existing initiatives, 298–314, 425–6
  fair procedures, 330–4
  harmonisation of domestic laws, 336, 337–47
  incorporation procedure, 395–8
  institutional criteria, 290–3
  institutional pre-conditions, 74, 81, 103
  institutional vehicle, 289–98, 370–1
  merger control, 85
  methods, 104
  minimum standard approach, 336, 348–55
  mixed architecture, 141, 418
  multilateral option, 396
  Munich Code, 300, 301–7
  negotiations, 395–412
  non-discrimination principle, 321–5
  objectives, 104, 315–18, 430
  obstacles, 140
  OECD treaty, 290, 298
  plurilateral option, 396, 398
  promotion of international trade, 221–3
  ratification, 397–8
  remedies, 103, 104
  Scherer proposal, 299, 301
  sectorial exemptions, 99
  selective convergence of domestic laws, 336–7, 369, 417, 431
  soft law, 360–4, 417
  stand-alone treaty, 290, 298
  and state entities, 98
  strategies, 139–43, 417–21
  substantive content, 336–69
  thesis, 2
  transparency, 327–30
  UN treaty, 290–4, 298
  WTO as optimal vehicle, 289–90, 293, 334–5, 429–30
  WTO as suitable vehicle, 147–84, 427
  WTO law amendment, 336, 365–8
international competition law
  alternative to anti-dumping, 271–83
  bilateral agreements. *See* bilateral agreements
  complementarity with international trade law, 163–76
  continuum, 107
  distributional fairness objective, 168–9
  efficiency objective, 167–8
  externalities, 43–51

international competition law (*cont.*)
    extraterritoriality. *See* extraterritorial jurisdiction
    fair competition, 169
    v international trade law, 170–6, 428–9
    justification, 175
    multilateralism. *See* multilateral agreements
    objectives, 167–9
    plurilateralism. *See* plurilateral agreements
    reconciliation with international trade law, 176–83
    regulatory methodology, 174
international conduct, 187, 188
International Court of Justice
    Barcelona Traction case, 388
    jurisdiction, 373
    sources of law, 360
international law
    application, 373
    soft law. *See* soft law
    sources, 360
international measures, 225
international relations theory, 164
international trade
    cartels
    effects of anti-competitive behaviour on, 187–91
    growth statistics, 35
    inter-firm trade, 37, 38–40
    intra-firm trade, 37, 40–2
    promotion by International Competition Agreement, 221–3
    strategic alliances, 37, 42–3
    trade liberalisation, 172
international trade law
    See also GATT; WTO
    1st competition regulation proposals, 151
    complementarity with international competition law, 163–76
    distributional fairness objective, 168–9
    and domestic trade measures, 226, 227–9

efficiency objective, 167–8
enforcement, 229
history of competition-trade links, 163
v international competition law, 170–6, 428–9
ITO failure, 150–3
justification, 174
objectives, 167–9
reconciliation with international competition law, 176–83
regulatory methodology, 174
scope, 226
International Trade Organisation (ITO), 150–3
Israel, 110, 213
Italy, 316

Jackson, J. H., 178, 197
Japan
    anti-competitive agreements, 95
    anti-monopoly laws, 91
    automobile VER, 243–4
    bilateral agreements, 110
    cartel exemptions, 99
    competition authority, 102
    cost of regulation, 32
    Daishowa case, 233–4
    'dango' bid-rigging, 205–8
    economic priorities, 27
    effects doctrine, 65
    enforcement of competition law, 103
    export cartels, 233, 235–6
    export promotion policies, 238
    Geneva Ministerial 1998, 402
    import cartels, 203
    inadequacy of competition laws, 208–12
    and Indonesian motor industry, 239
    keiretsu, 208–12
    Kodak-Fuji Film case, 191–201, 204
    merger control, 87
    priorities, 412
    public procurement, 205–8
    Seattle Ministerial, 404
    Semi-Conductors case, 196–7
    Singapore Ministerial, 399, 400

INDEX 493

US disputes with, 27, 179, 203, 205–12
US–Japan Automobile Trade Agreement, 211
voluntary export restraints, 242, 246
voluntary import expansions, 248, 250
and WTO competition agreement, 412
Jefferson, Thomas, 34
jurisdiction
  extraterritoriality. *See* extraterritorial jurisdiction
  territorial sovereignty, 1–2, 54
jurisdictional disputes
  mitigation, 378, 380–1
  resolution, 387–9
  rules of precedence, 380

Kajima Engineering, 207
Kaldor-Hicks efficiency improvement, 12–15, 175, 392
keiretsu, 208–12
Kennedy Round, 154
Kiewet Construction, 207
Kintner, E. W., 106
Klein, Joel, 352
Kodak-Fuji Film case, 191–201, 207, 211, 428

labour standards, 169
Laker litigation, 59–61, 424
law and economics theory, and WTO, 165–6
League of Nations, 148
least developed countries
  Geneva Ministerial 1998, 402
  lack of competition laws, 141
  and UNCTAD code, 130–3
  and Uruguay Round, 135
Leebron, D., 390–1
Levitt, Theodore, 35
liberal constitutional theory, and WTO, 164–5
licensing, Japanese public procurement, 206
lobbying, 269–70
Luxembourg, 65, 151

Magna Carta, 75
Malaysia, 73–4
market concentration, 79, 84–5
market conduct, meaning, 79
market contestability, 179–83, 185
market definition, 81–4
market deregulation, 29–30, 172, 326
market efficiency
  allocation of scarce resources, 8–14
  benefit of competition, 8–15
  imperfections, 14–15
  neoclassical microeconomic theory, 8–14
  Theory of Second Best, 14–15
market equilibrium, 10, 18
market failures
  causes, 14, 16
  and competition law, 73
  and trade-oriented industrial policies, 240
market power
  anti-monopoly laws, 16
  basic common concept, 78, 82
  effects, 16, 173
  identification, 16
  and price adjustment, 23
  rule of reason analysis, 81–4
market structures, 79, 84–9
markets, concept, 9, 11, 78, 82
Marrakesh Agreement
  competition provisions, 2
  incorporation of GATT, 159
  incorporation of International Competition Agreement, 395–8
Marshall, Alfred, 10
McDonnell Douglas, 51–3, 59, 115, 424
McGee, R. W., 270
MCI/Worldcom merger, 51
Melamed, Douglas, 353
merger control
  acquisition of dominance test, 88
  APEC countries, 84–9
  behavioural thresholds, 87, 88
  Boeing/McDonnell Douglas 1997, 51–3, 115, 424
  common concept, 78
  EU legislation, 127
  function, 79

merger control (*cont.*)
  GE/Honeywell, 51, 53, 68, 424
  harmonisation, 347
  notification procedures, 85–7
  over-regulation, 49, 51, 67–8
  pre-existing market concentration, 85, 89
  pre-notification, 86–7
  procedural convergence, 382
  public benefit assessment, 89
  regulation mechanism, 19–20
  standardisation, 85
  structural regulation, 16, 84–9
  structural thresholds, 87, 88
  substantial lessening of competition, 88
  thresholds, 87–8
mergers, state-mandated, 238
Mexico
  anti-monopoly laws, 91, 92
  Federal Competition Commission, 101
  merger control, 86, 87
  sisal traders, 62
  telecom dispute, 16, 83, 219–20, 221, 359–60
Miert, Karl van, 298
Milhar, F., 31
Millennium Round, 270, 403
minimum standard approach, 152, 336, 348–55
monopolies. *See* anti-monopoly laws
monopsony power, 204
Morgan, Clarisse, 282
most favoured nation treatment, 154, 212, 239, 321
multilateral agreements
  assessment, 140
  compliance, 375
  current initiatives, 129–39
  function, 141
  limitations, 138–9
  OECD Committee on Competition Law and Policy, 133–5
  unanimous consent, 138–9, 344
  UNCTAD Code, 130–3
  WTO Working Group on Competition, 135–6
multinational corporations
  definition of transnational corporation, 40
  inter-firm trade, 37, 38–40
  intra-firm trade, 37, 40–2
  rise, 36–43
  strategic alliances, 37
Munich Code
  critique, 307–14, 352
  elements, 301–7
  enforcement mechanisms, 305, 309–11, 372
  EU orientation, 306, 309, 313, 350–1
  institutional issues, 308–11
  International Antitrust Authority, 302, 305–6, 309–10
  International Antitrust Panel, 305
  majority principles, 304–6
  minimum standards approach, 349–51
  minority principles, 304, 306–7
  objective, 302
  origin, 300
  over-standardisation, 311–14
  plurilateral agreement, 303
  precedent, 430
  principles and standards, 303
  substantive issues, 311–14
Munich Group, 300
Murkowsi, F., 207
mutual legal assistance treaties, 113–18

Nakamura, Kishiro, 207
Nash equilibrium
national treatment principle
  GATT, 154
  harmonisation, 347, 367
  Kodak-Fuji Film case, 193, 194
  Munich Code, 304
  and trade-oriented industrial policies, 239
  WTO requirement, 321–2
nationality principle, 54
neoclassical theory, 8–14, 17–18
Netherlands, 58, 151
New Zealand
  anti-dumping law, 261
  anti-monopoly laws, 91, 92
  ANZ Agreement 1988, 118–20

INDEX 495

Australia–New Zealand CER 1983, 273–6
blocking statutes, 58, 62, 67
Commerce Act 1986, 273
co-operation agreements, 141
drug purchasing exemption, 99
electricity industry, 177
extraterritorial jurisdiction, 65
Geneva Ministerial 1998, 401
merger control, 86, 88, 89
objectives of competition, 316
recognition of Australian procedures, 381
shipping exemptions, 99
trans-Tasman provisions, 118–20, 274
vertical restraints, 97
Nickell, S., 22
non-discrimination principle
  and anti-dumping law, 229, 267–8
  de facto discrimination, 324
  de jure discrimination, 324
  GATT, 191, 194
  international competition law, 321–5
  price discrimination, 188, 264–5, 279–80
  and trade-oriented industrial policies, 239
  WTO, 214, 234, 318, 321–2
non-tariff barriers, 154, 178, 187
Norway, 58, 65
notification obligations, 85–7, 328, 329–30

objective territoriality principle, 55
OECD
  on Australian regulation, 31
  on benefits of deregulation, 32
  and bilateral agreements, 108
  Cartel Recommendation, 134–5
  on collusion, 20
  Committee on Competition Law and Policy, 133–5
  on competition institutions, 101
  Conflict Recommendation, 134
  Co-operation Recommendation, 134, 320
  on globalisation, 35–6
  Multilateral Agreement on Investment, 290
  and Munich Code, 307
  objectives of competition law, 77, 315
  origins, 130
  recommendations on competition, 134–5, 140, 220, 426
  structure, 133
  vehicle for International Competition Agreement, 290, 298
oligopolies, 23
oligopsony power, 204
OPEC, 62, 205, 212
Organisation of American States, 122
Oualid, William, 148–9, 150
over-regulation
  Boeing/McDonnell case study, 51–3
  and comity, 110
  effects, 46, 48–51
  and extraterritorial jurisdiction, 61, 67–8
  and globalisation, 1
  need for international competition agreement, 43
  recent merger examples, 51
  system frictions, 49–50
  trade disputes, 50–1
  and transaction costs, 48–9
  welfare consequences, 50

pacta sunt servanda, 190
Papua New Guinea, 74, 88, 91
Pareto efficiency, 12, 172, 175
Peru, 86, 91, 92
Philippines, 85, 91, 95, 101
plurilateral agreements
  APEC model, 123–4, 426
  assessment, 139–40
  building block theory, 128–9
  EU model, 128, 426
  function, 141
  harmonisation of competition laws, 123
  International Competition Agreement, 398
  limitations, 128–9
  models, 122–3, 426
  momentum, 122–9

Portnoy, B., 185
Portugal, 65
predatory behaviour, 187
predatory dumping, 265
predatory pricing, 277–9
Prewitt Enterprises, 215
prices
  discrimination, 188, 264–5, 279–80
  monopoly pricing, 17–18
  predatory pricing, 276–9
  price fixing, 94, 347
  price resale maintenance, 96
procedural disputes, 378–9, 381–2, 386–7
producer-consumer equity, 26
producer-producer equity, 26
producer surplus, 10, 11, 17, 84
producers, and competition, 9
product differentiation, 79
product substitutability, 82–3
productive efficiency, 13, 18–19, 21
public choice theory, and WTO, 166–7
public policy
  exemptions from competition laws, 97
  and merger control, 89
  trade-oriented industrial policies, 237
public procurement. *See* government procurement
publication obligations, 327, 329

Reagan, Ronald, 242
refusals to supply, 187
regulation, and market imperfections, 14–15
remedies
  anti-dumping as remedy, 268
  APEC countries, 102–3
  exhaustion of local remedies, 192
  standardisation, 104
reprisal, 374
result-oriented approaches, 80
retaliation
  coercive mechanism, 374–5
  effect of under-regulation, 211–12
  export cartels, 233–4
  GATT remedy, 156
retorsion, 374
Ricardo, David, 170–1, 187
Richardson, J. David, 347, 367, 369
Rio Declaration, 362
Ross, D., 19
rule of law, 330
rule of reason, 80, 81–4, 95
Russia
  anti-competitive agreements, 95
  anti-monopoly laws, 90, 91
  cartels, 93
  competition agency, 102
  merger control, 86, 87

Safeguards Agreement, 244–5, 246, 250, 368
scarce resources, allocation, 8–14
Scherer, Frederick, 13, 19, 23, 299
Scherer proposal, 299, 301
Schott, Jeffrey, 395
SCM Agreement, 239
Seattle Ministerial Conference 1999, 403–5
Second Best, Theory of, 14–15
sectorial exemptions, 99, 327
semi-conductors, 248, 250
shipping, 99, 162
Singapore, 88, 91
Singapore Declaration 1996, 136, 298
Singapore issues, 398, 409
Singapore Ministerial Conference 1996, competition negotiations, 398–400
Smith, Adam, 16, 19
social choice theory, 24–8
social justice
  distributional fairness of competition, 24–8
  v economic efficiency, 26–8
  welfare transfers, 25–6
soft law
  mutual recognition of procedures, 381
  principles, 419–20, 431
  regulation of extraterritoriality, 388–9

UNCTAD code, 132
value, 360–4, 417
South Africa, 56–7, 58–9
South Korea
  anti-competitive agreements, 94
  anti-monopoly laws, 90, 92
  chaebol, 238
  competition authorities, 101, 102
  export promotion policies, 238
  Geneva Ministerial 1998, 402
  Korean Beef case, 255
  merger control, 87
  Singapore Ministerial, 399, 400
  state entity exemptions, 98
  and voluntary export restraints, 242
sovereignty
  and extraterritorial jurisdiction, 54
  and international cartels, 216
  and international competition law, 400
  sovereign equality, 371
  sovereign immunity, 215
Spain, 65
special and differential treatment, 169, 413–15
stare decisis, 191
state sovereignty. *See* sovereignty
state trading enterprises
  detriment to international competition, 255
  exemptions from competition laws, 98, 254, 256–7
  generally, 254–7
  operation, 254–5
  and WTO, 254, 256
static efficiency, and competition, 15–20
steel, 243
structural regulation, 16, 84–9
structure-conduct-performance paradigm, 78–9, 84, 89, 173
Sweden, 58, 65
Switzerland, 62, 65
system frictions
  export cartels, 233–4
  extraterritoriality, 2, 55–6, 68
  Laker litigation, 59–61
  over-regulation, 49–50
  trade sanctions, 211–12
  Uranium litigation, 56–9
  welfare consequences, 50

Taiwan, 87, 90, 238
technical assistance, 415, 416
technology, and competition, 21, 23
telecommunications
  anti-competitive practices, 190
  GATS Annexe, 218
  Mexican dispute, 16, 83, 219–20, 221, 359–60
  negotiations, 397
  technological innovation, 23
  and WTO, 162
  WTO Basic Telecoms Agreement, 218–21, 358–60
Telmex, 219
territorial approaches, 1–2, 54
territorial restraints, 96, 188
Thailand, 98, 102
Tokyo Round, 154, 252, 263
total surplus, 11, 12
trade. *See* domestic trade measures; international trade
trade barriers, 173, 177, 178, 179–83
trade disputes
  See also WTO disputes
  Boeing/McDonnell Douglas example, 52
  and extraterritoriality, 68
  and over-regulation, 50–1
trade liberalisation, 172, 173
trade-oriented industrial policies, 237–40
Trade Policy Review Mechanism, 375, 377
trade sanctions, 211–12, 374–5, 389–93
trade unions, 99
trans-Tasman provisions, 118–20, 274
transaction costs, 48–9
transnational corporations. *See* multinational corporations
transparency, 327–30
TRIMS, and competition, 136, 159
TRIPS, 320, 330–1, 356
tying, 96, 187

UNCTAD
  Code on Restrictive Business
    Practices, 130–3, 140, 220, 426
  on competition, 20
  on FDI, 41
  objectives, 130
  origins, 130
  role, 418
  on TNC numbers
under-regulation
  and comity, 112
  examples, 185–7, 202
  meaning, 45–6
  need for international competition
    agreement, 43
  private anti-competitive behaviour,
    189
  and territoriality, 1, 65–7
  welfare consequences, 50
United Kingdom
  anti-dumping law, 261
  blocking statutes, 67
  cost of regulation, 32
  Darcy v. *Allen*, 74
  effects of competition, 22
  and Havana Charter, 151
  and ITO, 150
  Laker litigation, 59–61
  Statute of Monopolies 1624, 75
  Uranium litigation, 56–7, 58–9
United Nations
  Friendly Relations Declaration 1970,
    319
  vehicle for International
    Competition Agreement, 290–4,
    298
United States
  Alcoa case, 62
  anti-competitive agreements, 94, 95
  anti-dumping law, 261, 269–71, 279,
    400
  anti-monopoly laws, 91
  bilateral agreements, 109, 110
  Boeing/McDonnell Douglas merger
    1997, 51–3, 115
  Cancún Ministerial, 408, 409
  competition authorities, 101
  competition laws, 349

conduct-oriented approach, 80
cost of regulation, 31, 32
Daishowa case, 233–4
Doha Ministerial 2001, 406
effects doctrine, 61–4, 68
export cartels, 233
extraterritoriality, 54, 55, 61–4, 67,
  389
Foreign Sovereign Immunity Act
  1976, 215, 216
Foreign Trade Antitrust
  Improvements Act 1982, 63–4
and GATT, 155
GE/Honeywell merger 2001, 53, 68
Geneva Ministerial 1998, 401–2
Hartford Fire case, 63–4
and Havana Charter, 150, 151, 153
IAM v. *OPEC*, 215
and Indonesian motor industry, 239
International Antitrust Enforcement
  Assistance, 114
and Israel, 213
and ITO, 150
Japan, disputes with, 27, 179, 203,
  205–12
Kodak-Fuji Film case, 191–201, 204
Laker litigation, 59–61
mergers, 51
monopoly pricing, 18, 19
and Munich Code, 306, 307, 308,
  314, 352
mutual legal assistance treaties,
  113–18
oil import cartel, 205
and OPEC, 215–17
priorities, 24, 27, 316, 412
Seattle Ministerial 1999, 404
service industries, 32
Sherman Act, 61, 62, 75
Singapore Ministerial, 399
telecom dispute with Mexico, 219–20
Timberlane case, 63
Uranium litigation, 56–9
vertical restraints, 312
voluntary export restraints, 242,
  243–4
and voluntary import expansions,
  247–8

INDEX

and WTO competition agreement, 343, 344, 352–3, 412
universal jurisdiction, 54
Uranium litigation, 56–9, 424
Uruguay Round
  and anti-dumping, 263–4
  and competition, 135–6, 158–63, 183
  and LDCs, 135

Vermulst, E. A., 383–4
vertical restraints, 96–7
Vienna Convention on Law of Treaties, 138
Vietnam, 73, 91
voluntary export restraints, 229, 241–6, 347, 367, 368
voluntary import expansions, 246–51, 347, 367, 368

welfare economics
  1st Fundamental Theorem, 14, 172
  2nd Fundamental Theorem, 24–5
  Grand Utility Possibility Frontier, 24
  market efficiency, 11
welfare policies
  and competition law, 28–33
  direct effects, 28
  indirect effects, 28
Westinghouse Electric Corporation, 56–9
Westphalia, Peace of, 371
Williams, Brett, 199
Williams, Mark, 102
wood pulp, 233–4
World Bank
  on competition institutions, 101
  creation, 150
  on effects of competition, 20, 22, 23
  on exemptions from competition laws, 100
  on lack of competition law, 73, 74
  objectives of competition law, 77, 315
World Economic Forum, 148–9
world trade. *See* international trade
World War II, 149
Worldcom/MCI merger 1999, 51

WTO
  See also international trade law
  agreements. *See* specific agreements
  on competition, 20
  Competition Agreement. *See* International Competition Agreement
  competition amendments, 365–8
  competition proposals, 298–314
  competition provisions, 158–63, 228
  consensual processes, 295, 396–8
  co-operation principle, 319–20
  disputes. *See* WTO disputes
  and domestic trade measures, 227–9
  enforcement of provisions, 229, 297
  exemptions, 214–17, 251, 252–3, 325
  and export cartels, 232–5, 236
  incomplete coverage, 228, 326–7
  institutions, 296, 297
  instrumentation principle, 317, 318
  and international cartels, 214
  international support, 295–6
  and law and economics theory, 165–6
  and liberal constitutional theory, 164–5
  negative obligations, 191
  non-discrimination principle, 214, 234, 318, 321–2
  objectives, 167
  origins, 159
  plurilateral agreements, 303
  positive obligations, 190–1, 356
  and private anti-competitive behaviour, 189–91, 196, 201, 217–21
  procedural fairness, 330–1
  and public choice theory, 166–7
  public international law instrument, 190–1
  scope of regulation, 228–9
  Secretariat, 315, 377
  and state trading enterprises, 254, 256
  suitability as international competition vehicle, 147–84, 427, 429–30

WTO (*cont.*)
  theoretical rationale, 164–7
  and trade-oriented industrial policies, 237, 238–9
  transparency, 327–9
  vehicle for International Competition Agreement, 147–84, 289–90, 293, 334–5
  and voluntary export restraints, 241, 244–5
  and voluntary import expansions, 246, 249–50
  Working Group. *See* WTO Working Group on Competition
WTO disputes
  appellate reviews, 384–5
  Canadian Dairy case, 255
  Canadian Salmon case, 235
  consultative procedure, 382, 384
  Dispute Settlement Body, 297, 373, 376–7, 383–9, 394, 431–2
  dispute settlement system, 198–200
  impairment of WTO benefits, 193, 197–201, 229
  implementation of decisions, 385
  Japan–Semi-Conductors case, 196–7, 250
  jurisdictional disputes, 387–9
  Kodak-Fuji Film case, 191–201, 204, 211, 428
  Korean Beef case, 255
  Mexico-Telecommunications, 16, 83, 219–20, 221, 359–60
  non-violation complaints, 198, 199
  Oilseeds case, 201
  panel reviews, 384
  procedural disputes, 386–7
  Shrimp/Turtle case, 331
  situation complaints, 198, 199–200
  and *stare decisis*, 191
  substantive disputes, 385–6
  trade sanctions remedy, 389–93
  violation complaints, 198–9
WTO Working Group on Competition
  annual reports, 136
  on cartels, 212
  establishment, 2, 136, 398
  generally, 135–6
  mandate, 136, 400, 407
  progress, 298, 409

X-inefficiency, 18